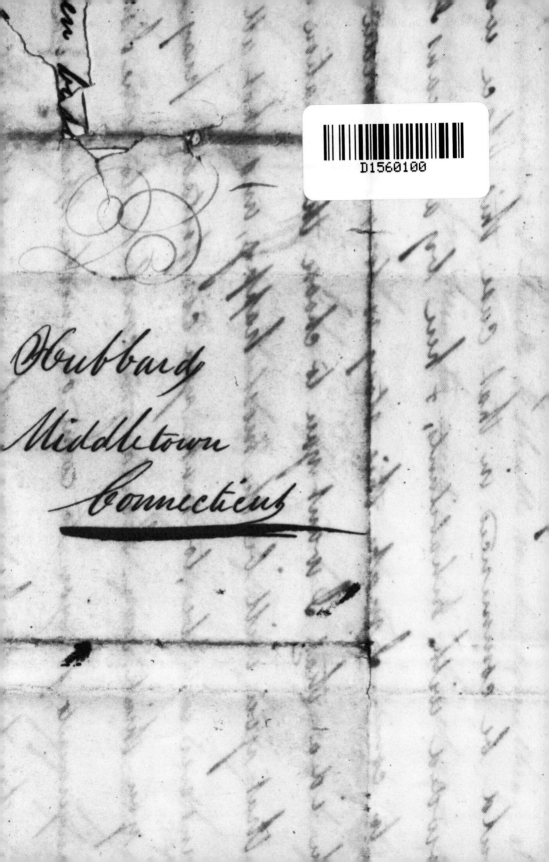

Hubbard
Middletown
Connecticut

LLOYD WENDT

'Swift Walker'

AN INFORMAL BIOGRAPHY OF

Gurdon Saltonstall Hubbard

Regnery Books
Chicago   Washington, DC

Regnery Books is a Division of Regnery Gateway, Inc.
All inquiries concerning this book should be directed to
Regnery Books, 950 N. Shore Drive, Lake Bluff, IL 60044.

Library of Congress Cataloging-in-Publication Data

Wendt, Lloyd.
    'Swift Walker': an informal biography of Gurdon
Saltonstall Hubbard.

    Includes index.
    1. Hubbard, Gurdon Saltonstall, 1802-1886. 2. Fur
traders—Northwest, Old—Biography. 3. Northwest,
Old—Biography. 4. Frontier and pioneer life—
Northwest, Old. 5. Pioneers—Illinois—Chicago—
Biography. 6. Chicago (Ill.)—Biography. I. Title.
F484.3.H883W46 1986 977'.02'0924 [B] 86-17886
ISBN 0-89526-581-8

Dedication

*To all those who share an appreciation
of the past, the lessons our heritage
holds for the present, the guidance
it offers for the future.*

ROYAL SOCIETY OF CANADA

La Belle du Rosier Blanc

Je m'en irai au Service
Je m'en irai au Service;
En Service pour un An
Et la belle Rose du Rosier blanc
En Service pour un An
Et la belle Rose du Rosier blanc

Combien gagnez vous, la belle
Combien gagnez vous, la belle
Combien gagnez vous par An
Combien gagnez vous par An?
Je ne gagne que cinq cents Livres
Je ne gagne que cinq cents Livres
Cinq cents Livres en Argent blanc
Cinq cents Livres en Argent blanc

La Violette Dandon, La Violette Dondé.

Quand j'étais chez mon Père,
    Petite Janeton,
Il m'envoyait à la fontaine
    Pour pêcher du poisson.
La Violette Dandon, oh! la Violette dondé.

Il m'envoyait à la fontaine
    Pour pêcher du poisson.
La fontaine est profonde
    Je suis coulée au fond.
        Chorus: La Violette, &c.

Il m'envoyait à la fontaine
    Pour pêcher du poisson.
Par-ice ils passerent trois
    Trois Cavaliers barons
        Chorus: La Violette, &c.

Voyaguers Songs from the Laurence Lande Collection
of Canadiana, McGill University Libraries, Montreal.

Contents

5

Preamble

When Gurdon Hubbard first saw Chicago in the autumn of 1818 it was an Indian crossing place on a route from Canada to the Illinois fur trade country and St. Louis. "Four and a half houses, a fort, and a Potawatomi town," he wrote his mother in Montreal. Indians claimed and held much of the great Northwest Territory then. Gurdon was sixteen when he crossed the dread Chicago Portage for the fur posts on the Illinois river with a brigade of French-Canadian *voyageurs*.

During Hubbard's often tempestuous lifetime, Chicago would rise to a population of nearly a million, the northwest would fill with farms and towns, the Indians would be driven into exile on reserved lands beyond the Mississippi. The Illinois fur trade would die. For more than a decade Gurdon lived among the Indians, trading with them, becoming the adopted son of Waba, chief of the Kickapoos, marrying Watseka, niece of Chief Tamin of the Kankakees. He could outwalk, outwork and outfight any Indian and was called by them Papamatabe, or "Swift Walker." He could outwork most whites, too, and was called by some "Indian Hubbard" or "Horse Hubbard," and by others "Yankee Hubbard."

An Illinois legislator from Vermilion county when he was thirty, Gurdon also was elected colonel of the Vermilion County Rangers; twice he led them to the relief of Fort Dearborn, in the Winnebago and the Black Hawk wars. At Vandalia, the Illinois state capital, he pushed legislation to make the Chicago Portage and river the eastern entrance of a canal to link Canada by water with the Gulf of Mexico. When the Indians lost their struggle to keep their land, and Hubbard's Indian trade diminished,

7

he moved to Chicago. There as much or more than any man, Gurdon Hubbard would make Chicago the great city it became. He kept it where it was, on the Chicago river at Lake Michigan, linked by the canal he helped to win and dig there, to Montreal on the north and St. Louis and New Orleans to the south.

   This account of Gurdon Saltonstall Hubbard and the people and events in his life is true, based on contemporary accounts, his letters and recollections, the reports of pioneers and local historians, and general historical documents and sources. Some of the dialogue is fictional, but evoked from actual events and incidents as recalled by Gurdon and those about him, the sources indicated within the narrative or in the end notes. The work of almost a decade, it was undertaken to correct accepted history and to set Gurdon Hubbard in the clear perspective of his remarkable career and his pioneering place in the forefront of Americans moving westward, especially in the establishment of Chicago, heartland city of the then-expanding United States.

1

In the month of April, 1816, my father procured for me a
situation in the hardware store of John Frothingham,
where I received for my services my board only. I was the
boy of the store—slept on the counter, worked hard, and
attended faithfully to my duties. . . .
Recollections,
Gurdon S. Hubbard

Outside Frothingham's in St. Paul street, on a cool bright April
afternoon in 1818, Gurdon Hubbard, errand boy of the marine
and general hardware store, hailed the stage to Lachine, a half
hour's drive out of Montreal. O'Shea, the driver, shouted at his
horses and leaned on his brake, his vehicle creaking and groaning to a stop a few yards from the lad. Timothy O'Shea had firm
instructions to halt at Frothingham's no matter who gave the
signal.

"Git aboard with ye, lad," O'Shea grumbled. "I'm late. It's
to the Ship Yards is it?"

"No, to Lachine."

"Well, git yerself loaded, no room for anything up here."

The passengers inside seemed as grumpy as their driver. But
they made room for Gurdon Hubbard to push his heavy packages among their filthy boots and accommodated him the best
they could as he pressed his lean body against them, drawing
between his own worn boots the snugly-sewn sailcloth bags
he'd brought, that he seemed to guard as treasure.

O'Shea shouted, the horses lunged against their traces, the
stage rattled over the cobblestones. In the doorway of Frothingham's a spare, white-haired man called after O'Shea, then
watched undecided as the stagecoach moved away.

Gurdon grinned at his fellow passengers. The pleasant, dark-
eyed boy who might have been French-Canadian spoke as if he
were English. "The Mackinac Brigade leaves early tomorrow,"

he told them. "I've got to get these to them now." He sought to spread his legs above the bags. The passengers in the seat beside him obliged with a bit more room.

Along St. Paul street Gurdon searched for a sight of Big John Dyde, his only close friend in Montreal, who, like himself, ran errands in the town when he was not helping out in his own family's boarding house. The stage's oilskin windows were not much for viewing. It clattered briskly through the town, past the Hospital and the Grey Nunnery, and into the countryside among the windmills slowly turning along the shore of the St. Lawrence. Gurdon knew most of the route, he had gone to Lachine on a provisioner's wagon before he became the boy in Frothingham's store.

He leaned back bracing against the carriage wall, his legs pressing the heavy bags he had carried from the hardware store, considering what he should do on reaching the docks at Lachine. He was on his own. Mr. West, chief clerk at Frothingham's, had by no means authorized him to take the baggage out of the store. Nor had there been time for Gurdon to explain that he knew precisely what was in them, since he had unloaded them from the steamer *Malsham* the day before and had inspected the bills of lading. One contained finishing nails, the other, steels for gun repair and flints-and-steel for the Indian trade. They had been ordered for the American Fur Company at Michilimackinac.

Obviously *voyageurs* from that outfit, almost ready for departure from Lachine, had left the most important items of their order when they picked up their share of the *Malsham* shipment that morning. Gurdon's father, writing up indentures and bonds for the Michilimackinac Brigade, had said at home that the brigade was already late. In charge of American fur interests at Lachine was Mr. William Wallace, who hated delay and could be most difficult. The boy of the store had said what he knew in fewest words possible: "Mr. West, it has got to go now!" Nevertheless West was hesitant.

"I must see Mr. Frothingham about this," Mr. West had said. "You wait here."

Then Gurdon had heard the noises of the approaching stage. He saw the need and met it. The bags each weighed near eighty pounds but he got both to the street in time.

Chapter 1

As West watched in astonishment from the Frothingham door while the stage disappeared from St. Paul street, he may have recalled that for weeks Gurdon Hubbard, their quiet, reliable boy, had talked of nothing but going west into the Indian country with the *voyageurs,* despite his parents' opposition. Mr. Frothingham, fortunately, said when informed of Gurdon's hasty errand to Lachine: "Good, let him do it."

*

Lachine without doubt was part of Gurdon's dream of the future. There he intended someday to take passage west and south into the Indian country. The little harbor was named, he knew, as an allusion to LaSalle's dream of discovering the route to China. It lay above the St. Lawrence rapids, where freight canoes and mackinaws could with relative safety begin their voyages southwest. The French explorers and traders for years had assumed and hoped the St. Lawrence, the great inland lakes, and the Mississippi could provide the way to the Orient and Far Cathay.

O'Shea got them to the little port town, on the cold and blue St. Lawrence, late in the afternoon, after a few stops to discharge passengers and freight. On the waterfront, near a long, low freight house that accommodated the American Fur Company, new to Montreal that year, they came among the *voyageurs.* There were scores, in buckskin pants and moccasins, stripped to waist despite the cool April day, loading the last of their trade goods onto the freight canoes, called mackinaws by the Americans, *canot du maitre* by the French and Canadians.

Gurdon, emerging from the stage, was happy to be among them. Since the days he first read Alexander Henry's account of voyageurs and fur traders, back in New England, he had yearned to become one of them, adventuring in the Indian country. Now his father was writing indentures for *voyageurs* and clerks sought by the new American fur company, yet his son could not go! At the moment such frustration dissolved in the excitement of Lachine. The voyageurs were vigorously preparing for departure, swarming over the docks and their boats. He knew from Henry's descriptions that tomorrow these sweating, laughing, bare-chested fellows would be dressed in their uniforms, blue or red shirts, buckskins with white gaiters, and *bonnets rouge,* their flop-eared red caps that distinguished the *voyageurs* from lesser men. They would be in their regalia and their boats would be dressed in flags and pennants as they departed Lachine, the first of the newly-formed American outfits to go that spring.

A young clerk came to his aid as Gurdon dragged his bags of trade goods from the stage. Gurdon asked in English where Mr. Wallace might be found, but the boy shook his head. Obviously the American Fur Company was not getting English-speaking clerks it was said to be seeking. He repeated his question in French, *"Ou est Monsieur Wallace?"*

The clerk lifted one of the bags, found it heavier than he had expected but managed to tote it as he led the way along the wharf. They soon came to a large *canot du maître,* fastened to the dock with hemp springers, where a grim, burly Scot in shirtsleeves was directing the stowage.

"Yes, what is it?" he said on seeing Gurdon with his clerk.

"These are for American Fur Company," Gurdon answered. "I just brought them from Frothingham's."

"So you did," Wallace said, inspecting the bags. "Good God!" he exclaimed. "I thought this was stowed hours ago. Goods ordered by Mr. Ramsey Crooks himself left at your store? Heads will roll! Tell me what you know of this!"

A bit shaken by the man's fury, when he had expected something better, Gurdon told Wallace what little he knew. He had himself carried the bags from the steamship *Malsham,* and had recognized them at the store long after Wallace's men had departed.

"Ah well, lad. You've done well. Mr. Crooks is in need of these nails to finish off his office. I expect he'll want you to have a bit or two for your trouble. Here, this will cover you and your fare." Wallace produced five Spanish bits, more than Gurdon had received in cash that entire month.

"I think Mr. Frothingham will pay the fare," the boy said.

"Then you'll be the better off for it," Wallace replied. "Come to think of it, lad, how will you get back? There's no stage returning tonight."

"I expect to go back by boat."

Wallace smiled grimly. "There's no small boat that will try the rapids this time of day. No, lad, you'd best stay here. You can mess with my men, we're camped down the shore. We lost two young Frenchmen like yourself two days ago trying those rapids at nightfall. The current is fierce this time of year."

"I'm not French. I'm American, Vermont born. You spoke to me in English. . . ."

"Aye, I did. I address all newcomers in English. We're an American company now, you know. You look French-Canadian, lad."

"Can I go with you to Michilimackinac, Mr. Wallace?"

William Wallace eyed him carefully. "American are you? What age?"

"Almost sixteen."

"Almost sixteen." Wallace laughed. "Come to see me, lad, when you're almost eighteen." He turned to his clerk giving an order in French. "We'll have blankets and a tarp for you. You'll be messing with us and staying the night," he said to Gurdon.

The temptation was great.

"Sir," Gurdon spoke reluctantly. "I can't stay. I can walk home. I'm expected home tonight. My mother will worry. My father. . . ."

"That's three leagues . . . ten English miles! It gets cold with the sun down. . . ."

"I'll cut across . . . about seven miles. . . . I walk a lot, I'll stay warm. Thank you."

"Then go, lad. And may God go with you."

*

Almost sixteen. Gurdon Saltonstall Hubbard was born August 22, 1802 in Windsor, Vermont, the first child of Elizur Hubbard, the son of George Hubbard, an officer in the Revolutionary army, and Abigail Sage Hubbard, the daughter of General Comfort Sage and Sarah Hamlin, of Middletown, Connecticut. They called the boy Gurdon Saltonstall for another illustrious forebear, the Reverend Gurdon Saltonstall, a graduate of Harvard College who became an ordained minister in the Congregational Church, the establishment of religion in Connecticut Colony, in 1691. Early in his clerical career, Reverend Saltonstall became advisor to Governor Fitzjohn Winthrop and the Connecticut Assembly. So valuable were his services that on Governor Winthrop's death he was chosen governor at a special meeting of the council December 17, 1707. Neither the English Crown nor the Board of Trade and Plantations in London were consulted. Thus Gurdon Saltonstall was said to be the first elected governor of a Crown Colony in America.

The Connecticut Saltonstalls and the Hubbards had been associated over many years. William Hubbard of Guilford joined with Richard Saltonstall as far back as 1659 to form a fur trade enterprise whose charter permitted it to explore and trade with the Indians in the Great Lakes area of the Northwest, according to colonial records. Authorized to trade for "Bever skins, (sic) Buck and Doe skins, Otter and Raccoon", the new company never engaged in any trading of record because the French dominated the territory.

Gurdon's great-grandfather, George, had lived in Guilford, as had his grandfather, George, the Revolutionary soldier. His father Elizur was born there, read in the law, married Abigail Sage in Middletown, and took his bride to Windsor on the Connecticut River. There their six children were born. Members of the Hubbard family had preceded Elizur and Abigail to the lovely Vermont town, that once had been the capital of the Republic of Vermont, accepted into the Union as the fourteenth state March 4, 1791. At first Elizur prospered. Windsor was known for its Yankee ingenuity and enterprise. The machinists, blacksmiths, millwrights and carpenters were superb in their manufacturing skills. Winsor became famed for its precision tools and machines. Elizur, one of five lawyers in the town, dabbled in politics and began investing in the burgeoning economy of the Windsor area.

Young Gurdon's earliest remembered experience, which he recorded in his diary of later years, was "the great eclipse," probably referring to a phenomenon related to the passage of Biela's comet between the earth and the sun in the summer of 1806. "The white stage horses passing appeared yellow," Gurdon remembered. He was with his mother in the garden. "Looking up to my mother, I discovered her face appeared yellow, as did all surroundings. I was so frightened I did not recover for some time.''

When he was about six, Gurdon entered the Windsor school conducted by Captain Joshua Dunham, who continued to use, as his reading textbook, the famous *New England Primer,* by then somewhat out of fashion. Occasionally Captain Dunham, who also edited the *Washingtonian Federalist,* one of the five weekly newspapers published in Windsor during Gurdon's boyhood, would visit the Hubbards for an evening meal and the boy was permitted to listen as his teacher and father discussed politics. There was trouble with England and with a terrible man named Napoleon in France, whose warships were interfering with American shipping on the ocean. The American Federalists, Elizur Hubbard's party, had tried a plan of withholding commerce from both France and England, bringing hardship to the shipping and export interests of New England. The plan ultimately produced disaster, causing Gurdon's father and his teacher to be bitterly critical of President Jefferson for doing nothing and then of President Madison for wanting to do too much. When Madison summoned a congress of "war hawks" a month early and blamed the country's economic troubles on England, Elizur Hubbard angrily abandoned his party and became something of a Tory. This posture was not popular in Windsor, although many of the farmers in the surrounding area were pro-British and sold their farm produce to the British forces in Canada throughout the war of 1812.

Whatever the reason, Elizur Hubbard came ultimately upon hard times, while the town of Windsor continued to prosper. There was a boom in 1810 as British wool imports were shut off by embargoes or by interference on the high seas. Spinning mills were built in the Windsor area to meet the demand for American-made woolen cloth. This brought on the great Merino sheep speculation in which Elizur Hubbard participated by liquidating his other investments and by mortgaging his home. America had begun the importation of Merino sheep from Spain and France years earlier since they produced a high quality of wool. This importation was cut off by Napoleon's activity at the same time British imports dwindled. Since Merinos had done well in Vermont and new mills were being built, the men of Windsor dreamed of huge fortunes to be made as Merino wool prices rose to $2 a pound. Merino rams brought as much as $1,000 each in the Windsor market. The great Merino speculation crashed when Napoleon's armies conquered Spain, releasing 24,000 Merino sheep for export to America within a few months. The new American woolen mills earned profits until the War of 1812 ended, but speculators in the Merino craze by that time had lost fortunes. Elizur Hubbard found himself heavily in debt and in trouble with his creditors.

Elizur and Abigail were compelled to reduce their standard of living. Their decision to send Gurdon to live with a relative at Bridgewater, Massachusetts was a difficult one, but he was the eldest and there seemed to be no alternative. Gurdon left home sometime in 1812. "My Aunt Saltonstall invited me to her house and influenced her son-in-law, the Rev. Daniel Huntington, to take me and a boy of about my own age to educate." Gurdon wasn't proud of his educational achievements up to that time. "I cannot remember at what age I commenced going to school, but the fact of dislike of books up to the age of thirteen I do not forget. I was always pleading to be excused and my indulgent mother too often granted my request. I was often truant and escaped punishment."

The boy enjoyed his stagecoach trip to Bridgewater, where he was warmly welcomed. After a period of homesickness passed, he began to enjoy his studies. The Reverend Mr. Huntington taught his pupils how to write and to cipher to enable them to find jobs as clerks at an early age, in addition to instruction in religion, literature and history. He encouraged them to read any of the books in his library. Gurdon chose books of travel and adventure, and he read and re-read Alexander Henry's *Travels and Adventures in Canada and the Indian Territories between 1760 and 1776* until he had memorized parts of it.

Gurdon showed some aptitude for figures, progressed satisfactorily in his study of religion and church history, and was made acquainted with Latin and Greek. In his later years he referred often to his lack of education, bemoaning his failure to take greater advantage of his opportunity with the Reverend Mr. Huntington. "I was very deficient in my education," he wrote, "but the winter passed pleasantly and I made fair progress with my studies." He knew nothing of his father's business affairs at the time he left home, but letters from his mother indicated that Elizur had lost his property, including their home. Since Gurdon undoubtedly would be required to find a job after he left Aunt Saltonstall's house, he sought hard to prepare for it. He wrote a good hand, learned to clip his own quill pens, and kept records of an imaginary hardware store. He wrote regularly to his mother and said his greatest pleasure came from her replies. But Abigail's letters became increasingly depressed, hinting of more and more family troubles. He wished desperately to go home to Windsor to help out, but was not permitted to leave Bridgewater, even in summer.

"My father's misfortunes continued, and he became very poor, which I felt so keenly as to make me miserable and discontented," he wrote in later years. "When, in the following winter (1815), I learned that my father had fallen into still deeper trouble and had determined to go to Montreal, there to practice his profession, I was inconsolable; and as I had lost all interest in my studies I was promised I should return in the spring."

He took the stagecoach back to Windsor in mid-April. He found that his parents, brother and four sisters were living in a rented house, where his mother was packing for the journey to Canada. Gurdon learned little about his father's difficulties, but Elizur evidently was in deep trouble with creditors. It was not unusual at the time for a victim of such a situation to flee to the western lands, where a man could easily become lost, yet find a new beginning. Elizur Hubbard, however, had a wife and six children and was determined to continue his practice of law. He could not lose himself in the wilderness, which had no appeal for him in any event, but he believed there would be great opportunity for citizens of the United States, especially those of the state of Vermont, in Canada following the end of the war. However, although he had discussed with Abigail during the winter his decision to go to Montreal, as she had in turn mentioned it to Gurdon, he had not taken the precaution to discover whether opportunities for an American lawyer actually existed there. He was unaware that no American could enter the legal profession in Canada until five years of residency had passed. "About the first of May, 1815, (we) started for Canada," Gurdon wrote a half-century later. "On reaching Montreal, my father learned that he could not be admitted to practice, as he was an American citizen."

Probably the Hubbards took a Connecticut river freight boat to a point where they could join one of the Vermont wagon trains carrying poultry and cheese to Montreal. The farmers of northern Vermont regularly carried their produce to the city, disposing of it through the provision houses. It was with such farmers young Gurdon immediately found work in Montreal, bringing in the first income the family obtained in their new home city. Once Elizur had received the news that he could not practice law, and that jobs were not plentiful in any field, Abigail suggested that they should start a board and room house, where the children could help her with the work while her husband searched for some kind of employment related to law. Their boarding house was situated at a considerable distance from downtown, at the foot of Mount Royal, but there were other such boarding establishments in the neighborhood and they felt they could get a share of the business. They were aided and advised by an American friend in Montreal, Horatio Gates, owner of a cigar store on Notre Dame street, a grandson of the American general with whom Elizur Hubbard's father had served in the Revolutionary War. He promised to become one of the Hubbard boarders.

When Gurdon, then fourteen, told Horatio Gates he was sure he could earn income for the family by purchasing unsold produce which the Vermont farmers still had in their wagons when the Montreal market closed and they were ready to return home, Gates was interested. "What would you do with it?" he asked somewhat suspiciously, since he was about to become a paying boarder at the Hubbard table. "I'd peddle it house to house, while it was still fresh," the boy replied. "We could be eating the eggs for breakfast before the stores even opened." Horatio Gates was so impressed he loaned Gurdon his starting capital. "My first winter in Montreal I was employed in small traffic, buying from Vermont farmers the remnants of their loads of poultry, butter, cheese, etc., and peddling them, from which I realized from eighty to one hundred dollars, all of which went into the family treasury. The capital with which I embarked in this

18

enterprise was twenty-five cents, and was kindly loaned to me by Horatio Gates.''

*

The boy loved his new life in Montreal. Some travellers called it a cold city of greystone houses and cobblestone streets, ruled by stern Scots who had made their fortunes in the fur trade and then dominated the mercantile and banking community. But Gurdon Hubbard found Montreal a city of color, beauty, noise and excitement, especially along the river front, where, in summer, the brightly garbed *voyageurs* of the fur trade mingled with sailors from the warm-water ports of the Caribbean, the clipper crews of the Oriental trade, the steamboat men of the Montreal-Quebec run, the trading farmers from Vermont, the Indians and fur traders hailing from south along the Mississippi to the cold shores of Hudson's Bay. Gurdon made friends with his fellow-countrymen in the farmers' markets, the French-Canadian housewives in the vicinity of the great Cathedral, and the servant women of the frowning stone houses on the approaches to Mount Royal owned by the great merchants, the recently deceased James McGill and Simon McTavish, the Frobishers, Hutchisons, and Alexander Henry, author of his favorite book. Soon cooks and housewives welcomed the boy inside on cold mornings and they usually found something to buy. He learned needed words of French and sometimes met the masters of the houses, who spoke English and learned of his love of books, so that in time he was able to borrow volumes in English and in French from their libraries. He discovered that his hero, the author Henry, still lived on St. Laurent street, but had no luck in seeing him. He kept much to himself that winter, except for his customers, and after helping his mother in the boarding house, he found time for his new fascinating hobby, reading. He sought out Alexander Henry's fur warehouse on St. Paul street, but found it temporarily closed. His mind buzzed with adventures such as Henry had known among the Indians of the west, living under the stars with the *voyageurs,* visiting Indian towns, hunting bear, and crossing the wide prairies.

Financial conditions improved a bit that autumn for Elizur, who discovered that a new law passed by the American congress, limiting fur trading in the Northwest Territory of the

United States to American citizens, might work out to his advantage. John Jacob Astor of New York City, owner of the American Fur Company, acquired some Canadian firms and was using them and the new law to expand his activity in the trade which France and French Canada had dominated for almost two hundred years. Some asserted that Astor intended to have a monopoly of the fur trade in the United States. He acquired Canadian companies, continued to operate them under the management of French-Canadians and Scots who previously owned them, and learned the truth of Alexander Henry's contention that no one but the *habitants,* the farmers of French-Canada, could or would endure the hardships of the wilderness.

So Astor had authorized his managers to recruit *voyageurs,* clerks and fur traders in the provinces of Canada, especially Quebec province, as they had done in the past. But it would be necessary to draft all contracts and agreements according to American law and it would be desirable to obtain a genuine American or two for the employment roster when possible. Thus Elizur Hubbard, unable to practice law in Canada, found work with Montreal solicitors having clients in the fur trade, drafting needed papers for those intending to work in the American territories. Elizur's new income, and the prospering boarding house, enabled Gurdon's parents to think about a trade for him. In the summer of 1816 an appropriate apprenticeship was found with John Frothingham's hardware store at 51 St. Paul street on the river, about three miles from the Hubbard home. Frothingham supplied fur traders and marine interests in Montreal and he had many customers among the home owners of the city. He was a major importer of heavy hardware shipped from Liverpool and Barcelona. Gurdon visited the store, found it a fascinating place and John Frothingham a pleasant, kindly man.

The apprenticeship arranged for Gurdon represented a sacrifice by Elizur and the family, since they no longer would receive the money Gurdon had been able to earn with his provisions business. It developed that the boy had quit his peddling at the right time for his own interests, however, since 1816 became known in much of New England as "the year without a summer." Cold weather with snow and ice persisted into July, few crops grew and the Vermont farmers had no provisions to sell in Montreal. Under the apprenticeship agreement there would be no pay for Gurdon, but he would receive training to become a hardware clerk, his meals, and the privilege of sleeping on a counter in the store whenever he worked late, which was most nights. The cold summer deprived Montreal of needed farm produce but did not otherwise depress its commerce. The exportation of furs and the supplying of the fur trade continued to be the city's chief business. Despite wars which redisposed control of the American west to Spain, France, England and the United States successively, the merchants, bankers and exporters of Montreal and Quebec continued to dominate the fur trade, maintaining their hold in the American northwest even after the United States won full control of the area by the Treaty of Ghent in 1815. Not until three years later was Astor ready for a genuine attempt to establish a monopoly, sufficiently strong to buy out the Canadian companies, themselves weakened or doomed to extinction by the new American laws. Prior to that, Montreal's long dominance had not seemed threatened.

Frothingham's hardware, selling at wholesale to the fur traders, provisioners and mariners, and at retail to the residents of Montreal, continued to do a thriving business when Gurdon became the boy of the store in 1816. Elizur Hubbard had chosen well for the training of his son, who once had kept accounts for an imaginary hardware store in Massachusetts as a school assignment. Gurdon ran errands, unpacked crates of goods, assisted clerks, and, in time, performed services for the bookkeeper. He learned to know merchandise, from the fine steel of Sheffield and Seville, to kettles, bowls, iron vats and sugar mills and iron shoes for plows arriving from Liverpool and Rotterdam. He grew strong lugging and unpacking heavy hardware, carrying kegs of nails to their proper bins, moving barrels of iron traps and horseshoes and crates of guns and tomahawks with tempered iron blades. He learned the terms, in French and English, for goods intended for the wilderness areas, from thimbles to iron vats for boiling sugar and soap, needles and lace, fine cloth made by the Stroud Company in England, axes, saws, skinning knives, and the ochre and vermilion grease used by warriors preparing themselves for battle.

When Gurdon was not helping to unload ships, checking manifests, bashing open boxes and crates in the warehouse, or toting kegs of nails, he delivered goods along the waterfront and in the residential areas, returning to aid a clerk or to sort invoices. In the evening he swept the store. He soon became well accepted, especially among the clerks, who were impressed by his eagerness to learn and his ability to cipher and do sums better than most. Also he could read and write in English and was always ready to help them with language problems, while they in turn taught him the French phrases required in the business.

When Gurdon delivered hardware to various Frothingham customers, he sometimes received a tuppence or a shilling for his service and was at last able to buy, from a friend of Horatio Gates, a worn French copy of Henry's *Travels*. Since he knew the English edition well, reading Alexander Henry in French aided him in learning that language. The clerks, observing his method, brought their own books to loan to him. He read at the store, when the sweeping was done, since he was allowed the use of a whale oil lamp as much as he wished before rolling out his mat to sleep on the counter. In time he came to borrow books from masters of the mansions on St. Laurent Street, but never did he find Alexander Henry at home. The leather-bound volumes entrusted to him concerned his favorite subject, French exploration and discovery in North America, from the writings of Louis Joliet and Father Claude Allouez, who sought the route to China, to the works of Father Louis Hennepin, the Recollect missionary, who had served as chaplain to La Salle and was sent to explore the Upper Mississippi. He was fascinated by Hennepin's descriptions of the western prairies, Indian towns, the vast Great Lakes, and Niagara Falls. Despite his contentment with his hardware store job, he longed to travel with the *voyageurs,* to see for himself Niagara Falls, the Illinois prairie, the island of Michilimackinac, called by Henry "The island capital of the fur trade, richer in furs than any other part of the world." He yearned to visit Indian towns, to trap beaver, wisest of the animals, to hunt deer and bear.

*

Yet Montreal was an eminently satisfying town. Gurdon learned from the newspapers, English and French that he and his father read together, not only the latest accounts from wilderness areas related by traders arriving in the city, but also that Montreal itself was the greatest fur entrepot on earth, an island city shipping more furs to England, Europe and to China than any other port in the world, although, following the war, the number had been declining. He learned from his books the history of Montreal founded on the site of Hochelaga, an Indian village, by Maisonneuve in 1642. There was no real town there, though, until Samuel de Champlain, geographer to the King of France and founder of Quebec, moved up the St. Lawrence to create a flourishing settlement below the Lachine rapids. The village was called Mont Rial, the royal mountain, for the height looming above it.

René Robert Cavelier, Sieur de La Salle, made Montreal his base in 1667, the seat of his planned seigniory and the island center of the fur trade industry he began. He expected to recoup his fortune from the Indian trade, established Fort Miami on the St. Joseph river, and portaged to the Kankakee and Illinois rivers. In time he pushed to the Gulf of Mexico and claimed all the southern Mississippi country for his king, calling it Louisiana. La Salle gave France an empire in North America and created a flourishing trade responsible for most of North America's exports, but France let it all eventually slip away.

When he came across the writings of Father Louis Hennepin, Gurdon found La Salle's adventures, as described by the priest who accompanied him, almost as absorbing as those of Alexander Henry. He yearned to visit someday the scenes of La Salle's explorations, in the country of the Iroquois, in the land of the Miamis and Potawatomis, where La Salle built Fort Miami on the St. Joseph river, and on to the Far West, to "the river called the Illinois by us, but called Che-cau-gou by the savages," where Fort Crevecour was built, and on to the reaches of the Mississippi river and the Gulf of Mexico. Meantime he was content to have seen the *voyageurs* at work at Lachine, and to have a few words in French with them when they called at Frothingham's to pick up supplies for their outfits.

He enjoyed also his opportunities to leave the store for errands along the Montreal waterfront and expected that sooner or later he would be sent to Lachine on official business, and might even be allowed to board one of those *canots du maitre* which the *voyageurs* called "mackinaws." He relished the smells and delighted in the sounds and movement of his town as ships from Europe and the spice islands discharged their cargoes amid the throbbing traffic, the shriek and moan of boat whistles, the shouts of stevedores and draymen, the clattering hooves on the cobblestones, the bellowing of ships orders in a dozen tongues from French and English to Scandanavian. Sometimes he boarded those European freighters to help unload cargo for Frothingham's.

The nights when he slept at the store were punctuated by the noises of revelry of sailors, *voyageurs* down from Lachine, the wagoneers from Vermont, and the flatboatmen from Lake Champlain, all sampling the somewhat austere joys of a town dominated architecturally and morally by the Catholic cathedral and the English church, the courthouse, and the jail. The *voyageurs* and flatboatmen and sailors were a joyful, good-natured lot who fought only at night, mostly in the grog shops, where Gurdon saw little of the action, since he was required to watch the store. Nor did he often have money for the day-time delights of the waterfront, where the shops and brasseries smelled of good things, tamarinds and preserved ginger and dried fruits from the West Indies, great mugs of beer brewed in the south part of town, frying clams, Indian corn soup, roasting lamb, stewed acorns. Now and then a lost visitor or a drunken sailor would pass him a coin for acting as guide, or for cleaning a man's dirty boots—he learned to carry a cloth and soap for the latter service. Thus he could spare a copper for Indian corn soup, his favorite delicacy. What little he learned of night life in Montreal came from John Dyde, who had become his friend, or from talk among the sailors that he overheard.

John Dyde, three years older than Gurdon, was also the son of boardinghouse keepers. They met when Gurdon was peddling provisions and quickly became companions on Sunday excursions around Montreal, after Gurdon had attended the Protestant Episcopal church with his parents. John was big for his age, knew the town, spoke French as well as English. Gurdon, although lithe and strong from his work in the hardware store, was somewhat undersized. John Dyde had no interest in books but both boys longed for adventure and John loved to hear Gurdon's stories of life among the Indians, which he recited from Alexander Henry's accounts. They went to see the Henry house on St. Laurent, but they saw only an occasional servant in the yard; Mr. Henry evidently was rarely at home. In good weather they sometimes climbed to the top of Mount Royal and found a pleasant spot where they could watch the traffic on the blue St. Lawrence below, beyond the twin towers of the Cathedral, the spires of the English churches, and the Nelson monument rising above New Market. There England's great sea hero stood, head bare, a spyglass in hand, looking inland! Sailors and visitors from seaward generally were astonished to find that the British admiral had been positioned to gaze ever landward, toward the Montreal jail. But the boys, fascinated by lore of the West, understood. The old sea dog, Lord Nelson, had he been in Montreal in 1818, would of course have looked inland, toward the Indian territories, and have yearned for adventures there as they did. Far below, even on Sundays, there were smoking steamboats on the Quebec run, sleek sloops and fat schooners, flatboats and York boats under sail and oar, carrying food from Lake Champlain and furs from Michilimackinac. The river, and adventure, called to them.

The boys wanted to travel, anywhere, but if at all possible to Michilimackinac, where the Indians and the fur trade came together. If they found it necessary to settle for less, Gurdon thought he could find them a job on the *Malsham,* an enormous steamship which, according to the *Gazette,* had carried on a single trip the entire 104th Regiment and its equipment. Gurdon had helped unload goods from the *Malsham* and was making friends with the crew. But Sunday a week later, when he arrived at the Dyde's to help peel potatoes for the boarders, he had not yet had another opportunity to board the *Malsham* and he found his friend John Dyde in a high state of excitement. John confided that he expected to get a job, a real job as clerk with the American Fur Company at Michilimackinac! William Matthews, agent of the company in Montreal, boarded with the Dydes. Gurdon and John had seen Mr. Matthews in the Dyde dining room, but he paid no attention to them. However, Mr. Matthews had told Dyde's father that he was still in need of

25

clerks and John had convinced his father to apply for such a job for his son, his father had done so and Mr. Matthews was considering it!

Gurdon at once pleaded with John to put in a bid for him. John shook his head. Gurdon was too young. The magic age was eighteen. Gurdon was fifteen. "Almost sixteen!" Gurdon protested. "You'd have to get your parents' special permission," John Dyde said. "You know they would never let you go."

Thereafter Gurdon pleaded with John whenever they met to give him a chance to make his own bid to Mr. Matthews. He was strong from his work in the hardware store. He was as big as most *voyageurs*. They came to the store to take away merchandise and he could carry with the best of them. He could speak French well enough to conduct the *voyageur's* kind of business which was important, since Frothingham's handled a great deal of fur trade goods. John promised to ask his father to speak to Mr. Matthews and later visited the store bringing Mr. Matthews' response, "No boy under eighteen will be considered." Gurdon went home that night to his own father, who was drafting the very kind of indentures he wanted to sign. Some of the work undoubtedly was for Mr. Matthews. He begged Elizur for help. He would be sixteen in August, he was strong if not big for his age, he handled bills of lading and did at the store the kind of work a fur company clerk in all probability would do at Mackinac. He recited the items received at Frothingham's that very day, from his own record of the invoices: 200 boxes of sheet iron, 220 boxes of tin plate, 10 tons of hoop iron, six tons of Crowley Shear Steel, 300 casks nails, 200 casks horseshoes, 4000 iron pots; also camp ovens, sugar kettles, sauce pans, tinned pots, sickles, sledges, anvils, plough-share moulds, crates of crockery, casks of wine and salt, cashmeres, Stroud blankets and threads. This cargo would eventually go to Mackinac Island he was sure, to Little York, to the Indian towns along the St. Lawrence, and to towns on the Ohio river. He had exactly the training Mr. Matthews was looking for, the boy insisted, and he was strong enough to stand any hardship.

Elizur Hubbard well knew that the kind of training his son had begun at Frothingham's was precisely what William Matthews required. He also knew that Gurdon was much too young.

"Do you know what a *voyageur* would get to eat?" his father demanded. "A pint of dried peas and a stick of tallow each day! Is that what you want? To sleep on the ground and work seven days a week? Are you mad? No son of mine will live that way." Elizur Hubbard assumed the matter was ended, but Gurdon's campaign for permission to apply to Mr. Matthews for a job was unremitting. His mother was appalled. His father was adamant. He made no progress. His cause wasn't helped when his father found in his files a copy of *Le Canadian Spectateur* reporting on a departure of *voyageurs* and clerks the previous spring, from which he translated for them: "On a recent Sunday a brigade of canoes bound for Michilimackinac started from Lachine when they were struck by a violent gust of wind near Pointe Claire. The lead boat was swamped, three boys were drowned, including two young brothers, Pierre and Joseph Cheval. The body of Louis Delorme was not recovered." Abigail shuddered at that year-old report, but Elizur was not finished. He had a fresh dispatch from the Indian country to the Montreal *Herald* which he read as the clincher: "A gentleman has arrived in the city from Sault Ste. Marie with a very disagreeable report from the Red River settlement. A dispute had arisen between Indians and some of the Hudson's Bay Company officers about an escort of provisions and the parties came to blows. In the contest, twenty one of the Hudson's Bay Company people were killed." And, for good measure, another report: "A party of Hudson's Bay traders, about twenty in number, were wintering on the Arathepascow Lake and it has now been learned that seventeen of them have perished from lack of provisions." Did Gurdon Hubbard, a mere child, think he could survive such hardships? Did he realize a clerk's indenture with the American Fur Company was for five years?

After such an onslaught Gurdon had no hope of persuading his mother to help. His depression and frustration became evident to the clerks at Frothingham's, so that Mr. West, his immediate superior who had befriended him, asked what his trouble might be with such solicitude that Gurdon broke down, weeping. "I told him my problem," he recalled. " 'Why, Gurdon, you don't want to go among the Indians,' West said. 'What a fool you are to think so. Stick by us and rise as you are sure

27

to do. Mr. Frothingham has not a word to say against you. He knows you have done your duty and in time will advance you.' Just then Mr. Frothingham came in and, noticing me, asked what was the matter. When West told him, he said I had a foolish notion."

That decided Gurdon. He requested leave of absence from the store for the rest of the day, and walked the three miles to his home. There he told his mother what had happened, repeating his account to Elizur when he arrived. "Boy, you are crazy!" his father exclaimed. "Crazy or not," Gurdon answered, "I want to go with Mr. Matthews if he will take me."

Such intemperance won him a reprimand, but then his father turned the problem over to Abigail, as he usually did when he became exasperated. "If your mother is willing, you can go to see Mr. Matthews," Elizur said. Abigail urged her son to wait until morning for her decision. Gurdon knew that she wished to pray over it, and he said a fervent prayer himself.

The following morning his parents agreed their son could apply for the job. He guessed that they had discussed it and decided that Mr. Matthews would certainly refuse to hire him. They were almost right.

William Matthews was a gruff, bulky man who recognized the boy on sight when Gurdon came to his office two days later. He was incredulous when Gurdon asked for a job as a clerk and spilled out his qualifications. The boy's father and mother had been at the office the day before, when Elizur had made out the last of the indentures for Matthew's recruitment quota, including his complement of twelve clerks. He didn't require another, though Gurdon Hubbard met his training specifications better than any boy he had hired. "You are too young and too soft," said Matthews. "There is nothing heavier than a keg of nails," Gurdon answered. "I carry them every day. I walk miles." The tough Scot, who had walked overland from Astor's ill-fated Astoria post in Oregon, most of the way to St. Louis, took another look at the boy. He understood the parents' ploy and he liked the lad's spunk. "Gurdon," he said, "if you can bring me written permission from your parents, I will engage you for five years and pay you $120 a year. This is more on account of John Dyde than anything else, as he wants you to go with him."

Chapter 1

Gurdon was jubilant. "I knew the negotiation was ended as I had my father's word, which never failed," he wrote later. "I sought my father and reported. He and my mother were sorely disappointed and grieved, but offered no further opposition. The agreement was soon thereafter signed and I drew $50, which my mother expended for my outfit."

Thus began actual preparation for the trip by freight canoe to Michilimackinac, scheduled to start at Lachine in mid-May. Each clerk would be allowed a small wooden chest and linen engagé bag for his outfit which, in Gurdon's case, included in addition to a buckskin shirt and leggings and moccasins and calico undershirts and cloth for breech-clouts, all acquired from the company itself, a swallow-tail coat and broadcloth pants and vest. Gurdon had not owned such regalia previously and insisted it would hardly be required in Indian country, but his mother assured him that a decent suit would someday be needed, even in the West. She had caused the broadcloth suit to be made much too large so that he might grow into it. She packed it into his chest, together with pairs of woolen socks—she had no confidence in the neips the company provided, squares of cloth worn under the moccasins in lieu of stockings—a box of Barclay's British Tooth Powder and a package of King's Odontalgic, in case of toothache. But the boy drew the line when his mother undertook to include Pullen's Purging Pills and a container of epsom salts recommended by John Beckett, the family's druggist. He was limited to sixty pounds and, beyond his broadcloth suit and mouth-care supplies, he would take nothing not to be found in John Dyde's outfit.

Gurdon kept back his tears when he said goodbye to his mother and sisters at the boarding house on the morning of May 13. He felt he would not see them again for five years. His father and brother Christopher accompanied him to City Tavern, where they took the stage to Lachine, along with John Dyde and other Montreal boys among the complement of thirteen clerks. At Lachine thirteen mackinaws were drawn up in the small harbor. *Voyageurs* in blue shirts, buckskin leggings and red-tassled caps were swarming over them, loading the last of the freight and sea chests and rigging the ensigns, flags and banners to be flown for their departure. Each *canot du maître,* except the lead boat, was thirty-five feet long, a bit over five feet in beam, and would carry a crew of eight oarsmen or paddlers, an *avant bout,* or conductor at the bow, and a *gouvernail,* or helmsman at the stern. In the distance lay a huge mackinaw, fifty feet in length and about seven feet wide, already dressed in flags and bunting. This, the boys learned, was the command boat, that would carry in addition to its crew of twelve *voyageurs,* Mr. Matthews himself, as *le bourgeois,* a Scotchman named Wallace, in direct charge of the expedition, and John Dyde and Gurdon Hubbard.

Gurdon and John knew that they were being specially favored by Mr. Matthews. Their boat was one of the new mackinaws built on Mackinac Island, constructed of wood rather than birch-bark, made of cedar, with a flat bottom and high bows and sharp, sloping sides, using oars and poles rather than the paddles employed to propel the rest of the *batteaux.* It was a kind of York boat, Gurdon's father explained, expected to become popular on the St. Lawrence, as the happy combination of a Lake Champlain flatboat and an Indian birchbark canoe. Matthews welcomed the boys. Wallace, busy with details, seemingly paid them no attention. But when he at last saw Gurdon, he nodded and smiled. "He was one of the party sent by Mr. Astor to the Columbia river on an expedition which was broken up by the War of 1812." Gurdon remembered. "He, with others, returned overland, their vessel, having been attacked by Indians, was blown up by one of the men aboard. He was a man of large experience and great energy and capacity and, like most Scotchmen, a strict disciplinarian, with a powerful will and undaunted courage."

Soon after nine o'clock, Wallace gave the command, "To boats all," and the jaunty crews boarded and pushed off. Then Matthews, as *Le Bourgeois* of the expedition, began the boat song, *"La Violette Dandon":*

> *Quand j'etais chez mon Pere*
> *Petite Janeton*
> *Il m'envoyait a la fontaine*
> *Pour pecher du poisson.*
> *La Violette Dandon, Oh! La Violette dondé.*

Gurdon vividly recalled that day in his *Recollections* written sixty-two years later in 1880: "The *voyageurs* in Mr. Matthews' boat started the boat song, which was joined in by all the *voyageurs* and clerks in the expedition. Stout arms and brave hearts were at the oars and the boats fairly flew through the blue waters of the St. Lawrence. . . . I cannot describe my feeling as I looked upon the forms of my father and my brother. . . . Nor did I, until that time, realize my situation or regret my engagement. The thought that I might never again see those most dear to me filled my soul with anguish. Bitter tears I could not help shedding, nor did I care to."

John Dyde looked upon his young companion with some astonishment. Dyde was thoroughly enjoying his experience. In a half hour the brigade was ordered ashore *"pour la pipe";* to smoke, rest and take lunch, which consisted of wine, crackers and cheese for *Le Bourgeois* Matthews, Wallace and the clerks, and for the *voyageurs* themselves, their usual pea soup and tallow. The *voyageurs* then stripped down to their working uniforms, breech-clout, buckskin leggings, neips and moccasins. The festive rigging which had dressed the boats for departure was stowed and the brigade paddled, rowed and poled up the St. Lawrence, against its powerful current, until four o'clock in the afternoon when Matthews and Wallace decided upon an early halt. The crew was having trouble with the big mackinaw, loaded with almost fifteen tons of freight, more than double the cargo of a large *canot du maître.*

While the *voyageurs* aboard the big boat re-stowed the freight for better buoyancy, Gurdon and John Dyde explored the riverbank and the canoes drawn up a considerable distance along the shore as their crews prepared for the night. Ordinarily the veterans did not even speak to the newcomers, the pork eaters *(mangeurs de lard),* but neither did they bar John and Gurdon from inspecting their *batteaux.* Gurdon was proud of his knowledge of Alexander Henry's book and he recalled the details of Henry's specifications for building a freight canoe: "The craft is formed of birchbark one-fourth-inch thick, lined lengthwise with small splints of cedar wood . . . strengthened with ribs of the same material, of which two ends are attached to the gunwhales. The small roots of a spruce tree supply the place of tar and oakum . . . spare wattap and gum are always carried in each

31

canoe." Gurdon asked a *voyageur* about the wattap, and was shown a bundle of spruce root, used for repairs. The cedar thwarts on which the men sat were slung from leather thongs. The eight paddlers sat crosslegged, like tailors at work, as did passengers. The *"bout"* on the bow of each boat was called the guide, or conductor, and was paid double the $100 a year paid to *engages* who paddled, rowed, poled, sailed, and sometimes carried the huge canoes.

"Our boat ain't birchbark," John Dyde said.

"No," Gurdon agreed. "My father said it is the kind they use in the west. They're trying it out from Montreal to Michilimackinac. It hauls three times as much."

"The men don't like it," John said. "They say nobody can get it over the portages." John understood the Quebec *patois* of the *voyageurs.*

"They got it down to Montreal."

"That was with the current," John said. "Now we're going agin it. The men don't like it."

They saw rabbits below a bluff, killed them with rocks and brought back five, John Dyde remembering that Mr. Matthews had liked fresh game at his family table. He was right. When the boys had dressed and roasted the meat, Matthews and Wallace had first choice, as was customary for the commanders of an expedition, and the clerks shared the remainder as an addition to their ration of peas and salt pork, they were momentary heroes. They concluded they would continue to do the hunting for the expedition and in the days following made slings and nets for that purpose.

The brigade moved out at dawn the next morning and the day went better. The cargo of the giant mackinaw and the freight canoes shook down satisfactorily and the contrary current eased. Gurdon and John became acquainted with the nature of their cargo, bales of goods wrapped in oil cloth, weighing eighty to one hundred pounds each, the maximum a man could handle on a treacherous portage. In addition to the bales for the trade, well protected against weather, each canoe carried dried peas and tallow and pork for *voyageurs* and clerks, with additional delicacies such as tea and coffee and flour and honey for the "bosses" and to supply the Sunday ration of pancakes and honey for all the men. Vital to the success of a trip was the provision of tobacco for the *voyageurs,* who stopped every six to eight miles when they were rowing or paddling, and not under sail, to smoke and rest, and the supply of eight gallons of rum for each canoe, rationed to last the journey.

The trade goods carried into Indian country in an ordinary *canot du maître* of six tons burden was worth about 500 to 600 livres, French pounds, or $1,200 to $1,440 at the time Alexander Henry made his trips and published his book in 1809. There had been little change since. Once at Mackinac Island, such a cargo increased in value to between $1,500 and $1,700. Converted into beaver pelts, worth $1 each in Henry's day, he estimated that the profit on a cargo of trade goods could range from 100 to 200 per cent and more if the Indians were cheated by the traders, as they often were. Now under the new American law, with which Matthews and his associates would cope, not only were foreigners excluded but the United States government opened "factories" to trade with the Indians, in competition with the companies, the factors, or managers, being instructed to fix prices and to restrict the amount of liquor any Indian could receive. These rules reduced the profits from the fur trade. Consequently, Astor's Scotch managers at Mackinac Island sought to lower costs and hoped to do so by using mackinaw boats that could carry double or triple the freight of a *canot du maître.* Matthews and Wallace and their brigade were in the midst of this experiment on the St. Lawrence run. Their new huge mackinaw, loaded with furs, had moved down the river to Lachine satisfactorily; going upstream and through rapids with a cargo less accommodating than furs, the heavy hardware of trade goods, was another matter.

Within days the problems became acute. The big boat was slowing the entire brigade and they were increasingly behind schedule. The men resented their hard duty at the oars, the conductor and helmsman had trouble keeping the craft headed into the current and all dreaded the portages ahead. In addition many of the farm lads recruited as *voyageurs* found the work more difficult than they expected, the food inadequate and the discipline exceptionally onerous. As the brigade proceeded through an area of French-Canadian farms and Indian towns, the disaffected men took advantage of the opportunities to desert. Gurdon and John Dyde in the emergency had volunteered to help with the rowing and poling of the big boat. The rest of the clerks were assigned to guard duty at night to stop the desertions. For this they were much resented by all the *voyageurs.*

"Our boats were heavy laden and our progress up the swift St. Lawrence was necessarily slow," Gurdon Hubbard recorded in his *Incidents and Events* published in 1888. "Some days when we had rapids to overcome, three to five miles was a full day's journey. And when the rapids were heavy, the crews of three and sometimes four boats were alloted to one, seven or eight of the men being in the water pushing and pulling to keep the boat sheering into the current, the rest on shore pulling on a rope attached to the bow. Yet, with all this force, the current at times was so strong the boat would scarcely move; and the force of the current would raise the water . . . even over the top of the boat. (Often) men and boat were dragged back until they found an eddy and chance to rest. The work was severe . . . from early morning until night, with only an hour at noon."

Desertions increased and Mr. Matthews multiplied the guard to stop them. As more men were missing, the work load grew. The recruits, including Hubbard and Dyde, could not stand the hard labor continuously and were allowed occasionally to walk into the countryside, where Gurdon and John were successful in killing game, some of which they traded, together with trinkets allowed them by Matthews, to the farms in the area in exchange for maple sugar candy, which they brought back to be distributed among the crews. But the clerks who stood watch at night were the enemies of the *voyageurs.*

The situation worsened as the brigade passed into unusually heavy rapids, where the lead mackinaw became almost totally unmanageable. Men from the following canoes were required to join the crew of Matthews' boat in pushing and hauling the huge wooden craft up swift currents and across rocky shallows, doing this work after they had portaged cargo and their own canoes. More than half the men detailed to the big mackinaw spent the long day in the near-freezing water, pushing and pulling, straining at the bow to keep the unwieldy craft into the current and away from the rocks. The *voyageurs* hated that boat.

Chapter 1

They fought it, cursed it, exhausted themselves, resting only when those on the ropes and poles could hold the mackinaw steady; then they began again. They cursed the company, the day they were born, their mothers' milk, and the madmen who forced upon them the lumbering mackinaw. They swore to desert in the night and to kill anyone who stood in the way.

At nightfall the grumpy, exhausted men took their pea soup and tallow in sullen silence, only a few veterans attempting to cheer them with humor and a promise that the worst might be almost over. They roused themselves momentarily when a veteran summarized the common view. "The man who built that boat," he said, "without doubt farted away his brains at an early age." They dried themselves and warmed themselves by fires built near the windbreaks they made of boats and tarpaulins to fend off the wind, cold even in early June, nursed their ration of rum, pulled on their pipes and sulked. Most were too tired to revolt or desert. They stretched on mats made of reeds and branches with a blanket for cover and slept through the pain of bruises and aching muscles. Not far away the dogs of an Indian village howled, probably at another deserter from Matthews' Montreal brigade.

As they moved into calmer and deeper waters a few days below Little York, the work eased and the brigade began averaging fifteen miles a day. Progress continued to be hampered however by further desertions. Wallace, a stern disciplinarian who was credited with bringing back his men through a killing winter in the Snake River country of the west on the return from Oregon, despaired of ending the near mutiny. Matthews summoned a meeting of his aides, the boat conductors and his trusted veterans, to announce a decision to change their route. "Instead of passing through Lake Erie by the way of Buffalo, as had been intended, we would proceed overland from Little York (Toronto) to Lake Simcoe," Gurdon recorded, "thus reaching the Nottawasaga river by a portage, and thence proceeding through Nottawasaga Bay into Lake Huron, and coasting the north shore of Lake Huron to Mackinac Island."

Matthews explained that the new route represented a short cut. Gurdon knew, from his father's explanation of Mr. Matthews' situation in Montreal, that the brigade was somewhat late in starting and it clearly had lost time after departing Montreal. Matthews had with him much of the trade goods needed at Mackinac before the various brigades could depart for their wilderness posts. He also had a dwindling supply of required *voyageurs* and clerks. The early explorers had used the route Matthews and Wallace now proposed and had even left records of the numbers of paces required for the Lake Simcoe area portages. Nevertheless the short cut would be a difficult one and all wondered how Matthews and Wallace would solve the problem of portaging the big mackinaw. Gurdon knew that the route from Little York, a village of three hundred, was near to the one used by Alexander Henry and somewhat on the pattern of that used by Champlain, La Salle and other emplorers, who went west on the Ottawa river, then entered the French river south into Georgian Bay. But those voyages were made with relatively light freight canoes. "The canoe is the only vessel which can be employed on this course," Henry had written. He said much the same of the St. Lawrence: "The St. Lawrence for several miles immediately above Montreal descends with a rapid current over a shallow, rocky bed, insomuch that even canoes themselves, when loaded, cannot resist the stream." The American Fur Company bosses evidently had not read Alexander Henry.

But Mr. Matthews had learned the truth of it. He had made the run with a large, new mackinaw of a kind Alexander Henry had not seen. He had accomplished it, but he wanted no more of it. They were a month late. And, Gurdon Hubbard suspected, they had decided to cross overland to Lake Simcoe and thence to follow the route of the early explorers to stop desertion. No one would contemplate escape in the rugged, dreary country along what was called Yonge's street west out of Little York. They were a month late, needed to hurry, and they waited expectantly for Matthews and Wallace to solve the problem at Little York. Matthews did it by purchasing wagons and yokes of oxen. He loaded the goods onto the carts, sent the carts and their drivers with the clerks to Lake Simcoe to establish a camp, then had the drivers return oxen and carts to Little York. There the carts were rolled under the large mackinaw, attached to it, and a harness was devised for the oxen to pull the craft on wheels across the roadless, rocky wilderness to Lake Simcoe. The clerks remained in camp on Lake Simcoe for two weeks until all of the cargo and boats were transported and loaded again on that clear and beautiful lake. Then, to the amazement of all, Matthews ordered two yoke of cattle into the big mackinaw for transportation across the lake. There was another, shorter, but more difficult portage coming up.

"We struck camp and proceeded to the other end (of Lake Simcoe) where the goods and the boats, with the help of the oxen, made the Nottawasaga portage into the river of the same name," Gurdon wrote. "Though this portage was only six miles, we were a week conveying our goods and boats across. We were in uninhabited wilderness over the low swamp lands . . . we were nearly devoured by mosquitoes and gnats. . . . Desertion among the men had ceased, for the very good reason that there was no chance to escape."

All went well after the portage was completed. Men recruited at Little York to replace deserters worked out well. The gentle current of the Nottawasaga river carried the boats easily on its course to the bay. *Voyageurs,* who doubted that mackinaws were ever intended to transport live oxen, plied their oars steadily and the cattle placidly stood in the center of the craft as Mr. Matthews predicted they would. "The worst of the journey was now over," Gurdon wrote. "With lightened hearts the *voyageurs* again lifted their voices and joined in the melodious boat songs. We descended the river to Lake Huron, which we coasted." Matthews could tell his associates at Mackinac all they needed to know about the big mackinaws, they were satisfactory going down river from Lake Ontario to Montreal, but of little use, or none at all, on return. The Indian freight canoes, carrying four tons of cargo, whether called North canoes, or mackinaws, or *canots du maître,* thereafter would continue to carry the freight from Montreal to Mackinac.

The afternoon of July 3, Matthews' Montreal Brigade came within sight of the island, lying to the southwest like a large dark turtle on the skyline. The Indians called it Michilimackinac, meaning "Great Turtle." The French pronounced it Mackinac, as they spelled it; the British and Americans called it Mackinaw. Early in the afternoon they landed at Goose Island, since the eight miles of open water to the big island was considered too rough for crossing, especially with oxen aboard the lead boat. "However," Gurdon recalled, "as the island abounded in gulls' eggs, we spent an agreeable evening around our camp fires, feasting on them."

2

July 4, 1818

At the time of our arrival on Michilimackinac, all the traders from the North and Great West had reached the island with their returns of furs collected from the Indians during the previous winter. . . . This island was the headquarters of the American Fur Company, and here I first learned something of the working and discipline of that mammoth corporation, and took my first lessons in the life of an Indian trader. . . .

Recollections,
Gurdon S. Hubbard

They were up in early dawn, washed in the cold clear water of Lake Huron, breakfasted, then dressed themselves and their boats in finery for the triumphant entry onto Mackinac Island. As the sun rose they heard the guns of the fort firing a salute. The *voyageurs* cheered, sure they were being welcomed, since they had seen a crowd gathering on the high bluffs of the eastern shore. Gurdon Hubbard, the lone American in the Montreal brigade, thought he knew better. The crowd on the bluffs might have gathered for them but the garrison at the fort was beginning its celebration of July 4, the birthday of the United States of America forty-two years earlier. "We all prepared to celebrate," he recalled, "not so much in commemoration of the day, as of our joy at the sight of that beautiful island where our wearisome voyage was to end, thankful that we had been brought in safety, without accident, through so many difficulties and perils."

They were seven weeks out of Montreal, well behind schedule and impatient to cross to Mackinac, but a strong west wind was blowing. Not until two o'clock did Matthews give the signal to start and Wallace called the command: "To the boats, all!" The high wind continued. Passage across open water took nearly three hours, they were unable to round the point of the island

and landed instead under the high bluffs at "Robinson's Folly."

There Ramsey Crooks, the stern and dignified manager of the American Fur Company, and his youthful assistant, Robert Stuart, were awaiting them, since they had anticipated the difficulty of the crossing. They were accompanied by *voyageurs,* company clerks, traders on the island for the summer, some of the wives of the *voyageurs* in the Brigade, and several Indians, all who could make their way down from the bluffs and onto the narrow beach. They received a warm welcome, though Crooks betrayed his chagrin at Matthews' long delay even as he expressed his relief at their safe arrival. Obviously, Matthews would be called upon for a few explanations as soon as the brigade was ashore.

That night they camped on the rocky shelf below the bluffs, Mr. Matthews and Wallace entertaining their superiors at mess, in which the clerks participated. As the usual supper of pea soup and salt pork was finished, Wallace broke out cheese, crackers and wine, while Matthews presented the *bouts* of the Brigade, the men at the bow and stern of the *batteaux,* and the company clerks. Ramsey Crooks stared long and hard at Gurdon Hubbard as he grasped the boy's hand and cast an inquiring glance at Matthews. "Gurdon Hubbard comes especially recommended," Matthews said. Possibly Ramsey Crooks was remembering his own beginning in the fur trade, when there was no company requirement that a recruit must be eighteen years old. Now a sturdy man of middling height and ample girth, his tousled black hair, large dark eyes, prominent cheekbones and large nose suggested he must have appeared remarkably like the boy now before him when he arrived in Montreal from Scotland at the age of sixteen in 1803.

Crooks no longer looked as grim as he had on meeting the boats. He shook Gurdon's hand warmly. "Come to see me," he invited. "I have a young helper about your age who will show you around. His name is John Kinzie." Gurdon nodded happily. He was not to be put down, or even sent back, because of his age. Mr. Crooks presented him to his senior aide, Robert Stuart, who reminded the boy of a painting he had seen in Montreal of a young English nobleman, tall and elegant, thin-faced with broad forehead and frosty blue eyes. Mr. Stuart was quiet and friendly, easy for the clerks to meet. Later, as they heard the company lore, Gurdon learned the stories of Crooks and Stuart.

In 1804, when he was not yet seventeen, Ramsey Crooks had been sent by his employer, John Gillespie, a Montreal merchant and fur exporter, to St. Louis to learn the bartering end of the fur trade. Crooks followed the trade along the Missouri river, setting up posts for Gillespie despite the efforts of the Missouri Fur Company to drive him out. John Jacob Astor, born in the German village of Waldorf, was introduced into the fur import business when he was sixteen by an uncle in London and worked briefly in the fur business in New York before starting his own American Fur Company in 1809. A year later, June 23, 1810, he organized the Pacific Fur Company and the following April established a trading fort called Astoria on the Pacific Coast at the mouth of the Columbia River. By this time he had recruited Crooks and Robert Stuart. Stuart, born in Scotland but educated in Paris, was with Astor's chief competitor, the Northwest Fur Company, organized in Montreal by the Frobishers, McTavishes and the Mackenzies, when Astor lured him away. Crooks and Stuart became Astor's partners in the Pacific Fur Company. When Astor's Pacific fur operations came upon troubled times because of British competition and difficulties with the Indians, Astor sent his new partners to the Astoria post, Stuart traveling on the *Tonquin* around the Horn, Crooks going overland from St. Louis.

Both Stuart and Crooks reached Astoria via their separate routes only to find that the trading company was in greater difficulty than anticipated. Although President Jefferson and his cabinet had encouraged Astor to engage in the fur trade in territory claimed by England, they did not support the effort with American influence or arms. When the *Tonquin* departed Astoria for Vancouver Island, it was ambushed by Indians and the crew massacred. Crooks and Stuart felt compelled to abandon the Pacific Coast project and departed overland with sixty-one men. The British army took over Astoria, renaming it Fort George. Crooks and Stuart ran into severe weather in the Snake River country and became the first white men of record to winter there, Stuart refusing to go on when Crooks became critically ill. After many months of hardship, during which they chewed on beaver skins when their food ran out, they reached the Missouri river and St. Louis.

Astor was determined to recoup his humiliation and losses following the War of 1812. Crooks and Stuart had formed the Southwest Fur Company in St. Louis in 1813 and he persuaded them to join his American Fur Company after the United States Congress passed the law forbidding foreigners to engage in the fur trade in American territory. They then took over the management of the Astor interest in the Great Lakes and Mississippi Valley areas and sent William Matthews to Montreal, "to engage *voyageurs* from the *habtans* (sic) of Canada," specifically seeking "young, active, athletic men who could pass under the inspection of a surgeon." He was also "to purchase at Montreal such goods as were suited to the trade to load his boats, principally the Canadian *batteaux*, carrying about six tons each."

It was when Matthews' orders were modified, to the extent that the freight canoes were overloaded and he was required to take the monster mackinaw, a boat used successfully on the Missouri, and could carry two yoke of oxen in an emergency, that the Scotch managers ran into trouble. It was that trouble they discussed under the bluffs of Robinson's Folly as they sipped wine and drew on their pipes the night of July 4, 1818.

*

What had been done on the Missouri river they could not do on the St. Lawrence, they all agreed that night. The Missouri-type mackinaw, built of hand-sawn cedar, could carry up to fifteen tons of freight, but was unwieldly against the St. Lawrence current and shoals, whereas the biggest of the birchbark freight canoes performed well and could be portaged by men. "When we must carry oxen for the portage we of course carry less cargo," Matthews said, an understatement that caused even Crooks to chuckle. They agreed that the cedar mackinaws could be used only for special services. The *canots du maitre* would continue to be the workhorse, especially on the St. Lawrence and at the most difficult of all portages at Chicago. "I am sure Antoine Deschamps would agree with this," Stuart said. Again chuckles. Deschamps, the most experienced and venerable of them all, had insisted that only freight canoes could be used at

Chicago "until the canal is dug." "He will live a hundred years just to see that canal," Crooks said.

Crooks and Stuart concluded to stay the night at Robinson's Folly and to accompany the brigade to the fur company landing in the morning. They wanted to see for themselves the cargo problems for the big mackinaw when oxen were of necessity included. "Let us go in fully dressed," Crooks said. "All Michilimackinac is eager to welcome you, even to the soldiers at the fort. Let us do it properly." And Gurdon heard the orders for Matthews that would change his life. "We will make up lost time by working all warehouse details extra hours the rest of the summer," Crooks told Matthews. "You will be in charge. Deschamps has returned from Quebec and he will help you. We can now send our furs directly to Buffalo by steamship. When the furs are ready, the steamship *Walk-in-the-Water* will be at our dock to receive them."

They were all up late that evening, as the sun dropping behind Mackinac Island continued to light the westward sky until well past 9 o'clock. Maxwell summoned his conductors and helmsmen to inform them that they would go into Mackinac in full regalia in the morning. "Step the stern masts and show our linen," he directed in French. Gurdon looked wonderingly at John Dyde, who shrugged. It was an order they had not heard before, but they learned its meaning in the morning. In addition to the sailing mast on the bow, a small mast was raised at the stern to carry a line on which would be hung, in addition to flags and bunting, Stroud calico and blankets, exhibits from the eagerly awaited cargo from Montreal. The cloth and blankets, woven by the Stroud company in England, held its dyes well and was especially prized by Indian women in vivid reds and green and was worn also by chiefs and warriors on ceremonial occasions. The stolid oxen in the lead boat were draped with garlands of hemlock branches and flowers.

They dressed with special care that morning, red tassled *capots,* red or blue shirts, depending on their order in the procession of canoes, buckskin leggings attached to the white sashes that also supported their otter skin pouches for flint and punk and their knives and tomahawks, the only weapon *voyageurs* carried. The clerks dressed as much like the *voyageurs* as they dared, but as sashes and bright colored shirts were not permitted, they kept to drab cloth near the color of buckskin. Nor did they have the white gaiters used by the *voyageurs* to snug down their neips above their deerskin moccasins. Matthews inspected them and told them he was proud of them. They were the first brigade to arrive from Montreal in full dress under the new company. Matthews himself marked the occasion by wearing a long blue coat with gold buttons and a tricorn hat decorated with red and gold braid so that he resembled a French admiral.

"*Marche au large, mes gens!*" Mr. Wallace called. Then, in French and in English, the familiar "To the boats, all!" With a shout, the men responded. The long line of freight canoes formed behind the lead boat, white waves gently spanking the narrow line of beach under the bluffs, the sun blaring across the blue water, lighting up the flags and Stroud cloth in a dazzling display of color. Above the ensign of the command boat flew the company flag on this morning. Crooks and Wallace joined with them as Mr. Matthews began the boat song:

> *Michaud est monte dans un prunier*
> *Pour treller des prunes. . . .*

The men responding:

> *Michaud a tombee?*

The fate of Michaud, who climbed into a plum tree and fell, or did not fall, was hilariously aired across the water, announcing to all Michilimackinac the arrival of boats almost seven weeks out of Montreal laden with goods from Liverpool, Le Havre and New York, Savannah and Barcelona, and with rum from the South Seas. The silly children's song was a favorite of the tough *voyageurs,* springing from the childhood of their ancestors, and it had helped to power the boat trains carrying merchandise from civilization into the remotest wilderness of America for almost two centuries. Now the beat sent the *batteaux* racing westward along the green Michilimackinac coast, the sea cobalt under the rising July sun, as they all sang in chorus:

> *Oh, reveille, reveille, reveille,*
> *Oh, reveille, Michaud est en haut.*

Chapter 2

The fort responded with the pounding of guns. They skimmed swiftly below the spray-splashed coast, Gurdon feeling a jolt of pride and pleasure as he glimpsed the flag of the United States flying high above the whitewashed walls, pickets and blockhouses of the fort on the hill above the green slope of the island. Men on the east and south walls shouted and there were shouts from the blockhouse and from the balcony of the officers' quarters. Women of the fort fluttered ribbons and kerchiefs and cheered them. Beyond the pickets of the fort, halfway down the island toward the waterfront, Gurdon saw the tall buildings of the American Fur Company, new and gleaming white, and below them the boatyard and docks, their destination. On high ground to the west spread the summer tepees and the lodges of a large Indian village. Mr. Matthews had told them there were more than 3,000 Indians on the island that summer, in addition to *voyageurs* and a village of permanent inhabitants and retired *voyageurs*. It appeared that the entire population, except those required at the fort, had come to the waterfront to welcome the Montreal Brigade.

Ramsey Crooks and Robert Stuart had departed Matthews' flagship early, using their own small passenger canoe, and they were now at the landing, flanked by officers from the fort and Indian chiefs. The formal ceremonies were brief, so that unloading of the cargo could be completed and the trade goods stored inside the warehouse that day. Young John Kinzie and other company clerks came early to the docks to make sure that choice goods intended for immediate sale should go at once up to the store in the cluster of company buildings. Matthews took time out to present Gurdon Hubbard to Kinzie, a tall, fair, blue-eyed boy, eager to make friends. Kinzie and Gurdon agreed to meet again that evening. "I live with Mr. Stuart at the Agency house," John Kinzie said. "It's next door to the clerks' dormitory. I expect you'll work unloading. When you are finished we can see the celebration tonight."

That afternoon, as the inventory of trade goods was checked out, the clerks received their work details for the summer. John Dyde, big and strong, sent to a crew assigned to cut wood on Bois Blanc Island; Gurdon ordered to report to Mr. Matthews at the fur warehouse next morning. He was saddened by his

45

separation from John Dyde and a bit envious of Dyde's assignment to work in the woods, which he saw as good preparation for a wilderness trading post. But the dormitory he entered that evening made his good fortune clear. It was new, clean and comfortable. The pork and peas were hot and good. He liked the idea of living with clerks of his own age learning the business. He thought that John Kinzie, though John was younger than himself, would prove to be a good friend. He looked out the dormitory windows, across the docks and boatyards and the gleaming water of the Straits to the mainland where Alexander Henry had lived within the walls of old Fort Michilimackinac, now gone. He decided to ask Kinzie to explore the ruins there and to find the cave on the island where Henry had hidden from the hostile savages.

That night Michilimackinac celebrated. The camps of the Indian town were ablaze with roaring fires where mutton provided by the company was roasting. The drums throbbed. On the compounds among the painted tepees and summer lodges the dancers of a half-dozen tribes competed, shrieking, howling, stomping to the beat of drums and the wailing of wooden flutes. Frightfully painted braves demonstrated their war and hunting prowess in leaping, strutting exhibitions. The rum and whisky were drunk, the frenzy of dancing and shouting mounted, the *voyageurs* joined in the fun with their own creations of chants and dancing. Gurdon and John wandered from camp to camp within the village, sharing the hot corn soup, enthralled by the noise and excitement. Kinzie spoke both the Potawatomi and Winnebago dialects and promised to help Gurdon learn those variations of the Algonquin language. John expected someday to prepare his own lexicon of the Winnebago tongue, which especially interested him.

In later years, Gurdon recalled those first days and nights on the island. "The force of the Company, when all were assembled . . . comprized about 400 clerks and traders, together with some 2,000 *voyageurs.* The clerks were assigned to varied duties in the warehouse, where all of the different 'outfits' were received to grade and count furs to be pressed and packed for Mr. Astor in New York, or were placed in charge of different gangs of men, or in wholesale and retail stores and offices. From these duties, heads of outfits were exempt. The Company had a yard which made and repaired their own boats (the famed mackinaws) and manufactured traps, tomahawks, and other articles from iron. Other parties of men were detailed to assist the mechanics in this work.

"Dances and parties were given every night by residents on the island in honor of the traders and they in turn reciprocated with balls and jollifications . . . (which) drained from the participants all hard earnings from the winter previous. In each brigade or outfit was to be found one who, from superior strength or bravery, was looked upon as the 'bully' of that crew of *voyageurs*. . . ."

The bully, who wore a black feather in his cap, was an excellent fighter. He maintained discipline in his own crew and took up the quarrels of any man in the outfit against any man of another outfit. There were fights on Mackinac almost every night, governed by rules of fair play, to settle arguments and grudges. The vanquished bully was required to give up his black feather to the victor. Generally, after the fight, which often drew large crowds of those who wagered on the outcome, "both joined with the lookers-on in a glass of beer or whisky as good-naturedly as though nothing unpleasant had occurred."

The majority of the inhabitants of Mackinac were of French and Indian blood. The married white men, except for company officers and officers at the fort, had Indian wives. Many of these women were well educated. A few were in the fur trade, operating posts or stores inherited from late husbands, and all participated in the social life of Mackinac, including the popular balls. Gurdon and John Kinzie, despite their youth, Kinzie was fourteen, were invited to such affairs, though Gurdon could accept only infrequently since he worked many nights as well as long days. But he became a favorite of several older women who looked upon him as a son, "Mrs. Mitchell, who carried on an extensive trade with the Indians in her own right"; Mrs. La Fromboise, "who could read and write and was a perfect lady in her manners and conversation . . . her husband had been killed by an Indian on the Mississippi River"; and Mrs. Chandler, a sister of Mrs. La Fromboise, "also noted for her ladylike manners, whose husband was an invalid, and whose daughter . . . was highly educated and considered the belle of Mackinaw." At those homes Gurdon learned to comport himself in the company of women and Mrs. Chandler's daughter Marie, a young widow, taught him to dance. He also received instruction "in the method of conducting fur trade with the Indians. . . . They called me 'their boy clerk' and my leisure evenings were spent with them, much to my pleasure and advantage."

Such other evenings as he had free, Gurdon spent in the company of John Kinzie, wandering through the Indian camps, especially those of the Potawatomis from Illinois and Michigan Indian territories, since Kinzie spoke their tongue well. There were also Winnebagos, Chippewas and Ottawas from the North, the western Sioux, and Sacs and Foxes, like the Winnebagos out of Wisconsin; and the Miamis and Delawares from Indiana and Ohio. Gurdon was especially interested in the Illinois territory, where La Salle had established his important trading forts, and he eagerly listened to Kinzie's stories of his home in Chicago, his experiences in the Indian camps, and of his escape from the Fort Dearborn massacre. Gurdon wanted to go into that territory, though his friend considered Chicago a dreary place. Both knew that a clerk had no choice of territoy. When the time came, he'd go where ordered.

Meantime the boys enjoyed together the summer nights when they were free. There were balls, celebrations and fights almost every night. "The *voyageurs* were fond of fun and frolic," Gurdon was to remember, "and the Indians indulged in their love of liquor. By exhibition of their war, medicine and other dances and sports, they made the nights hideous with their yells."

*

His second day on Mackinac Gurdon Hubbard discovered the man who would influence and guide him, aiding him with formal studies, in probing into history, which would become a passion of his life, and in dealing with the Indians in a fair and highly tolerant manner. He had been instructed to report to Mr. Matthews at the fur warehouse, a white, three-story building of hand-hewn beams and hand-sawn siding built in 1810. There worked the *voyageurs* at the kind of labor they detested, sorting, packing and pressing furs for shipment to the dealers and exporters in Montreal and New York. Each *voyageur* was required to serve one summer in the fur warehouse every four years. Gurdon, known by Matthews to be able with figures and proficient in writing English, was assigned to aid the acting chief of the warehouse although he was the youngest of the 400 clerks on the island. He was told to find Monsieur Antoine Deschamps, who spoke French and English, was superintendent of trading posts on the Illinois River, and had, that summer, in addition to fur warehouse duty, the task of instructing John Kinzie, Jr. in company lore and details of the fur trade. It had been Deschamps, a friend of John Kinzie's father, who had brought the boy into the company.

M. Deschamps was easy enough to find on the warehouse floor among the traders, Indians and *voyageurs* who were opening the dusty, insect-infested collections of furs for the sorting, cleaning, counting and grading that would determine the price the seller should get for his year's work. Deschamps towered above the others, a lean, graying, big-boned man who stooped to hear what was being said to him in the noisy room. His hair and beard were white and thin, like a fuzz of feathers fluffing from his tanned skin, stretched tight around his large skull. The tanned circle at the top of his head, gleaming in the shafts of sunlight from the high warehouse windows, gave him the appearance of one who had been scalped. His pale blue eyes bulged, his wide mouth seemed carved in leather until he smiled, flashing broad white teeth. M. Deschamps bent low to listen attentively, his eyes blinking, and hesitated as he replied, except when the answer was *"Non!"*, which he snapped out, ending all discussion. He shuffled a bit as he walked among the piles of furs, passing a word to the *patron,* or foreman, stopping to examine a fur being appraised, pausing to enter notes in a black book he carried. When there was a dispute between a trader and a *patron,* M. Deschamps stepped in to listen and then quietly settle it, speaking in French or in the Algonquin tongue, the basic language of all Indians in the Northwest fur trade. When Gurdon at last got M. Deschamps' attention by speaking to him in English, the gaunt old man turned on him, appraised him with blinking blue eyes as if Gurdon might have been a green bearskin, and then smiled a bit.

"Do you speak French?" Deschamps asked.

"A little, not well, sir," Gurdon answered.

"You will learn," Deschamps replied. "Do you write in English?"

Gurdon answered that he did. Deschamps sighed and handed the boy his black account book and pointed to an ink stand and a box of sand on a crate near by. "You write in English," he said. "You'll find quills and a cutter there. I'll tell you what to set down. Write in English, that's what's wanted now. If I lapse into French, remind me. Mr. Matthews tells me you clerked in an English hardware store in Montreal. You've come in the nick of time, lad." Deschamps smiled.

The work in the warehouse started early and lasted late six days a week. The traders watched as their furs were graded and appraised. The *patrons* were experienced and rarely overruled by Deschamps. Prices for the furs varied, since there were a number of grades: marten or sable was graded extra fine dark, number one dark, number two dark, number one brown and number two brown, and numbers one, two and three common. In addition some marten were rated out of season, bringing a bottom price, and some were rejected as worthless. As Gurdon kept the record of grading and appraisal and credited the trading post or individual trader with the price, he also began to learn how to judge furs on his own. A successful trader paid the Indian trapper a better price than any competitor would offer, but not more than it would grade at Mackinac, allowing for the necessary profit. Often there were violent disagreements. Deschamps' judgment was final. He was not usually required to work in the warehouse, Gurdon learned, but he had substituted for Matthews on his return from furlough in Quebec, his home city, and he agreed to continue after Matthews came back because of the emergency.

Gurdon learned rapidly and got on well with M. Deschamps. "The value of marten depends as much on color as fineness," he wrote in his own notebook. "Marten is found in greatest variety and is the most valuable, except for silver gray fox. Mink, muskrat, raccoon, lynx, wild cat, fox, wolverine, badger, otter, beaver, and other small fur animals must receive the same care as marten, but there are fewer grades. Exception is bear, where grading is as careful as for marten, being extra fine black *she,* number two ditto, coarse, and numbers one, two and three *he* bear. Deer skins require little skill in assorting, being classed as red doe, red buck, blue doe, blue buck, season doe, season buck, out of season, damaged.''

Each day was one of excitement and joy for him. He breakfasted at the first light with the fifty or so clerks who lived in the dormitory and was at work by six o'clock. He soon learned enough about grading furs to keep his own account in the various categories while another clerk recorded the count of the *patron.* If Gurdon's record corresponded with that of the *patron,* the furs were considered ready for shipment. They were placed in a wood frame by a *voyageur,* then pressed. This was accomplished by the *voyageur* who, using a mallet to drive wedges between the wooden forms of the frame, pressed them together against the pelts. The pressed frames were then marked according to grade and hauled to the shipping room. If Gurdon's count did not agree with the *patron's,* he was required to count again, and if the discrepancy remained a third person counted.

M. Deschamps was delighted with Gurdon's accomplishment in the skills of the grading and shipping room, but he was not pleased with his progress in French, a requirement for successful work with the *voyageurs,* or in Algonquin, equally necessary. Since Deschamps had undertaken the duty of perfecting John Kinzie in his languages and the lore of the fur trade as a service to the boy's father, he invited both boys to take their lunch, generally crackers and cheese, with him on the docks, where they could discuss with him any topics he chose in the language he selected for the lesson. Mostly they talked of history, Deschamps' favorite subject. He had known personally Gurdon's hero, Alexander Henry. They were together on Mackinac while Henry served on the government fur trade commission. Deschamps had been Henry's guest at the famous Beaver Club in Montreal. Gurdon read and re-read his French edition of Henry and he listened fascinated as the old man and young John Kinzie discussed events of the past—life in Chicago, the Fort Dearborn massacre, the importance of the Chicago Portage, the relationship of Indian history to the problems of the traders in

51

John Kinzie's territory. And Deschamps spoke often of his own hero, Louis Joliet, who in 1673 voyaged with Father Marquette from Point St. Ignace to Green Bay, up the Fox river, down the Wisconsin river to the Mississippi, and back north to the Illinois and east to the Chicago Portage.

Joliet was not only an intrepid explorer, but a man devoted to Father Marquette and the Catholic church. The boys understood M. Deschamps' loyalty to the memory of Joliet. Deschamps too, John Kinzie told Gurdon, had trained for the priesthood with the Jesuits, but had declined ordination because he did not feel he could keep the vows. When possible he attended mass each day, as had Joliet, and he even assisted the priest in the chapel on Mackinac and in the missions he visited. Frequently that summer he was asked to be present in the chapel as a witness to the solemnization of marriage rites for a *voyageur* and his Indian wife. It was not possible for legal marriages to take place in the wilderness, Deschamps explained. But the *voyageurs* and Indians converted to Christianity gladly travelled hundreds of miles to accomplish this purpose when possible, bringing with them their children to be baptized.

Sunday was a day of special joy for Gurdon and John Kinzie. They had pancakes with honey, pork and real coffee for breakfast. They went to church, where M. Deschamps often aided the priest, and then departed in Deschamps' canoe, provided with powdered corn, biscuits, cheese and a bottle of wine. Deschamps shot birds, rabbits and porcupine for his own evening mess and the boys fished for whiting, the Lake Huron delicacy. In time Deschamps taught them to load, prime and fire his double-barreled flintlock shotgun, made in England by the famous Joseph Manton, and to use the sling, spear, net and bow and arrow to obtain small game needed to survive in the wilderness. As a special favor to Gurdon, he took them across the strait to inspect the site of Old Fort Michilimackinac, where Alexander Henry had lived as a young trader in the days of the Pontiac war. The fort had been destroyed by the Indians, but stones and half-buried timbers still marked its location. Deschamps had recovered guns and tomahawks and war clubs there, which he had contributed to the wardroom of the new fort on the island.

Gurdon recalled for John Kinzie the events at Mackinaw on

the mainland, as Henry had related them, while Deschamps monitored his account. Henry, after serving as a sutler with the American army, had gone into the fur trade in Montreal following the French defeat by the English in 1760. Three years later Henry was a fur trader at old Fort Michilimackinac when Pontiac, the Ottawa chief, led an alliance of Indians in attacks on English forts and settlements said to have killed more than had died in the entire period of the French and Indian wars. But Pontiac had refrained from attacking Fort Michilimackinac.

So the garrison at the fort was relatively easy and Henry was at work on his accounts in his house inside the palisade on June 1, 1763 when a party of Chippewa braves came to the fort to invite all there to watch a game of baggattaway (lacrosse) between two tribes in a field just east of the fort. The Chippewas had challenged the best players of the Sacs. Baggattaway was rough and wild, a game in which a hundred players tossed a small leather ball, each team of fifty braves attempting to carry it past the goal of the other. Players were often injured and sometimes killed as the teams surged across the field. Captain Etherington, commandant of the fort, and his soldiers loved to watch and wager on the game. They accepted the Chippewa invitation.

The match took place beyond the open south gate of the fort, where a crowd of soldiers, traders, Indian braves and squaws gathered near the palisade to watch. It began with wild yells and furious charges. The players struck, pummeled, tripped and clubbed one another as the squaws shrieked and the soldiers cheered. In the midst of the fury a Chippewa warrior caught the leather pellet high in the air and swung it in a wide arc through the open south gate. The players rushed after it, their women handing them knives and tomahawks hidden in their clothing as the men passed. Alexander Henry, at work at his desk, heard wild yells, calls for help, and musket fire. He moved to his cottage window and saw the remaining garrison inside the fort being slaughtered. He noted that the Indians were attacking soldiers and English visitors, not the French workmen and *voyageurs*. With the help of a French neighbor, M. Langlade, Henry hid for a time, but then, fearing he would endanger Langlade and his wife, sought to escape. The Indians killed twenty-one soldiers and civilians that afternoon, and captured eighteen, including Henry.

"But then Henry's Chippewa friends saved him," Deschamps reminded them, as Gurdon paused in his account. "They saved him because he always treated them fairly and was a brother to them." Deschamps used his stories and theirs to point up a lesson or to correct a detail of history from his own observation and knowledge. He promised to take them on a search for the cave in which Henry was hidden by the Chippewas on Mackinac while a party of Ottawas sought him. The following Sunday they found the cave, in a grove on a high ridge above the fort. Henry had lived there several days, discovering that it was a sacred Indian burial place and that he had been sleeping among human bones. His friends brought him food and the trappings of a Chippewa warrior. A few days later he came down to the camp of the Chippewas as one of them. He had shaved his head with his hunting knife, leaving only a scalp-lock, painted his face with white clay, charcoal and vermilion, wore a blanket and carried a scalping knife on his belt. He lived on Mackinac with the family of his friend, Chief Wawatam, until he could escape from the island months later.

There were endless lessons for Gurdon and John Kinzie in their noon hours with Deschamps, when they talked in French and Potawatomi, the dialect best known to John, and watched the *voyageurs* continuing to arrive with cargoes from distant posts. On one occasion, they heard a steamboat whistle shriek and saw the staunch craft *Walk-in-the-Water* arrive from Buffalo. "There is our future," Deschamps told them. "Steamboats will serve your father at Chicago, John, when a cut can be made through the sandbar there. Steamboats will carry furs to Buffalo and when Governor Clinton gets his ditch, they will go all the way to New York City and Montreal will no longer be the fur trading capital."

They did not know about Governor Clinton's ditch. "He will have a canal from Lake Erie to the Hudson river," Deschamps explained. "He has seen the need of it and now has gotten the New York legislature to authorize it. Soon there will be a canal. I have told your father, John, that we must someday have a canal through the Chicago Portage. Joliet himself envisioned it. With such a canal we can travel from Montreal to New Orleans and never leave the boat.''

Deschamps desired his young charges both to envision the future and to respect the lessons of the past, and to appreciate the ways and traditions of the Indians. ''Alexander Henry loved the country and its inhabitants,'' he said. ''He knew the value of furs, he carried trade goods of high quality, he could judge the worth of a trader and of a pelt. He always dealt justly with the Indians. He was humble. After he had been received at the French court as a result of the fame of his book in France and was named a commissioner on the Indian trade by the government of Canada, he continued to treat as brothers the red men who contributed to his wealth and fame.'' Deschamps could suggest no better model for the young men than Alexander Henry, unless it should be Louis Joliet himself. They heard the lecture among the cedars, spruce and red oak guarding Alexander Henry's cave, where the dark opening to the sacred cavern of the Indian dead could still be seen.

There were teachings too on Indian history. The red man who first welcomed whites to America soon learned to fear and distrust them with good reason, Deschamps said, recalling the incident of the Walking Purchase, so often cited by the great Shawnee chief, Tecumseh, whom he knew well. The Delawares had ceded land to William Penn for his American colony, ''as far as a man could go in a day and a half.'' This was forty miles as walked by William Penn himself in 1686. But in 1737, when William's son Thomas Penn renewed the lease to the land, he had trained walkers ready who made sixty-six and one-half miles, from the Quaker meeting house at Wrightstown at the fork of the Lehigh and Delaware rivers to the Pocono Hills, encompassing an area almost double that of the original lease. When the Delaware owners protested, John Penn brought in the fierce Iroquois to drive them out.

It was the Iroquois, Deschamps noted, who first got guns from the Dutch to use in their own quest for land, after they had sold or surrendered their territories to the settlers. The Huron Indians surrounding Mackinac Island had fought first the Iroquois and then the whites. The Iroquois drove the Hurons westward and the Sioux drove them back into Michigan. The Iroquois harassed

the Algonquin tribes so successfully that the very name came
to mean "bark eaters," since victims of the Iroquois were
reduced to surviving on tree bark and roots when they were
driven from their hunting lands. In time, the victims of the Iroquois found some peace and well being in the Michigan, Wisconsin and Illinois territories, where their trading posts were
situated. The French who sought to trade with the tribes of the
Potawatomi confederation, the Chippewa, Sacs, Ottawa, Illinois
and others, were successful where English and Americans failed
because they were not seeking to seize Indian land. Nevertheless, even the French were long barred from Wisconsin rivers
by the Fox and Sac Indians, which forced them to use the difficult Chicago Portage.

Meantime the Delawares and Shawnees were pushed into the
Ohio country by the English and Americans seeking land. The
Delawares, who called themselves the Lenni-Lenape, or Children of the East (or Sun), were the peace keepers among the Indians, sometimes called the "Petticoat Indians," since their
women participated in tribal councils and even ruled a tribe,
as in the instance of Queen Alliquippa in Pennsylvania. The Delawares, however, became vassals after their defeat by the Iroquois and were used by them to conduct relations with tribes
hating and fearing the fierce warriors to the northeast. Thus the
Delawares became communicators and diplomats, as well as
teachers carrying their own and Shawnee and Cherokee culture
to the prairie and plains Indians. It was the Delaware chief
Netawates who established the custom, widely adopted, of ad-
dressing respected Europeans, such as the French in Canada and
Sir William Johnson, the British leader in America, as "Father,"
Europeans in general as "Brothers," and Chief Netawates himself in the term of highest respect as "Grandfather." Sir William
Johnson adopted this custom and it became widely used. "This
practice prevails where we trade," Deschamps said. "When we
speak to Indians in formal council we must remember to follow their ways."

Young John Kinzie and Deschamps sometimes clashed over
the old man's report and estimate of events. Kinzie insisted, as
his father did, that their log home and trading post in Chicago,
which young John called "the mansion," was the first perma-

nent building in Chicago. It was built by Jean Baptiste du Sable, a handsome black trader who claimed to be a Potawatomi chief but actually came from Santo Domingo, according to John Kinzie Sr. But, Deschamps said he had visited Chicago in 1776, when he was nineteen years old, with the trader Sara of St. Louis and there was only one log house there, the cabin of the trader Gaurie on the north branch of the river. All the rest was Indian. Deschamps did find pickets of a fort which once stood on the north side of the river. The French called the north branch the River Gaurie, Deschamps said. "We all called it that."

"Du Sable probably came in the following year," Deschamps continued. "I have read the records of the parish and of the fort at Mackinac, as well as the writings of the explorers. The first record of du Sable I have found is in the reports of Colonel Arent De Peyster, who took command at Michilimackinac on the mainland in 1779." Colonel De Peyster assigned scouts to investigate rumors of possible Indian uprising in lands around the Chicago Portage. On July 4, at l'Arbe du Croche, in an address to his officers and men, he denounced du Sable, describing him as "a handsome Negro, well educated, but very much in the French interest." De Peyster dispatched Lieutenant Thomas Bennet to the Chicago Portage to arrest du Sable, who was captured not at Chicago, but in Michigan territory. Lieutenant Bennet reported to De Peyster, "I had the Negro prisoner brought in from the River du Chemin." His message indicated du Sable was taken "at the St. Joseph's post on July 23 before the Potawatomis assembled."

Jean Baptiste Point du Sable impressed the British with his knowledge of Indian affairs and displayed a willingness to change his allegiance. When Lieutenant Governor Patrick Sinclair arrived to take charge at Michilimackinac and Detroit, he assigned the prisoner to operate his trading post, the Pinery, on the St. Clair river. Then, a year or two later, du Sable returned to Chicago, as a friend of the English. He expanded his log house, stocked it with trade goods and excellent furniture, according to an inventory he filed in Detroit, then the government seat for Chicago, and he married Catherine, a Potawatomi woman. He had risen from *villien* representing St. Clair to lord of the manor at Chicago. "I have talked with him," Deschamps said.

"He was a prepossessing, able man, charming, fluent in French and the Indian dialects."

"You have just proved that my father is right, du Sable was the first permanent settler," young John Kinzie said.

"It depends upon what you mean by 'permanent.' But we can agree that du Sable and your house have an excellent claim."

"Where did Monsieur du Sable come from? What happened to him?" Gurdon asked.

"His French leads me to believe he came from Haiti, a part of the island of Santo Domingo discovered by Columbus. It was under French rule for many years. In my time, I have seen French, Spanish, English and American rule in the St. Louis territory. I think the French brought in du Sable from Haiti. The Spaniards brought in a black named Glamorgan, who was Spanish speaking, and probably was from Santo Domingo. Both may have served at Fort de Chartres in Illinois country. We do know that du Sable and Glamorgan, who traded for furs in the Lake Peoria country, were friends. In about 1796, du Sable left Chicago abruptly and never returned. It is known that he went to live with Jacques Glamorgan on his land near St. Louis. His reasons for leaving Chicago are not known, but he sold his property to the Trader Le Mai, the property your father John Kinzie now owns."

"My father, too, left Chicago abruptly—twice," John Kinzie said bitterly. "Once because of the massacre and the war, when we were all seized by the British as spies for the Americans. Before that, because he was accused of murder."

"John," Deschamps remonstrated, "you must not speak so freely of such events. Your father was cleared in the killing of Joseph La Lime, who after all attacked him from behind. You are all now citizens of the United States in good repute."

John Kinzie did not share Gurdon's near-reverence for Deschamps and sometimes spoke of him in an uncomplimentary way. "He thinks he knows everything," John fumed on one occasion. "He talked my father into sending me here for training and said he'd watch over me each summer. He couldn't get my father into the company, so he got me. He thinks only the French know how to get along with the Indians. It is the English who know this. That is why the English still have an empire in America. My father has as many Indian friends as Antoine Deschamps.''

*

Early in July Gurdon had reported his Mackinac arrival to his parents in Montreal. On July 24 he wrote again in detail, a letter to his mother. He appeared confused as to the whereabouts of his family since he addressed the letter of the 24th to ''Mrs. Abby Hubbard/To the care of Jonathan E. Hubbard, Windsor, Vermont'' but then crossed out Windsor and wrote Middletown, Connecticut. Jonathan Hubbard was the patriarch of the Hubbard family in Windsor; Middletown was Abigail's family home. The letters Gurdon received from his parents in Montreal evidently contained news of a conflicting and disturbing nature. Clearly he assumed his prior letter from Mackinac had not been received, since on the 24th he repeated the details of his arrival there. He was confused; he referred to his arrival as occurring in June:

Dear Mother:

I now take this opportunity to write you a few lines by a Gentleman that is going to DeTroit, and will have the Goodness to put it in the post Office. We arrived here after Saturday the 27th of June after having a verry pleasent and favorable passage up. We did not come the route that we expected and consequently did not see all the Towns in Upper Canada. We came no farther than York . . . (He described the route via Lake Simcoe which he said was 400 miles shorter but through 200 miles of wilderness ''where we saw nothing but rocks and a few Indians.'')

Mackinac is a verry pleasent and healthy island with about 200 houses on it. I received a letter from you and father by Mr. Matthews . . . we do not have an opportunity to write very often . . . but do not feel anxious about me Dear Mother for I assure you that I will do real well. We are treated better than I expected by our employers. I have not heard from father as yet but I hope that he has found a profitable business and will be able to lay up some money. . . . I shall try hard to get a post near St. Lewis but I do not know where I shall go but I do not think I will go very soon.

59

I will certainly write you when I can. I have been very well and grow fat every day. . . . I hope I shall hear from father before I go and I hope I shall see you all next summer in health and prosperity. Please when you write direct the letter to Samuel Abbott Esq. (an American Fur Company man in New York) and I shall get it. I remain your most affectionate son.   G. S. Hubbard

In August he heard again directly from his family. "I received a letter from my father, written in Erie, Pennsylvania, in which he informed me that he and my brother were on their way to St. Louis, and they had waited a week there looking for the Fur Company's vessel, which it was expected would touch there on her way from Buffalo to Mackinaw, upon which they hoped to obtain passage, and thus visit me . . . but, fearing she had passed, and being uncertain whether they would find me on the island, they had reluctantly concluded to continue their journey by the way of Cincinnati."

This news totally desolated him. He did not know what had happened in Montreal to separate the family. He did not understand why his father would again abruptly leave the place in which he had settled, nor why he would take Christopher but not the rest of the family. Why was he going into frontier country? What was happening to his mother and sisters?

It was at this time Gurdon was informed that he would be assigned to the Lake Superior brigade and would be stationed at Fond du Lac. This doomed his hopes of going with Antoine Deschamps, or any possibility that he could travel to St. Louis to see his father and brother. In desperation he decided to take Elizur Hubbard's letter to M. Deschamps. "I had been told by M. Deschamps that he made a trip to St. Louis every fall, with one boat, to purchase tobacco and other necessities for distribution among the various traders on the Illinois river," he recalled. He dared not ask to go with Deschamps, but he was sure his boss would be glad to carry a message to his father. John Kinzie had told him no clerk could ask for assignment to a particular post. "You will have nothing to say about it," John said. "*They* decide where you go. *They* decide I must stay here so nothing can happen to me. I'm a prisoner here. You are not.

60

But you can't choose to go with M. Deschamps or to the Illinois country. That's not how it's done."

Gurdon did not really believe he could actually accompany Deschamps and thus get to St. Louis. He felt guilty at the thought. His wish to accompany Deschamps to an Illinois post came from his admiration for him. "He was an old man when I first knew him," he wrote in later years when he sought additional information about Deschamps for his own memoirs. But he learned little beyond what he already knew, that Antoine Deschamps was born in Quebec in about 1756, was educated by the Jesuits at the college there, and joined the Trader Sara of St. Louis when he was about eighteen years old. He then travelled into the Indian country. Gurdon found Deschamps' name appearing frequently in *The Parish Register of the Mission of Michilimackinac* as a witness to the marriages of traders and *voyageurs* but he discovered little more.

Gurdon presented his letter and his problem to M. Deschamps, who questioned him carefully and reassured him. Possibly his father had been offered a good opportunity to practice law in St. Louis, a most pleasant place, Deschamps suggested. "Of course we will get your letter to your father there," he assured his young clerk.

"John Crafts is to go this year in my place since he is ill and needs to see a doctor in St. Louis. He will await my arrival at Chicago. Gurdon, would you like to go with me if it can be so arranged?"

The boy eagerly seized upon this offer. "I begged for his influence and efforts to that end." He was advised that a clerk named Warner, also from Montreal, was detailed to the Illinois Brigade. "Now," said M. Deschamps, "if you can get Mr. Warner to consent to an exchange, I think I can get Mr. Crooks' permission, and, as I am the party mostly interested, I think it can be arranged with him."

Gurdon sought out Warner. To his astonishment he found Warner preferred to go north and was glad to make the change. "I reported to M. Deschamps, and he, seeing my anxiety, went immediately to Mr. Crooks, who gave his consent. Thus my desire of finding my father in St. Louis was the probable cause of an entire change in my destiny. . . ."

Since the Illinois Brigade would be the last to leave Mackinac, Gurdon Hubbard had almost a month to prepare himself for the Illinois country. The excursions and lessons with Deschamps and John Kinzie continued. They visited the grave of Father Marquette on Point St. Ignace, crossed to the wood-cutting base on Bois Blanc where Gurdon saw John Dyde for the last time, and travelled in Deschamps' canoe to Sault Ste. Marie. The excursions helped Gurdon to become proficient in handling a canoe, to gain experience in the woods, and to add to his knowledge of the history of the Indians, the country, and the fur trade. His friendship with John Kinzie had led him to have a special interest in Chicago and now John obliged with more stories of his life there.

*

On September 10, the Illinois Brigade, eleven *batteaux* and one hundred ten men, departed Mackinac for the Chicago Portage and the Illinois River country. The crowd that saw them off was subdued in contrast to those who cheered the earlier departures to the Lake of the Woods, the Upper and Lower Mississippi, the Wisconsin River and Lake Superior, the Wabash and St. Joseph Rivers and other posts. Gurdon Hubbard carried with him a package of gifts from John Kinzie to his family and a letter of introduction to John Kinzie, Sr. He also expected to find John Crafts in Chicago and to accompany him all the way to St. Louis where he would find his father and Christopher.

"M. Deschamps took me in his boat," Gurdon recalled. "He led the way, with his fine, strong voice starting the boat song." It was Deschamps' favorite, *La Rose du Rosier Blanc*. "The people on shore bid us 'God Speed' and joined us in our hope of a safe return next season. . . . The Islanders, more than anyone else, regretted our departure, as what few traders remaining would go in a few days leaving them to the monotony of their own surroundings. Even the Indians having departed for their hunting grounds."

3

1 October, 1818

Through my intimacy with John I had become familiar
with the appearance of the Kinzie family and their surroundings. . . . I knew that Fort Dearborn was located at
Chicago, then a frontier post; that it was garrisoned by two
companies of soldiers, and that on my arrival there I
should for the first time in my life see a prairie, and I felt
the new detail was to take me among those who would be
my friends, and was happy at the thought.
                    Recollections,
                    Gurdon S. Hubbard

They coasted westward through the Straits of Mackinac, camping the night on the south shore. Their eleven mackinaws were
low in the water, laden with guns and powder, tomahawks and
iron traps and cooking pots, casks of high wines and whisky and
crates of Stroud cloth and silver bangles and vermilion for the
trading posts and Indian towns of the Illinois country. There
were long hard drills into the wind until they turned south at
Waugoshance point and then more gruelling hours on the paddles as storms forced them to hug the shore, making forty miles
some days, though other days none; joyous relief arriving when
they could run before the wind, square sail hoisted, making seventy miles—twenty leagues—on a good day. Few boat songs
most days and no linen showing; no cheers for troubadours in
bright regalia singing children's songs and love songs for a lonely
outpost in the wilderness. They passed by the Indian towns.

The Illinois Brigade was now express from Mackinac to
Chicago and Fort Dearborn. Earlier departing outfits had reached
the villages and trading posts of Michigan, the Indians in the

north had received their supplies and departed for their hunting grounds. The brigade was late, but progress was slow. When the wind rose they dropped their sail and made for the nearest creek or river mouth. As storms broke they beached their craft, laid poles on the sand, hauled the boats out of danger and piled their freight on other poles, covering it all with tarpaulins. They spent the nights and days in the lee of their shelters until the storms ended.

"Sometimes we were compelled to remain in camp four or five days at a time, waiting for the storm to subside," Gurdon would recall. They raced, wrestled, played cards, hunted and fished until the storms passed "and all were jolly and content." Their trip around the lake took twenty days. "Nothing of interest transpired until we reached the Marquette River." There *Le Bourgeois* Deschamps ordered the boats ashore and led his men to the weathered, leaning cedar cross marking the spot where Father Marquette died. M. Deschamps dropped to his knees and his men crossed themselves and did likewise, Gurdon included. He knew that Father Marquette's body was now buried at St. Ignace, he had gone there with M. Deschamps and John Kinzie. He also understood that the *voyageurs* held this place sacred, some day to be called Ludington. After prayers, they reset the cross, Gurdon remembered. He would visit the site again, but did not find the cross. "It was covered by drifting sands the following winter," he wrote. "I doubt not that no white man ever saw it afterwards."

They coasted Lake Michigan south and west, passing rivers that would lead to Indian towns, such as the Grand in southern Michigan, without attracting attention. That country was traded by men not yet attached to the American Fur Company and well prepared to fend off competition. The American Fur outfit at Kalamazoo was required to deal with that problem. Deschamps, growing increasingly testy at each delay, was grimly intent on making Chicago by October. He was equally determined to settle an argument he long held with John Kinzie Sr. there, concerning the exact spot where Father Marquette had cabined in the Chicago area one hundred and forty years earlier. In Quebec that summer, Deschamps had visited the Hotel Dieu, where the nuns kept the copy of Father Marquette's journal, rediscovered in 1800, to recheck the records and he believed that he could now locate the site well south of Chicago, whereas Kinzie insisted Marquette had wintered on the Chicago River in 1674-75. Marquette, Deschamps found, did not cite the name Checagou in his journal nor on his maps; though Joliet, his companion, did. They used the Chicago Portage, Deschamps believed, but at flood stage, so that they portaged less than a mile. Thus, no one could have wintered along that flooded waterway itself in 1675. Deschamps hoped to prove it.

As they neared the mouth of the Little Calumet, they saw the smoke of many fires and knew a large encampment lay ahead. Deschamps signalled a turn to port and began a boat song. This good fortune took precedence over his desire for exploration and a triumph over John Kinzie. Business was business. Clearly they had come upon a hunting camp, bound for the trading posts of Chicago, hunters without doubt short of supplies. Deschamps concluded at once to supply them, crediting Johh Crafts, his own trader at Chicago, and John Kinzie, who got most of his supplies from the American Fur Company, with the goods disposed of. Generally hunters were required to call directly at the trading posts, where credit records were kept.

They received a wild welcome. The Potawatomis and Kickapoos enroute to Chicago had undertaken a hunt in the Sag woods that morning and had killed a fine, fat he-bear. Such a good omen required an immediate celebration, the shamans accompanying the expedition decreed. Surely the urgently needed supplies had arrived in Chicago as the medicine men promised. All the spirits, the *chasgieds* and the *wabenos,* were favorable. The bear had been roasting over the fires but an hour or so when a runner came into camp to report that mackinaws from the north were arriving! Runners were sent to the nearby villages inviting chiefs and headmen to the feast. When Wasachek, hunting chief of the Potawatomis, heard the boat song he knew the lead voice to be that of his old friend Monsieur Deschamps. There was joy in the camp.

The *voyageurs,* bringing songs and trade goods, were always well received in the Indian country. This year they were late and thus twice welcome. The concatenation of splendid omens was beyond expectation, greatly pleasing the shamans. The hunting would be good. Many of the braves consumed the last of their rum and whisky in anticipation, knowing that surely there would be ample fresh supplies. The women, mostly young squaws—second wives allowed to accompany their husbands on the hunt—were eager too. The Potawatomi women were known for their beauty and love of finery and for their good manners, which, among most nomadic tribes, included complaisant consideration for the lonely traveler. The Illinois Brigade arrived out of uniform—no time to dress themselves or their boats—but singing gloriously as they dipped their paddles. Their welcome was a tumultuous one.

*

Early that evening, while the women finished roasting the bear and cooked bear soup with its nameless condiments and herbs, as well as corn soup intended to placate the spirit of the deceased bear, and roasted nuts and roots for the feast, Monsieur Deschamps and his men completed their trading. Deschamps then broke out a good supply of rum, since only rum was proper for the sacred feast of the bear. He instructed his young clerk Hubbard to keep a record of the trade goods provided, to be credited to the accounts of Crafts and Kinzie at Chicago, and of the rum to be distributed, since all disbursements of company goods required strict accounting. The time for dancing and feasting had come when Chief Winnetuk arrived with his band of Peorias, laden with whisky and trade goods. Wasachek had no love for the Peorias, who had remained at war with the Potawatomis many years, only reluctantly making peace at the insistence of the great Shawnee chief, Tecumseh, then uniting the tribes to fight the Americans. Chief Wasachek especially disliked the arrogant and untrustworthy Winnetuk, but, since the young chief came on the eve of a sacred feast, on a day of many propitious omens, it was proper to make him welcome. The Potawatomi braves were pleased to drink Winnetuk's whisky, Deschamps' rum was being held for the feast, and when the dancing began, many of the young men were quite drunk. Some rude young braves staggered about, sneering and snickering, when the feast formally began with the head of the bear paraded to the stone dias raised for the occasion. Such behavior by the young men was a profanation of the ceremony, intended as a solemn sacrifice to the spirit of the bear. The older braves set the bear's head down among the green hemlock boughs, amid the gifts of tobacco, pipes, rum and corn soup, intended to assure the bear there was nothing personal in his abrupt demise. Then Chief Wasacheck invited the leading guests present, Waba of the Kickapoos, a white-haired, aging man; Tamin of the Kankakees; Winnetuk of the Peorias, and Antoine Deschamps and his aide, Vasseur, to join him in the place of honor. Old Waba, as he usually was called, was at the moment speaking in French to Gurdon Hubbard, old Waba saying he recently had lost a son of Gurdon's age. When he learned from Deschamps that Gurdon, in the month before, passed his sixteenth birthday without ceremony, Chief Waba clucked sadly. It was a grave omission, he said. In his sixteenth year a Kickapoo brave could paint and join the war dance!

Chief Waba was a venerable man, tall and thin, his coppery face a mass of creases, which wreathed his aging features as he smiled. His son had been born to him of his third wife when Waba was already old. His long, white scalplock fell in two braids on his shoulders. In them he wore the two eagle feathers of a war chief. On his belt he carried a silver-encrusted scalping knife and a handsome tomahawk of tempered iron, one of the best sold by Deschamps. "Welcome, friend of Deschamps," the old chief had said in French. "Thank you, I am glad to be here," Gurdon had responded. Deschamps, always alert to opportunity, told Gurdon he too would sit in the place of honor with Vasseur and himself and next to Chief Waba, whose tribe traded at Beebeau's post, to which Gurdon was being assigned. It would be good for the young clerk to know him.

All went well in the beginning. The women of the village brought in the stacks of steaming bear meat, bowls of bear and corn soup, and quantities of baked roots and nuts, fresh thorn apples and berries. The chiefs paid homage to the spirit of the bear and drank the rum with their braves. Then Winnetuk, uninvited, rose to speak. He was a strong, handsome bull of a man, who had been an excellent hunter until he took to drink, wild fantasies, and his crusade against Americans. Winnetuk began by boasting that he was well received when he carried his war belts to the Winnebagos in the north and to Big Foot, whose village north of Chicago comprised both Winnebagos and Potawatomis. They were ready to fight, he said, and would get help from Canada. Winnetuk now brought his belts of black wampum to the prairie Potawatomis and their allies and kin, Kickapoos, Kankakees, Miamis, and Ottawas. The time had come, Winnetuk said, to unite to drive the American robbers from Indian lands.

Chief Waba exchanged glances with Tamin as they declined to accept the black war belts. Winnetuk was making a mistake. The Peorias too long and too recently had been enemies of the Potawatomis. Winnetuk knew that Waba and Tamin were close friends of Black Hawk, the Sac (Sauk) chief who long had nursed an ambition to lead the tribes against the Americans. What Black Hawk so far had not succeeded in doing, surely Winnetuk could not accomplish. He appeared to think his potlatch gift of liquor and trade goods could buy the support of the young braves and influence the chiefs. But it seemed to Deschamps and Vasseur that Winnetuk's oration at the sacred feast of the bear could have an opposite affect upon the older men.

It was at this time that Gurdon, conspicuous, sitting among the chiefs, pressed by his solicitous hosts to consume vast amounts of bear meat and greasy bear soup, became sick, visibly pale beneath his tan. Deschamps whispered to Vasseur to take the boy out and to make sure that all men, boats and supplies were taken beyond the Little Calumet for a new camp. Deschamps did not like what he was hearing, the roistering young braves cheering Winnetuk while the old chiefs sulked. "Return with boats for me and our people," Deschamps said. Vasseur understood.

Winnetuk, with a sneering laugh, interrupted his exhortation to advise the departing "Little American" that he must not vomit the sacred bear meat, it would insult the spirit of the bear, who watched over them. The young men howled at this. Winnetuk resumed his discourse, his manner so scornful and insulting that the older Potawatomi braves grew wary and began to move stealthily toward the dias where they could best protect the chiefs. Winnetuk ignored this precaution. He scolded his Potawatomi hosts for including white men at the sacred rites that night, especially the young American, a symbol of their enemies. But then he mockingly excluded Deschamps, saying his grandfather, the Frenchman, was long known to them and would continue to be their friend if he ceased bringing Americans into their lands. "My grandfather is welcome, but not with Americans," Winnetuk said. He asserted that Neopope, the prophet and advisor to Black Hawk, supported Winnetuk, and at the proper time would bring English arms to them from Canada. Now they must unite: He invoked the spirits of Pontiac and Tecumseh and the most sacred Gitchie Manitou.

Winnetuk's impassioned speech, however badly timed, provided a challenge Antoine Deschamps could not ignore. He saw that while the young chief's insolence and effrontery had angered the older men, he also had made his points. The tribes and nations were outraged by new American laws and rules in violation of their treaties. Americans were moving in to seize and hold Indian lands. They pretended to come to advance the fur trade, yet most were not traders, but farmers. They broke their own laws, then accused the Indians of doing wrong. Main Poc, the Potawatomi chief, had put it to them in the days of Tecumseh, saying: "Whenever you do wrong, nothing is done, but when we do anything, you immediately take us and tie us by the neck with a rope. . . . Our young men upbraid us, they say, 'You give the Americans your hand and some day they will knock you in the head.' " The Indians preferred to trust the French and English traders from Canada, but the Congress of the United States had decreed that only American companies could engage in the fur trade in lands recently seized from England or purchased from France, lands the Indians insisted still belonged to them. Many young Indians were awaiting a leader who would seize the torch Tecumseh carried to his death. Deschamps feared Winnetuk might already have committed an act of war at Chicago. Yet he did not know how to accuse him credibly, but felt compelled to rise and, observant of tradition, tender the young chief a civil answer.

"My son hears false messages," Deschamps said, speaking from his place of honor. "He listens to bad birds. It is true that our father in Washington claims lands by right of treaties, treaties some of you have signed. I do not dispute this claim. I do not make or unmake treaties. You can see that we come among you as friends to trade with you as we have long since. I have come lately from Quebec and Montreal and I can tell you that there will be no guns or powder sent to you from Canada for the purposes of war. I have lived among you honorably many years. I have spoken with Tecumseh, and the great Peoria chief Gomo, and the great Potawatomi chief Main Poc. I speak with Shabona, and Keokuk and Black Hawk. I tell you that *they* do not listen to the bad birds. Nor should you. Your chiefs have made us guests at your sacred feast and we are honored. We give thanks to the spirit of the bear and to the spirits of our ancestors. We do not profane such an occasion as this. We give thanks to Gitchi Manitou, the supreme giver of goodness and good fortune for our good fortune. I am greatly pleased on this sacred and auspicious night that you have honored me and my men, including my son from Montreal, who, I fear, is a bit unwell, but who will recover. We now leave you with our thanks and our prayers for many moons of good hunting."

Shortly thereafter the fighting broke out, first grappling in the feasting circle itself when the visiting Peorias accused young, drunk Potawatomis of stealing their remaining whisky or of failing to share their rum, then the ill temper spreading through the camp and to the tepees and lodges where some of the young wives were entertaining guests. Warriors battled with stones, clubs and knives. Presumably those among them who saw *voyageurs* emerging from their lodges and tepees, where the visitors had been sequestered while the feasting proceeded, took bad temper out on them. Since few *voyageurs* could swim, Vasseur brought back several *batteaux* to rescue them and M. Deschamps himself. Most members of the Illinois Brigade reached the new camp beyond the Little Calumet before gunfire was heard in the Potawatomi camp to the south. The last of the *voyageurs,* arriving late, reported to M. Deschamps they had counted seven Indians dead and many wounded. They were somewhat battered themselves.

Chapter 3

*

They coasted silently northward that morning of October 1. *Le Bourgeois* Deschamps was about to make entry into Chicago on the first day of the month, as he intended. He was much concerned, however, about the trouble of the night before. How had Winnetuk, the renegade Peoria, and his band come upon the supplies, especially the whisky? Clearly they had not been hunting nor had John Crafts or John Kinzie extended credit. Winnetuk had no standing with any trader, though the Peorias generally were excellent hunters and reliable people. There was a possibility, though a remote one, that an Indian war already had started in the north and that Winnetuk had made a foray at Chicago, such as had occurred days prior to the Fort Dearborn attack and massacre in 1812, when a small band of marauders killed the dwellers at Lee's cabin, the post now occupied by John Crafts. Deschamps intended to proceed cautiously until he knew more. He was sending his young clerk, Hubbard, to the tallest tree of the highest oak hummock near the shore to spy out what could be discovered at Fort Dearborn and Chicago, some two leagues to the north. Gurdon knew, from his many talks about Chicago with John Kinzie and Deschamps that summer, the layout of the fort and the village. Also he was the only one among them who could swim well, most *voyageurs,* including Noel Vasseur, Deschamps' aide, could not swim at all. "The boy can outswim, outwalk and outclimb any of you," Deschamps had said pleasantly to Vasseur. "Besides, he wants to see the prairie and to walk to the fort, to visit the scenes of the massacre. If he sees soldiers fishing, or working in the gardens, we know we can go in showing our linen."

Noel Vasseur agreed. Vasseur did not hesitate to challenge a Kickapoo brave, or even an angry bear, but the water, on which he had spent most of his twenty-one years, terrified him. He did not worry as Monsieur Deschamps did about possible Indian trouble, but then, Vasseur was not responsible for all the Illinois River trading posts, the company's men and cargo. He knew the boy M. Deschamps had called his son the night before could quite accurately report all that might be going on at Fort Dear-

71

born and Chicago, providing he didn't confuse the village of four houses with the Potawatomi town to the west.

*

They proceeded quietly, without boat songs, in case unfriendly Indians might be near. As they approached the high bluffs along the lake, some five leagues to the east of the Chicago Portage, where Vasseur knew there were high oak hummocks beyond the sand dunes, Deschamps, standing tall and gaunt in the bow of his command boat, hand-signalled a turn to port. At his feet the boy crouched, naked except for breech clout, his engagé bag held ready as he awaited the command to jump. He might have been an Indian, his hair black, cheekbones high, body brown. But his feet shone white as he sprang kicking into the Lake Michigan whitecaps, responding to Deschamps' touch and the soft command, *"Maintenant, Gurdon . . . en avant!"* He struck the water hard, a belly flop, but he thrust his linen dufflebag high and swam with one arm and powerfully kicking legs. He found the rocky bottom of the lake and ran shoreward, swiping water from his hair and eyes. He climbed the bluff, saw the oak hummock Deschamps had chosen for him about half a mile away, and scurried inland, through sand and brambles.

As the mackinaws glided northward, the *voyageurs* raised a cheer for the boy, though some jeered good-naturedly: "Ho, Gurdon, where you go?" one shouted. "To dig a hole?" "To climb a tree!" another called, "To find a big fat bear!" The sallies brought shouts of laughter and an angry order from Deschamps. *"Taisez-vous! Fermez la bouche!"* Why did those dolts think they were proceeding without the boat song this fine October morning? Silence was the order of the day. Yet Deschamps grinned down at Noel Vasseur. The men were in a good mood after the uproar of the night before. Not a man dead, none wounded. And, after all, the boy Gurdon *had* got sick on fat bear meat at the Indian feast. He was not alone, many of them were digging holes in the sand that morning.

There continued to be possible danger. Seven Indians killed. The Peoria warriors responsible had brought vast supplies of whisky into the Potawatomi camp, liquor that could have been obtained only from the trading posts of Kinzie and Crafts who would not have surrendered such supplies readily. One always remembered the terrible massacre at Fort Dearborn, only six years past, in such circumstances. Deschamps did not really believe that Winnetuk, the young Peoria chief, and his renegade band could have attacked the entire Fort Dearborn garrison. But, if the troops had been away, or even if all present were inside the palisade John Crafts or John Kinzie, or both, might have been raided, their people slaughtered. Somehow the Peorias obtained much whisky, rum and trade goods very early in the season. Deschamps, long based in the Peoria country, knew that Winnetuk had an evil reputation and no credit with the traders. He could not have acquired the supplies honestly.

Inside the sheltered cove they were safe. Deschamps now called out quietly: *"A terre! A terre! Pour la pipe!"* The men drove their canoes high upon the sand and took their ease, relieving themselves along the beach, passing the punk to light their pipes, talking of the feasting and the wenching and the fighting of the night before. Deschamps, with his mariner's glass, and Vasseur climbed a sand dune, remaining in the shelter of its crest and waited to get a sighting on Gurdon.

"I know Winnetuk, you know him, and we both know the truth is not in him," Deschamps told Vasseur. "If he says the portage is wet, we may be sure it is dry. If he says he traded corn and deer hides for liquor, we may be sure he stole it, perhaps violently. If he says the Winnebagos are ready to attack Fort Dearborn, we may believe they are peacefully harvesting their corn. But we can't be certain. Winnetuk is too unreliable. Sometimes he tells the truth." Deschamps chuckled softly and continued, "Gurdon will signal the truth. He knows every foot of Chicago. That's all we talked of this summer. Gurdon, John Kinzie and I: Chicago, Fort Dearborn, the massacre, the Indians, and I must not forget, the prairie. That boy is mad about geography and history."

Vasseur, lean, brown, and young, eyed his aging boss with affection and understanding. "Is that why you claimed young Hubbard as your son last night?" he asked.

Deschamps sputtered. "Of course I lied to them," he said.

73

"They called him 'Little American.' That alone can get him killed in Peoria country. He is a good boy, Noel. He learns fast, he knows what to look for. They told me at Mackinac that he walked most of the way from Montreal to Lake Simcoe, keeping up with the boats, just to keep himself strong. And he carried on all the portages! His legs are strong, his eyes are sharp. You will find him a big help to you at Beebeau's post. He will get the books in order and he can write the reports in English, as must be done now. He is American and Americans we must have. How Winnetuk guessed that I myself cannot guess."

"One of our men told Winnetuk," Vasseur suggested. "He didn't know it would be harmful. All the men are fond of Gurdon Hubbard. He is the only *mangè de lard* I've ever known to be invited to mess with them the first trip out."

Deschamps, having spotted Gurdon on the oak hummock, handed the glass to Vasseur. He was pleased by Vasseur's comment. Ordinarily the veteran *voyageurs* would not accept into their company the newcomers they called "pork eaters." The *voyageurs* themselves ate only peas and tallow and were proud of it. They chose carefully whom they had to their mess. However, in truth, there were not many who craved that honor.

It was Vasseur who held the brass mariner's glass on Gurdon in the oak tree when the boy signalled. "He says all is clear at the fort," Vasseur said. "Good," Deschamps answered. "Give him the sign that we understand." Vasseur wagged the gleaming brass piece in a semi-circle.

"Tell the men to dress and to dress the boats," Deschamps ordered. "We will now go to Chicago in usual fashion. I'll follow shortly."

Deschamps knelt in the sand, praying his gratitude for their deliverance from danger, their safe journey from Mackinac, their fortunate arrival in Wasachek's village before the hunters departed. He sought forgiveness for sins, including his sin of lying about his son from Montreal. He prayed for guidance and for peace. As he walked back to the cove, he smiled to himself. That story of his son would spread quickly and widely, but not, he hoped, all the way to Quebec and Montreal. Some of those in the Illinois country, at St. Louis and Cahokia, would believe it he knew. He had trained for the priesthood but had failed of ordination, and they always suspected him. He had declined to take the vows since he feared he could not keep them, especially that of chastity.

*

High on his perch in the tallest oak atop the hummock, Gurdon searched again for any signs of movement across the stretches of sand, marshlands and highland groves that formed the land approaches to Fort Dearborn. There were none. A few canoes plied the river. Immediately to the south of the fort, men, bare to the waist, labored in the potato fields, harvesting the fall crop. The water gate to the north was open and a few men were washing their shirts. Beyond the gleaming, whitewashed palisade on the north bank of the river, behind a row of poplar trees and a neat white fence, stood the Kinzie "mansion" a large log cabin with a huge piazza across the front. Northwest of the Kinzie outbuildings was a cabin he knew to be that of Antoine Ouilmette, who worked for Kinzie and ferried soldiers and visitors in his rowboat. To the left, near the Kinzie house, a large two-story cabin was under construction, the new government Agency House that John Kinzie had mentioned. Farther west, along the North Branch, that Deschamps called the Guarie River, lay the Potawatomi village, ruled by Chief Billy Caldwell, the son of a British officer and a Potawatomi woman, who called himself "The Sauganash," meaning "The Englishman." There was little more to see, except the Burns cabin to the west of the Agency House, where Mrs. Kinzie was visiting Mrs. Burns, who was ill, the night she learned of the first Indian raid on Chicago in August, 1812. Chicago was not much, "just four and a half houses," Gurdon would write his mother a few days later.

His eyes followed the river westward. Along the south branch, called Portage Branch by Deschamps, a swamp area and a few oak hummocks and sand hills appeared. Deschamps called the biggest area of oaks "the Blue Island." About three miles down the south branch was the cabin he knew to be that of John Crafts, at Hardscrabble. There the Lee family had been attacked by Indians a few days before the massacre. They bashed the heads of children against the log walls and killed the adults they could capture. There was now no sign of life at the Crafts place.

Below Hardscrabble, the south branch lost itself in thick marsh grass. Gurdon's eyes followed it to the mound of high ground Deschamps called "The Summit." Below The Summit was Mud Lake, the swamp that stretched south westward for five miles. In times of high water a light canoe could float all the way from Chicago to the Desplaines and thence into the Illinois and the Mississippi rivers. But this was the dry season in a dry year. Gurdon saw only tan marsh grass, a few scrubby trees, expanses of bare earth and rock. He could detect the gleam of a few ponds of water in Mud Lake beyond the Summit. The extremity of the south branch also appeared dry. Without much doubt they would have to portage not only the five miles across Mud Lake, but another two or three miles of the South Branch.

Feeling himself prepared to report to Deschamps on the condition of the portage, Gurdon at last feasted his eyes on the prairie, spreading westward between the sand dunes and the river and on southwesterly beyond the river into the horizon, a golden, undulating sea of Indian grass and flowers, rippling in the sun. "The waving grass, intermingled with a rich profusion of wild flowers, was the most beautiful sight I ever gazed upon," Gurdon Hubbard would remember years later. "In the distance the grove of Blue Island loomed up, beyond it timber on the Des Plaines river, while, to give animation to the scene, a herd of wild deer appeared and a pair of red foxes emerged from the grass within gunshot of me." Alexander Henry had called the western prairie of America one of the world's great wonders. Father Marquette and Joliet, among the first to describe it, marvelled at the endless, treeless expanse of vegetation in which bison sank to their withers and elk could disappear. Later Gurdon would find the prairie to be tough, thick and mean, almost impenetrable to wagon traffic or to a wooden plough, a terrifying inferno when set aflame by lightning strikes in late summer. The prairie he gazed upon seemed tinder dry that morning, tawny, with only occasional patches of green where springs fed prairie marshes. Yet the lavendar and yellow wild flowers gave the prairie color and motion in the light morning breeze. It beckoned to him invitingly.

From a half mile away, where the wind tossed the blue lake into breaking whitecaps, Gurdon heard the voice of *Le Bourgeois* Deschamps beginning the boat song, the men soon joining in. John Kinzie said his father swore he could hear and recognize Antoine Deschamps' voice from four miles away!

The Illinois Brigade swung out from the cove and sped north along the coastline, eleven big mackinaws brightly dressed in flags and bunting, and the red, green and blue strips of Stroud cloth, so prized by the Indian women and soon to drape the shoulders of some of them. The *voyageurs* were in full dress, jaunty red caps, blue shirts, buckskin pants and white gaiters. They would go into Chicago in all the glory of their trade, troubadours, freight carriers to the wilderness, and, in their own opinion, eagerly awaited lovers. There they would discharge their freight-carrying responsibilities, set up camp for the repair of boats and the re-stowing of freight after supplying the Chicago posts. Gurdon thrilled at the sight of them, was proud to be a part of them, and somewhat sorry he was not to appear before the Kinzie family as one of them.

Yet he understood that as a clerk he could never be one of them, a true *voyageur,* who brought to the Indian villages and to the lonely forts and pioneer towns songs, joy and laughter, news and gossip, excitement and romance. But he was proud to be a friend of these hardy men, hired for $100 a year to ply the lakes and streams of the remotest parts of the country in fifty-foot bark canoes, living on a ration of rum, an ounce or two of tobacco, a pint of peas or lyed corn, a four-ounce stick of tallow, and, on Sunday, pancakes with honey. They slept in rude huts in winter, or by their boats in howling storms, sheltered by tarpaulins, otherwise they slept in the open, under the stars, cushioned by hemlock boughs or a quickly gathered mat of marsh or prairie grass. No wonder his father had said no boy of his could stand such hardship! He was eager to have his father to see him now, and hoped John Crafts would indeed take him to St. Louis. From his tree perch he heard a fragment of the boat song:

Il y un cog qui chante
des pommes, des poires, des raves, des choux,
des figues novelle, des raisin foux . . . .

Another children's song those tough *voyageurs* loved, most boat songs were, children's songs and love songs. He looked across to the Kinzie place, almost four miles distant. Sure enough, a man he guessed to be John Kinzie, Sr. appeared on the piazza, followed by women and children of the household. They listened, then turned back, probably to prepare for their long-expected visitors. The soldiers at the fort would hear the song and the news would soon reach to the Potawatomi village. Gurdon remembered the day and would write years later: "I saw the whitewashed buildings of Fort Dearborn sparkling in the sunshine. . . . Our boat flags were flying, the oars keeping time to the cheering boat song. I was spellbound and amazed at the beautiful scene."

*

Gurdon walked the Indian trail toward the fort, through scrub pine and brambles between the sand hills and the lake. It was the route the garrison and the wagon train bearing the women and children had taken when they departed Fort Dearborn that morning of August 15, 1812. John Kinzie, Jr. had not made the march, but he saw and heard a part of what transpired and learned the rest from his father and step-sister who survived the actual massacre. He was a boy of nearly nine then. His mother, with the help of friendly Indians, had hidden him, his brother Robert and his sisters Ellen and Maria, while the garrison moved out. John Kinzie, his father, had insisted on leading the wagon train himself, because his daughter, Mrs. Helm, was riding with it. Her husband, Lieutenant Lainai Helm, commanded a company of infantry protecting the train. At about the point where the attack began, a mile and a half south of the fort, Gurdon climbed the highest of a series of sand hills. The fort seemed very close, the soldiers in their potato fields could be heard joining in one of the boat songs as they worked. He recalled John's description of that morning of the massacre six years before. Captain William Wells was first out the gate, astride his horse, a tomahawk and scalping knife in his belt. He had blackened his face, a sure sign of trouble and death. Wells, part-Indian, was a famed Indian fighter and had come to aid the garrison because of his friendship for Captain Nathan Heald, commandant of the fort, bringing a band of Miami scouts with him. Eighteen of these warriors rode with Wells in the van of the procession, another eighteen in the rear. Captain Heald led his cavalry through the gate. John Kinzie preceded the wagon train accompanied by Margaret Helm, also on horseback. The infantry followed. There were two women and twelve children in the wagons. As the procession cleared the gate, nearly five hundred Potawatomis, Winnebagos and Kickapoos rode out, ostensibly to safeguard the procession to Fort Wayne, Indiana Territory. They had been given the fort's supplies for their service, all except the liquor and guns that Captain Heald had ordered destroyed.

Captain Wells was a man Gurdon Hubbard especially admired. He had spent his life in Indian country. He knew Indian ways. And he was sure as he rode out that day that the attack would come and he would die. Captain Wells saw his escort of Indians beginning to vanish from the column. He suspected they intended to regroup beyond the sand hills to the west and rode back to inform Captain Heald of his fears. Heald ordered Wells to lead an immediate charge, before the Indians could attack. Wells rode into the sand hills, but only Captain Heald and his Long Knives followed. The Miamis front and rear had disappeared. In the first volley of the fighting Wells, shouting insults at his enemies, was killed. Heald's charging cavalry met raking fire from the sand hills. In ten minutes of intense gunfire and hand to hand combat, the soldiers slashing with their sabers, the Indians wielding tomahawks and war clubs as their ammunition ran out, forty two soldiers and members of the wagon train died.

A warrior dragged Margaret Helm from her horse and raised his tomahawk. She seized his upraised arm with her right hand as she sought with her left to reach his scalping knife. She was losing the struggle when Black Partridge, a Potawatomi chief friendly to the Kinzies, saw her. He claimed her as his prisoner, yanked the attacking warrior away, sending him spinning. Black Partridge had saved her life and with other friendly Indians he took her and Mrs. Heald, wounded, to the place where they had hidden others of the Kinzie family. There John Kinzie joined them. Captain Heald, Lieutenant Helm, and soldiers still alive surrendered to Black Bird, a Potawatomi chief leading the attack.

The fighting ended but scenes of horror continued. Indians scalped their victims. An unborn infant, torn from the body of Mrs. Corbin, wife of a soldier, lay decapitated and the dying mother was similarly mutilated.

An Indian woman stabbed Thomas Burns, a soldier wounded in the fighting, with a stable fork until he died in agony. Four warriors cut the heart of Captain Wells from his body, divided it and ate it, expecting to gain his courage. Then they paraded his head on a pike. Friendly Potawatomis escorted the Kinzies and Mrs. Heald to the Kinzie house that night. Three days later all escaped to St. Joseph, again with Indian help.

*

South of the fort, where the sand spit ended and the Chicago River emptied into Lake Michigan, Gurdon cachéd his duffle bag under a clump of scrub oak, shed his buckskins, and went for a swim and bath. The lone blue heron fishing there watched disdainfully. The water was cold and clear. His reflection told Gurdon he was as brown as a Potawatomi, his hair, though somewhat sun-bleached, still as dark as his smoky eyes. He was beardless, like any Indian brave, and wore his hair long, tied in back at the nape of the neck, Indian style. He wondered why Chief Winnetuk the night before had called him "The Little American." He was as big as any of the *voyageurs* and he expected he would grow to the six feet of his grandfather, George Hubbard, the Revolutionary War soldier. He looked closely into his reflection to see if he should use his hunting knife to shave, but the white fuzz on his thin, brown face didn't seem to require it.

It was time to report to M. Deschamps and to go to the Kinzies. He dressed, breech clout of clean white cloth, freshly washed and dried in the wind, a blue calico shirt, buckskin leggings extending to his thighs and attached to a belt from which, on most days, he hung his hunting knife, tomahawk and the otter skin pouch in which he carried flint and moss and sometimes parched corn. He would have liked to appear at the Kinzies with all his accoutrements, including the tomahawk, but it wasn't possible. They had gone on to camp in his *voyageur's* chest, which contained his other belongings, his Bible and Alexander Henry book, soap and tooth powder, and the ruffled shirt, swallow-tailed coat and broadcloth trousers his mother had insisted on sending with him. He wrapped neips about his feet, tucking the corners of cloth up into his leggings so they held fast, and slipped his moccasins over them. He wore his hunting knife but, unlike most *voyageurs,* no silver ornaments.

A young soldier fishing near the wash house at the northeast corner of the fort watched impassively as Gurdon approached. Gurdon saluted him. "You kin talk," the boy said, "I got all the fish I want anyways."

"How can I get a boat to the Kinzies?" Gurdon asked. "I'm Gurdon Hubbard, a friend of their son."

"Sure," the soldier said. "I got a canoe. Ol' Ouilmette's got a boat some place but he ain't here. I kin take you over. I'm Seth, Major Baker's orderly. You with them *voyageurs?* How come they didn't fetch you?"

"I had a job to do back there."

"Wheah you from?"

"From Marriole," he answered as a *voyageur* would.

"Wheah's thet?"

"In Canada."

The soldier was satisfied. Someone at the Kinzie's saw them coming. When they reached the landing, John Kinzie, a chin-whiskered, blue-eyed, craggy Scot, greeted him. "Welcome to Chicago, lad!" He seized Gurdon's hand in a warm, firm clasp. Kinzie was not the grim, forbidding man Gurdon had expected from his talks with John Junior. "Come," Kinzie said, "we'll go to report to Deschamps. Then Mrs. Kinzie wants us to come up to the house."

Gurdon thanked the soldier, proferring a coin which was refused. "Can I come to see you at the fort?" he asked. The soldier nodded. "Seth gets back here in an hour or so," Kinzie said. "Major Baker is coming over to pay his respects to your boss and to have supper with Mrs. Kinzie."

The *voyageurs* had their camp set up in good order on the river bank, all cargo unloaded and the *batteaux* readied for repair. Vasseur prepared to depart for John Crafts' place and to inspect the portage if Gurdon's report indicated anything unusual. "I hope you're wrong about the low water in the Portage Branch," Deschamps said to Gurdon. "It will mean a league more of carry." Vasseur was instructed to make a calculation of the probable distance. But Deschamps' main worry was for John Crafts. "Something went wrong out there," he told Kinzie.

"Antoine, you're fretting because you remember that first attack there," Kinzie said. "Crafts wasn't feeling well. Maybe he thought he couldn't wait for you any longer."

"I know we're late," Deschamps snapped. "Crafts nonetheless was to wait for me. It is unlike him not to come in when the brigade arrives."

"Just wait for Noel's report," Kinzie advised soothingly. "I know there was no trouble with Winnetuk at Crafts' place. We certainly would have heard it. They would have heard it at the fort. . . ."

"But something has happened to John Crafts."

"He may have gone out to carry the last of his supplies to a hunting party."

"John," said Deschamps heavily, "Winnetuk got those supplies in Chicago. He didn't get them from you."

It was Kinzie's turn to be cross. "Damn it, Deschamps, if the Peorias are planning a ruckus I would know about it. Forsyth would have come up to tell me." He referred to his partner, Thomas Forsyth, trader in the Peoria country. "Wait for Vasseur's report. Come on now, to supper. Somehow or other, Mrs. Kinzie looks forward to seeing you."

*

Chapter 3

In his first letter home from Chicago, Gurdon recounted the
events to his mother, omitting only Deschamps' worries about
a possible Indian uprising. "As soon as our tents were pitched
on the north side of the river, we were called upon by the
officers of the fort, to all of whom I was introduced by M.
Deschamps as his boy. I presented my letter of introduction to
Mr. Kinzie and with it a package from his son. In the afternoon
I called at Mr. Kinzie's house and had the pleasure of meeting
Mrs. Kinzie, Maria, their youngest daughter, their youngest son
Robert and Mrs. Helm. As I had so recently seen John and had
been so intimate with him, I had much of interest to tell them."

The Kinzie log house, to which John Jr. usually referred,
somewhat derisively, as "the mansion," was built about 1776
by Jean Baptiste Point du Sable, the black fur trader from Santo
Domingo, who added sheds and cabins as his business
prospered. Kinzie bought the property at the lake on the north
bank of the river in 1803, attached the piazza and another cabin
to accommodate his own fur trade and silversmith work, as well
as his growing family.

This day Kinzie had with him Charles Jouett, the Indian agent
in Chicago, and two Indian chiefs, once allied with the British,
but now friendly to the Americans, "medal Indians" who had
sold out their people, some said; pragmatic politicians able to
cope with reality, others believed. Billy Caldwell, The Sauganash, continued to wear the silver gorgets given to him by
the British though he was now in the American camp. He was
a rugged, beaming giant of a man, towering over John Kinzie.
His father, a British officer, had married a Potawatomi woman.
The night of the massacre, John Jr. had told Gurdon, when they
thought they had been saved, a war party of Miami Indians invaded their home. Billy Caldwell charged in and ordered the
warriors out. "I see you are in mourning, you have blackened
your faces," he told them scornfully. "Mourn for your dishonor!
You are in the home of friends who never denied you your
needs. You need food? They have always given you food. Take
it now and go!" The Sauganash saved their lives, John Jr. believed, and none of them would forget it. Alexander Robinson,
the second of Kinzie's Indian guests, was a mild-appearing, little man, the son of a Scotch officer and a woman of the Ottawa

tribe, close kin of the Potawatomis. He was chief of the United Potawatomi Tribes and served at Fort Dearborn as Indian interpreter.

John Kinzie took Gurdon to met his wife Eleanor. She hugged him close. "You are the dear friend of our son," she exclaimed. "You are now in your Chicago home. It will be your home always!" She led him onto the porch and introduced her step-daughter, Margaret Helm. Gurdon was astonished that one so slight could have fought off an Indian warrior, as she did until Black Partridge rescued her. Yet she was as tall as Gurdon, a trim and lovely woman. She took his hand, welcomed him as a friend of her brother, and held his hand as she presented her youngest brother, Robert, and sister Maria. In the next hour the Kinzies gathered around him, asking Gurdon countless questions about John Jr., exclaiming in delight at every detail he could recall. He sought politely to direct his answers to Mrs. Kinzie, but found himself glancing whenever possible at Margaret Helm, the prettiest woman he ever had seen. He knew that she was the wife of Lieutenant Lainai Helm of the United States Army and that she was six or more years older than himself. But he had thrilled at her touch and wished to keep her close to him. He recalled all possible recollections of his friend John on Mackinac. He was elated when Margaret, on learning that he and John had gone to the dances at Mackinac that summer, announced that she would be his partner for the evening.

Margaret joined her mother and the Indian girls in getting the hot supper on the long table on the piazza, leaving Gurdon to her father, the agent Jouett and the officers from the fort who were gathered about Deschamps to hear the news of Mackinac, Montreal and the American Fur Company. When Vasseur appeared, to announce that John Crafts was not at his cabin at Hardscrabble, nor were there any trade goods left, Antoine Deschamps was again upset. John Crafts would have stored his goods at the fort before departing if he went voluntarily, Deschamps insisted. But Kinzie disagreed. John Crafts disliked Jacob Varnum, the factor, he said, and would not have called on him for help. As for leaving word with Kinzie, John ruled that out also. "John Crafts was ill," Kinzie explained. "He waited as long as he could for you to arrive, Antoine. He was ill. He sold the last of his goods and he has gone to St. Louis."

"Then how did the Peorias come by the trade goods, especially the spirits?" Deschamps demanded.

Kinzie couldn't say. "They might have robbed it all at Milwaukee," he suggested. But they all knew better. The Peorias had acquired their stock of whisky and trade goods immediately before arriving at the camp on the Little Calumet. It would not have survived a trip through Winnebago country, nor a visit to Big Foot, whose appetite for liquor was enormous. If Winnetuk was passing war belts in the north, he would have given up his rum and whisky trying to win friends, as he did on the Little Calumet. Deschamps knew the Peorias as well as any man. They had continued their hostilities against the Americans longer than any tribe, into 1815, after the Peace of Ghent ended the War of 1812. Renegade or not, Winnetuk would win some of the Indians to him, Deschamps believed. He would not have hesitated to rob John Crafts, to kill him, hiding the body. The Peorias, Deschamps feared, might once more be on the warpath.

They drank their whisky, mixed with cold water from the river, and dismissed the Crafts mystery for the evening. "I cannot send my men out to search for him," Major Baker said apologetically. "Nor can I send men to the Little Calumet to look into the killing of seven Indians. They get drunk and kill one another. Not one would admit that it happened. You know that, Deschamps."

Deschamps nodded. "I will look for John Crafts myself," he said. "There is a matter of missing supplies. Mr. Astor won't take that lightly, Major. I myself will go to St. Louis." He turned to John Kinzie. "Let me know what you need, John. I'll try to fill your list." And then to Gurdon: "You were to go to St. Louis with Mr. Crafts," he said. "Now you will go with me."

A ship's bell summoned them to the picnic supper on the piazza. Gurdon was delighted with Deschamps' words. Margaret Helm met him at the piazza steps, bringing plates and spoons and gourd cups for him and herself. "I hope you are hungry and that you really like to dance," she said. "My brother John hated it. I'm surprised he danced at Mackinaw." She pronounced it American style. "All brothers hate to dance," he told her. "But I'm most fond of it." They joined the others at the long table, piling food onto plates or clean cedar shakes, and into bowls and canteens. The table was spread with steaming platters of fresh venison roasted by the Indian women in the cook house back of the kitchen, fresh fish caught that afternoon, fried turtle and eel, boiled potatoes, kettles of corn soup, baked beans and squash, parboiled Indian corn called *petit blé,* and wild rice, *folles avoines,* as well as parched roots and nuts, fresh vegetables from the Kinzie garden, berries and wild apples. Margaret helped him choose the delicacies he might most enjoy and they sat together at the end of the piazza absorbed in their talk, again of John and then of Gurdon's assignment on the Illinois river. "I'm afraid my father doesn't care much for Mr. Beebeau," Margaret said. "He's a tyrant. . . . But I know you can stand up to him." Her view of Beebeau didn't dismay him as much as her next observation, "I'll be leaving Chicago, too, to be with my husband at Detroit. I hope you will come to see us when you return to Mackinaw for the summer. You and John must come."

His dream of her was shattered. "I had hoped to see you again here!" he exclaimed. She smiled at him, a bit sadly. "You will be too busy at Mr. Beebeau's to even think of me," she said. "But you must come when you get to Mackinaw." He pouted gloomily on the steps as she excused herself to help clear the tables. He watched her move gracefully about, lighting candles and directing the work of the women. When she appeared before him again, she seemed taller and he saw she wore dancing slippers, her eyes were very blue, like her father's, and the hurt of seeing her so close, so beautiful, and the realization that he might not see her again, saddened him. Margaret, however, was oblivious to his misery as she led him to the Kinzie lawn to join the squares forming for the quadrille. John Kinzie had brought out his fiddle and an officer from the fort stepped up to call. They pigeon-winged and double-shuffled, hoed corn and dug potatoes, as Kinzie's fiddle shrilly sang and Margaret's laughter sweetened the darkening October night.

The day following Gurdon returned to the Kinzie home for breakfast, bringing with him the suit of clothes and ruffled shirt, both still much too large, that his mother had sent with him from Montreal and other articles from his *voyageur's* chest he did not expect to use in the wilderness. Gurdon was to write of that morning, "As I sat down to the well-ordered table for the first time since I left my father's house, memories of home and those dear to me forced themselves upon me and I could not suppress my tears. But for the kindness of Mrs. Kinzie, I should have beaten a hasty retreat. But she saw my predicament saying, 'I know just how you feel, and I know more than you think; I am going to be a mother to you if you will let me. Just come with me a moment'."

She led him to the washroom off the kitchen, where he bathed his eyes in cold water. When he returned to the dining room, he saw the family had awaited his return. He glanced toward Margaret, who smiled understandingly. He spoke to Mrs. Kinzie before them all, "You reminded me so much of my mother I couldn't help crying." They resumed breakfast and he turned to the ham, smoked in the Kinzie smokehouse, and fried eggs and hot chunks of fresh bread made from real flour, coffee brewed from actual coffee beans, and realized he had been half starving for many months.

*

Within five days the brigade had refitted and repacked the mackinaws and was ready for the ordeal of the Chicago Portage. The requirements of Kinzie, the missing John Crafts, and Jean Baptiste Beaubien for their Chicago and Wisconsin posts reduced their cargo by two boatloads. Even Jacob Varnum, the government factor, had his needs met, as the new laws demanded. John Jacob Astor himself had sought to end the government factory system, sending his agents to Washington to lobby for repeal. But he had been unsuccessful. Traders in the northwest unanimously opposed the system, insisting that the goods the government offered in exchange for furs failed to meet the needs of the Indians, were shoddy and overpriced. The government retaliated by requiring Astor to sell to the factories his own trade goods at favorable prices. Thus Deschamps was compelled to supply Varnum, even after the record showed Varnum had sought to have John Kinzie and others barred from the Indian trade on the grounds that they had aided England during the war and were selling the Indians too much whisky.

Gurdon Hubbard kept the trading accounts for Deschamps while they were in Chicago, stood his watch at night, and also was put to work with the *voyageurs,* patching and stitching the birchbark skins of the canoes, wrapping the cedar ribs with deerskin thongs, lashing strakes to the bruised gunnels, caulking seams with pitch and resin. He saw nothing of Margaret Helm since the morning after the dance and suspected that Deschamps and John Kinzie had plotted to keep him away from the Kinzie house. Not until the morning of their departure, when a great crowd gathered to see them off, did he have a chance to speak with her again, and then she was with her family. Eleanor Kinzie hugged him close, reminding him that their home was his home. John Kinzie shook his hand firmly, urging him to look up his partner, Forsyth, on Lake Peoria. Robert and Maria ignored him to watch the *voyageurs,* in full regalia, board their flag-decked *batteaux.* Margaret surveyed him in full uniform, with his tomahawk and knife in his belt, smiling her approval as she took his hand. "Take care of yourself, Gurdon Hubbard," she said, then added pointedly, "Don't forget you have promised to come to Lieutenant Helm and me when you get back to Mackinaw." He understood that he was to remember her as Mrs. Margaret Helm. "I will come to see you," he promised again.

His romantic torment did not last long. That night they camped on a dry hummock two miles below John Crafts' post. Deschamps had stopped to inspect the cabin, returning grim and preoccupied. The men were in a fine mood, they had danced every night at the Potawatomi camp, and they talked freely of their conquests as they all messed together consuming the last hot pea soup to be had until they completed the portage. They set fires for the night with the wood brought from Chicago and bedded down early on tarpaulins laid on Indian grass to protect them from the marshy dampness. The air reeked with the odor of leek and wild onion, which the Indians called "Chegakou," coughing up the word as if to rid themselves of the smell by articulating it. Deschamps and Kinzie argued about that too, Kinzie asserting that "Chegakou" meant the region around Fort Dearborn, Deschamps insisting that Father Hennepin, the first to use the word in print, said "Chegakou" referred to the Illinois river area and the rest of northern Illinois, including the Chicago

River. They agreed it alluded to the wild onion, saying it also meant "a powerful odor."

Gurdon slept well that night on his tarpaulin spread over grass and reeds, with a single blanket against the early October cold. In the morning the portaging began, easy at the start. As the South Branch grew shallow all but a few carried cargo bags weighing from eighty to one hundred pounds held to their backs by chest girths. They followed the bed of the river for about two miles, sometimes through shallow water, often over slippery rock, then crossed the five miles of Mud Lake. The empty boats floated part of the way and were towed along the dry stretches of the river on cedar rollers cut for the purpose. As they moved into the oozing marshes surrounding Mud Lake, the going was hard. "Four men in each boat pushed with long poles to which branches of trees were attached to provide bearing on stones and tussocks of grass," Gurdon wrote. "While six or eight waded in the mud alongside, by united efforts they constantly jerked the boat along, so that from early dawn to dark we succeeded only in passing a part of our boats to the Desplaines River outlet, where we found the first hard ground."

The mud deepened, Mud Lake was aptly named. "All along the lake, grass and wild rice often reached above a man's head, so strong and dense it was almost impossible to walk. . . ." Men slipped and lost their balance, struggled to keep the cargo packages from going down in muddy water. Sometimes a package disappeared and the *voyageur* went down into the marsh mud to retrieve it. "They frequently sank to their waists and at times were forced to cling to the side of the boat to keep from going over their heads." They were in misery throughout the three days of the carry, muscles aching, welts growing on their bodies from the attacks of gnats, flies and mosquitoes. They plastered themselves with mud to keep the pests from biting. By night they emerged from the swamp as cold, black zombies, to drop their cargo into the portaged boats while they sought dry places to sleep after swallowing a ration of corn washed down with water from their canteens. On drying, they found themselves covered with slimy bloodsuckers.

"The lake was full of these abominable black plagues," Gurdon wrote years later. "They stuck so tight they broke in pieces if force was used to remove them. Experience had taught that a decoction of tobacco would remove them and this was used with success." It was the beginning of his tobacco habit. "Having rid ourselves of the bloodsuckers," Gurdon continued, "we were assailed by myriads of mosquitoes that rendered sleep hopeless. . . . Those who waded the lake suffered great agony, their limbs becoming swollen and inflamed . . ." Gurdon himself would suffer from the experience the rest of his life, with bouts of fever and rheumatism.

*

The portage was traversed within three days, the canoes reloaded, and the weary, beaten *voyageurs* proceeded by water toward the Isle La Caché in the Des Plaines river. They were able finally to cleanse themselves of mud and bloodsuckers, but they had to unload the boats again because of low water before reaching the high ground of La Caché, where they camped. Deschamps sent Gurdon, armed with a double-barreled shotgun, across the little island covered with prairie grass and a few trees. That night *Le Bourgeois* and his clerks had Canada geese in addition to their pea soup and pork. As they sat around the fire, enjoying their pipes after their first hot meal in three days, Deschamps told them how Caché Island got its name. His employer, Sara of St. Louis, was threatened by hostile Indians when he reached the island. Realizing he could not freely pass the Indian village, he hid his most of the cargo, burying it on the island during the night. He then wrapped a large bale of goods with bright ribbons, dropped a red orb of sealing wax onto the ribbon, "sealed" it with a medallion brought from Quebec, and took it to the Indian village under a flag of truce.

When the chief and headmen appeared, Sara offered them the impressive beribboned and sealed bale of trade goods, saying: "I had prepared this gift for you, it has the seal of my king. But the Great Spirit has told me that you intend to rob me." This the Indians denied. They wanted the gift. They were pleased when they opened it, since the bale held calico and fine Stroud cloth, tobacco, flints, powder and shot, and steels for striking fire. Sara informed them they would get another similar bale if they would help his men portage his cargo. The Indians agreed, brought up their ponies and dug up and carried the cargo over the portage. "They enjoyed Sara's strategy," Deschamps said. "It amused them. They got their second bale of gifts and we went our way unharmed." Deschamps taught them by parable, as Jesus did in the Bible, Gurdon realized. He had traded among Indians for forty years with little trouble. He respected their ways, they respected him. The boy understood the implication of the Caché Island story, that the Indians didn't mind being deceived if the ruse was a clever one, but he saw another lesson in the whole portage experience. Why not sink the boats near the south branch of the river, make the carry, and build new mackinaws on the Desplaines? He had seen a freight canoe built in a single day on Mackinac Island. Deschamps merely drew on his corncob pipe, ignoring Gurdon's question.

Their spirits revived as they paddled down the Desplaines to the Illinois, a wide, beautiful, tree-lined river where a strong current helped to carry them along. They passed thick forests of oak, hickory, pine and maple, and glimpsed beyond the woods the serene stretches of golden prairie. That evening Gurdon again climbed a tree for a view of the land. The wide prairie was laced with streams and ornamented with gleaming ponds where Indians still fished and squaws harvested corn. Along the Illinois and its tributaries, he could see the smoke of Indian villages: later they heard sounds of barking dogs, singing and the beat of the Indian drums, another harvest celebration. Deschamps sent men out to the villages to trade powder and tobacco for corn and venison, but no further barter was allowed. The Illinois Brigade was late that year and the Indians were eager to go to their hunting grounds. Nevertheless they were required to come into the trading posts for supplies they would require for the winter's hunt.

"Why is this?" Gurdon asked Noel Vasseur. "Why not give them their trade goods now? Why not take the goods to them in their hunting camps by using ponies?" Vasseur did not reply, but Deschamps, overhearing the questions, explained, "We make best time going directly to our posts. At each post our trader knows the worth of the hunters in his territory. He will allow as much trade goods to the hunter as he can expect the hunter to bring in by season's end. He can keep records and books at the post. You will go with Vasseur to Beebeau's post. He is sick and cannot go out to any village, but he knows more than any man the ability of the hunters in all the villages. He knows how much credit to extend. You will learn from him how to judge the worth of each hunter. When you have learned this, in a few years, you can become a trader.

"Now, as to leaving the *batteaux* at the portage. . . . I will not waste time discussing that. The boats could burn in prairie fires, even near the water. They might be stolen. It is good for you to ask questions, Gurdon, but don't bother Vasseur with them until you have improved your French, and don't both Monsieur Beebeau with them at all. He is not a patient man. But he does know exactly how many traps and how much powder and tobacco and how many knives and blankets a hunter can earn in a season. This you will learn. Be content that you can do what Beebeau cannot do, you can read and write."

*

The woods thickened along the Illinois river. South of Starved Rock they entered the rich hunting, trapping and corn country served by Antoine Deschamps personally, in addition to his responsibilities as superintendent of the Illinois River posts of the American Fur Company. That evening they drifted quietly into Beebeau's post, without flags or boat songs. Beebeau lived and traded in a log house on the Illinois at the mouth of the Bureau river, his retainers having their cabins a quarter of a mile away. Deschamps ordered Vasseur to take the brigade to camp a half mile south, to allow Beebeau the solitude and quiet he craved. There also was an Indian village not far from the camp site.

Deschamps took Gurdon Hubbard with him to Beebeau's cabin. A fat Indian woman came to the door, recognized Deschamps, and silently admitted them. The split log door had been closed early against the cool of the evening and the windows, covered with oiled paper, also kept out the setting sun, but in the lurid glow from the huge fireplace, Gurdon could see Beebeau lying on his bunk in the dark, foul-smelling room. He saw no more, since the trader growled a command and the Indian woman pointed to the open door, signalling the boy to leave. "Wait outside for me," Deschamps said. Gurdon was glad to escape the fetid smell of the sickroom. He was dismayed by his glimpse of Beebeau, a huge, fat, whiskery old man reclining on a bed of bearskins. Beebeau was sipping soup or a medicine as they entered. The boy saw stacks of trade goods and a pile of stinking pelts in the room and was sickened by the realization that this might become his workplace.

When Deschamps emerged he was in a cheerful mood. "Monsieur Beebeau regrets his indisposition," Deschamps said loudly as he stood at the doorway, keeping the door open. "He welcomes your service and says you may report to Monsieur Vasseur. Monsieur Beebeau himself will see you in good time." Deschamps beckoned the relieved boy to approach, so he could continue within the hearing of Beebeau. "We have agreed," Deschamps said loudly, "that we will build a house to serve as the trading store and your living quarters. Thus Monsieur Beebeau will have the calm he requires for his health. You will be responsible for the inventory and the records, at the direction of Monsieur Beebeau. Since you and I, Gurdon Hubbard, must go to St. Louis for tobacco, shot and powder, Noel Vasseur will begin the construction of the house as soon as the hunters have been supplied. The store in which you will reside and the books should be ready for you to take over on your return."

In the morning they unloaded supplies at Beebeau's, one of the best trading posts in the Illinois country, Deschamps said. Gurdon inventoried the goods and made out invoices, which were supplied to Beebeau, unable to read them.

Noel Vasseur and the boy discussed the house they would build and its location. Deschamps approved their plan, clearing it with Beebeau, and left a detail of *voyageurs,* who were told they would report to Vasseur on his return from the Opa post. As the boats were readied for departure, the Indian woman brought word that Beebeau wished to see his new aide. She escorted Gurdon into the house, which stank as much as the day before, and left him standing in the flickering light of the fire. Beebeau raised himself on an elbow, his face pale, his eyes bulging unnaturally, his jowl sagging. He studied the boy a moment, snorted disgustedly, then fluttered his pale, plump hand to signal dismissal.

*

The Illinois Brigade departed Beebeau's as silently as it came, leaving two boats and eight men detailed there, including a *voyageur's* son, Pierre, brought up from the Indian village nearby, who would aid Gurdon at the store and assist him with the Potawatomi language. They could live together in the new house if Gurdon so wished. Gurdon was delighted with his good fortune. He could tell his father, when they met in St. Louis, that he was eager to remain in the fur business. Not that he had a choice, he was indentured for five years. Still, his father had hinted that the contract could be broken if necessary. Gurdon was now sure it wouldn't be necessary.

They were bound for Mr. Beason's Opa post three miles south of Lake Peoria on the Illinois River. Mr. Beason, an aging, quiet man, and his Indian wife had joined the Illinois Brigade as passengers after spending the summer on Mackinac. His establishment at Opa exceeded Beebeau's or anything at Chicago. The American Fur Company had also leased added quarters for him at Old Fort Clark on the lake. Since Opa was sixty miles from Beebeau's and they had Indian villages to visit, as well as a stop at Old Fort Clark planned, Deschamps allowed two full days for the journey. The Illinois Brigade was proceeding slowly on Lake Peoria, against a strong wind, late the second day when Vasseur called attention to heavy smoke in the direction of the fort.

"As we rounded the point of the lake, we discovered Old Fort Clark was on fire," Gurdon Hubbard recalled. "Deschamps set the men paddling to increase their speed. We soon were abreast of the blazing log fort and headed toward the landing area. Upon reaching it, we found Indians to the number of about two hundred engaging in a war dance. They were hideously painted and had scalps on their spears and in their sashes, which they had taken from Americans during the war with Great Britain."

Deschamps was furious. He was certain that Winnetuk and his renegades were responsible for this new outrage, one clearly intended to intimidate the American Fur Company if not to precipitate war. He was determined to demand an accounting of such behavior. As the *voyageurs* brought the *batteaux* ashore, Deschamps leaped into the shallow water before his own boat had made fast. Leaving Vasseur in charge, he picked two veterans to accompany him in the direction of the dancers, vowing to find a responsible chief. Meantime, a band of young braves, brandishing tomahawks, moved down upon the boats.

Deschamps correctly guessed that the firing of the fort was considered by the Indians to be an act of defiance unlikely to produce reprisals by the American government, though American federal property was being destroyed. But it was an act of unthinking vandalism. He was sure that among so many he could find chiefs who knew the value of such a trading post. He hoped to persuade them that the path they had chosen could only harm their own welfare and might lead to war. He assumed that Winnetuk was responsible, and, seeing that arrogant young man in a cluster of older chiefs merely watching the fire and the dancing, he sent a *voyageur* to tell them he wished to parley at the boat landing.

As Deschamps returned toward the landing, the leader of the band of braves moving on the boats approached Gurdon Hubbard, who was standing beside Deschamps' canoe with a *voyageur* detailed to guard it. Gurdon saw that the warrior was one of those with Winnetuk at the Little Calumet. The young brave was in red, blue and yellow war paint, wore only a "fig bar" as the French called the leather apron warriors hung fore and after from their war belts, which supported also a knife, tobacco pouch, and a number of scalps.

"The young brave, having noticed me, inquired who I was and M. Deschamps replied that I was his adopted son from Montreal," Gurdon remembered.

The Indian impudently disputed this statement as Deschamps moved away to meet the chiefs, arriving in response to his message. "He insisted I was an American and endeavored to force a quarrel with me," Gurdon wrote. The *voyageur* in charge of the canoe acted as an interpreter for Gurdon. The Indian then took the scalps from his sash. "Showing them to me, one after the other, he told me they were scalps of my people. I was trembling with fear, which he observed. . . ."

The Indian took one of the scalps by the hair, lifted his fig bar, pissed on the scalp, and swung it by the long hair until "it sprin-kled the water on my face."

With a yelp of rage Gurdon dashed into the lake, splashed his face and eyes clean, and then remembered Deschamps' double-barreled shotgun, primed and ready, lying under a strip of oiled cloth in the canoe. Within seconds Gurdon had found the gun, lifted it carefully to avoid losing the powder from the pans, stepped from the boat and raised the heavy flintlock to his shoul-der to take aim at the Indian and his companions. "The *voyageur* with me, seeing my intention, struck up the gun and saved the Indian's life, and probably my own and others of our party," Gurdon recalled.

Gurdon pulled both triggers just as the *voyageur* struck his gun and there was a roar and recoil that jolted him back on his heels. His effort was no flash in the pan, the gun spoke from both barrels, blasts of shot and smoke and flame and sound that caused Gurdon's assailants to run howling back toward the fort while Deschamps whirled in his tracks to see what had hap-pened. The Indian chiefs approaching Deschamps froze in astonishment. The uproar at the boats attracted only minimal attention from the warriors dancing near the burning Fort Clark, but all *voyageurs* scurried toward the boats.

After a brief conference with Vasseur and his other aides, Deschamps shouted the order, "To the boats, all!" Then, "Step the masts." He intended to take advantage of the wind on the lake to outdistance any possible pursuit by the Indians. That meant they would turn back whence they had come toward the relative safety of Beebeau's post.

They made excellent time across the lake and half way back toward Beebeau's on the river, Deschamps, observing they were not noticeably being followed, ordered a stop. They camped that night under heavy guard, though Deschamps said it would be unusual for Indians to attack by night, and the old chiefs, in any event, probably did not want any more trouble. They had come upon the burning Fort Clark, they said, while going out with their hunting parties and did not wish to restrain their young men, who wanted to join the dancing. Winnetuk, they assured Deschamps, had no real standing with their people. Nonetheless, Deschamps was taking no chances. He said they would reach Mr. Beason's post by coasting the other side of the lake. Mercifully, he said nothing at all that night to Gurdon Hubbard.

4

November 6, 1818

I was permitted by M. Deschamps to accompany him to St.
Louis and Cahokia, where he would obtain tobacco and
other necessaries from the French people, whither he
went in one boat with picked *voyageurs*. . . . On November sixth, about 2 o'clock in the afternoon, we reached St.
Louis. Our boat was soon surrounded by friends of M.
Deschamps, among them were many priests, and all united
in a hearty greeting.

Recollections,
Gurdon S. Hubbard

The blustery, cold days of squaw winter buffeted them as they
departed Beebeau's post to cruise the eastern shore of Lake
Peoria, a cautious return to the Opa area, four miles below Fort
Clark. There they would leave Mr. Beason, the veteran trader,
and his fat Indian wife, who had accompanied them all the way
from Mackinac, and they would unload the bulk of their remaining trade goods, since Opa (later Peoria) was an important station. Enroute through the country of the Peorias they called at
the Indian villages, Deschamps taking extreme care to determine
in advance whether they were peaceful, because of the trouble they experienced at the burning of Fort Clark. Old Mr. Beason scoffed at such precautions, telling Deschamps repeatedly
that the young chief Winnetuk and his renegades no longer represented anyone of consequence in the Peoria community. But
Deschamps, knowing the Peorias well himself and remembering that the so-called Peoria War had continued well beyond
the defeat of Tecumseh and other hostilities of the War of 1812,
continued to be wary.

The final days on the Illinois were windy and cold, although
they were moving south. By night they drew their *batteaux*
ashore and rigged tarpaulins to cover the cargo and themselves
against the stinging, wind-blown rain and driving snow that

lashed them day and night. Deschamps and the Beasons and the clerks had tents for shelter, but the *voyageurs* slept in the open, sheltered by the tarpaulins and covered by a blanket. Squaw winter was vicious, but mercifully brief, a warning to the Indian women to complete the tasks of storing the last of the crops and preparing the lodges and wigwams against deep snows and storms. The last of the hunters had packed their gear. They would head for their hunting and trapping grounds as soon as supplies promised by Deschamps' runners reached Opa.

Squaw winter ended as abruptly as it came, followed by the warm, golden days of Indian summer. The flaming color among the sumac, hickory, maples and oak shone in the low slanting sun. Lesser trees had dropped their leaves and the Indian villages on the lake shore stood out in a sunlit glory that could be seen miles ahead. They were found to be peaceful by Deschamps' scouts, so the *voyageurs* decked their boats with flags and sang the boat songs as they approached. The village dogs yipped, the children, enjoying their last warm days of naked freedom, shouted in excitement, the women turned from their harvest labors and the waiting hunters, lolling in the late October warmth, roused themselves and moved down to the landing. There was a joyous reunion of the Indians and the Beasons. "Old Mr. Beason, a large, portly, gray-headed man" had been a trader among them for more than forty years Gurdon recalled. "His wife, a pure-blooded Potawatomi Indian, enormous in size—so fleshy she could scarcely walk."

The Indians wanted their over-due supplies that day and, since Beason was on hand, Deschamps agreed. That night a feast was proclaimed. The summer and fall had been good for crops, corn, peas, beans, potatoes, and pumpkins; and game was plentiful. A good hunting season was expected. The time had come for feasting and dancing. Deschamps was glad to comply. He admitted to Beason that his caution following the Fort Clark incident might have been excessive. So they camped and celebrated at the Indian village, though the Opa post was only four miles away. "The inhabitants of Opa were suspected by our government, wrongly I think, of being enemies and of aiding and counseling the Indians in giving assistance to Great Britain," Gurdon would write at a later date. The Peorias, Kickapoos and Miamis and the Beasons had been attacked for such alleged offenses. Ninian Edwards, governor of the Illinois Territory, personally led a mounted army of 800 men against the Indian towns along Lake Peoria, driving out the inhabitants, burning their homes. Edwards' undisciplined militia then turned into a mob, pillaging, vandalizing and killing without quarter. A second expedition completed the razing of towns. Not a man was lost in the attacks, Governor Edwards boasted. Fort Clark was then constructed. The Indians never forgot nor forgave those depredations.

Nevertheless the trader Beason was sure that his Indians would not again rise against the white man, as they had under Tecumseh and at Fort Dearborn in 1812. He was pleased at the show of friendship that night in the village above Opa, since Deschamps should be convinced that good trading times lay ahead. "I can understand your caution," he said to Deschamps, in reference to the circuitous route to his post, "but I know my people. They do not follow Winnetuk, that outcast disciple of Machtando (the Evil One). He speaks with forked tongue and leads his young men into wickedness. But they are few. Kinzie says his Winnebagos and Potawatomis will not follow Winnetuk. My Peorias will not. They are good hunters. They will bring in many pelts."

But Antoine Deschamps was superintendent of all the American Fur Company posts along the Illinois River and knew his duty. The company itself was on trial. Chief Winnetuk, outcast or not, was dangerous, his plan diabolical. He raided and robbed the American Fur post in Chicago and perhaps killed the trader, John Crafts, escaping without notice being taken at Fort Dearborn. He burned Fort Clark, abandoned as a military post, but leased to the American Fur Company as a trading fort. The wily Winnetuk was sure no government action would be taken, yet, with impunity, he had destroyed American government property and deprived the American Fur Company of a base. How better to inspire dissidence and followers?

Deschamps disclosed his fears to Vasseur, but also his confidence in Beason. He admired Beason's defense of his people, the Peorias, Kickapoos, Potawatomis and Miamis of the area. His veteran trader had lived so long among the Indians he

101

thought as they did, a quality Deschamps admired. He would rely on Beason, and they distributed guns, powder, traps, Stroud cloth and whisky to the villagers and assured them that tobacco and rum would be available at Opa as soon as Deschamps returned from St. Louis. Then Deschamps took his ease, joining his *voyageurs* in the celebration. The corn harvest was in and it was the night of the crane dance, when the young people husking corn that day kept the red ears for the maidens to present to the braves of their choice that night. The mating dance of the crane and the symbolic red ears of corn would announce the forthcoming nuptials of any young brave accepting an invitation to dance. It was a proper and beautiful dance, to the slow, muted beat of the drum and the mellow call of the flute, a favorite of the older Indians watching. As the dancing and feasting ended, pledged young couples wandered away into the woods, *voyageurs* and hunters departing early the next day left for the lodges and wigwams with their wives, or sought the forest with their conquests, and the old men sat late smoking and talking with Deschamps and the Beasons of the summer past, of former days and of the outlook for the season ahead.

The Illinois Brigade ended its journey from Mackinac at Opa landing the next morning, the bulk of the trade goods remaining there with the Beasons, individual crews receiving their assignments to the small posts in the area, Deschamps proceeding on toward St. Louis with goods for the southernmost stations under his direction. Late in the day *Le Bourgeois* and his picked crew of *voyageurs,* with Gurdon Hubbard as his clerk, were well south of Lake Peoria, cruising the Illinois river to the Mississippi. Since they were moving downstream, some of the time under sail, they made as many as seventy miles a day, gliding through gently rolling country of hardwood forests rimming river marshes and vistas of tawny prairie extending beyond the horizon. Occasionally they saw black gashes in the landscape where lightning had started prairie fires and they sometimes paused at Indian towns. Gurdon fretted because their speed kept him from disembarking to walk through the prairies. The *voyageurs* continued to be amused by his love of the prairie and walking. "You'll get your bellyful of prairie," they assured him. "One day you will get your ass burned in big prairie fire. Then you will wish to Sacred Heaven you had stayed in the boat with us.''

Deschamps was relaxed at last. He was going home to St. Louis and Cahokia after a summer in Quebec, Montreal and Mackinac, ending a year that had been a good one. That evening after their supper of peas and tallow, he chatted with Vasseur and Gurdon about his early days and about the history of the area as the men played cards and smoked and listened. Deschamps, contemplating the changes in his life, had given thought to leaving the fur trade. He had dealt with the French, Spaniards and the English in the Peoria country before the Americans came and he was growing weary. He was beginning to fear he would never see a canal through the Chicago Portage. La Salle had dragged the small boats he built on the spot across the Portage, the first of the mackinaws, Deschamps said. Tonti had hauled boats across on the ice in winter. La Salle never favored a Chicago portage, doubted a canal could be dug there, and had tried another portage in about 1867, from the St. Joseph to the Kankakee river. The Chicago Portage was an ordeal he, too, hated, Deschamps confessed. Gurdon Hubbard assumed this discussion of the Portage was mostly for his benefit. M. Deschamps now conceded that Gurdon's idea of building mackinaws on the Desplaines river had been tried and wasn't a bad one. On his own part, Gurdon vowed to himself that he would never again use the Chicago Portage if he could avoid it. Again he was grateful to M. Deschamps for not bringing up the Fort Clark incident.

Late the afternoon of November 5, they camped on a rise of ground at the confluence of the Illinois and Mississippi. Deschamps announced they would hunt for an hour or so to provide for their supper and for fresh game he wished to bring to his friends in St. Louis. Deschamps and Vasseur took their guns, inviting Gurdon to accompany them, though for once Gurdon would have preferred to stay in camp, marvelling at the broad river they had reached and the procession of traffic toward the city to the south where he expected to find his father and brother. But he was happy that Deschamps at last had forgiven the Fort Clark episode and his invitation, in any event, was a command. They made their way through the marshes to a pond where Canada geese, blue-winged teal and mallards were feeding. Deschamps, after bringing down a satisfactory number of birds, handed his shotgun to Gurdon. Gurdon took it gratefully, dropped shot into the barrels, rammed in the oiled linen patches, primed, sighted and fired. Sloughing through the marsh to retrieve his mallards, he glowed with pleasure. He loved hunting and knew that nothing his father could say in St. Louis would now dissuade him from staying in the fur trade, as close as possible to M. Deschamps and the wilderness. He had heard in Chicago that St. Louis had become a boom town of 3,000 persons, a place of great opportunities, but he wanted no part of it. As they made their way back to camp, they passed a meadow where the prairie had thrust into the marshes and Deschamps cut across. Soon they were waist deep in tough Indian grass, cord grass, big blue stem and prairie dropseed; and the sunflowers, goldenrod and wild aster which gave the prairie in autumn its soft rainbow colors.

The going was slow in the thick prairie growth, since they were loaded with birds, but the way was shorter. Deschamps identified the grasses as they moved through. A white-tailed deer broke cover and Deschamps dropped it. Gurdon was instructed to return to bring it in. "My priests love fresh venison," Deschamps said. They reached camp as the sinking sun fired the sky with orange and purple hues, silhouetting the forest to the west, beyond the Mississippi's opalescent glow. While Vasseur roasted a supper of birds, Gurdon and a *voyageur* went for the deer. When they returned, the ducks and corn soup were ready and Deschamps brought out cheese and wine. *Le Bourgeois* was then given his first choice of the meat, as was the custom, the *voyageurs* politely refusing duck, saying they preferred the corn soup and tallow. But then Deschamps persuaded them to try the game, they ate, smoked their pipes, and the stories and songs continued until Vasseur noted that Deschamps was propped comfortably before the fire in his reminiscent mood and brought out the cards for a game while they listened. Deschamps did not disappoint them. Again he talked of the early days, when St. Louis was a lively trade town and Chicago an Indian village where the only outsider was the trader Gaurie living on the north branch above the Chicago Portage. He spoke of his trips up the Missouri, of meeting Crooks and Stuart when they returned from more than two years in the wilderness, having become explorers and tough traders in the process. The men played quietly, gambling trinkets or river pebbles to keep their game interesting, as Deschamps talked sometimes in French, sometimes in English. They knew the stories were for the benefit of the lad they continued to refer to privately as "the little American." The old man was "going home" on the day following and bringing with him his foster son. They chuckled among themselves as they contemplated what the young priests and all the populace would think, knowing Monsieur Deschamps.

Deschamps had come through the Chicago Portage in early 1776, he said. It was months later that he learned of the great events taking place in Philadelphia and along the eastern seaboard that year. While he worked for Sara in St. Louis, he also had opportunity to spend time at the mission and to read the books there brought in by French and Spanish priests. St. Louis then rivalled Montreal, Mackinac, Detroit and even New Orleans as a center of trade. He drew from his purse a roll of bills and passed around the certificates, each bearing the engraving of a beaver. "These are Beaver dollars," Deschamps said. "When last I was in St. Louis, ten years ago, they were each worth one beaver pelt, two and a half Quebec livres, or four bits broken from a Spanish eight-bit dollar. I think that this money is still circulated in St. Louis." He passed two of the bills to each of the five *voyageurs* and three to Gurdon, and five to Vasseur. "I thank you for your loyalty to me," he said.

Deschamps then spoke directly to the boy he had called his foster son. "St. Louis will become a great city," he said. "It does not have the problems of extreme cold we find in the far north, it does not require a canal to flourish. You must point this out to your father, Gurdon, if he does not point it out to you. You must think of what you will do when your indenture ends. The fur business, I regret to say, may not flourish beyond that time. But St. Louis will be the center of the farming trade, the white men by then will have seized and plowed the Indian hunting grounds. The powers of the world have come thousands of miles to fight over this land, always forgetting that the oldest and best claim was that of our Indian brothers. We may be sure that the Americans will not stop until they have devoured it.

"This is the best land of all for farming, for grain and for cattle. Tecumseh, the greatest of the Indians, saw it. He united the tribes and fought well, but he was defeated. The Indians can no longer resist. Some of them think, like White Cloud the Prophet, that the English will help them regain their lands, but that is merely a dream. In this fertile valley, in hundreds of villages and for many thousands of years, our red brothers lived, hunted and tilled their fields and worked with metals and created a great civilization. I will show you the great mounds, Gurdon. We will visit Monk's Mound, greater than the Pyramids of Egypt, raised by ancient red men to honor their dead and their gods. The Trappists grew their turnips on the terraces when I was first there. Years before, La Salle saw the countless leagues of prairie and saw the great herds of bison and elk from that height. Tecumseh called such creatures 'the Indians' cows.' There, at the great Mound, I have found not only spearheads and arrowheads of flint, but copper, which can only have come from Lake Superior, and mica, which is found in Carolina, and objects of lead, from mines in Missouri and Illinois. What does this signify? That the red men who dwelled here were not just primitive people, as now is said, but were workers in metals who had a great commerce the length of the Mississippi, easterly along the Ohio, and into the Great Lakes by way of the Chicago and the Kankakee-St. Joseph portages. This was a great trading center for the ancient tribes. Until De Soto, who is said to have asserted obscenely that killing Indians was his favorite sport, came to the Mississippi with his troops and horses. Until the English hired the Iroquois to drive out the Delawares and then proceeded to drive all the tribes westerly. Until the Americans cheated the Delawares and the Miamis and then claimed all the west on the pretext that the Delawares and the Miamis once owned it. Until all the deceit and violence and lust for land destroyed most of our red brothers and dispossessed the rest, who have nowhere to stay and no safe place to go.

"It seems to me that many thousands of workers must have created the mounds we will visit in this valley. They are a great mystery, not solved even by Father Louis Hennepin, whose *Nouvelle Decouverte* we must find for you in St. Louis, in French, so that you can read it against your English edition and thus perfect yourself; not solved by Joliet, not solved by President Jefferson, who himself studied similar, smaller mounds in the east and concluded the Indians are an ancient, civilized people from across the Atlantic Ocean. Whatever the mystery has been, we have not solved it. Some say the Indians have sprung from the lost tribe of Israel that fell out of favor with God after being led safely to the New World. Whatever the mystery has been may never be solved.

"So this land we enter is shrouded with a great sadness, because we are guilty of so much injustice to our red brothers. They have always been caught in the midst of the white men's struggles for power, land and gold. The British and the Americans defeated the French and the Indians at Fort Louisburg and Fort Frontenac in this struggle for power and Indian lands; the Spanish defeated the British and the Indians at St. Louis in 1769 in the struggle for power and gold; then the Americans defeated the British and the Indians in 1815 in the struggle for power and Indian lands. Always the Indians lose and we have not seen the end of it. They lose their lands, they are robbed of their homes and their possessions, are debauched with rum and cheated. We speak of the massacre at Fort Dearborn in August, 1812, but we do not remember the massacre of the men, women and children of the Indian villages in this land we now visit by Governor Edward's lawless militia a short time earlier.

"We have provoked the Indians into anger and atrocities. We prate about the Noble Savage in our parlors and lecture halls in the east, but we despise him as our neighbor whom we should love. This is a great sadness. I fear the time will come when the Indians are driven from all this fair land east of the Mississippi. There will be no more hunting grounds, forests will be cut and the prairies will become farmlands. There will be no more trading in furs. Gurdon, my foster son, I am training you for a future that may not continue to exist! This too is a mystery. You must listen to what your father has to say to you should you find him tomorrow in St. Louis."

The *voyageurs* clucked and shook their heads and played their game, comprehending little of Monsieur Deschamps' sermon. They regarded one another and the boy and shrugged in resignation. Changing politics and the advance of the Americans westward by the thousands had aroused the Indians but had not touched the *voyageurs.* There had always been wars in the Illinois and Ohio and Michigan country. The Fox and their allies had fought the Sioux until all were exhausted and the Sioux departed, following the buffalo onto the great plains. The Miamis, Fox, Sacs, Kickapoos, Chippewas, all driven westward by the terrible Iroquois and the whites, united to crush the pestiferous Peorias, and then found themselves fatally menaced by the advancing Americans. They, too, moved west and south. Some like the Delawares, the diplomats gentled by the Iroquois and the Moravian missionaries, arrived peacefully, but only after white treachery and Iroquois terror had dispossessed them of their lands. Chief Pontiac of the Ottawas united the tribes for a heroic stand, and almost succeeded before the defeat came; then he was killed at Cahokia, across from St. Louis.

The defeat of Pontiac by General ''Mad Anthony'' Wayne on August 4, 1795 had won a treaty transferring Indian lands and authorizing forts, one at Peoria, so recently burned; one at the mouth of the Illinois river, where Deschamps and his men were now encamped; and one at Chicago, the latter provision stating: ''One piece of land six miles square at the mouth of the Chicago River emptying into the southwest end of Lake Michigan where a fort formerly stood.'' These forts were cancers to the Indian nations obdurately insisting that Pontiac had never been empowered to sign away their property. The defeat of Tecumseh at the Thames river in Canada in the War of 1812 confirmed the end of the Indian rights east of the Mississippi and the towns and villages of that vast territory were filling up with Americans, entrepreneurs, farmers, mechanics, and speculators. Deschamps thought that night that he was returning to a village of eight hundred or so, the old St. Louis. Actually, in the two years since 1816, it had grown to a city spread almost a mile along the river.

Le Bourgeois Deschamps finished his reminisence and prophecy and his pipe and arose from his place at the fire. ''Well,'' he said, ''tomorrow we will cross the Great Muddy and then hang out our linen and we will sing our songs and our friends will greet us, as they have done in the past. The more things change, the more they stay the same. Let us be in good voice, so that our friends may know, from far off, that we are coming.''

*

That morning they entered upon the Mississippi, the silted swift-flowing river Gurdon had known from Joliet, Hennepin and Deschamps. The current took them downstream into river-port traffic that seemed as diverse and thick as that at Montreal. There were freight canoes from the Wisconsin, Fox and Illinois rivers, huge mackinaws from the Missouri, flatboats and keel boats from the Ohio and New Orleans. Gurdon Hubbard, in his recollections, estimated the population of St. Louis as ''about eight hundred'' at the time of his visit, but actually it was more than three thousand, though widely spread. He was right about the ethnic division of the town, ''French, Indian, English, Spanish, American.'' St. Louis was in a boom. The *Gazette* reported more than a hundred houses built in 1818, plus stores and warehouses. It was in transition from a fur trade barter economy, in which peltries, whisky and lead were exchanged for manufactured goods, to currency trade, including the Beaver dollar, the Spanish dollar of eight bits, and United States treasury warrants paid to soldiers and civil servants. ''The demand for eastern goods constantly exceeded the value of the territory's exports,'' wrote historian James Neal Primm, ''keeping the local markets drained of currency.'' The void was filled with notes of chartered banks, called ''shin-plasters.'' Prices were high. Gurdon and his friends would find though that their Beaver dollars were still accepted, partly because Thomas Hart Benton, later a United States senator, and the Chouteaus, the leading fur traders, invaded the Bank of St. Louis at gun point, demanding that their Beaver currency be redeemed at face value. This was done for a time, until the bank crashed in 1819.

As they approached the port area in the afternoon, Deschamps gave no sign that he saw anything changed, though the port seemed overwhelmed with traffic. Within voice range of the mission, he raised the strains of *''Rose du Rosier Blanc''*:

Je m'en irai au Service
Je m'en irai au Service
En Service pour un An
Et la belle Rose du Rosier blanc
En Service pour un An
Et la belle Rose du Rosier blanc

Combien gagnez vous, la belle
Combien gagnez vous, la belle
Combien gagnez vous par An?
Je ne gagne que cinq cents Livres
Je ne gagne que cinq cents Livres
Cinq cents Livres en Argent blanc
Cinq cents Livres en Argent blanc
La belle Rose du Rosier blanc.

"Our boat was soon surrounded by the friends of M. Deschamps," Gurdon wrote, "among them many priests, all united in a hearty greeting. I knew my father and brother should be at this place, but where I could find them I could not tell."

*

It had been agreed with M. Deschamps that Gurdon would immediately be free to search for his father and brother, and that he could stay with them if he was successful, or return to camp with the *voyageurs,* while Deschamps attended to company business in St. Louis, searched for John Crafts or word about him, and visited the mission in Cahokia, across the river. Walking along the waterfront, Gurdon in some way felt he was back in Montreal, but mostly because of the French spoken, rather than a real likeness between the two towns. St. Louis was warm and relaxed and disorganized. Years later, Gurdon underlined in his copy of Washington Irving's *Astoria,* the New York author's impression of St. Louis in that day: "The old French houses engaged in the Indian trade had gathered round them a train of dependants, mongrel Indians and mongrel Frenchmen, who had intermarried with Indians. . . . All these circumstances

110

combined to produce a population at St. Louis even still more motley than Mackinaw . . . the hectoring, extravagant, bragging boatmen of the Mississippi, with the gay, grimacing, singing, good-humored Canadian *voyageurs.* Vagrant Indians of various tribes loitered about the streets. Now and then, a Kentucky hunter, in leathern hunting dress, with rifle on shoulder and knife in belt, strode along. Here and there were new brick houses and shops, just set up by bustling, driving, and eager men of traffic from the Atlantic states; while, on the other hand, the old French mansions, with open casements, still retained the easy, indolent air of the early colonists; and now and then the scraping of a fiddle, a strain of an ancient French song, or the sound of billiard balls, showed that happy Gallic turns for gaiety and amusement still lingered about the place."

He went at once to the nearest tavern to inquire about his father but no one knew Elizur Hubbard there. He began questioning men in the street, "Do you know of a man named Hubbard here?" None did. "I passed a gentlemen who seemed to notice me," he recalled, "and I turned to tell him I was a stranger in town in search of my father. He thought a moment and said, 'The name sounds familiar; I think I was introduced to him at Mr. Paddock's.' I asked him if Mr. Paddock was from Vermont and he nodded in the affirmative and directed me to the Paddock house, which I soon found." The attractive girl who opened the door told Gurdon that a Mr. Hubbard and his son boarded there, but that Mr. Hubbard was at Mr. Enos' nearby. Gurdon hurried over. "Here at last I found my father who did not recognize me, so much had I changed . . . though only six months had passed. I was then thin and pale . . . but with my outdoor life and exposure, I had gained in weight and height and strength and become brown as an Indian."

Gurdon recalled few details of the reunion, nor did he mention in any writings the reasons for his father's departure from Montreal. He asked about Christopher and his father took him to a drugstore near by, where Christopher was employed. "We found him pounding something in a mortar. Though I did not speak he knew me at once, and exclaimed, 'O brother! Brother!' bursting into tears. The meeting was a joyous one and I think the happiest day of my life." He joined his father and Christopher at Paddock's, their board and room house, living there until they departed. In later years Gurdon's nephews would write that while in St. Louis, or Cahokia, Gurdon Hubbard met Eleanora Berry, daughter of an Urbana, Ohio judge, the woman he would marry as his second wife, after Watseka, the Indian maiden. However, Gurdon did not mention such a meeting in his letters or recollections, nor did he again mention the girl who opened the door to him at Mr. Paddock's. Within a few days he said goodbye to his father, who left for Arkansas, taking Christopher along. "It was our farewell," Gurdon wrote, "I never saw him again."

Deschamps, meantime, had solved the mystery of John Crafts. As John Kinzie had suggested, Crafts had become seriously ill. He had awaited the Illinois Brigade as long as he felt possible, then packed his goods for transfer to the fort. It was at that time that Winnetuk and his men surrounded Crafts' cabin and seized the packed supplies, Crafts himself escaping in his canoe, with his *voyageur* who was to help carry the goods to the fort. Together they made the portage and went down river to St. Louis, where Crafts was receiving the care of a physician. Deschamps did not identify the illness nor discuss Crafts further; but the trader continued in good standing with the company and later returned to his post in Chicago.

*

Gurdon accompanied Deschamps to Cahokia, where most of their purchases were to be made, and where Deschamps had many friends. "M. Deschamps was a favorite of all and was treated as the distinguished guest of every family," he wrote. "There was dancing at some of the houses every night; and even the priests claimed his assistance in singing." Gurdon thought Cahokia had a greater population than St. Louis at the time, an error, and he preferred that friendly, snug town, saying, "This French village was then a jolly place." It fascinated him, a neat, handsome community, consisting of whitewashed houses built of logs set upright on their stone foundations, under steep roofs thatched with prairie-grass straw that flared widely at the eaves, in French-Quebec style. Behind the houses were gardens and green fields. There was a line of clean, bright shops packed with goods from New Orleans or produced by local artisans and overflowing with the products of the Cahokia farms, so that merchandise was stacked on counters in the street. Deschamps there made his purchases of flour, tobacco brought from Kentucky, and other items of supply and trade goods not available in Montreal. Gurdon kept the inventory.

Wherever they went, Gurdon was treated as M. Deschamps' son and warmly welcomed. The men and women of Cahokia dressed much alike, he noted, in blue garments trimmed with white collars, with white or blue kerchiefs on their heads. When cold weather came on, many wore white cloaks made from a thick woolen blanket, fashioned to provide a capote for the head. Gurdon used two of the beaver dollars Deschamps had given him to purchase such a garment. It was as warm as the finest Stroud and he expected it would provide him not only warmth, but excellent cover when he hunted in snow.

He went with Deschamps to the mission, also of upright, whitewashed logs, and saw that Cahokia, even more than St. Louis, was home to his boss. The priests welcomed him as one of their own. The mission was an ancient one—established in 1699 by an order from the Seminary of Quebec, where Deschamps himself had studied—on the site of an Indian town which had been the largest in America hundreds of years earlier, surrounded by scores of great mounds, including Monk's Mound on which the Trappist fathers had constructed their monastery. The mounds were built by an ancient people as fortifications for defense and for burial. Gurdon heard at the mission that Cahokia, governed for many years from Quebec, was sixty-five years older than St. Louis, one hundred and four years older than Chicago, nineteen years older than New Orleans. It was still fervently French despite the fact that many Cahokians had left with Pierre Laclede Liquest in 1763 to escape British control. They established the town of St. Louis in Spanish territory across the river and made it the southern capital of the fur trade under the leadership of Pierre and August Chouteau. The Chouteaus, Gurdon learned, now presented John Jacob Astor with the greatest competitive obstacle to the creation of the fur trade monopoly he planned.

Antoine Deschamps and his foster son drew the intense interest of Cahokia's society their few evenings of freedom in the town. M. Deschamps had been a most popular bachelor there in earlier days. Later he was reputedly wed to a Potawatomi woman. Now he presented the handsome foster son he called Gurdon Hubbard, who looked considerably like a fine-appearing, half-breed Indian! Gurdon nonetheless was welcome in the community noted for its liberal views. John Reynolds, the young Cahokia lawyer whom he met at a Sunday evening dance, described one of the excesses peculiar to the French which the priests at Cahokia condoned: "The young people of Cahokia dance with much decorum on a Sunday evening. The old people watch, enjoying the amusement with approbation." Gurdon saw Reynolds later at a ball in which Cahokia celebrated, with some resignation, the news that Illinois Territory, with forty thousand population, mostly in the south, was about to be admitted to the Union as the twenty-first state, the proclamation being made by President Monroe on December 3, 1818. They would meet again when Reynolds took office as governor of the new state of Illinois and Hubbard was elected to its legislature.

*

Within the week Gurdon said goodbye to Antoine Deschamps at the Beebeau trading post on the Illinois river. They had distributed trade goods enroute back from St. Louis and reached Beebeau's near mid-December. Deschamps appeared saddened and preoccupied. He worried about the situation in Chicago, since John Kinzie stubbornly refused to join Astor's company, Crafts would not return for some weeks, and Jean Beaubien in all probability was needed back in Milwaukee. There was no help for it, Deschamps felt compelled to take Noel Vasseur with him until such time as Beaubien could return to Chicago as a full-time agent there. Gurdon was being left alone with fat, mean irascible Beebeau, comforted only by the knowledge that Pierre Chabailler, son of Antoine, one of the *voyageurs* regularly assigned to Beebeau's post, would live with him in the house and store still under construction. Pierre, Gurdon's age, knew little about the fur trade, but could help with chores and problems of language, Deschamps suggested. Beebeau himself clearly had no intention of doing more than to unload his account keeping chores on his new assistant:

"The accounts had heretofore been kept in hieroglyphics by my ignorant master, who proved to be sickly, cross and petulant. He spent the greater part of his time in bed, attended by a fat, dirty Indian woman, a doctress, who administered various decoctions to him. M. Deschamps, after giving me particular instructions as to my duties, and opening the books, left me with his blessing."

Noel Vasseur somewhat brightened the outlook for Gurdon by promising at the last moment that he would return within two months, well before the time the first pelts would be brought in to be credited against the accounts in Beebeau's books. Meantime, Vasseur suggested, Gurdon should simply stay clear of Beebeau as much as possible and especially of the old woman. She was a witch, Vasseur confided, who made a medicine of mare's urine for Beebeau. This Vasseur knew, because his wife was required to obtain the mare's fluid for her. She no doubt also knew how to make poison from the root of the May apple. The fruit was good, but anyone who drank a broth made from its root died within a few hours. Do not eat or drink with Beebeau, Vasseur urged, and Gurdon assured him he would not.

Following the departure of Deschamps and Vasseur, everything changed astonishingly for the better, Beebeau himself aroused from his stinking bed and was up and about, after receiving an Indian runner the afternoon of the third day. He shouted at his woman to get his house in order and actually came to the door dressed in his buckskins, with his beard combed, to summon Gurdon, instructing him to remain close at hand in case he should be wanted. Through the doorway Gurdon could see that Beebeau had his best pipes and tobacco on the table, the drinking gourds were set out, and a container of whisky was at hand.

Soon a white-haired old Indian debarked from a canoe, followed by a splendid-appearing younger man. The old man was Chief Waba of the Kickapoo tribe, whom Gurdon had seen first at the Little Calumet camp. The young Indian was Shabona, of the Ottawa tribe, but married to Wiomex Okono of the Potawatomis, and therefore now a Potawatomi chief. "He was then about twenty-five and was, I thought, the finest looking man

I had ever seen," Gurdon would write. "He was fully six feet in height, finely proportioned, with a countenance expressive of intelligence, firmness and kindness. He was one of Tecumseh's aides at the Battle of the Thames, being at his side when Tecumseh was shot."

Neither Indian paid the slightest attention to Gurdon, if they saw him, but strode to Beebeau's house, where the old woman opened the door and they entered. Their meeting with Beebeau was brief. They emerged within a short time, shouting agreeably back to Beebeau in the Potawatomi tongue, that they thanked him and that they would find the one they sought without assistance. They were now looking directly at Gurdon, who nodded to them and led the way to his own incomplete cabin. Clearly he was the one they wanted.

Chief Waba spoke in English. "We have come to see the Little American brave," he said. He presented Shabona, his companion, who gravely inspected Gurdon, then followed Waba's example of extending his hand. Gurdon on his part presented his workman, Pierre, saying in Potawatomi that because of his own slowness with the language Pierre would remain to translate, if that was acceptable. Chief Waba nodded. They sat on puncheon stools outside the cabin and Chief Waba spoke in Potawatomi, English or French, seeking to gain Gurdon's understanding without translation, while Shabona, giving no sign he understood the English passages, continued to gaze intently at Gurdon.

Gurdon summarized the incident years later. "My trouble at Fort Clark, and the circumstances attending it, had become known to the Indians in the vicinity of our post. Their chief was Waba . . . who had shortly before this lost a son, of about my own age, and so, according to Indian custom, he adopted me in his stead, naming me Checomocomones, 'the Little American.' "

Gurdon was by no means sure it would be proper for him to accept the honor. M. Deschamps had warned him against making known his American nationality in the Peoria area, but, after hearing of the bravery of Chief Billy Caldwell, who proclaimed himself English even when being Indian might have provided less risk, Gurdon had determined he would be an

American whenever his identity might be directly questioned.
So he was pleased to be recognized as an American and to accept his Indian name, as translated by Pierre. Yet he hesitated.
Shabona signalled that he wished to talk with the Little American alone and Chief Waba assented, strolling back to call on Beebeau again.

The young chief spoke only in Potawatomi, Pierre translating. Chief Waba was showing him great honor, Shabona said.
His courage was recognized. He would enjoy many benefits as
a foster son of Waba. He would be free to invite Waba's other
son to live in his house to aid him with Indian ways and they
could hunt together. He would always be welcome at Waba's
lodge and at Shabona's lodge. He would be showing an act of
appreciation and friendship that would speak well for him
among all the tribes.

Gurdon thanked Shabona, still hesitating. He wanted to be
a brother to this young chief who had fought with Tecumseh;
he wished to understand Indian ways, to learn the Potawatomi
language . . . yet . . . he nodded toward the Beebeau cabin. Shabona smiled. "Beebeau is honored by Chief Waba's choice,"
he said. "He will be most pleased if you become Waba's son."

"But I am unworthy of such honor," Gurdon protested.

Shabona brushed aside this objection. The Little American had
proved his courage. He had won the honor and now should take
it. Chief Waba was a great and good leader. He desired to send
his son to live with the young white brave as John Kinzie had
sent his son to Mackinaw, to learn new ways. Little Elk would
some day become a chief, not among the Kickapoos but in another tribe, the tribe of his wife. He could learn now the wisdom of white man's ways. The Little American could help his
own chiefs with their trade and could himself learn red man's
ways.

Gurdon agreed at last. Chief Waba returned to learn the boy
was honored to become his son and to bear the name Checomocomones and would seek to make Chief Waba proud he
had conferred the honor. Waba smiled his pleasure and led them
all back to the cabin. There, in the presence of a grumpy Beebeau, Chief Shabona took a flint and touched its point to Waba's
thin wrist and then to a vein in Gurdon's arm and the old chief

laid his arm across Gurdon's so their blood mingled. Chief Waba then clasped Gurdon and held him back to smile a wrinkled smile. "I am most happy," he said. "When you can come to my lodge you will meet my other son, who will come to stay with you as you please."

Beebeau drank a whisky with Chief Waba, Shabona declining. When the chiefs had departed, Beebeau growled at Gurdon, "Do not think this will make a difference. Get to work." But it did make a difference. Gurdon worked as he pleased and where he pleased, but got the work done. "I was disgusted with the disagreeable and filthy habits of my master," he wrote. "As I had little to do in his house besides keeping books and being present when sales were made on furs or on credit, I fairly lived in my own house and in the open air with my two comrades."

Gurdon's memoirs would speak of his deep friendship with Chief Waba and his close companionship with Pierre and Little Elk that winter. But he reserved his highest praise for Shabona, whom he called the noblest man he ever knew, even after he had become a friend of Abraham Lincoln and worked for his election to the presidency in 1860. From Shabona he would learn much.

*

That winter and spring of 1819 Gurdon Hubbard learned the work of the trading post, hunted with his new companions, and visited often at the village of Chief Waba, from whom he heard the story of the life of his new hero, Shabona. Waba spoke English and could write his name, Shabona could not, or would not, more probably, because of a vow he had taken. Shabona's mark would appear on many treaties, his name would be spelled and translated in many ways. The French called him Chaubonner, (Shabonay) the "Coal Burner," either because he was the first man to burn the coal in the Illinois country or because his Indian name sounded that way in French—or both. Some Indians called him the stone burner. Gurdon wrote his name Shaubenee and translated it "Made Like a Bear." Shabona was born into the Ottawa tribe, excelled at hunting and war sports, was allowed to paint when only fourteen, and wore the eagle feather of a war chief when he was eighteen. He visited the Potawatomi village at Chicago after a hunting trip, met and wooed Wiomex

118

Okono, daughter of a chief. Thereafter Shabona lived among the Potawatomis and became their war chief while continuing also to hold this rank among the Ottawas. He was also okama, or judge, among the local towns. In about 1809 he came to the attention of Tecumseh, the great Shawnee chief, and joined Tecumseh in organizing the tribes against the whites. Shabona drilled the young braves for war, becoming Tecumseh's chief military aide.

In the lodge of Waba, when Shabona was present, the talk often was of the past, to the glory days of Tecumseh. Like Shabona, Tecumseh of the Shawnees had been a wanderer. He learned the dialects, the dances and the traditions of many tribes. He trapped beaver in the north, shot buffalo in the west, fought with the Cherokees against the encroaching settlers in the south. He saw the wagon caravans crossing the Indian lands and stopping to settle and to plow Indian land. He fought against George Rogers Clark and General St. Clair's army to check such advances. He led the Indians against General "Mad Anthony" Wayne at Fallen Timbers and lost, so his people signed a new treaty ceding more lands. Tecumseh himself refused to attend the signing of the treaty that gave up a million square miles for a small mound of trade goods and petty annuities to the tribes and he denounced the chiefs who did sign. Thereafter Tecumseh travelled widely in a fierce effort to correct the sporadic strategy of the Indians and to unite and organize for war. Shabona, his second in command, drilled the growing number of warriors.

Tecumseh seemed on the way to success when he was summoned to appear before General William Henry Harrison, governor of Indiana Territory in August, 1810. Why was the Shawnee chief conspiring and seeking to evade the treaty? Tecumseh arrived with 400 warriors in eighty canoes, passing below Fort Knox enroute to Harrison's headquarters at Vincennes. Harrison accused the handsome, haughty chief of intruding on treaty ground purchased from the Miamis and of conspiring for war. Tecumseh, flanked by his brother Tenskwatawa and Shabona, spoke:

"I do not make war, but it is impossible to remain friends

with the United States unless they give up the idea of making settlements farther to the north and west and unless they acknowledge the principle that the Western Country was the common property of all the tribes, not alone the Miamis. . . . The Great Spirit gave this land to his red children. He placed the whites on one side of the Big Water. They were not contented with their own but came to take ours from us. They have taken it upon themselves to say that this tract of land belongs to the Miamis, this to the Delawares, and so on; but the Great Spirit intended it to become the property of all.

"How can you ask the Indians to give up or sell this land? Would you have us sell the clouds? The great sea? The sky? The whites wish our prairies for their cows. Our cows are the elk, and they occupy these prairies. The deer are our sheep.

"How can we have any confidence in the white people? When Jesus Christ came on earth, you killed him and nailed him on a cross. You thought he was dead, but you were mistaken. . . . Everything I have said to you is the truth. The Great Spirit inspires me."

There was an awesome tension in the darkness beyond the crackling flames and the glow of pipes as the men surrounding old Chief Waba heard such words repeated. Sometimes Shabona was present, or Black Bird, or Black Hawk, once all three. The Kickapoo had been fierce warriors when Waba was a young man and he maintained war-like traditions. Black Bird had been a leader of the assault on Fort Dearborn. Black Hawk recalled his own time of the fighting with Tecumseh, predicting another prophet would arise signalling a new united strike against the whites. But Shabona did not agree.

Shabona had been Tecumseh's lieutenant at Tippecanoe, when The Prophet Laulewasikau, a tall, one-eyed medicine man, grotesque in white and black paint, brass earrings and a high-feathered headdress that added to his great height, cravenly betrayed them.

Laulewasikau, also a brother of Tecumseh, was an eloquent orator and Indians flocked to listen as he visited tribes with Tecumseh, preaching a revival of Indian fighting zeal, denouncing the white man's thievery and treaties. Tecumseh and his brothers established Prophet's Town at the confluence of the Tippecanoe creek and the Wabash river in Indian territory where Indians gathered to revive their war-like spirit. General Harrison at Vincennes vowed to put an end to such practices. In September, 1811, Harrison moved north with one thousand soldiers, well trained and equipped. They built a fort at Terre Haute to control the land route to the west, a fort Harrison named for himself. On October 29 he resumed the march north and a week later he was arrayed for battle before Prophet's Town.

The Prophet meantime had been exhorting the Indians to a fighting pitch as Shabona worked on their military training. The Prophet swore that American bullets would not kill them and asserted that the Great Spirit would strike the enemy at the time of battle, dementing them so they could not fight. Shabona called for a conference with Harrison, who agreed, but the movement of his troops before the town led Shabona and his chiefs to fear that Harrison intended to attack. The Prophet, as a brother of Tecumseh, outranked Shabona, and after a night of oratory, dancing and yelling in which the warriors worked themselves into a frenzy, The Prophet ordered them to attack. The warriors hid among the willows along Tippecanoe creek during the rainy early morning hours and when the drums at Harrison's camp beat reveille, they thought it was for an attack and the Indian forces charged. In fierce fighting Shabona's men broke through the American lines but in daylight General Harrison's cavalry counter-attacked. It was then that The Prophet and his closest advisors broke and fled. General Harrison won the great victory of Tippecanoe. Shabona checked the rout of his forces regrouping them a distance away but the battle was lost. "It was a complete victory, dearly purchased," said General Harrison's report. He lost sixty-two killed, one hundred twenty-six wounded, and estimated Indian casualties at between six and seven hundred. Harrison retreated to his new fort at Terre Haute.

Shabona wanted no more of prophets. When Tecumseh returned to his ruined village, he summoned his brother and Shabona. He embraced Shabona, thanking him for saving most of

121

their warriors, then seized his brother, less tall minus his head-dress, and pushed back The Prophet's head, as if to snap his neck or slit his throat. Instead he shook Laulewasikau until the brass rings pulled from The Prophet's ears and blood spurted from his nostrils and he fell like a crumpled bag of corn husks when Tecumseh let him go. The angry Tecumseh then strode away, taking Shabona and Black Hawk with him, to seek out the British in Michigan and to offer them his services in the coming war with the Americans. General Harrison would one day become president of the United States as a consequence of his Tippecanoe victory.

Shabona himself related the story of his days with Tecumseh, Chief Waba translating as needed. Neither Shabona nor Tecumseh knew details of the fall of Fort Dearborn or the capture of Mackinac, but, for a time, they believed the British and Indians were winning the War of 1812. Then General Harrison took charge of American forces, Commodore Perry drove the British from the Great Lakes, and Harrison prepared to take Detroit. Tecumseh with six hundred warriors joined British General Henry Proctor. They were pushed by Harrison into Canada. General Proctor favored a further retreat. Tecumseh insisted on making a stand at the Thames River. Harrison sent his cavalry against Proctor's infantry, who checked the advance with heavy gunfire. The Americans reformed to charge again, Proctor's line broke and his force surrendered. Tecumseh with Shabona, Black Hawk, Chief Billy Caldwell and his six hundred warriors kept fighting, firing from behind trees and fallen logs.

The night before, Tecumseh had a premonition of death, stripping himself of all regalia signifying his rank. Now he fell, a rifle ball in his heart. Shabona and Mad Sturgeon, another of Black Hawk's brothers, were beside him. They and Black Hawk, Robinson, and Big Foot of the Winnebagos, the other chiefs, kept up the firing after they had ordered their warriors to slip away through the woods, the Indian fire continuing long after Proctor's surrender. Black Hawk and Shabona were among the last to fade into the woods. On that day Shabona vowed to the Great Spirit that he would not again lead his people against the unequal odds the white man could bring against them. Black Hawk, on his part, vowed to some day renew the struggle

Tecumseh had lost. General Harrison vowed he would not make peace with the Potawatomis, calling them "our most cruel and inveterate enemies." Soon, however, Harrison relented and on October 14 an armistice was signed. It was a peace Shabona would strive to keep.

*

Gurdon found excuses that winter to carry items of trade goods to distant hunters. His trips through snowy woodlands and prairies took him often to the village of Shabona, to the west of Waba's Kickapoos. Late in winter he combined a delivery to a Kickapoo hunting camp on the Wabash with a visit to the Tippecanoe battle site. "I told the Indians that I had read in a book that they had deceived General Harrison, pretending to be friendly and getting him to camp in an exposed position where they would have advantages in an attack. They laughed heartily, saying that was contrary to the truth. He had selected the strongest natural position in all that country; that in any other place they could have conquered him." The Kickapoos loaned Gurdon a pony and three warriors took him over the battlefield. "The trip was a successful one," he wrote, "and, having sold all our goods, we (his interpreter) hired ponies to transport our furs and peltries and returned home, where I was warmly welcomed by my young companions (Pierre and Little Elk), who were glad to have me rejoin their hunts. A day sufficed to decipher Beebeau's hieroglyphics . . . and write up the books. . . ." What Beebeau thought of his new way of trading, Gurdon didn't record.

*

Gurdon was proud of his house at Beebeau's post. He would build other houses, a fur trade compound, the first brick courthouse in Danville, Vermilion county, and the first three-story brick building in Chicago, but, in his handwritten manuscript of recollections covering the early years of his life, it was his first house at Beebeau's that received hundreds of words of description. "Our cabin was built of logs, those forming the sides laid one upon the other and held in place by stakes driven into the ground," he began. This was Indian style, the notched logs much used by white settlers were introduced to America by Swedes settling in Delaware territory. And it was Vasseur, not

123

Gurdon himself, who began the walls. "The logs forming the ends were of smaller sizes, driven into the ground perpendicularly, the center ones being longer and forked at the top." This was in crude imitation of the Cahokia houses. "Upon the forks rested the ridgepole. Straight-grained logs were selected and split as thin as possible, and laid with one end resting upon the ridgepole, the other on the logs forming the sides, and were fixed with wooden pins, the extension of the logs forming the eaves. The cracks were then filled with a cement made of wood ashes and clay." The roof was thatched with tough prairie grass, an idea also borrowed from Cahokia. The floor was of puncheons, split logs "dressed with a common tomahawk." The door, also of split logs, was hung on wooden hinges and fastened by a wood latch lifted from the outside by a cord that then could be withdrawn.

Gurdon's directions for building the fireplace were provided in great detail: "At the center of one side of the room four straight poles were driven into the ground, the front ones being about eight feet apart, and the back ones about five feet; then small saplings, cut to proper lengths, were fastened by withes at each end of the upright poles, about eighteen inches apart. Then came the mortar, made from clay and ashes, into which was kneaded long grass so as to form strips ten or twelve inches in width and four feet long; the centers of these strips were then placed or hung on the cross poles and pressed together to cover the wood, and in this way the chimney was carried to the top of the upright poles and then three or four feet above the roof . . . a second coat of mortar, about two inches thick, was then thrown on, pressed to the rough first coat and smoothed with the hands; the hearth was made of dry stiff clay, pounded down hard, and the structure finished."

Thus Gurdon, then sixteen, and his companions of about the same age built the house in which they would live on a site opposite the future town of Hennepin where, a century later, a huge steel plant would stand. The furniture was early Hubbard, bunks made of puncheons split as thinly as possible and resting on sapling poles inserted into auger pits bored into the logs of the cabin. The bedding consisted of prairie grass laid lengthwise. "At the head the grass was raised so as to make a pillow, and to each man was allowed one blanket for cover.''

The house and furniture were built with the only tools allowed to each fur trading outfit, an ax, a two-inch auger, a crooked knife used for skinning animals, and a tomahawk. "The table with round sapling legs and puncheon top and a three-legged stool completed the furniture of the mansion. . . . Some of the men did excellent work with our simple tools. Our kitchen utensils were few and primitive, consisting of a frying pan, a couple of tin pots, one very large Indian bowl made of wood, and several smaller ones. Table knives and forks we had none, and our spoons were of wood, ranging in capacity of a gill to a pint.''

Wood blazed in the fireplace and the cooking kettle hung over the fire from the ridgepole, that also supported a horizontal pole from which depended thongs used to roast game. "The game was suspended over the fire and it was the duty of one man, with a long stick, to keep it whirling rapidly until sufficiently cooked when it was placed in a large wood bowl on the table, and each one helped himself by cutting off with his knife as much as he desired. Usually we had nothing else on the table except honey. The wild turkey was used as a substitute for bread, and, when eaten with fat venison, coon or bear, is more delicious than any roast can be. One of our luxuries, which was reserved for special occasions, was corn soup, and this was always acceptable.''

Gurdon and his friends lived in snug comfort that winter in the cabin serving as their home and retail store. When Gurdon was not keeping accounts, or engaging in trade with Indian hunters, he joined his companions in supplying food for themselves and Beebeau's establishment, including Vasseur's wife and children. Mrs. Vasseur had an iron bake-pan and received a ration of flour, so that she could bake pancakes for the young men from time to time, and a dish of chopped meat and flour pie, called "*avingnols* . . . a dish not to be refused by kings.'' Gurdon eventually acquired skill as a cook himself and provided his own recipe for a superior *avingnol* supper:

"To one pound of lean venison, add one pound of the breast of turkey, three-fourths of a pound of the fat of bear or raccoon; salt and pepper to taste, and season with the wild onion or leek, chop up or pound fine (the meat), and mix all well together; then make a thin crust, with which cover the sides and bottom of the baking pan; then put in the meat and cover it with a thicker crust, which must be attached firmly to the side crust; now put on the cover of your bake pan and set it on the hot coals, heaping them on top, and bake for one hour, and you will have a delicious dish!"

They hunted game, fished the ponds from which they also gathered the lotus seeds that they used for coffee, while the "ever-filled honey-trough" furnished the sweetening. They worked long hours by daylight and at night smoked, talked, made oars and paddles to replace those broken, and otherwise prepared for spring departure.

To allow himself more time in the woods, Gurdon also worked on his books at night by fire and candlelight. Since they spent all of their time among the Indians when not hunting or working at home and Little Elk corrected his Potawatomi, Gurdon learned the dialect well that winter. He had lessons also in tracking and woodcraft. "I became accomplished in the Indian language by spring," he remembered. "I also became proficient in hunting and could discern animal tracks on the ground and tell what kind they were and whether they were walking slow or fast or running. I could detect the marks on the trunks of trees made by such animals as the raccoon or panther, if they had made it a retreat within a month or so."

His companions laughed at his awkwardness and ignorance, he recalled. They hunted, wrestled, played jokes on one another, and worked. Only in walking did Gurdon outdistance Pierre and Little Elk in the beginning; soon he excelled them in stalking game and shooting, and when spring came and he went into the ice-strewn Kankakee river to save an Indian hunter, he proved he could outswim them also.

*

In March Beebeau received orders by a runner from Deschamps to instruct his men to prepare the fur cargo for Mackinaw. Vasseur and Gurdon also stocked up on game, smoked venison, raccoon, panther, bear and turkey and added swan, geese and crane when their notched stick in the company store told them that time for arrival of Deschamps was near. The forenoon of March 20 they heard Deschamps' voice singing a boat song and Gurdon and his friends were at the landing when the *batteaux* rounded a point about a mile below. "His ensign was flying in the breeze," Gurdon wrote. "Little sleep was had that night which was spent recounting events since our parting. M. Deschamps had flour and tobacco, we feasted and smoked and talked and laughed, and a happier party cannot be imagined." The day following, they loaded their furs, supplied game to all boats of the Illinois Brigade "and, to the music of the boat song, we started our long journey."

This time high water and floating ice and logs caused problems. They made the familiar camp sites under Starved Rock and at Caché Island, on the Desplaines they were able to hoist sail for the first time and, to their delight, they crossed Mud Lake, filled with water, to the South Branch without portaging. They camped on the north side of the Chicago river, at a point near the Agency House, later State street. Again Gurdon visited the Kinzies', concealed his disappointment at finding that Mrs. Helm was no longer there, and was pleased that he had grown too tall for the suit his mother had sent with him. "Seeing Mrs. Kinzie again brought my mother vividly to my mind," he wrote. "I was all the more anxious to see her and my father . . . ."

They coasted Lake Michigan south and east, arriving at the mouth of the Grand river (Grand Haven) in Michigan early in May, at a time when the Indians of the area gathered there to feast and honor their dead under the May moon. There were several Indian camps near the mouth of the Grand, surrounding a burying ground selected for the ceremony. It had been cleaned and small poles flying white cloth had been raised to mark many of the graves. Some of those present had brought their dead from hunting camps and villages for burial. They had been kept safe from wild animals by resting on scaffolds high above the earth through the winter. The camps were solemn and quiet, all but the smallest children blackened their faces with charcoal, and nothing was eaten for two days. At night there were sounds of mourning in the wigwams and tepees and the dogs howled.

After the two days of fasting, the mourners cleansed their faces, put on their decorations and feasted and visited from one wigwam to another. They also set out bowls of food on the graves. Then they played and watched "their celebrated game of ball, intensely interesting, with even the dogs becoming excited and adding to the commotion by mixing with the players. . . . Then it was announced that a Canadian Indian, who had killed the son of a Manistee chief the previous autumn, had returned to give himself up, since he had not been able to trap sufficient pelts to pay indemnity to his victim's family. The murderer had promised the brothers of the slain man that he would return during the Feast of the Dead." Deschamps advised the men of his brigade that they should find places early the next morning to witness the ceremony.

Traders, *voyageurs* and Indians gathered on the sand hills the day following and soon heard the thump of an Indian drum and the mournful voice of the Ottawa brave, chanting his own death song. Gurdon watched from a hillside with Vasseur and Deschamps: "Then we beheld him marching with his wife and children, slowly and in single file, to the place selected for his execution, still singing and beating the drum. When he reached the spot where sat the chief (the father of the slain Indian) he placed the drum on the ground, his wife and children seated themselves on mats prepared for them. He then addressed the chief, saying, 'I, in a drunken moment, stabbed your son, being provoked to it by his accusing me of being a coward and calling me an old woman. Here is the knife with which I killed your son; by it I wish to die. Save my wife and children, I am done.' "

The chief took the knife from the confessor's hand, handed it to his eldest son, and gave the order, "Kill him." The young brave receiving the knife placed his left hand upon the shoulder of the condemned man, made a few feints with the knife, then plunged it handle deep and withdrew it. No sound was heard. No word was uttered by the victim, nor his wife or children nor any witness. "All nature was silent, broken only by the singing of the birds. . . . Every eye was turned upon the victim, who stood motionless with his eyes firmly fixed upon his executioner without the appearance of the slightest tremor

. . . . For a few moments he stood erect, the blood gushing from the wound at every pulsation; then his knees began to quake; his eyes and face assumed an expression of death, and he sank upon the sand."

His family had been silent, but now threw themselves upon the prostrate body with loud lamentations, and a murmur of sympathy ran through the crowd and a few traders were seen to weep. Gurdon, near to tears, blinked them back and turned angrily upon Deschamps, "down whose cheeks tears were trickling." "Why didn't you save that noble Indian?" the boy demanded. "A few blankets and shirts, a little cloth would have done it." Gurdon referred to the indemnity the Indian failed to pay because of his bad luck trapping. Deschamps showed no resentment of Gurdon's anger. "Oh, my boy," he answered, "we should have done it."

At last the Manistee chief, avenged for the loss of his son, spoke to the weeping wife of the victim. "Stop, woman. Your husband was a brave man, and was not afraid to die as the laws of our nation demand. We adopt you and your children in place of my son; our lodges are open to you; live with any of us; you shall have our protection and love."

There was a rising sound of approval among the Indians, who began to call out, "Che-qui-ock! Che-qui-ock! . . . That is right!" "The scene is indelibly stamped on my mind, never to be forgotten," Gurdon wrote.

They proceeded on to Mackinaw without difficulty, arriving in mid-May, among the first of the outfits to return. Gurdon found letters from his mother in the company office, one of them reporting the death of his father Elizur: "He was taken sick while on the circuit, shortly after arriving in Arkansas. Having been but a short time in the territory, he had formed but few acquaintances, and those mostly lawyers. My little brother Christopher, thus suddenly left, was kindly cared for by R. P. Spalding, an attorney of the Territory." In the winter Spalding, whose parents lived in Norwich, Connecticut, took Christopher home to Middletown, delivering him to Abigail. "My mother had left Montreal and returned to New England, and had with her, her youngest daughter, Hannah, while my other sisters had been placed in school, one in Windsor, the others in New Lon-

129

don, thus were those most dear to me, and to each other, cast upon the world without home or protector. This news made me very sad."

He was approaching seventeen, had grown tall and strong in his year away from his family, and he now believed firmly that his duty was to return to Connecticut to reunite them and provide for his mother, brother and sisters. The return of the Lake Superior Brigade brought the news that John Warner, who had traded places with Gurdon and gone north to the Fond du Lac post, had been lost in a blizzard and frozen to death. Gurdon felt God had spared him to replace his father. He considered asking Deschamps to appeal to Ramsey Crooks to release him, but thought his old friend might instead seek to dissuade him from leaving the company. He discussed his problem with young John Kinzie, who urged him to go directly to Crooks, to whom Kinzie himself then spoke. There were five hundred young clerks in the company. They were required to go through channels with their problems and Crooks rarely heard of them, but he agreed at once to see Gurdon Hubbard. On this occasion Mr. Crooks seemed a mild man, Gurdon remembered. He shuffled the papers on his desk, looked keenly at his young visitor who more than ever must have appeared as Crooks did at a similar age, tall and brown, dark eyes, long black hair drawn back and fastened with a silver barrette, Indian style, high cheekbones and a somewhat prominent nose. Finally Mr. Crooks spoke:

"I know why you are here, Gurdon. I know why you feel you must leave the company. I am sorry about your father. However, even though there are reasons that seem to you compelling, I must remind you that you have contracted your services to us for five years, as of May last year."

The boy flared angrily, "Sir, I do not think you understand . . . ."

Mr. Crooks raised his hand, silencing him. "Gurdon, your duty to your mother, to yourself and to us is to remain. You are paid $120 a year and found. What can you earn in Middletown? You can help your mother more as a clerk with the American Fur Company. As a clerk seeking work in Connecticut, with times as they are, you could become a burden to your family."

Gurdon thought it over and decided that Ramsey Crooks was

right. He knew also that he did not want to leave the fur trade, but that desire no longer created in him a sense of guilt. He realized that he could not even ask to go briefly to his mother, for it would cost money and take time, neither of which he could afford. Abigail Hubbard had by now made adjustments for her family and, he understood, had opened a select boarding house in Middletown. She had not pleaded with him to come back, though she had written of her yearning to see him. His mother had always been the strong one.

"Mr. Crooks," he said, under a compulsion he did not himself understand, "I would like to go to Middletown. . . ."

"I know you would, my boy. I fear we can't arrange that. I must go to New York myself, and if at all possible I will go up to Middletown to see your mother. Also, we can provide for payment in advance to you on next year's wage, if you so wish."

Thus Gurdon was able to send his mother $90, adding together what remained after deductions from his first year's pay and a portion of the advance toward the year ahead.

The day following he reported for work under Mr. Matthews in the fur warehouse.

5

September 10, 1819

I had supposed I should again be detailed to the Illinois River Brigade with my old leader M. Deschamps and was much surprised and grieved, when the time arrived to select the goods and make ready for departure, to receive a summons from Mr. Crooks to meet him in his private office, when I was informed that I was not to go to my old post, but, in company with a Frenchman named Jacques Dufrain, take charge of an outfit on the Muskegon River.

Recollections,
Gurdon S. Hubbard

It was a time of woe, worry and exceedingly hard work for Gurdon that spring and summer of 1819. He mourned the death of his father and was deeply concerned about his mother, Christopher and his sisters. He felt increasingly a responsibility for the series of tragic events leading to his father's death. Had he not quarreled with his parents, insisting, against their better judgment on leaving Montreal, he would have been with them when their troubles came. As the eldest son he could have gone with his father to St. Louis, and into the Arkansas wilderness, and might have saved him from the overexposure said to have caused Elizur Hubbard his fatal illness. He was gnawed by guilt. He selfishly shipped with the *voyageurs* to satisfy his own desire for travel and adventure; he failed to listen to his father in St. Louis, when Elizur suggested that his son might be able to terminate his indenture with the fur company. He had not tried hard enough to find a way to help his mother in Middletown. A letter from his sister Elizabeth gave him some comfort. She was in school in New London and said their mother and the rest of the family were doing well.

M. Deschamps was not at Mackinaw that summer, but had gone to Montreal. This irked Mr. Matthews, who became testy and mean. He often left Gurdon in sole charge of the fur ware-

house and when Robert Stuart appeared there, evidently checking up—Stuart directed the outside work on the island—Gurdon
clashed with him. "He often gave unnecessary orders and was
quick tempered," the boy noted. Gurdon himself was not on
a slow fuse. "My work commenced at five o'clock in the morn
ing and lasted until sunset," he added by way of explanation
of his own short temper. "My duties did not end with the sunset, however. I had to lock up before I went to my supper and
write up the accounts of the day, which often took until
midnight."

Gurdon's only close companion that summer was John Kinzie, Jr., who joined him on Sundays, to share his gloomy mood.
Kinzie too was having problems. Gurdon was to remember well
their walks about the island, their discussions of shared miseries, and possible futures, and the meaning of death and life. They
ate their crackers and cheese along the shore those Sunday fore-
noons, sometimes killing game to be roasted over a camp fire
as they talked, the smell of smoke mingling agreeably with the
sweet odor of arbutus, so that Gurdon called the flower his favorite, despite the sad memories its fragrance evoked. He took
along the Bible his mother had given him and read aloud to John,
selecting with morbid satisfaction passages that suited their
mood. " 'When I cry and shout he shutteth out my prayer,'. . ."
he read from *Lamentations*. " 'He was unto me as a bear lying
in wait, and as a lion in secret places. He has turned aside my
ways, and pulled me into pieces; he has made me desolated. He
hath bent his bow, and set me as a mark for the arrow.' "

He marvelled that the experience of the Prophet of Israel
could be like his own, and they speculated on the Indian prophet
who guided, or misguided, Gurdon's friend Shabona in the Indian country at the Battle of Tippecanoe and whether the Bible
was intended also for the Indians as Deschamps so intensely believed. But mostly they discussed the Company and their own
unjust fate. John Kinzie, in his second year on Mackinaw, also
could not go home. He too had trouble with the company and
Robert Stuart. He not only worked for Mr. Stuart, he also *lived*
with the Stuarts. "I made out a 10-page invoice for him," John
complained. "I did every page with special care, in good commercial style, and gave it to him. He read it, sheet after sheet.

On the last page he saw a blot. 'Do you call this well done?' he says to me. 'Do it over!' He tore it all up, every page!''

They were comforted by their common misery. Gurdon asked John often whether they could go to Detroit. "Why do you want to go to Detroit?" John would respond, knowing the answer. "To see the Helms." "But you don't know him," John would object. "You only know my half-sister. What's so great about her?" Gurdon's agony of unrequited love actually gave him a kind of pleasure, particularly since he treasured it to himself, being unwilling to confess to John his actual thoughts about Margaret Helm. He said he was considering the possibility of asking for a permanent assignment to Mackinaw Island, since he would be closer to Middletown, and perhaps he could obtain a leave to visit his mother once the outfits had departed for their winter posts. John scoffed at this idea. "Look at me," he advised. "I'm stuck here at the store and Chicago is a lot closer than Middletown, Connecticut. My father is supposed to have influence with the company. Either he doesn't want me to come home, or his influence means nothing to Mister Stuart. It's all the same to me."

Mr. Matthews was equally inflexible. He would not discuss Gurdon's future. Hubbard would find out where he was going when he got his orders. He could not expect again to get special consideration. Gurdon knew that well enough. M. Deschamps was not there to help him. He felt that he never would get a leave to go to Middletown, no matter where he might be assigned. The summer continued grim. There were no visits by night to the Indian camps, where the noisy celebrations went on as usual, and no opportunity to accept invitations to the homes of the women who had befriended him a year earlier. There were few lunch hours to enjoy with John Kinzie, since Gurdon felt required to give that time to the clerks he supervised in the fur warehouse and the *voyageurs* who labored there and welcomed him to their mess. He found his troubles eased among the men, they hated the warehouse as much as he did, and shared his increasing dislike of Stuart, relating their own experiences with him. On an occasion when Stuart believed two men from the woods crew were stealing liquor, and they answered his charges with curses, he seized a length of log lying near and knocked both men down, almost killing one. Mr. Stuart then summoned Dr. William Beaumont, the new surgeon at the fort, and stayed solicitously with his victim, caring for him into the following day, until Dr. Beaumont said the fellow was out of danger. Did Stuart have a streak of kindness in him, or merely fear of a possible murder complaint? Gurdon understood why John Kinzie would not go to him with personal problems. He decided to solve his own problem by going directly to Mr. Crooks. "He was a mild man, rarely out of temper, governed more by quiet reasoning and mild command than by dictation," he remembered. Again Mr. Crooks received him and heard him out. Again he reminded Gurdon that he was under a five-year contract, that he was doing well, that both Mr. Matthews and M. Deschamps spoke well of him. "I am saying, Gurdon, that we cannot accept your resignation. If you agree, we will advance, against your next year's wage, one-half the amount of your present credit. This may enable you to increase the amount you wish to send to your mother."

*

It was settled. He would remain with the company and go where the company ordered. Antoine Deschamps returned in September, looking fit; full of stories of Montreal and Quebec. Again with their old friend, Gurdon and John Kinzie planned a Sunday of freedom and, after attending mass with Deschamps, they cruised to Bois Blanc island where Gurdon saw John Dyde for the last time. John had gone to Lake of the Woods and hoped to return there. He pleased Gurdon when he said, "You've growed a lot, you're getting bigger than me!" They planned to see each other the following summer, but Gurdon did not again mention John Dyde in his recollections.

He assumed he would be given leave from the detested warehouse job to assist M. Deschamps when *Le Bourgeois* of the Illinois Brigade began his preparations for departure into the Illinois country. But when the time neared for the brigade to leave, Ramsey Crooks summoned him to his office in the Agency House. "Gurdon, you are going to be placed in charge of your own outfit," Mr. Crooks said. "Your post will be on the Muskegon River in Michigan."

Gurdon heard this announcement in stunned silence. He was

still wrathful about the treatment he had received during the summer. Despite the proffered promotion, he was dismayed to learn that he would not be going with Deschamps. Even another year at Beebeau's would have been acceptable. He had not thought of heading his own outfit, nor did he yearn for it. And there was his mother . . . when would he see her? Crooks read his thoughts: "I will indeed go to see your mother shortly, since I will be visiting Montreal before going to New York, and can pass through Middletown."

"Thank you," Gurdon said respectfully.

"You will be the commander of your outfit, Gurdon," Crooks continued. "Jacques Dufrain, who knows the territory well, will be your advisor. Your base will be on the Muskegon River. You are young and inexperienced, but you have done your work well. Mr. Matthews says you know how to judge furs and you can manage men, despite your age. M. Deschamps vouches for you. Dufrain cannot read nor write. All invoices will be sent to you. You are to listen to Mr. Dufrain, but if you disagree with his judgment after giving it full consideration, then your decision will be final. I myself will make this clear to Mr. Dufrain. We are sure you can assume this responsibility, Gurdon. Mr. Stuart has been watching your work this summer and recommends you highly." The boy stood before him silent, struck dumb with astonishment. Mr. Crooks appeared pleased with himself. "Now, Gurdon, does this satisfy you?" he asked.

"Sir, thank you, but I had hoped to go with M. Deschamps."

"Yes. You may be sure M. Deschamps and I talked this over. He thinks you can take charge and I know you can rely on Dufrain for both his honesty and his judgment. You will be paid $150 year. Now, you may depart with M. Deschamps and your friends in the Illinois Brigade if you choose, going as far as the Muskegon. Then you will go to your own headquarters sixty miles northeast."

Gurdon left the Agency House half swooning with excitement and initial delight at his good fortune. He was to be paid $150 a year! This staggering increase of $30 would allow him to send his mother almost as much as he had earned previously in a year! Mr. Crooks had been right. He could help his family more by remaining with the American Fur Company. He was sorry he had misjudged Mr. Stuart's reason for looking in on him at the fur warehouse. He would have some time with M. Deschamps enroute to his new post. He was satisfied and he hoped his friend John Kinzie would have equal good fortune. He even found it in his heart to praise Robert Stuart years later. "He was quick tempered and wholly fearless," Gurdon wrote. "The clerks knew his commands were to be obeyed to the letter but if their duties were properly performed they would receive full credit and be treated with kindness and consideration."

He was at once freed of warehouse duty to collect trade goods and supplies for his own Muskegon River outfit. He wrote his mother of his good fortune and told her more money and news would arrive with Mr. Crooks. Mackinaw again was beautiful. He and John accompanied M. Deschamps to dinner with the officers at the fort and to the homes of the matrons who welcomed Deschamps back and were pleased to see that Gurdon, their "boy clerk," had grown tall. They had heard too that he had received a promotion and would head an outfit, though he just passed his seventeenth birthday! They claimed some of the credit for themselves. Mrs. Chandler, noting Gurdon's pleasure at again seeing her daughter Marie, back from school in Montreal, archly suggested that he was getting to the age and position where he should be thinking of marriage. Mrs. Chandler's widowed daughter was amused. She had met the man she intended to have as her second husband. "She afterward married Mr. Beard, a lawyer at Green Bay," Gurdon recalled.

He had second thoughts about his own ability to command an outfit. He was not at all sure Dufrain would be content to leave him in actual charge once they were alone in the wilderness, among people Dufrain knew well. "Mr. Crooks' offer was a bitter disappointment to me," he wrote years later. "I had counted very much on seeing Mr. Kinzie's family, for whom I had formed a great attachment. I had hoped for M. Deschamps' permission to spend two or three weeks with them and the officers at Fort Dearborn. . . . But, as there was no other alternative, I received my goods with good grace, and, about the middle of October, 1819, started with the Illinois Brigade on my second trip into the Indian country."

Gurdon, Jacques Dufrain and their *voyageurs* had but a single mackinaw for their Muskegon River assignment, but they left the island with Deschamps and his brigade and Gurdon was relatively happy. He felt he had an excellent assistant in Dufrain, who spoke no English and but little French. He was part Ottawa Indian, married to an Ottawa woman. Gurdon visited their lodge on Mackinaw and found that his knowledge of basic Algonquin enabled him to speak with them in a mixture of that tongue and French. He was glad he'd be forced to use the Ottawa dialect, almost the same as Potawatomi, at his Muskegon post. This he felt would enable him to converse easily with his friend Shabona when he returned to the Illinois country, as he was determined to do. Deschamps assured him this would be possible in a year or two. "I am getting old," Deschamps said, as they chatted after mess on their coasting route along the Lake Michigan shore, enroute to the Muskegon. "I will need another assistant. You may be sure I will ask for you."

When the Illinois Brigade reached the Little Traverse Bay, after a slow trip from Mackinaw because of heavy storms, M. Deschamps advised Gurdon to buy a small canoe for his personal use around his trading country and also to take a supply of corn which could be had from an Indian village about ten miles distant. Gurdon dispatched Dufrain to the village to make the purchases, providing him with trade goods to barter for the canoe and sufficient supplies for the winter. He was also to acquire native help, if any could be had. It was October and most of the hunters in the area had already departed for their camps.

Two days later Dufrain returned with a canoe, well filled with Indians, and about eight bushels of corn and two of beans, which he insisted was all he could obtain. Gurdon suspected that Dufrain and his crew had themselves consumed most of the rum he had sent out for trading purposes. By this time Deschamps had departed with the Illinois Brigade and Gurdon Hubbard was on his own. He doubted Dufrain had got all the corn and beans he should for his trade goods, including the liquor, but accepted his aide's explanation that it was all they could get at any price. "Having paid for it, we got ready to leave," he wrote. "When morning came we found the wind blowing strong from the northwest, for ten days blowing a gale." Thus it was November before they started. Then Gurdon discovered that all but two of the Indians Dufrain had brought refused to go into winter quarters with them. Thus they were reduced to four to man their large freight canoe. They were detained further by storms at Grand Traverse and on the Calp River. It was December before they reached the Muskegon River where Jacques Dufrain declared it would not be possible to reach their post on Muskegon Lake. "The lake was frozen, the weather was very cold, and the coast Indians had all left for their hunting grounds in the interior," Gurdon recalled. He feared that his expedition and the trading season were failures before they got under way. The Indians would need supplies, but would not return to their villages since they had no knowledge that an American Fur Company outfit had arrived. If they sought the old trading post on Muskegon Lake, there would be no message or sign for them.

Gurdon had taken trade goods to the hunters from Beebeau's post, refusing to follow the practice of waiting for the customers to come in. He felt now that they must do the same in Michigan country, despite the intense cold. But some kind of shelter was required as their base. Dufrain recalled an abandoned trading post near the entrance to Muskegon Lake and suggested it could be made into a winter quarters. The log house was fifty or sixty miles from the probable Indian hunting camps and thus most inconvenient, but it was the best site they could reach. They broke the ice of the lake to make way for their mackinaw, and slowly and with much labor found the abandoned cabin on the lake shore, under the protection of a rise of timbered hills.

"We suffered from cold and were worn with toil," Gurdon recalled. "We had often been in great peril, shipping water, and narrowly escaping wreck." But they rallied their strength and began the work of reconditioning the cabin, plugging holes with bark and moss, cleaning the fireplace for use, placing oiled cloth over the window openings. By day's end they had cut firewood, melted ice, made corn soup, and were warm and snug and again optimistic that they could find the hunting camps. "We made up an assortment of goods into three packages of about sixty pounds each, which, with a blanket apiece, were to be carried by Jacques and the two *voyageurs* who constituted our force,"

Gurdon wrote. He felt compelled to agree with Jacques Dufrain that he alone, as the boss, should stay at their base while Dufrain and their remaining *voyageurs*, who knew the country and the language, would search for the hunting parties—all recruits brought in by Jacques had left. He considered Dufrain a man of judgment and honesty, despite his unfortunate choice of candidates for their crew. They had been hampered in all things by the lateness of the season. They needed to get out with their trade goods as rapidly and effectively as possible. Dufrain and his men could tell any Indians they met nearby where they could find the well-stocked trading post. They had not seen an Indian in two weeks, but Jacques believed they might not be far from the nearest hunting grounds.

Gurdon was satisfied to stay. He was not accustomed to the unusual cold. He had built a house and furnishings at Beebeau's and could be usefully employed in preparing their base to accommodate four men, or six if more could be hired. He could use his gun to obtain a supply of game. He had brought along three books, including *Nouvelle Decouverte,* which he intended to read several times that winter to improve his knowledge of French as well as history. He intended to lay up a good store of firewood and meat. They had acquired a drowned deer enroute to the cabin and skinned it, the deerhide providing Gurdon a bed in front of the fireplace until the bunks were built. Dufrain told Gurdon he had not been able to find game near the house, but his young commander did not at first believe him. After two days alone, he realized that Dufrain had been right. He trudged miles through two feet of snow in the vicinity of the cabin and found nothing to shoot. Yet he was unworried. In time, he felt, he would be sure to find at least rabbits and squirrels.

"I expected Dufrain and our men to return very soon and concluded to remain indoors and to keep up a good fire. . . ." The fireplace was broad and deep and took in large logs. Gurdon ate hot corn soup and read his books by the faint light through the oilcloth windows and from the blazing logs in the fireplace and was content another few days.

Then the blizzard struck, a day and a night of howling winds and driving snow, followed by intense quiet, a stillness relieved only by his crackling fire. Gleaming snow in huge drifts covered the roof, the earth, and the lake so deep he could no longer discern where the shore ended and the ice began. The drifts packed against the eaves of his cabin and his glazed windows. The heavy silence perturbed him so he left the cabin, after pushing away snow that half blocked his door. He required firewood and he hoped to hear a sound of some living thing. The world outside was silent. The cold seemed to set his blood. He wore his white coat and capote purchased in Cahokia which kept his ears from freezing and hurried about to start blood circulation as he searched for wood. There was little to be had that would keep a fire long. He saw he had erred in working on the bunks before laying up a good store of fuel. Now he had to climb a nearby hill, cut wood, and carry it to the cabin, an ordeal in the intense cold and heavy snow. But the work warmed him and mercifully occupied him. He worried about Dufrain and his men, but thought their prolonged absence was partly due to the storm. He assumed they must have found hunting parties and had moved farther out and now were prevented from returning. At least they would be sheltered by the hunters.

Inside the warm cabin he rested and made sure his nose hadn't been frost nipped. He had been told to rub frosted skin gently with snow, before applying a warmed cloth. He satisfied his hunger with corn soup, then hastened outside once more to build up his wood supply. The snowfall had resumed, a steady, implacable, deepening white. This made the transportation of heavy logs from the hill increasingly difficult and he sought a solution. He made a sled by wetting the deerskin that had been his bed, wrapping it around a three-foot length of log that would go into his fireplace, tieing it tight with grapevine, then sliding the frozen cylinder down the hill. "I found I had a pretty fair sled," Gurdon wrote. "My downhill path became hard and smooth, and my load would frequently slide down to the bottom with me astride it."

He had solved his firewood problem, but the deep snow prevented him from finding game or venturing farther in search of it. He had no snowshoes at the cabin. He did not want to use up the corn, beans and flour since he knew the supplies were to last the winter, as they might, with game added. The absence of Dufrain and his men now worried him. Surely Dufrain would not have ventured too far without sending one man back for added trade goods and to inform Gurdon of their plans. Clearly something might have gone wrong. He worried, but then concluded that men of Indian blood who knew the country would surely survive. An Indian in the wilderness was always at home, he knew. He devoted himself to further efforts to find food. He recalled reading in Alexander Henry's *Book of Travels in the Northwest* that Canadian Indians fished through a hole in the ice, covering their fishing hole with a small tepee to keep out the light so they could see the fish. The occupant of the shelter over the ice hole dangled a small fish in the water while holding his spear at the ready. This bait attracted a larger fish, which then was speared. It seemed easy. But Gurdon had no small fish for bait and no spear.

He worked most of the day carving the fish he needed from a piece of wood and colored it by searing it with a hot iron. He also drilled a hole to be filled with melted lead, so the fish would sink in the water. He attached trade beads for eyes and a leather thong to be used to dangle it beneath the ice. He made his spear from a pole to which he fastened his hunting knife and attached a thong to ensure he would not lose the spear if he missed his fish. He melted some shot, poured it into the hole in his small fish, and tried bobbing it in a bucket of water. It worked fine.

The next morning he was ready to fish. Cutting the hole in the ice with an axe was no problem. He thrust tree branches into holes in the ice and covered them with a blanket to form his shelter. As he lay flat on the ice, with his head over the hole, he dangled his "little pet" in the water. Soon a large fish appeared and darted at his decoy. He saw it well, but was in no position to cast his spear. He tried again from a sitting position. The fish returned. He hurled his spear and missed. He retrieved the spear. There were plenty of fish but the light was deceptive and he continued to miss. "And thus every few minutes for more than two hours I repeated the operation with the same results, when, mortified and angry, I returned cold and hungry to my solitary home and made a dinner of corn."

That night he re-read Alexander Henry's description of the ice fishing, concluding that he simply needed more practice and a better estimate of the effect of the water and ice on the light. He lowered the poles holding his blanket to darken the fishing area and after an hour or so of effort, he speared a large lake trout. He took it immediately to his house, cleaned it and boiled it in the camp kettle he had ready. "Never before or since did fish taste so good," he wrote. "After that I had no trouble taking all the fish I wanted."

*

His problem of food supply had been solved. But he ventured outside to hunt since he could not endure the silence of his cabin. Nothing stirred. The slate sky was free of clouds and the pale sun transcribed a low arc in the south, but the snow lay thick on the lake and land, piled high in impassible drifts, and now and then snapped a tree limb with a crack as loud as a gunshot, shattering the stillness. Yet no animal appeared. Then, in the loneliness of a wakeful night, Gurdon began to realize he had a visitor. The moss and bark filling the cabin cracks had blown away in the storm, and through a crack he saw a large timber wolf, silhouetted against the phosphorescent glow of snow under the full moon. The animal had discovered the remnants of Gurdon's lake trout and was devouring the icy bits. Thereafter each night Gurdon remained awake to await the coming of the wolf. "I could easily have shot him, but he was my only companion. . . . Thus I lived for thirty long, dreary, winter days, solitary and alone, never once during that time seeing a human being, and devoured with anxiety as to the fate of Dufrain and his men, who I feared had met with some serious mishap, if, indeed, they had not been murdered. My anxiety for the last two weeks had been most intense, and at times I was almost crazy. I could not leave my trade goods, and knew not what I should do."

He felt responsible for the fate of his men and perceived himself to blame for the ill fortune that had come to his outfit because of a too late start. Clearly the company had been late in selecting him for the post, but he did not, in his recollections, seek to place any part of the blame on the company. He saw himself as too young and inexperienced for his job and expected to return to Mackinaw in disgrace, should he survive. "I would be the object of ridicule among the traders and would incur the

144

lasting displeasure of my employers, and this was to be the end of all my bright anticipations for the future.'' But he was seventeen, innately optimistic and had become inured to the cold and could no longer stand his inaction. He made increasingly wide circles about his cabin when the snow settled so that he could walk and find his way around the drifts. He found rabbits again, varying his menu of fish and enabling him to store up food against the day Dufrain and his men might return. He regained hope though he continued to be half mad with worry and remorse. The wolf, finding the menu gradually improved, returned each night, stealthily without sound, only the noises of his feeding audible through the cabin crack. Then, one night, there were wolf howls in the distance and the visits ended. The pack was hunting again.

And Jacques Dufrain and his men returned, accompanied by three Indians, all on snowshoes, all bearing bales of furs. They were joyful, eager to report on their good fortune and exploits. They were utterly astonished at the barrage of angry words Gurdon hurled at them. When the frustrated, cabin-sick commander had cooled down, Dufrain explained that he had been ten days finding the first Indian hunting party. It had been visited by a trader who had supplied them for the rest of the winter and cleared their camp of available furs. The trader also had informed the Indians that no other trader was coming to the Muskegon area. The Indians were sorry that Dufrain had arrived so late, he was a great favorite with them, but they had no choice but to take the goods offered earlier. Gurdon allowed for Dufrain's good opinion of himself, since he knew it was justified, and awaited the rest of the details.

Dufrain and his men had pushed on, to make sure they would reach other hunting parties ahead of their competitor; also they had run short of food but could not take time to hunt for themselves, since they wished to reach the camps in urgent need of traps and powder. Again Gurdon understood Dufrain's reasons, and urged him to get on with it, while he prepared their roast rabbit and corn soup. Dufrain had sent an Indian runner to tell Gurdon of their plan. The Indian had badly injured his foot enroute to Gurdon's base and returned to the hunting camp after Dufrain and his men had departed. Thus, without Dufrain's knowledge, Gurdon had been left in ignorance of Dufrain's plan. Mentally Gurdon forgave Dufrain for all the doubts he had harbored while he was in the cabin alone. He asked forgiveness for the evil words he had flung at them on their return. He had been crazy with worry.

They forgave one another and opened the bales of pelts Dufrain and his men and his hired Indians had brought back. "The expedition had been one of great success," Gurdon wrote. "The goods had all been disposed of and in their place they brought the finest and richest of furs—marten, beaver, bear, lynx, fox, otter and mink making up their collection. At the sight of such rich treasures all my gloomy anticipations fled, and joy and satisfaction reigned in their stead. All was joy in our little household. The men were as glad to return as I was to welcome them. I feasted them bountifully on corn soup and fish and rabbit and I listened to the recital of the incidents of their trip."

The day following they made plans for the distribution of more trade goods. There was a large camp Dufrain had heard of, but not seen, where trade goods were required and a large store of furs awaited. Gurdon announced that he would make the trip. One of the Indians would be detailed to watch the cabin. Dufrain objected, insisting that his young boss could not stand the hardship—"that never having travelled on snowshoes I would have the *mal du raquette,* or become sick, and thus detain them." Gurdon was adamant. He was going on the trip. Nothing could be worse than the loneliness he had endured. He had to learn to use snowshoes sometime. The accounts would be in good order before they departed. This trip would not last thirty days. Dufrain gave in at last, providing Gurdon would carry only half a pack of trade goods. It was agreed.

They set out after accounts and food and wood supplies were in order. The day was clear and cold, the snow crunching under their feet as they swung into the rhythm required by the snowshoes. The sky seemed a sheet of pale blue ice above them. The country was rough, covered with underbrush half hidden by snow. Gurdon fell repeatly, "usually landing full length, burying my face in the snow." His companions helped him up, but he soon fell again. Once more Dufrain urged Gurdon to go back. No man could learn to use snowshoes while carrying a pack on a long trip, he insisted. Gurdon refused. That night, after making only six miles, they camped in two feet of snow, without shelter. They scraped clear an area about six by ten feet beside a fallen tree and started a fire with flint and steel, after piling green wood to the windward. They cut hemlock boughs for bedding, covered them with a blanket to keep them in place, and set their packs to windward to protect their heads from the cold. They had killed two porcupines during the day. These they now dressed and then toasted on long sticks over their blazing fire. The pounded parched corn they carried was mixed with melted snow and served with their hot meat, and they pronounced the meal excellent. They hadn't eaten since their breakfast of corn soup and salt pork. After supper they smoked and talked a bit. They were weary and the three, Dufrain, the Indian *voyageur*, and Gurdon, loosened their clothing and lay down on their hemlock bough beds, covered themselves with two blankets and slept, their feet to the fire.

Gurdon soon awakened. His muscles ached, his ankles were swollen, his feet throbbed with pain. From time to time during the night he replenished the fire while his companions slept. There had been no need to decide who would share this chore; they all knew it would be Hubbard who would sleep fitfully. Dufrain and the Indian awakened refreshed, shared with Gurdon the rest of the porcupine meat and a handful each of lyed corn. Their march resumed, but Gurdon was so obviously lame that Dufrain turned back to him. "Let us all go back," he pleaded. "Or let me go part way with you, you go back to our house and send out Baptiste. I will wait for him."

"At first I thought I would agree with him and turn back," Gurdon recalled. "But the recollections of the lonely month I had passed there determined me to go on with the party, and all of Dufrain's arguments failed to change my purpose. I had caught the knack of throwing out the heels of my snowshoes by a slight turn of the foot and my falls were less frequent." That day, he said, they made three leagues, or a little more than nine miles. His leg muscles loosened as he walked, so that his agony concentrated in his feet, but he kept on. During the day they saw rabbits scurry into a hollow tree. They cut them out and had roast rabbit for supper.

Dufrain had thought they might find the Chippewa camp they were seeking by the end of the second day, but he was wrong, though he found signs of an old camp at the site he had in mind. Snow fell and the wet flakes stuck to the wide, webbed snowshoes, making them heavy. When Gurdon removed his moccasins and neips that night he found that his feet were badly swollen, red and bruised where the straps held the snowshoes in place. Dufrain looked and shook his head, *"Mal du racquette,"* he said. By morning the swelling had increased and the pressure of the snowshoe straps caused excrutiating pain. But they had to go on, and Gurdon suppressed any complaints and sought to keep up. Towards noon they heard dogs barking. They saw distantly the Indian camp they were seeking, the *voyageur* pressing ahead at Dufrain's order, while Dufrain walked behind Gurdon, who hobbled, blinded with pain, and seemed about to fall. They rested, and resumed the march, and rested again.

*

They were welcomed to the hunting camp by Indian women, who took them to the lodge of the young hunters, where they were served hot venison and corn soup. An old woman, observing Gurdon's condition, told him to remove his moccasins and neips. She poulticed his swollen, bleeding feet with herbs and he at last slept for a while. He awakened to learn that the hunters were returning, bringing in a good supply of furs. It was a large hunting party, but the lodge was an ample one, made of logs and reeds, which provided cover from the snow and wind but stood open to the sky, a log fire burning across the leeward end. The northern Indians, the Sacs, Foxes, Ottawas and Chippewas, constructed such large shelters for a long winter season in permanent camps to which they returned year after year. Women did not stay in such a lodge, which Gurdon and his companions were welcomed to share as long as they wished. The Indian woman, old and fat, who had attended him, returned to change the dressing on his feet, after bathing them in warm water. Gurdon was grateful. The young men, coming in from the hunt, recognized his malady with good-natured laughter. They were taught to ignore pain themselves, and watched suffering without sense of sympathy. While Gurdon rested, he and Dufrain inspected the pelts offered to them and disposed of much trade goods. Gurdon finished the required book-keeping and instructed Dufrain to pay the old woman in goods for her services to him. More trappers and hunters were expected back, so they remained five days with the Chippewas.

"The old squaw poulticed my feet with herbs and I practiced every hour or so on my snowshoes," he wrote. "When I left these hospitable people I had no trouble keeping up with the others, nor was I tired at night, and we made fifteen miles the first day."

Runners had gone out from the Indian camp to others in the area, thus on their approach to the next camp, in addition to the usual welcome of yapping dogs, they were met by a delegation of hunters who warmly greeted Dufrain and informed them they were to be guests that night "at a grand feast, partly in honor of our visit, at which all the meat and broth set before us must be eaten, and the bones saved and buried with appropriate ceremonies, as an offering to the Great Spirit, that he might favor them in the hunt. The offering was a fat bear. . . ." Gurdon was ready, he had been through it before. This was an Ottawa camp, where Dufrain was welcomed as an honored son, and his young master, the trader, was treated with due respect. They were informed that afternoon of the circumstances relating to the slaying of the bear, an exceptionally fine beast, weighing about five hundred pounds. Hunters had discovered the bear two days previously in a large pine tree, the trunk torn by claws, the upper branches broken. The two days were required to get the bear out, since the tree was huge, with a girth of more than twenty feet, and fires were built at the base of it. When the she-bear emerged, they shot her neatly through the back of the neck, cutting the spine, and were delighted by the fineness of the pelt, which was quickly removed. The fat was six inches deep and six hunters were required to carry the meat, the head and the bearskin into camp, while others guarded the remaining carcass in the woods. That these arrangments were completed just as the trader arrived with Dufrain, the son of an Ottawa woman, was considered by the hunters to be an exceptionally good omen.

The feast that night was limited to the Ottawa men, a party of Huron hunters and the traders, whose timely arrival signified that the spirit of the bear did not resent the abrupt loss of its earthly home, the trade goods coming when they were most urgently needed. Dufrain advised Gurdon to present to their hosts a new Stroud blanket, never before used, which would cover the scaffold in the chief's lodge where the bear's head would be placed. Around the head were distributed medals, gorgets and armbands worn by the hunters who killed the bear, plus the usual sticks of tobacco and several pipes. By evening, when the bear meat was cooking in a lodge nearby, more guests arrived from a camp a few miles distant, they were led by the Ottawa Chief Masquat in an appeal to his manitou, or personal good spirit, who was requested to explain to the spirit of the bear the necessity for taking its life. Then Chief Masquat and his hunters and guests in turn lighted their pipes and passed in procession before the head of the bear to blow smoke into its nostrils, enabling it symbolically to participate in the feast.

Gurdon Hubbard remembered the Little Calumet feast and knew what would be required of him. He insisted that Dufrain should have the place of honor, while he removed himself to a relatively darkened part of the lodge, an act of modesty which won the clucking approval of the Ottawas and their Huron guests. Dufrain warned they must eat everything, "Eat it all or you will insult them," he insisted. "I can't," Gurdon protested. "They have given me more than anyone." Dufrain set the example, falling to with gusto. "The fire was low and in my location not even Dufrain could watch my movements," Gurdon remembered. "I wore my French (Cahokia) capote. I took my first opportunity to slip a piece of meat into the hood." He ate slowly, tearing the bones away from the meat and placing them back in his bowl while slipping the meat into the cowl thrown back from his head. Even so, he was sickened by the amount of bear meat he felt obliged to consume. He excused himself, left the lodge, and gave his hidden meat to the dogs. He thrust his fingers into his throat, trying to vomit, but without success. There was a roar of laughter from the Indians when he returned to his place in the lodge and began eating once more. Gurdon beamed at them and consumed his final helping.

The speeches began. The feast was a success. The Hurons invited Gurdon to their camp to trade and spoke of other hunting camps still unsupplied. It would be wise to cover the territory as rapidly as possible. Gurdon and Dufrain agreed that they should go on to the Huron camp while their *voyageur* and Indian runners carried their fur collection back to their base on Muskegan Lake, returning with more trade goods. Thus they could cover all possible camps despite their late arrival in the Michigan country.

They had visited several camps, had replenished their supplies and the season at last was a sure success. He and Dufrain had been gone nearly a month, Gurdon estimated, and they turned back in excellent spirits, carrying only their personal gear and two extra blankets. They even sold the last but one of their flint and steel pouches, complete with punk and tinder. On the third day of their return trip, travelling through deep snows, Gurdon saw a strangely leaning tree that had attracted his attention earlier that day. He knew they were walking in a circle and told Dufrain they were going the wrong way. "Dufrain replied sharply that if I knew the way better than he I had better take the lead; thus rebuked, I followed on in silence." They were out of food and had seen no game. When they stopped at night, Dufrain reached for their flint steel and tinder he carried and discovered he had lost it. That night they bedded down on hemlock boughs and covered themselves with the extra blankets they carried, but there was no fire and no food. "Soon the ice on our bodies began to thaw, and we fell asleep," Gurdon wrote. A second day and night passed. They were warm under their blankets and did not want to arise when the sun awakened them. "We were no longer hungry. We felt more like laying where we were and awaiting death rather than making a further effort. . . ."

Gurdon at last roused them both. He had been thinking of his responsibility for the outfit and of his mother, sisters and brother. Dufrain at last admitted he was lost and he had no hope. He refused to move from his warm spot. Gurdon, promising to return, went out seeking a route that might lead them to help. About a mile distant, under a fresh fall of snow, he found snowshoe tracks and followed them to a blaze on a tree. Clearly the tracks were not their own and had been made within hours. He had found a trail. He returned to Dufrain, who was indifferent to their possible good fortune, but agreed to follow. They found a path of broken twigs on the new fallen snow and more tree blazes. "Dufrain seemed not to understand," Gurdon remembered. "He stopped frequently, crossed himself while he moved his lips in prayer, and it required much persuasion on my part to get him to move slowly forward, he protesting that he could not move another step."

They lost the trail and, in frantically searching for it, Gurdon lost Dufrain. When he had found the tree blazes again, he retraced his snowshoe tracks to a spot where Dufrain, wrapped in his blanket, lay asleep in the snow. Gurdon sought to arouse him. Dufrain briefly responded. "Leave me," he said, then relapsed into sleep. Gurdon dug away the snow, wrapped blankets around Dufrain, and hurried back to the tree blazes, where he discovered further tracks. He hastened on, hoping to find a camp before dark so that Dufrain could be rescued. He heard the barking of dogs and came upon a single cabin, crudely made of bark and skins. He called for help. The squaw who lifted the door of skins signalled that he could enter. Inside, before a warm fire, her husband sat, his arm wrapped with thongs and sticks obviously pulling together his broken bones. Gurdon felt faint. "I reeled like a drunken man. I told the woman I was hungry and had not eaten for days and nights," he remembered. "She exclaimed, 'nin guid muck-a-ta-minna baein,' meaning, 'It is not good for us . . . we too are hungry.'" Her husband had broken his arm and was unable to hunt. Their son had gone out, seeking game. "She opened a sack and from their small store of corn, all that remained of their winter's supply, she took some, boiled it and offered it to me," he recalled. It frightened him when he found himself unable to swallow it. They made a place for him on the floor of the hut and he promptly slept. When he awakened minutes later he remembered Dufrain and announced he was going back for his companion.

As he spoke, the Indians' son returned proudly bearing a slain bear cub, his first kill of big game. The Indians insisted that Gurdon was too weak to go to help his friend, the squaw volunteering to go with her son. "Only I know where to find him," Gurdon told them. "I only can get him to come with us." It was agreed he and the Indian boy would go, while the woman prepared bear meat for them all. They rigged a snow sled and brought back Dufrain and the woman and Gurdon nursed him. "The poor fellow was ruptured," Gurdon wrote. "It was several days before I could push back the protruding parts." He constructed a *train-de-clese* and with the help of the Indian boy he hired to accompany him, he got Dufrain back to their base.

Dufrain survived the slow sled trip but thereafter he was listless, or in pain, and did not leave the cabin again through the winter. They could not travel to Mackinaw with him, but cared for him in the cabin as well as possible while they collected the furs from their territory. Their freight canoe was well filled with pelts when the ice went out and they could depart for Mackinaw. Dufrain remained reluctant to venture outside. They placed him on a litter and carried him to the mackinaw, resting the litter on the thwarts. "There was a light wind blowing the day we started," Gurdon remembered. "The motion of the canoe caused Dufrain to vomit and before we could reach a harbor at White River he died. We buried him in the bluff."

*

That summer Gurdon was given little time to recover from the ordeal of the Michigan snows. He spent a few weeks in the retail store with John Kinzie and then, when Mr. Matthews arrived, he was ordered back to the job in the fur warehouse. He had been commended for his work in Michigan, but he had lost a man and he felt under a cloud. The messages from his mother and sister Elizabeth were reassuring; he again sent money to his family. When Mr. Crooks informed him he would return to Michigan and not to Illinois with M. Deschamps, he felt in no position to protest. This time he departed in a fifty-foot mackinaw with a crew of four camp aides and five *voyageurs.* "My chief aide was Cosa, well and favorably known among the Indians for his bravery and intelligence . . . he was paid $100 for his winter's service, an unusually high fee, but he knew the country, he had a good reputation as a leader, and he furnished two horses besides the services of his wife."

Frequently the bosses of small outfits did not know their precise territory until they were under way, when those who could read opened a letter of instructions, or they were informed by the leader of their brigade. Gurdon knew in advance he would not go back to the Muskegon river post, but to the Kalamazoo, "near the site of a city of that name," he wrote in his recollections. There he would be in competition with those traders on the Kalamazoo and St. Joseph rivers who had not joined the American Fur Company.

After his Muskegon troubles, the Kalamazoo post provided a relatively easy life for the young trader, now past his eighteenth birthday. Since Cosa owned horses, could hire others, and his wife would watch their supplies, Gurdon was able to send his entire crew out to the hunting camps with pack ponies, greatly expanding his trading area. They even penetrated into the territory of the powerful trader William Burnett, who had settled in the Michigan wilderness in 1769, but only because Gurdon Hubbard wished to learn from Burnett if he could portage freight from the St. Joseph River to the Kankakee, possibly by using ponies. He found that he could pack goods across the portage, but not the mackinaws. Mr. Burnett, old and portly, was not interested in such a venture himself.

Gurdon's only trouble that winter came from Cosa. His solitary vice, like Dufrain's, and so many of the Indians, was drinking too much. Cosa usually abstained when he was working, but when he indulged in ardent spirits he did not care to drink alone and was generous with his friends. Consequently the stock of this necessity had run low on an occasion when Cosa told Gurdon an important trade with a tribe on the St. Joseph River would depend on the supply of whisky available. "We had only a two-gallon keg of high wines, watered one third," Gurdon recalled. He declined to produce the liquor when the trading began, although many traders preferred to deal with the Indians after they were drunk. Instead he hid the keg even from Cosa. But Cosa's friends had some whisky of their own and when Gurdon returned from an errand he found the trading party, including Cosa, drunk and still thirsty. Cosa instructed his boss to produce their hidden keg. Gurdon refused and Cosa and his friends advanced on him. "I told them it was my property and not theirs," Gurdon remembered. "They desisted, but Cosa, to show his independence of me, began to search for the keg. When he found it and sought to reach for it, I seized him by the throat, threw him on his back, and, placing my knees on his stomach, choked him so he could neither move nor speak." The other Indians fled, but Cosa continued to yell for whisky whenever Gurdon released the pressure on his throat. "At last Cosa understood there was to be no more liquor. I let him up, conducted him to my quarters, covered him up, and laid down by his side. . . . Cosa was considerably injured but he slept well. The next day Cosa hoarsely begged me to tell no one what had taken place. . . . He was afterward very faithful and attentive to his duties."

*

The following spring at Mackinaw Gurdon found letters from his mother awaiting him, "telling of her loneliness and great desire to see me." He had completed his third year of service, and again was assigned to the fur warehouse job with Mr. Matthews, a duty the leader of an outfit was not required to perform more than once in four years. Mr. Matthews, however, informed him that conditions had changed. Gurdon had an alternate suggestion. Why do all that tedious work on the island? Why not provide fur presses to the various trading posts so that pelts could be graded, counted and packed during the winter as they were received? There were many objections to this procedure, Matthews thought, but he promised to consider it. Two years later, Gurdon would take such a press to his own post in Illinois. His *voyageurs* were thus able to spend the summer at home with their wives and families and to plant gardens. This, however, did not please the *voyageurs.* Despite their complaints about work in the fur warehouse, they preferred to spend their summers doing whatever was required of them on Mackinaw Island.

Warehouse duty went no better for Gurdon than before. He knew he was being treated unfairly and determined on a showdown with Mr. Crooks. He was summoned to the Agency House and informed he again would be assigned to the Michigan territory. Gurdon reconstructed the scene: "I asked to be discharged, giving as my reason that my mother was a widow and my brother and four sisters were all younger than myself and needed my services and protection. I was then eighteen and felt myself a man in all things." Mr. Crooks, jolted, brought out a letter he had received from Mrs. Abigail Hubbard, Middletown, Connecticut. Far from wanting her son to leave the company,

155

she had expressed her appreciation of the opportunities the company was giving her son, Crooks said. She did not wish to interfere with her son's career. Abigail, it appeared, had written Mr. Crooks to thank him for forwarding money and news. Thus, Mr. Crooks had not visited Abigail Hubbard personally as he had promised Gurdon he would try to do. Mr. Crooks nevertheless prevailed upon his young employee to remain with the American Fur Company, but felt obliged to change his assignment to Illinois, possibly because Antoine Deschamps, hearing of Gurdon's defiance, insisted on it.

So, in September, 1821, Gurdon returned to *Le Bourgeois* Deschamps and the Illinois Brigade: "I was again with my old companions, all of whom gave me a cordial welcome." He was almost as tall as Deschamps now, bronzed and toughened and sure of himself. The trip to Chicago was fast but dull—"row, row, row all the way," he wrote—but his welcome by the Kinzies was a joyous one, and at the Kinzie home he had the incredible good fortune to meet Dr. Alexander Wolcott, the new Indian agent at Chicago, who was from Middletown, knew his mother Abigail, and had met his sisters. In this young government bureaucrat Gurdon Hubbard found another teacher, with credentials complementary to those of M. Deschamps, and Gurdon found he could aid Dr. Wolcott in his work. The two became close friends.

Dr. Wolcott did not practice medicine in Chicago, though he had come west as a medical officer assigned to a commission under Governor Lewis Cass of Michigan Territory empowered by the federal government to study Indian problems in the northwest. A graduate of Yale University, Dr. Wolcott had studied anthropology as well as medicine and also the subject of Indian treaties. He accompanied Cass and Henry R. Schoolcraft, a minerologist and student of Indian life, on a survey trip to the headwaters of the Mississippi. In 1821 he was appointed Indian Agent for the Chicago area and directed the drafting of a treaty with the United Potawatomis that was signed at Chicago on August 29 of that year. Wolcott was a cheerful, opinionated, forceful young man who did not mention his medical background to Gurdon. As Indian agent, he moved into the new Agency House, which he dubbed "Cobweb Castle." He invited

Hubbard to share his bachelor quarters there, confiding that he didn't expect to be alone for long, since he was courting Ellen Kinzie, who lived next door. "I try to see her every minute her father will allow," Wolcott said, "but that's not many. John Kinzie seems to hate anyone connected with the government. I hope you don't feel that way, Hubbard. I hear you are a good friend of the family and I need a friend there."

Gurdon was never happier. The Kinzies continued to welcome him as a member of the family. Maria teased him, Robert asked to hear his Indian stories, Ellen was pleased that he and Dr. Wolcott had become immediate friends, and even John Kinzie, Sr. seemed ready to make peace with the American government at last. Eleanor Kinzie welcomed Gurdon warmly as usual, eager for his stories of her son John at Mackinaw. She ruefully produced the clothing Gurdon had left with her three years earlier and displayed the broadcloth suit to the family. "You've outgrown it without wearing it once," she mourned. Gurdon reported the scene in letters to his mother and his sister Elizabeth, promising he would never rest until he could bring them all to Chicago, or at least to Mackinaw.

The evenings of their week in Chicago, when Doc Wolcott had returned from his visit to the Kinzie mansion, Gurdon and Deschamps and sometimes Kinzie himself talked of Indian affairs and of the fur trade. Wolcott fascinated Gurdon. He was an aristocrat, like Stuart at Mackinaw, a fastidious man of letters, but affable. He designated the Indians under his jurisdiction, "my prairie Potawatomis," and was pleased to learn of their ways from Deschamps and young Hubbard. "I told Governor Cass in my report this month that the Potawatomis are a handsome, relatively cultured people," he said. "Yet of all the tribes and nations that people this globe, the Potawatomis have the least that is peculiar in their manners, or customs, or, I fear, interesting in their history. The only prominent trait in their character I have so far discovered is their universal and insatiable love of ardent spirits, and that is common to all tribes that are so lucky as to live in a state of frequent intercourse with Christian men."

Deschamps was amused. "Did you really write that to Cass?" he asked. Deschamps often denounced easterners who "came west prating of the noble savage, then turned at once to fleecing him." He obviously did not rate Dr. Wolcott as one of these, but rather a man of humor. Gurdon Hubbard was shocked and at once defended the people with whom he traded. "Father Allouez, who knew them well, called the Potawatomis the best-mannered tribe he knew when he saw them in Wisconsin," Gurdon said. "He called the men good-humored and their women modest, and said they were especially skilled at games and the hunt. Sure, they have been hurt by whisky. It is the worst enemy the whites have brought to the Indians."

"After smallpox, possibly," Wolcott replied. "We must not forget our sainted forebears gave them that devastating and decimating plague. And we must remember that the Dutch sold the Iroquois their first guns; that Thomas Penn hired Iroquois to drive the Delawares off the land he had acquired from them by fraud. Yes, the trader has done his share of deviltry, and, like the Pharisee, I thank God that I am not as one of them. I fear that we may not rest until disease and the gun-and-whisky trade have totally destroyed the Indian. But also, I must admit that I am not without guilt. My forebears, the Pilgrims, all but exterminated the Indians who welcomed them, and put the head of Metacom, son of Massasoit, on a pike as the reward for his father's somewhat indiscriminate hospitality."

"You omit the farmer and the meddling American government from the list of offenders against the red man," Deschamps suggested. "The trader has not attempted to reorder the Indian's way of life. The trader simply makes it easier for the Indian to live in the way he chooses. The Indian brave will wear a dozen silver gorgets, one over the other, and many silver arm bands and other ornaments, but no breeches. The trader sells him the ornaments and the traps and guns by which he makes a living, but does not require him to buy breeches. We sell him the wire screws he uses to pluck his beard. We did not teach him to pull out his whiskers, nor do we urge him to wear a beard. We sell a silver gorget for a pelt. The government awards the Indian silver medals then steals his land. We traders sell the Indian what he wants and needs. This is something not yet learned in the government factories."

"I appreciate your candor," Wolcott said. "I hope to learn

to know the Indians well. I will come to visit you both, if you will have me."

John Kinzie, who hated the government factory system and generally quarreled with his prospective son-in-law on the subject, was at the door and Deschamps quickly changed the subject. "It is time for me to propose a toast," he said when John had entered. "I have with me a letter, written by Mr. Ramsey Crooks. Gurdon, your next post will not be with Beebeau, as you had anticipated, but you will have your own station on the Iroquois River! I am authorized to go with you to help select the site. I wanted you to hear this news with our good friend John Kinzie. And we welcome Dr. Wolcott into our select company, and urge him to visit our stations any time."

*

The water was low at the Chicago Portage. "We were compelled to carry our goods and effects from the South Branch through Mud Lake to the Desplaines River, encountering the usual fatigues," Gurdon wrote. He vowed once more that he would find another way to get his trade goods into the Illinois country, pending the time a canal could be built. They stopped at Beebeau's post. "Mr. Beebeau was still in charge, though much more feeble, nor had his temper and disposition undergone any change for the better." Pierre, who had lived with Gurdon at the post three years before, begged to be taken to the Iroquois station. "I am a man," Pierre said. "I have prayed and seen my vision in the forest, found my manidog, and my medicine is as good as any Indian's." Gurdon wanted Pierre with him, but Deschamps would not permit the change. "He is your friend, your equal, keep it that way," Deschamps said. "Noel Vasseur will go with you to the Iroquois as your assistant."

They chose a site on the Iroquois near the mouth of Crooked Creek, far to the east of Beebeau's station, and Deschamps departed. Gurdon was ill, but he assured Deschamps he would recover quickly. He and Vasseur, using the experience gained at Beebeau's three years previously, built "a good-sized trading house" and storage pens and a dock. As the house progressed Gurdon's illness became worse. By the time they had completed the walls and roof of the room that would serve as the store, and had distributed trade goods to most of the hunters, Gurdon was too ill to stand long at a time. He wished desperately to go to St. Louis for medical help, as John Crafts had done, but he knew he could not make such a trip alone, nor would he spare a man to take him. "I felt symptoms of ague, loss of appetite and chills. . . . My fever increased. I was unable to sit up, and daily grew worse."

It was at this time two white hunters stopped at his post, their large *piroque* loaded with game. They spoke French, said they were from St. Louis and had been hunting ducks and other game for the St. Louis market. "Their arrival seemed Providential," Gurdon recalled. He begged them to take him to St. Louis, but they exacted harsh terms. In addition to paying them liberally for his passage, he was required to buy the amount of game his presence in the *piroque* would displace. Gurdon agreed, ordered the St. Louis pair to be provided with corn for the trip, and told his interpreter of his plans, instructing him to send word to M. Deschamps, asking for orders, if he did not return by a certain day. The men then removed the game he had purchased and placed Gurdon in the boat, making him as comfortable as possible.

A few miles from his Iroquois River station, he was unsure of the time or the distance, "the river became very rough, the motion of the boat caused me to vomit excessively and I became unconscious. The men carried me along until they came to a settler's cabin, and, supposing me to be dying, took me ashore, left me there, and pursued their journey."

The events of the next ten days or so Gurdon remembered vaguely and in various ways. He did not know how long he had remained unconscious. When he awakened he found himself in a bed in a crude cabin, according to one recollection, and on a bed of blankets in a glade near the river in another. Also he recalled lying for a time on soggy reeds, the coolness of the water reviving him, and drawing himself up the muddy bank, where he lay exhausted. The two women who found him, he thought them to be mother and daughter, spoke a strange tongue. They wore Indian garb and were deeply tan, but their eyes were blue and their sun-bleached hair indicated they were white women. When he again awakened they had drawn him up the slope and placed him under a roof fashioned of leafy twigs and branches tied with vines. He lay on a blanket spread across hemlock boughs and was covered with a blanket. The girl of the two, possibly the age of Maria Kinzie, about eight or nine, was cooling him with a maple leaf fan. When she saw he had awakened she hurried to bring the older woman, her mother or possibly a sister, who reminded Gurdon of Margaret Helm. He had sought to move while the girl was away and discovered himself naked except for an Indian breech-clout of buckskin which they had belted about him. His bed was the kind the Indians made for their sick, the branches covering a hole in the earth to be used for natural relief. He realized they had removed his buckskins and breech-clout and cleansed him.

As the older woman knelt above him, smiling gently, he saw that her eyes were as blue as corn flowers and her breasts were pale and again he knew she could not be Indian. He tried to speak but she touched her fingers to his lips and shook her head. He slept again. He awakened some time later to find the girl sitting guard over him. A cool, wet strip of deerskin lay across his forehead and he smelled the herbs and bear grease that had been used to anoint him. He spoke to the girl in English, French, and Potawatomi, but she merely shook her head. She turned her attention to a gourd containing a mixture he guessed to be an Indian poultice of herbs, horse chestnut and butternut mixed in corn flour, an ointment he sometimes made himself. Soon the girl's mother appeared bearing a dipper containing a decoction used at Mackinaw for dysentery that he knew to contain blackberry juice and *geranium maculatum*. While the older woman raised him slightly, supporting him against her firm body, the girl gave him medicine from the gourd. He smiled his thanks. They spoke a language he thought he had heard aboard one of the ships docking at Montreal, probably Scandinavian. Neither wore ornaments, except for a small, carved head each had hanging from a chain about her throat. This he recognized as the replica of an image he had seen somewhere in the villages of his trading territory.

In the days that followed he was given medicine, cooled with water-soaked deerskin when his fever flared, and provided with hot corn soup. His nurses created a new bed for him, helped him to move onto it, and kept him clean. On the third day, or so, he asked the woman in French, "Are you *Lenni-Lenape?*" She understood the Indian word for Delaware and nodded. He pointed to the carved wooden head, dangling at her breasts. *"Wsinkhoalican?"* he asked. He knew she was surprised at his utterance of the Delaware name for the beson protecting one's health. She laughed and drew back as he excitedly sought to rise, as if to touch her. He moved his hands, seeking to tell her he wished to have his clothes and his pouch containing flint, steel and tinder. He hoped the St. Louis hunters had left this with him, since he had hidden in it two Spanish *reals* he wished to give to her.

Gently she thrust him back, holding his shoulders firmly. He realized she had misunderstood his attempt to communicate with his hands, but he now had a fervent wish to touch her as she was touching him, and to draw her to him. His fever flared again. The woman applied cool buckskin. He saw that she nervously scanned the river from time to time, sometimes going to the edge of the glade to do so. He watched her as she moved about, thinking again of Margaret Helm. When he slept again he dreamed. He was packing furs at Mackinaw. He was in the store with young John Kinzie, and there saw the idol *"Wsinkhoalican"* and the carved wooden heads worn by women. A Delaware talisman, a beson used to protect the wearer from illness, Dr. Beaumont, the young surgeon from the fort, told them. Half awake, he dwelled in his thoughts of the girl and the woman. They were white and Delaware. Some time back, he remembered John Kinzie in Chicago had told him that his first wife had been a white woman carried into the Ohio country as a prisoner of the Indians. Kinzie was a young trapper then and he had arranged her release and had married her. Margaret Kinzie Helm was their daughter. So that was it! There were Delawares in Gurdon's new trade territory, they had come west from the Muskingum area of Ohio. The woman and her daughter helping him could be prisoners of the Delawares and he could free them to repay them for their kindnesses. If prisoners, why didn't they flee? Where could they go? Possibly they had been adopted into the tribe and the woman might be the wife of her captor. Perhaps, like his friend Pierre at Beebeau's, he too was having visions.

Chapter 5

_____

But the girl caring for him returned, and she was real, though she made no response to his questions. Later in the afternoon her mother appeared. He tried a few Delaware words he knew. Were they from the Muskingum country? He mixed Potawatomi with the Delaware word *Muskingum,* which meant Elk's Eye. She nodded, smiling at his efforts to learn more of her. *"Choan-schican?"* he persisted, meaning the country of the Big Knives, the East. Again she nodded. *"Woapanachke?"* he asked, meaning people toward the rising sun, the true *Lenni-Lenape.* She smiled assent. Thus he decided she had come from the far Delaware country to the east, and was perhaps Swedish, since the Swedes had settled early in Delaware and had taught the Indians there to build log cabins.

He grew excited and again wished to have her fetch his clothes and the pouch with the coins. She sought to calm him and pressed close to him. That night he dreamed of her. She came past his bower, went on to the river and he heard sounds of splashing and swimming. When she returned, she carried her deerskins and moccasins and she was pale and tall and beautiful in the moonlight. He knew that she was coming to him. He knew nothing of love beyond the talk of the *voyageurs* and what he had read in the Holy Scriptures. As she moved toward him in the beauty of the night he remembered that King David, walking upon the roof of his house, had seen Bathsheba, bathing, and she was very beautiful. And he remembered that later, David, too, laid ill, and that they had gone to find a lovely damsel and had taken her naked to the bed where David lay naked, and thus determined that the king was, indeed, dead. His own illness departed and he flung aside his blanket and she was with him and in his delirium of delight they became one as in the Scriptures and he did not wish to let her go when dawn came.

He was weak and fevered again that day, but now had little interest in demonstrating recovery. He ate his corn soup and cleansed himself with water the girl brought from the river, and awaited the night, when he was sure the woman he much loved would return and he was not disappointed. On the sixth day of the ten days he estimated later he had been with them, they gave him his clothing, and he got into his once tight buckskins, and also found that his leather pouch with its coins was gone.

When he sought to rise to his feet he learned that he had over-estimated his strength, and they returned him to a fresh bed of hemlock boughs and fed him corn soup.

Then, on the tenth day by his estimate, he saw that an Indian in a canoe had arrived. The woman went to meet him and the girl followed. They were ready for departure, carrying deerskins and their few personal belongings. The Indian did not look beyond the summer lodge of saplings and bark where the woman and the girl had awaited his coming. They departed without a glance toward the forest that hid Gurdon.

"I was able to start on foot for my trading house, about 35 miles distant," he recalled. "I arrived there in two days, to the joy and astonishment of my men. I cannot conceive why I have lost from my memory the name of those . . . who nursed me so kindly. . . . I never saw them but once afterward."

6

Michilimackinac
20 June, 1822

The company is about to establish a house at St. Louis for
the outfits of the south, which post, if I continue on the
Illinois (I) will make my headquarters . . . if the company
will consent to my proposal. I think my prospects for the
next year will be verry good (sic). I think myself as capable
of transacting Indian traid (sic) as traiders in general.

I have been trying to find an opportunity of speaking
with Mr. Matthews of the necessary experience being
found in me.

Gurdon S. Hubbard
to his mother Abigail

Gurdon Saltonstall Hubbard was twenty, grown to six feet, arrow straight, toughened by the hard work of the fur warehouse
on Mackinaw Island and in the wilderness of the Indian country, his endurance on the trail well proved. He had been tested
at the Chicago Portage, in the woods, marshes and prairies of
Illinois, and by the harsh, cruel winter of Michigan Territory. On
his return to Illinois in the fall of 1821, the Indians of Hubbard's
trading territory saw that Chief Waba's name for him, Checomocomones, meaning Little American, was no longer appropriate.
Young Indian males generally received their names on the basis of their appearance, or by achievement, or in the case of Sacs
and Potawatomis, they were encouraged to pick their own,
usually that of an animal, fish or bird. Such a name was chosen
by ritual: the fledgling brave went alone into the forest, remaining there, fasting, until he experienced a vision, guiding him in
his choice of a name and the collection of requisite articles for
his beson bundle—his good luck charms or medicine. Thus
Black Hawk of the Sacs carried the feathered skin of a sparrow
hawk with him all his life and his brother Namah, or Sturgeon,
toted pebbles from his namesake's habitat. Gurdon Hubbard

165

was not inspired by fantasy in choosing a new name, but earned it. Chief Tamin gave him the name of *Papamatabe,* or "Swift Walker," after he had carried medicine and food to Tamin's northernmost village among the frozen Kankakee marshes during his third tour of duty in the Illinois country.

By 1822 Gurdon's solid qualities were well recognized by the Indians, but not, he sometimes felt, by anyone in the Company except M. Deschamps. He had worked for Messrs. Crooks and Stuart for four years. He had grown strong and tough and sure of himself, a man who knew as much as anyone in the Company, other than Antoine Deschamps himself, of the problems of the Illinois fur trade and their solutions; the ways of the Indians; the vagaries of travel on the lakes, unexpectedly turbulent and unpredictable in storms; the treachery of the rapids in the rivers and streams; the often unmanageable mackinaws, too frequently overloaded. Gurdon could lead a brigade of mackinaws when called upon. He could find his way in the wilderness, paddle a canoe, swim icy rivers, clip the backbone of a bear or beaver at a hundred paces with a single shot, and barter powder and guns, traps and tomahawks with the canniest of the Indians. Gurdon S. Hubbard was not a young man who undervalued himself and the Company knew from Deschamps' reports that his self-esteem was soundly based. This knowledge it kept secret, but the Indians and the settlers alike were fond of the boy and let him know of their admiration. Papamatabe, known as "Our Gurdon" to many whites, was respected for his quickness and compassion, his fierceness in combat; his serene good nature only occasionally marked by quick anger; his fairness and honesty; his wide grin and hearty laughter at rude fontier jokes. Such qualities were valued by the Indians and by the settlers thronging into Illinois from the south. The settlers relied on him, as the Indians did for trade goods, for his knowledge of the new frontier as well.

Gurdon had recovered rapidly from his illness of the fall of 1821 and for a time grew content, seemingly stronger and more confident than before. He confided in no one his experience with the St. Louis hunters and its aftermath. After getting his books in order, he began a series of personal visits to the Indian camps. He walked fifty miles a day, carrying a pack of trade goods on his back, as well as his gun, to extend the limits of his trading territory by supplying any outlying hunters' camp he could find. When the rivers and creeks were open he traveled in his personal black-walnut canoe. In time he began using ponies to pack and portage his goods. He loved his life as boss of an "outfit" in the Indian country and was well-pleased with his house and his housekeeping skills. "It was finished with puncheons (the flat split logs that sealed it against cold and heat)," he boasted. "The window at the end was nicely covered with greased foolscap paper, the clay fireplace would take logs six feet in length." He built his furniture, including Hubbard-style bunks, plugged into the walls for support. Despite his bad experience with visiting hunters, he again invited a pair "one a future governor of Illinois (John Wood)" to his home and they vowed the dinner he prepared for them was the best they ever ate. He felt this tribute entirely justified. "I have never tasted any roast turkey that seemed to me so excellent as those fat wild ones I killed and prepared with my own hands. . . . I used to hang them by the fireplace, suspended by a string, gently turn them with a long stick until they were done, and then with fat raccoon or bear meat boiled, I had a dinner fit for a king."

Gurdon Hubbard's rugged qualities impressed Chief Tamin of the Kankakee Potawatomis even before the young trader personally delivered needed supplies to his village over the ice and snow of the Kankakee marshes in the winter of 1821-22. When he chose to name the young man *Pa-pa-ma-ta-be,* for this and other similar feats, Chief Tamin invited his own family and retainers and the family of Chief Waba to his lodge for the ceremony. It was a proper and happy family occasion. Tamin's young people sang, danced and told stories while the assembled families, including the women, drank whisky and sweet wines and were served venison and wild turkey and Gurdon Hubbard's favorite food, corn soup. The children sang so well the songs celebrating their woodland and prairie lives that Gurdon at first assumed they must have been trained by M. Deschamps himself, but then he remembered that Alexander Henry had heard such children's choruses in the Indian villages half a century earlier. All present were well pleased with the performance except Tamin's half-brother, Chief Yellow Head, a sulking, hard-drinking warrior who brought both of his wives to the feast but appeared to resent all aspects of it.

Following the entertainment, Chief Tamin presented the members of the troop. His own daughters were plain, ungainly girls who held back shyly, but the little minx who attracted Gurdon's attention earlier as she merrily played the wrong notes on her willow flute or boldly sang the words of a song while the sisters merely mouthed them, now cast a mischievous smile upon the honored guest and giggled happily when he smiled back. She was called *Watchekee,* or, in English, Watseka. She was Tamin's niece, Gurdon was told, daughter of his sister, Monoska, and a Delaware brave said to have been killed while fighting with Tecumseh before the child was born. Chief Tamin ended the formal festivities with a fitting oration, praising Papamatabe, and citing a few examples of his own exploits in war and peace. Then the women and children departed. While the men talked, smoked and finished off the ceremonial liquor, Chief Tamin quietly suggested to Papamatabe that he might now wish to take Tamin's eldest daughter in marriage. "Such a request made by the chief of a tribe had something of the same force as a command of royalty," Henry Hamilton, Gurdon's grand-nephew and biographer, would write many years later. "The daughter was of mature years and quite devoid of personal charm," he added. "Therefore, Hubbard softened his refusal by promising to marry Tamin's niece when she became of marriagable age."

It was a politely civil response on Gurdon's part, but one that satisfied Chief Tamin. The public benefits of the potential union became effective with Tamin's announcement that immediately followed. The chiefs and retainers hearing of the intended nuptials were pleased, with the exception of Chief Yellow Head, who merely belched. Yellow Head had his own village to the north, but resented the intrusion of any outsider who might gain influence with Tamin. Although Yellow Head had two wives, sisters as was often the Indian custom since this helped to keep the peace in a lodge or wigwam, he may have coveted the child Watseka for himself. This would have been repugnant to Potawatomi tradition, but Yellow Head was known for his flouting of established ways.

Chapter 6

Chief Tamin spoke with commendable candor to Gurdon about his attractive niece. Since she was about eleven she would not be eligible for marriage for four more years, he said, which was fortunate, since she had much to learn. Watseka had not yet justified her name, which meant "accomplisher of many things." She did not wear down her teeth chewing on deerskin to soften it for clothing. She did not bead moccasins, or weave baskets, or mold and fire clay bowls. She had not learned to play the flute well either. Her uncle thought that Watseka served better the alternate meaning of her name, which was "Child of the Evening Star," though Tamin confessed he did not himself know what that meant. He promised, however, that the comely Watseka would learn to take care of her man as well as any Indian woman. His squaws would see to that. The wedding plans were told in many Potawatomi villages, and Gurdon was content. He did not expect he would be in Tamin's territory four years hence.

*

His fame as Swift Walker was soon matched by his reputation as a fighter. Early in the season, he and Vasseur had checked out the trade goods against the credit of the hunters, supplying them for the season's harvest as was the custom. "Without such credit it would have been impossible for the Indian to hunt or trap," Gurdon noted. The conditions of the credit were well known. If an Indian failed to pay for two years, he got no more credit. Vasseur, in the absence of Gurdon, had stopped credit for a hunter he knew to be two years in arrears at Beebeau's post. The hunter, a Kickapoo man, had gone on to camp, expecting his companions to share their supplies, but they refused. Thus he returned to the Iroquois post after vowing publicly to kill Papamatabe, the trader, as the one responsible for his bad fortune.

"I was sitting before the fire in my cabin, on a three-legged stool made of puncheons, reading a book," Gurdon recalled. "The Indian stole into my room, up behind me, with his tomahawk raised to strike me. I did not hear him, but saw his shadow, and threw up my left arm, striking the handle of the tomahawk . . . ." The blow was deflected, the tomahawk knocked from the attacker's hand, but not before the razor-sharp blade had cut through Gurdon's fur cap and gashed his forehead. Blood spurted down into Gurdon's eye as he leaped up, turned, and clutched his assailant in a bear hug by clasping the wrist of his numb and paralyzed arm with all the strength of his right hand. His attacker was unable to reach his scalping knife, as he was seeking to do. They fell and rolled on the floor, Gurdon maintaining his bear hug by his tight grip on the wrist of his injured arm. "My grasp was weakening, yet I clung on, afraid to trust my lame arm," Gurdon recalled. "My opponent was breathing very heavily and I knew he was exhausting his strength in his efforts to rid himself of my embrace, while I was saving mine. . . . I was bleeding from my wound, the blood blinding me and I sought to wipe it away on his naked body. When my numbed arm had recovered, and we had rolled up to where the stool lay, I let go of him, and seizing the stool struck him a stunning blow upon the head." In his rage Gurdon followed up the blows until the Indian lay unmoving, then he dragged the fellow out of his house and called for help.

Gurdon's men arrived and so did the Indian's squaws. Their master had left their village on a pony after returning from the hunting camp, saying he was going to kill Hubbard, and they had followed on foot. Gurdon ordered them to care for the fallen warrior and was greatly relieved when he saw the Indian open his eyes. "I regretted I had punished him so severely," Gurdon wrote. "My men were alarmed, as the incident could cause trouble with the entire tribe." Gurdon dispatched Dominick Bray, his interpreter, to the hunting camp to explain the incident to the young Chief Kanakuk. In a day, Kanakuk arrived, heard Gurdon's version of the incident—his Indian opponent was still unable to speak—and agreed that Papamatabe was within his rights, but should nevertheless supply the family of the injured man with necessities, since now he obviously would be unable to hunt or trap. This Gurdon refused to do, and so it stood for the time, the Indian being taken away by his friends, who returned to their hunting grounds.

*

Gurdon's southern post served a great expanse of territory and since he sought to increase it, he was away from his Iroquois base a considerable part of the time. The camps he covered extended from the headwaters of the Little Wabash River in the south, to the Kankakee on the north. In 1878, in a letter to B.F. Shankland which subsequently became a part of the Iroquois county historical record, Gurdon suggested that his trips from his trading post below the Little Wabash River to a base on the Kankakee River began the route from southern Illinois to Chicago that became known as Hubbard's Trail and eventually the first Illinois state road to the north. The Indians hunted on the Iroquois and its tributaries during October and November, then moved south to the Vermilion, Okaw, Embarass and Wabash rivers, and Gurdon followed them with trade goods. In the spring they returned to their villages and brought their furs to the Iroquois post or to another of Gurdon's bases.

At some time in the spring of 1822, Chief Black Hawk of the Sacs came to visit in the Kankakee and Iroquois territories. Black Hawk had served in the War of 1812 with Shabona, the Potawatomi chief and okama, or adjudicator, for the tribes of that area, but the two disagreed politically, Black Hawk seeking to unite the tribes for war, Shabona insisting they must find a way to live at peace with the white man if they were to survive. Thus Black Hawk came to visit at the village of Waba, leader of the warlike Kickapoos, but without Shabona. Chief Waba arranged a feast for Black Hawk, ordering dogs killed, since such meat was a delicacy in the view of Black Hawk, though Indians generally killed their dogs for food only in times of famine. Gurdon Hubbard, as Papamatabe, was invited to the feast honoring Black Hawk, together with his interpreter, Dominick Bray.

The weather was cold, but the festivities were held in the open air, among the camp fires and cooking fires. Mats were placed behind a windbreak at one side of the village compound for Black Hawk and his party, together with chiefs and their aides from the area, and for Gurdon Hubbard and Bray. There was high excitement among the people, since Black Hawk not only was a hero for having fought with Tecumseh, but it was believed that he led forces at the Fort Dearborn massacre. This latter report Black Hawk himself rejected in later years. He arrived in the vicinity of Chicago after the attack was ended, he said then, and he interceded for Captain Heald and other prisoners who ultimately were ransomed.

Black Hawk was not fond of white men, but he understood the need for fur traders and was civil to Gurdon Hubbard, having learned the young trader was the foster son of Waba and had well earned his name, Papamatabe. Black Hawk was well past middle age, a lean, ascetic man, who only occasionally indulged in dog feasts and ostentatious display of medals and ornaments. This night he wore the silver gorgets given to him by the British for his services in the War of 1812, also silver and gold cords and chains of beads about his throat, and silver bracelets. Into his scalp lock was thrust an elk's tail and at his side, under his Stroud blanket, he carried the feathered skin of the sparrow hawk from which he took his name. His leggings were of fine buckskin, well-beaded, and he wore the buckskin breechclout of the Potawatomi. His earlobes glittered with small jeweled ornaments. Black Hawk looked like an Oriental potentate pictured in a book of Chinese history. He was a war chief, not an orator like Keokuk, nor a mystic such as the Prophet White Cloud of the Winnebagos, who advised him. He had been devoted to Tecumseh's cause. He believed someday he would lead a united people against the whites.

Gurdon Hubbard was given a place of honor near Black Hawk as the festivities began. The drummers and singers of the tribe filed into the square to the beat of war drums and Black Hawk smiled his thin, weary smile as the first dancer entered. He was known to favor war dances and endlessly saw them. The warrior, tall, sinuous, and grotesquely painted, advanced in powerful crouching leaps, his feet seeming to shake the earth, his cries fierce as the drumbeats mounted to frenzy. He wore fig bar and belt, gorgets and arm bands of silver, carried a spear which he flung into a war post with deadly aim. With now stealthy steps he kept to the slowed beat of the war drums, then shouted horrible cries to stultify his foe with fear, then charged, swinging his war club. He struck his blow and drew his scalping knife. He danced the beginning of a war dance, portraying the brave scout who first found, flushed and slew the enemy, a tribute to Black Hawk, who was known to have personally dispatched, in single combat, nearly a hundred foes. The dancer was applauded with shouts and the crowd called for Black Hawk to rise, as he did. Other dancers followed, each demonstrating an aspect of battle, hunting skills and valor. Then the braves of the tribe who were warriors and hunters joined in the dancing and the young women of the tribe, dressed in their finest silver ornaments and bright Stroud cloth and feathers, danced about them. Some of the younger men watched glumly from the sidelines, unmoving and silent as the fever of the crowd rose. Black Hawk, pleased with the exhibition, smiled his thin, but pleasant smile, and explained to Gurdon the plight of the young men. "They have not been out on a war party and have not killed an enemy," he said. "So they are not allowed within the circle. I remember that I was ashamed when I was a young warrior and had never fought a battle. What a pleasure it is to an old warrior to see his son come forward to tell his story of the battle. See, now the old warriors will step forward to tell their tales of glory." Black Hawk arose, applauding the veterans, and the chiefs and Gurdon joined him.

When Black Hawk was told by Dominick Bray that *Le Bourgeois* Hubbard had become betrothed to the young niece of Chief Tamin, the Sac war chief expressed his pleasure. "You do well, Papamatabe," he said. "I will tell you the custom of our people when the time comes to claim your maiden. Our young men go to her lodge where all are asleep . . . or pretend to be asleep . . . he strikes a light with his flint so he may find his intended, it is not the time for a mistake! He finds her on her mat in the lodge, awakens her, shines the light on himself so that she may know him, after which he holds the light close to her. If she blows it out the ceremony is ended and he appears in the lodge next morning as one of the family. If she does not blow out the light, but leaves it burning, he leaves the lodge."

But all was not necessarily lost, the chief said. The young man should persist. "The day following, if the light is left burning, he may return and play his flute before her lodge. All the young women of the village will appear to hear him. He may find a young woman even more suitable to him. The young women go one by one to see if she may be the one, and he will change the tune if he finds her. Or the young maiden of the night before may come from her lodge in response. He quits playing whenever the result is favorable. Now they are one, the brave and his squaw. During the first year, they determine whether they can agree with each other and be happy; if not, they separate and each looks for another companion. If we were to live together and disagree we would be as foolish as the whites," Black Hawk concluded, smiling.

Gurdon thanked Chief Black Hawk for his lesson. They agreed to go together to watch the beaver trappers the next day. The beaver ponds were frozen, traps had been set, and the harvesters would include veterans who could follow the trail of the beaver under the ice to the runways of their underwater homes and drag them out with bare hands. "We believe the beaver is wisest of the creatures," Black Hawk said. "Once the beaver had the gift of speech, but Gitchie Manitou took it away to keep beaver from conquering all the earth."

*

The season ended, the fur harvest sparse, but most of the Indians paid up their accounts. When the Kickapoos returned from their hunting camp, Gurdon was visited by three men, one whom he had vanquished in the fight in his house, all with their faces blackened, the sign of death. Gurdon recalled John Kinzie's story of his family the day of the Fort Dearborn massacre, menaced by Miami warriors similarly painted, until Chief Billy Caldwell arrived to save them. Gurdon wished that Vasseur and his men were near, but he was alone.

"They demanded of me that I pay the man for his injuries," Gurdon wrote. "I again refused, telling him that it was his own fault, that he had come upon me stealthily and would have killed me had I not discovered him just in time to save myself."

Now it was Chief Black Hawk who arrived in time to save the white man. Chief Kanakuk, leader of the Kickapoo hunting party, on learning that some of his braves had painted and gone to see Papamatabe, foster son of Waba, found Black Hawk at Tamin's village. The visiting Sac chief agreed to act as okama, or judge, in the absence of Shabona, the tribal adjudicator for the area. Thus Black Hawk and a band of Kanakuk's men reached the Iroquois station as Gurdon was lecturing the three Indians threatening him: "I came among you with goods for your accommodation, to trade. I have as much right to do as I please with my goods as you do with the pony you ride. . . . Should anyone attempt to take him by force, would you defend your-

174

self? Or would you, like a coward, give him up? Say, would you?" And the Indians answered, "No!"

Black Hawk had paused outside the store to hear the dispute and to assure Vasseur, who had just come up, that his mission was friendly. Now he entered the store and took charge. "The trader Hubbard, who has won the name of Papamatabe, lives among us and must live by the laws of our people," Black Hawk said. "He who kills unjustly the provider for women and children must pay them what has been lost, even to taking them into his lodge as a part of his family. But no one has been killed. The trader is right. The goods were his. Papamatabe would not trust you because you did not pay," he said. "All here say this is true."

Hubbard and the injured Indian stood silent. "The Indian extended his hand to me, which I took," Gurdon remembered. " 'Now we are friends,' I said. 'I wish to give you evidence of my friendship, not to pay you. I am sorry, not for what I did, but for the result of it, causing the loss of your winter's hunt. I will make you a present of the goods you need.' We all had a smoke, and so that difficulty was ended, much to the satisfaction of my men, who were fearful that great trouble would result from it."

*

They found Antoine Deschamps worn and ill when they met the Illinois Brigade at Opa, but without incident made the journey to Chicago where Deschamps seemed better. "As usual I found a warm welcome with the Kinzie family and the officers of the fort," Gurdon reported. He spent much of his time with Dr. Wolcott, exchanging experiences, then departed with the Illinois Brigade, arriving at Mackinaw early in June. He anticipated assignment once more to the fur warehouse and was determined to have a showdown with Crooks and Stuart. Instead he was ordered to assist his friend John Kinzie, Jr. in the company's retail store. He was pleased, since he felt deficient in that area of the company business. Within hours of his arrival he witnessed an incident that became celebrated in medical history, one Gurdon would recall vividly more than half a century later: "On the sixth of the month I was present when Alexis St. Martin was shot, and am probably the only living person (in 1880) who witnessed the accident. . . ."

St. Martin was an American Fur Company engagé who came to the store with friends to inspect the guns there. One of the party was holding a shotgun, Gurdon insisted, though others said it was a musket, which accidently discharged, "the whole charge entering into St. Martin's body. The muzzle was not over three feet from him—I think not over two. The wadding entered as well as pieces of his clothing; his shirt took fire; he fell, as we supposed, dead."

Gurdon helped to place St. Martin on a cot and to cut away his clothing. He saw a gaping hole in the abdomen, oozing blood. Someone went to the fort, returning soon with Dr. Beaumont, the surgeon, "within three minutes," Gurdon estimated.

Dr. Beaumont examined the victim, saw that the charge had torn away the wall of St. Martin's stomach. He removed as much of the charge as he could find and dressed the wound. As an army surgeon he knew stomach wounds were the worst and most painful a man could take. St. Martin was nineteen years old, had lived in the woods all his life, and had endured much, but Dr. Beaumont did not expect him to live more than a few hours. He returned every three hours during the night to see his patient. In the morning when Gurdon and Kinzie returned to the store, Dr. Beaumont was there and St. Martin was still alive. "Take him to my quarters," Dr. Beaumont ordered. They fashioned a litter and obeyed the command.

There at the fort Alexis St. Martin continued to live. Dr. Beaumont found that he could look directly into the man's stomach. "He used his instruments, getting more of the shot and clothing, cutting off the ragged edges of the wound," Gurdon wrote. "He informed Mr. Stuart in my presence that he thought he could save St. Martin." The wounded man continued to improve, but the gaping hole in his stomach did not close. Dr. Beaumont then began the series of experiments, leading to understanding of the digestive process, that would make him and St. Martin world famous. In time a flap grew over the stomach opening, but did not close the wound completely, so Dr. Beaumont could lift the flap to suspend food by a thread through the orifice, watch the stomach's action, collect the gastric juice, then study the action outside the body. After three years of such experimentation, Alexis St. Martin wearied of it, ran off to resume his life in the woods. Four years later Dr. Beaumont saw him at a trading post at Prairie du Chien in Wisconsin. Except for the stomach hole, the young engagé was in good health. Dr. Beaumont contracted with him for further study and meticulously kept notes on the effects of anger, sleep and temperature on the flow of gastric juices and in 1833 published his famous paper, *"Experiments and observations in the gastric juice, and the physiology of digestion."* Twenty years later, Dr. Beaumont was killed in a fall in St. Louis. Alexis St. Martin survived him, dying in 1873, and was said at the time to have been the father of twenty children. "I knew Dr. Beaumont very well," Gurdon wrote. "I think that the experiment of introducing food into the stomach through the orifice purposely kept open and healed with that object, was conceived by the doctor very soon after the first examination."

*

In the fall of 1822 Gurdon had entered his fifth year with the company. He had finished the summer on Mackinaw in the fur warehouse as usual, being requested by Matthews soon after the St. Martin incident, but no longer was in rebellion. Times in the fur business had changed, as Mr. Matthews liked to say, and bosses of outfits could not dictate their working conditions. The Illinois Brigade was a month reaching Chicago. M. Deschamps was in poor health. Gurdon again lodged with the Kinzies and for a time with Alexander Wolcott. There also he found Pierre Chouteau, Jr., of the St. Louis fur company, who offered him employment at St. Louis or on the Missouri River when his period of service with the American Fur Company should end. Gurdon was prepared to consider it, in the two weeks they were together at Chicago he and young Pierre got on well.

Gurdon now had become chief aide to Deschamps and was to take charge of Beebeau's post, as well as his own, since the trader had died during the year. He installed Vasseur as acting agent on the Iroquois, built a new story-and-a-half log house for himself there, near the site of the town of Bunkum on the Iroquois River, and then returned to Beebeau's place, where his chief competitor was Antoine Bourbonais, a trader receiving his goods from St. Louis, who "was possessed of a foxy sharpness, was fond of his cups, and when under the influence, inclined to be quarrelsome. . . . But we became friends, and treated each other with respect."

Bourbonais had five or six horses, while Gurdon Hubbard had none. He arranged to match Bourbonais in reaching the camps by sending out his own men with lighter packs than before and carried such packs himself to the hunting camps when ice closed the waterways. This system worked so well, Gurdon recorded, that Bourbonais agreed two years later to sell out to the American Fur Company. "With a light load my men could travel as fast as horses," Gurdon wrote. "They did not depend for their existence on foraging for half-dead grass on the bottom lands."

The young trader spread wide his fame as Swift Walker that winter and spring. In March, 1823, when the ice was breaking, he visited Big Woods, seventy-five miles north of Beebeau's post and after completing trades prepared to return to Beebeau's, later called Hennepin. An Indian asked to accompany him and Gurdon agreed. They started early, he recalled, and the Indian seemed especially eager to make time, though the ground was soft and muddy. This was unusual. Gurdon knew the Indians usually could outwalk and outrun all others if they cared to, but rarely was an Indian that concerned with an urgent schedule, except in war. He might start a trip late, then dally on the way, much to the exasperation of whites. This Indian wanted to race, Gurdon decided. "I kept on as fast as I could and got a distance ahead of him. When I reached the Illinois River above Hennepin, I discovered that the canoe I had left there had been stolen . . . I swam the river, which had become much swollen, and reached my post about dark."

Gurdon had walked seventy-five miles that day, much of the distance through slushy marsh country, and then swam through the ice floes, an ordeal the Indian did not attempt. In the morning he sent his men to learn what might have happened to his companion. "They found him with a party of others on horseback, much chagrined." There *had been* a race, a group of Indians at Big Woods betting that no man could be found who could outwalk Papamatabe. Those wagering on Hubbard had won. His fame spread, but Gurdon himself claimed no record, recalling instead: "Pierre La Claire, who carried the news of the

War of 1812, being sent by Major Robert Forsyth to his uncle, John Kinzie, at Chicago, walked from the mouth of the St. Joseph River to Chicago, a distance of 90 miles, in a continuous walk."

*

That fall when the Indians had departed for their hunting grounds and he and Bourbonais were getting on together, and Waba and Shabona came often to see him and Vasseur reported that all was well on the Iroquois, Gurdon became reasonably satisfied with his life in the fur trade. He was comfortable in the old cabin. He rehabilitated Beebeau's quarters as his store, with Pierre in charge. Late in November a runner arrived to inform him that Dr. Wolcott would spend a week with him on his return from St. Louis, providing the rivers stayed ice-free, since he was travelling by canoe. Gurdon sent word to Deschamps, Shabona, Tamin and Black Hawk, inviting them to come to a feast he would prepare for the Indian agent. The chiefs, he knew, wanted to air grievances.

Early in December they gathered at Hubbard's place, together with his interpreter, Dominick Bray. They smoked and talked and drank company liquor and Gurdon prepared his specialty, *avignols.* While Gurdon did the cooking, Dr. Wolcott and the chiefs worked their way into a discussion of the antagonism that lay between them because of Indian treaties generally and the Treaty of Chicago of two years before (August, 1821), which Wolcott himself had drafted. The night outside was cold, an icy rain drove against Hubbard's oil-cloth windows, but they lodged in comfort, the cabin was snug and warm. They smoked Dr. Wolcott's tobacco, fresh from the Carolinas, and drank his port, up from New Orleans, and consumed the potatoes, brought by Shabona, which had roasted in the hot embers of Shabona's burning stones. He had contributed a bag of coal and another of herbs and potatoes from his farm. Dr. Wolcott sat on a puncheon stool, like a schoolmaster among his pupils, the Indians sprawling on their blankets, while Deschamps sat cross-legged, *voyageur* fashion, on pelts spread across the floor. Black Hawk raised himself on his elbow to lecture them as Gurdon joined the group. His thin voice gave a cutting edge to the soft gutteral of the Algonquin tongue, the basic language of the northwest tribes. He was scornful of whites and treaties, angry at the injustices to his people, contemptuous of his superior chief, Keokuk, famed for oratory, but not for courage, he asserted, yet respectful of Shabona, still a thick, tough bear in fighting trim, who, even more than Keokuk, urged caution in dealing with the whites. Black Hawk did not forget that Shabona stood first as war chief under the great Tecumseh, Black Hawk himself arriving only for the final battle and defeat.

Black Hawk was pleased to have Dr. Wolcott at hand for this denunciation of the Treaty of Chicago, he said. "Who spoke for the Sac at Chicago?" he demanded, spitting out the name of the place as if the word itself connoted evil. "My people do not accept this treaty. There have been treaties upon treaties, lies upon lies, each twisting tighter the thongs about our throats. Little Turtle of the Miamis at the Treaty of Greenville in the days of my father (August, 1795) spoke to General Wayne of the injustice of it: 'You have pointed out the boundary line between the Indian land and the United States,' he said. 'I now take the liberty to inform you that the line cuts off country which has been enjoyed by my forefathers from time immemorial without question or dispute. The prints of my ancestors' houses are everywhere in this region and are well known to all my brothers present.' But the treaty was signed, the land was taken."

Shabona dipped his smoking potato into the salted bear fat, savored it and joined with Tamin and Waba in uttering approving "Humphs" to Black Hawk's words. Shabona had no quarrel with the Sac chief's notions of history and law, nor with many of the essential beliefs of White Cloud, the Winnebago prophet who advised Black Hawk. But Shabona opposed a war policy as futile. He now spoke softly, yet resoundingly in the small room, and Gurdon regreted Shabona had not chosen to become an orator, like Keokuk, the great chief on the Mississippi: "My brother speaks of our days with Tecumseh. I remember well his words on the treaty, 'Sell our country? Would you sell the clouds, the sky, the sun, the great sea?' It is true that we are cheated by the white man's treaties. Our brothers the Lenni-Lenape tell us of the treaty made in their land of the rising sun, called Delaware by the white man. In good faith they deeded land extending as far as a man could walk in a day and a half. They knew the distance to be that walked by William Penn. But then his son found those men who could walk many leagues further in such a time . . . it is good they did not have you to walk for them, Papamatabe! . . . Our forefathers were cheated. When they refused to leave the land thus taken from them, the white man paid the Iroquois, the enemies of the Delaware, to drive them from the land. And then the Iroquois were deceived and driven out, or killed in white men's wars, or by white men's plagues. Black Hawk speaks the truth. We are cheated. There are lies upon lies. Our young men are debauched by the white man's whisky that rots their bowels and sickens their souls. When we fought beside Tecumseh, Black Hawk, our white allies fled like rabbits, leaving us alone to meet the Americans. it was a final act of treachery. When Tecumseh died and I made my escape, I vowed to the Great Spirit never again to lead my people in wars we can only lose.''

Black Hawk responded vehemently. "If it must be so we will fight without my brother Shabona. I give you again the words of Little Turtle, when he had fought and defeated his enemy: 'We met, I cut him down, and his shade as it passes on the wind shuns my walk.' It is the spirit of Little Turtle we must follow. The treaty cheating has not ended. Our brother, Wolcott, who comes from our Great White Father, had drawn a treaty he thinks good, but it is filled with falsehood and the Sac does not sign it. There was the treaty of Portage des Sioux, after the War of 1812, signed by the Fox and the Missouri Sac, but not by us. And what has happened? The whites come upon us thick as grasshoppers, into our villages and hunting grounds to take our land for their plows. These plowshares are spears into our hearts. I have gone myself to our father in Canada to say to him: 'I hope I may not be obliged to dig up my hatchet. I know these Big Knives have sweet tongues. I fear they have again cheated us all. Our father in Canada wants justice for us and will help us. I say to my brother Wolcott, undo the mischief you have done before the prairies are again ablaze with war! Papamatabe gathers us here that we may talk together as brothers. Not many moons ago you gathered the tribes for the Treaty of Chicago. Black Hawk was not there. The Sac did not sign this treaty. I tell you in the presence of all that we will fight again. Shabona will someday see that the evils will not end of themselves. The white man's plow will devour our land. Shabona and his Potawatomis will join us, as will the Miamis, the Fox and the Winnebagos, and I will have an army like the leaves of the forest and will drive the palefaces like autumn leaves before an angry wind. I tell you this, Wolcott, in the presence of my brothers, red and white, so that you may know and undo the mischief, as I believe you may be trusted by our White Father, who says he wishes to keep the peace.''

Dr. Wolcott was momentarily silent and Deschamps hastened to speak. "I am an old man. I have said to Gurdon Hubbard that the days of our work among you will be much changed and perhaps ended, though not in my time. I wish to speak the truth as I know it. It is true, my brothers, that we have betrayed you, my people of France and Canada have done so in their own way. We have bought your furs, enticed you from your land, not because we French coveted your land but we wanted your pelts in trade, and some of us wanted your immortal souls. Now, I agree with Shabona, who has urged the red man to join his women in farming. The way to save your land, my brother, is to farm it as many of your kinsmen to the south are doing. When God created the Earth, He did so in six days, and you say He sent the Great Turtle to find the earth upon which His people might dwell in productive harmony. How God did this is not agreed by white and red men, but we do agree He put the tribes upon the earth to hunt and trap for their sustenance and also to till the soil, raising crops and herds against the insufficiency of the hunting. When God promised Abraham that 'in thy seed shall all nations of this earth be blessed,' Abraham had no land of his own in which to bury his dead; but Abraham and his descendants paused to till fields, to plant crops, to pasture sheep, and to build towns. Thus they won the land. The day of hunting and taking wild game will end and the market for furs will diminish. But the planting of corn and grain is endless. Shabona is right in staying with his groves and corn fields and raising sheep and horses. The Indian, who is of the seed of Abraham also, since all nations are thus blessed, must till his fields, not make war. I know the people of Canada. Do not expect help from Canada, my brothers.''

Black Hawk, less than a decade younger than the old man,

regarded Deschamps intently, fixing his dark eyes upon him, smiling his tight, cynical smile. "My grandfather has taught us much," he acknowledged. "I do not like therefore to be compelled to remind him that Tecumseh once said to General Harrison himself that it was not the Indian, but the white, who killed the White man's god, nailing him to a cross. I do not think your Great Spirit can guide us, unless also he can guide the white man. The Indian has cause to know most white men do not believe in their God. Nor do they obey him. Grandfather, it is said among us that the Great Spirit made the white man and the Indian. He did not make them alike. He gave the white man a heart to love peace and the arts of a quiet life. He taught him to live in towns, to build houses, to make books. It would be good for all if the white man lived in the way he has been taught; but it must not be done at the expense of the Indian. The Great Spirit gave to the red man a different character. He gave him the love of the woods, a free life, of hunting and fishing and making war with his enemies. The white man does not live like the Indian, he covets the land, to plow it, to own it. The Indian shares the land and the fruits of the chase. He does not covet white man's land. He has not crossed the great ocean to seize another's land. He does not begrudge the white man his freedom. We think, that if the Great Spirit had wished the Indians to be like the whites, he would have made us so.

"Each of us has our place and we should keep to it. My grandfather need not regret that his people trade for our furs, teach us their ways, and dwell among us. We intend no harm to those who do not harm us. It is true that the buffalo have left us and that the wise beaver are fewer. It is also true that the Delawares, who grew corn and potatoes and built towns of log lodges, as my grandfather suggests, are now few in number, driven again and again from their lands, and are scorned by many as the petticoat Indians. I think, Grandfather, that we do not keep our land and our freedom by growing corn and building towns; we must also fight for them."

*

It had been a good year though a difficult one. Gurdon was satisfied. "We had accumulated more furs and peltries than our boats could carry up the Desplaines River," he recalled. M. Deschamps consequently dispatched him with four boats to Chicago, to unload the pelts and then return, a quadruple crossing of the portage in that year! Gurdon arranged for the storage of his cargo at Fort Dearborn; the garrison had left and Dr. Wolcott had been named caretaker of the fort in addition to his duties as Indian agent. Wolcott was jubilant. The removal of the garrison by the War Department would reduce tension, he believed. He had concluded after the meeting in Gurdon Hubbard's cabin that Black Hawk was no real threat so long as Shabona, Billy Caldwell and Alexander Robinson opposed his views. The War Department evidently had agreed with him. Dr. Wolcott also had been successful in his courtship of Ellen Kinzie, they would be married in July. Hubbard, meantime, had made the Chicago Portage six times in that season, endured much hardship and, aside from the boon of friends such as Wolcott and Kinzie and Shabona, had achieved nothing. He was near the end of his five-year indenture and continued to be dissatisfied with his treatment by the company. He had worked long and hard seven days a week all those years. He had accepted responsibility for wilderness posts. He had labored in the accursed fur warehouse every summer. His wages had been increased by a total of $50 a year in all that time. He was now back in Chicago garbed in buckskin as he was the first time he came there on October 1, 1818, all he owned save for the clothing and a few personal articles he had left in a chest with Mrs. Kinzie. That night, at the Kinzie house, he got out the broadcloth suit and tried it on. "Five years before it looked on me as though it was my father's; now it looked like a half-grown boy's. To have fitted myself in a manner to have been presentable to the society of Middletown would have cost me all my accumulated funds!" He swore to himself he would never again cross the Chicago Portage and he was determined to leave the company when he consulted with John Kinzie and Dr. Wolcott about his future.

They urged him to stay in the fur trading business, either with the American Fur Company or under a more favorable arrangment with Pierre Chouteau, Jr. at St. Louis. Wolcott reminded him he had discussed Gurdon's prospects with Chouteau when he was in St. Louis and received favorable response.

"I will not take a job that will force me into competition with

M. Deschamps,'' Gurdon said. ''That wouldn't be necessary,''
Dr. Wolcott responded. ''Chouteau would send you to a post
on the Missouri River if you wished. He will pay you a good salary. Demand of the American Fur Company a fair consideration
of your abilities. If they refuse, you have Mr. Chouteau to fall
back on.'' John Kinzie agreed. ''If both these possibilities fail,''
he said, ''then you are well enough known in the Illinois territory to obtain credit for your own outfit and take chances on
your own account.''

Gurdon recalled these discussions in later years. ''I had not
settled in my mind what was my duty and interest,'' he wrote.
''My inclination led me to my mother, struggling to support her
four young daughters. My brother had secured a position in
Henry King's hardware store in New York City, receiving only
his board for his services. It was now five years and I was reaching my majority with no knowledge of the world outside the
wilderness and with no business experience except in the fur
trade. . . . I had no opportunity to improve my mind by intercourse with refined society excepting during the short time I
passed in Chicago and in Mackinaw, but at the latter place, more
than half my time was devoted to hard labor. In my boyhood
I had no love for books and now that I felt the need for improving my mind, I could find no opportunity for doing so. For the
past year I felt more than ever the waste of my life and the mortification my ignorance caused me.''

But there were other considerations. In the Indian towns, in
the lodges of chiefs such as Waba, Shabona, Tamin and Black
Hawk, Gurdon Hubbard, by whatever name, was received as
a man of importance, deserving respect. He was very good at
most things Indians did. At his wilderness post he was The
Trader, directing men, making decisions. He was Deschamps'
No. 1 aide, sometimes acting as *Le Bourgeois* of the Illinois Brigade. He was appreciated as a friend in Chicago, where his peculiar knowledge was sought out by a man such as Dr. Wolcott,
a graduate of Yale. He exchanged Indian lore and the understanding of Indian history and myth for Dr. Wolcott's teachings
of books and world affairs. He desired to find a way to improve
his future at Chicago. There he was happiest. He needed a way
to earn wages in the town, but he would not compete against

John Kinzie any more than with Antoine Deschamps. He urged Dr. Wolcott to think of a way for him to live in Chicago.

It was not likely that Gurdon thought at all about his putative obligation to Chief Tamin and the child, Watseka, to whom he was pledged, however lightly he may have taken his promise at the time it was given. Watseka was a pretty, spoiled child, he had concluded at the time of the feast in Tamin's village. More recently, when Vasseur told him that the little girl was growing up and was said by the women of the village to be putting on airs because she was to marry The Trader, Gurdon grew testy and didn't wish to hear more. He realized then that Vasseur, like the Indians, did not doubt that he would honor his promise to Tamin at the proper time. He had never confided to Vasseur that he might have thoughts of love for Margaret Helm or for the woman who found him half-dead along the river, a woman he could not again find, nor even name. It would not have mattered to Vasseur or the Indians if he had said he was already married, with a wife in Middletown, Connecticut. Many Indians had two wives if they could afford them and so did traders, a wife at the wilderness post and another in Mackinaw or Montreal.

On May 18th the schooner *Chicago Packet* arrived from Buffalo and Mackinaw, bringing in Dr. Wolcott's mail pouch a letter to Hubbard from his mother and Elizabeth. He replied the day following:

Chicago May 19th, 1823

Fond Mother:

After a tedious and toilsome winter I am again permitted to return to a civilized world. I wintered on the Iroquois River.

I was myself out all winter trading with the natives . . . although I had a good tent I frequently suffered with the cold, the winter was verry (sic) severe, the depth of snow was great for that quarter . . . our poor horses were obliged to paw through the snow to find subsistence and the loss of a horse made it necessary for us to walk. Although they were lightly loaded, the horses would frequently give out and, when in a prairie, leave us to carry their loads, and bear them until we could get to timber, where we could camp; for months we have lived mostly on corn and grease.

I called on Dr. Wolcott last evening and was verry agreeably surprised on his giving me a letter from you and Elizabeth. I have been in excellent health but I do not know what my prospects will be with Mr. Crooks who is in St. Louis. . . . About the first of July . . . I shall not make arrangments at Mackinaw until I see him, thinking he may make me a better proposition. Necessity my dear Mother will oblige me to forget the unexpressible (sic) pleasure of seeing you in Middletown this summer but I hope . . . to spend the summer with you next year.

I think that if the Company does me justice they will give me a situation that will hereafter enable me annually to add more to your support. If they do not I shall not stay in their employ.

Your truly affectionate son
G.S. Hubbard

Again Gurdon coasted with M. Deschamps and the Illinois Brigade to Mackinaw, pausing at the mouth of the Marquette River in Michigan to search unsuccessfully for the cedar cross marking the site of Father Marquette's grave. Deschamps persisted in his futile effort despite his weariness and serious illness. "M. Deschamps knew that he would not soon come that way again," Gurdon wrote. When they reached Mackinaw, Deschamps urged his aide to at once present his resignation to Mr. Crooks if he intended to do so. But Crooks was away and he saw Robert Stuart instead. "Mr. Stuart seemed very much surprised. He said he thought it was settled that I would remain in the employ of the company. 'No sir,' I told him. 'I consider my services worth more than you and Mr. Crooks offer me. Therefore I intend to leave you. I will go east to see if Mr. Astor wants me in his New York store.' "

Robert Stuart glared at his obstreperous young trader. "I cannot alone alter any offer made jointly by Mr. Crooks and myself," he said coldly. "This, I should think, would be clear to you."

"Then I will sail on the next schooner to Buffalo," Gurdon answered.

Ramsey Crooks arrived on Mackinaw a day later, but he and Stuart allowed their rebellious employee to stew in possible self-doubt. Not until the schooner was ready to sail did Crooks send a messenger calling Hubbard to his office. There he treated Gurdon with kindness and said they would surely satisfy him. Gurdon did not record the offer in his letters. He would be required to serve one year more at the company's fur warehouse. It was too late to make changes. He would return to his Iroquois River post in Illinois. But his situation with the company would be improved.

Gurdon presented his own conditions. He was to use his own judgment in choosing which route to follow in carrying goods from Mackinaw to the Iroquois River. He would not use the Chicago Portage, he said. He could leave the *batteaux* in Chicago and carry the goods overland by pony to the Kankakee, where they could be distributed directly to the hunting camps enroute to the post on the Iroquois. Once based on the Iroquois, he would use small canoes, ponies and men walking to take trade goods to the hunting camps farther south. He wanted company assistance in acquiring land for a farm near the Iroquois post where he could pasture the horses he intended to use. That would make him independent of the Indians. Since M. Deschamps had already approved his aide's plan for avoiding the Chicago Portage, Hubbard's terms were accepted. He was assured a share in the profits of his Iroquois River outfit as well.

Gurdon, well content, returned to the detested fur warehouse, now as manager, succeeding Matthews. "All the furred skins, except muskrats and wolves, had each to pass my inspection. I was furnished with two assistants, who, after I assorted the furs, counted and delivered them to the packers to press, tie, mark and store, 100 *voyageurs* being detailed to this duty." Gurdon instituted shorter days for the men than he had been required to observe under Matthews. "The roll was called at six in the morning . . . an hour's intermission at noon, our labors were incessant until six at night." The manager, Mr. Hubbard, however returned to work after his evening meal to make up accounts showing a total of the day's labor. There was no visiting at the homes of Mackinaw's widows, nor the Indian camps, for him that summer either. "I was glad to reach the close of the summer's duties. It was very fatiguing work."

In September Gurdon, his assistant Noel Vasseur and the men assigned to them, left Mackinaw with Deschamps and the Illinois Brigade as usual, coasting the eastern shore of Lake Michigan until they entered the St. Joseph River. Deschamps had agreed that Hubbard could try the long portage from the St. Joseph to the Kankakee and promised to explain to the Kinzies and Dr. Wolcott and his bride that Gurdon would walk overland from his Iroquois post to visit them sometime during the winter. They camped not far from William Burnett's trading post on the south bend of the St. Joseph and learned from him that an Indian camp near Bertrand's trading post a few miles to the south could supply the ponies Gurdon would require for his experiment.

Both Burnett and Bertrand were in competition with the American Fur Company but they assisted Hubbard. It was Burnett, he said, who suggested that they could carry the fifty-foot mackinaws by lashing poles athwart the gunnels, extending on either side so the *voyageurs* could lift the heavy craft. Burnett provided them details on the waters of the Kankakee, which were low. Gurdon modified Burnett's suggestion. Since he was hiring the Indian ponies to carry the bales of trade goods across some fifteen miles of portage, he intended to use them to haul the boats overland as well. The Indians were glad to rent their ponies and to participate themselves. The squaws joined their men in cutting the poles to be lashed to the mackinaw boats bow and stern. Larger trees were felled to provide the rollers which would be placed under the heavy mackinaws. "We then wove and tied the ponies' tails securely to the poles at the stern, and tied their heads to the bow," Gurdon explained. "In order that the boats might move more easily, we placed the rollers under them. Then the Indians and squaws commenced urging the ponies forward. For a time they were stubborn and awkward, some would pull, others would not, but by patience and perserverance, the men also pulling, we finally got them started and to advance for a hundred yards." Then the ponies stubbornly refused to go farther.

But Gurdon was now sure his plan would work. They had negotiated much of the sloping rise from the water. There were fifteen miles of rough earth, stones, trees and brambles ahead.

They rearranged the harnesses, devised with leather thongs and ropes, so that several horses could be used to tow the boats along the rollers, which the Indians picked up and re-laid ahead of the on-moving craft. Some rollers were too long, and got in the way of the ponies' feet. Trees ahead were felled. Finally they again were ready to proceed. Men shouted, whips cracked, *voyageurs* cursed, the Indians, lacking any words of profanity in their language, laughed and yelled, especially the women who appeared to enjoy the novelty of their braves working hard beside them. Soon the strange procession moved a quarter of a mile at a time, as the log track almost miraculously appeared ahead of the forward-moving *batteaux.*

"In this manner we passed our boats over and launched them into the Kankakee," Gurdon Hubbard recalled. "We found the Kankakee narrow, and crooked, with sufficient water to float our boats, but with very little current." The conditions were as described by Bertrand. Gurdon was disappointed. He had hoped that on a second attempt he could pass the boats over fully loaded, but this would never become possible. He saw again that the only solution for the passage of freight regularly from Lake Michigan to the rivers to the south, including the Mississippi, would be by the way of a canal cut through to the Desplaines River somewhere near Chicago, the solution proposed by Joliet a century and a half earlier, but scornfully dismissed by La Salle as "Joliet's ditch."

They made excellent progress thereafter, reaching the mouth of the Iroquois River, which they ascended to a landing "a short distance below the present village of Watseka, which was our destination." Thus Gurdon concluded his description of the portage experiment a half century later. It was his only mention of Watseka in any of his writings; oddly that was not the name of his stopping place. Instead, as Hubbard disclosed earlier to Hiram Beckwith, for Beckwith's *History of Iroquois County,* and re-confirmed in a letter to B.F. Shankland, he had reached a landing between Old Middleport and the site of the village of Bunkum. The latter place was subsequently called Concord, while Old Middleport was renamed Watseka, in honor of the Indian girl who became Gurdon Hubbard's wife.

Hubbard's Iroquois River Station expanded and prospered

that winter. He had created the Hubbard Trail south into the Wabash country in 1822 and he continued to add more hunting camps. In the spring, as soon as the fur collections had been received and accounts with the Indians were settled, he instructed Vasseur to take the *batteaux* downriver to Opa, there to join M. Deschamps and the Illinois Brigade. Gurdon himself walked to Chicago along a northerly route he intended as an extension of Hubbard's Trail. Within three days he had arrived at Dr. Wolcott's quarters in the government Agency House on the north bank of the Chicago River. Thereafter he would use the trail to carry trade goods from Chicago to the south and furs north. Hubbard's Trail would become the Illinois State Road, its Chicago terminus known as State Street.

In 1830, after twelve years in the Indian country, where he
was called *Papamatabe* (Swift Walker) and wore
buckskins, Gurdon Hubbard travelled east to visit his
widowed mother. He bought store clothes, had his hair
cut, and sat for Anson Dickinson, the famed miniaturist
working Connecticut towns that spring. At age twenty-
eight, Hubbard was a man of substance, a respected trader
in the West, the chosen leader of the Vermilion County
Rangers, and soon to be elected the county's
representative in the Illinois legislature.
Courtesy Chicago Historical Society

Gurdon Hubbard departed Montreal for the Indian country with French-Canadian voyageurs in 1818, bound for Mackinac Island in Michigan Territory. Birchbark freight canoes (called *canots du maître* in Canada, mackinaws in the American west) carried eight tons of freight and could be portaged miles past rapids by the husky voyageurs who powered them. Craft built at Mackinac Island were decked fore and aft and carried sailing masts. Some, made of cedar splints, could carry up to fifty tons of freight. Frances Ann Hopkins painted the Canadian passenger canoe (above left).

Courtesy Public Archives Canada

C. Butterworth used a Frances Ann Hopkins painting for his engraving "A fur trade canoe on the Mattawa River, Ontario" (left center), which illustrated a book on Canada published in London in 1840. The light, fast *canots du maître* could sometimes negotiate dangerous rapids. Most mackinaws were portaged. Gurdon Hubbard's voyageurs used heavy mackinaws, carrying from eight to fifty tons. They made forty miles a day by paddle, pole and oar; seventy-five under sail; and sometimes, on a difficult portage, only a few hundred yards in a day.

Courtesy Public Archives Canada

The freight canoe of the voyageurs served as their shelter from storms and cold, windy nights. Since their heavily laden craft were not seaworthy in bad weather, the men spent much of their time ashore. Gurdon Hubbard described such experiences: boat repairs, hunting, fishing, games and songs occupied the men known for their rugged endurance in the wilderness. Camp cooking wasn't much unless fishing was good, with the staple diet of the voyageur consisting of peas or lyed corn and tallow. Frances Ann Hopkins' painting shows voyageurs in camp (lower left).

Courtesy Public Archives Canada

For more than two centuries mackinaws, *canots du maître,* North canoes and York boats served as freight trains for the Canadian and American west as Indian trade flourished, military posts were supplied, and farmers pushing into Indian lands required trade goods. A train of light passenger and freight batteaux is shown above, coursing the Mattawa River in Ontario. Fixed transportation rates were established by the mackinaw operators; in the early 1800s the round trip from Montreal to Mackinac Island cost a passenger twenty-five beaver skins.

Courtesy Archives of Ontario

Black Hawk (Makataimeshekiakiak), Chief of the Sac and
Fox tribes, served with Tecumseh in the War of 1812.
Leading a united force against whites in 1832, he again was
defeated. Charles Bird King's painting of Black Hawk
appears by permission of the Warner Collection of Gulf
States Paper Corporation, Tuscaloosa, Alabama.
Courtesy Warner Collection

Watseka (Watchekee, Daughter of the Evening Star), first
wife of Gurdon Hubbard. Her mother, Monaska, was a
sister of Tamin, chief of the Kankakees. "We called her a
princess because she behaved like a princess," a Vermilion
county pioneer told historian Beckwith. She and Hubbard
separated after the death of their daughter, Lowanen,
heeding Black Hawk's advice, "Don't live together, like
foolish whites, if you disagree." After 1834, Watseka went
into exile west of the Mississippi with her people. The
portrait by Laura Hunt Eaton is probably based on a
photograph taken late in Watseka's life when the town of
Middleport was renamed Watseka in her honor.
Courtesy Watseka Public Library

Keokuk, Sac and Fox chief, famed as an orator and peacemaker, was a friend much trusted by Hubbard. From a daguerrotype taken in 1847, a year before Keokuk's death.
Courtesy Smithsonian Instituion

Shabona (Made-Like-a-Bear), chief of the Potawatomi-Ottawa tribes and military aide to Tecumseh, vowed to stay at peace with whites after defeat by the Americans. Hubbard called "Shaubenee" the noblest man he knew.
Courtesy Smithsonian Institution

Alexander Robinson (Che-che-pin-qua), chief of the United Potawatomi, Ottawa and Chippewa nation. Son of a Scottish officer and an Ottawa woman, Robinson was the interpreter—helpful to Hubbard—at Fort Dearborn.
Courtesy Chicago Historical Society

Dr. Alexander Wolcott, Yale graduate, medical doctor, treaty expert, and Indian agent at Fort Dearborn, taught Gurdon Hubbard much while learning of Indian ways from the young trader.
Courtesy Chicago Historical Society

Gurdon Hubbard's Chicago 1826–1836—

A.T. Andreas map on pages following

A.T. Andreas, historian and cartographer, adapted a United States Land Office map showing original land patents issued between 1828–1836 for the first volume of his *History of Chicago* (published in 1884). On this he superimposed other Chicago developments, including Hubbard's Trail, shown entering below the South Branch of the Chicago River —**1** and crossing State Street to enter the west gate of Fort Dearborn —**2**. Hubbard carried his trade goods to southern Illinois and the Wabash country of Indiana via his trail, and drove hogs and cattle up the trail to Chicago for slaughter along the marsh west of the fort, an area now within Chicago's famed Loop. "Hubbard's men stored the meat on the frozen river and no one touched it because they knew who owned it," Indian Agent John Fonda wrote. Hubbard brought his Vermilion County Rangers up his trail to the relief of Fort Dearborn during Indian troubles in 1827 and 1832.

While representing Vermilion county in the Illinois legislature at Vandalia, Hubbard pushed hard for Chicago as the eastern entrance to a proposed Illinois and Michigan canal. He in effect commuted from his southern base at Danville to Chicago. In the absence of the garrison, he leased space in the Fort Dearborn barracks for his fur trade warehousing, freight forwarding and ship lighterage business, and he obtained a contract to supply the fort with meats and other provisions when the garrison returned. In 1833 he built a three-story (later four) brick warehouse on the south bank of the river for his activities, including packing, and ultimately real estate, banking and insurance. To some, this immense brick structure amidst log and deal houses and stores was known as "Hubbard's Folly"—**3**. With Dr. William Fifthian of Danville and other partners, Hubbard became owner of Chicago land. He also urged Mrs. Eleanor Kinzie, mother of his close friend John Kinzie, Jr., to send her son, Robert, to the downstate land office near Danville to register their claim to Chicago property, though Robert insisted much of the acreage was worthless—**4**. Hubbard decided Chicago should become home for himself and his second wife, Eleanora. He purchased a cabin from Indian Chief Billy Caldwell on Lake Michigan north of the Kinzie holdings—**5** and built a house there. He induced eastern associates Russell and Mather to join him in buying acreage northwest, beyond the north branch, an area considered worthless by most, which he called the Russell and Mather Addition—**6**.

By 1835, Hubbard had sold his warehouse on South Water Street and was building a new one and a "grand" hotel, to be called the Lake House, on the north bank of the river at Rush Street—**7**. In the east to visit his mother, he stopped in New York City and auctioned off part of the Russell and Mather Addition at a handsome profit, thus spurring the great Chicago land boom. Back in Chicago, he was named one of three canal commissioners to begin the digging of the Illinois and Michigan canal to Lockport—**8**. Chicago, which had a population of thirty in 1826, had grown to 3,000 within the decade, according to Andreas. During Hubbard's lifetime it would grow to a million—on a base he did much to create.

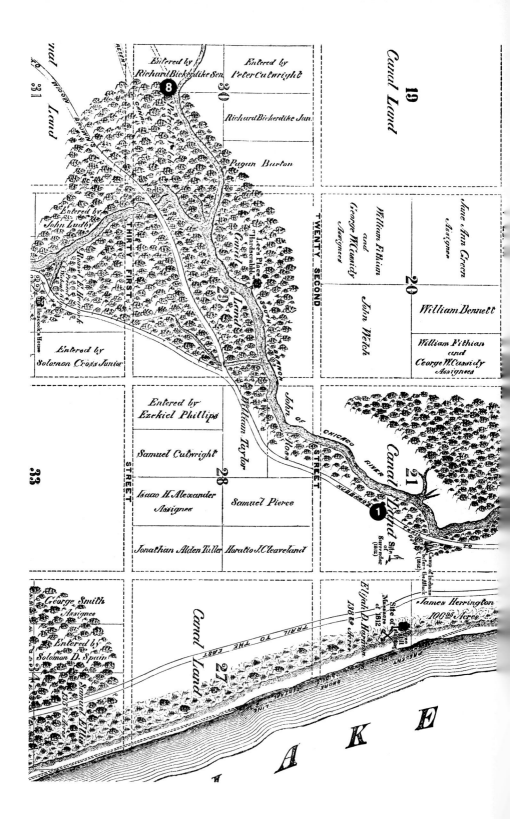

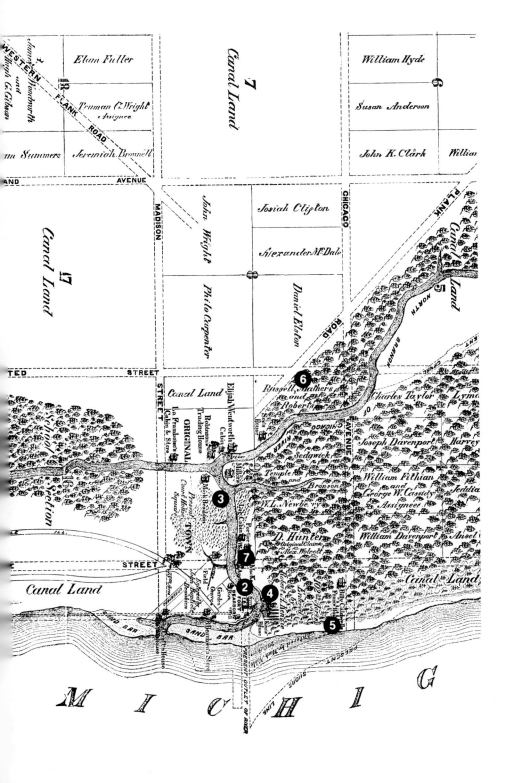

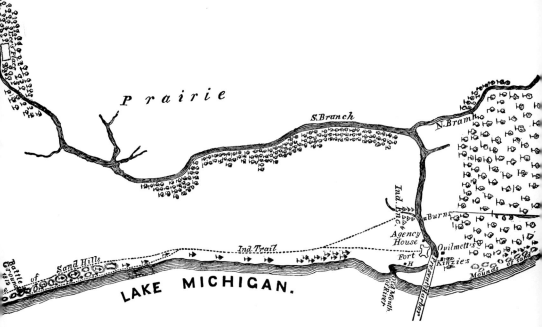

Late in life "Uncle Gurdon" Hubbard took young Henry R. Hamilton down Hubbard's Trail to various sites of his early days in Illinois. Later Hamilton aided Hubbard with his memoirs. In 1930 Hamilton incorporated them into his own recollections, creating the Illinois map (opposite page) showing the trail, from Vincennes to Chicago, and the sites of Hubbard's fur trade posts and various adventures.

Andreas' map of Chicago at the time of the Fort Dearborn massacre depicts the area much as Hubbard first saw it from his tree perch on October 1, 1818. He then walked the Indian trail through the sand dunes where the 1812 battle occurred, later cruising the south branch of the river to the Chicago Portage beyond Lee's place.

In 1820 Henry R. Schoolcraft accompanied Governor Lewis Cass of Michigan Territory on a federal expedition into Indian country including Chicago in 1820. Standing on a Lake Michigan sandbar, Schoolcraft sketched this view of Chicago, much as it was when Hubbard first was there in 1818, a few log houses added.

Courtesy Chicago Historical Society

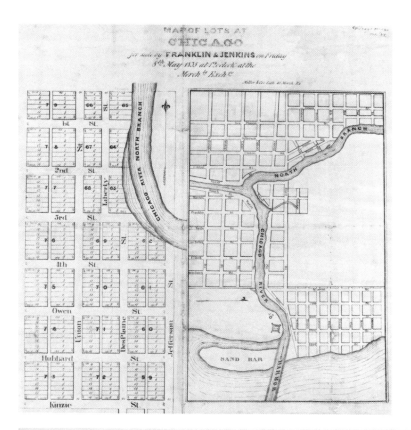

In New York in May, 1835, Hubbard abruptly arranged a Wall Street auction of some of the Chicago lots he owned with Russell and Mather. He drew the needed maps from memory, then had them recorded and lithographed. Franklin & Jenkins conducted the highly successful sale, which precipitated the Chicago land boom.

Courtesy Chicago Historical Society

While in the east, Hubbard inspected hotels so to guide him in constructing the Lake House on the north bank of the river. Hailed as Chicago's finest, the Lake House ultimately failed. Civic strife prevented a Rush Street bridge from being completed for many years. Hubbard provided a ferry, but still lost the hotel in the 1837 panic.

Courtesy Chicago Historical Society

The John Kinzie home on the north bank of the Chicago River, expanded from a cabin built by fur trader du Sable in about 1776. Juliette Kinzie, who lived there, sketched the "mansion" for her book *Wau Bun* (published in 1856). Hubbard often stayed there as the Kinzies' guest.

Chicago at Wolf Point as it appeared in 1830, from a description provided by Hubbard, according to Andreas. Elijah Wentworth built Wolf Tavern (so-called after he killed a wolf in the kitchen) on the west side of the North Branch, earlier known as Gaurie River. Samuel Miller built the two story inn on the east bank, where James and Robert Kinzie added stores. From Andreas, *History of Chicago,* vol 1.

John H. Kinzie, Jr., became Hubbard's lifelong good friend on Mackinac Island.

Júliette, wife of John, who knew life with Indians, shared John's friendship·with Hubbard.

Judge Richard A. Hamilton, lawyer from Kentucky, joined in Hubbard's land ventures.

William Ogden, lured West by Hubbard, became his lawyer and, later, Chicago's mayor.

Feisty Long John Wentworth was Hubbard's political foe until Lincoln united them.

A friend from Black Hawk
War days, Abraham Lincoln
often stayed with Hubbard in
Chicago.

Stephen A. Douglas and
Hubbard clashed early over
canal plans but became
friends years later.

Hubbard, chairman of the Building Committee charged with completing
Chicago's convention hall in record time, had the Wigwam ready in three
months. A fervent Lincoln supporter, he helped with convention strategy
that won the Republican nomination for 'Honest Abe'. Alexander Hesler
photograph.
Photographs above courtesy Chicago Historical Society.

Hubbard (here photographed in 1870) at age 69 lost his home, his papers and most of his other possessions to the Chicago fire of 1871. Relatives and refugees, panicked by the approaching flames, gathered at the Hubbard mansion on the north side, and he led them to safety as his home burned. Then in the hard days ahead, Hubbard returned to work, seeking to rebuild his fortune.

Courtesy Chicago Historical Society

Gurdon Saltonstall Hubbard died September 14, 1886. His widow, left with moderate means, in 1906 commissioned Chicago sculptor Julia Bracken Wendt to create the bronze plaque pictured above to memorialize Hubbard's arrival in Chicago in October, 1818. The oak trees symbolize the tree young Hubbard climbed to gain his first view of Fort Dearborn, the village of Chicago and the prairie. She presented the plaque to the Chicago Historical Society shortly before her death in 1909.

Courtesy Chicago Historical Society

Iroquois River Station, Illinois 1825

Hubbard himself wedded an Indian princess, called (in the Potawatomi language) Watch-e-kee (but called Watseka by the whites). Her mother Monoska was an Illinois Indian; she was the niece of Chief Tamin. She was dignified and intelligent. Her complexion was light, her form small, lithe, slender and comely.
                    Beckwith,
                    History of Iroquois Country

In the fall of 1824 Antoine Deschamps, grown old and weary in the fur trade, resigned his post as Superintendent of the Illinois River Trading Posts of the American Fur Company. On Deschamps' recommendation, Gurdon Saltonstall Hubbard, just past his twenty-second year, was appointed to succeed him. Hubbard received a magnificent increase in salary, from an amount somewhat under $200 a year to $1,300 a year. He could now care for his mother and sisters in Middletown, have funds to spare for his own personal needs and for investment. He also was given permission to continue his experiments intended to improve company efficiency in transporting trade goods to the wilderness and furs back to Mackinaw.

Ramsey Crooks and Robert Stuart had not been favorably impressed when they first learned that Hubbard had managed to get the huge mackinaws, capable of ten tons burden, from the St. Joseph River to the Kankakee by harnessing them to the tails of Indian ponies. However, the returns on the Iroquois River business that year were excellent, Hubbard's costs were down, and Deschamps swore by the young man. So Gurdon was permitted to experiment further. That fall he carried out a project he had considered from the first time he crossed the Chicago Portage. He unloaded the boats when they arrived at the portage from Mackinaw, scuttled them in the slough, and used Indian ponies to carry the trade goods. "In this manner," he wrote, "the long, tedious, and difficult passage through Mud Lake, onto and down the Desplaines River, would be avoided, and the goods taken directly to the Indians in their hunting grounds instead of being carried on the backs of men."

Having bypassed the portage successfully, Gurdon experimented further. He sought a shorter and better way into southeastern Illinois. He sank his boats along the Little Calumet River and again used pack ponies. A canal could be cut from the Little Calumet to the Desplaines, he noted, but he soon abandoned his Little Calumet base to return to Chicago, where he could leave his mackinaws and quarter and warehouse men and goods at the abandoned fort. There the *batteaux* were used by the *voyageurs* to lighter cargo from ships anchored in the lake. The sailing schooner *Chicago Packet* was calling regularly at Chicago and Gurdon expected other sailing ships and steamboats would ply those waters in time. "There is no good harbor on Lake Michigan," he wrote. "By cutting the sand bar, one could be had at Chicago." Army engineers would make a similar recommendation. Such a channel was dug by soldiers in 1828, but the cut was narrow and frequently silted over, so ships could not often enter the Chicago River. Hubbard's *voyageurs* at Chicago continued to have work to do, carrying cargo across the sand bar in their shallow-draft boats, and storing it in the warehouse space he leased from the government.

Hubbard's main base continued to be the Iroquois River Station but he took pleasure in his increasingly frequent trips to Chicago, one hundred twenty-four miles north. Dr. Wolcott and Ellen had moved into the commandant's house at the fort, facilities provided to him as caretaker. Since Wolcott had added to his responsibilities, he had obtained the employment of his father-in-law, Kinzie, an Indian sub-agent. He was apologetic to Gurdon for failing to consider him for such a job. But John Kinzie's house was falling into ruin, he could not afford to restore it, and the Agency House was available to him as sub-agent. Kinzie also would receive $500 a year and could continue in his declining fur trade, Wolcott explained. He knew Gurdon would have liked such a job.

Hubbard spent much of the spring and fall at Chicago, but in winter he travelled out of his Iroquois post, using his small black walnut canoe when the rivers were open, horses when the ground was free of snow, and going on foot when conditions were totally bad. His trading posts extended from Black Hawk's territory along the Rock River to the Mississippi, east to the lands of the Miamis and Kickapoos on the Indiana border, and south into the country of the Piankeshaws to Vincennes, west along the Illinois to the Mississippi. "The winter of 1825 I passed at my Iroquois post," he wrote in later years. "The hunting had been unusually good and large quantities of goods were sold and many fine furs collected." Henry Hamilton, who undertook to help Gurdon Hubbard write his memoirs of those early years a half century later, would complain that he could learn little of Gurdon's personal life in the late 1820s. He discovered the reason when he visited southern Illinois with his grand-uncle in about 1875 and they met the local historian, Hiram Beckwith. Beckwith demanded to know the details of Hubbard's life with the Indian woman, Watseka. Gurdon complied. Beckwith soon published what he learned of the story but Hamilton refrained until he wrote his autobiography, including the early life of Hubbard, published in 1932.

*

In late 1825 Hubbard was invited to Chief Tamin's village not far from his Iroquois post for the corn harvest feast, which, he was told, Shabona and Black Hawk also would attend. He knew that Black Hawk was travelling widely among the tribes since they met often. He suspected there was secret war talk when the chiefs gathered. He was not much concerned about Indian politics, except that he generally resented the continuing intrusion of the white settlers into the hunting grounds, from which they were excluded by the treaties. Like Dr. Wolcott, Gurdon felt sure that Black Hawk would not succeed in uniting the tribes for war so long as Shabona and Billy Caldwell and Alexander Robinson opposed him. Chief Tamin, whose country extended from the Kankakee River to the Iroquois, also preferred to remain at peace with the whites. Tamin expected the kind of alliance he had arranged for Hubbard and his niece, Watchekee, would help to maintain it. Yellow Head, Tamin's half-brother, whose lands were north of the Kankakee and Big Foot, based on a large lake (Geneva) northwest of Chicago, were fervent disciples of Black Hawk and his prophet, White Cloud, the Winnebago. Gurdon rarely saw Big Foot and he had no wish to see Yellow Head. However, at Tamin's village, he would be required to be civil to all who attended the feast.

The truculent Yellow Head brought their difficulties to a showdown prior to Tamin's festival. Yellow Head and a few of his hunters came to the Iroquois River Station seeking whisky for his band well in excess of the supply Gurdon had allocated to them for the winter's hunt. As the new superintendent of the American Fur posts in Illinois, he had cut the liquor ration generally on the practical ground that widespread drunkenness was ruining the Indian trade. Plenty of whisky could be had by the Indians from the settlers coming into the territory who brought large supplies, but Yellow Head preferred to make an issue of Hubbard's announced rationing policy. Vasseur and his men were away from the store, which was locked, and Gurdon himself was again the victim of severe rheumatism and had gone to his bunk. Early in the evening of the Indian summer day, Gurdon heard shouts and pounding in the vicinity of the store. He reached the door of his cabin as Yellow Head arrived, flanked by his men.

Yellow Head, so named because his father had evidently been a blond white man, called upon the trader to open his store and supply liquor on credit. Otherwise he would break open the store and take the liquor they needed. Gurdon curtly refused. He shut his door against Yellow Head's threats and ranting, went back to his bunk, and then realized the drunken Indians had gone off toward the store to carry out Yellow Head's threat. "I got up from my bunk, took my rifle, and thrust it through the oiled paper which served as window glass," Gurdon remembered. "As Yellow Head had reached the store, I drew a bead on him and called to him to go on and break in."

Yellow Head knew Gurdon Hubbard's reputation as a sharpshooter. He could bark a squirrel on a tree limb, sending it tumbling to its death, or cut the spine of a running bear at a hundred paces with his rifle bullet. Yellow Head moved back from the store building while his men jeered at Gurdon from a safe distance. Gurdon returned to his bunk, using a crutch as his rheumatic joints were causing him agony. He had opened the door of his house to watch the apparent retreat of the Indians and now left it ajar to enable him to hear any further sounds of disturbance. Soon he heard stealthy steps on his puncheon floor. Yellow Head was aptly named. His scalp lock gleamed a saffron glow above his plucked, lemon-colored head as a shaft of setting sunlight caught him. He closed upon Gurdon's bunk, brandishing his knife.

"Lame as I was, I jumped up, seized the knife, took it away, pushed him out the door." Yellow Head was drunk, but strong, and Gurdon suffered a slashed hand in the struggle. Outside, he found that several squaws had been attracted by the disturbance. Indian women usually feared the worst when their men were drinking. Beyond the door was a mortar and a large ironwood pestle, used for pounding corn. Balancing on his crutch, Gurdon seized the pestle and handed Yellow Head's knife, wet with blood from his own slashed hand, to one of the squaws. "Give the old woman his knife," he told her. The insulted and humiliated chief was reaching for a second knife, hidden in his legging. When he saw Hubbard above him with the heavy pestle poised, he thought better of it, took the bloodied knife and slunk away, still muttering that he would kill Hubbard. Presumably his men led him to the medicine lodge in Tamin's village, where the whisky could be sweated out of him.

Thus Gurdon went early to Tamin's village on the day of the corn festival a week later. He intended to explain the incident to Tamin and to settle the feud in council with Shabona and Black Hawk, if they would agree to hear him. This was the custom, Shabona being okama for the area, and Black Hawk a visitor of similar rank. Gurdon wished also to inform his host of his respect for him, despite his trouble with Yellow Head. If Tamin agreed, their trade would not diminish, but his half brother could be included only if he changed his ways. Liquor would not be sold on demand. Hubbard did not understand all the reasons for Yellow Head's enmity, yet he was prepared to effect a truce and to correct his own behavior if he had transgressed on Indian rules. But he would not attend Tamin's feast unless the feud with Yellow Head was first ended.

There was no problem. Yellow Head had departed Tamin's village. His half brother knew of the fight. He approved the limitation of liquor sales, as most responsible chiefs did. Tamin knew of no other reason for Yellow Head's animosity to Papamatabe. Years later it was asserted by some that Yellow Head was the father of Watseka and disapproved of her planned marriage to Hubbard, Yellow Head considering himself to be victimized by miscegenation. This inference seems unlikely. Many half-breeds were honored chiefs among the Indians. By Potawatomi custom, the father of a girl, if alive, arranged her marriage. Yet it was Tamin, brother of Monoska, Watchekee's mother, who pledged the girl to Hubbard, saying her father had been a Delaware brave. It was Delaware tradition, one common to many tribes, for the son of a chief to marry into his clan in another tribe. Thus had Shabona, son of an Ottawa chief, become a Potawatomi. Tamin, it turned out, was little concerned that Hubbard had fought with Yellow Head. He was meeting with Shabona and Black Hawk, but the matter need not be discussed with them. Tamin expected Papamatabe to occupy his place of honor at the feast that night.

*

Gurdon respected the good sense of Tamin. He knew that the council that afternoon was secret, that there would be talk of Black Hawk's endeavors among the tribes to unite them for war. He expected Tamin and Shabona would prevail. He looked forward to the corn festival, the happiest of the Indian celebrations. He wandered toward the fields where the young braves and maidens, while shucking harvested corn for storage, were searching for the red ears which would be used in the mating ceremony that night. Their laughter and shouting rose to the timbered high ground of the village that sparkling Indian summer afternoon. The young would dance and love that cool autumn night. The older squaws were busy at the cooking fires, a party of young hunters shouted greetings on arrival from another town, the old men lounged near the lodge where Tamin was meeting the visiting chiefs. The soft laughter of contentment rippled through the village.

The young women of marriageable age, those who had spent

their first days and nights in the huts to which they were banished for the time the moon affected their blood, now sought joyously the red ears of corn they would present to their prospective mates in the crane dance that night. The young men, Chief Tamin had said wearily, had been playing their flutes before the lodges of their beloved night after night for nights on end, while the dogs howled and sensible people lost sleep. But Tamin and all the chiefs loved the corn festival and the crane mating dance. The tribes needed and loved children.

Gurdon walked near the mounds of corn where the sounds of merriment were centered. Several young women who had obtained their red ears of corn were moving off, toward the village square to assist the older women attending the cooking fires. One of the maidens differed from the rest, she was dressed in the buckskin shirt and skimpy skirt of the unmarried woman, but she lacked the feathers in her hair denoting the woman who had been to the menstrual hut, and, instead, wore a single turkey feather in her long black hair and the beaded headband of a chief's daughter. He saw that she was young and fair, and he was sure she was Watchekee, or Watseka as her name was said in English, her impish laughter as she responded to gibes of her friends reminding him of the bold little girl he had seen in Tamin's lodge years before. When she saw him there was no sign of recognition. She flounced from their mutual path, lengthening her stride to move quickly from him, her bare thighs flashing in the late afternoon sun. Her companions, glimpsing Gurdon, obviously marked him as The Trader and ran off too, giggling and shouting to Watchekee.

The cooking fires burned brightly in the warm, smoky haze of Indian summer. The moon was rising, bright and cold, forecasting the winter season soon to come. The raw bluster of early November, called Squaw winter, had warned all that the storehouses must be filled with corn, roots, squash and pumpkin, sun-dried berries and nuts, smoked venison and fish. The remaining hunters and trappers would soon depart, a few taking with them a favorite wife, to the winter hunting grounds. Some young men already at the camps were allowed to return for the festival, joining their young brothers who would find their mates that night and later would call upon them in their family lodges.

The village thereafter would have quiet days, only Tamin and the old men, women and children remaining. By spring, in the course of events, the hunters would return laden with pelts and fresh kills of meat and the young braves, hunting and trapping their first season, in all likelihood would come back to pregnant squaws.

The crane dance was the celebration of the harvest and of fecundity. All summer long the young women to be honored that night had prepared the finery they would wear, petticoats dyed with powdered earth from Vermilion Creek, red, burned ochre, and orange, sewed with dried-deer-tendon threads and over-skirts made of Stroud, the fine English cloth famed for holding brightest dyes of red, yellow and blue, skirts that would be removed during the dancing. As the men moved toward their places in the square, the young women could be seen at the doors of the lodges, arraying themselves in ribbons and feathers, wearing their loose-fitting diaphanous blouses of white or pale green or pink, the texture of flower petals, revealing the fulsomeness of their nubile breasts, the effects enhanced by the shadowing of their bosoms with ochre paint. All were bedizened with collected family ornaments of silver and beads, feathers and wampum shells in which Potawatomi women gloried and for which they were widely famed. The drums and flutes began as the spectators took their places, Gurdon sitting with the older chiefs, next to Tamin's own family. Yellow Head was absent, as promised. The dancers disappeared into the lodges for their final preparations.

The throb of the drums increased, the flutes sobbed an insistent cadence as the dancers appeared, advancing slowly, in a long sinuous line. The older girls had wrapped themselves above their bright skirts with wide bands of white linen, ornamented with silver buckles and thin strips of lavender wampum. They had painted their faces bright vermilion and as they unwrapped themselves, coming foward sensuously swaying and lowering their linen wraps, it could be seen that they had also rouged their dark, firm breasts with vermilion in mystic designs of their own fancy. The youngest of the dancing girls were nude to the waist, customary for a girl child at an age when her brother ran about naked, with only a leather belt to accustom him to the fig bar he later would wear. All of the young women wore red or blue leggings, made of fine cloth ornamented with porcupine quills, and shells and coral brought from distant shores and sold by the traders. Beaded moccasins completed the dancer's attire. Into her hair was braided the brightly colored feathers Gurdon had seen that afternoon, a sign of marriageable age; a single turkey feather if she was not. Thus it was easy for him to pick out Watseka.

As the dancing proceeded, the drums increased their beat and flutes shrieked wildly, the noises that made Chief Tamin complain. Older women joined in the circle of dancers, while the marriageable maidens dashed to a pile of husked corn in which the red ears, found that afternoon, had been hidden. The single turkey feather worn by Watseka was conspicuous among them and Gurdon sensed the displeasure of Monoska, the mother of Watseka, sitting near him, as she whispered to her brother, Tamin. The maidens, including the ineligible Watseka, quickly found the red ears, the symbol of fertility and good fortune, and rejoined the dance. The steps of the crane-mating rites began, the younger women portraying the male crane. The music grew fierce, the sensuous steps of the dance intense, the boys and men among the spectators pounded out the rhythm and shouted and prodded one another as they professed to see special significance in the color, size and quality of the ears of corn the maidens displayed. Gurdon watched for Watseka at each turn of the dancing and saw that she danced as a marriageable maiden, brandishing a red ear of corn, a divergence from ritual that continued to cause signs of angry disapproval among some of the women. Chief Tamin himself merely frowned and grimly awaited developments. Watseka, observing that Papamatabe watched her closely as she spun by, smiled boldly at him, her small white teeth flashing in the lurid light of the fires.

Amid the rising excitement of the dance, the marriageable maidens removed their topskirts to disclose the beribboned petticoats beneath. Then, flaunting their red ears of corn in unmaidenly triumph, they rushed upon their favored braves sitting among the spectators, who leaped up in glad expectance. Watseka, approaching her uncle and her mother, turned suddenly to Gurdon Hubbard. She paused smiling before him to ask, "Do you remember me, Swift Walker?"

He arose quickly, standing tall among them, and eagerly accepted the ear of corn. "I remember you, Watch-e-kee," he said, using her name in Potawatomi form. "I have never forgotten you." He glanced at Chief Tamin, who remained inscrutable, and at Monoska, her mother, who showed signs of inexpressible relief. "I claim my ear of maize," he said, taking it from her, and, forgetting his recent aches and pains, he joined in the crane dance with the other young men. Since leaving Mackinaw he had danced only at the Kinzies, but he had seen the crane dance and now considered he could be good at it. He accompanied Watseka readily, shouting and leaping with the best of them, as the young braves celebrated the glorious ending of their weeks, even months of courtship. He had danced sedately at Mackinaw and with the Kinzies but the wildly improvised steps of a happily betrothed Indian brave was no problem. He had not courted Watseka, he was aware she was not ready for marriage, that she had flouted the rules of her tribe that evening, but he was happy. There was no doubt of it, Gurdon Hubbard had fallen in love that night of the crane dance. His Indian friends congratulated and complimented him.

When the young people dashed away into the woods in completion of their ritual, Gurdon ran with them and found Watseka to be as elusive as an antelope and wild as a panther when captured. He returned her to her lodge, where her mother was waiting. Hubbard, too, had violated the courtship traditions of the tribe. He had not slipped into the young woman's lodge to find his way to her bearskin sleeping place with a lighted candle, staying the night only if she recognized him and blew it out. He had not brought to her mother the requisite gifts: pelts, game and finery to symbolize his ability to care for a wife and children. But Monoska forgave him. Watseka, too, had ignored their laws and tempted Hubbard, and, in the end, they could have done no more than often occurred among young people in the forest. Once pledged to one another, they were expected to remain faithful, a requirement more often observed by the Potawatomis than others, it was said. Gurdon was forgiven and Monoska without doubt expected he would meet all the requirements of courtship in good time. Gurdon returned to the feasting where he was greeted joyously and with understanding by the chiefs. He had become one of them. Black Hawk and Shabona, who, as they bore the burdens of age also added to their drinking exploits, undertook to advise Gurdon on the way to enjoy life best as the husband of a pretty squaw. Both chiefs practiced monogamy, Shabona especially being widely celebrated for his faithfulness to Wiomex Okono.

It was advisable, Shabona said, to have but one wife at a time for one's peace of mind. When one travelled, he suggested, the reason for the travel should be uppermost in the mind. Black Hawk agreed. "It is not necessary to take a favorite tree into the forest," he said. "You will find an old woman who will sell you a proper beson to keep your woman's love. Watch-e-kee without doubt has obtained such a beson and has proved its power. This will make it easy for you to remain faithful while you are among us."

"We leave the management of our household affairs to our women," Black Hawk advised. "She must cook two meals a day. If she does not, say nothing, but go to the home of a friend. You will always have food there, even a stranger is given food, and she will come to realize her error. Do not cut wood nor keep the fire, except when there are guests. This is woman's work. If your wife longs for meat, and hints of it, you must go out early without food and do not return until you have game. Put down the game, saying nothing. She will dress it and share it with friends, after first giving her husband corn soup, if that is what he desires." This amused Shabona, Waba, and Tamin. Gurdon's love of corn soup was known even to Black Hawk.

"It is most important you give much attention to the first year of your marriage," Black Hawk continued. "That is when you must learn whether you can agree with one another and be happy." Gurdon remembered that Black Hawk had counseled him in this manner previously.

"If we were to live together and disagree, we would be as foolish as the whites," Gurdon prompted, remembering.

Black Hawk laughed. "You listen well, Papamatabe. We must live together in good companionship for our peace of mind, as Shabona has said, and for the sake of our children. And no man should look too closely at the past behavior of his wife, since he expects the same consideration from her. Among our people, no indiscretion can banish a woman from the parents' lodge. It does not matter how many children she may bring home, the kettle is on the fire to feed them."

Chief Black Hawk's discourse on marriage and the family was delivered to the young white trader in the company of good friends. Gurdon recalled it, disclosing the scene years later to Henry Hamilton, after he had kept the secret of his marriage to Watseka most of his lifetime. Hamilton, in turn, did not publish any mention of Watseka until after the death of Mary Ann Hubbard, Gurdon's third wife. The secret was well known among the Indian tribes, however, and to the whites of Vermilion and Iroquois counties, where the story of Hubbard's romance with the "The Princess Watseka" was first told in print by Beckwith while Gurdon was still alive. The young trader knew the Indian traditions well enough. Women planted crops, harvested them, cooked meals, cared for children. The children were rarely disciplined yet were generally well behaved, respectful to elders and obedient to tradition. Men fished, trapped, hunted, traded and made war. Fathers announced arrangements for a child's marriage, but women attended to the details. Indian men took more than one wife if they chose and could afford it. Boys entered the forest to experience exhaltation and visions which guided them in choosing their animist spiritual guide and their besons. Girls were sequestered in a hut, fasting, and were kept away from any contact with others during their first menstrual period and at such times thereafter. They were then ready for marriage and, if pledged, their mothers delivered them to the lodge of the intended mate following an exchange of presents. Prior to formal marriage young Indians had a considerable sexual freedom.

Some weeks after the feast in Tamin's village, Monoska brought her daughter to Hubbard's house near Sugar Creek. Gurdon had presented Monoska with gifts symbolic of his prowess as a hunter and provider. He had not, however, gone to Monoska's lodge with flint and steel to light a candle which Watseka might or might not extinguish. Such recalcitrance was ignored by the prospective mother-in-law. Gurdon had vowed his love for Watseka. And in the cold and snowy December of

1825, he forgot his promise to the Kinzies and Dr. Wolcott that he would come to Chicago for Christmas. He remained at his Iroquois River Station. He allocated to Noel Vasseur many of the trips to the hunting grounds and to the villages of the chiefs that he had undertaken himself in the past. By May Gurdon and Watseka had enjoyed their first major quarrel and reconciliation when she would not agree to accompany him to Chicago and Mackinaw, saying she would be happier among the people of her village. Gurdon left her, trying to understand her reluctance to join other Indian wives in those white communities, but promising to return as soon as possible.

At Chicago he found that letters had arrived from his mother and his sister Elizabeth. "I am seeking a wife for you," Elizabeth had written earlier and he had responded, "I feel I will always remain a bachelor," adding, "Suppose you found one who did not go to the Episcopal church, how would it look if she went to one church and I went to another?" It was an on-going joke between them, his Episcopalianism. He had written that Mrs. Eleanor Kinzie required him to attend the Episcopal services she conducted in her home. He called her "the Episcopal bishop of Illinois." Now, in May, Elizabeth had written, "I have found the perfect wife for you," a young Middletown woman she described as "a perfect Episcopalian." "Do not search further for a wife for me," Gurdon answered. "I am in love!" He did not indicate that his inamorata was an Indian girl.

Temporarily Gurdon had given up his plan to make his major trading base Chicago or Mackinaw or Peoria. He had forgotten for the time M. Deschamps' warnings that the end of the fur trade in Illinois was approaching and his own prior realization that this was true. He liked his life as it was that spring and refused to contemplate change. He knew that the settlers were pouring into southern Illinois, seizing and plowing the land, keeping pigs and cows. He was preparing to do the same himself. With Watseka as his wife, all things seemed possible. He could maintain his station in the Iroquois country, he could farm, he could open a store for the settlers in Danville. He could take Watseka to Mackinaw, Chicago or St. Louis, she would be welcome. He refused to see that even in the Chicago portage country the land was attracting settlers; he refused to hear talk that all the Indians would soon be required to move further west even when Dr. Wolcott said so.

He was proud of Watseka, her beauty, her poise, her fiery temperament, and he was sorry she had refused to go north with him. But he did not mention her to Wolcott or to the Kinzies, nor to his mother, sisters or brother. In Chicago he possibly recognized that the Kinzies had not married Indian women, nor had Dr. Wolcott. John Kinzie Jr., now secretary to Governor Cass of Michigan and hoping to become an Indian agent since he was becoming known as a specialist on Indian affairs, was in love with a girl in the East introduced to him by his brother-in-law, Wolcott. Juliette Magill, a descendant of the Connecticut Wolcotts, attended Emma Willard's famous school for females at Troy, New York. John Kinzie, Sr. had married a woman who long had lived as an Indian, but she too was white. At Chicago and at Mackinaw Gurdon kept secret his romance and marriage. A half century later, when Hiram Beckwith was preparing his *History of Iroquois County* and confronted Gurdon Hubbard, then the famed Chicagoan, with the story of Watseka, Gurdon talked freely about her, though it was for print. "Yes, Watseka was my wife," he said. "She gave me beauty and delight and happy years. She bore me a child, who died in infancy. I had promised to wed her when she was offered in marriage to me as a young girl. Her mother brought her to me. She was then about fifteen or sixteen. We were happy together."

Beckwith was a respected historian whose work appeared in scholarly publications of the northwest, those of the Wisconsin, Chicago, and Illinois historical societies among them. Beckwith's histories of Iroquois and Vermilion counties were among the best of that genre published. Yet the account of Watseka's life as written by Beckwith, or possibly an associate named B.F. Shankland with whom Gurdon corresponded, was filled with the bias against the Indians prevalent at the time. "Watseka declined to mingle with the common herd of redskins," said the sketch in Beckwith's history. "She was anxious to learn the manners and customs of her more favored pale sisters. A romantic story is told of how she became endowed with royal distinction (she was known as an Indian princess in the Danville area), but this is only a tradition. By this union Hubbard greatly strengthened his relations with the Indians, and it is known that he placed more reliance on the fidelity and friendship of the Potawatomi chief, Was-sus-kuk, than on any white man. With the influx of the white population, Hubbard himself was confronted with the alternative of divorcing his Indian wife or of losing caste. . . ."

Watseka in her later years *was* called an Indian princess by the press of southern Illinois. She did not seek to emulate the ways of white women, however. At the time of her marriage to Hubbard, she had not seen a white woman. The pioneer white women who later knew her at Danville said Watseka "put on airs," but during her relationship with Gurdon she made quite clear to all who knew her that she preferred her Indian ways to those of the whites. When, years later, after she had gone into exile with her people, Watseka returned to Illinois to visit Middleport, the town that had been renamed Watseka in her honor, an old settler provided a probably accurate appraisal of her to newspapers: "Watseka was not like other Indian maidens, she considered herself different, better than the rest; we called her princess because she behaved like a princess."

Watseka had one white woman friend during her years with Gurdon. He had hired Allen Baxter to farm his eighty acres next to his trading post, and in 1826 Baxter went back to Indiana to return with his bride, the first white woman in what would become Iroquois county. Mrs. Baxter taught Watseka something of white ways, and Watseka aided the young bride through her first years in Illinois. Contrary to Beckwith's history, it was not Gurdon Hubbard who decided to separate from Watseka. She requested it, saying she could not live as a white woman, and she intimated that she was in love with another man. Possibly Watseka acted in belief that their union was not favored by the Indian gods; or she wished to save Gurdon from a life that might result in exile, her ultimate fate.

Throughout his life Hubbard protected the secret of his marriage to an Indian woman until he was directly challenged by Beckwith. According to one "grand nephew", Alfred Holt, he almost killed a blackmailer in Chicago who threatened to disclose his secret on the eve of his third marriage. Throughout his life Gurdon defended the chastity of all Indian women.

Henry Hamilton, the other "grand nephew" who helped with his memoirs, noted that Gurdon wrote in the margin of a book that attacked the virtue of Indian women: "I have never found this conduct; young or old, generally chaste." However Gurdon must have known from the writings of Henry and missionaries, both Catholic and Protestant, that his marginal commentary wasn't entirely so. Promiscuity was widespread among the Indians, as reported by Fathers Membre and Allouez, and the Moravian, David Zeisberger. Allouez did credit the Potawatomis with better behavior than most. Indian sexual mores simply differed from those proclaimed by the whites. Promiscuity was condoned by most nomadic societies that regarded women as property. This Gurdon must have known from experience and as a student of history and Scripture. He often marvelled at the similarity between ancient civilizations and the American Indians and was aware of the accommodation western nomads made to fellow travellers, sharing food, shelter and women. He did not consider polygamy immoral, since it was a practice of tribal people in Scripture. He would one day visit Prophet Joseph Smith, leader of the Mormons, at Nauvoo, Illinois, possibly to inquire about Smith's view of such matters and the assertion that the American Indians were descended from the Biblical Israelites, representing a lost tribe.

*

In the spring of 1826, John Kinzie, still in the fur trade in Chicago while also serving as Indian sub-agent, sent a runner to Gurdon asking him if he would go to St. Louis for supplies, since Kinzie had run out, especially of such necessities as whisky, rum, wines and tobacco. Gurdon agreed. He was almost out of trade goods himself. His available freight canoes were in Chicago, but he arranged to lease a large mackinaw at Peoria and instructed his men, Vasseur and Jacques Portier, to go to Lake Peoria to get the boat ready. For the first time, Noel Vasseur refused to obey an order, saying that the rivers were extremely high and that Portier could not swim. Gurdon demanded that they obey him. "I assured them they did not need to swim as they could head all the streams on the route," he recalled. When this argument failed, he threatened to fire them. "That was the only time they refused to obey my orders," he noted. When Vasseur and Portier finally departed, Hubbard remained at his Iroquois station to complete the building of his new house. "It was a nice, hand-hewn log house, a story-and-a-half high, situated about a half mile north of Bunkum" (later called Concord, but at that time the site of one of Chief Tamin's villages).

The house "had a loft for storage of smoked venison, corn and other supplies, or could be used as a place where children could sleep." He knew that Watseka suspected that she was pregnant. Their new house was on the river, yet high enough to remain clear of spring flooding. It was convenient to his eighty acres of land, which he had pre-empted under existing land laws and soon would own free and clear, and it was close to Watseka's people. When John Hall, an assistant to John Kinzie, arrived to supervise the Iroquois station, Gurdon, taking Jacques Jombeau and another half-breed *voyageur* with him, left to join Vasseur and Portier for the journey to St. Louis. Hall had brought with him an interesting letter from Dr. Wolcott, sent evidently with the knowledge of Kinzie. After a better than usual winter of trading and with the expectation that he could open a Chicago retail store with his son Robert, John Kinzie intended to resign as Indian sub-agent. Wolcott, clearly pleased with this development, intended to offer the job to Hubbard.

"We passed very pleasantly toward Peoria until we reached a small stream on the prairie that had overflowed its banks," Gurdon wrote of his trip. "The upper ice was not strong enough for a man to walk on, but my men lay down and slid themselves across. I rode my horse to the stream and, reaching out with my tomahawk, broke the ice ahead of him." They progressed to the middle of the creek, his horse Croppy walking on the under ice, Gurdon chopping away at the upper crust. Then the horse slipped, the saddle girth broke and Gurdon was pitched between the layers of ice and carried downstream by the swift current. "I made two attempts to regain my feet," he wrote, "but the current was so swift and the space so narrow I could not break through the ice. I had given up all hope when my hand struck a willow branch near the bank." He grasped the willow and held fast. This gave him purchase for another attempt to stand. He reared up, his head breaking through the top ice. "My men," he said, "were much astonished to see me come up through the ice."

Beyond such travel difficulties the St. Louis trip was relatively placid and uneventful. Gurdon was astonished by the growth of the town. Shipping thronged the riverfront though it was March. Many of the big Missouri mackinaws had arrived from the north, joining the Ohio keelboats and the flatboats, loaded with pigs or logs that had negotiated the flooded southern streams, bringing urgently needed supplies for the boom town. Huge brick and stone buildings were under construction, vast warehouses and docks stretched along the riverfront. When they docked, among flatboats loaded with squealing pigs and bawling cattle and piers piled high with logs and lumber, furs, cotton bales, casks of whisky, bags of corn and crates of Kentucky tobacco, Gurdon was told that St. Louis had become a city of 5,000.

Crowds of men were in the streets, not only the trappers and hunters he had seen eight years earlier, but scores of farmers in denim and dirty boots, in town to sell the last of their stores of corn and potatoes. He remembered the waterfront of Montreal and saw that St. Louis now had visitors from Europe, too, mostly Germans he thought, and farmers and planters from the southern states, in a few cases travelling with their black slaves. Missouri was in a frenzy of settlement, especially by planters from the south, who felt reassured by the second Missouri Compromise that Missouri would remain unrestricted as to slavery. Gurdon and his men slept aboard their mackinaw since the town's inns were filled. He called on Pierre Chouteau, Jr. and promised to consider his offer of a fur station on the Missouri, a new one deep in the Dakota Indian territory. "It has been named Pierre for my father, not for me," Chouteau said.

Gurdon wrote his mother from St. Louis, mentioning the offer from Chouteau, without discussing the considerations that might take him further into the Indian country. "I cannot come to see you this summer," he said. "I know you would not want me to endanger the prospects I must consider at this time." He endlessly made excuses to his mother, it appeared, but it was a spring and summer of decision for him. He knew that the fur trade was changing. It was Chouteau, not Astor who was winning the battle for monopoly of the Indian trade in the Mississippi Valley.

The Indian trade was in fact dying in the country east of the Mississippi. There were fewer Indians, fewer animals to be taken and less demand in England and elsewhere for beaver, bear or even marten pelts. "What is happening here and in Europe affects our trade," Gurdon wrote. He may have been aware that the British hatters were finding substitutes in the manufacture of beaver hats exported and sold throughout the world. There were those in England who refused to buy such hats made of beaver when it was disclosed that arsenic used as a stiffening agent caused insanity among workers who shaped the hats, the phrase "mad as a hatter" becoming widely used. Whatever the reason, British and French importers no longer vied for beaver pelts, bearskins declined in popularity, and the English used buffalo hides, rather than deerskins, for shoes. Marten continued in demand for ornamentation of the very rich, including the emperor and nobility of China, and buffalo robes and coats were popular. But generally, heating stoves and better windows for houses made furs less attractive as a means of keeping warm indoors. Gurdon had been considering the possibility of opening a "white goods store" somewhere near his Iroquois post to supply the settlers. In St. Louis he saw that English textiles, crockery and glass for windows were widely available at reasonable prices. The price of bearskins had dropped to $1.60, but a buffalo skin brought $4. The German shoemakers in St. Louis also had found that buffalo skin was better than deerskin for shoes, Chouteau told him. Thus Chouteau's western trading posts would offer great opportunity. He expected a shoe and leather industry to grow rapidly in St. Louis and he intended to supply that market. Buffalo, Chouteau needlessly pointed out, could now be found only in the west.

The opportunity to go with Chouteau, the cheerful, ambitious son of one of St. Louis' first families, tempted Gurdon, but, he confided to his mother, Dr. Wolcott had offered an opportunity also in Chicago. John Kinzie was making a comeback in the fur and silver business and intended to resign his post as sub-Indian agent. If Gurdon was interested, Wolcott said, he could have the job. "It would pay only $500 a year," Gurdon told Abigail, "but I could engage in other activity not inconsistent with the post."

*

In Cahokia, still a sleepy village, Gurdon saw his friend John Reynolds, who had himself passed up St. Louis opportunities to go into Illinois politics, winning election to the legislature. He spoke with Reynolds about his problem of planning a future, suggesting that Chicago could become a boom town like St. Louis if a canal should be built there.

"Of course a canal should be built," Reynolds said. "We have discussed it at Vandalia. It will be up to the State of Illinois to push the federal government into it. You say you discussed it with Pierre Chouteau and found no interest. What did you expect? Chouteau is interested only in the growth of St. Louis, where he will soon dominate the fur trade and where he is making a fortune selling St. Louis land at ten-fold profit. Illinois needs a canal, and that could benefit St. Louis, but Chouteau fears otherwise. Perhaps our canal would extend from the Wabash to the Mississippi, by way of the Illinois. That leaves out Chicago, of course, but, keep this in mind: Chicago may be taken from us by the people of Wisconsin, they want to seize the top tier of Illinois counties! They could succeed. We could build a canal from the Calumet to the Illinois River, and thus hold the northern territory. I want to be sure we have an Illinois ditch."

"The short way is from the south branch of the Chicago River to the Desplaines," Gurdon said. "I know all the routes well. If you should have the eastern terminus on the Calumet it would be on the Indiana border. Wouldn't Indiana get the most benefit of that? Joliet and Marquette and the Indians all used the short route because it's best. Joliet proposed a canal there."

"Joliet didn't have to dig it."

"The digging would be through rock there," Gurdon agreed. "But you can use the rock to build the canal. M. Deschamps says they found much rock digging the Erie. Get the Erie diggers. The Erie is already a success. Now we can ship our furs directly from Chicago to New York City by way of Buffalo and the Erie canal."

"We can get the Erie diggers, those who know how to go through hard rock," Reynolds said. "What we need to get is money. That is what's hard to come by. We are authorizing a study of this in the legislature. Vandalia is not far from your Iroquois country. I'll have a committeeman talk to you. Better yet, get into the legislature yourself."

"How could I do that?"

"You say you are thinking of a store in Danville. Get it going. That could be a better bet than Chicago. First chance, run for the legislature. What's your party?"

"The party of Henry Clay."

"Good! I see you know something of what's going on in Washington. Only Clay will help us to get our roads and waterways. Since you are such a friend of Kinzie, I thought you might be a Jacksonian . . . Old Hickory, man of the frontier . . . my party . . . but Old Andy don't know our need out here for internal improvements."

"John Kinzie is for Governor Lewis Cass for president," Gurdon said. "His son John has become the governor's secretary and Indian expert."

"Party don't matter that much in the legislature. We all must be for roads and river and harbor improvements, such as a harbor at Chicago. When we were fixing to mark a state road, and we saw that there was a Hubbard Trail, I couldn't believe it was you doing that, a mere boy when I met you here . . . when was it?. . . . How old are you anyway?"

"I'm twenty-three," Gurdon said. "My wife is a Potawatomi woman. What does that mean, running for the legislature?"

"Jesus Christ!" Reynolds exclaimed. "Why did you have to do that?"

"I love her. She is my wife. She is going to have my child."

"Well," Reynolds said, "I don't know what that might do in politics. I don't think anybody around here has ever tried it. Even so, I'll have that committeeman see you . . . and I want to see you when I get to Vandalia. Your Indian girl must be some woman! Gurdon, I intend to help you if I can."

*

Watseka remained stubborn in her refusal to go to Chicago and Mackinaw with her husband that spring. "This is not the time," she told him, speaking always in Potawatomi, though she used both English and French as well as Indian dialects when she helped out in the company store. "I will be well here. You will be back in time, my husband."

"I will bring you many presents," he promised.

"Some silver only," she said. Like all women of her nation, she covered herself with bracelets, necklaces, bells, buckles and silver bangles on occasion. "Bring a gift from Mackinaw for our son."

*

At Chicago in June he found he could indeed have the opportunity he sought there if he wished. John Kinzie appeared to have come to an end of his bad times in the fur trade, but he was weary and ill. He had moved his family into the comfort of the Agency House since his "mansion" next door had fallen into ruin despite efforts to save it. But he still had no liking for a bureaucrat's job. He preferred to quit the government and rely on the fur trade once more. Dr. Wolcott, the Indian agent, had married daughter Ellen, son John had joined the staff of Governor Cass, daughter Margaret was the wife of an officer, and little Maria had grown up and was being courted by Lt. David Hunter. "I can't have everybody in the the family working for the government," Kinzie said. "The sub-agency job is yours if you want it. Talk to Doc Wolcott." Dr. Wolcott, much pleased at this, reminded Gurdon that the sub-agency appointment for him was his own idea in the first place. He promised Gurdon he would have it as soon as his father-in-law actually had quit. Gurdon wrote his mother of these developments while yet in Chicago, saying that he was embarking for Mackinaw Island. On the day he was leaving Chicago, Dr. Wolcott, much agitated, found him at the dock. John Kinzie had come to tell him he had changed his mind about resigning as sub-agent. He gave no reason for his abrupt reversal. "He had submitted his resignation to Washington," Dr. Wolcott said. "I can't believe he'll now be permitted to stay on. But if he is, if he is permitted to withdraw his resignation, there is nothing I can do. I'm sorry." Wolcott handed him a letter from Mr. Crooks, which had arrived in his mail pouch that day. It told Gurdon that his sister Elizabeth was on her way to Mackinaw with Mr. and Mrs. Crooks and that they had invited her to stay with them for the summer.

On his arrival at Mackinaw, Gurdon completed the letter to his mother. He now bitterly denounced John Kinzie, Sr. for his vacillation. "He has forced me to change my plans," he wrote. "I am now going to go directly to Mr. Astor to see if I can get approval for the opening of a retail store in Danville. If I can succeed in doing so, I will have you and the girls come to Danville to live. Maybe I will open a store in Chicago. I do not need to worry any more about not competing with Mr. Kinzie." After a tearful meeting with Elizabeth, his favorite sister who had grown to womanhood while he was away, Gurdon gave her his letter, instructing her to write a few words quickly, since the schooner was about to leave:

My Dear Mother,

Gurdon brought his letter to add a post-script. I am in haste and have not much time to write. I was very much surprised at seeing him for I looked for the vessel as we went to Sunday School & it was not in sight but on our return the vessel was anchored and Gurdon came immediately to shore.

I suppose you would like a description of him. He is hardly as tall as Christopher or rather stouter which makes him appear so. Black hair & eyes and somewhat sunburned but not an Indian by a great deal and not as awkward as I expected to find him. He has concluded not to go to Middletown as I am here.

Love to all friends tell the girls they must write

in haste your affectionate daughter
Elizabeth

Gurdon directly proposed to John Jacob Astor, with the approval of both Crooks and Stuart evidently, that the company get into the business of selling at retail to the white settlers. His letter was receiving favorable consideration, Mr. Crooks told him. Several "inland" stores might be possible, serving farmers and agricultural towns. He surely would be authorized to start such a store at Danville and thus was permitted to buy goods as an experiment. Elizabeth was working for Mr. and Mrs.

Crooks through the summer at Mackinaw, but Gurdon departed early with Vasseur. He reduced the Illinois Brigade to five *batteaux,* each capable of ten tons, and shipped the remainder of his inventory via schooner to Chicago. They again coasted Lake Michigan, dropping some of their freight on the St. Joseph for portage to the Kankakee; the boats then carried the remaining cargo to Chicago and remained there for lighterage duty.

At Chicago Dr. Wolcott sought to explain John Kinzie's change of mind about resigning. "He has been in ill health," Wolcott said. "He didn't feel he could give up the comfort of the Agency House to find another place. He is a relatively poor man, Gurdon; he has many acres of Chicago land, but John and Robert and I fear most are valueless."

"The land will have great value if a canal is built here," Gurdon said. "Think of what is happening at St. Louis. I really never expected to get the sub-agency job anyway, but I'm glad you offered it. I believe I'm supposed to go into business for myself."

Somewhat reluctantly, he rode out to Big Foot's town to buy fifty Indian ponies. Shabona raised a few ponies, only for his family. Gurdon believed Big Foot to be a potential trouble maker, but he was the sole source of supply. He also hired Indians to help his *voyageurs* with the pack trains into southern Illinois. If the Indians couldn't trap and wouldn't farm, he felt they ought to be given a chance at other work. He called on Eleanor Kinzie and her family, choosing a time he knew John would be away. The silver gifts he took south for Watseka had been purchased at Mackinaw, not from Kinzie's silver shop.

*

Watseka was big with child but in excellent health and eager to join him in walks and short hunting expeditions and canoe trips on the river and Sugar Creek. The days were warm, the maples glowed with color, the nearby prairie acres of Gurdon's farm a sea of tawny grass and lavender and yellow flowers. His men fenced a pasture for the pack horses. Baxter, his farmer, had planted plum trees and cleared a plot of ground for corn. Watseka said she had made herself strong helping Baxter and his wife cultivate the corn that summer. On Gurdon's arrival,

Baxter inspected the new steel-shod plow he fetched from Mackinaw, then announced he would break five acres of prairie the following spring. "Git me a team of cattle and I'll make it five acres sure, maybe ten," Baxter urged.

"You can go for the oxen yourself," Gurdon said. "Take Mrs. Baxter back to visit the folks in Indiana. Watseka and I will take care of things here."

He was happy and content once more, having settled the decisions for their future. He and Watseka could live at the Iroquois River Station and rear their children there as long as the fur trade lasted and they could stay on as farmers thereafter. He would get more land. Chief Shabona had been urging the Indians to farm, as he was doing, and some were responding. The Delawares in the area were experienced farmers, taught long ago by the missionaries, and were good at it. Gurdon offered Watseka the alternative of going with him to Danville where he would build the store or remaining at the Iroquois post until their baby was born. He knew what her answer would be. He would come out to the station often. He was glad to be alone in Danville to concentrate on the problems of the store. Dan Beckwith saw what he was doing, erecting a structure of hand-hewn logs, with puncheon doors and siding, and ordered a building like it, plus a house which he said he would rent to a doctor interested in moving to Danville.

In late October Gurdon was back in Chicago, where he expected a cargo of trade goods for the new store. He had not reconciled with John Kinzie, he wrote Abigail and Elizabeth, but he sent greetings from the Wolcotts and Eleanor Kinzie. "Doc Wolcott seems to be quite mortified at Mr. Kinzie's decision to have the agency job continued to him," he wrote. "He does not seem to be aware of the offense to me. Doc Wolcott thinks it will be entirely impossible for him to continue holding it after once resigning." But Gurdon no longer expected to go to Chicago.

*

His white trade goods did not arrive, only more goods for trappers. He left Chicago disappointed, travelling alone since he in-

217

tended to hunt on the Kankakee marshes to replenish the food supplies at home. Squaw winter came early and was severe, alternating cold and snow, thaws and floods. Game was scarce. By night the wolves howled and the panthers screamed in frustration. The Indians were reduced to eating possum and ground hogs, as well as some of their dogs. Gurdon carried to the hunting camps supplies he could pack in his small canoe, mostly gun powder, shot and traps, and made camp *voyageur* fashion, on an island among the drowned lowlands during a thaw, building a driftwood fire. In the night he awoke in an agony of painful joints and fever, replenished the fire, and slept again.

By morning the pain in his legs was so intense he could not make his way to his canoe, but fell short of it. An Indian hunter found him, placed him in the canoe, took him to the lake shore, about a day's march from the Iroquois Station, and agreed to go to the trading post for help, to include a horse and harness. Gurdon hoped that the tough little canoe could withstand dragging across the barren, rock-strewn land covered with patches of ice and snow. When his men arrived they tried it, but he found he could not stand the pain of being jostled in the canoe. It was a repetition of the malady that had struck him earlier, and again he feared he could die from it.

He wrote later:

"I sent back to Iroquois for two more men, which necessitated my camping for another night. On their arrival they constructed with poles and a blanket a litter on which they bore me safely and quite comfortably home. I had a severe attack of inflammatory rheumatism, which confined me to the house for three or four weeks, and from which I did not fully recover for 18 months. I doctored myself with poultices of elm and decoctions of various herbs."

Gurdon did not mention his wife in recounting his experience. However, Watseka, like all Indian women, knew well the remedies for rheumatism, a common ailment among the Indians and all who lived much of their time without shelter in the wilderness. Zeisberger found the Delawares using as many as twenty different roots in obtaining relief and sometimes total cure. The Potawatomis also had bathhouses where they sweated away miseries. Watseka accomplished the same for her husband by dropping hot stones into leather buckets of water and covering the steaming water and the patient with blankets. There was no doctor nearer than St. Louis, since the surgeon at Fort Dearborn had departed with the garrison, and none had yet arrived at Danville. Gurdon evidently was unaware that Dr. Wolcott was a medical doctor. He refused to allow Chief Tamin's shaman, or medicine man, to visit him, wisely without much doubt, since Zeisberger, after living long among the tribes, called the medicine men charlatans. The Indians were generally poor nurses, Zeisberger also said, but Watseka cared for her husband solicitously, applying their mutual knowledge of treatment by roots, herbs and berries.

Despite his suffering, Gurdon had a happy time with Watseka those weeks, teaching her English, reading to her from his Bible, demonstrating his own cooking skills when he felt better. Watseka told him of her religion. *Chibiabos* and *Wiske* ruled the spirit world, under guidance of the Gitche Manitou, the Great Spirit. It was *Wiske* who gave them their foodstuffs, pumpkins, squash and corn, and also tobacco. He ruled over the helpful *manidogs,* or spirits, while *Keganzi,* the great fish with horns, led the evil ones. The shamans spoke the language of the spirits, propitiated them, obtained their help in times of trouble. There were also *Chasgied,* spirits to be called upon in times of illness, and the *Wabenos,* who controlled weather and crops, sometimes appearing as fireballs; when angry they sent bolts of lightning to fire the dry prairies. That winter, in the final days of Watseka's pregnancy, Gurdon made furniture, snowshoes and canoe paddles, and directed the pressing of incoming furs on the equipment he had brought from Mackinaw, while Watseka fashioned a cradle board of hickory bark, lining it with soft furry rabbit skins, and gathered into cedar bags the spagnum moss she would use to diaper her child. She also sewed beaded garments of deerskin, using deer tendons frayed into thread, and sturdy moccasins of buffalo hide for her husband. She kept from him her fear that the child she was carrying had become exceptionally quiet.

When her pains began and continued long without further sign that the child was soon to arrive, Gurdon hobbled from his lodge to the village to find Monoska, who angrily upbraided him for not coming sooner. Monoska went at once to the house with collections of besons and charms and two shamans, whom Gurdon ordered out. Watseka pleaded that they should stay. He remembered Alexander Henry's account of an Indian woman in bad labor whose father had gone into the woods, killed a snake, let its blood flow into a gourd cup, then supplied the blood to a shaman who rubbed it on the woman's thighs. Her anguish soon eased and the baby was successfully born. Gurdon then touched Watseka gently, saying the shamans could stay, and walked into the winter night to the store. He was there, pacing painfully before the fire, hours later when Monoska came to him, bringing Chief Tamin along for his comfort. The child had been born dead, a son, she told him. Watseka was doing well now. Vasseur would help to place the infant on its burial scaffold in the woods until Gurdon arranged the burial ceremony. None was required if he so chose, Tamin told him.

"I will go to Watseka and follow her wishes," he answered. Watseka took his hand and told him her wish. He must release a spirit to guide the wandering spirit of their child, not yet ready for life on earth. Against Tamin's protest that he was too unwell, Gurdon left early with Vasseur, who led him to a bend in the river where he had seen huge whooping cranes, there strangely in mid-winter, clearly for a purpose. Gurdon shot a large crane, still waiting in the snow, releasing its spirit to find and guide the spirit of his child to *Chibiabos,* who would guide it to heaven. He again shook with ague, his bones ached, but he was grimly satisfied when he returned to the cabin to tell Watseka what had been done. They marvelled that the crane had been sent to them.

"It was known to *Chibiabos* that our child was to be called back," she told him. "There will be other sons, my husband."

That night Chief Waba, informed of the death of the child by Vasseur's runner, rode in to the Iroquois Station to join them for a brief ceremony, one not usual for a stillborn child. In the darkness of the lodge, Waba prayed to the spirit of the crane and to *Chibiabos* assuring them his prayer had been heard and that the spirit of the child was in good care. Gurdon relighted the fire and the candles and Monoska set out venison, parched corn, and baked turkey, hot corn soup and ceremonial cups of

220

rum. Watseka was grateful that her husband had gone beyond the requirements of religion for their child.

*

The winter continued severe, the worst in half a century, it was said. Game was scarce. The trouble had been caused when the annual prairie fires spread into the timbered land and the dry marshes along the streams in the year of drought, killing game and clearing the way for spring floods. By planting time, after the exceptional winter, Indians and settlers alike were in an ugly mood, each blaming the other for their troubles. Yet the immigrants continued to arrive, by wagon train, on ponies, even afoot. All wanted Indian land for farming. The fame of the rich black soil of Illinois somehow had become known beyond America, all the way to Yorkshire and Normandy and Bavaria, and the farmers of Europe came when they could make it; came to the southern Illinois country ignorant of the problems of the frontier and the burned-out prairie, which would bloom gloriously once more in spring, over a root structure tough as thongs of buffalo hide and impervious to an ordinary wooden plow. The softer land along the streams, land long claimed by the Indians, was coveted.

Following his recovery, Gurdon hunted again, sometimes on snowshoes, as the famine worsened. When spring arrived, the Indian women dug for green dragon and dogtooth violet bulbs for food, hunted toothwort and skunk cabbage, and mashed roots to feed their children so they could use remaining corn for seed. The newly arrived settlers, who had no iron shod plow or yoke of oxen, found they could not break the prairie sod. A few began their own gardens in small clearings using seed Hubbard supplied to them. None entered the Iroquois River area, but they were thick about Danville and they patronized Gurdon's new, one-room store, most buying on credit he allowed them. His letter to Elizabeth, written from Danville, Vermilion County, April 5, 1827 was cheerful and somewhat optimistic:

Dear Sister

I had the pleasure a few days ago of receiving your letter, which was the first since we parted, but as I have neglected

221

writing you this winter past I therefore cannot reproach you. I have been verry unsuccessful in trade this winter. I intend to spend a week at this place to recreate my spirits and then to Chicago as fast as oars and wind will carry me. . . I am glad you have succeeded in forming a society though I doubt it will be of much help or profit to the missionaries, but (I hope) you will find pleasure at your Episcopal parties. As regard to my shirts I shall be glad to have you send them to me at your convenience. I have been tormented for a month (this winter) with rheumatism so bad I could not walk without crutches, caused by exposing myself so much in the Indian trade. I am determined to quit it, let the consequences be what they may and nothing but sickness or death will prevent me from visiting Middletown in the fall. I beg you to excuse the imperfections of this letter but the mail is waiting. I beg mother to take care of her health.

Your affectionate brother
G.S. Hubbard

P.S. Your advice on love matters comes too late. I have felt the sensations of Love and my heart is so warm that it cannot be! I am subdued! Suffocated! Enthralled in the chains of Love. Amen.

8

Danville, July, 1827

I will say here that a better man than Mr. Hubbard could not have been sent to our people. He was well known to all the settlers. His generosity, his quiet, determined courage, and his integrity were so well known and appreciated that he had the confidence and good-will of everybody, and was a well-recognized leader among the pioneers.

Hezekiah Cunningham to Hiram Beckwith
The Winnebago War

At the breaking out of the Winnebago War in July, 1827, Fort Dearborn was without military occupation.

Gurdon S. Hubbard
Fergus Historical Series

Hubbard returned to Chicago briefly that spring, confirmed what he already knew by letter from Dr. Wolcott, that Kinzie would not be required to give up his appointment as Indian sub-agent, then went on to Mackinaw by the schooner *Chicago Packet,* which carried most of the winter's harvest of furs. To Noel Vasseur he assigned the duty of *Le Bourgeois* of the Illinois Brigade, instructing him to transport the rest of the cargo and to bring in the *voyageurs* for their island duties. Vasseur himself was to remain at Mackinaw for the summer as Hubbard's representative in the fur warehouse, sorting and counting the Illinois fur collections. There Vasseur followed Gurdon's practice of studying the parish records and, with the aid of a priest, discovered his family name to be Le Vasseur, that he was born in southern Canada in 1798 and had been sent to Mackinac Island by the Hudson Bay Company in 1816. Thereafter he proudly bore the name of Noel Le Vasseur.

Gurdon learned that summer of the many changes contemplated for the American Fur Company. John Jacob Astor was planning to retire from the fur trade to devote himself to his real estate interests which, it was reported, had made him the wealthiest man in America. Ramsey Crooks was to go to New York to become president of American Fur, but meantime he had been negotiating with Pierre Chouteau at St. Louis for the sale of the Astor fur interests east of the Mississippi and south of the Michigan and Wisconsin territories. So Chouteau had a special reason for offering Gurdon Hubbard a job. If he had removed the superintendent of the Illinois posts from Astor's ranks, he could have weakened the company and lowered his bid. So Gurdon believed. He concluded he must look out for himself after such experiences with Chouteau and John Kinzie. He made his own bid for the Illinois territory and he found that Crooks and Stuart were interested. He knew the fur trade was in decline. The Indian tribes would be inevitably pushed west of the Mississippi. Crooks and Stuart had in fact written off the Illinois territory and their discussions with Chouteau were not progressing well.

Thus in the late spring of 1827, while he was twenty-four, Gurdon S. Hubbard became the owner of an American Fur Company franchise in Illinois. Crooks and Stuart set out to shore up the company operations to the north. Gurdon left early in June for Chicago where he knew he would have the cooperation of Dr. Wolcott in expanding his quarters and warehousing facilities at the fort. He prepared to handle the increasing amount of freight he expected at Chicago, since the *Chicago Packet* and other vessels would be calling there regularly. He was optimistic about his future when he wrote his sister Elizabeth. His fur properties were not much, he admitted, a few log cabins scattered along the rivers, a cluster of mackinaw boats at Chicago, and a half hundred Indian ponies. But also there was his new store at Danville, for which he would now have the proper trade goods, and his eighty acres of land at the Iroquois River Station. He had received liberal credits from the American Fur Company and estimated his stock of new white goods would be worth $8,000. He instructed his family to henceforth send mail directly to Danville, Vermilion county, Illinois, via Terre Haute.

He found Watseka happily employed at the many tasks of an Indian woman and in the Iroquois post store, where Vasseur's son, Antoine, assisted her. She was again pregnant. He had urged her to hire a girl to aid her at home, but she stubbornly refused. She was cultivating corn on his return and she sought to help him carry the game and packs he brought from Mackinaw and the Kankakee marshes, saying it was a woman's duty. She was pleased with the necklaces, bracelets, Mackinaw candy and fine Stroud cloth and white women's dresses he brought her. She was equally proud of the vegetables and herbs she could serve him from her garden. It was a fine reunion, they saw no one for days, and they planned a hunting trip together. But when he spoke to her of plans for life in Danville, she showed little interest. She carefully packed away the gowns he had brought from Mackinaw and wore a dress woven from the hair of buffalo, her deerskin leggings, stained with dyes gathered on the Vermilion, ornamented with porcupine quills, and the moccasins she herself had beaded.

So Gurdon went alone to Danville to stock his store and to add to it a living space, to confer with Dan Beckwith about the new buildings he wished built in his town of Danville, and to join the Vermilion County Battalion of Militia, which elected Achilles Morgan its captain, and Gurdon S. Hubbard, lieutenant in command of mounted rangers. "I have two orders for houses when I finish the store," he wrote his mother exultantly. "They don't worry much about architectural style around here."

There were rumbles of trouble early that summer. The desperate attempt of the whites to hunt and trap the prior winter had not added much to the fur harvest but it upset the Indians. In the spring the settlers discovered they could not break the tough prairie unless they had a steel shod plow and a yoke of oxen, which few could afford. Consequently they sought to move into lands along the rivers and creeks where the rich soil long had been cultivated by the Indians. The first whites in the Danville area had come from Indian country to the south and were experienced in dealing with redskins. Recent newcomers from the eastern seaboard and Europe were ignorant of Indian ways, feared them, but were no less determined to acquire Indian land. A few were ready to buy, so long as they could trade whisky for it.

By July there had been many rumors of Indian uprisings planned. The settlers became frightened, some to the point of panic. Hubbard received reports regularly from his agents along the rivers and from the villages of Waba, Shabona and Tamin. They indicated general dissatisfaction with treaties and annuities and acute unrest in the north and west, along the Illinois River and especially in the Lake Peoria area. There were also disquieting reports from the Sangamon River territory, where incoming Anglo-Saxons had supplanted the French. He made a quick trip to the Opa post and at Peoria saw Thomas Forsyth, half-brother of John Kinzie and Kinzie's long-time partner in the Indian trade. "The newcomers are causing the problems," Forsyth said. "I have told John and Doc Wolcott about this. They trade whisky for furs and for rights of lands the Indians don't individually own. It is truly shameful that such quantities of liquor are sold and traded among the Indians, all along this river. Almost every settler's home is a grog shop. But traders will get the blame for it if trouble comes."

James Latham, the government's sub-agent for Indian affairs at Peoria, agreed with Forsyth. He had been working with Chief Shabona in an attempt to reduce the liquor traffic. The result had been that the new white settlers banded together to demand that Latham be removed from his job. "They want all the land," Latham said bitterly. "They accuse the Potawatomis of stealing horses and killing hogs. These new people coming in have got no sense. They have gone into the Indian hunting grounds and encroached on Indian farms. Some of them are going to get themselves killed."

In August Gurdon went to Chicago, where the Indians were assembling for treaty payments, to discuss the situation with Shabona, Wolcott, Kinzie and Billy Caldwell. He feared that an incident could cause real trouble, like the lightning touching off a prairie fire in a dry summer. It was time for responsible whites to damp down the embers of resentment among the tribes. Few whites understood the limitations of the treaties opening up Indian lands. There were government laws to be obeyed, Indian rights to be respected. Most of the tribes owned land in common, an Indian rarely could claim a plot of ground to himself. When a man died, his weapons, clothing and ornaments were buried with him for his needs in the next world, the remainder of his belongings were divided among kin and friends. He did not own land. That was given by the Great Spirit to all Indians, as were the clouds, the sky, the lakes and oceans. Tecumseh and Little Turtle had sought unsuccessfully to make the white man understand. The white scramble for Indian land after the War of 1812 brought gnawing fear to the tribes. Gurdon wondered what Black Hawk might be doing.

*

When he reached Chicago, Gurdon shook hands with John Kinzie in an unspoken truce. Kinzie was worried, as was Dr. Wolcott, who planned to report to Washington in the course of his vacation trip east, to follow immediately after the payment of annuity monies. They too had heard reports of troubles in the north, near Galena, and along the Mississippi, where the Winnebagos announced they intended to continue to levy tolls on white shipping, including the vessels supplying forts in Minnesota. In the Chicago area, and in some part of the territory to the south, the tribes remained friendly. Wolcott and Kinzie did not doubt the loyalty of Shabona, Alexander Robinson (Chechepinqua), Billy Caldwell, Waba or Tamin. A few miles to the north, Chief Mawgehset, known to whites as Big Foot, ruled a tribe of Potawatomis and Winnebagos strongly antagonistic to the whites. Immediately to the south was Yellow Head, who hated all whites, and especially Gurdon Hubbard; Black Hawk, to the west, had for years been seeking to unite the Indians for war; the Sioux might return. The Chicago pioneers suspected what a respected historian of the Potawatomis, R. David Edmunds, would document many years later. "Big Foot met secretly with the other chiefs (in the Chicago area) and presented them with an invitation from the Winnebagos and the Sioux to join in a war against the Long Knives," Edmunds would write. Big Foot had held his secret meeting the week of the August treaty payments. Representatives of the Potawatomis south of Chicago attended the council but refused the Winnebago war belts, Edmunds found: "They were strongly influenced by Shabona and returned to their camp south of the river." In Chicago itself Chiefs Robinson and Caldwell "urged their people to refrain from joining in the Winnebago plot." The warning letters from Wolcott and Kinzie survive in the National Archives.

The Potawatomis, "my prairie people," Dr. Wolcott called them, gathered for their annuity payments. Since many of Big Foot's people were Potawatomis, they also were present and it did not attract particular attention when Big Foot left some of his Winnebagos in town after he departed on a trip west to see Black Hawk and the Sioux. Dr. Wolcott and the government representatives in Chicago for the payments left soon after Gurdon arrived. Wolcott had heard that Governor Cass of Michigan Territory, which until 1825 had included Chicago, was enroute to Green Bay for the Winnebago payments. He undoubtedly would look into reports of unrest there.

Gurdon was invited to stop with the Kinzies, as in the past. Robert and Maria were at home and Mrs. Margaret Helm had returned to visit her family. Whether any of them attended the dance at the fort the night following the annuity payments, Gurdon did not say in his account of the events of that night and the succeeding days written in a letter to his mother, dated August 25, 1827.

"The night following the payment of the annuities there was a dance in the soldiers' barracks, not then occupied by the soldiers, during the progress of which a violent storm of wind and rain arose. About midnight those quarters were struck by lightning and totally consumed. . . ." Gurdon was asleep in the Kinzie home when the storm hit. He awakened when he heard a cry of "Fire!" and realized it was Margaret Helm calling out. She had been awakened by the storm, then saw the flames from her window and assumed that Indians had once again attacked Fort Dearborn.

Gurdon dashed from his room, briefly comforted Margaret, then called Robert and John Kinzie and ran to the river "only partially dressed." He found the Kinzie canoe, drawn up on the river bank, was half filled with water. He shouted to Robert to bring help and buckets. Then he swam the river, to find that Winnebagos were at the north gate of the fort, sullenly watching the flames, yet making no move to force the gate open. He remembered the burning fort on Lake Peoria years before, though this time there was no war dance. Like Antoine Deschamps at Fort Clark, Gurdon did not hesitate to advance upon the Indians to demand an explanation. He did not at the time know the cause of the fire. The Winnebagos merely glared at him and turned back to watch the flames. While they obviously had not started the fire, they also were doing nothing to help save the fort.

Gurdon shouted to those inside the palisade, many of them his own men, to open the gate. Robert Kinzie had also swum the river after summoning help. He now joined Gurdon at the gate. John Kinzie and others soon crossed in the Kinzie canoe, bringing buckets and wash tubs. The north gate swung open and Gurdon ordered the men at hand to join the Kinzies in a bucket brigade. He and Robert entered the palisade. "We saw the situation at a glance. The barracks and storehouse being wrapped in flames, we directed our energies to the saving of the guardhouse, the east end of which was on fire. Mr. Kinzie (Robert) rolling himself in a blanket, got up on the roof. The men and women, about forty in number, formed a line to the river, and with buckets, tubs and every available utensil, passed the water to him; this was kept up until daylight, Mr. Kinzie maintaining his position with great fortitude, though his hands, face and portions of his body were severely burned."

*

The behavior of Big Foot's braves on the occasion of the fire frightened the townspeople, including the Kinzies. The Winnebagos had remained in Chicago after the annuity payments for a purpose, it was said. Some believed the Indians started the blaze in order to observe the reaction of those within the fort and in the town. The threat of the presence of the Indians near the gate had kept those inside from opening it and calling for help in time to save more of the buildings. "The strangeness of their behavior was the subject of discussion among us," Gurdon recalled. Big Foot's warriors had, at the least, discovered that there had been no one inside the fort willing and able to defend it, even from fire.

Within the week, Hubbard and the Kinzies received the jolting news that the Winnebagos were on the warpath in Wisconsin, following their heavy loss of men in an attack on a government supply boat on the Mississippi near Prairie du Chien. The news came from Governor Lewis Cass himself.

"While at breakfast at Mr. Kinzie's house, we heard singing, faintly at first. . . ." Gurdon recalled. "Mr. John Kinzie recognized the leading voice as that of Bob Forsyth." They soon saw a birch bark canoe, manned by thirteen *voyageurs,* keeping time to a Canadian boat song as they paddled. It bore Governor Cass of Michigan, who also was superintendent of Indian affairs for the government, and his secretary Robert Forsyth, though not Kinzie's own son John, also a Cass aide. "From them we first learned of the breaking out of the Winnebago war, and the details of the massacre on the Upper Mississippi," Gurdon wrote. The army supply boat had been drilled with bullet holes, two soldiers and fourteen Indians had been killed, and many were wounded. Cass had arrived at Green Bay for a treaty council with the Winnebago and Menomonee tribes, but the Indians failed to meet him as scheduled. Hearing that hostilities already had started, Cass "procured a light, birch bark canoe made purposely for speed," portaged into the Wisconsin and within days had passed into the Mississippi and on south of St. Louis to Jefferson Barracks, the Missouri army base. There he arranged for soldiers to move north by steamer. He left this contingent at the Illinois River, came up the Desplaines, and crossed the Chicago Portage to warn the Chicagoans of the danger. "This trip from Green Bay was performed in about thirteen days, the Governor's party sleeping only about five to seven hours, and averaging sixty to seventy miles a day," Gurdon marvelled. "They passed several Winnebago camps without difficulty, since they did not stop to parley, but passed by rapidly, singing their boat songs. The Indians were so taken by surprise that before they recovered the canoe was out of danger."

Governor Cass quickly convinced the Kinzies and Gurdon Hubbard that the danger was great. A council with the Potawatomi chiefs in the area was arranged. "They acknowledged that messages had been sent to them by the Winnebagos, but assured us of their friendship," Gurdon said in the letter to his mother dated August 25, in which he urged her not to worry about the dire reports of the Winnebago uprising she might read in the newspapers. "The Governor left here yesterday for Green Bay," he wrote. "He will send a company of troops on here immediately to take possession of this fort. We expect them in twenty days. I will not leave here until I see my friends out of danger. You shall hear from me again shortly, in the meantime do not be uneasy as to my safety. We have vigilant scouts out, and get notice of any party of Indians before they could surprise us, although I do not think . . . they will make the attempt."

Gurdon was much less sanguine about the safety of Chicago than he admitted. Nor did he disclose to his mother that he had volunteered to ride that night through one hundred and twenty-five miles of potentially hostile country inhabited by Indians but no whites to his Iroquois River Station and on into Vermilion county, where he hoped to induce Captain Morgan and his militiamen to come to the defense of Chicago, pending the time government troops promised by Governor Cass might arrive. There had been a consultation at Fort Dearborn earlier that day. No government official remained in Chicago except the Indian sub-agent, John Kinzie, unless it might be Archibald Clybourne, a former butcher at Fort Dearborn, who had been named Chicago constable by the Peoria County Court in June, 1825. Peoria had become the county seat for Chicago, supplanting Detroit. The conferees at the fort concluded that the Winnebago threat was a federal matter. Thus Kinzie was the ranking man present. Not a single soldier was stationed at the fort, even Wolcott the caretaker was away. It was agreed that a militia should be organized.

"In our consultation I suggested sending to the Wabash country for assistance, and tendered my services as a messenger," Gurdon recalled. "This was first objected to, on the ground that the majority of the men at the fort were in my employ, and, in case of an attack, no one could enforce their aid or manage them but myself. It was decided, however, that I should go, as I knew the route and all the settlers."

*

Shabona, Billy Caldwell and Alexander Robinson and a Kankakee chief named Shamaga had agreed to go to Big Foot's village to find out what they could about his intentions. Though Big Foot was reported to have departed his town, probably on his way west with a small party of warriors to confer with Chief Black Hawk, or the Sioux, Shabona agreed with Gurdon that they would calm all concerned by making the trip north and they might gain further useful information. When the chiefs reached Big Foot's town (Fontana, Wisconsin) they found the earlier report was true, Big Foot had left. They continued on to the Winnebago town on Lake Koshkonong. There it was decided that Shabona should enter the village alone. Billy Caldwell would accompany him as far as possible without attracting notice, remaining at that point in hiding. Thus Caldwell could get word back to the others if it should turn out that the town was unfriendly.

The precaution served them well. Shabona was seized by the Winnebagos as soon as the barking of the dogs announced his arrival and was accused of being an American spy. After holding him prisoner overnight, the Winnebagos relented, agreeing to release Shabona if he would promise to go directly to his own village, avoiding Chicago. To make sure, the Winnebagos assigned guards to accompany Shabona home. As he left the Koshkonong town, Shabona loudly discussed the terms of his release with his guards so that Billy Caldwell would hear. Caldwell, remaining in his hiding place, got the message. He and the others on the mission returned to Chicago to report on the Winnebago hostility. Hubbard and Kinzie estimated that they would have at least a week before Chief Big Foot could consult with Black Hawk, report back to his Winnebago allies, and assemble forces for an attack.

Fear among the Chicago populace was great. Those most involved in the action to be taken, the Kinzies, the Clybournes, Jean Baptiste Beaubien, who had been elected captain of the newly formed militia, and Gurdon Hubbard, knew well the stories of the Fort Dearborn massacre, which had occurred while a full complement of troops had been stationed there. Newcomers also had heard the stories from the Kinzies, the principal survivors. Among those who recalled the grisly details were Mrs. James Galloway and her two daughters, who had arrived in Chicago while her husband sought a plot of land he might acquire in northern Illinois. When the women failed to find shelter in Chicago, Chief Alexander Robinson befriended them, renting them the old Lee cabin at Hardscrabble, which John Crafts had occupied and Robinson had bought the previous summer. It was there the Indians killed two men and bashed out the brains of children against the log walls preliminary to the 1812 Fort Dearborn attack. At some time prior to the Winnebago trouble, Mrs. Galloway and her daughters thought they were under attack. They heard Indians shouting outside the cabin. "We had two axes," Mary, the eldest daughter, recalled. "Mother took one, gave the other to me, and told my sister to open the door a crack. We intended to get one Indian before they got us." The Indians merely wanted to arouse John Crafts, the fur trader, to buy whisky, and fled from their hostile reception. But all in Chicago who heard the women's story shuddered.

*

At five o'clock on a steaming August afternoon, Gurdon Hubbard departed the south gate of Fort Dearborn to begin his long ride south. He had instructed his *voyageurs* to take orders from Captain Beaubien in his absence. They were not American citizens and could not be impressed into a militia, but they were ready to defend the fort, giving Beaubien a total of about forty men, since settlers flocking in from the terrified countryside also agreed to help. Gurdon Hubbard mounted an Indian pony he recently had purchased from Chief Big Foot. It bore Big Foot's mark and Gurdon intended to say he had come from a business talk with him if accosted. He planned to avoid trouble if at all possible. He carried no weapon except his knife and tomahawk, the latter needed to cut away branches and brambles which sometimes obstructed his trail. His route was through Indian country mostly friendly to him in ordinary times, yet possibly hostile in the current situation. Yellow Head, chief of the Potawatomis based below Blue Island, continued to be his prime enemy, having sworn to kill him. He intended to shun that place.

A heavy wind and rain storm broke as he rode among the dunes south of the fort. He forded the Kankakee River in the blackness of night, the rain pounding him. There were no guiding stars; the trail was soggy and treacherous, strewn with downed tree limbs and often flooded. He continued to move south through the night, dismounting to swim raging creeks, drawing his unwilling horse across with his right hand on the mane and bridle, while using his left to swim. By morning he was bone-weary, hungry, and wet.

"On my reaching Sugar Creek I found the stream swollen out of its banks and my horse refusing to cross. I was obliged to wait until daylight, when I found that a large tree had fallen across the trail and made fording impossible." He was dripping from the night-long storm, his rheumatic joints ached, but he packed his wet clothing into a saddlebag, freed his horse, swam the creek, and went on afoot.

He stopped briefly to see Watseka, at work in the store early though she was far gone in pregnancy with their second child. She quickly got him hot food and dry clothing and, while he ate, she summoned Noel Vasseur's son. Gurdon told Watseka only that there was an emergency in Chicago; he would have to return there at once, after first going to Danville. He instructed her and Antoine to round up Baxter and the *voyageurs* to prepare guns, powder and horses for the militiamen he expected to bring out from Danville. Some of them would have neither guns nor horses.

Watseka asked no questions. She laid out the buckskin leggings she had prepared for him, as part of his lieutenant's outfit. They were beaded, brilliant with dyes, and decorated with porcupine quills. He thanked her with a kiss. He reached the home of his friend, Peleg Spencer, at noon, outlined the situation, took food, and rested. "Mr. Spencer started immediately to give the alarm, asking for volunteers to meet at Danville the next evening with five days rations."

Gurdon had ridden through a hundred and twenty-five miles of prairie, woods and marshlands, crossed flood swollen rivers and creeks, passed through country without white habitation, travelling mostly in darkness, with no clear trail in the storm-struck country, in about nineteen hours. It was a feat to match that of Governor Cass and his *voyageurs* in their trip for help in a fast express canoe.

Hezekiah Cunningham, a member of the Vermilion County militia, gave his account of the march from Danville to Chicago to the relief of Fort Dearborn to Historian Hiram Beckwith for his Winnebago war report. Nearly one hundred men were mustered, double the number Hubbard had hoped to raise, though some dropped out early, for lack of horses and the hardship of walking the wet trail. They departed Danville on Sunday, half of them mounted, the rest on foot, "each man carrying his five days of rations, including a pint of whisky, essential to mix with the slough water we would drink on the route. . . . Abel Williams, though, was smart enough to bring only coffee, and on the way back we all did the same."

It was a ragtag body of men assembled at Danville, toting shotguns, Kentucky rifles and old army muskets, knives and tomahawks or hatchets. Captain Achilles Morgan commanded the force; Hubbard, with the rank of lieutenant, leading the way with his mounted rangers. They would follow the Hubbard Trail. Most were in buckskin, or butternut-dyed homespun, good camouflage in the prairie or woods. Gurdon kept his new brilliant leggings in his saddlebag. The company reached the Vermilion River about noon. "The river was up, running bank ful about a hundred yards wide, with a strong current," Cunningham recalled. The men sought to drive their horses across after sending the marchers and all supplies over in canoes. But the frightened animals were turned back by the swift current.

"Mr. Hubbard, provoked at the delay, called to Jacob Hester, 'Give me Old Charley,' a horse he knew to be steady, and stripping off his shirt he mounted his horse and rode into the stream, the other horses being crowded after him. The water was so swift that Old Charley became unmanageable, when Mr. Hubbard dismounted and seized the horse by the mane, near the animal's head, and, swimming with his left hand, guided the horse in the direction of the opposite shore."

They feared Hubbard would be pushed under his horse by the current, but he crossed safely and the other horses followed. "Mr. Hubbard got by without damage, except wetting his broadcloth pants and his moccasins." They forded the North Creek at Bicknell's point, where some of the walkers and two of the riders dropped out, and late that night camped near Sugar Creek. "It was a wilderness of prairie all the way, except a little timber we passed through near Sugar Creek and at the Iroquois." The next morning they reached Hubbard's Iroquois River Station and there they saw many gun-bearing Indians, on the river bank and lurking near the trading post. Some of the men feared the trading post had been captured and were reluctant to cross.

235

Gurdon had gone ahead the night before, to make sure that Baxter and his *voyageurs* were ready with food, guns, powder and horses, and to check on Watseka, whose time was near. When he returned to the river and found the militia on the other side, he was at first furious. "We feared the Injuns might stampede our horses and steal them," they told him. Hubbard understood. All Indians were potential enemies to the settlers. "Mr. Hubbard assured us that these savages were friendly, and we afterward learned that they were Potawatomis, known as Hubbard's Band, from the fact that he long traded with them." The Indians had heard rumors of troubles to the north and had gathered at the Iroquois Station to protect it in case of any trouble. The crossing by the militia was soon effected.

"It is proper to state that we were deficient in arms," Hezekiah Cunningham remembered. "We gathered up squirrel rifles, flintlocks, old muskets, or anything like a gun that we might have around our houses. Some of us had no firearms at all. I myself was among this number. Mr. Hubbard supplied those of us who had inefficient weapons, or who were without weapons. He also gave us flour and salt pork. He had lately brought up the Iroquois River a supply of these articles. We remained at Hubbard's Trading House the remainder of the day, cooking rations and supplying our necessities."

The following morning they started early for Chicago. They swam Beaver Creek and crossed the Kankakee River at the rapids. "We passed 'Yellow Head's Village' . . . an old chief with some old men and squaws were at home . . . the young men had gone." Cunningham incorrectly thought the old chief was Yellow Head. Gurdon wondered if Yellow Head might be leading his men to join Big Foot. It was too early for them to be away hunting; their absence could be an ominous sign. They camped that night about five miles from the village and posted sentries. The following day the company reached "a branch of the Calumet River west of the Blue Island," Cunningham recalled. "We followed old Indian trails." Again Cunningham was in error. They had followed Hubbard's trail east of Blue Island. The side trails were made by animals. It rained almost every day. The muck sucked at the bare feet of the marchers when they removed their moccasins to wade through swamps. "The streams and sloughs were full of water. We swam the former and travelled through the latter almost by the hour. Many of the ponds were so deep our men dipped up the water to drink as they sat in their saddles. Colonel Hubbard (Cunningham used the rank Gurdon received later) fared better than the rest of us, he rode a tall, iron-gray stallion. . . . We reached Chicago about 4 o'clock in the evening of the fourth day, in one of the most severe rainstorms I ever encountered . . . we were without tents. But it was the water we took in that hurt us more than what fell on us . . . many of us were sick."

The people of Chicago had feared an Indian attack at any hour, although none of the scouts posted beyond the town on Gurdon's advice had reported signs of hostile activity. Captain Beaubien's militia now numbered fifty men, incoming settlers contributing to the numbers. "They were mostly Canadian half-breeds interspersed with Americans," Cunningham said. "The Americans, seeing we were a better-looking crowd, wanted to join us. This caused quite a row, but the officers finally restored harmony, the discontented men going back to their old command." The men of the Vermilion County Battalion, as they called themselves, joined Captain Beaubien's men in standing guard in Chicago "for eight to ten days" until a messenger from Governor Cass at Green Bay arrived to tell Kinzie and Hubbard that Cass had concluded a new treaty with the Winnebagos. "The citizens were overjoyed at the news," Cunningham remembered, "and in their gladness they turned out a barrel of gin, one barrel of brandy, and one barrel of whisky. Knocking the heads of the barrels in, everybody was invited to take a free drink, and, to tell the plain truth, everybody did drink."

There were women present who treated the men well too, Cunningham said. "They gave us all manner of good things to eat. They loaded us with provisions and gave us all those delicate attentions that the kindness of a woman's heart would suggest. Some of them, three ladies who, I understand, were recently from New York, distributed tracts and other reading matter among our company, and interested themselves in our spiritual, as well as temporal, welfare."

Not a shot had been fired by any militiaman in Illinois in the course of his duty in the Winnebago campaign, but the men from Vermilion county said proudly ever after, as Cunningham did, "We were out in the Winnebago war." Some historians scoffed, calling it "the Winnebago scare." But Henry R. School-craft, the most respected writer on Indian history of his time, in his *History of the Indian Tribes of the United States,* published in 1857, found the settlers to be well justified in their fears, and later careful writers of Potawatomi history, such as R. David Edmunds and James A. Clifton, found, via reports in the National Archives and the accounts of pioneers, that Winnebagos were passing war belts and in all likelihood would have attacked widely had it not been for prompt action taken by Cass, Hubbard and others. No community of pioneers could ignore the threat of an Indian outbreak, Schoolcraft said. He found that the Indian attack on the goverment supply ship was made in an attempt to re-establish the Indians' asserted right to collect tolls on Mississippi shipping, an act of war.

Chicago historians later compared Gurdon Hubbard's ride with that of Paul Revere. Hubbard had travelled the one hundred and twenty-five miles through hostile country and brought back the militia. Paul Revere, who alerted the patriots to the march of British troops, travelled slightly more than fifteen miles before he was captured; his mission also successful. "No textbook heralds to a rising generation the fame of Gurdon Hubbard's ride to Danville to bring troops to imperiled Chicago," complained Milo M. Quaife, the distinguished historian of America's northwest. "Yet, in comparison with it, the midnight ride of Paul Revere was merest child's play." Epic poems were written to commemorate Hubbard's ride, one, composed by William A. Roundy, was remembered for a time after it appeared in the *Chicago Tribune* in 1903, but all lacked the sprightly cadence of Henry W. Longfellow's celebration of Revere's midnight ride. Governor Lewis Cass was a hero of the Winnebago scare, subsequently backed for the American presidency after he had served as secretary of war. But Gurdon Hubbard named Shabona, the Ottawa-Potawatomi chief, as the real hero of both the Winnebago and Black Hawk wars, eulogizing his Indian friend in reporting on those matters: "I cannot close this communication without adding my testimony regarding the character and services of that noble Indian chief, Shaubenee. From my first acquaintance with him, which began in the fall of 1818, to his death (in 1859) I was impressed with the nobleness of his character. . . . He was remarkable for his integrity, of a generous and forgiving nature, always hospitable. . . . He was ever a friend of the white settlers, and should be held by them in grateful remembrance. . . . He had a perfect knowledge of this western country. Had he been favored with the advantages of an education, he might have commanded a high position among the men of his day. It ought to be a matter of regret and mortification to us all that our Government so wronged this man, who so often periled his own life to save those of the whites. . . ."

*

Gurdon returned to Watseka, finding her serene and contented, and not much interested in the consequences of his ride from Chicago to Danville to raise troops against the Indian people. Her own family accepted their fate placing them among the whites, though it was said her father had died fighting with Tecumseh. Watseka desired only to live close to her people and to rear her child among them. She was momentarily expecting a birth that would be successful, since this time she was scrupulously observing all signs and conditions which would ensure the well-being of the child. She was satisfied in her consultations with her mother and the shamans and merely laughed when Papamatabe suggested a last-minute trip to St. Louis to see a doctor. "No, my husband, I will stay here," she told him. Indian women who worked in the cornfields had no difficulty delivering a child, often going into the woods alone. It was needed only to stay in good health, to possess the proper besons, and to have arranged with the shamans for the correct propitiation of the spirits. She had failed previously because of inattention to such details, failure to work sufficiently in the fields, to carry her share of burdens with the head girth which strengthened the abdominal muscles, to acquaint the confused spirits with the fact that Watchekee had taken unto herself a white man as husband; this time she would not fail. It did Gurdon no good to plead. She was loving and considerate and adamant. She would stay, tend the corn, and bring forth a strong child. She even suggested that if again he felt required to make war, or to go to Danville or to Mackinaw, he could choose another wife to accompany him. She would help him choose.

Gurdon was exasperated but he felt he understood. He had hurt her by not disclosing to her the true situation in Chicago. But he had his duties and responsibilities also. Now he was needed at Danville to supervise the expansion of his store and the construction of buildings for Dan Beckwith. He had come to an agreement with Dr. Wolcott to bring supplies to Fort Dearborn when the troops returned; Wolcott was sure he would receive a permanent contract. There was also the necessity to be in Chicago when his white goods arrived and his promise to his mother and Elizabeth that he would come to Middletown that fall. None of these obligations required the presence of Watseka. He felt relieved that she did not wish to participate in them but his sense of guilt was great. He understood now that Watseka would never go with him to live among the whites. Yet he refused to contemplate a possible alternative.

In September their child was born, a girl, wrinkled and dark and puny, but Watseka and her mother seemed satisfied, even joyous. They told him she would become a strong and beautiful daughter. Gurdon had behaved correctly, leaving the house when the shamans arrived. The signs had been right, Watseka would choose a good name for the child, and her husband could give a name feast at the proper time. Meantime, Watseka would devote herself to nursing and caring for their baby. A bit of the umbilical cord had been sewed into the buckskin wrapper provided for the child; she also was blanketed with soft rabbit skins and diapered with spagnum moss. Thus the child was protected from evil while the problems of name and besons were considered. Obviously Watseka could not even consider a trip to Chicago and Mackinaw.

*

The season was late, the need compelling, so Gurdon departed alone in September, promising he would return shortly with the Illinois Brigade. He could not leave to Vasseur nor anyone else the selection of goods for the store, since it was an arrangement between John Jacob Astor and himself. If the Danville plan succeeded, Astor would finance other stores on easy terms. He gave up the idea of visiting Middletown, despite his promise, assuring himself he had a prior obligation to return as soon as possible to Watseka and his child. In Chicago he was told of the death of the infant daughter of Dr. Wolcott and Ellen and the Kinzies required him to break the news to the child's parents when he met them at Mackinaw. They had been away to the east that summer. It was a sorrowful duty and a bad omen for him.

"I had the disagreeable task of communication to them the news of the death of their little daughter the 16th of last month," he wrote to his mother and Elizabeth from Mackinaw. "Her poor mother was much afflicted, more so I presume than she would have been had she been present at her death. . . ." He realized that Watseka had been right in staying with their child. She would nurse their baby for two years, by Indian custom, and he vowed to himself that he would remain close to them as much as possible thereafter. He told his mother he had offered a job in his Danville store to Christopher, but had received no response. Nor had his mother acknowledged receiving money he had sent to Christopher for delivery to her. He was vexed by their behavior. Abigail had pleaded with him to help Christopher. He now withdrew his offer to him, saying "Times are tough here. Four houses will oppose me in the Indian trade on the Iroquois." Dr. Wolcott had spoken to him of seeing Abigail. "Doc Wolcott says you look younger than you did years ago," he added. The rift between Gurdon and Christopher was never fully closed.

*

Watseka dutifully welcomed him on his return from Mackinaw. She had chosen the name Lowanen, meaning Child of the North Star, for their daughter, and it pleased him. "Let us have Shabona to the name feast," he proposed. "The name Lowanen honors him, since it is of the Constellation of the Bear." Watseka agreed, although it was possible she had thought of her own name, meaning Child of the Evening Star, in choosing for her child. Shabona and his wife, Wiomex, attended, and Chief Tamin wove the name Lowanen into a speech in which he made reference to Shabona, and also alluded to the fact that Papamatabe, the father, was from the north. Gurdon awkwardly held his daughter, grown plump and lively, who sucked a stick of maple sugar candy and searched for sight of her mother, gurgling happily when she saw her. Watseka herself sipped a decoction made from poke berries to increase her supply of milk. He felt guilt ridden as he sensed the depth of her love for the child and his own relative unconcern. He recalled the anguished cries of Ellen Wolcott when she learned her daughter had died while she was away. There was something to be said for Potawatomi ways, he decided. Watseka would not leave her child, but kept her always near within the protective rabbit skins of the cradle board. He knew also that while Watseka nursed her child, and even after, he would no longer be a part of her life as before. But he had not meant to take her away from her child. He hoped they could become reconciled. He would be kind to her. They could live in Danville by way of compromise.

In the late fall, after Indian summer arrived and the crops were in, Watseka at last accompanied him to Danville to inspect the new store, the structure of squared logs to which he had added a large living space they could occupy. It was now well stocked with supplies for farmers and their women, as well as trappers and hunters, and it drew a heavy trade, so that he had trained two *voyageurs* to act as clerks. The only competitor was Dan Beckwith's Saddle Bag store on the edge of town, so-called because it sold only goods carried in saddlebags from Terre Haute, Indiana. Beckwith actually welcomed his competition, since he was interested in selling Danville lots and in developing the salt deposits near town. He and Hubbard had become good friends.

Watseka agreed to stay. She could have her child with her at all times. The store was not greatly different from that at the Iroquois Station. She got on well with the male customers as she did at Iroquois and few women entered. Most had not yet heard of the new inventory of goods which included in addition to such items as plows, fire steels, gun flints, whisky and scalping knives, an excellent array of woman's goods: Irish linen, worsted hose, calico handkerchiefs, laces, London Scots gartering, embossed brooches, printed cotton shawls, ivory combs, embossed serge, tow sheeting, nun's thread and white wampum. Watseka soon knew the stock, she was intelligent and eager to please, and was knowledgeable of the needs and problems of the hunters and trappers if not those of a white housewife. She was a pretty, lissom, ripe young woman, much appreciated by the men. She kept Lowanen nearby at all times and, when required to do so, publicly fed her at her breast, as did most pioneer women. At such times the males stole appreciative glances. Watseka was obedient, but she also had a sense of humor about her role, responding to Hubbard's commands with a bemused, "Yes, my husband," and "No, my husband" as she executed his orders, or ignored them, according to her best judgment. Watseka soon became known in Danville for her ability and charm, but it was not to her advantage.

It did not please wives at home to hear of the beauty and virtues of the Indian woman Watseka, seemingly an ideal mate and mistress in the view of any frontiersman, a woman who looked good, obeyed orders, worked hard, and stayed home without complaint when her husband was required to travel. When the wives got together, somewhat infrequently if they dwelled on lonely farms, those who had visited Hubbard's store mimicked Watseka's imperfect English, scoffed at the title of "Princess" their men had given her, and accused her of putting on airs and thinking she was better than they were. An irked female customer passed along these accusations to Watseka at the store in the presence of other clerks and openly sneered at her child. Hubbard's wrathful wife loosed a torrent of Potawatomi that scared her critic into quick departure. Then Watseka herself left, packing her baby on her back in the cradle board as she rode a pony to the Iroquois Station where Gurdon that day was getting together the corn, provisions and hogs he expected to drive to Chicago in December.

Watseka's homecoming was an explosive one. She pointed out to her husband the irony of their situation. He had said he wished them to be together. He was at Iroquois, her preference, while she was kept in the Danville store. She had no intention of returning to Danville. She would assist at the Iroquois store, though she had no great love for that occupation either, but it would aid her husband and it was near her own people. He sought to understand why her anger was directed against him. He had not complained of her work in the store. He was well satisfied with it. She should have stood her own ground, remaining in the store, not retreating under a white woman's scorn. It would be the way to win the friendship and respect of all whites.

"I do not wish to win the friendship of the whites," Watseka told him. "I am an Indian woman and I have the respect of Indians and that is what I wish to have. I wish my child to live a happy life. That will not be in a white village. I want my child to live among my people, who will love her as an Indian child is loved."

"She is our child," Gurdon said.

"You do not seem to think so. You are more interested in your pigs."

"You must cool off, Watchekee. It will do no good for our child if we quarrel."

"I have only our child in mind," she replied. "I do not wish to go back to the store. I wish to be here, where she can grow up with her people. Do you not see? What is life for her or me with white people? Do they sing, dance, play games? Can their women make thread of deer tendons, clothing of deer skin, spoons of mussel shells, dishes and baskets of bark? No. They are helpless. They do not help their men. They make nothing."

"That is why we have a store for them, Watseka."

"We do not need your store. Come with me to my village. Dance and sing with us. And go to war, if you love war so much, with my people, who are much wronged."

He angrily left and stalked to the company store, where Antoine Vasseur was supposed to be working, but which was unattended. There he saw the post cat gnawing at the meat left on one of the pelts improperly prepared for packing. He had observed such damage to skins previously and at last knew the culprit. As the cat ran through the door to escape his angry shouts, Gurdon lifted his rifle. He clipped its spine neatly. He took the cat to the camp cook, according to his recollection given to Henry Hamilton, suggesting the cook might wish to use the skin for a tobacco pouch. It had been a difficult winter, his hogs had just arrived, and his *voyageurs* had only corn to eat that day, no tallow or meat.

"Just before dinner I went out to ask the cook what he had done with the cat," Gurdon recalled. "He answered by pointing to the kettle in which the corn soup was cooking for the men's dinner. I laughed and said nothing." When the men came in they smelled the savory stew and offered Hubbard the choice bits of meat always provided to the boss. Hubbard refused, saying he was unwell and not hungry. "They ate it with relish," he remembered, still enjoying, a half century later, his appreciation of this incident of frontier humor. "The men believed it was wildcat. They were greatly astonished when I told them they had devoured our Tom cat."

That was not the way Watseka recalled the story, according to Hubbard's other editor, also his "grand nephew" Alfred Holt (though neither he nor Henry Hamilton were Gurdon's blood kin). Gurdon brought the dead cat to Watseka, Holt wrote, suggesting she could use the skin to make mittens. When he sat down to his evening meal he greatly enjoyed the corn soup and stew. At some time during the evening he asked Watseka if she had trouble skinning the cat. "Oh, no, my husband," she replied. "But I do not need mittens and I will give the skin to my mother. And I am glad you enjoyed the stew."

*

In December Gurdon led his *voyageurs* on their first major overland trek north over his trail with a herd of hogs and wagons loaded with provisions for the garrison newly arrived at Fort Dearborn. It was the beginning of the caravans north that would bring swine, cattle and emigrants to a village destined to become the hog butchering capital of the world. He had stationed boats at the streams to be crossed, in case the ice was thin, but a cold snap made them unnecessary. Within two weeks, a few days before Christmas, the soldiers at Fort Dearborn and the people of Chicago heard cries of drovers and the crack of whips and creak of wagons that would resound for generations along the road into Chicago to become known variously as Hubbard's Trail, the Wabash Trace, and the State Road, culminating at the Chicago River as State Street.

The arrival of a food supply for Chicago provided cause for celebration that bleak and cold winter. Hubbard employed Jonas Clybourne and his sons, the fort butchers, to slaughter the pigs at his camp along the marsh to the west of the fort, a site to become part of Chicago's famed Loop. The sides of pork were then stored on the ice until they were required by the cooks. Pigs had been killed at Chicago before, on a large scale at times by the Clybournes, but Gurdon Hubbard's arrival and his simple method of icing pork, and later, holding it for sale in the spring, marked the beginning of the meat packing business in the town. He would thereafter call regularly with supplies and thousands of drovers and wagoneers and job seekers would move up his trail. He wrote his mother from Chicago on January 2, 1828: "I arrived here on the 23rd of last month in the company of thirty-five long-faced gentlemen who I do promise were gratefully received for the inhabitants of this place were quite out of pork, and they came in at the right time for sausages and black pudding. I succeeded in selling them all and have made a clear profit of $125." He also received a contract from Wolcott to supply the Fort Dearborn garrison when it should return. He added that he was staying with the Kinzies, and with them "partook of a Christmas meal and a New Year's dinner for the first time since I left Montreal. I must observe that when I am in Indian country I never eat but two meals a day."

He and John Kinzie were friends once more which, in retrospect, was most consoling. John Kinzie died that winter. Gurdon described for his mother and Elizabeth his new arrangement with the American Fur Company. "You had wished to know the details of my co-partnership. The company has agreed to furnish me with necessary goods for my trade both with the whites and the Indians at cash and interest of the money, with the addition of five per cent commission on the total amount of disbursements. I am to have sole charge and conduct of the business, and, as you might say, in lieu of wages receive one half of the profits." He also wrote of his special interest in a canal, to extend from the Chicago Portage to the Desplaines, "which would communicate the waters of Lake Michigan to the Illinois River and the Mississippi." He indicated that he again was considering the possibility of making his home in Chicago, where "if Providence should favor my exertions so as to be able to give you a comfortable home, to have you come . . . I think you could be happy here."

He was suffused with holiday happiness and ignored the dismal aspects of the little town, pristine under a snowfall at the moment, but described earlier that year by Mrs. Clybourne, wife of his butcher, as "a black and dreary expanse of prairie with patches of timber. At the mouth of the River (the foot of Madison Street) stood the cabin of Jean Baptiste Beaubien (then Hubbard's fur trader) . . . where the river turned south stood Fort Dearborn, and across from it was a double log house occupied by the Kinzies (the Agency House), near this the blacksmith shop of David McKee and Joseph Portier. At the forks of the river was a cabin used as a store by James Kinzie (a cousin of John)." Mrs. Clybourne forgot the old Kinzie "mansion" occupied by the Jonathan N. Bailey family despite its ruined condition, and the cabin of Antoine Ouilmette. Early in 1828 Samuel Miller was building a log inn at the forks of the river and James Kinzie had under way a similar structure he would rent to Elijah Wentworth. These would become the Miller House and the Wolf Tavern. The soldiers at the fort were digging a channel through the sand bank to admit ships from Lake Michigan directly into the Chicago River, a development of special interest to Hubbard. There were a few cabins at Hardscrabble on the south branch. The Clybournes lived on the north branch of the river. Altogether fourteen cabins and their occupants comprised the village. John H. Fonda, the Indian Agent at Prairie du Chien, passing through Chicago, wrote his brother, prior to the return of the garrison, "Chicago is merely an Indian Agency. Gurdon Hubbard of the American Fur Company occupies the fort. The staple business seemed to be carried on by Indians and run-away soldiers, who hunt ducks and muskrats in the marshes." Those hunters were probably Hubbard's *voyageurs*. To Gurdon that Christmas, Chicago appeared, blissfully, home; the Kinzies and Wolcotts were there.

*

Gurdon's letter seemingly indicated that he had made a decision to part permanently from Watseka, since she had made it clear she would not leave the country of her people. However his plans included his store at Danville and his fur trade activities, as well as provisioning the fort from his southern base. Possibly he intended to maintain his marriage to Watseka, basing at his Iroquois River Station, living with her and the child when he was not at Chicago or Mackinaw, or visiting his scattered trading posts. Watseka in effect had suggested such an arrangement, allowing him a second wife if he so chose.

He continued to offer excuses to Abigail and Elizabeth for his failure to come east to see them. The regular visits of Dr. Wolcott and his wife to Middletown undoubtedly emphasized in Gurdon's mind his own remiss behavior. Since he was essentially honest, his sense of guilt about his deception concerning his personal life was great. Again Elizabeth had suggested finding a wife for him, evidently, for he told her "I do not think I can become interested in the Miss Gordon you describe." He closed his extended letter with a final excuse and the provision of funds. "There are a great many obstacles to prevent me from seeing you this spring. I have advised Mr. Astor on this subject," he said, relative to the money included. He had asked Astor's New York office to send any moneys due him to his mother should a fatal accident or illness befall him.

He had not hestitated to leave Watseka and his child for his long stay in Chicago that winter. The Christmas holiday would concern Watseka little, since her people had not been converted by the missionaries as were the Delawares living in the area. He had felt compelled to drive his hogs to Chicago in time to feed the incoming garrison. He also had Indian trade work to do in Chicago, even in winter, and it was his purpose to visit some of the hunting camps on his return south. He brought gifts of silver for his wife, making his purchases from John Kinzie once more, and he intended to restore their good life together. He returned to find much excitement at the post and fears for his safety.

The Kinzie trouble was past, but the feud with Yellow Head, which Gurdon did not want and failed to understand, flamed again. Once more Yellow Head announced publicly that he intended to kill Hubbard. Again he went to the Iroquois Station, this time directly to Hubbard's lodge. Watseka had taken her child to Tamin's village, as Gurdon was in Chicago. Dominick Bray occupied the house, sleeping in the large bunk bed. Yellow Head and his braves broke in, spraying the wall above the bunk with bullets. Bray rolled to the floor, crawled across the room in the darkness to escape through the open door while the Indians continued shooting. "The Indians pillaged the house and the store," Gurdon wrote. Yellow Head, after learning he had shot at the wrong man, departed shouting that he would surely destroy Hubbard when they met. A few days later they learned that Yellow Head had himself been killed in a drunken fight.

Watseka's concern for him rapidly vanished, it appeared to Gurdon. She accepted his gifts with small sign of pleasure. She refused to discuss plans for a return to Danville. She pointed out that he would not be there anyway, since he intended to visit the hunting camps on the Little Wabash. She made it clear that his absence was no deprivation for her. She was nursing their child and would continue to do so for some time. She again suggested that Indian men often sought other companionship at such times. She exasperated him by her insistence that she did not intend to change her wilderness ways. She preferred the work of an Indian woman. She would not take food from the *voyageurs'* cook. She carried her child in her cradle board, keeping it close, scrupulously making sure that all required besons were with her. She went often to her village where she consulted, through the shamans, both *chasgieds* and *wabenos,* concerning the baby's health. Gurdon would not allow the shamans into his house, though he knew Watseka was convinced the child might require their medicine.

Late in March, as he returned from his trip to the Little Wabash country, he was met by a runner sent by Tamin. Watseka's premonitions and fears had been realized. Lowanen, their daughter, was dead. He hurried homeward, bitterly remorseful for his indifference to Watseka's worries and angrily resentful that the gods of the Indians and the God of the whites could not together have protected his child. Chief Tamin had come up from his village, bringing all of his medicine men, and he said he had sent for Waba.

"What of Watseka?" Gurdon asked.

"Watchekee is well, but she is speaking with the spirits at all times, and will do so until the feast of purification is observed," Tamin answered. Gurdon nodded. "She chose the name Lowanen in the sign of the bear," he said. "It is good you sent for

Waba. I will see Watchekee. You stay with her and I will take
Vasseur and Waba to find a bear.''

"She will not see you, Pápamatabe. She will see no one."

"I will see her," Gurdon answered roughly as they neared his
lodge. He pushed open the puncheon door against the objections of Monoska and found his house well occupied by the
family of Tamin and his shamans, all chanting in mournful voices
as they shook gourds and bells. Monoska, understanding finally
that he did not oppose the ceremony, allowed him to approach
Watseka, sitting on a mat of cat-tails in the semi-darkness. The
child, wrapped for burial, lay upon a bed of furs placed on a cat-
tail mat. Gurdon knelt beside his wife and placed his arm gently
about her, but she sat rigid and unresponsive, staring at the
besons strewn across the tiny form swathed in pale Stroud cloth.

Gurdon rose and spoke to Tamin. "Tell her I will return when
the spirit of the bear is set free," he said. Outside Vasseur was
waiting with Waba and his son Wabanin. They had anticipated
his wish. "We have found a tree with bear," Vasseur said. "We
will show you."

Gurdon was grateful. "What caused her death?" he asked.

"It was phlegmon," Vasseur answered. "Watchekee used
onion poultice and powder of horse chesnut, but the fever was
very great. The shamans were called, but the fever was indeed
great."

A she-bear was soon found and dispatched. Gurdon returned
to his house to inform Watseka. The feast of the dead would
be held that night, he decreed. The child had expired of pneu-
monia the previous day and had been ill a week. Watseka had
taken almost no food in that time. Monoska, Tamin and Waba
were at hand. There was no need for delay. Monoska at once
began the preparations.

That night, in full darkness, the fire extinguished despite the
raw cold, they prayed the ritual of the feast of the dead. Chief
Tamin offered bear meat to placate the angry spirits and
reminded them that the Great Spirit always recalled the shade
of a child not yet ready for the world of men. Waba spoke to
the spirits, and Gurdon reminded himself that Jesus Christ had
said, "Suffer the little children to come unto me, for of such is
the Kingdom of Heaven." When the old chiefs assured them that

the spirit of their daughter was being guided safely to Heaven, Watseka, racked by weeping, at last allowed her husband to comfort her in his arms.

"She must eat now," Monoska said gently, "but only a little corn soup. And you must eat, Papamatabe. Then all must rest. The child will be safe on her scaffold under the North Star."

They knew after the night that their marriage had died also. In the days following they treated each other with elaborate kindness and courtesy, but they slept separately.

*

The bleak winter ended, the snow collapsing into rivulets as the sun flared through scudding clouds driven by the winds of late March. The streams and rivers flooded, the earth smelled of new life and the prairie began to green. The hunting parties came to the Iroquois Station with their pelts. Gurdon and Vasseur supervised the counting and packing of the furs, Watseka helping them.

"Come with us," Gurdon urged often. "Come on to Mackinaw."

But she answered, "No, my husband."

"I will come back from Chicago," he offered.

There was no response.

"I will go on with Vasseur to Mackinaw then. But you cannot continue this way. I have wronged you greatly. I should have gone with you to the village to arrange for the attentions of the shamans. I am sorry."

"Yes, my husband. I know that you are sorry. The Great Spirit knows that you are sorry. And your God knows that I am sorry for you."

When he returned from Mackinaw early in June, leaving Vasseur behind for the summer's work, he found Watseka laboring among the squaws in the corn fields. She seemed well and strong, but remained aloof.

"You have come back soon, Papamatabe."

"Yes, Watch-e-kee. I have come back to live with you. I will make you happy again."

She smiled sadly, shaking her head. "We cannot be happy again, not together. The Great Spirit has told us this."

"It was because of my stubborness. I would not believe. But I know we are all one, all people. I believe in the Great Spirit, the Supreme Being, God. I will live with you."

"You will not become Indian. I cannot become white woman. You have told me of the woman Ruth, in your Bible, but I cannot be Ruth. You have told me Black Hawk said we should not live together when we cannot agree. You must seek another companion."

"And you? You will find another companion?"

"I have found one, my husband."

"And who is that?" he demanded angrily.

"He is Noel Le Vasseur."

"Vasseur? Good God! You and Vassseur? Le Vasseur? What is this 'Le' Vasseur? Has he become *Le Bourgeois* also? What has been going on?"

In black rage he turned to leave. He could not believe what she had said, but he knew that she was done with him; their life together was finished.

"Wait, my husband," she called softly.

"I am not your husband. No more. Black Hawk has spoken."

"Do not be angry, Papamatabe. Do not blame Le Vasseur. Nothing has been going on. He knows nothing of this. But I love him for his kindnesses. He is lonely and has not found a wife. He is loyal to you, *Le Bourgeois* Hubbard. He calls himself by the new name he found at Mackinaw, because it pleases him and he believed it would please you. But you did not even notice! You are free. I will marry Noel Le Vasseur if he will have me. If I am free, he will come to love me."

"I will go to speak with Tamin and with Waba," he told her. "I will come back to you when my mind and heart are clear. I do not blame you. What has happened is my fault, Watch-e-kee. But I am angry. I am angry at my God and your God for letting this happen. I will come back to speak with you."

In three days he returned. She gave him a supper of venison, vegetables from her garden, planted with the advice of Mrs. Baxter, and corn soup. They spoke of the store and their earlier days, of the failing health of Tamin and the remarkable vitality of Waba. He said he would go alone by pony all the way to Mackinaw. He wished to explore the possibilities of another land trade route. She understood his need to be alone.

"I will speak to Noel Le Vasseur at Mackinaw, to say I will replace him at the fur warehouse, and that Watchekee and Hubbard have said farewell according to the laws of Tamin's tribe," he said. "If he wishes to return at once, it will be done. Noel Le Vasseur will be my manager in the Iroquois country as long as he and I live. And I will love you Watchekee, as long as I live. But I know I have not loved you well enough."

In the morning Gurdon Hubbard departed, taking his favorite horse Croppy and a supply of parched corn, salt pork and venison jerky cured in the sun.

He saw again the battlefield at Tippecanoe where Shabona had fought with Tecumseh and the station near the town of Niles, Michigan where John Kinzie engaged in the fur trade, the grave site of Father Marquette near Ludington, the cedar cross no longer to be found, and the woods along the Thames where Tecumseh died and Shabona and Black Hawk vowed to go their differing ways. He knew that time was ending for the Indian in the country he had come to know well. They would inexorably be driven west.

At Mackinaw, six weeks later, Noel Le Vasseur heard Gurdon Hubbard's statement of their new relationship without comment. He would take charge at the Iroquois River Station at once. Hubbard would base himself at Danville in October. They would work together, but separately. Gurdon doubled Le Vasseur's wage. "You may wish to marry," he said.

"Since you have spoken," Le Vasseur answered, "I would wish to marry Watchekee."

9

July, 1828

I have no information as to Mr. Hubbard's life during the years 1828-29, further than that he engaged in general business at Danville, and retained his trading post at Iroquois . . . he had contracts for furnishing beef and pork . . . to Fort Dearborn . . . he kept the pork on ice (the Chicago River) until the arrival of barrels in the Spring.
Henry E. Hamilton to
Caroline M. McIlvaine

He was submerged in gloom on his return to Chicago in the fall of 1828. Again he had not found an opportunity to go to his mother and sisters at Middletown. Instead he shared with Eleanor Kinzie her grief in the death of her husband and spent as much time as he could with the Wolcotts, who were back at the Agency House after troops returned to Fort Dearborn in October. Eleanor now lived with the Wolcotts and Margaret Helm had come back to visit her Chicago family. Gurdon found himself delaying his departure from Chicago. Noel Le Vasseur was on duty at the Iroquois River Station, clerks tended the Danville store, and Gurdon was not immediately responsive to Dan Beckwith's note saying he had rented one of the log houses to a Dr. Fifthian from Ohio and required more buildings at once.

Gradually Gurdon was healed by Dr. Wolcott, Eleanor Kinzie, and the very presence of Margaret, though none of them discovered the true reasons for his sadness, attributing it to the death of Antoine Deschamps that fall and the earlier death of John Kinzie. Dr. Wolcott also suspected that his friend was dismayed that he had undertaken a contract with the American Fur Company at a time when the approaching end of the Indian fur trade in Illinois seemed obvious. Actually, Gurdon's despondency was increased by the discovery that Dr. Wolcott himself feared he was seriously ill of a heart ailment that kept him from joining Hubbard and Captain John Fowle, the new commandant at the fort, in hunting and fishing excursions. Only then had Gurdon realized that Doc Wolcott was a medical doctor as well as an expert on Indian treaties and tribal relationships. Dr. Wolcott had not sought to practice in Chicago and confided his regret that he could not help Eleanor Kinzie, ill with cancer. "We must take her east with Margaret when she will go," he said. "You should go with us, Gurdon, and visit your mother. She really wonders why you have remained away so long."

But Gurdon could not go to Middletown that summer or fall. He had contracted for the American Fur Company holdings and had to pay off his debts. He agreed with Dr. Wolcott's prediction that Andrew Jackson would become the next American president and would remember his own troubles with the Indians and Jefferson's plan to remove the Indians to lands west of the Mississippi. The Cherokees, Delawares, Kickapoos and Creeks had already been pushed west and the southern Indians had agreed to cross the Mississippi, Wolcott pointed out. The prairie Indians would surely follow. The Great Plains with their buffalo and abundant small game lay open to the Indians and were unsuitable for farmers, it was believed. Let the Indians go there. John C. Calhoun, secretary of war, had made a precise recommendation to President Monroe, but Monroe had been reluctant to act. Jackson would act, Dr. Wolcott said. "My prairie Potawatomis will be gone before I am," he added wryly. Gurdon was shocked at his friend's fatalistic contemplation of death. Dr. Wolcott, it turned out, was wrong in his prediction. He died in 1830; the Potawatomis departed the Illinois country four years later.

It seemed that Chicago was permeated with sadness and the imminence of death, yet Gurdon stayed on as long as possible. Margaret Helm scarcely had spoken to him, though she smiled somewhat primly when he was near. He thought he understood. When she saw Fort Dearborn ablaze on the stormy August night the year before and called for help, shaken by her remembrance of the earlier Fort Dearborn horror, Gurdon had dashed to her side in his breech clout in which he slept and for a moment comforted her in his arms as he saw for himself the flames beyond the river and the Winnebago warriors at the gate. Then he was running to the river and the Kinzie canoe, having grabbed his buckskins enroute. Margaret, recalling the hideous Fort Dearborn massacre, had shuddered close to him and was calmed in his embrace. He knew that she did not want to be reminded of that splinter of time, which he would never forget. He was free now, Margaret Helm was not. They were brought together often that late summer and fall when he called at the Wolcotts', joined them at the fort to hear a Sunday sermon by the new blacksmith there, the Reverend William See, or came to Wednesday night prayer meeting, led by Eleanor Kinzie herself, but Margaret continued aloof. He watched her furtively when he was a guest at the Wolcott table and saw that she was still beautiful, but wan and remote. Her extended absences from Lieutenant Helm went unexplained. She was devoted to Eleanor Kinzie, a hopeless victim of cancer. In his letters home that year, Gurdon said little about the troubles of his Chicago friends. Dr. Wolcott and Ellen were planning to go east, he said, but he could not be with them. He promised to see them in another year. He continued to refer to Eleanor as "the Episcopal bishop of Illinois" and said she was planning to establish a church in Chicago. He had promised to help.

*

He found his own release in his long talks with Dr. Wolcott, evenings at the Agency House. Wolcott even found strength to accompany him on a trip to the Desplaines and into the Sag woods to study the possible route for the Lake Michigan-Illinois River canal. But Gurdon alone went fox hunting in the dunes with Captain Fowle and his officers. Fowle had been much pleased that Hubbard had arrived promptly with needed supplies for his troops in their first cold months in Chicago. They had become friends. Captain Fowle was interested in building a military road along the route of Hubbard's Trail to Vincennes; he also urged Gurdon to follow John Reynold's advice to push for a Chicago canal, and provided him with the army engineering reports on canal proposals. Lieutenant Allen, in preparing for the ditching of the sandbar the previous year, had come upon all the prior harbor and canal studies made by the Corps of Engineers, including those of Chief Engineer Justus Post and that of Major Stephen Long, which especially impressed Gurdon. The army engineers found the Chicago Portage route to be much preferred, despite the difficulties of tough rock formation. It was the short route. Dug deep enough, the Lake Michigan waters could flow into the Illinois, affording a waterway that could also drain the marshes of the area. It would be possible to take a mackinaw from Montreal to New Orleans without leaving the boat. Gurdon was greatly excited by his studies and decided he definitely would try for election to the legislature, as John Reynolds had advised, on his return to Danville.

In their evening discussions of canals, harbors and military roads, Dr. Wolcott did not agree with either Hubbard or Captain Fowle that a canal and a military road would solve Chicago's supply problem. "You are leaving out a most important factor," he warned. "There are months when the best of roads will be under water, and a canal and the rivers and even a part of Lake Michigan will be frozen over. What we need to do is to develop a large warehouse facility at Chicago, to store food and supplies for the winter season. When my friend Henry Schoolcraft was here with the Indian commission eight years ago, he pointed out the problem. As we know, there is no harbor in the southern part of Lake Michigan, as Schoolcraft stated in his report. 'Every vessel that passes into that lake after the month of September runs into the immediate hazard of a shipwreck.' I think I quote him precisely. Until you can maintain your ditch through the sandbar, Captain Fowle, we'll have no harbor here. Once the ditch is really finished, and I commend you on starting it, we must also have docks and piling and warehousing, then we'll have a harbor and requirement for a canal."

"The canal will bring the harbor," Gurdon said. "I agree that the harbor must come also. It will. Meantime, I'm ready to keep my mackinaws here, with *voyageurs* to man them, and to expand my warehousing effort, if Captain Fowle will lease me additional space in the fort. If you'll rent me quarters for my men and needed floor space for goods, we'll have a bigger warehouse right now."

Captain Fowle smiled. The fort was half empty. The rent would be reasonable. "You keep the beef and pork coming to my troops throughout the year and I assure you Dr. Wolcott and I will guarantee your lease," he said.

"I'll supply your needs," Gurdon promised. "I'll also supply John Reynolds with all the information he wants on a Chicago canal route. I'll even make a try for the legislature. It won't be easy to get support at Vandalia though. Right now no one in southern Illinois, except John Reynolds, gives a hoot whether Chicago is open to water shipping or a road. A lot of northern Illinois people still want to see a canal across state east to west from the Wabash to the Mississippi, by way of the Kankakee and the Illinois. That's not the right place for it. The Kankakee is too twisting, rocky and shallow. We need the shortest possible route from the Lakes to the Mississippi."

"We also need Fort Dearborn," Captain Fowle said. "This must be realized in the south."

"I don't think southern Illinois wants to pay for any improvements in the north," Gurdon responded. "Maybe we can bring the interests of the north and south together. In those papers you loaned me, Captain, I find that President Madison years ago called for a canal along the Chicago Portage route. The army has always been for it. John Reynolds once told me we'd never get action until Illinois pushes Washington into it. Looks like that's what we've got to do."

"The pushing has to come from southern Illinois, Gurdon," Dr. Wolcott said. "You can do it better than anybody. Get into that Vandalia legislature as Reynolds advised. We correspond now and then and I know he intends to run for governor of Illinois one of these days. Join up with him, Gurdon. We need everything here at Chicago, a road, a canal, a harbor and warehousing. Captain Fowle and I can talk to Washington. Lewis Cass will surely help us. You know the problem and the solution. Go for that Vandalia legislature!"

"Well," Gurdon said, "down in Vermilion county some people say I'm already in too much. They may not want to vote for a Yankee. But I'll go for the legislature if I can. So I guess I'd better go home and see about tryin' to get elected."

*

He left Chicago in the dead of winter, proceeding south with trade goods in canoes mounted on sled runners, as Henri de

Tonty, La Salle's lieutenant, had done a century and a half earlier. All was well with Le Vasseur at the Iroquois post. Allen Baxter took in the ponies Gurdon had used to haul the boats along the frozen rivers and ice trails and promised he would have plenty of corn under cultivation the spring following. He learned from Baxter that Le Vasseur and Watseka had married under the laws of Tamin's tribe and she was living at Le Vasseur's cabin on Sugar Creek. He called on them, wished them happiness, provided wedding gifts from Mackinaw and the late John Kinzie's store in Chicago. He urged them to make their home in the house he had built for Watseka, near the trading post, the farm and her village. "I will be working with Baxter as well as you," he told Le Vasseur. "It will be more convenient for me." It was agreed. Gurdon went on to Danville, carrying supplies for his store and the southern trade posts. He felt that he really was going home.

*

Dr. William Fifthian, a burly, powerful, abundantly cheerful man, was already popular in the frontier town and surrounding Vermilion county. He would ride anywhere to help a patient and was quick and sure at setting broken bones and dislocated shoulders, common injuries among the men felling and hauling logs, poling boats on sometimes unmanageable rivers, and breaking the prairie with inadequate plows. Dr. Fifthian also was gentle with his women patients, it was said: his chuckle and good cheer were widely known as his best medicine. At forty-nine he was youthful, ebullient, optimistic and convinced that most ailments, including those of the mind, would respond to his remedies and will. He had heard the story of Gurdon Hubbard and Watseka and understood Hubbard's general malaise when the young trader, attacked by rheumatism, called on him for help. Dr. Fifthian told Hubbard frankly that he expected the Indians knew more than he did about treating rheumatism. He produced his favorite remedy, developed by the Delawares along the Muskingum, a mixture of powdered roots "including the rind of dog-wood . . . better than Jesuit-Bark sold in the apothecary shops," Dr. Fifthian rumbled. Soon he had prodded from Gurdon the story of his life and family, and in turn provided his own history, asserting that he was the first white child born in Cincinnati, April 7, 1779. He recently had married the daughter of Judge Elisha Berry of Urbana, Ohio, "much too young for an old goat like me." When Alethea Fifthian entered, a tall, blonde woman who had absented herself from their cabin so that her husband would have privacy with his new patient, Gurdon saw that she was indeed much younger; fair, blue-eyed, her cheeks glowing from the cold, her smile warm.

"Thea, this is Gurdon Hubbard, the man who built our house," her husband said.

Alethea smiled, urged Hubbard to sit, and brought coffee. "I want to compliment you on the best fireplace I've seen," she said. "It really draws very well."

They became instant friends. It was Alethea who decided that she and Dr. Fifthian should take a boarder, a common practice among pioneer couples needing cash and yearning for companionship in a new town. Dr. Fifthian's fees were modest and usually paid in produce, if at all. When Thea suggested to him that Gurdon Hubbard might like to board with them, her husband warmly agreed and Gurdon was glad to accept.

Soon the moody young trader spent most of his free evenings when in Danville at the Fifthian cabin, enjoying the pleasures of conversation, entertaining them with his stories of the wilderness, the Indians and the *voyageurs,* while they gave him news and gossip of the settled and civilized world of central Ohio. Canals were being built throughout the east, many were planned for Ohio, Dr. Fifthian said. The Baltimore and Ohio railroad was under way. President Jackson was attempting to buy Texas from Mexico. President John Quincy Adams had ruined the south and west by signing a tariff law, strongly opposed by President-elect Jackson, already known as "The Tariff of Abominations." Gurdon's hero, Henry Clay, had fought a duel with John Randolph over Randolph's charge that Clay had entered "a corrupt bargain" to help Adams win the presidency. Neither duelist was hurt and Clay was now a leader in the Congress, Jackson's most formidable opponent. Dr. Fifthian held Clay to be a law-breaker, a high-living Kentuckian who liked fast horses and fast women. He only accepted Clay at all because he was a southerner who appeared willing to compromise on slavery.

Hubbard, always practical, was uncritical of Clay. "I'll vote for Clay for president if I get the chance," he said. "I'd like a ticket of Henry Clay and Lewis Cass. We've got to have improvements in the West. With Clay and Cass we'll get harbors and canals and roads." Dr. Fifthian fiercely opposed such pragmatism. "No damned politician can be allowed to break any law," he declared. Sometimes Dr. Fifthian was so firm in his views, and stated them with such force, Gurdon was inclined to dispute them, even if they essentially agreed. Alethea was amused when they came to the brink of anger in their discussions. They remained friends. When Gurdon asked their opinion of his chances to win a seat in the legislature, Dr. Fifthian was staunchly for him. "You'll be elected without doing a thing," he said. "You just say the word and I'll spread it."

They clashed mostly over the slavery question, though both opposed the evil. Gurdon put the Indian problem first. "But the Indians are free!" Dr. Fifthian objected. "Let's keep them free, then find ways to free the slaves," Gurdon replied. "Andy Jackson wants to drive the Indians from their hunting grounds and to pen them up on reserved lands west of the Mississippi. How can we expect to free black slaves at the very time we're creating red slaves?" He knew the Indians themselves had held slaves, sometimes treating them cruelly, as Alexander Henry had recorded. But generally, the Indians ceased to keep slaves because it didn't work for them. The same would be the experience of the whites in the north, he insisted. Farmers in Illinois, Indiana and Michigan needed oxen and plows, not slaves. Dr. Fifthian sputtered at this. Equating black slaves with oxen turned his stomach. "The problems of the Indians are greater and more extensive in my mind," Gurdon said patiently. "If the powerful Creeks are now being forced from their lands in Georgia it will be the signal to all the tribes that all will be driven west beyond the Mississippi. There will be Indian wars again in the United States. There will be an Indian war here in Illinois. We are closer to war now than we were when Governor Cass quieted the Winnebagos in Wisconsin. The discontent among the Indians is wider and deeper. I have seen it even as I came south from Chicago and I know it is far worse in the north and west. Black Hawk now regrets he did not join the Winnebagos two years ago. He is watching for the right time. He does not intend to repeat Tecumseh's mistakes. He will strike without warning. We were saved from a war two years ago by Shabona. We may not be so lucky this time. We whites must mend our ways.''

They were impressed by his concern and the hopelessness of the situation if he was right about Black Hawk. "Gurdon, you know the land pressure of the whites will never cease," Dr. Fifthian said. "The Indians themselves must know their cause is hopeless. You are right about the Creeks. They will have to go, General Jackson is determined on it. You say slavery will end because it doesn't pay in the north and west. You may be right, but don't you see, it's the same with the Indians! They cannot or will not farm, putting the land to highest and best use. Thus they will lose it. They are uneconomic in this territory. That's why Jefferson wanted to reserve land for them west of the Mississippi, land not needed and not wanted for farming, land the federal government owns. President Jefferson wanted to benefit the Indians, not pen them up. The Indians should know and understand this."

"Yes, Doc, we take away their homes and we say it benefits them and we want them to understand, and they do not. Or, maybe they do understand, but they do not accept. Some chiefs, like Shabona, I'll admit, have accepted, they see no choice. Shabona urges his people to farm and he farms himself. Billy Caldwell accepts the move west, because there is no other choice. But there are young chiefs coming up who do not accept these things. They do not believe their cause is hopeless. They agree with Black Hawk that to keep your land you must be ready to fight for it. It is to them that Black Hawk now speaks and they listen. Maybe Black Hawk, like Pontiac and Tecumseh, has waited too long. But, if chiefs like Shabona and Keokuk, the only old chiefs who can reach Black Hawk now — if they cannot prevail, Black Hawk will fight."

Dr. Fifthian studied his friend. "You are captain of rangers in our militia," he said. "You are adopted into Waba's tribe. You are closer to the red man than any white man I know. Will you fight your friend Black Hawk?"

"Yes, because I think like Black Hawk. I must go with my own people. But first I want my people to change their ways. We don't need war, we can avoid it even now."

"After what you've just said, how will that be possible?"

"There is plenty of land. All of the Illinois prairie can be farmed. It is the settler pushing into the timber and river lands — the hunting grounds of the Indian — who causes the trouble. This is because he doesn't want the hard work of breaking the prairie. Let the *white man* cross the Mississippi! There is plenty of prairie in Kansas and Missouri. But the cry is 'Across the Mississippi . . . for the Indian!' The Indian will not go farther without a fight. Hopeless or not, Black Hawk, if he lives, will fight."

"What can any of us do?" Alethea asked.

"I once thought it would be enough to trade with them," Gurdon answered. "Our goods for their goods. I know now that neither trade nor treaties protect them. I still think they can hold their land by farming it, as Deschamps used to say. I could buy pigs from Indians. They have corn and can feed pigs. They can herd pigs on their lands and drive them to market. My *voyageurs* live on salt pork and corn. All hungry people can do it, if we could get to them the corn and pork the Indians could raise."

"You forget something you have told us, coming from your friend Black Hawk," Dr. Fifthian said. "The Great Spirit meant the Indians to be hunters not herders of pigs and goats."

Gurdon nodded. "Yes, that is what Black Hawk says. But my friend Chief Shabona has adoped the ways of the white men; he raises corn and ponies, if not pigs. Up to now there has been no market for pigs. No one has tried to teach the Indian to eat pork. But they raise ponies and dogs and they can raise pigs and sheep. We need time to get them to do it."

*

Little time was left. In the summer of 1829 immigration swept across the prairies of eastern and southern Illinois and into the north. The farmers entered Illinois by the southern rivers, a population of forty thousand gradually filtering inland after spreading along the Ohio and the Mississippi and moving westward from the Wabash. Ten years after Illinois had become a state, December 3, 1818, the white population had quadrupled.

264

Between 1830 and 1850 Illinois would get more than its share of twenty-four million immigrants entering the United States. Most were in the south. Chicago, where Hubbard slaughtered his cattle and warehoused his goods, kept a few of them, but the sandbar cut through by the army soon silted over. Harbor prospects faded. The schooners continued to stand off-shore, the captains warily watching for squalls, while Gurdon Hubbard's *voyageurs* used their shallow-draft mackinaws to lighter passengers and goods ashore. Chicago could provide few new jobs, little opportunity. Most immigrants arriving via the Erie canal and the Great Lakes were not looking for jobs. They sought land, like the others. Chicago kept a few in 1829, rising from under ten families that year to about forty families in 1830. Generally the immigrants departed Chicago as quickly as they could to search for farmland beyond the sand dunes and marshes.

Yet Gurdon prospered in the years 1828-29. He was the owner of "the franchise and good will" of the American Fur Company in Illinois, had been granted liberal credits, and the fur harvest was good. He complained to his mother, however, that he lacked sufficient cash for his needs. "I keep things going by holding my personal expenses to $125 a year," he wrote in January, 1829, possibly to discourage the increasing demands made upon him by his family in the east. "By the bye, you do not acknowledge receiving the $50 paid to Christopher for your use. I am mortified at not having any more money to send you but you can expect something during the winter." He was as happy with the Fifthians in Danville as he had been with the Wolcotts and Kinzies in Chicago and credited Dr. Fifthian with restoring his health. "Doc says he had nothing to do with it," he wrote, "but says that I feel better because I eat Alethea's cooking and no longer sleep on the ground." He was sleeping on two bearskins in the loft of his store as the rest of the space was used for trade goods. He criticized the company for not sending him the kind of goods required by his white customers.

He was into construction activities too, bidding with a partner named Norman Palmer on the construction of a brick bank building and the Vermilion county courthouse. He had travelled to the colony of Harmonie on the Wabash river, where he ex-

265

pected to buy brick, and learned that the Lutheran colonists there had returned to Pennsylvania. They had left a few brick-makers behind, however, and he found he could obtain regular supplies of the brick he would require. In his letters home he was modest about his architectural achievements. "You will perhaps laugh at the idea of building three houses in so short a time (a month)," he wrote, "but I must remark that we are not particular about architecture around here . . . they are composed of a square of rough logs with a hole cut for a door big enough to get in and get out. . . ." Actually his structures, including the bank and courthouse, showed knowledge of architecture and engineering he evidently gained from close observation of such work in St. Louis and Cahokia.

*

In late fall 1829, Hubbard was ill again, despite the best efforts of the Fifthians to keep him well and strong. He wrote his mother from Danville on December 12: "I left on the first of last month for Chicago but was taken sick at Iroquois River and confined to my bed for 15 days, and it was not until a few days since that I recovered my strength to return." Evidently he was at the Iroquois River Station during the period of his illness, possibly in the care of his men, the Baxters, or perhaps the Le Vasseurs. He found that all was going well in his store in Danville. His *voyageurs* recruited from Danville, his Iroquois post and his trading posts in the Little Wasbash area, were driving pigs to his farm and hunting a bit enroute, as he also did. Game was still abundant. Hunting parties shot hundreds of squirrels and scores of wild turkeys in a day. Frontiersman George Grogan of Ohio once boasted that a good hunter in the Ohio valley could keep a hundred men in meat. It also was necessary to kill squirrels and turkeys to keep them from destroying crops. Hubbard's store provided the settlers with guns, powder, bullets, nets and fishing tackle, and his men were instructed to teach the settlers to hunt. Wild turkeys, weighing up to fifty pounds, and catfish, as much as one hundred pounds, got the pioneers through a hard winter. Yet, increasingly, they were coming to rely on pigs and cattle, especially at Chicago.

Gurdon personally directed the wagoneers and herdsmen who drove loads of corn and scores of hogs north along Hubbard's Trail. He stored fresh pork on the frozen Chicago River and adjacent icy marshes until it was required at the fort. He began to think about building a warehouse in Chicago where he might keep his provisions and also receive trade goods lightered from ships by his *voyageurs* in the mackinaws. "We shall leave as soon as the waters get low enough to ford," he wrote Abigail in March of 1830. His iced supplies at Chicago had run out, though he had expected to have enough on hand to ship to the east and had ordered barrels from Detroit for such purpose. No ships had arrived with the barrels and Chicago was out of pork. His December drive had totalled three hundred hogs. The demand for pork was growing fast, he said. His butchers, the Clybournes, were killing some hogs on their own.

In the spring of 1830, Gurdon found he had much company along the trail north. His caravans of Pennsylvania farm wagons and herds of hogs and cattle were followed by others also engaging in such trade and the Conestoga wagons of families heading north to seek farmland. More settlers entered the Danville and Iroquois river areas. "Six families from Cincinnati, dependant on what the men can kill for subsistence, are spending the winter here, without shelter except for what their waggons (sic) afford," he wrote. Hiram Beckwith, in his histories of the area, credited Gurdon Hubbard with supplying game and food to such newcomers while he taught them to hunt. Once more Gurdon promised his mother and Elizabeth he would come to see them, and this time he meant it. "Do not expect me in Middletown before the last of March," he wrote early in the winter, "business will make it necessary for me to go via Vincennes, Louisville and Cincinnati . . . as I do not expect to go again verry (sic) soon I shall take some time to *look about*. . . ." He promised to visit his Aunt Saltonstall, who had cared for him in Bridgewater, and reported on the possibility of a boarding school in Danville:

"I have spoken with a number of people and they think a small school could be had immediately and could be increased in a few years to as large a number as could be attended to, on this subject we will talk when we meet. . . .

"Tell E. I am quite impatient to see *that wife* she so minutely describes. She should have omitted her religion, for I am not a great admirer of the Episcopal form and to see me go to one church and her to another would look rather odd. I like the picture well, but could such a lady have a man who has spent his life in the wilderness? I have got the name of being a bachelor in this country and, from present prospects, I am bound to remain so."

He returned to the possibilities of a school in Danville, a project for his sisters previously discussed. "Some verry respectable families are coming in." At the same time he assured his mother that he would be able to take care of all of them, without the necessity of a boarding school venture, in the near future.

Elizabeth was not alone in her concern about Gurdon's bachelor status. Alethea Fifthian had assured her husband that she would find a wife for their boarder and she had a candidate in mind, her sister Eleanora, who was teaching school and caring for their father in Urbana. By that time Judge Berry himself had found a second wife, so Eleanora felt free to accept her sister's invitation to come to Danville for a visit. Alethea learned that Elizabeth Hubbard, too, was busy in her brother's matrimonial interest. Possibly Gurdon let her read his correspondence; it was not unusual for pioneer families, hungry for news, to exchange private letters or to read them aloud when families gathered with friends. Alethea urged her friend Hubbard to exercise restraint and care in judgment on his eastern trip.

"Eleanora is coming this summer I'm sure," she told him. "She is blonde, like me, but taller, younger, better looking and much more intelligent." She urged Gurdon to withhold decision on "the widow in Middletown." Gurdon promised. He intended to withhold all judgment on his future until he could attend the wedding of his friend of Mackinac days, John Kinzie, at Middletown that summer. Kinzie was marrying Juliette Magill and in his letter of invitation to Hubbard, he had mentioned that Margaret Helm would be there. Gurdon told Alethea there would be plenty of time for applicants to present themselves. "I told my mother I won't marry until I'm forty," he said.

"Then you may not marry ever," Alethea warned. "Eleanora is as shy and stubborn as you are. I shall expect you to remember that when you meet her.''

*

Gurdon's visit east, his first since his departure from Montreal for the Indian country twelve years previously, was in many ways disappointing. He had foregone his buckskins for a broadcloth suit and white shirts on his arrival to Middletown, Connecticut, and abstained from chewing tobacco, but his mother nevertheless found his dress and deportment somewhat rough. She complained of his neglect of her, was unhappy when he invited his two young sisters, Abby and Mary, to accompany him back to Danville and upbraided him for bad treatment of his brother Christopher. He was hurt and much angered by Abigail's attitude. He pointed out to her that he could not accommodate all of them at Danville at once and that she, in any event, had refused to move to the west. He was leaving Elizabeth, her oldest daughter, and Hannah with her. Sister Mary was in ill health and he hoped her health might be benefitted by life in the west, where she could help sister Abby open the proposed boarding school, which if successful, might provide a living for Elizabeth and Hannah as well, should Abigail agree to move west. As for Christopher, Gurdon had offered him a job at Danville and did not even get an answer for months. When he sent money to Christopher in New York City for delivery to Abigail, he sometimes never learned whether it was done. He had stopped in New York City, enroute to Middletown, but Christopher had not met him there, as requested.

Gurdon dutifully visited the various family relatives in Middletown and Hartford, attracting considerable attention since he continued to wear his hair long, Indian style, twisted tightly at the nape of the neck and fastened with a silver barrette and he also wore moccasins after trying shoes briefly. The kinfolk and Elizabeth's friends welcomed him with enthusiasm, were eager to hear firsthand stories of the Indian country, and wanted to know of the opportunities in Illinois, especially for the acquisition of land. Many of the Hubbards and Sages and Hamlins of the area were prosperous businessmen, others had sons needing jobs. Gurdon met men who would become his partners in land buying and other ventures in the west, the Russells, Mathers, Litchfields, Campbells and Hinsdales, as well as more Hubbards. Some authorized him to buy land in southern Illinois, others recommended him to their business friends in Hartford and New York City. None at the time were interested in Chicago, though Gurdon sought to convince them opportunities existed there, especially if the canal should be dug. He met Juliette Magill at Middletown and learned that John Kinzie, her fiance, had spoken of him often to her. John Kinzie had been delayed, and the wedding postponed. John's mother was not expected because of illness nor would Margaret Helm be there. Nevertheless, the wedding would take place in Middletown and Juliette urged him to stay. Since she and John would go west to a new assignment in Wisconsin, and they could meet later in Chicago, Gurdon declined. He had many to see in New York City and had promised Abigail he'd try to repair the rift with Christopher.

In the beginning his reception in New York was little better than at Middletown. He did not at first find Christopher, who seemed to be avoiding him, and Ramsey Crooks, now president of the American Fur Company and based in New York, seemed exceptionally cool. Gurdon decided to terminate all relations with the company after making one further effort to obtain a better position in an area where the fur trade might be expected to continue strong. He had heard a man named Borup, the company agent on Lake Superior, was about to resign. Not so, said Crooks coldly. "I did expect him to resign but he has agreed to remain. There is no vacancy in that quarter nor do I see a present chance of any opening for you anywhere else." Nor was John Jacob Astor interested in possible opportunity for investment in Chicago real estate should a canal be built, nor in supplying different trade goods for white farmers and store keepers moving west. "If we invest in western real estate it will not be in Chicago," Ramsey Crooks said. "Mr. Astor is withdrawing from business. That is why I am here. We do have an interest in land opportunities and similar activity in the west, but at Green Bay or Milwaukee; certainly not Chicago." Then Crooks assured his young trader that they wished to keep him on the job in Illinois and would, in fact, sell him all the Illinois assets, supplementing the franchise he already held. "You seem to have friends here in New York and in Connecticut," Crooks said. "Perhaps they will wish to join you in such an adventure."

Gurdon, dejected, promised to consider Crooks' proposition. As he was about to leave New York for Mackinac, his brother Christopher sought him out, bringing a letter from their mother. She had concluded he was right about taking his sisters to Danville and would send them to New York to join him. He reconciled with Christopher, writing Abigail: "I received your favor by Christopher this morning and was glad to hear that you had got nearly through your trouble in out-fitting the girls, whom I hope to see with Mrs. Wolcott this Sunday. You complain, my dear mother, of my neglect in not writing Christopher. . . ." He now stated that Christopher had satisfactorily explained that he had been merely careless about forwarding Gurdon's letters and money to their mother. He had forgiven Christopher, but had no intention of taking any blame to himself. He had been doing his own buying in New York for his Danville store, he said, since he could not get the company to supply what was wanted by white settlers. He regretted missing a Mr. Wm. Hinsdale, who evidently had planned to meet him in New York and was interested in Illinois land. He told his mother of Crooks' offer, saying, "I find everywhere those willing to make advances . . . could get any amount on a 12 month cdt." He had received a letter from Danville, reporting that new settlers were pouring in, "a number of families have settled on the Iroquois River where my farm is."

He had been bitter over his treatment at Middletown and by the company in New York, but he was ready to forgive them all. He assured Abigail that he truly understood "the grief that the separation (from Mary and Abby) will give you." He urged her to allow Elizabeth and Hannah, his sisters remaining at home, to accompany Mary and Abby as far as New York to experience the excitement of a city. "It will cost you but little." He did not mention the candidate for wife Elizabeth had promised. He named a man in New York he knew who would be returning to Middletown and would accompany Elizabeth and Hannah back home.

*

He was at last at peace with himself and ready for a new future. He arranged with Christopher to become his New York agent for land dealings and to represent Gurdon to the various companies that had expressed interest in opening agencies in the west. He at last understood his mother, he thought, her ill temper with him was not unlike his own with Dufrain in Michigan, when the trader showed up in good health and spirits after he had needlessly worried over him. He had decided to go into business for himself, but was in no hurry to inform the company. He had found some in Middletown interested in Illinois farm land, others in Hartford and New York City. Since there was a government land office at Palestine, near Danville, he could go into the land business readily. His store would be well-stocked with the kind of goods required by white settlers, he had construction work ahead in Danville, and meat packing and warehousing in Chicago. He sent Ramsey Crooks of the American Fur Company an offer he was sure the company would refuse.

On his arrival at Chicago, a crisp letter from Ramsey Crooks, datelined Milwaukee, awaited him. "Dear Sir . . . I had intended to pay you visit . . . but I cannot spare the time now . . . in the present circumstances of the company we desire to realize the whole of our property, and will sell it cheap for money payable all by 1843. . . . If you think this will suit your friends, address me at Prairie du Chien and I will name you a price . . . Mr. Abbott (at Mackinac) gave me to understand you would require several years' credit . . . but you are without doubt aware that will not answer in our present situation. Cash, or short credit only, will be required now."

Gurdon wasn't interested. He offered to sell back his rights to the name and goodwill of the American Fur Company in Illinois for $1,000, an amount to be deducted from his debt to the company, an offer promptly accepted. Pierre Chouteau, Jr. of St. Louis then purchased the remaining American Fur Company interests in the Mississippi valley, arranging with Hubbard to operate a few of the posts as an independent agent. Gurdon placed Noel Le Vasseur in charge of his remaining fur trade interests on the Iroquois and at Bourbonais and kept John Crafts as his assistant in charge of the *voyageurs*, the mackinaws and the warehouse facilities in Chicago, when Hubbard himself was not there. He chose Danville as his own base, though he would be much at his farm on the Iroquois, after rounding up cattle and hogs for drives to Chicago.

Earlier in the year he had learned of the death of his friend, Dr. Wolcott, distressing news confirmed by Ellen, when she arrived in mourning for her brother John's wedding in Middletown. Since the wedding had been delayed, Ellen had accompanied Gurdon and his sisters back to Chicago, by the way of Mackinaw. There he found Margaret Helm at the Kinzie place, helping care for Eleanor Kinzie, still too ill to go east. It was a house full of widows with Robert succeeding to his father's place as the head of the family, but there was no doubt about Eleanor's domination of them all. She informed Gurdon that he was to continue to make their house his home whenever he was in Chicago. Gurdon helped Robert to open a Wolf Point store as the new Kinzie family business. He advised Eleanor to send her son to the government land office at Palestine, to file claim to the Kinzie acres in Chicago, which extended from Lake Michigan almost to Wolf Point, along much of the north bank of the river. Robert delayed action, declining to pay for a survey of the westerly fifty-two acres because he did not consider them worth having. But Eleanor and her advisor prevailed and the family became legal owners of land on which a century later would be constructed some of Chicago's most famous buildings.

Gurdon lingered in Chicago as long as he decently could. Margaret, who would loyally care for her stepmother until Eleanor Kinzie's death early in 1834, continued remotely sweet, carefully putting between them their ten years' difference in age, until he understood at last that Margaret Helm was to remain like a sister, nothing more.

*

In the late summer he led his pack train south, distributing trade goods as usual, though the bulk of it would arrive later. Gurdon was deep into the concerns of change but discovered that his growing independence from the company had prepared him well for the final separation. A market of furs would continue to exist. Indians and settlers would continue to trap. Chouteau

273

left Hubbard free to deal with the Indians as he chose, since his own interests were largely north and west. Gurdon could leave to Le Vasseur the direction of his remaining posts on the river. His own preoccupation was with the Danville store, his farm on the Iroquois, his meat packing and freight warehousing operations in Chicago, and the possibility of running for the state legislature in 1831.

He was pleased on his return to Danville to hear that the Fifthians, expecting a child, had invited Eleanora Berry, Alethea's sister, as promised. Tall and blonde, she searched him quizzically with lustrous, gray-blue eyes as he stood before her, resplendent in his dark broadcloth suit and his shining white stock, in which he had hoped to dazzle the Fifthians when he appeared uninvited at their open door on a warm August evening. "You're Eleanora Berry," he stated as the young woman responded to his call. "Alethea has told me about you. I'm Gurdon Hubbard."

"Well, I'm Eleanora," she agreed. "But you surely cannot be Gurdon Hubbard!"

"Good God Almighty!" Dr. Fifthian exclaimed as he reached the door. "Come at once, Thea! See what Providence, Rhode Island, has wrought! Gurdon Hubbard is back, in disguise!"

Eleanora was lovely, spoke softly but in the clear, crisp tones of a teacher and she was sturdy and long-limbed and walked easily at his pace. She loved the Indian country, the fishing and the hunting, and pointed out to him in the woods and along the streams some things he knew and many he did not, the difference in blueness of the asters, the texture of the sunflowers, the best yellow ochre for achieving the brightest vermilion; the reason why loons didn't walk on land (their feet were too far back); the varied uses of spagnum moss, the signs of Indian potatoes, which really were artichokes; the habits of wrens, larks, wagtails and titlarks, creatures previously too small for his attention. She loved fishing for the giant pike, known in Ohio to sometimes exceed a hundred pounds, she said, and netting catfish, walking through the thick prairie, and simply listening in the sunset for the lonely call of the loon. When she in turn asked for the identity of a slatey blue sparrow hawk, and he told her it was not only fastest of the hawks but was Chief Black Hawk's beson, she urged him to tell her of his life among the Indians. He sometimes wore his buckskins when they walked out, but only at her request, after she began to call him "her wilderness man." She corrected his grammar and his letters, suggested how he could display his trade goods in a manner more appealing to the women who visited his Danville store, and he gave up chewing tobacco, substituting his carved pipestone pipe. When Eleanora returned to Urbana to her pupils for their six-month school year, Gurdon accompanied her east to meet her father and stepmother, and she promised to come back to Danville in the spring to marry him.

*

The winter of 1830-31 was the worst in the memory of the oldest settlers in the Danville area, "the most severe one I ever experienced in the Indian country," Gurdon himself wrote, "the winter of the big snow." On November 7th, he began a drive of several hundred hogs and wagons carrying corn and camping equipment for the drovers. The snow was seven inches deep at the start of the journey and continued to fall until they reached Beaver Creek, when snow turned to rain. "By dark we reached the Kankakee and camped in a little hollow, having left the hogs a mile or so back. It rained hard a portion of the night and then the wind changed and it began freezing. The water gradually worked its way under the blanket and buffalo robe in which I wrapped myself, and, on attempting to arise, I found myself frozen to the ground, and had much difficulty freeing myself."

The drive along Hubbard's Trail was successful, Gurdon and his men reaching Chicago in ten days. They slaughtered the hogs on land west of Fort Dearborn, the Clybournes, butchers at the fort, assisting, fulfilled Gurdon's government contract, sold pork to the civilian settlers, and piled the rest on the frozen Chicago River, awaiting arrival of barrels from the east to be used to pack the meat for shipment by schooner. The Mackinac strait froze over early, and remained frozen late, so no ships arrived in the early spring, thus again Gurdon Hubbard missed being the first to export pork from Chicago, since the local populace bought and consumed it all. George W. Dole, who arrived in Chicago on May 4, 1831, won the honor by barreling and shipping pork, after wintering it on the ice Hubbard-style, until lake navigation opened, in 1832. Dole also built the first retail store building in Chicago to compete with Robert Kinzie, who sold his trade goods from a log cabin on Wolf Point. Dole complained that Gurdon Hubbard dominated packing and trade, saying "Hubbard hires more men than may be found in the garrison of the fort."

Hubbard's pack train went south along his trail in December without the trade goods he had expected. It was again a trip fraught with hardship and danger. Floating ice jammed the Kankakee River, making it impossible to ford. They had with them a single Pennsylvania box wagon, filled with blankets, buffalo robes and their food. They chinked the wagon box with snow, poured water over it, allowing it to freeze, creating a water-tight boat. Into it they packed the harness of the horses. Gurdon, Le Vasseur and two *voyageurs* clambered aboard. They rowed the wagon box across the river, the horses swimming after them, dried themselves and the horses at a camp fire, and proceeded on south at a rate of five to eight miles a day until they reached Beaver Creek overflowing its banks.

*

Thousands of others followed the Hubbard Trail from Vincennes to Danville, and north to Chicago, in the years following. Droves of hogs, herds of cattle, hundreds of Pennsylvania and Conestoga wagons moved up the trail each year, the drovers camping along the creek west of Fort Dearborn immediately north of the marshes along the south bank of the Chicago River. The sounds of their shouting, fighting and roistering grew increasingly obnoxious to other Chicago settlers in ensuing years, but the men who followed what was variously called Hubbard's Trail, the Wabash Trace, and the Illinois State Road were nevertheless welcome. They mingled with the *voyageurs*, the remaining Indians, and the sailors who brought Great Lakes shipping and Wisconsin and Michigan lumber schooners to the rude frontier town as it grew into a city. Growth was slow those first years. The sandbar across the river mouth and the hard dolomite rise of nearly fourteen feet between the south branch of the river and the Desplaines effectively shut off Chicago from its true trade potential.

Schooners and some steamships arrived at Chicago when the ice was gone, however, and other entrepreneurs followed Hubbard's example of bringing herds and provisions north. Gurdon initiated a regular freighting service, integrating his pack trains with the lake shipping via his stevedore and warehousing service in Chicago. One of his regularly employed drovers, Micajah Stanley, described the experience of freighting along the trail in the 1830s for Beckwith's *History of Iroquois County:* "Mr. Hubbard employed me and some other men to go to Chicago for goods. He engaged four teams. I took five yoke of oxen. At that time there was nothing between Chicago and here in the shape of a white family. When we got to the Kankakee the river was full. We had to ride on the middle cattle (the oxen) and drive the head ones, and the water ran into our wagon boxes. When we got to Chicago we found no goods there, so we had to stay three weeks before the schooner came in. . . . We were three to four weeks getting home. Sometimes we had to hitch ten yoke of oxen to one wagon to haul it through quicksand. We ran out of food on the way back and Henry Hubbard met us on the way with provisions." Gurdon's cousin Henry had arrived in Danville from Middletown that spring to aid Gurdon with his growing southern business.

*

In May, 1831, when Eleanora Berry arrived from Urbana, Ohio, to marry Gurdon, she found his house full of Hubbards, his sisters Mary and Abby and his cousin Henry, but she got on well with all of them. She and Gurdon were wed on May 17 by the Reverend Edward Kingsburg, minister of Danville's new Presbyterian church. Then Gurdon and his bride rode off to Perrysville, Indiana, where they caught the riverboat *Prairie Queen* for their wedding trip to Louisville. There Gurdon acquired a supply of trade goods for the white settlers which he and Eleanora hauled back "by teams and waggons." Back home in Danville they lived with Gurdon's kin in his enlarged house, a series of attached cabins in the John Kinzie style, where his sisters also conducted a school. Soon Eleanora was involved in Hubbard's multifold enterprises, the Danville store, the book-keeping for his construction projects, including the new stone and brick Vermilion county courthouse and the new Palmer-American bank building for Norman Palmer; the farm, the roundup and driving of hogs and cattle.

Often by night the Hubbards, Fifthians, Palmers and their neighbors from far into the back country gathered in the open air for talk, barter, and exchange of news and to sing the *voyageur* songs taught to them by Gurdon, or the hymns led by Eleanora, or to dance the Virginia reel and the quadrille. Gurdon had taken to heart Watseka's complaint that the white people generally did not sing and dance and enjoy life. Eleanora loved the fast-growing, prospering frontier town and the trips into the wilderness with her fast-moving husband. She accompanied him to St. Louis to buy supplies, including iron hinges and locks for the Palmer bank vault, to the Baxter farm, and into Little Wabash country, where she rode with the men rounding up cattle and pigs for the December drive to Chicago. She assisted Gurdon with his books and letters; his spelling, grammar and diction quite obviously improving.

In July Gurdon announced his candidacy for the Illinois Assembly, as John Reynolds, the new Democratic governor of Illinois, had urged him to do long before. He had little time to campaign and little need. Hubbard was known to all Danville residents and to the settlers in Vermilion county, most of whom called him "Our Gurdon," according to Hiram Beckwith, the county historian. Hubbard was a Whig, New England-born, running in territory largely inhabited by Jacksonian Democrats. He favored the construction of a canal through the Chicago Portage and deplored President Jackson's attack on the Bank of the United States. His constituency had no interest in a canal in northern Illinois and actually had helped to defeat such legislation, even though it was favored by John Reynolds; few cared about the bank controversy in Washington, though they revered Jackson. Gurdon Hubbard nevertheless won election easily.

Early in December, 1831, Gurdon rode alone from Danville en route to Vandalia, where the eighth general assembly of the legislature was scheduled to convene. Eleanora had suffered an illness and was content to remain at home where she could have the care of Dr. Fifthian and could aid in the store and help the

Hubbard girls with their school when her health improved. Assemblyman Hubbard was in his buckskins again, but carried his broadcloth suit and white shirts in his saddle bag as he headed southwest to the once-sleepy river town on the bluffs above the Kaskaskia, a place saved from oblivion when it became the capital of the state in 1820. The legislature and the Illinois Supreme Court now met in a two-story brick building once occupied by a bank. Gurdon saw it and the spire of the Presbyterian church rising among the neatly spaced cabins, taverns and stores lining wide streets in the well-timbered town, pleasant even in winter. Vandalia had a population of about eight hundred, making it one of the larger towns in the state and was thronged with legislators, lawyers and visitors, a stage from Springfield clattering in, horns blowing, just as Gurdon arrived. The plank sidewalks were crowded, men milled before the taverns, greeting old friends, and women alighted from the stage and from carriages to join the crowds. Some verteran legislators had brought their wives and daughters for the Vandalia social season. Most were farmers who came alone, as Gurdon did, and lodged in the few available room and board houses, where he also found accommodations; the taverns were packed.

He returned to the Lee Tavern taproom, seeking friends, and was soon found there by a messenger from Governor Reynolds, who escorted him to Reynold's office. "Well, Hubbard, you took my advice," Reynolds said, extending his hand. "I hear you've married again. Congratulations. Now sit a spell, we've got some talking to do." The governor looked tough and sure of himself, but not unfriendly. Gurdon sat quietly, wondering at the reason for his summons. "I keep track of things," Reynolds explained. "When I saw the returns from Vermilion county I was much gratified — you followed my advice. I almost congratulated you then, but my own supporters wouldn't have been pleased. They thought I should have helped Tim Lacy." Lacy, a Democrat, the owner of the new inn at Bunkum, had provided Hubbard with faint opposition.

"We have work to do that requires both sides of the house," Reynolds said. "I have a personal and official but secret mission for you. I'm glad you kept your hair long and that you still look half-Indian. Don't cut it." He pushed his hand through his own thick shock of dark hair. "First things first," he continued. "I know you wanted to be on the internal improvements committee. But you will be better off on the committee on finance and banking, and that's where they'll put you, you'll learn faster there, and, in time, when you're needed, you'll have much more power. I, myself, will appoint you to a special joint committee on public lands and roads."

Gurdon understood what the governor was doing, but was not quite sure why he, a Whig and a newcomer, was being picked. They had discussed Hubbard's background at Cahokia; Reynolds now indicated that he knew of Hubbard's Trail. That explained the road and public land committee. But, finance and banking? The governor soon made his plan clear. There could be no internal improvements whatever until Illinois finances improved. The finance committee would be involved in discussion of the Illinois state bank in the forepart of the session; the committee on public lands and roads would handle legislation on lands, roads, bridges, and canals.

"You will learn the problems first," Reynolds said. "Then we'll start looking for answers. By the time we can even think of canals, you'll have some experience. Dr. Wolcott writes me that you have been studying the matter."

"Yes sir, I'm more sure than ever that Chicago is the place for it. Captain Fowle let me have the Army Engineer reports. Major Long has made a good study of the problems. The water divides about thirteen miles southwest of Fort Dearborn, the elevation there being about thirteen feet above Lake Michigan; the Portage route is eleven miles long, to Mount Juliet." He quoted Major Long: " 'Of the practicality of the work, and the sufficiency of a supply of water, there can be no doubt.' "

"I agree that the Chicago Portage provides the shortest route," Reynolds said. "I also fear that the legislature is right about the cost, as much as $8,000,000. That is for a deep ditch through which the water would flow freely."

"We can have a shallow cut for a third of that amount, according to Major Long," Gurdon said. "He estimates $2,000,000 for a shallow ditch and a half million more for locks and machinery."

"I see you really have been studying it," Reynolds said. "Keep it up. Spread the gospel. Your words will be much respected, but don't underestimate the opposition here in the south. Don't forget that the cut must be through dolomite rock.''

Gurdon nodded. He understood the problems; they had gone over them before. However, he also knew that, by the Treaty of St. Louis in 1816, to which Black Hawk so strongly objected, the government had obtained a strip twenty miles wide along a possible canal route from Chicago to a site called Ottawa to the southwest, ''covering the navigible route to the Illinois and Desplaines Rivers and the Portage of the Chicago River.'' So, the government of the United States already had committed itself. The government owned the land and would undoubtedly pay part of the costs.

''You speak of Black Hawk,'' Governor Reynolds said. ''That brings me to the next item for our meeting. I want you to do something for me and the State of Illinois, quietly and confidentially. I want you to see your friends among the tribes to find out what Black Hawk is up to. You can do this as a member of the public lands and roads joint committe; you can go anywhere, openly. If you need to do more than that, why get back into your buckskins and become an Indian for a time.''

''I would not spy on my friends!''

''Dammit man, why not? How else are we going to know what best to do? You have told me long ago that your friend Shabona opposes Black Hawk. Surely you do not want him to unleash a war on us? Governor Cass was able to prevent the Winnebago war from spreading because he learned in advance what was brewing. I need to keep myself in a similar position. You, Hubbard, are the right man to do it and you know it.''

''I did not get elected to become a spy,'' Gurdon said firmly.

''You are a soldier in the militia and an officer,'' Reynolds replied. ''I am commander-in-chief of the Illinois militia. I can command you, but instead I urge you to volunteer. George Rogers Clark sent his man Ben Linn into the British post at Kaskaskia and he sent Sam Moore to Cahokia to find out the lay of the land, and General Clark took both without firing a shot. What's wrong about that? You are the one who can best do this; you are an officer of the Vermilion County Rangers and I am commander-in-chief of Illinois Militia. You'll be serving your state and helping

281

your Indian friends.''

"They might not think so.''

"The time has come, Gurdon, when all of us must decide what side we're on," Reynolds said firmly. "*You* already decided that when you chose to ride for help against the Winnebagos. I understand your reluctance. When the legislature breaks for Christmas, go home and see your wife . . . then see your friend Shabona, and maybe Keokuk . . . and come to see me when you get back. . . . Learn all you can, and continue to study up on our canal project. We'll bring that up at the proper time.''

*

Gurdon Hubbard of Vermilion county moved swiftly into the committee work of the Eighth General Session, while the Assembly itself mostly marked time with general discussion and debates through December, as Governor Reynolds had predicted. Gurdon found Eleanora and his sisters in good health when he returned to Danville. Again Eleanora was content to remain at home while he called on his trading posts and inspected possible roads to the west. He visited Tamin, Waba and Shabona and was reassured by them. Since the Congress of the United States had passed the Indian Removal Act, and it had been signed into law by President Jackson, even Black Hawk realized that fighting would be hopeless, his informants said. They predicted that Black Hawk himself, already holding lands in Iowa, would obey the removal law; he had agreed before witnesses to do so. The friendly chiefs asked Hubbard to seek to delay their eviciton as long as possible. He promised to help, assuring them that Governor Reynolds' voice would be heard in Washington. He went on to Chicago to seek out Billy Caldwell and to consult with Col. Thomas J.V. Owen, the new Indian agent there, and his friend John Kinzie, Jr., now Indian agent among the Winnebagos. They jointly sent an appeal to Lewis Cass, once Kinzie's boss, now secretary of war, urging him to delay the actual removal of the Illinois Indians. But, in the south, the Creeks, Choctaws and Seminoles had signed treaties finally ceding their lands east of the Mississippi and were preparing to depart. While in Chicago, Gurdon learned from Kinzie that Black Hawk was in Winnebago country, with his

282

prophet, White Cloud, seeing potential allies. At Prophet's Town, on the Rock River, White Cloud advised Black Hawk not to give up his land in Illinois "for the whites to plow up the bones of our people."

Back in Vandalia Gurdon reported to Governor Reynolds on this final bit of intelligence. It was possible that Black Hawk would recross the Mississippi with his warriors. Shabona and Billy Caldwell doubted this would happen. "If he crosses, it will be the beginning of war," Reynolds said.

*

Gurdon found himself welcome in the councils of the Illinois House. He was comfortable there, though he was a newcomer and a Whig among Democrats. The house met on the first floor of the crumbling old bank building in a large, bare room filled with long plank tables and spindleleg chairs, each seat provided with a sand box and quills and sheets of foolscap for those able to write and inclined to take notes, and sand boxes on the floor for tobacco chewers. Plastering had fallen from the ceiling and some walls, especially over the presiding officer's desk and podium where the oratory and shouting sometimes became loud and fierce. Iron Franklin stoves provided the heating; there were supplies of candles for dark winter days and evening sessions. Hubbard, who had brought a tailored suit back from the east, found himself to be among the better dressed of the representatives, mostly farmers and young lawyers from the country towns, garbed in homespun, coarsely woven stocks about their throats to guard against the cold, thick woollen coats hanging low over their blue denim pants. Most wore as much clothing inside the room as they did out. On the floor above sat the senators, older and richer men, dressed in the manner of eastern gentlemen, as was Representative Gurdon Hubbard in his dark broadcloth suit neatly cut, his stock of white silk, his white cuffs showing. He continued to wear Indian moccasins and his black hair was long and held tight to his neck by the Indian barrette. The well-dressed women who occasionally came to the visitors' gallery of the House found him a pleasant young man to watch. He presented a committee report or two and generally his utterances on the floor were few and to the point. Hubbard ter-

283

minated much of the discussion in the two years of his service, the record shows, by his motion "to lay on the table" the measure under consideration, thereby killing it. At the same time, Hubbard's own major contribution to legislation, a proposal to require the existing canal commission to make a study of the Chicago Portage alternative, got nowhere. As the session neared its end in March, 1832, Governor Reynolds again summoned him.

This time it was Reynolds who had fresh intelligence concerning Black Hawk, received from the army commanders at Jefferson Barracks, Rock Island, and Prairie du Chien. "I worry about that Indian," he said. "He has been in touch with the tribes all the way to Texas and into Iowa and Missouri and Wisconsin. The Winnebagos are said to be with him. The question is, when and how will he strike? Governor Harrison had his worry about Tecumseh, brought him in to talk. When that settled nothing, Harrison moved, and the Battle of Tippecanoe settled it. But I have no regular army. There is no garrison at Fort Dearborn. Illinois is laid open if Black Hawk chooses to strike. You are my scout, Gurdon. I must know now what is going on."

Gurdon was not pleased. His remarkable rise in the legislature appeared to be due to Reynolds' requirement of a good spy. Yet he understood the need of spies, remembering that when God told Moses to take the land of Canaan, Moses chose trusted men of the tribes and "sent them to spy out the land." Gurdon knew that he was specially qualified for the mission. He knew the country, the languages, the chiefs; but the Indians, for the most part, were his friends. He was determined not to betray their trust. He felt he had done good work on the governor's select committees, earning his way as a legislator. He resented being asked to pay for his opportunities by spying. He also understood that his own project, the canal, was at stake. Should Black Hawk loose an attack, it could doom the canal for months or years. Thus he felt compelled to accept Reynolds' assignment, but first he defended Black Hawk. "He had just cause for complaint," Gurdon told the governor. "He did not sign the St. Louis Treaty nor the Chicago Treaty. He has been robbed of his land. Not only Sacs are unhappy. All the tribes are unhappy. Their treaties are violated, their lands taken, their hunting grounds filling up with squatters. And now you are saying that if Black Hawk recrosses the river it will be an act of war!"

"It is not your place, nor mine, to decide the justice of this," Reynolds responded hotly. "Our sworn duty is to protect the citizens of this state. Whatever Black Hawk's justification, he must be stopped, overwhelmed. It must be ended quickly. You and I can't stop history from happening, but we can make it less painful.

"The Indians will be better off west of the river. This country in Illinois is intended by God for farmers. Look at our prairies! They exist because the God of Nature sends fire to destroy them in proper season. Thus there is new growth, but no trees can grow. The prairies have been awaiting the white man's plow. The Indians have been here a thousand years, but they have not tamed the prairie. They have not tried. It is the manifest destiny of the white man to do it."

Governor Reynolds was justified in his view, Gurdon believed. Deschamps had said the same thing. So, in effect, had Black Hawk. The Indians themselves called the prairie *maskolis,* meaning place of fire, where no trees could survive. Black Hawk and Reynolds thought alike, but arrived at differing conclusions. The Great Spirit sent fire to prepare pastures for buffalo and elk, in the Indian's view. God had reserved the prairie for the white man's plow, said Reynolds. Let the Indian and the white man do that which the Great Spirit intended each should do, Black Hawk intoned.

"As Governor of Illinois I must know what Black Hawk is thinking," Reynolds persisted. "I have waited for you to volunteer. Since you don't, I now order you, as an Illinois militia officer, to this duty."

"Governor, I don't have a commission from you. I am a volunteer and I can volunteer to quit. You honor me with your friendship, but don't put a knife to my throat."

Reynolds was content. He tossed off his port, rose, and held out his hand. "I know your duty," he said. "There is not much time. Let me know what Black Hawk is doing. You are my friend."

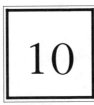

10

Belleville
State of Illinois
April 17, 1832

To the Hon. Secy of War, of the United States

Sir: The State is again invaded by the hostile Indians and
the country is in imminent danger. This is made manifest
to me by Official Communications a part of which I here-
with transmit to you. . . . The regular troop under the
command of an excellent officer of the U. States Army
Gen. Atkinson is too small to pursue the Indians . . . the
frontier is in great danger.
                                                    John Reynolds

Late in March Gurdon Hubbard was in the north, moving up
from the Peoria and Sangamon territory, toward the Rock River.
A few days earlier he had visited Chief Keokuk on the Mississippi and had stopped at Chief Shabona's village. He learned
from them that Black Hawk *(Ma-ka-tai-me-she-kia-kiak)* seemingly planned to move soon against the whites. Should the Sac
chief and his warriors cross the Mississippi for any reason, he
would be in violation of the treaty he signed June 7, 1831, in the
presence of Governor John Reynolds and Major General Edmund Gaines. Black Hawk, leader of both Sac and Fox tribes,
had been a reluctant signer. "The Great Spirit made the land for
all men, red as well as white, and has placed the red men on this
land where they now lived, and the women were tilling the corn
fields until they had become easy of cultivation and they were
unwilling to leave them," Black Hawk had said. But General
Gaines replied that there were prior treaties obliging the Sacs
to leave their corn fields and villages and their cemetery on the
bluffs overlooking the Mississippi at the mouth of the Rock
River. "They must now move, within three days, across the river
into Iowa." Thus read the official report. "Whereupon Black
Hawk replied that if the chiefs of his tribe consented, he would

no longer oppose.''

On April 5, 1832, Black Hawk violated all treaties including the June agreement, by crossing the Mississippi at the mouth of the Iowa. He became an "invader" of lands his people long had claimed.

Governor Reynolds knew in advance that Black Hawk intended to return to Illinois and that he would not have the aid of the Potawatomis there, nor would he be helped by Keokuk, the powerful chief in Iowa, though some of Keokuk's braves might join him. Nonetheless the potential for a widespread Indian uprising was great. The young men of all the tribes had heard much of the grievances against the whites and saw their lands being taken. They had heard more of the glories of Tecumseh than of his defeats. Many of them were ready for war. Since their own chiefs were aging and timid, they prepared to join Black Hawk, a white-haired warrior himself, but a chief with courage, who had been advised by the young prophet, White Cloud, that the British in Canada would come to his aid once he began the fighting.

Gurdon Hubbard kept in close touch with Keokuk and Shabona in the days when Black Hawk personally visited those chiefs in his effort to whip up war fever. Black Hawk himself never mentioned the name of Shabona in his own account of the war, dictated while he was in military prison, but he did admit the failure of his visit to Keokuk, and he also alluded to conferences with various Potawatomi chiefs. Henry R. Hamilton, who included Hubbard's memoirs of his early years in his own autobiography, describes these meetings in considerable detail, evidently obtaining the information directly from Hubbard, as well as from Drake's biography of Black Hawk.

Black Hawk, accompanied by his entire band of braves and warriors, came to Shabona's town at Paw Paw, in DeKalb county, Illinois, after sending runners to all the Potawatomi villages "urging attendance of every chief, brave and warrior" at the war dance he proposed to hold in "Shaubenee's" village, according to Hamilton, who used Hubbard's spelling of Shabona's name. This would have put the time after April fifth. "When all had assembled, Black Hawk himself rode up on a white horse, dressed in the uniform of a colonel of British cavalry, with a cavalry sword and belt, followed by Neopope (his leading advisor and military aide) also in British uniform, and other Sac chiefs and their warriors, the latter beating tom toms and singing war songs.'' They were armed with lances, spears, war clubs, bow and arrows, as if going to battle. Black Hawk's guns evidently were few in number, so he showed none of them.

Black Hawk clearly expected to infect the Potawatomis with war fever sufficient to override the objections of Shabona and his chiefs. He intended to arouse a spirit of vengeance among the young men that would sweep before his advancing warriors, setting the villages against their peace-keepers, turning loose the fighters he would arm with British weapons which, White Cloud had assured him after a trip to Fort Malden in Canada, would be brought to him at Milwaukee. Black Hawk's braves, singing their songs, set up a war post in the village circle before Shabona's lodge and called upon the Potawatomi warriors to join their dance. At this moment Shabona himself emerged from his lodge, followed by Billy Caldwell, Tamin, Waba and other chiefs who long had opposed further war and who obviously intended to remain friendly to the whites. Possibly Hubbard himself was at Shabona's village that night, in war paint, or within Shabona's lodge. Shabona greeted Black Hawk with cold civility, a sign to his own young men that, although they had painted, they should not join the dance. Soon Black Hawk realized that only his Sac and Fox braves and some neighboring Kickapoos constituted the leaping, shouting circle around the war post.

Black Hawk angrily rode through the line of dancers, hurled his tomahawk into the war post with a force that sunk its steel blade deep. His signal stopped the dance. Black Hawk was then sixty-seven years old, his scalp lock into which an elk's tail was woven was almost white. He slid gracefully from his pony and stood beside the war post, his gems, silver medals and ancient accoutrements of war oddly contrasting with the British uniform. Black Hawk was not an orator, nor powerfully built like Shabona or Keokuk, but he was lean and hard and clearly ready for battle. He recited the wrongs inflicted upon the Indians by the white man. He described the territory once held by the Sacs, Potawatomis and Winnebagos, reaching from the Illinois river to Prairie du Chien and Green Bay, some seven hundred miles, land long held from the domination of the whites by the victories of Tecumseh; land that teemed with buffalo, moose, elk, deer, bear and varieties of game, where the rivers and lakes were filled with fish. "The Great Spirit gave us elk and deer and corn and berries and squash. Never was an Indian child to know hunger. Food was in plenty, we shared it with one another and with the white traders among us. No stranger, red or white, entered our lodges without finding food placed before them. Gitchie Manitou created this land and its plenty for his children and they were happy here until the palefaces came to drive them away." There was a further listing of specific wrongs, and Black Hawk recalled the Sac wars with Indian enemies, especially the Osages, who also sought Sac and Potawatomi land, and the battle in which his father died. "I assumed command, killed three men, wounded many. I now fell heir to the medicine bag of my fathers . . . (The skin pouch holding besons, his good luck charms) . . . I blackened my face, fasted, and prayed to the Great Spirit for five days. . . ." Black Hawk recounted his own acts of valor, totaled the costs in lives of Sac and Fox warriors. Always their hunting grounds were sought by voracious whites, first the Spaniards, then the Americans, the latter with false promises as much as by force of arms. "They asked us to pull down our British flags and to give back our British medals . . . this we declined." But the British, too, betrayed them at the battle of the Thames.

Black Hawk described American treachery and broken treaties. "I took my rifle and shot in two the cord by which they hoisted their flag," he boasted. He recalled Fort Dearborn, saying he had helped to free those American prisoners because they had fought well. He paid tribute to Gomo, the great Potawatomi chief who had fought the Americans. He described the final despoilation and humiliation of his people when they were driven from their homes, their corn fields and their national cemetery while their hunters were away, leaving the women, the aged and the children at home. "They burnt our lodges, destroyed our fences, plowed up our corn, violated our women, brought whisky into our country, made our people drunk, and took from them horses, guns and traps."

Black Hawk turned to his old friend, Shabona, who had fought so well with Tecumseh. "Shabona, if you will permit your young men to unite with mine, I will have an army like the trees in the forest and will drive the palefaces like the autumn leaves before the angry winds."

And Shabona, thick in girth, ten years younger than Black Hawk, but somehow seeming older, answered clearly with the words he had so often used in replying to Black Hawk in the past: "Yes, Black Hawk. But the palefaces will soon bring an army whose numbers are like the leaves of the trees, and they will sweep you and your army into the great ocean beneath the setting sun."

*

No warriors from Shabona's village, nor from eastern Illinois, nor from Chief Keokuk's territory joined Black Hawk in the early days of April, but some two or three hundred came to him later. He blamed Keokuk especially for the failure of the young men to respond at once, which would have created waves of recruits, in his opinion. "Keokuk has been the cause of my situation," Black Hawk would say in his autobiography, though without doubt, Shabona and his allies had withheld far more men. Keokuk, the orator, had spoken impassionedly, "I will lead you, my people, upon Black Hawk's path only if we first put our wives and children, our aged and infirm, gently to sleep in that slumber that knows no waking, since we cannot take our dear ones with us, and we dare not leave them behind."

Gurdon Hubbard could report to Governor Reynolds on Black Hawk's movements after crossing the Mississippi, a route northeast up the Rock River, towards Prophet's Town and into Winnebago country. The Tippecanoe situation, seemingly, was being repeated. Save for two hundred or so of Kickapoo and Potawatomi braves, and a hundred or fewer of Keokuk's men, Black Hawk would have to fight alone, with his Sac and Fox warriors, so long as he remained in Illinois. Black Hawk had taken with him the women and children, the aged and infirm. "Our women and children were in canoes, my braves on horseback," he said in later years. "The Prophet (White Cloud) came down to join us on the Rock River." Black Hawk up to that time used

291

the excuse that he had re-crossed the Mississippi to help The Prophet's people plant crops. From White Cloud, Black Hawk learned that General Henry Atkinson, commander of Jefferson Barracks in Missouri, was personally bringing soldiers north. In a few days a runner sent by Atkinson found Black Hawk encamped on the Rock River north of his own ancestral village, Saukenkuk. He was ordered to "re-cross the Mississippi at once." Had General Atkinson then called for a conference to discuss the situation, the war might have been avoided.

"I sent him (General Atkinson) word that I would not recognize his right to make a demand," Black Hawk recalled. "I was acting peaceably and intended to go to the Prophet's Village, at his request, to make corn." Moving on up the Rock River, past Dixon's Ferry, due west of Chicago, Black Hawk passed near Shabona's territory and may at that time have visited his village, as stated by Hamilton, or called in Potawatomi chiefs, his own recollection, or perhaps both. Near the Kishwaukee River he was met by emissaries from the Winnebagos, promising help if he was ready to fight. "During this council, a number of my braves hoisted the British flag, mounted their horses, and surrounded the council lodge." This demonstration was to impress a suspected American agent, who arrived with the Winnebagos. Actually he was Henry Gratiot, son of a Wisconsin fur trader. Possibly Black Hawk earlier had some suspicion that Gurdon Hubbard was checking his activities. In this instance he evidently wanted an inspired report to go back to the Americans: Black Hawk was ready for a fight. "I concluded to keep up the river and see the Potawatomis and have a talk," without the presence of Shabona and his chiefs. He asked the Winnebagos if they had heard or seen signs of British guns and supplies arriving at Milwaukee. They had not. "The next day the Potawatomi chiefs arrived at my camp. I had dogs killed and made a feast. I received news that three or four hundred white men, on horseback, had been seen eight miles off." Black Hawk sent out eight braves, three under a flag of truce, five to watch proceedings from a hillside. He intended at this time to discuss a return to Iowa, according to some historians. Again there was the chance that war could be averted. White soldiers of Major Isaiah Stillman's command, Illinois militia, opened fire on Black Hawk's emissaries, pursuing some of them into an ambush at Black Hawk's camp. The Black Hawk War was on.

*

There was panic in northern Illinois. Governor John Reynolds and his militia felt they were ready for war but the populace generally did not know earlier that Black Hawk had crossed the Mississippi "prepared to ravage the countryside." Up to the time of the attack on Black Hawk's truce party, actual hostilities might have been avoided, Black Hawk himself would say in later years. "I concluded to tell my people that White Beaver (General Atkinson) was after us, no news had been brought to me of guns and supplies at Milwaukee, that it was useless to think of going on." But the soldiers attacked his truce team, killing two. "I was preparing my flags to meet the war chief," Black Hawk recalled. "Nearly all my young men were ten miles off . . . I started with what I had left (about forty) before we saw part of the army approaching. I raised a yell . . . we saw the full army coming at full gallop . . . we thought all our truce party had been killed. I placed my men in front of the bushes, that they might have the first fire. . . ." The enemy halted. "I gave another yell and ordered *a charge upon them!*"

Black Hawk said he expected he and all his men would be killed. But it was Stillman's force that retreated, an ignominious defeat. Twelve of Stillman's 234 men died. The battle was fought near a creek, or run, in what would become Ogle county, Illinois. Black Hawk himself killed at least one soldier. "I threw my tomahawk and struck him in the head, he fell to the ground, I ran to him and with his own knife took off his scalp." Black Hawk returned to camp with his men, giving up pursuit of the whites after riding six miles. They brought in stores of provisions, guns, ammunition and some whisky and empty whisky kegs from Stillman's camp. "I was surprised to find that the whites carried whisky with them!"

Possibly Black Hawk did intend to sue for peace, before the skirmish at Stillman's Run, as he later stated. The Winnebagos had convinced him that no British help was at hand, contrary to the promise of White Cloud, (*Wabokieshiek,* the Prophet). He knew he had been deceived. Perhaps he recalled that Tecumseh, too, was betrayed by his Prophet. But his victory over the Americans convinced Black Hawk to go on, ending any chance of his peaceful return to Iowa. President Jackson ordered the chastisement of Black Hawk. The settlers in the northwest demanded it. Governor Reynolds in his communication to Secretary of War Cass on April 17, had indicated the determination of the whites: "I have called out a strong detachment of Militia to rendezvous near the frontier on the 22nd. inst., this is within three or four days march of the enemy, and this is a place where supplies can be furnished by water. While the Militia is organizing, I hope to see General Atkinson and know the precise situation and intention of the Indians. I am satisfied that the country requires the movement and I hope the Militia will not be ordered home before these Indians are chastized. I will march with the Militia and go to all lengths of my constitutional power to protect the frontier by chastizing these insolent and restless Indians."

Major Stillman's defeat was an isolated skirmish, a defeat to be avenged. Walter Havighurst, respected historian of the Northwest, suggests in his *Land of Promise* that "the foolish and tragic Black Hawk war could have been averted by a modicum of white man's patience and coolness of mind. But in that troubled summer a fear and fever swept over the Middle Border." Donald Jackson, editor of the 1955 edition of Black Hawk's autobiography, states flatly that "Black Hawk tried to surrender," just before the Battle of Stillman's Run. But Black Hawk was doomed from the time he crossed the Mississippi. The whites had long been prepared finally to disperse the Indians from eastern United States after two hundred years of struggle. Black Hawk, like Pontiac and Tecumseh before him, could not stop the inexorable process. The whites coveted the Indian lands and meant to have them. Black Hawk merely speeded the inevitable end.

*

General Henry Atkinson, on reaching Fort Crawford at Prairie du Chien, had sent his scouts into the Winnebago and Menominee country of Wisconsin and into the Sioux country of the Great Plains to the west, intending to check any assem-

294

bly of allies in support of Black Hawk. Atkinson himself reconnoitered southwestern Wisconsin to the Illinois border, where Galena, the largest northwest settlement, was situated, Galena being vital to the army and the nation as the source of lead for bullets. Atkinson was in a relatively strong position; he had two companies of the First Infantry at Fort Atkinson; two hundred soldiers were moving up the Mississippi by steamboat from his base at Fort Jefferson in Missouri, and he could call upon troops at Galena, and those under Major Zachary Taylor at Prairie du Chien, as well as the Illinois and Wisconsin militia. Black Hawk had fewer than 1,000 warriors, though the numbers were growing, the warlike Kickapoos alone sending one hundred. There was always the possibility that the Winnebagos and Sioux would be aroused. Black Hawk had the impediment of his women and children and aged, the entire population of his Iowa village, and he lacked sufficient guns and supplies. Keokuk had warned him specifically on both. "The British Father is at peace with the Great Father in Washington and neither knows about you," Keokuk had told him at the council in Keokuk's village. "Will our cousins on the Illinois River rise up to help you as the false prophet tells you? . . . They are at terms of peace and goodwill with these white settlers. You are told that when the watch fires are kindled at Saugenkuk they will begin the slaughter. Where are their great chiefs tonight? You have been deceived, cruelly deceived. If you persist in going to war, then we must say farewell to Black Hawk, whose protecting spirit has forsaken him in his old age. . . ."

*

Gurdon Hubbard had returned to the Iroquois country and Danville sometime in April, having discharged his legislative duties and his mission for Governor Reynolds. He was not called up with the militia until May and then with the rank of second lieutenant in Captain Alex Bailey's company in the regiment of Col. I.R. Moore. Hubbard subsequently was elected colonel by his own Rangers, a scouting force, which addressed him as colonel throughout the war, the custom at the time. After the war he would be appointed colonel on Governor Reynolds' staff and paymaster for the Illinois militia.

As the Vermilion County Battalion prepared for war in the weeks prior to muster in late May, other Illinois enlistees, among them a jobless ex-clerk named Abraham Lincoln of New Salem, gathered at Reynolds' staging base at Beardstown for training. Young Lincoln was elected captain of his company, a mounted force like Hubbard's. "Even after his nomination for the Presidency, he remembered this as the most satisfying honor of his life," biographer Benjamin P. Thomas would write. Lincoln drilled his men hard at Beardstown, attempting to whip into shape the undisciplined band, most of them his friends. Twice Lincoln was required to drill with a wooden sword as punishment for the misadventures of his men. "In the intervals between drilling they sang, roistered, wrestled, and played rough pranks," Thomas wrote. Lincoln, good at wrestling, nonetheless lost his match. Gurdon Hubbard's mounted company was relatively well-drilled in advance, ready for the order to proceed to Fort Dearborn, again without a garrison. Terrorized settlers to the west had been seeking supposed safety of the fort. Some, to the south, were fleeing towards Danville.

*

The roles of Hubbard and the Potawatomi chief, Shabona, in the early days of the Black Hawk "invasion" are not clear. Whether Black Hawk held council with Shabona at his Paw Paw village, as stated by Henry Hamilton, or whether he was called to council at Black Hawk's camp on the Rock River, as reported by Schoolcraft, the result, so far as Hubbard, Shabona and subsequent events were concerned, were the same. Shabona risked his own life to save white settlers. "He stole forth from the council of war in the dead of night. . . . He had decided he would save the lives of frontier settlers from the terrible torture of the tomahawk and scalping knives. He saw death like a pall hanging over the white settlers; nor did he stop to consider long." Thus Hamilton's version, based on the Paw Paw council, details probably from Hubbard. Shabona knew the whites well enough to understand their suspicion of his motives when he rode to warn them that Black Hawk was on the warpath. He knew also the possible consequences of betraying his own people. Yet he rode through the night from Bureau Creek, according to one account, with his son Pyps and a nephew, dispersing them to make sure they reached as many settlers as possible, along a hundred-mile route towards Chicago. His message was succinct, "Me Shabona. Black Hawk come!"

George Hollenbeck, one of the settlers saved by Shabona, would recall the ride of his Indian friends. "There were no roads or bridges, they were pursued by Sac spies. . . . They called on settlers' homes and most so warned, fled." Some did not and instead reviled Shabona for disturbing them when he pounded on their doors. Some who knew him suspected he was drunk, since Shabona was known to drink much whisky in his late years. At Hollenbeck's place, Shabona's horse foundered, and then died. Shabona was a heavy man and had ridden hard. He carried the bridle and saddle to Hollenbeck's door, and the settler, knowing him, gave him a fresh horse, then gathered his own family for the ride to Fort Dearborn. "Every settler along the whole frontier was warned in time to speed for safety," Hollenbeck remembered. "But, alas, there were a few who failed to heed the warning."

He referred to the massacre at Indian Creek, twelve miles north of Ottawa, unrelated directly to Black Hawk, except that he had aroused the young Indians. William Davis, known for his hatred of redskins, had built a dam on Indian Creek that obstructed the flow of water to the Powatatomi village downstream, ruining the fishing. The Indians demanded that Davis should remove his dam, but he had refused. While Black Hawk ranged further north, a war party of sixty Potawatomis and a few Sacs on May 20 raided the Davis outpost, killing sixteen adults and children. Two young women, the Hall sisters, Rachael and Sylvia, were taken prisoner and later freed. They said they were decently treated.

Shabona, age fifty-seven, rode thirty hours without sleep, through country hostile to his purpose, in his successful effort to arouse the whites to danger. Most whites soon forgot what he had done; he was later treated shabbily by the American government, and Neopope, Black Hawk's chief aide, and his warriors twice tried to assassinate him in later years for betraying his people. Gurdon Hubbard, however, would remain Shabona's trusted friend through the remainder of his lifetime.

*

In mid-May, Hubbard had led the vanguard of his Vermilion County Rangers back to Fort Dearborn. Once again the fort was in the charge of an Indian agent, this time Col. Thomas Owen, but the command of the militia there was divided between Jesse B. Brown and Richard J. Hamilton, the latter adjutant to Governor Reynolds. Colonel Hamilton had just arrived; evidently his chief mission was to find and deliver instructions to Gurdon Hubbard, since there were only thirty-seven militiamen under two colonels at the fort prior to the arrival of Hubbard, who brought only one hundred men, not the three hundred expected. The people of Vermilion county also had been panicked by the news from the north, especially after a postman carrying the mail from Chicago reported that he had been followed by hostile Indians all the way to the Iroquois River. Settlers fleeing western Illinois were coming east through Vermilion county en route to Indiana, despite the fact that Black Hawk, starting from an area near Fort Madison, Iowa Territory, had gone north to the Rock River, not directly east or south. So Vermilion county retained a part of its battalion for its own protection. Such terror and panic were not unusual on the frontier. Henry Schoolcraft, in his *History of the Indian Tribes,* would summarize the situation: "The effect of an Indian War on the frontier is always appalling, a few hundred Indians having the power of alarming the inhabitants and disturbing the settlements through a wide extent of the territory."

Gurdon Hubbard, having been elected colonel of his mounted Rangers prior to departure for Chicago, arrived at the gates of Fort Dearborn with men who previously had come to the salvation of the fort and town, thus they were welcomed with great joy. Colonel Hubbard himself was resplendent in a uniform of his own design, which Judge Henry W. Blodgett, who witnessed the scene, described at a meeting of the Pioneers of Chicago some years later: "I think, without exception, he was the nearest to my ideal of a frontier soldier of anyone I have ever seen. Splendid in physique, six feet and something more in height, he rode a splendid horse, and dressed in just enough of the frontier costume to make his figure a picturesque one. He wore buckskin leggings, fringed with red and blue, and a jaunty sort of hunting cap. In a red sash about his waist was stuck, on one side, a silver-handled hunting knife, on the other, a richly mounted tomahawk. His saddle and accoutrements were elegant, I might say, fantastic, and altogether he made a figure to be remembered.''

*

That first battle of the war, which even the whites soon denigrated as "Stillman's Run," was a disaster for whites generally and especially for Governor Reynolds, now functioning as commander-in-chief, Illinois Militia, who on April 16 had informed General Atkinson, "I have ordered General (Isaiah) Stillman of the Militia to organize four companies of mounted men of fifty each. And for him to command them as Major. The Battalion is ordered to range on the frontier under Major Stillman's command from the Mississippi eastward. In order to be ready for war or peace, I have judged it proper to call out about 1,200 of the militia, who will be mounted and will rendezvous at Beardstown (on the Illinois River below Peoria). . . . Should the Indians commence hostilities, the militia can be marched in a few days to the scene of the action.''

Major Stillman and his battalion had reached Dixon's Ferry when reports came in that Black Hawk was to the north, somewhere near the confluence of the Kiskwaukee and Rock rivers. Stillman asked permission to go after the hostiles and permission was granted. Major Stillman boasted that he was starting out "with a fixed determination to wage a war of extermination wherever he might find any part of the hostile band,'' reported the newspaper *Galenian*, published at Galena. It added maliciously: 'They had with them a full commissary, including a barrel of whisky, and the authorities are quite numerous in saying that many of them were inspired by maudlin courage they imbibed.''

Major Stillman would give his name to a creek flowing into the Black River about thirty miles above Dixon. His disparagers would attribute the name of his battle, Stillman's Run, to the nature of his defeat. When Stillman and his fleeing soldiers reached Dixon, after he had lost two officers, Major Perkins and Captain Adams, and ten men, General Whiteside in command of the main force of militia returned to the scene of the battle. Nothing remained for them to do but to bury the mutilated dead. Among those who helped was Private Abraham Lincoln, newly assigned without rank to a mounted "spy" force commanded by Captain Jacob M. Early. That was as close as he got to the fighting, Lincoln would later say. But he would not forget the scene of death and mutilation.

The Stillman disaster convinced Governor Reynolds and General Atkinson that they were dealing with an elusive, resourceful and brave foe. Black Hawk could move rapidly and secretly to strike at points of his own choosing. They were required to protect vital areas on a broad perimeter. Black Hawk in effect controlled a vast country through which they needed to communicate regularly, and Reynolds said he had a way to do it. He sent his adjutant, Colonel Hamilton, to Chicago with orders to Gurdon Hubbard of the Vermilion County Rangers to report to Reynolds with a few men of his choosing. Since Gurdon gave up his command, as Lincoln had done, he too lost his elective rank, and became a lieutenant in the scouting and spy force. His orders instructed him, "find the seat of the war." As he was about to leave Fort Dearborn, a messenger arrived with the news of the massacre at Indian Creek. Colonel Hamilton ordered Hubbard to go at once to the scene of this attack before reporting to Commander-in-Chief Reynolds.

Lieutenant Hubbard reported on two such guerilla attacks: "The victims (at Indian Creek) had all been scalped and the bodies mutilated. The children had been hacked to pieces, the bodies of the women being nailed, suspended by their feet, to the walls of houses." Gurdon and his small band buried the dead. "At Holderman's Grove, about sixteen miles northeast of Ottawa, conditions were similar to those at Indian Creek," he reported. The following morning, Fort Beggs, at Plainfield, was abandoned and the settlers were sent to Fort Dearborn under an escort of Hubbard's Rangers, adding to the terror-stricken throng already there. Their stories of massacre and horror increased the panic.

*

Lieutenant Hubbard's activities and precise whereabouts during this period are sketchily recorded in regular army annals. He was no longer connected with his own militia company other than to communicate with Commander-in-Chief Reynolds and Colonel Hamilton. The Vermilion County Battalion, including his Rangers, remained at Fort Dearborn. The nature of Hubbard's mission thereafter is indicated by a note to Governor Reynolds, signed by Brig. Gen. H. Atkinson, Headquarters Right Wing West Depot, Ottowa (sic) 7th June, 1832: "Sir, I have received your letter yesterday by Lt. Hubbard." Followed by an order: "I have to request that after assigning a company to cover the settlement on Hickory Creek at DuPage, that you will march the residue of your force to the fort as early as practicable." The dispatch was to Captain William Moore, 27th Illinois Regular Militia. Moore was an officer Gurdon Hubbard had restrained earlier from indiscriminately killing Indians, including friendly Potawatomis, according to a letter commending him for it, written by Colonel Owen at Fort Dearborn, and was under direct command of Reynolds. It is doubtful that Hubbard spent much time with the officer he previously had countermanded and criticized, however, since the records indicate he was carrying messages from Atkinson to and from generals Edmund P. Gaines and Henry Dodge, the commanders in the west, as Atkinson began to close in on the elusive Black Hawk.

The militiamen and regular army officers seemed to be free spirits who disobeyed orders, flouted their superiors, and communicated outside channels with some impunity. Lt. Col. William Jackson, at Galena, in a near hysterical letter sent directly to President Andrew Jackson in Washington on June 19, reported that "a hostile army of 900 is said to be at Mud Lake (the Chicago Portage). . . ." Colonel Jackson also feared that Black Hawk might prove himself able to seize the lead mines at Galena. Should Black Hawk succeed, Colonel Jackson wrote, "millions of dollars will not reinstate the condition (of) 14 years ago . . . a great number of troops will now be needed to conquer and destroy those hostile Indians."

The lead mines were in potential danger, but there were no Indians immediately menacing Chicago and Fort Dearborn, as General Atkinson learned from the courier, Lt. Hubbard. In riding through Indian country dressed in buckskin with no insignia, Gurdon could pass as an Indian, as Governor Reynolds long before had noted when he advised his friend not to cut his long, black hair. Gurdon was armed Indian-style with rifle, knife and tomahawk. Again his mission was not to fight but to carry messages and to observe. He evidently was the communication outlet for Colonel Early's force, since he met Abraham Lincoln during the latter days of the Black Hawk war, and they became lifelong friends, Lincoln sometimes making Hubbard's home his residence when he visited Chicago.

As a courier among the commanders, Gurdon rode mostly by night, along the Indian trails, which were generally deserted since no Indian would travel in total darkness if he could avoid it; evil spirits were about. In daylight he hid when he saw potentially hostile scouts. He investigated what he could without risking capture. If caught he hoped to be taken before Black Hawk and to be treated as a prisoner of war, and even expected to use his friendship in an attempt to persuade Black Hawk to surrender. On the trail Gurdon carried the familiar supplies of his fur trading days, parched corn, dried venison, and tobacco. Since there was little time to stop for a pipe, and he couldn't light up in the darkness without risk, he began chewing tobacco again, a habit that would persist the rest of his life. Each mission was filled with danger, since he crossed country where only Indians roamed. The regular army mostly kept to its forts and bivouac areas after Stillman's Run. Gurdon saw nothing of Black Hawk, but found signs of his encampments and indications that his food supplies were exhausted. Bark had been pulled from the trees, roots dug, areas cleaned of berries. Black Hawk continue moving north, up the Rock River, and finally into the swamp region around Lake Koshkonong in Wisconsin. When he reappeared it was in the vicinity of Four Lakes, west of Koshkonong.

*

By July, General Atkinson believed that Black Hawk would soon emerge from his hiding places in the Wisconsin swamps and marshes since food would be required for his women and children as well as his fighters. But Atkinson said he would need no Illinois help in destroying Black Hawk. Governor Reynolds took advantage of this news to release some of the militiamen, needed on their downstate farms. Captain Early's scouts evidently were included, since Private Lincoln was one to go back. Black Hawk's forces had, in part, broken into small guerilla bands carrying on terror raids in eastern Wisconsin and northeastern Illinois, sometimes bringing down the wrath of Winnebagos as well as the whites. Their need of food had become desperate. "In the style of savage warfare, they are devastating the settlements, robbing, destroying and murdering in sweet revenge for the outrages of Stillman's men," said a report quoted in Andreas' history. The writer referred to Du Page county, Illinois, specifically. General Atkinson came under strong criticism in Washington for failing to find and destroy Black Hawk's force. John Reynolds induced John Kinzie, the Indian agent in the Winnebago country, to return to Chicago to organize a force of Potawatomi warriors for the defense of the town and Fort Dearborn, enabling him to free more men for work in their southern Illinois cornfields.

General Atkinson concurred with Reynolds' decision. Through Hubbard they were coordinating their efforts. Atkinson knew that Black Hawk had emerged from the swamps and was heading west. Atkinson had neutralized the Sioux to the west and would be ready for the final battle with Black Hawk.

Gurdon Hubbard succinctly summarized his own duties in the Wisconsin area in later years for the Wisconsin Historical Society. Responding to a query, he wrote: "I was on Gen. A.'s campaign from the time I left the Illinois River . . . and conversant with every movement."

*

Early in June a new disaster befell Fort Dearborn and Chicago. General Winfield Scott had been ordered by General of the Army Alexander Macomb to take over the conduct of the war since Washington was dissatisfied with General Atkinson. Scott and his hastily gathered force reached Fort Dearborn July 10, aboard the steamer *Sheldon Thompson*. "The morning after their arrival, it became known that cholera, in its most fatal form, was a passenger on the ship," wrote Henry Hamilton, a son of

Colonel Hamilton, who was then commanding the militia at the fort. "The soldiers died like flies, and corpses, too numerous for formal burial, were unceremoniously hustled into common graves." In days more than a hundred soldiers and civilians died within the palisade walls. The terrified settlers now fled the fort, preferring to take their chances with the Indians after Lieutenant Hubbard arrived to report that Black Hawk, quite definitely, was in western Wisconsin. On July 16, General Scott, a victor over the Chippewas at Lundy's Lane in the War of 1812, led his ill and weakened force to the Des Plaines river, west of Chicago, for ten days of recuperation, and then started north to join Atkinson's forces, where, presumably he would carry out his orders to take over the conduct of the war.

General Atkinson, meantime, found Black Hawk now attempting to escape across the Mississippi, it was assumed, and troops under Generals Henry and Dodge were stationed to block his way. They came up to Black Hawk's force July 21, on the south bank of the Wisconsin river, about twenty miles from Fort Winnebago. There was a battle lasting six hours, until darkness fell, Black Hawk losing sixty-eight dead and many wounded. The troops and militia volunteers under James D. Henry and Henry Dodge had marched forty miles, fought six hours in heavy rain, and their weapons and powder were wet. "They were not in a condition to continue the pursuit that night," said the official report. The next morning they found that Black Hawk had escaped in canoes with his entire force including the women and children. Lieutenant Jefferson Davis would say that Black Hawk's river crossing, under fire, was the most brilliant exhibition of military tactics he had ever witnessed.

*

Black Hawk sought to retreat across the Mississippi. Atkinson's troops blocked him. On August 3, Black Hawk divided his force, part of his band descending the Wisconsin river while his own contingent approached the Mississippi along the Bad Axe. The Wisconsin river group met army regulars with Menominee recruits from the Green Bay area and was wiped out. Neopope, Black Hawk's chief aide, protecting the rear, failed to come up,

304

though a few of his men got through to Black Hawk. At the mouth of the Bad Axe, the army steamboat *Warrior* blocked the way to the Mississippi and opened fire. Black Hawk and his people disappeared into the thicket along the rivers. The day following, white settlers, troops and militia found the Indians. They attacked men, women and children. Black Hawk lost one hundred and fifty killed at Bad Axe while the army reported eight dead and sixteen wounded. It was the end of the Black Hawk war. Black Hawk himself surrendered. Some two hundred of his force escaped across the Mississippi.

Later General Winfield Scott apologized to the Indians for the killing of women and children at Bad Axe, saying they could not be distinguished from warriors as they hid in the thicket. However, some of the casualties were women attempting to swim the river with children on their backs, according to Black Hawk. In his official report to President Jackson on the successful campaign against the Indians, Commanding General of the Army Alexander Macomb declared that they had undoubtedly been well chastized for crossing the Mississippi. "There was clamor for Black Hawk's blood," wrote Henry Schoolcraft, "but President Jackson refused, saying Black Hawk was a prisoner of war. He was taken on a tour to see the military works at Fort Monroe and returned to his people a better and wiser man." Prior to the tour, however, Black Hawk and some of his chiefs were imprisoned in irons at Jefferson Barracks for several months.

*

The defeat of Black Hawk signalled the end of the Indian struggle to retain their land east of the Mississippi. The way was open for a flood of immigration, especially into northern Illinois and southern Wisconsin. The war lasted only fifteen weeks; casualties, especially for the whites, were light; most of the troops called up never met an Indian in combat, but the consequences were great. The government could proceed to move the Indians into permanent exile without further hindrance. The whites could lay claim to the best farmlands in the United States without fearing the redskins.

The lives of many young men directly involved were

changed. The young Indians were forced into reservations west of the Mississippi, until such time as they would be pushed farther west. Hundreds of soldiers and kin of the soldiers would return to claim bonus lands in the west. Some of the leaders in the war would go far in politics: Abraham Lincoln and Zachary Taylor, the latter the commandant at Fort Howard, would become presidents of the United States; and Lieutenant Jefferson Davis, president of the Confederacy. Major General Scott would become General-in-Chief of the United States Army. Lieutenant Albert Sidney Johnston would command the Confederate forces at the Battle of Shiloh. Joseph Duncan, Thomas Ford, and Thomas Carlin would become governors of Illinois; Colonel Henry Dodge, governor of Wisconsin; Private Orville H. Browning, a United States Senator. Gurdon Hubbard knew most of them and would become involved in their lives, but he sought no political advantage for himself, though Governor Reynolds made him a colonel and state paymaster of the Illinois militia. Colonel Owen, commandant at Fort Dearborn, and Colonel Richard Hamilton, commanding the militia there, would become Gurdon's lifelong friends and his close associates in activities at Chicago.

Black Hawk became a celebrity in the east for a time. He was taken before President Jackson in April, 1833, then set free after an eastern tour in which he and his son Nasheaskuk were shown the mighty works of the white man. Then Black Hawk returned to Iowa, where he died October 3, 1838. Years later whites erected a fifty-foot granite memorial to him on land whites had stolen from him on the Rock River.

*

When the Illinois General Assembly met December 3, 1832, Gurdon Hubbard was present as a politician of considerable skill and power. He was a member of the House finance committee and two House-Senate select committees, one on banking, the other concerned with audits of Illinois finances, which were found to be in deplorable disarray. He exploited his new-found political strength by extending the purview of his House Committee on Roads and Bridges to include canals. He recommended that the House approve further study of the proposed

Chicago Portage canal route, which had been abandoned, and that a new board of canal commissioners be created. His proposals resulted in legislation which ultimately would reverse the anti-Chicago bias of the legislature, some based on high cost of a canal cut at the Chicago Portage, some representing the indifference of southern Illinois to problems in the north, particularly Chicago.

Hubbard also won approval of his proposal for a new county to border Vermilion county on the north, no mean achievement since Vermilion county had claimed territory all the way to Chicago as recently as January 15, 1831, when the Illinois legislature authorized the creation of Cook county, Chicago until that time having its county seat at Peoria. The Vermilion country claims preceded those of Peoria or Detroit, long the repository of Chicago records, dating back to the days when Illinois was a part of Virginia. Cook county, named for Congressman Daniel P. Cook, a fervent advocate in Washington of a canal for northern Illinois, was organized March 8, 1831. The county commissioners, meeting in Chicago, created a plan for public roads and selected a site for the courthouse, south of the river and west of the fort, on land where Gurdon Hubbard had been penning his cattle and hogs prior to slaughter. To pay for the projects, Cook county authorized the auction of ten acres around the courthouse site. Hubbard purchased several of these lots, where Chicago's famed Loop would rise, for about $5 each, all ten acres going for a total of $1,153.75.

*

Gurdon had begun the creation of his own barony on the Iroquois River, to the north of Vermilion county, in September, 1831. There he owned much of the land not claimed by the Indians or the United States government and he employed most of the settlers. He had appeared before the Vermilion county commission to offer a proposal from the Iroquois river dwellers: "This day Gurdon S. Hubbard presented a petition of sundry inhabitants praying for the election of one justice of the peace, and one for constable; and that all elections be held in the house of Allen Baxter (the house on Hubbard's farm). Ordered, that Isaac Courtright, Allen Baxter and Isadore Chabert be, and they are, appointed judges of the above election district, and that an election be held in said district on the 15th day of November next." All three judges were employed by Hubbard. At the June, 1831 session of the commissioners, an election was ordered held in the house of Toussant Bleau, for a district "on the waters of Sugar Creek and the Iroquois and their tributary waters." Toussant Bleau also worked for Hubbard.

On February 12, 1833, as Representative to the Illinois Assembly from Vermilion county, Gurdon Hubbard procured passage of "An Act Establishing Iroquois County," extending to the new Cook county line on the north, along the Kankakee river. The judge of the Circuit court of Vermilion county in Danville was instructed to proclaim the Iroquois area a county by granting an order for the election of county officials whenever he deemed it had 350 inhabitants. This election took place February 24, 1834. Gurdon Hubbard was not a candidate himself, since he had departed his fiefdom by that time to become a resident of Chicago.

But Gurdon's major political proposal, the canal bill favoring the Mud Lake route between Chicago and the Illinois river via the DesPlaines, failed of passage by a single vote early in 1833, the deciding vote being cast by Zadok Casey, president of the senate, to break a tie. "Southern counties could see little advantage to them of a canal across Mud Lake, or in the platting of a town on Lake Michigan," wrote John Clayton in his *Illinois Fact Book.* "There also was debate as to whether the canal should be a shallow-cut plan with feeder canals from the Calumet, Kankakee, Desplaines, Du Page and Fox rivers, or a deep cut which would reverse the flow of the Chicago river." Hubbard had gained several votes for his canal proposal by offering a companion measure for the study of a state railroad plan. This bill survived and began winding its way through the legislative labyrinth. Gurdon had lost, temporarily, but also he had made important gains. In February, 1833, he was named to a select committee to study "An Act Incorporating the Illinois and Michigan Railroad." In the hearings he pointed out that a railroad, running north and south across Illinois, and a canal at the Chicago Portage would tie the Port of Chicago, planned by the Army Engineers, to the rest of the state. A canal terminus on the

Calumet river would not do, he asserted, since the city and port which would develop at such a terminus would be partly in the state of Indiana. On March 1, 1833, Hubbard proposed a new canal bill which would include the construction also of a railroad. However, no further action was taken on internal improvements in that session.

*

Gurdon had been away from his personal affairs for almost a year while he served as a legislator, on missions for Governor Reynolds, and as a soldier. Evidently Eleanora and his cousin Henry Hubbard did well at the Danville store, and Noel Le Vasseur and Allen Baxter likewise at the trading post and the farm. Le Vasseur even participated in politics a bit, being named to the commission which selected a site for the Iroquois county seat they called Iroquois, for which service he was paid $20. That summer of 1833, Hubbard selected two men to carry on his canal fight in the state legislature. Dr. Fifthian agreed to run from Vermilion county, Isaac Courtright from the new Iroquois county; both were elected. Also in the summer of 1833 Hubbard was named one of the official witnesses to treaty payments to be made to the tribes served by the Indian agency at Chicago, the Potawatomis, Ottawas and Chippewas, and, at the request of the chiefs, he agreed to serve as a trustee for some of the Indian children who were to be paid, since their parents had died.

He persuaded Eleanora to accompany him to Chicago though she was not in good health. He told her the gathering of the Indians would be a spectacular event and it might be the last in Illinois. He could make her comfortable since they would travel with one of his pack trains increasingly making the trip from Vincennes to Chicago. "Hubbard's pack trains made a standard route . . . which gathered the travel from many miles on either side, as far south as Vincennes," Beckwith's history would say. The trip was far from easy, however. The route was long, dusty and intensely hot across the prairies in late summer. The sun blistered the paint on the wagons and forced frequent stops to rest and water the heaving horses. Heat waves shimmered, creating mirages of lakes and cool groves that did not materialize. Bull whackers cursed their laboring oxen and mules. Eleanora, sickened by the heat, rested in a wagon as Gurdon rode to the head of the column to order an early afternoon stop at Beaver Creek. The heat and dust choked animals, bull whackers and horsemen alike; the women were made comfortable while the wagons and animals crossed at the ford, then the women mounted horses and rode across, being delightfully cooled as they forded the deep stream. None hestiated to splash their faces with the pure creek water and to lower ladles into it for drinking.

The following day Eleanora felt better and she accompanied Gurdon to the head of the column. They were being joined constantly by Indians, Potawatomis, Ottawas, Chippewas, Kickapoos, Delawares, and Miamis, all having some relationship to the United Potawatomi nation, which was ceding the last of the lands, and receiving annuities from past treaties. When they reached the Kankakee river they were joined by Chief Tamin and his headmen and many of their women. Tamin and Hubbard continued to be good friends. As the train lumbered over the final miles to Chicago the creaking of labored wheels, cracking bullwhips, angry shouts of drovers and the squeal of pigs and the bawling of cattle was relieved by the melody of silver bells, clinking weapons, straining harness and greaves as the chiefs of distant villages came up, then passed the freight caravan and Tamin's modest band on their way to Chicago.

Another of the white travelers to Chicago that September was Charles J. Latrobe, an English writer, who provided a vivid description of the Indians and the town. "Within five miles of Chicago we came to the first Indian encampment . . . five thousand Indians were said to be collected around this little upstart village for the prosecution of the treaty by which they were to cede their lands in Michigan and Illinois. I have been with many odd assemblages of my species, but in few, if any, of an equally singular character as with that . . . in Chicago. The little mushroom town is situated upon the verge of a perfectly level tract of country . . . open prairie land . . . at a point where a small river enters Lake Michigan . . . no harbor, however, vessels must anchor in the open lake. Fort Dearborn, a stockaded enclosure with two block-houses (and a lighthouse near by) is garrisoned by two companies. . . . We found the village on our arrival crowded to excess; and we procured, with great difficulty, a

small apartment, comfortless and noisy. . . . The Potawatomis
were encamped on all sides on a wide level prairie beyond the
village, beneath a shelter of low woods . . . they consisted of
three principal tribes with adjuncts of smaller tribes.

"The village presented a most motley scene. The fort contained within its palisades by far the most enlightened residents,
in the little knot of officers. . . . Next to the officers, the residents, a doctor or two, two or three lawyers, a land agent, five
or six hotel keepers and merchants." For the rest: "Birds of passage, horse dealers and horse stealers—rogues of every description, white, black, brown and red; half-breeds, quarter-breeds,
and men of no breed at all; dealers in pigs, poultry and potatoes, like our friend Snipe (who sold pigs the wolves had killed
and partly eaten); creditors, sharpers of every degree, pedlars,
grog sellers. The little village was in an uproar from morning
until night, and from night until morning, when the housed
population of Chicago strove to obtain repose in the crowded
plank edifices of the village; the Indians howled, sang, wept,
yelled, and whooped in their encampments. With all this, the
whites seemed to be more pagan than the red man." The whites,
said Latrobe, were to blame for the sale of whisky to the Indians.
He paid his compliments to Mark Beaubien, landlord of the Sauganash, Chicago's best known hotel: "Within the vile, two-story
barrack, which, dignified as usual by the title of hotel, afforded
us quarters, all was in a state of most appalling confusion, filth,
racket. The public table was such a scene of confusion that we
avoided it from necessity. The French landlord was a sporting
character, and everything was left to chance. . . ." Thus Latrobe
began the creation of Chicago's reputation.

Eleanora Hubbard fared better than Latrobe. The Hubbards
were guests of the Kinzies and she was soon comfortable among
them as a member of the family. She became a friend of John's
young wife, Juliette Magill Kinzie, who would herself describe
the Chicago scene in much gentler terms in the pages of her clas-
sic story of travel *"Wau-bun" The Early Day in the Northwest,*
first published in 1856 (Wau-bun meaning dawn or break of
day). The ladies of the Kinzie household probably didn't venture forth much in the September heat. John and Gurdon Hubbard were busy with treaty affairs. Gurdon, looking into land

311

purchase possibilities for Dr. Fifthian and eastern friends, wrote briefly to Fifthian on the eve of the treaty signing: 'There are many thousands here for the treaties. . . . The Indians are not well satisfied. Great interest in the lots on which I will give more later. Eleanora is not well." But a cooling rain and the breezes off Lake Michigan brought them comfort and they were some distance from the new town growing up at the forks of the river and the Indian camps west and north. Eleanora soon recovered. John and Robert Kinzie and Gurdon Hubbard donned Indian garb and staged their own Indian war dance for their women in the Kinzie front yard.

*

Charles S. Butler, arriving in Chicago that August with his friend, Arthur Bronson, both of New York City, had come to Illinois to look into the possibilities of real estate investment for William Ogden, Butler's brother-in-law, a young New York lawyer, financier and politician. They had heard of the beauties and possibilities of northern Illinois from their friend, General Winfield Scott. In a long letter to Ogden, Butler described Chicago as he saw it just prior to the great Indian council. "We approached Chicago on a beautiful day in August. . . . A small settlement, a few hundred people all told, the houses, with one or two exceptions, the cheapest and most primitive for human habitation, suggest the haste with which they have been set up. A string of these buildings are erected without much regards to the (property) lines on the south side of the Chicago river (South Water Street) . . . on the north is a single house previously occupied by Kinzie (probably the Agency House, the Kinzie house had been partly destroyed by fire) . . . the government has just entered upon the harbor improvement of the Chicago River."

Butler and Bronson stayed at the new hotel being built by James Kinzie near the forks of the river, where a new village was beginning to grow. Called Green Tree Tavern because a single large oak stood in the yard, Kinzie's inn was not yet completed. Latrobe was at the better known but older hotel, the Sauganash, operated by Mark Beaubien, famed for the dances he conducted there, his race horses, which he ran along the river in summer and on the ice in winter, encouraging all to bet, and his boast, "I keep hotel lak hell!" There was also the Wolf Tavern, at Wolf Point, kept by Elijah Wentworth, who, it was said, once, with an axe, killed a hungry wolf trying to steal meat from his kitchen, and Samuel Miller's tavern.

Chicago without doubt was a hot, miserable place, filled with the stench of leek and wild onion and the festering rot of the marshes at the end of summer, but Butler showed understanding of the frontier town and its people, suddenly overwhelmed with visitors, and treated them with relative kindness. "The house (evidently Green Tree) is crowded with people . . . many of them could find sleeping room only on the floor. The east window of my bedroom looked out upon Lake Michigan in the distance, Fort Dearborn lying near the margin of the lake, the buildings very low structures." He and Bronson liked the resident Chicagoans they had met, as well as the officers at the fort. "We made acquaintance of the principal men of the place, Richard Hamilton, the Kinzies, John H. and his brothers Robert and James (James was a cousin), Mr. Wright, Dr. Temple, Gurdon S. Hubbard, Colonel Owen, and George W. Dole."

Gurdon Hubbard would become closely associated in Chicago not only with Butler and Bronson and William Ogden, later to become mayor of Chicago, but also with the others Butler named: Colonel Hamilton, a former Kentucky lawyer, soon to hold simultaneously all of the Cook county offices except commissioner, the only man ever to do so; Dr. John T. Temple, the preacher from Washington, D.C., who would also carry the mail from Green Bay to Chicago, for whom Chicago's great skyscraper devoted to religious activities would be named; George Dole, first to build a retail store; and John W. Wright, builder of a reaping machine and one of the famed Chicago boosters, but then a merchant, who had described Chicago succinctly earlier that year: "It contains 150 people exclusive of the garrison, two framed stores, no houses except of logs."

Eleanora Hubbard, made welcome by the Kinzies, became a good friend of Eleanor Kinzie, who urged her to come to Chicago to join her planned Episcopal church, since she was of that faith. Again Gurdon agreed to help. When he learned that the army was under way with harbor improvements, he was eager to make the move north. Eleanora was not precisely pleased. Though accustomed to oppressive heat at Danville, she objected to the Chicago smells, winds and noise. "I can't believe Chicago is intended for permanent habitation," she told him.

He knew that she was unwell and under a strain, despite the kind hospitality of the Kinzies. He thought, too, that she was experiencing Chicago at its worst, for which he could only blame himself. "October is beautiful," he told her. "We should have waited for October, but it wasn't possible. That smell is from wild onion and leek, and is only bad at this time of year. That's why it's called Chicago by the Indians. It ends in October. The heat can end any time the wind changes."

"Let the wind change soon," Eleanora implored.

"Sure, we'll have problems here, but there'll be good times too. Let's try it again before we decide. You'll grow to like Chicago. The Kinzies are our friends, the Beaubien and La Framboise families want to be. You'll like Billy Caldwell and Alexander Robinson when they get free of their treaty negotiations. Chief Robinson is half Scotch, as kind a man as can be found, yet he rules the United Potawatomi nation. He and Billy Caldwell will remain here when the tribes leave." He ignored the probability that when the Indians departed permanently all those he mentioned except the Kinzies might depart too, since the French families were closely intermarried with the Indians.

Gurdon worked late at the fort, on the treaty problems and the distribution of his trade goods in from Mackinaw. The Indians were causing problems. They had not understood that the government intended this treaty to require the surrender of the last of their lands, except for a few small reservations, and grants of farms to individuals for special services to the American government. They were not ready to sign away their last claim to lands east of the Mississippi. Yet, after the defeat of Black Hawk, they were ordered into permanent exile in lands reserved for them to the west. Some of the chiefs had ridden their ponies west to inspect those lands and they did not like what they saw.

On September 21, Gurdon wrote again to Dr. Fifthian, who was in Ohio, seeking funds he planned to use to buy Hubbard's Danville store and Chicago lots. "The Indians are not content with the treaty but will sign. . . . I expect to sell some of my trade goods while we are here. I hope that your trip to Urbana will help to bring our concern to a close. I am looking at purchases for our (land) concern here. Eleanora has been quite sick but she is getting better. The treaty will be concluded soon. Love to Fanny and kiss little George (Dr. Fifthian's children) for me.''

On Sunday they went with the Kinzies to a religious service at Wolf Point, conducted by the Reverend William See, a Methodist preacher and the blacksmith at Fort Dearborn, recently arrived from Washington, D.C. There they met Mr. and Mrs. Forbes, who had come to Chicago to start a school, and thus got on especially well with Eleanora Hubbard. As they walked back to the Kinzies', Eleanor Kinzie reviewed the sermon: ''Mr. See should have asked forgiveness for murdering the King's English.''

Eleanora Hubbard soon concluded she really would wish to make her home in Chicago, as her husband so urgently desired. He promised to build her a house on a high oak summit north of the river, near the lake, away from the miasma of the swamp, where cool lake breezes could reach them. The time was right. The army was moving ahead with harbor plans. Dr. Fifthian was obtaining funds to buy the store. Gurdon planned a large brick warehouse on two of his lots on the south bank of the river. Hopefully, when he sold the remaining lots, he would have funds for the operation of his business and a good house. John and Juliette Kinzie would be their neighbors. Gurdon had letters from the east asking about the advisability of buying farmland in northern Illinois. He would have a real estate as well as a lighterage and warehousing business and could continue his fur trading operations through Le Vasseur. They'd visit Danville often when he went south for pigs and cattle. Eleanora did not doubt that they would do well in Chicago.

11

September, 1833
The red man had been deceived, robbed, driven from his possessions. This I have seen, indeed, I have assisted in driving them from their homes.
John H. Fonda, Indian Agent
Wisconsin Historical Collection V5

They had come to Chicago, the dreary frontier town with its gleaming, whitewashed fort now guarding land once their crossing place from the Great Lakes to the Mississippi. They had come to surrender the last of their precious possessions, the land. They wore their finery, feathers and beads, fringed buckskin, silver gorgets, medals, bracelets and bangles, glittering gemstones in nose and ears. They were barbarians who refused to live in the white man's way, saying their God decreed otherwise. Their chiefs had declined to give up their land and homes cheerfully and even now stubbornly resisted signing the warrant ordering them and their people into permanent exile. They had been defeated, destroyed, and decimated in two hundred years of fighting for their country, their freedom, their rights, their way of life. When Black Hawk dared to explode in furious rage at the centuries of misdeeds, and to engage in acts of savagery and terrorism, his people had been ravaged and destroyed. They had been chastized. Now their kinsmen were assembled, friend and foe alike, to acknowledge once again they had learned their lesson and to promise they would depart their land forever. Still, stubborn aborigines that they were, they resisted.

Late in the afternoon of September 21, the high chiefs and headmen of the United Potawatomi Nation, a people entrusted by the tribes as the keepers of the sacred council fire, gathered at Chicago to hear last words of wisdom and remorse from their advisors and the statement of government terms before putting their marks to still another treaty; this one immutable and final. They had been summoned by the Government of the United States that, having vanquished them, now appeared to mock them in their adversity by treating them as a sovereign nation, whose treaty obligation would be duly reviewed by the Senate of the United States, then ratified, then signed by the President. They had been defeated for the last time east of the Mississippi. Now they were given the conditions of their inescapable fate, which no amount of parleying, feasting, dancing, chanting and praying, nor of drinking white man's whisky, could further delay or change.

It was true they had sold much of their land, or parts of it, many times over, usually after they had lost another war. It was the way of the world, acquisition by conquest: To the victors belonged the spoils. It was true that the conquerors offered payment, from trinkets and baubles to needed food, clothing, guns, medicine and silver. Between 1778, when the United States made its first Indian treaty between two nations, and 1880, the government paid Indians an estimated $187 million "for the extinguishment of Indian land titles" according to a federal report in 1883. This was considerably more than the $100 million paid France, Spain, Mexico and Texas for territory west of the Mississippi and east along the Gulf of Mexico into Florida. President Jefferson had been villified for paying far too much for that Louisiana Purchase, so his plan to exchange some of the land thus acquired for Indian land, by means of an amendment to the constitution of the United States, initially was doomed. But, in time, the country saw the wisdom of President Jefferson's Indian policy, as he had expressed it to his friend Samuel Kercheval, "bribe them into peace . . . and retain them by eternal bribes." Land, good land, it was said, was made available in Missouri, Kansas, and Iowa.

Chief Black Hawk's unwise lunge against the whites, ending in fifteen weeks with the destruction of his people in the Bad Axe thickets, provided the right conditions for the final extinction of the red man's claim to lands east of the Mississippi. This was a reality perceived by Gurdon Hubbard and all who attended the Grand Council of the Potawatomi, Ottawa and Chippewa nation, all except the Indians. Earlier, according to historians of the Potawatomis, their chiefs in the Iroquois river area had come to Gurdon Hubbard at Danville to ask his help in delaying expulsion from their lands. Hubbard himself said he passed along their appeal. No record of such an appeal has been found but there was delay. Hubbard, like any Indian trader, preferred to keep his customers about him and so had incentive for such an attempt to help his red brothers. But also without doubt he shared the conviction of the Indian agents, the Kinzies, father and son; Wolcott, Fonda, Owens; and Gholson Kercheval, sub-agent at Chicago, that the expulsion of the Indians from Illinois was inevitable. Antoine Deschamps had warned the redskins long before that they could not hold their land unless they farmed it, while Black Hawk, citing the Delaware example, insisted they could not hold it, even as farmers, unless they fought for it. Chief Shabona tried farming and failed. Black Hawk tried fighting and failed.

Now Gurdon Hubbard sat among the twenty-seven government representatives and witnesses gathered around the Potawatomi council fire on the north bank of the Chicago river. Governor G.B. Porter of Michigan, representing President Jackson, informed the Indians that their Great White Father knew that they wished to sell their land for annuities and in exchange for lands west of the Mississippi in Iowa, Missouri and Kansas. He called upon the chiefs to consider, sign and adhere to the treaty as promised.

Chief Alexander Robinson of the United Potawatomi, Ottawa and Chippewa tribes signalled to Chief Topenebee, representing the tribes on the St. Joseph River in Michigan, that he would be heard. Topenebee, a tall, white-haired old man, benign as a village parson except for his fierce black eyes, arose slowly, loosened the folds of his blanket, looked about him in quiet dignity, and spoke: "The Great White Father in Washington has heard lies. We are not ready to consider nor to sign a treaty. We are not prepared to leave our lands. We have come here since the Great White Father has called this council, to speak with you on general things."

The general shock of disbelief was brief. Only the carpetbaggers from the East, newly arrived with whisky and other trade goods for the redskins, were really fooled. Veterans who knew Indians merely exchanged knowing glances. Governor Porter sighed and spread his hands in exasperation. Gurdon Hubbard and the other traders present had anticipated this, Gurdon saying in his letter to Dr. Fifthian that very morning that there might be a brief delay, since the Indians obviously were not satisfied. Porter glanced good-humoredly at his fellow officials and said that the council would resume when the chiefs were ready. The delay would cost a few more days, a few more kegs of whisky, a few more hideous nights of howling and dancing. God had made the world in six days and Porter expected the Indians could be prevailed upon within less time to relinquish their share of it. Once again it would be necessary for the Indian agents and sub-agents, and all white friends of the Indians, to explain to them that they would get excellent lands west of the river in exchange for their marks on the treaty paper.

So again the chiefs conferred with one another and with their advisors and the agents. The young braves resumed their celebration. B.J. McClure, a young army man, and Charles Latrobe, the English writer, wandered through the encampments by day, when they deemed it safe. "Scenes of drunkenness, debauchery and violence occurred," McClure would recall in later years. Wild redskins, mounted on their ponies, sometimes two braves to a mount, charged down upon them, laughing derisively at their fear, Latrobe remembered. "Far and wide the grassy prairies teemed with figures, warriors mounted or on foot . . . whooping, yelling like fiends." The young men visited the encampments of tepees and shelters made of branches and blankets, saw children and squaws and dogs in great numbers, listened to "a grave conclave of chiefs seated on the grass in consultation. . . . It was amusing to wind silently from group to group, noting a raised knife, the sudden drunken brawl quashed by good-natured and even playful interference of neighbors. . . ."

Latrobe, like McClure, complained of the hideous nights as the howling braves celebrated. He was strongly critical of the American govenment for allowing so much whisky to be sold and drunk, asking how the United States could be exculpated of charges of "cold and selfish behavior toward the Indians" under such conditions. "Day after day passed," he noted. "It was in vain that the signal-gun from the fort gave notice of an assemblage of the chiefs. . . . The council fire was lighted. . . . There might be twenty or thirty chiefs assembled (by late afternoon). The palaver was opened by the principal commissioner (Governor Porter). He requested to know why his colleagues were called. . . . An old chief would arise . . . answering one question by proposing another . . . why had their White Father called his red children together? . . . A young chief arose, and spoke vehemently to the same purpose. One or two tipsy chiefs raised an occasional disturbance." Governor Porter angrily assailed the chiefs for playing a dangerous game with their Great White Father in Washington, using "vehement Jacksonian discourse," Latrobe said.

On September 26, the chiefs capitulated. They assembled to append their marks to a treaty providing that "all the lands of the United Nation of Chippewa, Ottawa and Pottawatomie (sic) Indians along the western shore of Lake Michigan and between this lake and land ceded by the Winnebago Indians (in Wisconsin by the Treaty of Fort Armstrong . . . and the Treaty of Prairie du Chien in 1829) would become property of the United States and open to settlement by whites." Topenebee was the first to make his mark. It was Gurdon Hubbard's duty, evidently, to identify the chiefs he knew personally as they drew their rude crosses. He said later that Shabona did not sign in person but authorized Billy Caldwell to act for him. All three of the friendly chiefs left only their marks, though both Billy Caldwell and Alexander Robinson were able to sign their names.

The treaty provided for the exodus of the Indians to new lands, money for provisions, annuities, the payment of claims to creditors and for the establishment of farm equipment repair and blacksmith shops the Indians would require if they concluded to at least try to live as white people did; and for an Indian school that would teach reading and writing in English. That the Indians did not want these latter boons was of no consequence. Their cosmogony and theology were ignored. So the Great Spirit did not intend whites and reds to live in different ways? The epoch of the nomad in eastern America neverthe-

321

less was ended.

Critics would later say that excessive claims against the United Potawatomi Nation were entered by fur traders, at least one historian a century later naming specifically the American Fur Company, John Kinzie and Gurdon Hubbard as major beneficiaries. John Kinzie, the fur trader, was dead in 1833; Gurdon Hubbard received $125 for his own account, according to Bureau of Indian Affairs records. The American Fur Company collected $25,000 directly and through agents. The John Kinzie family, six members, received a total of $26,516. These later accounts were billed as accumulated debts of Indians to traders over a period of years; James Kinzie, a cousin of John, Sr. long a trader in Milwaukee, got $6,125 of the Kinzie family total. Gurdon Hubbard received $400 as trustee for "the child of Isadore Chabert." No money was paid to anyone for almost four years. The Senate ratified the treaty May 22, 1834 but Congress failed to appropriate the necessary funds for payment until 1837. The Indians in Hubbard's territory in southern Illinois didn't mind, they had extra time to stay on their land.

*

The Hubbards remained in Chicago well into October, Eleanora appearing to recover her health. Gurdon was pleased with the prospects there. The army engineers were again digging the channel through the sand spit, to open the way to lake shipping. Lieutenant James Allen, in charge, told Gurdon he would build a five-hundred-foot log pier this time to keep the channel from re-silting. It wasn't ready in November, McClure reporting that when the schooner *Marengo* from Detroit arrived, "there being no harbor she anchored out in the lake a half a mile from shore to unload . . . this could only be done by the aid of small boats, crossing the bar at the mouth of the river." The boats were Hubbard's. Nevertheless Gurdon could now report to the Illinois state legislature, when it assembled in December, that Chicago would soon have a harbor. His good friend Thomas Owens had been elected president of the Chicago town trustees on August 10, 1833, all twenty-eight citizens eligible to vote casting their ballots. Hubbard promised Owens that he would continue to push hard for the canal legislation, even though he was no longer a member of the legislature. He had two sure canal votes from southern Illinois in Dr. Fifthian and Isaac Courtright and was confident he could get others. Owens showed him his proposed plat of the town of Chicago, covering seven-eighths of a square mile, bounded by Jackson on the south, Jefferson and Cook streets on the west, Ohio on the north, and State street, the terminus of Hubbard's trail, on the east. Gurdon, on his part, said he'd send Henry Hubbard, his Danville manager, to Chicago to start construction of a large, three-story brick warehouse.

*

That fall back in Danville, Gurdon completed his plans for an early return to Chicago. Dr. Fifthian was prepared to take over Hubbard's store, as well as his seat in the legislature, while also continuing his medical practice. Noel Le Vasseur would manage the fur posts, eventually moving his base to Bourbonais Grove. Allen Baxter, in addition to farming, would collect pigs and cattle for the drives to Chicago. Hubbard himself would direct all the operations, act as the state militia paymaster, and serve as an unpaid lobbyist at Vandalia for the Chicago canal project.

He found Governor Reynolds in a black mood when he arrived at Vandalia in December. Reynolds had been blamed for the mistakes of the militia in the Black Hawk war. "They said I ordered the militia 'to shoot the first redskin you see'," Reynolds fumed. "I issued no such damn fool order. They blame me for the killing of Indian women and children at Bad Axe. The fools! Don't they know the governor of Illinois can't send his militia into Wisconsin?" Gurdon himself had been sent into Wisconsin repeatedly and some of the Illinois militiamen volunteered to go, but Reynolds was right, Gurdon Hubbard and the others were serving under General Atkinson. Reynolds' real fault was bad selection of officers such as Moore and Stillman, who allowed their men to fire wantonly on friendly Potawatomis or on Sacs bearing a flag of truce. Governor Reynolds' political hopes had died. He intended to resign from office early so that he could run for Congress from his own safe district.

"Who will take over?" Gurdon asked. "My interim successor won't count," Reynolds replied. "My ultimate successor I expect to be Congressman Joe Duncan."

Gurdon was well pleased. He knew Duncan from the Black Hawk war. They thought alike politically, so far as internal improvement matters were concerned, though Duncan was a Jacksonian Democrat and Gurdon was a Henry Clay Whig. Congressman Duncan had served as a canal commissioner, had favored the Chicago route, and was dismayed when the legislature threw out the Chicago plan as too costly. Gurdon called on Congressman Duncan, preparing to leave for Washington. "I expect to be a candidate for governor of Illinois," Duncan said. "However, I will continue to serve in Congress and will not campaign in Illinois. If I am elected, I will call a special session of the legislature to pass canal legislation."

"Do you still favor the Chicago plan?"

"That I do," Duncan answered. "I know that John is wavering, he doubts the legislature will ever back the Chicago cut, too expensive. I know he's asking you to study a railroad along the Illinois river; we've discussed this as an alternative. I think you should bring in a fair report. For myself, I will always remember that railroads last about fifteen years, a canal will last forever."

"We need both," Gurdon said, "but a railroad from the south to Chicago."

"Of course, but built with private capital," Duncan said. "I studied canals when I was commissioner. I know their limitations. I know the cost of a deep cut. I know it would drain farm lands as well as providing transportation. Perhaps we'll have to settle for less. Try to see the Erie canal if you can, that's a shallow cut and a great success. Enormous capital must be invested in a canal before you get a return, therefore a government must do it. Let the government build the canals and private capital the railroads. I don't think Illinois can afford to do both."

*

On January 3, home in Danville, Gurdon Hubbard wrote his customary New Year's letters to his family and business correspondents. One, of some length, was to Edward A. Russell of New

York City, who headed a group of eastern investors interested in Illinois land. Hubbard had recommended southern Illinois acreage to them, and now hoped to interest them in Chicago and northern Illinois as well. It was freezing cold in Danville, he wrote, so cold the ink froze and his hand was numb though he sat near a roaring fire. He had sent his cousin Henry to Chicago to get his new warehouse started. This, he said, showed his own confidence in Chicago. He would start for Chicago himself the day following, driving hogs and cattle despite the intense cold. He had a few recommendations for land buys in southern Illinois and would look into others in the north. "The purchase of Illinois farm land at this time is a hazardous business," he warned. "It is thought by the best lawyers that titles to (Indian) lands are illegal."

He offered recommendations, however. "I can purchase ten 80-acre lots from the postmaster at this place (Danville) at $50 each, upon which taxes have been paid regularly; also (farm) land situated on the Spoon river, a tributary of the Illinois. These are in a good section of the country, well located, very excellent lands, should you advise purchase, they can be had at any time. The flood of immigration is so great in the northern section of this state that squatter claims, unproved, are selling for some $200 to $300 for 80 acres. The risk of getting land cheaper is great unless the government throws them into land auction. The Hickory Creek purchase is good timbered land and will command purchase of the prairie adjoining it." Since timber was already becoming scarce in the area, "by cutting the timbered lot, money to pay for the adjoining land could be had."

"I will leave for Chicago tomorrow," Gurdon concluded. "I shall go by the way of the rapids of the Illinois river with a view to getting information on a railroad on the Illinois. I am of the opinion there will be a good opening for investments but do not think I shall make more purchases until I see you, but am desireous (sic) of being in possession of every information you can require of me." Russell, agent of the Connecticut Insurance Company in New York, also owned an interest in a wholesale provision company and Gurdon indicated his intention to buy supplies from Russell's house for his western operations when he visited New York.

Gurdon's letters reflected the influence of Eleanora as well as his growing experience in business. His spelling and diction had improved, his knowledge was specific and sound. He was ready for the Chicago challenge. He was now thirty-one years old, ranked as colonel and paymaster in the Illinois militia, well established as a politician in southern Illinois and warmly welcomed in Chicago. His relations with his suppliers of goods, the American Fur Company at Mackinac, Pierre Chouteau, Jr. in St. Louis, and Edward Russell in New York City were good. He had trusted deputies in Henry Hubbard and Noel Le Vasseur, Dr. Fifthian, and Eleanora, to whom he would shortly entrust special missions in the east, and he had a working relationship with Christopher. He stood six feet tall, spoke quietly in a voice described both as "deep and rough", and as "pleasant", and rarely if ever used profanity or expletives, once explaining, "The Indians have no swear words, they don't require them, why should I?" Gurdon had about him the vitality of the woods, it was said; women "saw fires in his eyes." Many settlers called him "Our Gurdon"—some "Indian Hubbard" or "Horse Hubbard." He would bring to Chicago little formal education, but a wide experience and knowledge, and the respect of all the pioneers who knew him.

*

They departed January 4, 1834, Eleanora and Gurdon, at the head of a caravan of sleighs, cattle and hogs, and a few hardy immigrants hoping to make their way across snow-covered prairies in their canvas-covered wagons. Since the creeks and rivers were frozen, and the sleds broke the way for the heavy Conestogas, a trip ordinarily impossible for the immigrants during the winter season became relatively easy. Within six days they came upon the village of Chicago, below the rise of Blue Island, the white walls of Fort Dearborn and the white tower of its neighboring lighthouse looking like a tiered wedding cake on a white porcelain plate. The growing little village to the west seemed a black and dreary blot in the snow spreading from the north and south branches of the river to blue Lake Michigan on the east. There was a cluster of log hotels at the forks of the river, the Agency House and the ruins of the Kinzie mansion on the

north bank, several stores lining the south bank. Gurdon pointed
out to Ellie the stone foundations and beginning brick walls of
his building, rising near South Water street to the west of two
new plank stores. That would be his warehouse, the lower floor
to be ready by the time the ice went out of the river. It would
have a large room with specially prepared walls, allowing "dead
air space", a room for the storage of meat, where ice blocks cut
from the river would retain their properties under a blanket of
sawdust through much of the summer. He had remembered that
ships at Montreal used such means to carry ice to the Spice Islands. The prior April George Dole had shipped pork in barrels
to Detroit, after keeping it on ice on the river, as Hubbard had
done. Gurdon expected to preserve his pork and beef into May
or even summer, should the Mackinaw Strait remain ice jammed
well into spring.

Enoch Chase, of Detroit, arriving in Chicago later that year,
sent back a description of what he saw. "On Lake Street and
South Water Street was the main village. It boasted one brick
block, which belonged to either Yankee Hubbard, Horse Hubbard, or Indian Hubbard, depending on who you asked. It was
quite an imposing structure. Clybourne's butcher shop was not
far from it, also Jim Kinzie's store, P.F.W. Peck's store, Harmon's
and Loomis'. . . . Between Stile's log tavern on the west side of
the South Branch and a tavern at the crossing of the Desplaines
(the Portage route) there was not a vestige of civilization. . . .
The only houses between Chicago and Milwaukee were Ouilmette's at Grosse Point (Wilmette), Sunderland's west of Waukegan, and Jack Vicaw's at Skunk Creek."

John H. Fonda, who passed through Chicago enroute to his
Indian agency at Prairie du Chien, reported that "Yankee" Hubbard's three-story brick building was called "Hubbard's Folly"
by Chicagoans even before it was finished. "What will he put
in it?" they asked. "Nobody said it directly to Yankee Hubbard,
though," Fonda added. "He was killing pigs and packing pork
on the frozen river, and nobody touched it all winter because
they knew who owned it."

*

Gurdon and Eleanora were happy in Chicago that long, cold

winter. They chose Jim Kinzie's Green Tree Tavern, managed by David Clock, as their home. It was new, warm and relatively clean. Their whitewashed room, twelve by twelve, had a chair, a washstand and a comfortable bed, and Ellie could spend much of her day in the adjacent family room, which both Clock and Hubbard used as their workroom. Few visitors arrived in Chicago in winter, though a four-horse stage began coming from Niles, Michigan, twice weekly when it could get through, bringing the mail and sometimes a passenger. Eleanora's furniture was stored in a cabin Gurdon had purchased from Chief Billy Caldwell north of the old John Kinzie "mansion", where he intended to build their home. She had her books and needlework at the inn and helped her husband with his letters. Henry Hubbard also lived at the Green Tree and they shared a horse and cutter, so that Ellie was free to go to the Kinzie home during the day when she chose. Mostly they saw the Kinzies by night, John and Juliette, Robert, and Maria and her fiance, Lieutenant David Hunter. They held weekly prayer meetings in John and Juliette Kinzie's new home, the old Beaubien cabin, just south of the fort, on a site Gurdon once claimed. Eleanor Kinzie and Margaret Helm were in the east, where Mrs. Kinzie sought treatment of her illness. After the death of Mrs. Kinzie from cancer early in 1834, when Margaret Helm returned to Chicago, they would organize St. James Episcopal church, Gurdon Hubbard assisting as he had promised; he was elected a vestryman, together with Eleanor's son, John. The first new communicants were Mrs. Margaret Helm and Mrs. Juliette Kinzie.

Gurdon and Eleanora entertained their guests in the Green Tree family room. Edwin O. Gale, also a resident in the hotel, described it: "On the east and west sides were the inevitable puncheon benches . . . scattered around the room was an assortment of wood chairs, near the north end was a bar counter, useful not only for the receiving of drinks, but overcoats, whips and parcels. The west end of the bar was adorned with a large ink-stand, placed in a cigar box filled with No. 8 shot, in which were sticking two quill pens . . . at the other end were a dozen or more short tallow candles, each placed in a hole in a two-by-four block, standing like mourners around circular graves . . . ." Beneath the bar was a bootjack and a tinder box. The men reached into the latter for the splinters of wood they could touch to the fire to light their pipes and cigars. "On the south wall of the family room was a long trough, tilted to drain to an open-headed keg below . . . at the top stood a half dozen wash basins and a pail of water." As befitted a manager named David Clock, a large Connecticut clock stood above the tinder box, beneath its dial, encased in glass, a rude painting of a plowman in green shirt and yellow trousers driving a purple horse drawing a blue plow.

The Hubbards' guests were glad enough to escape from their snug log houses into the capacious rooms of the Green Tree. Noontime dinner was served in the dining room on two long tables, covered by green-checked oil cloth. After Gurdon Hubbard arrived with pork and beef, the hotel's menu afforded some variety; in the early fall the Green Tree, according to Gale, served for supper a uniform menu throughout the hunting season: roast wild duck, fricasse of prairie chickens, and wild pigeon pot pie, with bread and coffee and dessert. The price was 25 cents, two English shillings, or two Spanish bits. The coffee was creamless, but could be sweetened with granulated maple sugar. A pint of rum, wine or brandy cost a quarter.

During the winter the Hubbards and all the young residents of the village and the officers and soldiers at the fort were invited to the town's annual ball, held that year not in Mark Beaubien's Sauganash hotel as usual, but at the new, still unfinished, Mansion House. Charles Fenno Hoffman, like Latrobe a writer of travel books, had come in by the four-horse stage and was, the very evening of his arrival, invited to the ball, and was glad to accept. "We were ushered into a tolerably-sized dancing room, occupying the second floor, and having its unfinished walls ingeniously covered with pine branches and flags borrowed from the garrison, so that, with the whitewashed ceiling above, it presented a very complete and quite pretty appearance. It was not so warm, however, that the fires of cheerful hickory, which roared at either end, could be dispensed with. An orchestra of unplaned boards was raised in the center of the room; the band consisted of a dandy negro with his violin (Nelson P. Perry), a fine, military-looking bass drummer from the fort, and a volunteer citizen who alternately played accompani-

329

ment upon flute and triangle.

"As for the company," Hoffman continued, "it was such a complete medley of all ranks, ages, professions, trades and occupations . . . now for the first time brought together, that it was amazing to witness the decorum with which they countermingled on this festive occasion. Here you might see a veteran officer in full uniform balancing to a tradesman's daughter still in her short frock and trousers, while there the golden aiguilette of the handsome surgeon (Dr. Philip Maxwell) flapped in unison with the glass beads upon a scrawny neck of fifty. In one quarter, the high-polished buttons of a linsey-wooly coat would be dos-a-dos to the elegantly turned shoulders of a delicate-looking southern girl; and in another, a pair of Cinderella-like slippers would *chassez* across with a brace of thick-soled brogans . . . those raven locks, dressed a la Madonne over eyes of jet . . . tell of lineage drawn from the original owners of the soil; while these golden tresses, floating away from eyes of heaven's own color over a neck of alabaster, recall the Gothic ancestry of some of 'England's born.' How piquantly do these trim and beaded leggins peep from under the simple dress of black, as its tall but brown wearer moves through the graceful mazes of the dance."

Gurdon, dancing with Eleanora, and Maria, and Margaret Helm, thought of the old days at Mackinac and the Kinzie home, where John Kinzie played the fiddle and Margaret completed his social education, such as it was. "Eleanora is lovely . . . we are all to glad you have come here to live among us," Margaret told him. She was even more beautiful in stark black, they had prevailed upon her to come despite the recent death in the family since the winter was a dreary one and they all were still young. Like the Kinzies, Gurdon mourned Eleanor Kinzie. She had been mother to him, as she promised, her illness had been a long one and she bore it without complaint. She would have wanted them to dance, as much as to organize a church, as they were doing. The Indian chiefs and their squaws sat on the puncheon benches, as in the old days, watching stolidly while their daughters danced with the soldiers and the new whites, constantly arriving; the Indian girls, severely plain as was their custom in the company of whites, contrasting with the young wives in their ball gowns carefully sewn over long winter weeks. Mark Beaubien came over from the Sauganash to make the calls in his customary mangled English; Hoffman, the writer, solicitously attended Juliette Kinzie, proferring her a cup of punch. He would encourage her to write the story of her life among the Indians.

Margaret was beautiful, even in black, but Gurdon was especially proud of Eleanora. Her shimmering green gown and slippers, made in New Orleans and bought in St. Louis, brought the sparkle of spring to the evening. She wore beaded leggings and Indian necklaces and bracelets. Tall and blonde and tanned, even in winter, she was the prettiest woman there. The temperature had dropped to 28 below that winter but Eleanora was in excellent health, glowing from their excursions on the frozen river, among the sand dunes, and in the woodlands to the north, where they hunted wolves. He saw that Hoffman watched her intensely and suspected that the visitor may have thought she was part-Indian, despite her blue eyes, since he knew that he himself looked Indian to many strangers and was called Indian Hubbard by some.

"Never did I expect to see such elegance and so many beautiful women in the wilderness," Hoffman wrote later. He dined then with the Hubbards and the Kinzies at the Green Tree. He got from Gurdon and John their dream of Chicago, as evidenced by his own estimate: "As a place of business, its situation at the central head of the Mississippi Valley will make Chicago the New Orleans of the North. . . . There is one improvement to be made however, I allude to a canal from the head of Lake Michigan to the head of steam navigation on the Illinois, the route of which has long been surveyed. The distance to be overcome is something like 90 miles and when you remember that the head waters of the Illinois arise within eleven miles of the Chicago river, that a level plain of not more than eight feet is the only remaining obstacle, you can conceive how easy it would be to drain Lake Michigan into the Mississippi by this route, boats of eighteen tons, (mackinaw freight canoes) having actually passed over the intervening prairie at high water. . . . St. Louis then would be brought comparatively near to New York, while two-thirds of the Mississippi Valley would be supplied by this route. . . .

This canal is the only remaining link wanting to complete the most stupendous chain of inland communication in the world."

This was the message, less dramatically put, that Gurdon Hubbard had been attempting to impress upon the Illinois legislators for more than three years; one he would continue to push upon the senators and incoming representatives until such a canal was authorized. That spring, when flood waters swept the remaining sand from the channel, Lieutenant Allen and his men were digging, lake schooners entered the Chicago river for the first time, the *Telegraph* taking on 300 barrels of beef and pork and fourteen barrels of tallow packed by Dole for the eastern market. Gurdon Hubbard rejoiced with George Dole and Oliver Newberry, Dole's partner, and Lieutenant Allen, over their successes. His warehouse was finished and filled with packed meats for the town and the fort. Chicago was ready for the canal. That summer Joseph Duncan announced his candidacy for the governorship.

*

Gurdon's letters to Edward Russell were mixed caution and optimism. The town had tripled in population, but still was a wilderness place. Land sales were slow. He advised great care in land selection, yet he appeared confident that Chicago would become a prosperous town, regardless of canal prospects: "As Chicago will be a market for the whole northern part of our state, which affords greater facilities to stock raising than any state east of the Mississippi, it will be a point where quantities of beef and pork will be packed for the Atlantic market, and these water lots (along the north and south branches of the Chicago river) are well adapted for business, there being a sufficiency of water to admit vessels of any burthen for several miles up this (south) branch at all seasons of the year. I am of the opinion they will be used exclusively for that purpose & will command cash at any time at a considerable advance."

Hubbard demonstrated a good amount of prescience as to the value of the lots in future, but some lack of candor if he meant to suggest the river could actually be used for navigation "at all seasons", including winter. He and Eleanora had been sledding on the ice and he used the frozen river to store his beef and pork.

Since Russell was aware of this, evidently he understood the limitation of "all seasons." The south branch property Gurdon recommended would become, in a few years, the site of scores of docks and lumber yards comprising the country's biggest lumber market. The north branch would serve warehouses and factories. That summer the Chicago harbor was used for the first time by a large schooner, the *Illinois,* which crossed the sandbar via the channel in July.

*

He built a big house for Elenora and himself and a few Hubbard kin on an eminence overlooking the lake, that he later designated as 300 Indiana avenue. Not far from the old John Kinzie home, it soon accommodated Henry George Hubbard, Gurdon's warehouse manager, Henry's sister, Harriet, and Ahira Hubbard, Gurdon's bookkeeper, as well as serving such visitors as his sisters and their husbands, the Fifthians from the Danville area, and Chief Shabona and wife and a selected child or two from their large brood. Shabona and Wiomex Okono were not comfortable in the Hubbard home, however. They preferred to live in the wood house, formerly Billy Caldwell's cabin, when they were in Chicago, and they sometimes stayed there for weeks at a time.

Gurdon Hubbard appeared to be prospering in Chicago that summer, though he frequently complained in his letters to Russell in New York. He admitted, however, that his brick warehouse was almost fully utilized and he expect to rent the last of available space for a branch of the Illinois State bank, which he was helping to organize. Chicago needed a bank and he particularly required such a facility as paymaster of the Illinois militia. The increasing water traffic continued to require his stevedoring facilities and he was making a few land sales. Yet he insisted that business was bad. The trouble, he said, was that Congress had not appropriated any funds to pay for Indian lands under the 1833 treaty. "In consequence of there being no appropriation, money is scarce and will continue to be so until annuities are paid in September (under prior treaties). . . . Also, no harbor funds have been put into circulation." That referred to $25,000 owed to the civilian workmen involved in Lieutenant

Allen's dredging and dock projects. "The spring immigration has ceased but the fall months we expect to bring a great many more. There are no transfers of lots owing to the scarcity of money, but no new changes of price except for those compelled to sell. The improvements are going on with astonishing rapidity. Water Street is building up fast with generally good buildings."

That summer Gurdon expanded his wholesale mercantile house supplying stores in Illinois, Indiana and Michigan with white trade goods; and his freight forwarding business, utilizing his *voyageurs* to lighter freight and passengers from schooners and steamboats still anchoring in the lake and to carry goods from his warehouse to various towns and camps along the waterways. As immigration increased in the fall, and land sales picked up, he organized a Chicago real estate syndicate of his own, with John and Robert Kinzie and Col. Richard Hamilton, the southern Illinois lawyer assigned by Governor Reynolds to command the militia at Chicago in the Black Hawk war. Hamilton had made a disastrous choice of Chicago real estate himself, acquiring 420 acres at a point he assumed would become a canal terminus. He turned out to be wrong, but his later association with Hubbard would become immensely profitable. Following the death of his wife, Hamilton joined the Hubbard family, wedding Gurdon's cousin Harriet on March 25, 1835 at the Hubbard home.

Gurdon kept Russell and George Mather informed of his activities. Early in the fall he reported on the canal situation: "The subject of a canal instead of a railroad is now in agitation, and is most popular in this section. The candidate for our legislature has rcd. a large majority in this precinct (the 6th) the other precincts have not been heard from but I presume he is elected. I think the people have decided in favor (of the canal). I hope you lose no time in seeing Bronson and others on this subject and would advise you to consult on a plan . . . in case the railroad bill should fail . . . eather (sic) is a grand speculation . . . a railroad bill will give much greater profit. Col. Hamilton, Col. Owens (the town president) and myself meet on that subject every few evenings, and we will send by Mrs. H. (Eleanora) a letter directed to Bronson, yourself, and others which we hope will be considered by you; we will get you news on the subject as early as possible. We shall organize ourselves and we shall attend the legislature.''

He was covering all the possibilities, a railroad and a canal, but he was for the canal as the best primary transportation for Chicago and the country. Arthur Bronson of New York acted for William B. Ogden, the financier politician and lawyer much interested in railroads. Since his visit to Chicago in 1833, where he and Charles Butler, Ogden's brother-in-law, met Gurdon Hubbard, Bronson was rising as a financier and an expert on internal improvement bonds. Gurdon did not completely trust him, but maintained good relations. John Kinzie had told him that Bronson and Ogden had bought a large part of the Kinzie and Wolcott addition to Chicago, extensive acreage on the north side of the river that Gurdon had urged reluctant Robert Kinzie to acquire by filing with the government land office years earlier (Ellen had inherited the Wolcott holdings). He feared that Bronson and Ogden might want to acquire all of the Kinzie land and that they might favor a railroad over a canal. He cautioned Russell ''. . . to prevent Mr. Bronson from playing any tricks on you, be on your guard and have all transactions with him perfectly binding.''

The three Chicago colonels, Hamilton, Owens and Hubbard, did not exclude railroads from their consideration of Chicago's future. Hubbard's own canal strategy had included an Illinois railroad as early as 1833, when his amended canal bill provided for a state-sponsored venture. That measure had failed to pass by a single vote. Now he thought he could induce Galena-area legislators to favor the canal if he could promise support for a Chicago-to-Galena railroad. Joseph Duncan, a Democrat but a most independent man, was the new governor of Illinois, and he knew Duncan to be a friend of the Chicago canal terminus plan. Canals and railroads would be uppermost in the minds of all the legislators when they assembled in December. Gurdon Hubbard would be there, lobbying for the Chicago town trustees. Evidently his plans were too secret and friable to be entrusted to Elijah Hubbard, his new young bookkeeper, who also was going east. Gurdon again told Russell they would be confided to Mrs. H., Eleanora, who would proceed from New

York to Middletown to visit his mother and sisters.

His business affairs were now in excellent shape, he wrote: "We have been full of business since we opened (his expanded wholesale house) and our stock is getting quite thin, particularly groceries, which Elijah will purchase largely & I hope yr. house will sell him the greater part. . . . We now command half of the southern trade and a fair portion of the other sections."

*

While Eleanora spent the late summer of 1834 in the east, her husband was heavily involved in Chicago civic affairs and the canal lobbyist project. The second town election was held August 11, the voters choosing John H. Kinzie, G.S. Hubbard, E. Goodrich, J.K. Boyer and John Hogan as the new trustees. They met promptly, naming Kinzie president. Their first official act was to provide for the drainage of State street at a cost of $60 and they created a Chicago seal and authorized Hubbard to study the town's canal and railroad prospects. The records of the meeting were destroyed in the Chicago fire, but Hubbard later recalled that the town's first board of health was established, since all the trustees vividly remembered the cholera epidemic of 1832, and, like himself, some were victims of the ague, a misery said to be caused by the miasma arising from the river and marshes.

The legislative session at Vandalia was a shambles, so far as progress on railroads and canals was concerned. Democrat Joseph Duncan had been elected governor by 17,330 over 10,224 votes for William Kinney and 4,320 for Robert McLaughlin, Duncan's uncle, a small victory margin. Congressman Duncan remained in Washington throughout the campaign, as he had told Hubbard he would do; John Reynolds was elected to succeed him in the Congress, as planned. Stephen A. Douglas, a new Democrat in the Illinois legislature, bitterly opposed Duncan as an anti-Jackson man who refused to follow the party line. "Illinois has got a traitor for governor," Douglas wrote his brother. When Governor Duncan in his inaugural address called for the establishment of a permanent system of common schools in Illinois, including a college program, and "the construction of a canal from Lake Michigan to the Illinois River," there was little prospect that the heavily Democratic Illinois House would give him quick action on either proposal.

So there was much talk and few laws passed at the December legislative session. Gurdon Hubbard was there to attend his lobbying duties, meeting with the handsome, flamboyant but politically purist Joe Duncan, who had publicly asserted that "always voting the party line is either weak or wicked," and another friend of Black Hawk war days, the shy and somewhat morbid Abraham Lincoln, the New Salem Whig. Gurdon introduced Lincoln to Dr. Fifthian, who would later become Lincoln's law client. Abe Lincoln favored canals for Illinois, including one in his own district, but he was not inclined to make speeches on canals or any other subject his first session. Gurdon sought out Senator J.M. Strode of Galena, vehemently opposed to a Chicago canal terminus. He suggested to Strode that a railroad from Chicago to Galena would be the correct connection for that town to the east. He proposed getting in touch with easterners interested in such a project. "Go ahead," Strode said. Few bills became law, nothing relating to the canal was accomplished, but a new Illinois State Bank would be created in February.

*

Gurdon returned to Chicago, again driving up pigs and cattle, after a few days at Vandalia. He arrived for a meeting of the town trustees shortly after another major fire had struck; as usual, a citizen carrying red-hot coals to start a fire at a home had dropped some from his shovel. The trustees passed a set of rules: Live coals could be carried only in a covered earthen or fireproof vessel; fire wardens had the right to draft anyone in sight to the duty of carrying fire buckets to douse a blaze; and each house was required to have a serviceable fire bucket. The following week the Chicago *Democrat* reported: "We understand that G.S. Hubbard has ordered on his own responsibility a fire engine with the necessary apparatus to be sent to Chicago immediately from the east. Individual responsibility being the only means offered for obtaining this important instrument of protection, we trust our citizens will avail themselves of this convenience by establishing a fire company without delay." Not until much later, however, did the town trustees authorize the creation of a town fire department, a hook and ladder company, to assist the volunteers who manned Hubbard's Fire King No. 1, a handsome pumper of red and gleaming brass, made by the John Rogers company of Baltimore, which had arrived earlier that year. Both Chicago newspapers, the *Democrat* and the newly established *American,* urged that Gurdon Hubbard should be named Chicago's fire marshal, but he declined. Henry Hubbard had become a volunteer fireman and Gurdon himself would join a volunteer company in later years. The Chicago *American* praised Trustee Hubbard for his gift: "He swam the Chicago River to extinguish the flames at Fort Dearborn in 1827," the paper said. "We are glad to know that his new engine is being put to use as Fire King No. 1."

*

The inability of Governor Duncan to get action on a Chicago canal bill, essentially the Hubbard bill which had lost by a vote in 1833, seemed for a time to doom Chicago prospects. The Galena *Advertiser,* then considered to be the most powerful newspaper in Illinois, continued to attack the Chicago plan. Early in 1835, Benjamin Mills, editor of the *Advertiser,* shocked Chicagoans when he joined southern Illinois legislators and some southern Illinois newspapers in strongly urging a canal or railroad from the Wabash river through the central part of the state to a connection with the Illinois River. John Calhoun, editor of the Chicago *Democrat,* previously no friend of the canal project, furiously attacked Mills' position, insisting that it was part of a nefarious plot on the part of certain northern Illinois citizens to secede from the state to join Wisconsin, about to apply for statehood. Thus Chicago would become a Wisconsin town, leaving Galena unchallenged as Illinois' largest and wealthiest city. This somewhat wild inference had some basis in fact. Though Illinois citizens could hardly benefit themselves by embracing Wisconsin at the urging of Galena, many Wisconsin residents were known to covet the port of Chicago. Long John Wentworth, later editor of the *Democrat* and for years a congressman and a leading Chicago politician, declared that Wisconsin emissaries offered to make him a United States senator from Wisconsin if he would lead a secessionist move. "They held that this was the intention of the Northwest Ordinance of 1787, creating the potential of five northwest states," Wentworth said. "Wisconsin, being out of the Union, could only come into it with boundaries prescribed by the majority of the states in it." Wentworth at the time was a congressman from Illinois. "And I lost the honor of being a Wisconsin United States Senator," he wrote.

Indiana, too, wanted the Illinois and Michigan canal terminus, as Governor Duncan had pointed out to Hubbard months previously. It was too late for Indiana to annex Chicago, but canal benefits would be obtained by that state should a Calumet-Sag route be created. It was Hubbard who demolished the efforts of out-of-state politicians to take the terminus benefits from Chicago and northern Illinois by his lobbying efforts and by his testimony before a joint committee of the Illinois Assembly. "The Hon. Henry M. Blodgett states that Illinois owes a debt to Mr. Hubbard which has never been accredited to him, namely the settlement of the question of the location of the terminus of the canal," wrote historian Caroline McIlvane in 1911. "It had been urged that it would be cheaper to follow up the Calumet to the valley of the Desplaines, than to cut through the hard ground between the South Branch of the Chicago River and the Desplaines. After hearing the argument on this point, Mr. Hubbard took a map and called attention to the fact that the mouth of the Calumet is within a few yards of the Indiana state line, and suggested that it was expected that wherever the canal terminated, a great city would grow up, and pertinently asked, 'Were it as desirable that the coming city should be as much of the state of Indiana as the state of Illinois, when the entire expense of construction would devolve upon our state?' This practical view of the question settled it, and the mouth of the Chicago River was made the terminus instead of the mouth of the Calumet."

On February 10, 1835, the Illinois legislature, summoned into special session to consider canal legislation as Governor Duncan had promised, approved the canal route between Chicago and Ottawa, Illinois and authorized Governor Duncan to appoint a new canal commission and to create a State of Illinois corporation, to be called the Illinois and Michigan Canal Company, empowered to issue stock and to borrow $500,000 to start digging. But the canal difficulties were far from over. Eastern banks relied upon as a market for the bonds refused to touch them. Duncan sent representatives east and to Europe to call upon financiers for aid and also sought aid from Gurdon Hubbard. Gurdon agreed to visit Arthur Bronson, on whom he had reported most unfavorably a year and a half earlier, but who now was acclaimed as a leading New York expert on internal improvement bonds.

*

In March, 1835, Gurdon completed the purchase of eighty acres of Chicago land in behalf of himself and his eastern associates, Edward Russell and George Mather—the Russell and Mather Addition to the Town of Chicago. It lay along the west bank of the north branch of the river, from the forks to Chicago avenue on the north, a bleak, desolate area, devoid of any building, though, on the opposite side, the Clybournes had built an elegant house and their new packing plant. Gurdon expected the river would become an important docking area once a canal and the Chicago harbor were created and he planned to locate his own packing plant there. The purchase price of the entire eighty acreas was $5,000. He informed Russell of his acquisition and told him and his brother Christopher, the latter acting as his New York agent in some matters, that he was coming to New York with Eleanora late in April enroute to Middletown.

He planned to study the Erie canal and New York hotels enroute, since he was investing heavily in a projected Lake House hotel on the north bank of the Chicago river, yet he also assumed it would be a leisurely vacation. He told Ellie they would visit Niagara Falls, which he had longed to see since boyhood, and perhaps Montreal. They would pass along the Erie canal, descend the Hudson, see New York City, cruise Long Island Sound to the Connecticut river, and ascend to Middletown. Since Eleanora got on well with his mother and sisters, she could stay there the summer, away from the rank heat of Chicago.

Chapter 11

They boarded the steamer *James Madison* for Mackinac Island, where Gurdon showed Ellie the scenes of his early fur trading days—the gleaming white buildings of the American Fur Company, Alexander Henry's cave, and the sweet-smelling pink and white arbutus above the landing at Robinson's Folly. A few days later, with no further mention of Montreal, they caught a schooner to Buffalo, experienced the awesome beauty and wonder of Niagara, returned to Buffalo, and there boarded a fine, thirty-one ton canal packet which passed serenely among the green hills and meadows of New York state to Albany—the Grand Canal, Governor Dewitt Clinton had called it. Ellie was never happier and Gurdon was rarely busier, spending his time acquiring information and inspecting boats, traffic, lands and locks enroute while she enjoyed the greening pastures and spring flowers only yards from her deck chair. The Erie was forty feet wide and four deep, Gurdon told her. It extended 362 miles, had 77 locks, and carried 20,000 packets, barges and bullheads, the latter boats hauling up to 75 tons of freight, in a season. The Chicago canal problems would be different, requiring a deeper cut, or the pumping of much more water into the locks to raise and lower boats. Gurdon consulted with captains, engineers, bargemen and ordinary travelers seeking canal information.

They rode a creaking railroad train of cars a few miles out of Albany, then took a stagecoach back, glad to be free of the dirt and smoke from the noisy locomotive, which pulled freight as well as passenger cars. "We will see William B. Ogden in New York, I hope," Gurdon told her. "He thinks railroads are the way of the future. I want to get him interested in a railroad for Chicago."

The descent of the Hudson delighted her. They were again leisurely and comfortable in their swift packet, cruising down a river teeming with steamboats, sailing ships, and huge rafts with log houses on them, called "floating log cabins." Gurdon saw no future for them. "They go down river just like Missouri mackinaws. They go down, but they can't come back. They're sold for old lumber at the end of the line." A federal warship slipped past, her cannon roaring a salute to the rising sun. Half of all the shipping they saw going south carried pork and beef

341

and provisions from the west, her husband said; half going up river would carry manufactured goods for the western lands. The west was the way of the future. A quarter of it all, both ways, would pass through Chicago, once the canal was built, he estimated.

They entered a maelstrom of marine traffic where Liverpool packets and the majestic clipper ships from the China seas swept down upon them, merging with keelboats, Hudson packets, the floating log cabins, and darting tugs escorting canal bullheads to their piers. They entered a slip above the Battery, under the skyline of six-story, steepled and gabled buildings, all in the Dutch style, and saw the great ships of the Canton tea run close at hand, their white spars gleaming in the early morning sun, their flying jib booms thrusting above the third-story windows of the buildings on the waterfront as they warped to their wharves. Eleanora had visited New York before, but never had she thrilled to it as she now did with Gurdon guiding her eyes and senses. The shouting, the shrieking of steam whistles, the rattle and creaking of carts and barrows, the smell of steaming clams and rotting fish, of spices and cinnamon, reminded him of Montreal in the spring, he said.

No one was there to meet them at the wharf—they had come in days early. "We'll have some time to ourselves," he told her, but she was not deceived. Two men lugged their baggage—she was prepared for the summer at Middletown—and Gurdon quickly found a hansom driver; they packed their trunk and luggage about them and were off over the cobblestones, savoring the smells and sounds and excitement of New York.

That evening they supped elegantly at Delmonico's, Eleanora in some discomfort at finding herself the only woman present, but Gurdon said it was because they were early, city folks ate late. He wanted to take her to see the New Jersey shore just after sundown, when the Hudson looked like the wide Mississippi, and to drive past the Tontine Coffee House to the foot of Wall street, and thence toward the market at Fulton street, where they saw the ferry boats, packed with weary, dazed people, depart for the Brooklyn Heights. They were back at the Park Place Hotel, which Gurdon's brother Christopher had recommended, as dusk deepened and the gas lamps were being lighted along

Broadway. Christopher, the slim, tall and somewhat petulant younger brother, awaited them, having been summoned by a runner Gurdon had sent to find him that afternoon. The brothers shook hands gravely, Gurdon presented Eleanora, who had not met Christopher on her prior trip, then the two men sat in the hotel family room to plan the days ahead while she retired to their new, comfortable room to rest. She was pleased that Gurdon and Christopher had become reconciled, but was confused by their remaining remoteness.

They arose early to drive in the park below the hotel and on north through the city to the Harlem River, where Gurdon promised a picnic breakfast. He had gone ahead into the hotel kitchen for the basket lunch, at the same time making an inspection. Christopher had chosen the Park Place Hotel for them because it was relatively new and Gurdon could get ideas for his new Lake House in Chicago. They passed the site of the Astor hotel, well under way. He would not see old Mr. Astor, Crooks had blocked that. Brother Christopher had brought mail and messages, including a confidential note from Ed Russell, saying it was rumored that Crooks had gone west to Milwaukee or Green Bay to decide on an important Astor land venture.

They saw the vast new city, and the countryside beyond, and were back in the hotel in time for the afternoon meeting Christopher had arranged for his brother. Eleanora was glad for a chance to rest and to prepare her wardrobe for the visit to Middletown. She was pleased that Gurdon had not mentioned the doctor he wanted her to see while in New York, a man who had treated Eleanor Kinzie on her visit East. She was determined not to see him, and she actually felt better. Christopher's note, saying Edward Russell, Charles Butler and Arthur Bronson wanted to meet him that afternoon obviously had driven all thoughts of anything else from her husband's mind.

*

Gurdon was much pleased to discover that Bronson had brought with him his principal investor, William B. Ogden, the sharp-eyed, genial upstate lawyer, a recent member of the legislature, like Gurdon himself, and a man said to be much interested in railroads. Ogden, he knew, was descended from a colonial governor as he himself was; his grandfather, like Gurdon's, an officer in the Revolution. Ogden's father had been a man of wealth, but lost his fortune shortly before his death, Ogden leaving school to go to work when he was sixteen. Ogden was now about thirty, three years younger than Hubbard, a man liberally educated, elegant and soft spoken. After dining on good western steaks that Bronson provided, they took their coffee and cigars in a private room and Ogden undertook a friendly cross examination of Hubbard. "You are planning to dig a canal at Chicago, Mr. Hubbard," he began, his dark eyes intent upon Gurdon, a slight smile softening the severity of his manner. "You have received Mr. Bronson's opinion that you cannot sell your bonds unless the full faith and credit of the state of Illinois is pledged. Do you expect that condition will be met?"

"I think Governor Duncan believes in the Illinois canal as much as Governor Clinton believed in the Erie," Gurdon answered. "He may have as many difficulties, but, yes, I am convinced we will do what is necessary to sell our bonds."

"As you know, I own a bit of Chicago land, thanks to Mr. Butler," Ogden continued.

"Yes, half the Kinzie and Wolcott addition," Gurdon answered.

"Should I sell it?"

"I would sell a part of it. President Jackson's specie circular will reduce the price of federal land being sold and that will probably bring down your land soon. However, when the canal is built, it will go up again."

"Mr. Bronson tells me you are a Whig?"

"Yes, a Henry Clay Whig, a clay ball they call us in Chicago. And you, sir, are a Democrat?"

"Aye, but not a Jacksonian. I don't like what President Jackson is doing to the Bank of the United States any more than you do. His policy of demanding hard money for government land is OK, as he is said to put it. That will hold down inflation. Bronson tells me that you should test your Chicago land prices right here in New York, putting it up for auction."

"Yes, Mr. Bronson mentioned that to Mr. Russell and me. We will consider it. And my recommendation to you is that you see your Chicago land and auction it. Now is a good time."

"Let's see your test here in Wall Street," Ogden countered. "New York is land-crazed and canal-mad. If we can sell Chicago lots at good prices, that will suggest we can sell canal bonds, properly underwritten. If your test works, I will go to Chicago. New Jersey farmers are trading their mortgages for bonds in Wall Street auctions these days; you can sell your land here I'm sure."

The day following, with Russell's concurrence and his assurance that George Mather would agree, Gurdon drew a plat of the Russell and Mather Addition from memory, parcelled it into lots, and called upon Franklin and Jenkins in Broad street, who agreed to call the stock at auction. They directed him to an engraver who shortly printed his maps. On May 8, 1835 Gurdon Hubbard sold out all the available lots of the Chicago tract, bought two months earlier, for $80,000, a profit of $77,500 on the forty acres sold, before expenses of the sale! He also sold three of his canal lots, bought for $66 in 1831, to Arthur Bronson for $1,500 and agreed to sign a contract with Bronson to represent him and his associates, including Ogden, in the purchase and sale of Illinois lands.

William Ogden, learning the results of the test, promptly called upon the Hubbards to ask them to his farewell dinner at Niblo's the next evening. "I am going at once to Chicago," he said. He brought along his sister, Athena Butler, to show Eleanora the shops and stores, while he occupied Gurdon Hubbard's time the rest of the afternoon. Arriving in Chicago the next week, with letters of introduction from Hubbard, and finding that news of Hubbard's New York auction had preceded him, William Ogden went to see his land on the north bank of the river. There had been heavy spring flooding. Ogden sank to his shoetops in mud and water and he sent a fiery letter to Butler back in New York, accusing him of being an idiot. But then Ogden reconsidered. He had bid contract work on the Erie and knew what could be accomplished with shovels and scrapers. Within a week he had his land drained, lot markers down, and some rough maps drawn, though there were no engravers in Chicago to print them. The government was opening its new land office in Chicago on May 28 and crowds of land buyers were in town. Ogden arranged with Augustus Garrett, the auctioneer, to conduct the sale of half his lots, as Hubbard had done in New York. Within three days the lots were snapped up and William Ogden had a profit of $100,000. He sent Charles Butler an immediate letter of apology. "He still could not see where the value lay," Butler would write years later. "He thought the people were crazy and visionary."

When Ogden returned east he found that Gurdon Hubbard had come back to New York after visiting his mother and sisters in Connecticut. Ogden had decided by then that Chicago visionaries might not be crazy. He had thought about Chicago all the way back, he said. Clearly a canal was needed there, and, if the bonds could be sold, he would himself be prepared to bid on the construction of one or more sections; he could provide the services of men who had cut through rock in building the Erie a decade earlier. He also wished to consider the possibility of railroads. He had himself been responsible for obtaining New York state backing for the New York & Erie road, he said. It could be done in Illinois. Gurdon urged consideration of a line from Chicago to Galena, the leading city of Illinois. "It would tie Galena to the east by a shorter route than the Erie, Ohio and Mississippi waterways, it would tie Illinois' best cities together, complementing a canal."

"You sell those canal bonds and I'll be ready," Ogden answered. "I like the way people work out there. They drained my marsh in days. First time I was west of Niagara in my life. Bronson says you are with us. I like that. I may join you in Chicago myself.

*

Gurdon returned to Chicago alone. He knew that Eleanora would be happy and better off in Middletown with his mother and the girls during the heat of the summer. She had agreed to see a doctor recommended by Abigail though she did not wish to seem disloyal to Dr. Fifthian, who told her the pregnancy problems could end of themselves and her breathing would improve away from the swamps. He found the great Chicago land craze well under way and he was welcomed back as a hero. The Chicago *Democrat* called him "a bold speculator in land," but it was a compliment he did not appreciate. Augustus Garrett, the auctioneer, who was making a fortune—he would sell $500,000 of lots in 1835 he said—offered to buy Gurdon's brick warehouse on the south bank, to which had been added a fourth story. Gurdon also sold his Danville property for $22,000 and could at once begin construction, on the north bank of the river, of a new warehouse and the Lake House. "Chicago's first really grand hotal," Andreas would say of it, "three stories and basement, elegantly furnished, costing $100,000." John H. Kinzie and Colonel David Hunter, Maria's husband, were among Gurdon Hubbard's partners.

Hubbard urged caution on his eastern backers, however, writing Russell on July 5 not to believe all he heard about the Chicago boom. "I very much doubt that all your property can now be sold advantageously," he said. "In your postscript you say, 'If I can get $10,000 for 40 feet of water lots you may sell them.' I think they may command that if speculation is high . . . (but) $15,000 is the highest price that has been paid for a lot 80 by 150 in Chicago. . . . I urge you to be patient, the reported land prices are exaggerated." The best outlook for Chicago land would be realized when canal construction got under way, he advised. The best prospects lay ahead.

12

November, 1835

As soon as we arrived . . . we noticed a rather large man,
put up in fine shape for an athlete, with dark hair and
eyes, prominent nose, high cheekbones, large firm mouth,
and strong face, showing great force of character, but,
withal, a voice and smile so pleasing that we took to him
at once. . . . " 'Who is he?' we asked a by-stander. 'Why,
that is the proprietor . . . Gurdon S. Hubbard. He is just as
nature labeled him. He can out-run or outwalk any Indian,
takes difficulties as you would dessert after dinner . . . is as
true as steel, with a heart as tender as any woman's. He's
worth 500 ordinary men in any town.' "

Reminiscences of Early Chicago,
E.O. Gale

Gurdon was seen frequently on the docks and at his warehouse
in those days. He exulted in hard work with his *voyageurs,* now
turned stevedores, and was a cheerful, smiling host to the
hundreds of travellers arriving at the rude town in the boom
years. Earlier there had been complaints about the surly welcome given many visitors, whether they came by boat or stage.
Too many innkeepers were in competition. Their draymen were
known to seize the baggage of a newcomer and haul it off to
one hotel or another where it was held for ransom should the
visitor fail to like the inn or couldn't afford it.

The practice had prevailed years before Town Trustee Hubbard went to work on the waterfront himself and confirmed
what was going on. Mary Galloway, later Mrs. Archibald
Clybourne, recalled her family's experience. When they reached
Chicago aboard a schooner from Detroit, they were landed
"near the foot of Madison Street." Mary's father, James, said at
once he couldn't afford Mark Beaubien's hotel. A drayman
nonetheless seized their baggage to take it to a "warehouse,"
actually the home of Jean Baptiste Beaubien. Big Jim Galloway
wanted to fight, but he was outnumbered by draymen. Then

349

Alexander Robinson and his band of Indians happened by. They heard Galloway's complaint and took his property from the Beaubiens, Chief Robinson providing the Galloways shelter by renting them his cabin at Hardscrabble on the South branch. The evil practice of preying on newcomers continued however. When Hubbard became a town trustee, Chief Robinson told him of it. Gurdon took to patrolling the docks while he supervised his *voyageurs* turned stevedores at times when he was in town. He pounded a few heads together as the *voyageurs'* bully did in early days, some said, and improved the behavior of the draymen and the innkeepers. Not all Chicagoans approved Hubbard's methods. While some called him "Yankee Hubbard," or "Horse Hubbard," others said he had been a squaw man and called him "Indian Hubbard," though not in his presence.

When freight and passengers were not being received, Gurdon tended his various enterprises, warehousing and freight forwarding, meat packing, construction, his new Lake House hotel, Indian trading posts, cattle drives and pig droving, white goods stores, real estate, his job as state militia paymaster, his duties as town trustee, and the canal lobbying assignment. When his term as town trustee ended he refused to run again. Governor Duncan had urged him to keep himself ready for a state job in the upcoming year.

In his letters to Edward Russell, his New York associate, Gurdon complained that he was overworked. "I am asking Christopher not to send me any more agencies or commissions for a time," he wrote in the fall of 1835, after disclosing that he had opened an insurance agency, representing the Howard Insurance Company of New York, issuing the first policy on his own household goods. "I have sold the house and lots in Danville. Our town is very healthy, but provisions and grain of any description are scarce and high." He said he was helping to organize a Chicago branch of the Illinois State Bank, with John H. Kinzie and Colonel Richard Hamilton, now married to Harriet Hubbard, Gurdon's cousin, and Elijah K. Hubbard, whom he had brought to Chicago from the east to become a partner in his insurance business. All, including of course Gurdon himself, would become directors; John Kinzie was named president.

By the time the Illinois State Bank opened for business in

December, Gurdon had sold his warehouse to Augustus Garrett and was building a larger structure on the north bank of the river, near the site of the old Agency House. The new bank was an immediate success, averaging $700 a day in deposits after three months, according to the Chicago *American*. The *American,* too, was new, having come to town in the spring of 1835. Gurdon, pleased with its Whig politics, gave subscriptions to his friends, and advertised some of his varied activities in its columns. "I am sending you a subscription to the new *American,*" he had written Russell in September, "it will help you to follow the developments here." He had reorganized his freight-forwarding company by 1836 and had moved into his new $44,000 warehouse on the north bank, while locating his freight-forwarding terminal in a new, smaller structure on the south bank of the river.

*

In his annual message to the Congress early in 1836, President Jackson foresaw the departure of the Indians from all territory east of the Mississippi. "The Indians have surrendered their land for $5 million, and expenses of removal, and (new) land," the President said with some satisfaction. "All previous experiments for the improvement of the Indians have failed. It seems now to be an established fact that they cannot remain in contact with a civilized community and prosper." He noted that the Indians were being treated with magnaminity by the government, receiving annuities totalling as much as $30 for each individual of the tribe "in some instances." Whites were to be barred from the Indians' "reserved territory", and, for the protection of the redskins, who had learned to love liquor after long contact with civilization, the President assured the Congress that "summary authority has been given . . . to destroy all ardent spirits found in their country, without waiting for the doubtful result and slow process of legal seizure."

In September the Potawatomis gathered for the last time in Chicago to receive their munificent bounty. They were to be removed the next week into the protection of the government on land west of the Mississippi by Captain J.B.F. Russell, who would manage provisions and logistics while escorting the

Potawatomis from Illinois and adjacent states to the reservation assigned to them in Clay county, Missouri, opposite Fort Leavenworth. Some 5,000 Indians, it was estimated, gathered at Chicago for the payment of annuities, as they had in 1833, when the final treaty was signed. The Indians announced a war dance to precede their eviction. Newspaper and magazine writers flocked in. The Hubbards and the Kinzies, depressed by the proceedings, nonetheless gathered at the old Sauganash Hotel along the line of the dance. The Indian warriors, some 800, mustered on the north bank of the Chicago river at a point where the Rush street bridge and Gurdon Hubbard's Lake House were being built. "They appreciated it was to be their last war dance on their native soil," an anonymous eastern reporter observed, ". . . that it was a sort of funeral procession of old associations and memories, and nothing was omitted to lend it all the grandeur and solemnity possible." The writer vividly described the dance itself:

"All were entirely naked, except for loin cloths. Their bodies were covered with a great variety of brilliant paints. On their faces they seemed to have exhausted their art of hideous decoration. Foreheads, cheeks and noses were covered with curved stripes of vermilion, edged with black points, giving the appearance of a horrid grin. Their coarse black hair was gathered in scalp locks, decorated with hawk and eagle feathers. . . . They were principally armed with tomahawks and war clubs, and were led by what answered for a band of music, which created hideous noises. They did not advance in a regular march, but a slow dance, proceeding along the north bank of the river . . . and crossed on the old bridge (Dearborn street) and passed in full view of the windows of the Sauganash Hotel . . . a fashionable boarding house and quite a number of young married people had rooms there. . . ."

Gurdon Hubbard preserved the clipping from the out-of-town newspaper and recalled his own presence at the Sauganash years later. Evidently he considered the report, in a publication not identified but not local, a colorful and accurate one. The war dance experience had been a terrifying one for most observers, the writer said. Some young women, new to Chicago, watched in fascinated horror as the dance proceeded. "The noise redoubled. The morning was warm and perspiration poured from the dancers almost in streams . . . their eyes were wild and bloodshot. Their countenances had assumed an expression of all the worst passions which can find a place in the breast of a savage—fierce anger, terrible hate, dire revenge, remorseless cruelty—all expressed in their terrible features. Their muscles stood out in great knots, as if wrought by a tension that would burst them. Their tomahawks and clubs were thrown and brandished about in every direction, with most terrible ferocity. Their yells and screams were broken up and multiplied and made more hideous by a rapid clapping of the mouth with the palm of a hand. To see such an exhibition by a single individual would have excited fear in a person not over-nervous. . . . Eight hundred such, a raging sea of dusky, painted, naked fiends, presented a spectacle absolutely appalling."

A few of the women spectators became ill and fainted. Most shrank back from their Sauganash viewing points as the dancing warriors glanced up at them in hateful fury. "Hell itself was depicted on their faces," the journalist wrote. "They seemed as if to make a real attack . . . we had a picture of hell before us, a carnival of damned spirits."

No one was actually harmed in this final, despairing demonstration by the United Tribes of Chippewas, Ottawas and Potawatomis gathered in Chicago as the Potawatomi Nation for the last time. There could be no doubt of their hatred and frustration, nor of the futility of such emotion. Gurdon and John Kinzie took their women home, then went to the Indian encampment that night to talk with the chiefs, Shabona and Billy Caldwell, who had agreed to accompany their people to Missouri to help with the initial settlement on the reserved lands. Shabona and Caldwell, like Chief Alexander Robinson, held title to Illinois lands, Shabona owning a farm and grove near Morris, Illinois, and they planned to return to Illinois. Shabona for the first time had come to Chicago without calling at Gurdon Hubbard's place. They found him bitter and depressed, at the camp north of Wolf Point. Yet he shook hands warmly and took Gurdon aside. "My son, Pyps, is dead," he said in the Potawatomi tongue. "Killed by Neopope's men."

"Because he warned the settlers!" Gurdon exclaimed.

"My son, Smoke, will find Neopope."

"The government is looking for him, too," Gurdon said. "No one will hide him. Even Black Hawk has called Neopope a traitor."

"I do not depend on your government."

"I know, my friend. Your son Pyps was a brave man. He is now hunting well, beyond the Western Star."

"Watchekee will not go with us," Shabona said. "She is well cared for by Vasseur."

Gurdon took the hand and arm of Shabona in his own strong hands. "I am sorry for you, my old friend," he said. "But I am glad that Watseka found Le Vasseur. Come to my house when you next come to Chicago."

Shabona nodded.

Abruptly that week, Chicago ceased to be a French and Indian town as many of the old families and *voyageurs* followed their Indian wives and kin west. It would soon become a city.

*

From among his *voyageurs* remaining, Gurdon selected a small crew of veterans to man the mackinaw that would carry him and Eleanora to Green Bay, reversing the route that Governor Cass had taken in the Winnebago crisis. He had concluded while in New York that he should go to Green Bay to see for himself what was attracting John Jacob Astor's interest there. Besides, he knew that his eastern associates needed to be reassured that they had been right in placing their faith in Hubbard's investment judgment, rather than in that of New York's most famed and rich citizen. They coasted north, stopping *"pour la pipe"* as in the old days, and made about twenty-five miles when Gurdon called, *"A terre! A terre!"* that evening at a suitable camping place on high ground. He led Eleanora from the sandy beach to the steep bluff above the shore and showed her the expanse of great oaks, not yet changing color, but a dark sheltering green. "We'll build a cabin here," he told her. "A day's canoe run from town. We'll get away from the summer heat in Chicago." The morning of the third day they reached Milwaukee and found that Ramsey Crooks had recently visited there and had gone on to Green Bay.

They were well over a week coasting Lake Michigan and portaging into Green Bay. There Gurdon found James Duane Doty, Astor's fur trader for the northern Wisconsin territory, who had accomplished with Astor what Gurdon Hubbard could not—he had convinced the American Fur Company and its retired owner that Green Bay in Wisconsin Territory was the Northwest's city of the future. Ramsey Crooks had brought the authorization to go ahead all the way from New York. Doty was to start construction of a new town, to be called Astor, at the mouth of the Fox River, just south of Naverino (later Green Bay). There would be a business center around the civic square to be bounded by Washington, Adams, Astor and Mason streets. John Jacob Astor had donated lots for church and school sites. Doty was elated that his plans for the future had been approved. Astor was America's richest man, he told Gurdon, and had made his fortune from wise real estate investments as well as from the fur trade.

Gurdon was sure that Ramsey Crooks and Robert Stuart had made the choice for Astor. The old man had never seen Green Bay; he had never in fact been to Mackinac. Ramsey Crooks had used the trade route through Green Bay ever since he went that way enroute to Astoria on the Pacific Coast, proceeding down the Fox and Wisconsin to the Mississippi. Crooks in years thereafter ignored the Chicago Portage, leaving it to Antoine Deschamps. Hubbard continued to rely on his own judgment that Chicago would be the city of the future. He wrote in confidence to Edward Russell, describing Astor's plans, after first offering a profitable tidbit for Russell himself:

"I have purchased for you a one-third interest in the Vermilion Salt Works (located near Danville). I am confident it will be a good investment for you. You may be sure of my orders from that source (for his meat packing operations). We have come to Green Bay and I have talked with Doty. . . ." He provided details of the "Astor plan" for Green Bay, scheduled to be well under way in the spring of 1836. Hubbard did not himself see Green Bay as "the entrepot of the fur trade" in the future, nor as a major center of business in general. Chicago, Milwaukee, Grand Haven on the eastern shore of Lake Michigan, or Toledo on Lake Erie, seemed to him to be better prospects to become "first city on the Great Lakes", he wrote. "Green Bay," he concluded, "is destined to be no more than the 2nd town on Lake Michigan."

Enroute home, Gurdon, Eleanora and the *voyageurs* might have taken the rivers south to Dixon, Illinois, the route followed and recommended by John and Juliette Kinzie, but instead they proceeded by way of Galena, where Gurdon reported to Senator James Strode on his talks with William Ogden about a possible railroad from Chicago to Galena, as he had promised Strode he would do. They returned to Chicago in golden October, Gurdon well satisfied that he would be able to tell Governor Duncan that Senator Strode was prepared to support legislation putting the full faith and credit of Illinois behind the Illinois-Michigan canal bonds.

The Illinois State Bank at Chicago opened December 5. The day following Gurdon and Ellie departed for Danville and Vandalia, where Gurdon would consult with Governor Duncan and attend the special session of the legislature. He also was authorized to file for the incorporation of the Chicago Hydraulic Company, with capital of $250,000, organized by George W. Dole, as president, and Hubbard and Maria Kinzie's husband, David Hunter, a member of Gurdon's new insurance company, as directors. The firm proposed to create a network of hollow logs and a pumping station that would lift pure water from Lake Michigan into a tank from which it would flow through the logs to subscribers fearful of the increasingly contaminated Chicago river water.

*

Vandalia, clean and bright under a fresh fall of snow, buzzed with legislators, lawyers and lobbyists such as Gurdon Hubbard, that December. The Illinois Supreme Court also would be in session, and the town was packed with visitors interested in the flood of one hundred and thirty-nine bills introduced by representatives and senators refusing to be limited to the subject of Governor Duncan's call, canal legislation. There were, according to Lincoln biographer Benjamin Thomas, eighty-one bills relating to railroads, five to navigation, and three to canals, one of these Abraham Lincoln's own project, the Beardstown and Sangamon Canal, in which he owned a few shares. Most of December the legislators discussed national politics as committees wrestled with the internal improvements bills, the Whigs pushing for attention to their favored presidential candidates, General William Henry Harrison, the hero of Tippecanoe, now quietly farming in Ohio, or, Daniel Webster, of Massachusetts, favored by a few. The Jacksonian Democrats were strong for Vice President Martin Van Buren, sure to continue the policies of Andrew Jackson. "They sicken me," Joseph Duncan grumbled to Gurdon. "I could almost turn Whig."

Backed by fellow members of the Long Nine, legislators from central Illinois, all over six feet tall, Abraham Lincoln was chosen the Whig floor leader in the House. Gurdon Hubbard soon determined that all of Lincoln's stalwart Whigs would back the Chicago canal bill, provided northern Illinois legislators would support their drive to move the state capital from Vandalia to Springfield, and, of course, such local projects as the Beardstown and Sangamon Canal. Stephen A. Douglas, the squat, plump, fast-talking Democrat from Jacksonville, also favored canals generally, but he firmly opposed a deep-cut plan for the Illinois-Michigan project, citing its $8 million cost. Hubbard himself favored the deep cut, which would allow water to flow from Lake Michigan to the Gulf of Mexico, but he listened carefully to Douglas' concept, a shallow cut "to terminate at Lake Joliet, with dams and locks on the Desplaines and Illinois rivers." Douglas obviously had studied the problem and the terrain. He was also familiar with Governor Clinton's specifications for the Erie, surely the world's most successful canal. Douglas' plan would cost millions less, initially at least, though it would not drain the marsh areas as planned by the deep-cut advocates. Governor Duncan insisted that the deep cut was to be preferred and would pass; compromise was not required. Hubbard stayed with Duncan and the deep-cut plan.

The canal bill squeaked through both houses on January 9, 1836, winning by a single vote, 28-27, in the House, where Lincoln provided a favorable vote, and in the Senate, where James Strode of Galena, for many years opposed, carried the day. Representative Douglas had excoriated the deep-cut idea before voting favorably for it rather than delay the canal longer. He angered backers by "apparently insinuating that those who supported the deep cut did so because of their interest in town site speculations," according to his biographer, Robert W. Johannsen. "His speech supporting the canal but opposing the deep cut was said by his opponents to be unequalled for its ridicule, exaggeration and abuse," Johannsen wrote. Many legislators owned lots along proposed canal routes, among them Abraham Lincoln, whose property consisted of forty-seven acres near the "paper" town of Huron on the planned Beardstown-Sangamon Canal. In the end, Douglas caused "a crucial delay in the construction of the canal," Johannsen noted, "a factor which would render him unpopular among some of the strong supporters of the canal." In time, after delays and financial difficulties, the canal was completed as the shallow cut urged by Douglas.

*

The long fight for the canal was over January 9, so it seemed, a victory greeted with a wild celebration in Chicago. "News of the event arrived by stage," said the Chicago *Times* years later. "By evening every able-bodied man was at one or another of the lounging places on South Water Street. An old howitzer was brought from the fort, stationed at Lake and Dearborn Streets where the Tremont (hotel) now stands, and the thunder began . . . . The boys blazed away and the old roarer got pretty hot . . . all of a sudden J.K. Botsford was very much astonished when a hand and an arm struck his shack. . . ." The howitzer had fired just as a visiting sailor was ramming down the shot.

Governor Duncan moved fast when the canal victory was won. On January 12 he announced the appointment of the three canal commissioners who were instructed to get the work started: "William F. Thornton, Shelby county; William R. Archer, Clark county; Gurdon S. Hubbard, Cook county are hereby appointed canal commissioners for the construction of the Illinois and Michigan canal, subject to the confirmation of the Senate," the Senate *Journal* recorded. "William F. Thornton to be president of the board; Gurdon S. Hubbard to be treasurer." All were promptly confirmed. "General Thornton and Colonel Archer are retired army engineers well qualified for the work," said the *Sangamon Journal* at Springfield. "Colonel

Hubbard is paymaster general of the Illinois militia and a well-known Chicago Whig.''

The commissioners met and agreed upon the selection of William Gooding, formerly an engineer on Erie canal construction, as chief engineer. Gooding arrived shortly in Chicago, met with the commissioners and announced plans that were warmly received by the press and the populace. "The Erie Canal was built too small," Gooding declared. "What the commissioners want, and I will give them, is a big canal, sixty feet wide at the top, thirty-six feet wide at the bottom, minimum depth of six feet, which will take Lake Michigan water into the Illinois river and take big boats with it."

Commissioner Hubbard wanted the deep cut if they could get it, but he had been impressed with Stephen Douglas' argument and he knew better than the engineers, from his personal experience, some of the difficulties ahead. He also knew, directly from Governor Duncan, that in addition to safeguarding and dispensing funds, it would be his duty to help raise them, and that wasn't going to be easy. A deep cut would be costly, in the neighborhood of the $8 million Douglas had cited. He warned his fellow commissioners that canal lands in northern Illinois were not going to bring the prices that had been anticipated. It had been stated in debate at Vandalia that canal lots and acreage available for sale, as a contribution of the federal government, land taken from the Potawatomis by the St. Louis treaty, would easily cover the cost: 250 canal lots in Chicago should have a value of $312,000, while fractional lands in Cook county and the acres along the canal route, all the way to Ottawa, would bring more than $2 million; lots at Ottawa, the western terminus, were estimated at $50,000. The State of Illinois was to provide the rest by selling canal bonds.

Arthur Bronson and others expected to provide the market for such bonds in the East had been given the required guarantees that the State of Illinois would back them with its credit, but, meantime, land prices had plunged. President Jackson's requirement that specie, or cash, payment must be made on government land purchases had depressed such sales and the price of land generally. The canal lots would no longer return the expected revenues, Hubbard warned. Nevertheless the Commission felt compelled to proceed. It called for construction bids on June 6 for the eastern sectors of the canal, and held a sale of lots on June 20. The result was a double disaster. Canal lots were bid in at low prices and the construction bids were so high all proposals were rejected. It appeared the digging could not proceed, though the building of a construction supply line was already under way. The commissioners scurried to Vandalia. They told Governor Duncan they would be required to expend all available funds on the supply road, from Bridgeport, formerly Hardscrabble, southwest of Chicago, to the proposed site of the major locking system at Lockport, a distance of thirty-one miles. Before canal digging could start, they would require additional funds. Governor Duncan agreed to provide them.

*

Work on the construction supply route was well under way in late June. The commissioners alerted the contractors to prepare for the major work. When Chicagoans learned that Commissioner Archer had bought up most of the land in the vicinity of Lockport, where a headquarters building was put up, the first canal scandal broke. The supply route was derisively called Archer's Road, a name that would stick. It was soon lined with the shacks of Irish and Scandanavian laborers, rude huts put up by the men themselves from scrap, reeds and a few sticks of sawn lumber, already scarce because of the building boom in the city. The Chicago terminus at Bridgeport shortly became the scene of struggle between immigrants assigned to attack with pick and shovel the tough dolomite underlying the supply route and the elite specialists from Indiana and coastal states who could handle blasting powder and the cement that had been developed for the Erie canal, or drive the mule-drawn scrapers, and who therefore got more pay for their work. Among the skilled newcomers was Matthew Laflin, who rumbled into Chicago with a wagonload of blasting powder he was promptly required to store in the Fort Dearborn magazine. Laflin and other experts had been lured to Chicago by William Ogden, Hubbard's New York friend, who lowered his construction bid to obtain one of the canal contracts. Soon Laflin and his men would go to work, blasting the seams of rock for the Hoosier muleteers

360

to attack with their scrapers. They were fewer in number than the pick and shovel men and they received not only the best pay, but the only available housing put up at the direction of the commissioners. Their top wage of $30 a month was considered exhorbitant by the citizens of the town as well as by the pick and shovel men getting only $20. Food prices shot up, working a hardship on the residents of the town and the unskilled men who had brought in their families. That summer pork would soar from $20 to $30 a barrel, flour $9 to $12, while potatoes brought 75 cents a bushel.

Thus before the canal commissioners and the Chicago town trustees could announce a grand Fourth of July celebration to mark the beginning of the canal itself, and the country's birthday, there was strife and even fighting in the construction boomtown on the southwest between the Irish and the Hoosiers, the Swedes and Norwegians joining in on one side or the other from time to time. Gamblers and prostitutes and more whisky sellers also had come to town to share the expected new wealth. The failure of the commissioners to let the first round of contracts delayed the expenditure of money, and the quarreling newcomers were mostly trying to live off one another as the June days passed. There was fighting and roistering in the construction camps and along South Water Street, where the Hoosiers gathered, almost every night. The noise was worse than when the Potawatomis came in for their treaty money, oldtimers complained.

Yet the grand canal earth-turning festivities of July 4, 1836 were eagerly awaited by all. The commissioners and the town trustees had agreed on July 4 as the date, but they agreed on little else. Politics took over, the Whigs and the Democrats vying bitterly for control. Finally a neutral celebration committee was named, with County Judge Richard J. Hamilton, a Democrat, as chairman. Chicago was Whig, but the state and county administrations were Democrat. Judge Hamilton chose Captain J.B.F. Russell, a Democrat who recently had escorted the Indians to their western lands and who was erecting the Saloon building on Lake Street, as marshal of the day. Col. Gurdon Hubbard, Chicago's own canal commissioner, Col. David Hunter, and Robert Kinzie, all Whigs, were named assistant marshals. Judge

Theopolis Smith of the Illinois Supreme Court, a downstate canal supporter, was to be speaker of the day, and Gurdon Hubbard also was invited to say a few words. Dr. W.B. Egan, a charming Irish Democrat trained in medicine in Dublin, but at that time better known in Chicago as an elocutionist, was chosen to read the Declaration of Independence.

Judge Hamilton's selections did not at all please another Chicagoan, Peter Pruyne, the new druggist, who aspired to leadership of the town's Democrats. Pruyne organized a rival celebration inducing the Irish along the south branch of the river and the Hoosiers along Wabash Avenue to declare a temporary truce in their labor difficulties in order to participate properly in the canal and Independence Day observances. Pruyne intended to have a parade and to mark the occasion that night with fireworks, gunfire and burning tar barrels. He was backed enthusiastically by John Calhoun's Chicago *Democrat,* fervently Jacksonian, and now supporting the presidential candidacy of Vice President Martin Van Buren.

Gurdon Hubbard was accustomed to the peaceful politics of Danville and Vermilion county, where he merely announced his candidacy for office and was elected. He admitted to Ellie that he knew something about practical politics too, since all the officers of Iroquois county, which he created, were on his payroll or under contract to run his wagon trains to Chicago. Yet he was appalled and angered by the vicious partisanship injected into canal contract and celebration proceedings. Though he was a Whig and a Henry Clay man, he had loyally worked with Jacksonian Democrats to get the canal. The Democrats John Reynolds and Joseph Duncan had taken the position that he did; Illinois internal improvements were not to be an area for partisan exploitation. Gurdon himself had brought in not only William B. Ogden, a leading New York Democrat, to bid on contracts, but also Arthur Bronson, like Ogden a supporter of Martin Van Buren, to seek canal contracts. Gurdon was disturbed by the political conniving and bickering under way and suggested to Ellie that she should stay away from the canal festivities planned for the Bridgeport site. There could be trouble, and he would be uncomfortable enough, trying to make a speech. He knew Peter Pruyne well, the druggist who was a fellow director in the new bank, and also an ambitious politician. While Pruyne professed to be uniting the Hoosiers and the Irish, Gurdon feared he might be merely stirring up more trouble.

*

July 4, 1836 dawned bright and beautiful. The Kinzies and David Hunter agreed with Gurdon that trouble could erupt at the canal festivities and the women of all three families compromised; they would attend the ceremony planned for the Dearborn street bridge in Chicago, allowing their husbands to go alone to the earth-turning event at Bridgeport. Gurdon was genuinely concerned, not only that Peter Pruyne's attempt to unite the warring Hoosiers and Irish could misfire, like the Fort Dearborn howitzer in a prior celebration, but that the great crowd trekking across the prairie would raise dust storms harmful to Ellie. Thousands were reported enroute to the Bridgeport festivities overland in wagon caravans. There might be a clash of Peter Pruyne's wagon train and the official canal party and the excursionists enroute by water, when all reached the construction site. The send-off for the celebrants planned for the Dearborn street bridge seemed safe enough. Possibly the entire day would pass without conflict, since Pruyne was, after all, gaining for the workmen some of the recognition denied them by the official committee. The wives, on their part, were content. No need to carry the children out to Bridgeport.

Chicago was aroused early that morning by the firing of three howitzers at Fort Dearborn. Soon after, the populace gathered at the Dearborn street bridge, where the steamer *Chicago* and two schooners, the *Sea Serpent* and the *Llewelyn,* bright with bunting, awaited the dignitaries and those with tickets who would be carried to the construction site by water.

"There was an immense attendance of strangers," wrote Frederick Cook in the Chicago *Times* years later, his account based on interviews with participants. "It was the most marked event that had ever taken place in the West, and every man took a personal interest in the success of the (canal) scheme. The entire Wabash Valley seemed depopulated for the nonce." Peter Pruyne was distributing a liberal supply of Smith's Ohio whisky.

The town south of the river "swarmed with butternut Hoosiers. They were getting ready *their* fleet of 'schooners,' the Hoosier boys putting their steers under yoke while the *ton* of the town were hurrying down to the river to take boats for Bridgeport," Cook wrote. "The streets were filling up with gaily ribboned oxen, for Pruyne's emmissaries had distributed cotton bands of red white and blue among them. Tom Towbridge, livery stable keeper, supplied Peter Pruyne with a really noble-looking span of cream-colored horses, covered with ribbons and other gay caparison, which he mounted."

Hundreds of Hoosiers in butternut pants, calico shirts, cowhide boots and wide-brimmed black hats drove the prairie schooners, or marched in the wake, singing, shouting, cat calling. "It was 'G'iang, Gee, Haw . . . hundreds of drivers howling to their full capacity," said Cook. Whips cracked, wagons creaked, musicians aboard strummed their banjos and played their mouth harps or harmonicas; women in gingham and calico gowns and cloth sunbonnets waved and shouted. Near the civic square the gunners had set up the old howitzer that had caused such problems in February and commenced firing. Tar barrels flared and smoked. The skipper of the steamer *Chicago* tied down his whistle. The band at the pier, recruited from the soldiers at the fort and a few civilian newcomers, began playing. Judge Hamilton presented Captain Russell, who read off the orders of the day as Hubbard and Kinzie, worried about the confusion that could result when Pruyne's procession, moving along rutted Lake street, reached the gathering crowd along Dearborn, urged the *Chicago's* captain to prepare to cast off.

The official celebration flotilla moved out as the Hoosier parade approached. The band continued playing, the crowds cheered, Gurdon and David Hunter and Robert Kinzie told their women and children in surries near the docks to get on home, as they themselves boarded the *Chicago*. Captain Ordway blasted his whistle, the little sidewheeler got under way, followed by the festooned schooners, towed by horses, and a brigade of Hubbard's mackinaws, all packed with passengers bound for the construction site. "The Hoosiers (ashore) enjoyed the fun immensely," Cook would write. "And, on the auguey banks of the Wabash River, of a winter evening, they undoubtedly told their grandchildren of the grand time they had at Chicago at the canal celebration."

The official regatta moved out slowly, some of the crowd aboard the boats shouting jeers and insults at the Hoosier celebrators. Several were sampling the kegs of whisky reserved for the on-site festivities. Along the south branch of the river, crowds of workmen, Irish, Scandanavian and Hoosiers, demanded to be put aboard the boats and were answered with abuse as well as the plain truth that there was no room. Some of the drivers of the horses towing the schooners were threatened and pelted with rocks. Colonel David Hunter wanted to charge the offenders at once. Gurdon Hubbard, remembering Governor Cass' run through hostile Indian country in a mackinaw, told Captain Ordway, "Keep moving, we can't stop now."

The crowd at Bridgeport was tumultuous but friendly. Thousands had found their way to the site, it seemed, driving across the prairie since there was as yet no road. The whisky kegs were broached. A militia company fired a 56-gun salute, honoring those who voted for the canal bill. What followed was variously reported. Some said that "lemons and sugar were poured into the spring for the temperance people." Others declared that whisky also was poured into the spring. Clearly there was confusion, since in contemporary reports, four different men, Captain Russell, Judge Hamilton, Gurdon Hubbard and Judge Theophilus Smith were credited with delivering the oration of the day. Captain Andreas, in his *History of Chicago,* and Frederick Cook, who interviewed participants for his account in the Chicago *Times,* provided differing, but probably near-accurate accounts. They agreed that Judge Hamilton, chairman, presented Captain Russell, marshal, who presented Dr. Egan, renowned as a declaimer of Shakespearian sonnets, who read the Declaration of Independence, "then urged all celebrants to 'Drink Deep or Taste not the Pierian spring . . .' before he was gently escorted off the platform . . ." according to an account in Andreas, or "Judge Smith read the Declaration of Independence followed by an eloquent address delivered by Dr. W. B. Egan," per Cook. Andreas and Cook agreed that Gurdon Hubbard made a short address, "contrasting the settlement with what it was 18 years before, when he first ascended the river in a canoe." "I first saw this place from an oak hummock and then from a canoe," Hubbard said. "There wasn't much to see but a fort, a lot of Indians, and some people I came to know as good friends . . . no man ever had better friends. Now we see building here a town with a great future because the ditch that Louis Joliet dreamed of 123 years ago is at last going to be dug."

Then, according to Cook and some others, Judge Smith delivered the main oration, standing on an empty whisky keg so that the vast crowd could see and hear him. "Judge Smith was a great orator and a great friend of the canal," a citizen recalled. "He indulged in wild prophecies, that in ten years the town would grow to a population of 10,000, in twenty to 20,000, in fifty years to 50,000, and in one hundred years to 100,000 . . . ." Finally Captain Russell , the marshal of the day, pulled Judge Smith from the whisky barrel and whispered, "You are making a fool of yourself, Judge. If you keep on you'll be claiming a million!" But the judge was right, another long-lived witness asserted. "There had been much celebrating of that event with liquor," he noted. "The story at the time went that while the barrel Judge Smith was standing on was empty, the judge was full." According to Andreas' history, Colonel Archer, the canal commissioner, for whom Archer road would be named, also delivered a speech and then Archer turned the first spadeful of earth. Frederick Cook wrote, "General Thornton came next and then, with an assumption of importance, Capt. J.B.F. Russell, the marshall of the day, stepped forward to put in his little 'dig'. But the crowd wouldn't have it so, and began to cry out lustily, 'Hubbard,' 'Hubbard,' and Gurdon S., ever modest, stepped forward and did his share of the work. After that, Russell came in order, and during the day about everybody on the ground enjoyed the felicity of assisting in digging the great Illinois and Michigan canal."

All reports of the July 4 canal celebration concurred in one respect, a considerable amount of whisky was consumed. Cook said Captain Russell was jeered, undoubtedly true. Henry R. Hamilton, grandnephew of Hubbard, credited Gurdon Hubbard with turning the first spadeful of earth, and wrote that his own grandfather, Hamilton, after giving the main speech, "was jeered and greeted with cries of 'Town Lots!', Judge Hamilton being reputed to be the largest landholder in the state." The Chicago *American* provided details of the Bridgeport observance, but the *Democrat* didn't mention it, covering instead Pruyne's parade as if it was the opening of Van Buren's campaign for the presidency. But all agreed that there was a grand fight along the south branch of the river that July 4 afternoon.

Hubbard and his friends anticipated trouble as the ships returned to Chicago. "No one then expected that Bridgeport would someday lie within the city," Cook noted. Colonel David Hunter, husband of Maria Kinzie and Gurdon's insurance partner, had promised he would lead a sortie to punish offenders if anything further happened. It did. Near the point where the officials and excursionists earlier had refused passage to the workmen, at the site of a brick works, the steamer *Chicago* came under a fusilade of bricks and stones. The schooners obviously would not be able to proceed. Charles S. Winslow, in *Early Chicago,* provided an account of the incident:

"Most heads were cleared by a satisfying fight on the riverbank. As the party in the steamer and schooners (had) moved up the river to the celebration a party of Irishmen was waiting on the bank at Adams street and insisted on being taken aboard . . . on their return the Irishmen were waiting with brickbats and a merry battle resulted, with quite a number hurt on both sides." Winslow quoted a participant: "We beached our boat and Colonel Hubbard and others dashed into the crowd of rock throwers and there was a fight and they pursued and caught six of the rock throwers and carried them off to jail." Chicago's log jail at the corner of Clark and Randolph streets was well filled for a time that night of July 4. It accommodated twenty-eight prisoners at once, but the locks were faulty. Prisoners frequently escaped if they cared to. No record survives of any rock thrower being captured or charged or brought before County Judge Richard J. Hamilton. The canal, thereafter, got well under way. The commissioners would spend $49,000 on construction in 1836, mostly for the road and the facilities at Canalport, and $300,000 the year following before depression and panic caught up with Illinois and Chicago.

*

The land craze raged throughout that summer. Harriet Martineau, the English novelist, arrived, with friends, and was told that the packed inns were intolerable. She took her troubles to Juliette Kinzie, who quickly arranged to accommodate Martineau and her friends in the Kinzie home and two other unnamed Chicago families, "who had the art of removing all our scruples about intruding on perfect strangers . . . none of us will lose the lively and pleasant associations with the place." One of the families was probably the Hubbards, whose large house was near the Kinzies, since Juliette and Eleanora were close friends. Martineau described the land boom:

"I never saw a busier place than Chicago was at the time of our arrival. The streets were crowded with land speculators, hurrying from one land sale to another. A negro, dressed up in scarlet, bearing a scarlet flag, riding a white horse with housings of scarlet, announced the time of the sale. At every street corner where he stopped, the crowd flocked around him; and it seemed as if some prevalent mania infected the whole people. The rage for speculation might fairly be so regarded. As the gentlemen of our party walked the streets, store-keepers hailed them from their doors, with offers of farms, and all manner of land-lots, advising them to speculate before the price of land rose higher.

"A young lawyer of my acquaintance there (Joseph Balestier) had realized $500 per day, the five preceding days, by merely making out titles to land. Another friend had realized in two years, ten times as much money as he ever before had fixed upon as a competence for life."

The second friend who at the time fitted Martineau's description probably was Gurdon S. Hubbard, who had invested his windfall of profit made at the New York auction in land that brought further profits, or possibly William Ogden, who lived in his suite in the Lake House at the time, though it wasn't quite finished. Hubbard had supervised the sale of canal lands in Chicago that summer, but had grown cautious. Some sources of Martineau's information on Chicago conditions were greatly exaggerated. "A poor man in town had a pre-emption right to land for which he paid $150 one morning and in the afternoon sold it to a friend for $5,000," she wrote. "A poor Frenchman (Jean Baptiste Beaubien) married a squaw, had a suit pending while I was there, which he was likely to gain, for the right of purchasing land by the lake for one hundred dollars, land which would immediately become worth one million dollars."

Martineau referred to the Beaubien suit, but it did not turn out as she and others anticipated. Beaubien, married to Josette Framboise, daughter of a French trader and his Indian wife, came to Chicago from Milwaukee, acting as an agent for the American Fur Company in both towns. He entered a pre-emption claim to seventy-five acres of lakefront adjacent to John Dean's property south of Fort Dearborn, which Beaubien then bought for $94.61 in 1817. The claim had been allowed by the government, but was declared faulty when Beaubien attempted to sell a part of it. Circuit Judge Thomas Ford ruled for Beaubien in 1836, but the decision was appealed to the United States Supreme Court and Beaubien lost. His property was put up for auction in June, 1839. Chicagoans, angered by the perceived injustice, refused to bid on it, but the land was bid in by James H. Collins, a former government attorney, at the government's land sale, for $1,049. The litigation had produced documents proving that part of Beaubien's land had been owned by John Dean, who had sold parcels of it to various persons, but not to Beaubien. Ultimately, the land, lying west of Michigan avenue and south of the Chicago river, did sell for many millions of dollars.

Harriet Martineau provided vivid and accurate pictures of Chicago life. "Chicago looks raw and bare, standing on the high prairie above the lake shore," she wrote. "The houses all appear insignificant, and run up in various directions, without any principle at all. There was much gaiety going on . . . as well as business. There is allowable pride in the place about its society. It is a remarkable thing to meet such an assemblage of educated, refined and wealthy persons as may be found there, living in small, inconvenient houses on the edge of a wild prairie." She found some of her Chicago friends "have the art of making themselves absolutely Indian in their sympathies and manners as the welfare of the savages among whom they lived required. They were the only persons I met with who, really knowing the Indians, had any regard for them."

*

That summer of 1836, Gurdon and Eleanora were busy helping the Kinzies raise funds for an Episcopal church edifice to be built on land contributed by John Kinzie. They had promised Eleanor Kinzie before she died that such a church would be built. The Hubbards and the Kinzies, including Robert, and David Hunter and his wife Maria Kinzie, had been members of the Episcopal congregation meeting in Kinzie's Tippecanoe Hall since 1834. By fall funds had been raised and the brick Gothic structure, 40 by 64 feet, rose at the corner of Cass (Wabash) and Illinois streets, and would be called by the newspapers the grandest structure in Chicago when Bishop Philander Chase arrived to dedicate it on June 25, 1837.

By fall commissioners had let contracts for twelve sections of the western division of the canal, including a steamboat turning basin to be located at La Salle. The work moved slowly however. The commissioners were plagued with trouble. They had been under criticism ever since it was disclosed that Commissioner Archer had bought up much of the land on the Lockport route. Hubbard himself was innocent; his partner, Judge Hamilton had lost heavily because he chose acreage in the wrong place, and Gurdon had sold his canal lots in New York long before the canal was authorized. But he shared the public wrath. Floods in the Desplaines valley held up road construction through the marshes. So much lumber and labor were required in Chicago that costs were bid up. Contractors worked their men long hours, as much as fourteen hours a day, and the workmen complained, threatening to strike. It was charged that contractors were selling Lockport rock, needed for the locks and turning basin, to Chicago builders who required foundation stones. Canal properties were vandalized, some blamed tramps angered when they couldn't get jobs, others said workmen dissatisfied with their hours and pay were responsible. The workmen charged that their foremen were brutal, demanding they should be fired. Most of these complaints were aired in the Chicago *American,* suggesting that Hubbard himself might have disclosed the troubles. He spent so much of his time along the canal and at Lockport that Ellie complained. He told her his business was suffering because of too many public demands on his time. He intended to quit.

*

The opening of the Lake House on the north bank of the river at Rush and Kinzie streets became a second major event of Chicago's social year. "We now have a hotel that is really grand," boasted the Chicago *American*. Gurdon had four partners in the enterprise, all eager to demonstrate that their town could well support a truly graceful inn. The Lake House was of brick, three and a half stories, and furnished in sedate luxury. Its bar was said to be the most elegant in the west. Hubbard brought Jacob Russell out from Middletown, Connecticut to become the manager. Menus were printed in French and fresh seafood, including oysters, hauled over frozen rivers and snowy trails, was served. Senator Daniel Webster of Massachusetts, the Whig candidate for president, was an early distinguished guest and a ball for him was given there. The Lake House, however, was situated on the wrong side of the river, since residents of Chicago's booming south side refused to vote taxes to pay for the completion of an adequate bridge at Rush street. Hubbard established the Lake House ferry, and in the beginning the Lake House did well. The panic of 1837, however, brought the Lake House to bankruptcy. Hubbard and his partners, John Kinzie, General David Hunter—Hunter had received a promotion—Dr. William Egan and Maj. James H. Campbell learned that Chicago's old guard, mostly Whiggish, could no longer successfully influence Chicago's voting or dominate its business affairs.

The lesson was repeated in November. William B. Ogden had come to Chicago to live in 1836, and for a time was a guest at the Lake House, but he soon moved to a boarding house on the south side of the river. Ogden, Hubbard's lawyer from the time of his arrival, and a partner with Gurdon in various land ventures, also had his own land company and acted as agent for eastern financiers. Ogden had told Hubbard in New York that he was not a Jacksonian Democrat, but he strongly supported Martin Van Buren, Jackson's chosen candidate for the presidency, who promised to continue President Jackson's policies. Ogden allied himself with Peter Pruyne, the druggist who had organized the July 4th parade. Hubbard and the Kinzies backed General William Harrison, the Whig, for the presidency, even though Daniel Webster had honored them by staying at their hotel. Vice President Van Buren carried Chicago by five votes of some 1,200 cast and Peter Pruyne won election to the Illinois senate. William Ogden, barely eligible to vote in Illinois, emerged as the boss of Chicago's Democrats, including the Jacksonians.

*

Early in 1837, the Illinois legislature passed a grandiose internal improvements act pledging the 400,000 residents of the state to spend more than $10 million on roads, railroads, bridges and canals. The Democrats formed an alliance with Whigs, led by Abraham Lincoln of the famed Long Nine, to ramrod the legislation through. Lincoln also "led the 'Long Nine' in finding the votes in the legislature to pass a bill moving the capital of the state from Vandalia to Springfield," Lincoln biographer Carl Sandburg would write. "A few members voted for the bill because they liked Lincoln, but most of the votes came through trade, deals and 'log rolling.' " The log rolling was with the internal improvements bill supporters, critics of Lincoln said, though Paul Simon, in his excellent study of Lincoln's legislative career, doubted that any trades were needed or made for passage of the internal improvements bill. "Public sentiment was overwhelmingly for internal improvements," Simon declared, "Illinois did not need any capital relocation bill to force approval. . . ." Gurdon Hubbard was in Vandalia, looking after Chicago canal interests though the Illinois-Michigan bill had been passed earlier. "The people are insane on the subject of improvements," Congressman John Reynolds complained. Reynolds predicted Illinois was headed for bankruptcy. Gurdon agreed. He was having trouble getting the money to keep the canal moving and was in town to get help from Governor Duncan. Duncan sent Reynolds and Senator Richard M. Young to Europe to attempt to sell state of Illinois bonds. The appointments were a disaster. Reynolds was accused of merely touring Europe. Young arranged "on controversial terms" to get a million and a half dollars from a London house that went bankrupt before the deal was completed.

Work on the canal continued, although by mid-1837 the financial panic which felled scores of New York City banks and business houses had spread to the West, including Illinois. The Whigs blamed the anti-bank, hard-money policies of the Jackson and Van Buren administrations for the troubles, but William Ogden, writing to his New York associates, blamed the Illinois legislature for ruining the state's credit with its excessive internal improvements program. Chicago continued to grow, despite tight money and interest rates rising to 25 percent. The estimated population passed 4,000 and the mushrooming town became increasingly unpleasant as a place to live. The frail balloon shacks trestled over marshes had walls so thin it was said a man could smash through them with his bare fists. There were insufficient sanitary facilities for humans and no requirements for the disposal of manure and garbage, or the offal of slaughtered animals. Some sewage remained in the streets and the few drainage ditches until rains washed it into the river or the lake. The wealthy residents could afford to subscribe to the Hydraulic company's hollow-log water service, which brought relatively fresh water from deep in the lake; the ordinary citizens took their water from the increasingly polluted river, or bought it from vendors at one cent a bucket. The streets were morasses in the spring flood season, rutted and rocky lanes choking riders and passengers with dust the rest of the year. Drovers continue to pasture their cattle along Wabash avenue and State street, slaughtered inside the city limits, and dumped the offal into the streams.

Gurdon Hubbard had begun his meat packing on the river and continued it from his new plant on East Water street along the north branch of the river. He had taken Sylvester Marsh of Concord, New Hampshire as his partner in the packing business in 1833. "We went down to the Wabash country, as we called it, and bought cattle and hogs and drove them up to Chicago," Marsh told a Senate committee in Boston years later. "We did not ship them in. We killed mostly beef for the local market. We were first in the market." Hubbard and Marsh processed

5,000 hogs in 1834. They ended their partnership early in 1836. "In 1836 they commenced building the canal and in that year I packed 6,000 hogs, mostly for home consumption," said Marsh. "They were building the canal then, and the contractors in 1837-38 took the pork for their men. Then the state failed to pay . . . state bonds went down to 25 cents on the dollar, and the state issued what was called 'canal scrip' to pay contractors what they were owed for work they had done. . . . The thing all burst up."

Hubbard evidently dissolved his partnership with Marsh to avoid a conflict of interest when the packing company began supplying the canal contractors. He formed a new partnership with George W. Dole and continued packing operations from East Water street, where he and Dole employed seventy-five to one hundred workers. Presumably they handled their disposal problem like the rest. Hubbard's records and correspondence relating to his packing activities were lost when his new plant was destroyed by fire in 1869. In 1845, the *Gem of the Prairie,* a weekly newspaper, reported that Gurdon Hubbard was slaughtering 105 cattle and several hundred hogs a week, paying $21,000 a year for salt and barrels. Most of his pack was sold in New York, Boston and New Haven by that time, the paper said.

Chicago became a city under a charter approved by the legislature on March 1, 1837 and the first city election was held May 8. Despite his close business relationship with William B. Ogden, who had formed his alliance with Peter Pruyne shortly after moving permanently to Chicago in 1836, Gurdon announced that he would support John Kinzie for mayor. The Ogden-Pruyne Democratic organization put forth its candidates: Ogden for mayor of Chicago, though he had been in town but a year, and Pruyne candidate for the Illinois state senate. Neither Kinzie nor Hubbard were much concerned with the Ogden-Pruyne announcement. They continued to believe they needed to do no more than speak quietly to friends to win. But Ogden had worked in the efficient Van Buren political organization in New York state. He proceeded to organize all six of the Chicago precincts and carried them all against Kinzie, including Kinzie's and Hubbard's own, the 6th, by one vote. The Chicago *Amer-*

ican, firmly Whig, declared that "unwholesome influences, namely unnaturalized foreigners" gave Ogden his margin of victory. Hubbard and Kinzie accepted the defeat gracefully. Hubbard, after all, had Ogden as his lawyer and he continued to do land business with him.

Gurdon was unhappy with his role in politics and wished to withdraw from his canal activities. By March the canal treasury had a healthy balance of over $1 million from loans and lot purchases, but the lots were moving slowly and some purchases were forfeited. Hard times struck by midsummer and so did cholera, especially attacking the canal workers. Chicago again was in panic. Gurdon sent Eleanora east to be with his mother at Middletown and promised to meet her there in August. The original canal plan, attacked from the beginning by Stephen A. Douglas as impractical, was again under fire when engineers reported that the estimated cost of $8 million for the project was far too low. The Illinois legislature brought in Benjamin Wright of New York as a special engineer to re-examine the route and plans and the construction under way. Wright's report strongly supported the canal commission. "The Illinois and Michigan Canal, as now projected and under construction, may truly be considered as one of the greatest and most important in its consequences of any work of any age or nation," Wright wrote. He said the route chosen was the best possible, "shortest with least leakage . . . it will justify by its revenue any outlay which may be put upon it."

On his return from the east, Gurdon Hubbard submitted his resignation from the commission nonetheless. On October 23, 1837 a new board was named, General Jacob Fry replacing Gurdon Hubbard and Colonel J.A. McClernand replacing Archer. General Thornton continued on the new board which ordered a study of a shallow cut alternative, raising the canal to a bottom level of twelve feet above Lake Michigan. Gurdon Hubbard was through as a commissioner, but, at the request of both Mayor Ogden and Arthur Bronson, he continued to represent canal interests at Springfield, the new state capital, and in New York.

*

Immediately after his return from Middletown, on September 23, Gurdon signed partnership papers with Henry Hubbard and Daniel S. Griswold for the establishment of a steamship company to be called the Eagle Line to engage in Great Lakes trade. The partnership arrangement was to begin "on the first day of March next and to continue for a period of ten years. . . ." Gurdon had arranged with Arthur Bronson in New York for financing. William B. Ogden was the attorney. The ships to be purchased or leased included the brigs *Illinois, Indiana* and *Queen Charlotte;* the schooners *Lewis Golin, Moses and Elias, Franklin, Tom Hart, Pacific, Oregon* and *Constitution* and "the steamers *Milwaukee* and a steamer now building in Chicago." The partnership would provide the first major freight line based in Chicago. The *Illinois* had been in the Chicago-Cleveland run since July 12, 1834. It was built in Sackett's Harbor, New York with funds from George Dole and other Chicagoans and Oliver Newberry of Detroit.

Throughout that summer and fall, Gurdon's warehousing and freight operations went well from his new base on the north bank of the river near his Lake House. The *American* declared that "Chicago has become the distributing point for the whole settled country. Hubbard & Company is the largest of four firms here, delivering to destinations in Iowa, Minnesota, Wisconsin, Michigan, and Indiana as well as Illinois." Soon the paper would report that "The brig *Indiana* of the Eagle Line, has arrived bringing goods from New York in 17½ days. The goods are bought principally in New York, and are shipped to this point via the Hudson River, Erie Canal and the lakes." The *voyageurs* still in Gurdon's employ then off-loaded the freight into Hubbard's warehouse, whence they were sent by stage, wagon train and canoe to their final destinations. The Lake House was then doing well. It was, said the newspapers, "the most elegant public house in the west, with a French cook, printed bills of fare and various other innovations," one of them being "the importation of fresh oysters from the east coast, shipped partly by fast sleighs," during cold winter weather.

*

Gurdon was intensely worried about Eleanora in the late fall of

1837. Her ailment was more than the ordinary morning sickness of a pregnant woman he was sure. Ellie could not retain food, nor even water, on many days. She was becoming thin and frail, though she sought to convince him that her problem was not unusual. He had been happy on first learning that they were expecting a child but guilty feelings soon assailed him. Ellie reluctantly saw Dr. Egan, Gurdon's partner in the hotel business, who had interned in the Dublin Lying-In hospital and was cavalierly told that her illness was in her mind. Dr. Egan recommended a caudle of ale with eggs, gruel and spices to give her strength, but the remedy worsened her illness. When in desperation Gurdon called upon Dr. Egan to demand that Eleanora be given more than cursory attention, Egan haughtily dismissed him. The distraught Hubbard seized the doctor by the shoulders and shook him, as Chief Tecumseh once shook his errant medicine man and prophet. Dr. Egan thereafter refused to see or speak to either Eleanora or Gurdon Hubbard. In October, Gurdon sent a pleading letter to Dr. Fifthian in Danville, asking him and Alethea to come to Chicago. By December, Dr. Fifthian, still unable to make the trip, urged that Eleanora should come to Danville, where she would be well cared for in their new home until the baby arrived, but Eleanora refused to go.

"Mr. Hubbard has been absent seven weeks," Mayor William Ogden wrote to Democratic politician and steamship operator, Edwin Croswell, Esq. of Albany, New York, on January 30, 1838. "I have pretty much made up my mind to go to Washington to attend to harbour interests and the city's interest in the Beaubien claim. . . . By the bye, Gen. McClure would like very much to be collector of this port when made a port of entry . . . nothing would gratify me more. . . ."

Mayor Ogden and Gurdon Hubbard had continued to be closely associated in business, canal lobbying matters, and as lawyer and client. Gurdon's reasons for remaining out of reach were unknown to Ogden, but evidently related to the illness of Eleanora, plus troubles attending Hubbard's various enterprises as a result of the panic. He had in January signed over his various insurance policies to Arthur Bronson, to whom he was indebted. On February 22, after two months of absence from Ogden's attention, Gurdon appeared in Ogden's office. "I have a son," he told the mayor. Ogden beamed and congratulated his friend and shook his hand, but found that Hubbard trembled from emotion and was fighting back tears.

"Ellie . . . won't live," he said.

Mayor Ogden was shocked but saw there was nothing he could do or say that would help. Gurdon composed himself and instructed his friend to make out a power of attorney form for him to sign, enabling Ogden to act for him in various pending business matters. The papers were signed the day following, with W.W. Saltonstall, one of Gurdon's business associates, acting as witness. Then Gurdon Hubbard disappeared again, so far as his friends could ascertain.

Eleanora died of peritonitus and complications the doctor said, January 28, 1838, six days after the birth of their son, whom they named Gurdon Saltonstall Hubbard. Gurdon was inconsolable. In his black, angry mood he wanted no consideration from family, friends or church. He was prevailed upon to care for the details attending death in the family, but remained apart, sitting alone with Eleanora's body, sullenly arising to accept condolences from kin and friends he seemed not to recognize. His consultation with the Reverend Isaac Hallam, rector of St. James church, left Hallam confused and dismayed. Hubbard seemed not to understand what was required and was unwilling to accept the consolations of his faith. The funeral services were held at St. James and Gurdon conducted himself correctly, but again disappeared. He saw his son frequently, yet left the care of the child totally to the wet nurse Alethea acquired, to Alethea, and finally to his sister Elizabeth, who came to live with him. Then he again disappeared for some days, as he had when he and Watseka parted, in a mood black as that his friend Lincoln had shown the first winter they were together in Vandalia. It was said that he went hunting in the Sag marshes and that he had gone to visit Shabona. The managers of his various enterprises seemingly heard from him, as did Elizabeth and Alethea. They waited patiently for his return.

*

By the summer of 1838 work on the Illinois and Michigan canal was well advanced, the commissioners working with a fund of nearly $2 million. Few lots were sold during the period of panic, but prices and labor costs fell and some contractors accepted Illinois scrip, called "Jackson money" by some, which was widely used. Yet the state was moving toward bankruptcy, as John Reynolds had predicted it would, because of the costly internal improvements act. Canal work would slow to a halt after peak spending of $1,470,000 in 1839. "The legislature has disgraced our state, we are bankrupt and ruined," William Ogden wrote Capt. L.S. Jameson March 22, 1839. There were other such letters, in which Ogden damned the legislature, his party and the people generally for the troubles in Illinois; publicly he was confident of the future, and risked his own fortune, as Gurdon Hubbard was doing, to hold on to his business interests and lands. "The canal is a desert and will remain so for four more years," Ogden wrote Charles Butler, but then he summoned Hubbard, dragging him from his "slough of Despond," as Gurdon called it (he had been reading Paul Bunyan) to find ways to revitalize the canal. Together they worked on new legislation and they sought the aid of Arthur Bronson in New York.

In October, 1839, Governor Thomas Carlin summoned a special session at Springfield, the new capital, to deal with the internal improvements problem. His solution: concentrate all effort on one waterway and one state-subsidized railroad. The Chicago *American* sneered at the idea. "Will Governor Carlin say which one?" it demanded. "All agree in thinking Governor Carlin honest, but few think him capable." Abraham Lincoln, the Whig leader, proposed that the state in effect form partnerships with private interests to complete selected projects. This was similar to a plan Hubbard and Ogden had been developing with Arthur Bronson. The problem again was, how to choose which projects would be saved. Ogden and Hubbard, attending the session as lobbyists, urged adoption of Lincoln's plan, one they may have suggested. Representative Edward Baker presented a bill diabolically proposing that Governor Carlin should pick the projects to be completed. A legislative wag proposed handing to Wisconsin the fourteen northern Illinois counties. The measure actually came to a vote in the House, losing 70 votes to 11.

Mayor Ogden continued to be disgusted with the legislature.

"Internal improvements for Illinois are dead and buried," he wrote Butler in January. "The state is disgraced and bankrupt, but party rules, tho the state may be ruined. What patriotism! What public disgrace for the sake of party!"

Canal work stopped, but the Ogden and Hubbard negotiations with Arthur Bronson continued, and the campaign of Russell E. Heacock, a dweller along the canal, for resumption of the work on a shallow cut basis, produced results in the spring of 1842. "As if by magic the right man seemed to spring up at the right time," said Andreas' history somewhat naively, for in that year (June, 1842) Arthur Bronson came west to look over his property and was interviewed by citizens on the best means for procuring funds. Bronson had devised a finance plan that he believed would be accepted by eastern bankers and had been urged by Ogden and Hubbard to come west to present it. Bronson's plan, simplified, provided that canal scrip, down to 25 cents on the dollar in value, could be used at face value to buy canal lots. When this plan was adopted, canal scrip was eagerly bought, canal credit was restored, canal lands were sold at rising prices, and canal construction work resumed.

The Illinois and Michigan canal would be finished and opened to traffic six years later. ". . . Despite limitations, the canal was a major factor in the extraordinary growth of Chicago in the next two decades," historians Mayer and Wade would say in 1969. "Creating a water opening to the southwest, it drew more and more of the surrounding country into the city's commercial orbit . . . trade could now move north to the Lakes as well as south to the Gulf. . . ." When Illinois ceded the canal to the federal government in 1915, it had paid its bills and earned profits from tolls, attaining a peak traffic in 1882. Contrary to the belief of many, Chicago did not have a single mile of railroad traffic when the canal opened. Mayor Ogden, in his letters, credited Gurdon Hubbard with assisting him in bringing canal work resumption about, but Hubbard himself sought no credit, insisting instead that his public life was over.

13

June, 1845
Chicago is in fact the first and great city of the
prairies. . . ."

Personal Memoirs. . . .
Henry R. Schoolcraft

"I didn't throw that man all the way downstairs. I only
threw him part of the way, he fell the rest. . . . I didn't
throw him over the heads of his gang. They got out of the
way."

Gurdon S. Hubbard to
Henry R. Hamilton

He found politics repugnant but necessary, Gurdon Hubbard
sometimes said. He preferred to "stop talking and get on with
it." He admired his friends in politics, feeling that William Ogden
could persuade and Abe Lincoln could inspire. But he was no
Ogden nor a Lincoln. He dreaded speaking in public. It was the
example of his friend Shabona, who persisted in good works
despite all adversity, including the ravages of rum, that restored
Gurdon after the death of Eleanora; Shabona, the ministrations
of a young pastor from St. James, and eventually the call of politics, demanding that he do his duty.

Gurdon's letters to his mother Abigail almost ceased from the
time his sisters moved west and could give her the news, so little of his private life in Chicago in the 1840s has been disclosed,
except for the writings of youthful kin so much with him they
were generally thought to be his grandchildren—Henry Raymond Hamilton and Anna Holt. They were the grandchildren
of Gurdon's trusted friends, Judge Richard Hamilton, whom he
had known from Black Hawk war days, and Devillo R. Holt, a
Wisconsin fur trader and timber cutter who had set up a flourishing lumber business in Chicago. In the ensuing years Hamilton
and Holt wrote of life with Gurdon. They were brought into

381

a close family relationship as kin of his third wife, Mary Ann Hubbard, and seemingly knew "Uncle Gurdon" better than did his own son, Gurdon Junior.

Immediately after the death of Eleanora, Gurdon's favorite sister Elizabeth had come out from Middletown to take over from Alethea Fifthian the care of Gurdon, Jr. Elizabeth and the wet nurse were left much alone with the infant. Her brother sought solitude, disappearing for days as he fought his feelings of grief and guilt. Usually he brought in game when he returned. Elizabeth wrote her mother that Gurdon evidently had been with Indian comrades, hunting in the Sag marshes. She had urged his white friends who called at the house to join him on his excursions. Devillo Holt and the Reverend W.F. Walker, assistant rector of St. James church, in time persuaded Gurdon to include one of them or the other on his hunting trips, as did Judge Hamilton and Henry George Hubbard, Gurdon's cousin and warehouse manager.

Responding to the persuasion of Reverend Walker, Gurdon returned to church, but not St. James in the beginning. Devillo Holt was a member of Second Presbyterian, known as Bross Church, for Deacon William Bross, the bookseller, who described the modest edifice as "a balloon-built, shanty-like structure on Randolph street east of Clark, patched at one end to meet the needs of an expanding congregation." Bross, soon to become a newspaper editor and one of Chicago's leading boosters, became Gurdon's close friend. Gurdon also met at Second Presbyterian an attractive, intensely devout young woman, Mary Ann Hubbard, the daughter of Ahira and his wife Sarah. Ahira, a cousin, worked for Gurdon. He had previously seen Mary Ann when Ahira's family stayed at his Lake House, shortly after their arrival in Chicago, but he had forgotten her. Gurdon was near forty when he saw Mary Ann again; she was twenty-two.

He continued in mourning for some months, finding some relief in discussing his melancholy with Devillo Holt and the Reverend Mr. Walker. Walker evidently was an ardent and able hunter. When he was summoned to the church trial that resulted in his resignation from St. James some months later, the specification against him read: "When visiting outlying parishes on Sunday he did take with him his gun and did return with his buggy well laden with game." Charges against the Reverend Mr. Walker were formally lodged by Bishop Philander Chase after a period of evil rumor. Though Justin Butterfield, the attorney, defended him, Walker was found guilty. He left St. James after the Easter Sunday service in 1844. Gurdon Hubbard was not directly responsible for Mr. Walker's Sunday indiscretions, if at all, but such strict imposition of church law by his one-time friend, Bishop Chase, further alienated him from St. James. He continued to be an Episcopalian, but he was no longer Anglican, he said.

It was Henry George Hubbard, long his business associate, who lured Gurdon back into Chicago social and political life by inducing him to join the town's volunteer fire department. Gurdon became an honorary marshal of Henry's company and in 1843 he helped to organize Engine Company No. 3, to become known as "The Kid Glove Company," that would own a new-fangled two-crane-neck piano-style engine, drawn by "flaxen lines so clear that the white gloves of the firemen would not be tarnished." Fire companies were the most elite men's organizations in Chicago and politically powerful. They conducted sports events, picnics, social dances and national fire company competitions. Chicago Engine Company No. 3 became famed for its ability to run five hundred yards with its heavy pumper to make a three-hundred-yard connection in one minute and seven seconds! Company No. 3 also held the town's most colorful and elegant dances in the new Saloon building on Lake street, to which, said the *American,* only "the *bon ton* of the city" were invited. The *Bon Ton Directory,* issued for some years, later became Chicago's social guide.

Gamblers, crooks, con men, convicted criminals and prostitutes flocked into Chicago in the boom days, but were mostly kept to segregated districts, one south of the river, not far to the west of Bross' church, which became known as "Hairtrigger Block", and another on the north bank of the river, known as "The Sands," an area near Hubbard's Lake House and his new warehouse. Usually Gurdon was a proper, law abiding man. He was abstemious, though he maintained a good table and had excellent wines in his cellar. He didn't gamble, nor even cuss, except rarely, and there was no suspicion that he ever entered any of the town's brothels. His recreation was hunting, reading and running to fires. His so-called grandnephew, Alfred Holt, would write that Gurdon slept with his fireman's gear near and that he responded to the fire alarms even in his sixties. Holt's information evidently came from Mary Ann Hubbard, young Holt's blood kin. Gurdon also went to the firemen's balls. Ernest Poole, in his Chicago profiles, states that Hubbard squired various Chicago beauties to these affairs and agreed with Alfred Holt that at one ball a hoodlum with political ambitions who failed to get an invitation attempted to crash the affair. Holt said the man was Big Jim O'Leary, the gambler, but O'Leary would have been about six years old at the time. Henry Hamilton provided the most reliable account, related to him by Colonel Dick Taylor in Hubbard's home. "A certain gambler" had been refused admittance to the ball and reappeared with his gang as the grand march began, Taylor said. "They trooped up the stairs, shouting and cursing and discharging their firearms." Gurdon left his position at the head of the marchers, hurried to the door just after the hoodlum had pushed it open. "Without wasting words in parley, he grasped the man about the middle, swung him off his feet, and threw him over the heads of his followers so that he fell to the landing below, blood gushing from his mouth and ears," Hamilton wrote. The gang picked up its bruised leader and left. "Uncle Gurdon was visibly discomposed during the progress of this tale," Hamilton recalled. " 'Dick, that story is very much exaggerated,' he said. 'I didn't throw that man all the way downstairs. I only threw him part way, he fell the rest of the way, and I didn't throw him over the heads of his gang, they got out of the way.' "

*

It was late in 1839 that Gurdon responded to friends urging him to participate in the campaign to elect General William Henry Harrison, the Whig, president of the United States, and John Tyler, vice president, the famed "Tippecanoe and Tyler Too" political team. Abraham Lincoln, Gurdon's friend from Black Hawk war and Vandalia days, sent him a circular, written by Lincoln himself, urging subscription to a new publication, *Old Soldier,* that, according to Paul Simon, Lincoln was helping to edit.

"Every Whig in the state must have it," Lincoln's circular urged. "Copies will be forwarded to you." Hubbard joined cause with Lincoln and Chicago Whigs. He was elected delegate to the Whig convention at Springfield and helped to launch an Illinois political crusade that became known as the "Log Cabin and Hard Cider" campaign. The Whigs, long on slogans and short on issues, presented General Harrison as a great victor in the Indian wars and a man of the people, a man born in the log cabin, and also a soldier who returned to the land, in the tradition of Roman generals, while portraying President Martin Van Buren, the Democrat, as an effeminate dandy who dressed in fancy clothes and favored the rich. When Van Buren asserted that he himself had been a farmer, his Whig enemies sneered: "Van Buren pompades his hair and combs his yellow whiskers *a la Paris* when he hauls his cabbages to market."

Despite Gurdon's reluctance to re-enter politics, and his dislike of the political newcomers to Chicago who tended to repudiate the old-guard Whigs, he joined his cronies, the Kinzies, William Bross, George W. Dole, and David Hunter in the management of the Harrison drive in Chicago. He liked General Harrison and he hoped to crush the ambitions of his personal foe, Long John Wentworth, editor of the *Morning Democrat,* who attacked not only Whigs, but Gurdon's favorite Democrat, William Ogden. Even the Indian chiefs Billy Caldwell and Shabona were induced to join the Whig campaign, though they could not vote. They dispatched from Council Bluffs, Iowa, on March 23, 1840 a letter stating, "We found General Harrison was a brave warrior, humane to his prisoners. . . . We had many friendly smokes with him." Presumably Billy Caldwell sent the missive as Shabona could not write.

Gurdon's friends not only wished to nominate and elect General Harrison president, as they had vainly attempted to do four years previously, they also desired to impress Springfield and the rest of Illinois and the northwest with the continuing importance of Chicago, the Queen City of the Lakes, the city of the future. As convention delegates, they planned to take with them, to symbolize their town, a "fully-rigged ship," actually a mackinaw freight canoe, mounted on a Conestoga chassis, complete with cannon. The gun was to be from Chicago's famed

Fort Dearborn armament, "the old cannon," a brass piece the Indians threw into the Chicago river when they destroyed the fort. The cannon had been raised from the river by workmen clearing the Chicago harbor. Mayor Buckner Morris, a Whig, authorized the use of the cannon aboard the proposed prairie schooner which would lead the Chicago Whig caravan to Springfield.

Anything the Whigs wanted, Long John Wentworth's *Democrat* opposed. Wentworth clashed early in the campaign with Hubbard and the Kinzies, writing in his paper that Harrison was supported in Chicago by those who had defrauded the Indians in the fur trade and had stolen their land. General David Hunter, infuriated by the charge, which sullied both his father-in-law Kinzie and his insurance partner Hubbard, if allowed to stand, marched into Wentworth's office and laid a brace of pistols on the editor's desk. Wentworth refused this challenge to a duel, but kept the pistols, exhibiting them in his office thereafter as symbols of the hazards in the life of an honest and courageous editor. Wentworth now denounced the use of the Fort Dearborn cannon, a revered relic, in a partisan political exhibit, but the Whigs ignored him. The cannon was mounted on the Whig float. But when Democrats obtained a court order requiring the Whigs to surrender the gun, it could not be found. The Whigs hid it in a grain bin in one of Dole's elevators, where it sank to the bottom and was not recovered until grain ships were loaded later.

The gun incident occupied the attention of the town's newspapers for several days, creating extra publicity for the Harrison campaign. In the end the Whigs concluded that the gun couldn't have been carried on their float, it was too heavy, but the "full-rigged brig, a canal boat on wheels" was readied for its dry-land journey. The procession left Chicago early in June for the Springfield rally and convention, the delegates and their retainers travelling in covered wagons, led by the mackinaw boat on wheels and several baggage wagons loaded with "hard cider" and other necessities. Democrat John Palmer recalled meeting the caravan as he travelled across Illinois with Stephen A. Douglas: "In the lead was an immense team of some eight yoke of oxen attached to a wagon upon which was a canoe forty feet long. Other teams were drawing log cabins ornamented with living coons, coon skins and gourds and other backwoods articles. . . ." When the leader of the column saw Palmer and Douglas, "he proposed three cheers for 'Tippecanoe and Tyler Too,' which were given and taken by the column; and then he called for three groans for Douglas and Palmer. This call met with a prompt response and it seemed to me that for miles across the prairie a wave of groans followed. . . ."

The Springfield Whig gathering was said by the Chicago *American* to have attracted 15,000 persons, whose encampment covered seventy-two acres of ground. Abraham Lincoln was one of the speakers, but most of the Chicago delegates insisted that S. Lisle Smith, a young lawyer from their own caravan, made the outstanding oration. Reported the *Illinois State Register* of Springfield: "We write . . . surrounded by log cabins on wheels, hard-cider barrels, canoes, brigs of every description . . . which, if a sober Turk were to drop in among us, would induce him to believe we were a community of lunatics."

But the Whigs lost Illinois in 1840, all five of the state's electors going to Van Buren by a margin of roughly 47,000 to 45,000 votes. Abe Lincoln of Springfield and Mayor Buckner Morris of Chicago were both losers. William Henry Harrison nevertheless carried the country, receiving 234 electoral votes to 60 for Van Buren.

*

Like others broken by the 1837-38 panic, Gurdon Hubbard lost much of his wealth and felt obliged to sign over his insurance to Arthur Bronson and Charles Butler, his chief creditors. His Lake House was a conspicuous failure. But, under Jacob Russel, its Middletown, Connecticut manager, the Lake House had succeeded for a time in providing frontier Chicago with the amenities of the effete East. "In 1838 the hotel manager announced a party for the whole set of 200 North Side aristocrats," wrote Emmett Dedmon in his *Fabulous Chicago*. "There was Bordeaux claret, champagne and oranges and grapes it required weeks to get from the East. . . . The last dish the Lake House manager put before his guests was new to most of them—it consisted of a piece of lemon peel floating in a tumbler of water and was served with a small glass bowl. Most guests thought it was lemonade and drank it." Juliette Kinzie, however, let the water from her glass trickle over her fingers into the bowl, then daintily dried with her linen napkin. Despite such fastidiousness, or because of it, the Lake House was bankrupt in 1839 and ultimately became a board and room house.

William Ogden handled Gurdon's legal problems and some of his business affairs. "Mr. Hubbard prefers the New York plan of settlement, since it won't affect his bankstocks," wrote Ogden to an eastern correspondent. "Hubbard and Dole are interested in the quarry," he wrote another. The quarry was the source of the pink granite widely used in Chicago construction. By 1843 Gurdon Hubbard had regained his fiscal, physical and mental well-being. He evidently left the care of his young son mostly to Elizabeth and to the other Hubbards constantly in his home. He had many responsibilities, his mother, sisters, uncles, aunts and cousins seemed to be dependent on his enterprises, and his brother Christopher in New York worked as his agent there. Friends, too, were again welcome to the Hubbard home after 1840, some of the neighbors complaining that Indians appeared to be living with him. Actually, Shabona and his wife and sometimes a grandchild or two dwelled in the Hubbard wood house and stable, where there were accommodations for servants or guests.

Gurdon was thirty-six when Eleanora died and, as grand-nephew Holt and Ernest Poole and others have suggested, he was a most attractive man to the young widows of the town. He was rich, six-feet tall, hard-muscled, darkly handsome, with a wide, flashing smile, and, from his canal negotiating experience, he spoke increasingly in the calm, reassuring, but reserved manner of a diplomat. He was a partner in the elegant Lake House. He had learned courtliness with Eleanora, and something of social life among the Kinzies, especially after Juliette Kinzie came to town. He had learned to be respectful of the opinions and desires of women as a boy on Mackinac. He listened intently and patiently to others for he was powerfully aware of his own ignorance. He sought the views of those who would add to his knowledge or to provide a reference for what he knew. He had learned history from Deschamps, trained in a Quebec seminary, and Dr. Wolcott, schooled at Yale College. He remembered that Black Hawk spoke wisely and with winning candor and that Keokuk intonated the language of poetry. Gurdon sought to emulate those he admired and tried always to make up for his lack of education which distressed him. But, mostly, he was a man of splendid silences, honored among his friends for his wise reticence, for his reserved judgment and fair decisions. Few in his later years knew that Gurdon Hubbard had been short in temper, but those attending the firemen's ball in the second-floor ballroom of the Saloon building discovered it. Other versions than Hamilton's recorded that incident.

Wrote Poole in *Giants Gone:* "He was chief of a volunteer fire brigade; and when the brigade gave a dance for their daughters and wives in a small hall above a saloon, Hubbard and a budding society leader led the grand march. Because they were all nice people, a noted gambler had been kept out, so he got together his gang and whooping and shouting they made a rush up the narrow stairs. Excusing himself from his partner, Hubbard stepped quickly to the doorway, seized the gambler by his shoulders lifted him high and swung him around and threw him downstairs, on his gang, knocking them down like nine-pins . . . ."

Alfred Holt said Gurdon's partner was "the widow Hogan." More likely she was Mary Ann Hubbard. Probably the hoodlum was Cap Hyman, a mean gambler who in later years took over the Tremont hotel at gun point, holding all the guests hostage for several hours until police dislodged him. There was no "saloon" in the Saloon building, but city and federal government offices. There was a ballroom on the second floor.

*

Mary Ann Hubbard was born November 2, 1820 in Middleboro, Massachusetts, "of Pilgrim ancestry and environment," and was eighteen years younger than Gurdon Hubbard. She had come to Chicago with her parents, Mr. and Mrs. Ahira Hubbard, late in 1836. Ahira was to follow his son Henry in working closely with Gurdon. The family first stopped at the Hamiltons—their daughter Harriet was married to Judge Hamilton—then they resided for a time in Hubbard's Lake House. They later settled on Chicago's south side, where they became members of Second Presbyterian church. "Mary Ann brought her New England ideals and standards of religion with her to Chicago," wrote her cousin and close friend, Anna Holt Wheeler. Gurdon probably saw her at the Hamiltons' or at his hotel. Mary Ann was a pretty blonde with a golden glint in her hair, her eyes deep blue, her complexion fair; her nose somewhat prominently Hubbard. She was aloof and self-possessed and intensely religious. She was active in the Sunday school, mission work and the charitable activities at Second Presbyterian, where she and her parents were regular and devout worshippers.

Mary Ann Hubbard was almost twenty-three years old in 1843 when her Uncle Henry and Judge Hamilton concluded she would be an appropriate wife for Gurdon Hubbard. She had never seemed interested in silly boys or men and marriage. Her voice was cool and sweet and well assured when she discussed matters of salvation and the soul, but Mary Ann was shy and not many had heard her musical laughter. Possibly Gurdon would have courted Mary Ann without encouragement, since he knew her moderately well by 1843, but it didn't seem likely. Gurdon was forty-one, he had vowed publicly that he wouldn't marry again, and it is doubtful that he escorted as many belles to firemen's balls as stated by Alfred Holt and later Ernest Poole. Not all Chicagoans agreed that Gurdon Hubbard was "a good match," though he was a man of impeccable reputation. He was too friendly with Indians, allowing them to live in his home. He was known to be critical of his church. Some thought that Ahira Hubbard and his wife Sarah were not especially pleased in the beginning when Gurdon Hubbard asked their permission to escort Mary Ann to a firemen's dance, though it was Chicago's most social occasion. There was some truth in what was whispered. Ahira and his wife had not expected such frivolity on Mr. Hubbard's part, nor did they anticipate that Mary Ann would enthusiastically respond. Ahira may have heard the ugly rumors of Gurdon Hubbard's past. There was the problem of blood kinship, Mary Ann and Gurdon were second cousins. Still, the marriage of full cousins was not unusual on the frontier; middle-aged widowers sought young brides, and Mr. Hubbard, after all, was Ahira's boss.

Ahira had visited his son Henry in Gurdon Hubbard's home in Danville some years earlier and there had known Eleanora. Possibly in Danville he heard the dark rumors of Hubbard's liaison with an Indian girl. In Chicago, Gurdon had been called "Indian Hubbard" and he allegedly had beaten a fellow who called him "Squaw Man." Whatever the rumors and gossip, Ahira had to admit to himself that Gurdon was definitely a middle-aged widower, while Mary Ann was a very young woman. It was a father's duty to protect his daughter. Yet Ahira and Sarah, deeply loving Mary Ann and wishing for her happiness, agreed that she could not soon find a better man than Gurdon Hubbard. She was no ordinary girl; he was no ordinary man. Ahira never disclosed Gurdon's secret to Mary Ann nor to Sarah, if he knew it. It was enough that his daughter wished to be in the company of a man almost twice her age who had a five-year-old son. Mary Ann took care of children in the mission school and told her parents she was sure that she would get on well with Gurdon Junior. It soon was obvious to the Hubbards that their wondrously radiant, happy daughter was genuinely in love and that Gurdon Hubbard was serious. Ahira and his wife prayerfully joined the Henry Hubbards and the Judge Hamiltons and the Devillo Holts in helping to encourage a match quite clearly arranged in Heaven.

*

Gurdon Hubbard himself appeared astonished that he could so easily fall in love with Mary Ann, a naive, sheltered girl young enough to be his daughter. He had believed his emotions and capacity for love had died with Eleanora's passing. Mary Ann fascinated him and amused him. In the beginning she had appeared somewhat dour and dowdy, and a bit plump, as compared with Eleanora or Margaret Helm. But then she cast shy glances at him, responded to his smile, and when he talked with her she burst from her preoccupation with Scripture and devotions and became a blithely cheerful creature, her unexpected laughter delighting him. He saw that she was young, in ripe good health, and in her way quite beautiful, her hair like ripening wheat, her eyes the violet blue of cornflowers. She was fair and demurely sweet and reticent until she had known him a while, when she thrilled him with eager, breathless excitement in all things new, and also by her surprising, quick bursts of temper. She was a beauty too, when her mother allowed her to wear a low-cut ball gown, which Gurdon himself did not quite approve, but which she displayed in triumph at the firemen's ball, seemingly oblivious of the stares she attracted, or the glances they received as a couple. Gurdon found Mary Ann surprisingly receptive to any of his suggestions for their entertainment. They rode his cutter on the frozen river, fished through the ice, skated at night among blazing tar barrels; she even insisted on joining him on a wolf hunt. Mary Ann, who at first seemed entirely preoccupied with her church life and mission school, now passionately enjoyed each new experience Gurdon offered her.

Chicago at the time was not a place where anyone of fine moral and Christian character would be likely to discover vicious temptation or violence. Thus Ahira and his wife may have been shocked to hear that their daughter had watched her stalwart escort throw a ruffian down the stairs of the Saloon building and actually cheered him on. But they continued to allow her considerably more freedom than courting couples of good family generally were allowed. Only the religious beliefs of Gurdon and Mary Ann stood in their romantic way. Finally they compromised, Mary Ann would not attempt to lure Mr. Hubbard into Second Presbyterian membership, he would not ask her to become Episcopalian. He was allowed to take Mary Ann to his own Lake House, where there was a public bar fifty feet long, to a supper for men and their wives. She even accompanied him to William Ogden's grand bachelor mansion on the north side in company with other Ogden friends and their wives. Chicago was not yet a wild town, but it was somewhat free thinking in its ways.

"In those days the comparatively small circle of business and professional men, and others of note, were generally well acquainted," Caroline Kirkland noted in her book, *Chicago Yesterdays*. "Every man stood on his own merits. . . . Chicago was not a fertile spot for amusements of a public character. . . . Chicago was a one-horse town, and had not begun to step toward . . . all the attending evils of a great city." Those who contributed their recollections to Kirkland's book did not speak of the whisky drinking in the town, even the Temperance House had a bar; nor of the gambling and prostitution in The Sands or the shootings in Hairtrigger Block, nor of the fighting and hell-raising in the construction camps, and among the drovers and mule drivers along Wabash avenue. Chicago, as Caroline Kirkland had observed, was a relatively quiet frontier town. Not many could afford commercial sin. Wheat sold at 43 cents a bushel, corn at 20 cents, oats at 13 cents. Barreled beef brought only $6, butter was eight cents a pound. Hundreds of Chicagoans had filed for relief under the national bankruptcy law passed in 1841. Wages for common labor had fallen to $16 a month. Gurdon Hubbard himself had paid off most of his debts, but was continuing to suffer from the general hard times.

When Gurdon told his sister Elizabeth that he was thinking of marrying Mary Ann Hubbard, his second-cousin, she welcomed the idea. Mary Ann was good with children, Elizabeth told him. Gurdon Junior appeared to be fond of her. Elizabeth was eager to return home to Middletown. Ahira Hubbard was agreeable when Gurdon asked for his daughter's hand. He had long since dismissed the numerous impediments to such a marriage. The difference in age did not matter, Ahira said, nor was it of concern to him that Mary Ann would remain Presbyterian while Gurdon was Episcopalian. Gurdon proposed to Mary Ann and was accepted.

Then Mary Ann Hubbard shocked them all by insisting, like a giddy girl of eighteen, on a formal wedding at Second Presbyterian church. Her father, Ahira, not yet recovered from the financial panic, couldn't affort such an affair, and Gurdon Hubbard didn't look forward to a public event with any pleasure, but Mary Ann would have her way. Judge Hamilton, Gurdon's good friend, had stood ready to perform the ceremony—he now agreed to serve as Gurdon's best man.

"I was married to Gurdon Hubbard on the Ninth of November, 1843," Mary Ann would write years later. "We had a large wedding but *no* presents, we afterward returned some gifts. My bridesmaids were Miss Cornella Brown and Miss Towner. A few wedding parties were given, at which I had to represent both of us, as about two weeks after the event the groom went to

Peoria, engaged in packing, and was gone until Christmas. We remained at home until my parents moved into their own house, when I went to housekeeping on Indiana Street, with a lovely garden, where we lived about nine years. . . ." Mary Ann's reference to her husband as "the groom" may have indicated her continuing pique at Gurdon's inconsiderate treatment. It was characteristic of their marriage that Gurdon's young bride would always address him as "Mr. Hubbard," and never as Gurdon, while he called her Ann, or "Wifie," according to the Holts and the Hamiltons.

*

Several reasons for Gurdon's abrupt departure from Chicago could have accounted for his secrecy about his movements and activities, but "packing" in Peoria could not have been one of them. Sylvester Marsh, his former partner in the packing business, said that he and Hubbard bought their livestock downstate and packed in Chicago. After the dissolution of their partnership, Gurdon built another plant on the north branch of the river, where beef and pork were packed. They might have arranged for the purchase of livestock at Peoria, but more likely Gurdon merely provided Mary Ann with an easy answer for those who would inquire about her missing groom. Other possibilities for his somewhat secret trip can be found in the writings of Alfred Holt and the letters of William Ogden.

Shortly after his marriage, Gurdon had trouble with a blackmailer, according to Alfred Holt, a nephew of Mary Ann who indicated that some of his information about Hubbard came from her. Holt declared that Gurdon told Mary Ann about his marriage to Watseka. He also asserted that Gurdon thrashed a man called "Bagwell" who demanded $5,000 as his price for the suppression of an account Bagwell said he had written of the Watseka affair. This encounter probably occurred, if at all, near the time news of Hubbard's marriage to Mary Ann appeared in the papers. If Gurdon had seriously hurt "Bagwell," he might have left town until the outcome was not in doubt. However, had Gurdon told Mary Ann about Watseka, as Holt stated he did, it would seem doubtful he had much to fear from a blackmailer. Holt was a blood relation of Mary Ann, and obviously had details of Gurdon's life from her. Yet, Henry Hamilton, who lived with the Hubbards from time to time, and had himself heard the Watseka story when the historian Beckwith discussed it with Hubbard at Danville, carefully refrained from publishing any hint of it while "Uncle Gurdon," Mary Ann and Gurdon Jr. were living. It does not seem likely that Mary Ann or Gurdon Jr. knew of Watseka. But if he accosted Gurdon Hubbard, Bagwell probably suffered for it.

More likely, however, Gurdon departed Chicago early in December, 1843 on confidential canal lobbying business and in the course of it became involved in an even more secret mission. The Illinois-Michigan canal was in deep financial trouble because the Illinois Internal Improvements Act, passed in 1837, had brought the state to the brink of bankruptcy. William Ogden and Arthur Bronson believed that the Chicago canal could be saved financially if Governor Ford would abandon the rest of the internal improvements program, for which Illinois could never fully pay. Since the Illinois-Michigan Canal Act was separate legislation, passed in 1836, the Chicago canal could then survive. Such scuttling of statewide internal improvements would prove to be politically unpopular. Yet, said Bronson, only by such a reversal could the Chicago canal be saved. He and Ogden urged Gurdon Hubbard to help. Thus, in December, Gurdon joined a group of Chicagoans for a discussion of their plan with Governor Ford.

The governor welcomed the self-appointed Chicagoans who called on him at Springfield and agreed that the Chicago project should be saved even though drastic action would be required. But Ford's concern about the Illinois Mormon situation took precedence. Ford was a Democrat, elected with strong Mormon support. The Mormons had established colonies along the Mississippi river in Illinois after being driven from Missouri when white settlers there not only objected to their religion, but also accused their leader, Prophet Joseph Smith, of conspiring with Indian chiefs to foment an uprising on the reservations newly established in that territory. When the Mormons first arrived in Illinois they were welcomed. They settled in Hancock and Adams counties and soon had created the largest and most prosperous town in the state, called Nauvoo. Initially, the Mormons voted for the Whig political candidates in Illinois, providing them with a winning margin. But after Thomas Ford, then a justice of the Illinois Supreme court, denied efforts of Governor Boggs of Missouri to extradite Joseph Smith and his brother, Hyrum, to Missouri, to face highly dubious charges, the Mormons backed Ford in his campaign for governor and gave the Democrats a victory.

Governor Ford that December thus was concerned for his Mormon friends, who had come under attack in Illinois as they had in Missouri. Ford now heard rumors that Joseph Smith had summoned a conference of Indian chiefs, including chiefs still in Illinois, to be held in Nauvoo. It was also said that Smith was raising his own powerful army and might attempt to make his colonies an independent territory. Ford wanted to know the truth of the reports he was hearing. He also knew from former Democratic governors John Reynolds and Joseph Duncan that Gurdon Hubbard had served them in getting information from the Indians. Ford too apparently sought Hubbard's help. Gurdon was in no position to refuse, nor could he disclose to Mary Ann why he absented himself from her for weeks immediately after their marriage without obvious reason. He was not "packing" in Peoria as she later would write. He probably was visiting Chief Shabona in his Paw Paw Grove village and other chiefs.

Gurdon himself knew something of the Mormons. An aide to Joseph Smith had sought out Arthur Bronson and Charles Butler in New York to request a loan to help finance the Mormon movement. His friend and associate Dr. Fifthian had known the Saints when they settled in Ohio before continuing west to Missouri. Joseph Smith had received revelations from angels which led him to establish his Church of the Latter Day Saints, Fifthian said. Smith had only five followers when he organized his church in New York state in 1830, but the number had grown to hundreds, then thousands. The Mormons, so-called because Prophet Smith entitled his revelations *The Book of Mormon,* prospered in Ohio but were discontented there and moved, to Missouri Territory, which some said Joseph Smith believed to be the site of the Garden of Eden.

In Missouri the Saints, by their zeal and industry, grew wealthy and powerful. Their critics and foes feared they soon would own the state and it was said they intended to give Missouri land to the Indians. There were armed attacks on Mormon settlements and rumors that Smith might start an Indian uprising. In 1838, Governor Liliburn Boggs of Missouri ordered that "Mormons must be treated as enemies, and must be exterminated or driven from the state if necessary . . . their outrages are beyond all description."

It was then Prophet Smith and his Elders decided to locate in Illinois. They purchased the town of Commerce, on the east bank of the Mississippi, and petitioned the Illinois legislature for a charter creating the city of Nauvoo, as well as Nauvoo University. Soon both Whigs and Democrats were courting the Mormon towns in Adams and Hancock counties. Stephen A. Douglas was especially popular among them, aiding them with legal problems. By 1843, the Mormons were acknowledged to have provided the margin of votes electing Ford governor and Douglas to Congress. Other Democrats, among them Long John Wentworth of Chicago, took all but one of the Illinois seats in the Congress in the Democratic victory.

Gurdon Hubbard called upon his Indian friends. What he learned enabled him to reassure Governor Ford. The Mormons might have raised a militia, as reported, but they were not conspiring with the Indians to start an uprising. It was true that Prophet Joseph Smith had conferred with the Potawatomi chiefs at Nauvoo, but only to discuss with them the dispatch of Mormon missionaries to the Indian reservations in Iowa, Missouri and Kansas.

Governor Ford was well pleased by what he learned and agreeable to the Chicago group's canal petition. He evidently indicated to Gurdon Hubbard that more intelligence missions might be offered. Gurdon agreed with Ford and his colleagues to return to Springfield in the winter of 1844. This time he took Mary Ann with him. They stopped briefly at Mr. Hubbard's favorite inn at Peoria and she was appalled by the place. "I expected to board there with your uncle," she wrote to Anna Holt, "but it was so badly kept our friends, Mr. and Mrs. Curtenius, would not allow us to remain, but invited us to visit their bright and cheerful home." Thus Mary Ann began her narrative of the Hubbards' eventual visit to Nauvoo, five weeks before Joseph

Smith and his brother Hyrum were murdered in the Carthage jail by an Illinois mob on June 27, 1844.

Mary Ann did not suspect at the time that her trip to Springfield early in 1844 was the beginning of her Nauvoo experience. She evidently was confused by the sequence of events and knew little of her husband's real purpose in taking her with him to Springfield and later to Nauvoo. They did not stay in Peoria but left soon for Springfield accompanied by Norman Judd, the Chicago Whig leader and lawyer much interested in canal and railroad projects, and William Brown, agent for Chicago school lands. All purported to be en route to the capital for a Whig strategy conference, but Gurdon additionally would call upon Governor Ford relative to Mormon matters.

Gurdon by this time had improved his knowlĕdge of the Mormons and was much impressed. He had in his library *The Book of Mormon,* Joseph Smith's translation from golden plates provided to him by the Angel Moroni: *The Book of Mormon,* an account written by the hand of Joseph Smith, Jr. published 1840. Mary Ann, in 1871, found the book among the many volumes on Indians in the library of their Locust street home, just prior to the Chicago fire, in which all of Mr. Hubbard's books and records were lost. *The Book of Mormon* had been addressed to the American Indians, the Lamanites, in Prophet Smith's translation. The Lamanites had come to the New World, but had abandoned their faith, Mr. Hubbard had told her. Thus, in writing of their Nauvoo visit after her husband's death, Mary Ann noted that Mr. Hubbard might have contemplated joining the Mormon church.

*

The trip to Nauvoo in May, 1844 was undertaken with some dissemblance by Gurdon Hubbard, whatever the reason. The Hubbards left Chicago in a two-seated carriage belonging to a Mr. Blackstone, who accompanied them part of the way, Mary Ann recalled. "I think it took four days to reach Peoria." Her husband might have utilized a river boat via the Desplaines and Illinois to reach Peoria, but he chose the more difficult overland route. At Peoria they met Norman Judd and Joseph Gillespie, leader of the Whig caravan to Springfield in the Harrison campaign of 1840, and one of the earliest backers of

Abraham Lincoln "for any office, from governor to President of the United States." So, a political meeting of some sort evidently took place in Peoria.

The Hubbards then proceeded due west to Galesburg by buggy. This didn't suprise Mary Ann, since her husband had told her in the beginning that they would go to Burlington, Iowa to visit his relatives, the Alfred Hebards. Reaching Galesburg, they stopped at an inn, then "we went out to Jubilee College, Bishop Chase's home," Mary Ann recalled. Gurdon evidently had reconciled with the Episcopal bishop who once had been his friend, but from whom he had been alienated after the death of Eleanora. They did not stay with Bishop Chase, but Sunday were back at the inn, which Mary Ann found congenial, "quiet, comfortable, a good table with quiet, gentlemanly boarders." The landlady told Mary Ann they did not cook dinners on the Sabbath. "That will just suit us," she had replied. The hotel at Peoria, however, had been abominable as usual, she now noted. Evidently the Hubbards did not stay with friends in either Peoria or Galesburg; Gurdon's route may have been somewhat hastily arranged. Their visit to the two towns was not a social one.

Although Hubbard had told Mary Ann that they were headed for Burlington, Iowa, they turned south before reaching the Mississippi. She discovered at last that they were en route to Nauvoo, the Mormon town on the Mississippi. She was surprised and fearful. There had been articles in the newspapers about Mormon troubles in Illinois and Missouri. Mr. Hubbard did not confide in her his reason for abruptly turning south toward the place called Nauvoo. The road was muddy, running through flooded country, and the trip was difficult, but they kept on, even though they had to buy another horse, since one of their animals "couldn't stand the trip."

*

Nauvoo, along bluffs overlooking the river, was a thriving town of log houses, brick stores and a great stone temple, rising on the heights, that had become "the most imposing building in Illinois" though its tower was not yet complete. Mary Ann was frightened. Her husband told her not to fear, they would be protected by the Nauvoo Legion. "I saw no sign of any Legion," she wrote. The newspapers said that the Nauvoo Legion was the best uniformed militia in the state, a deserved reputation, but the men protecting the town when the Hubbards arrived were not visible. They proceeded to the Nauvoo House, where Prophet Smith dwelled and they were well received, almost as if they had been expected, Mary Ann recalled. Mr. Hubbard had an appointment with Joseph Smith, she learned, and she was to accompany him. "I did not want to meet Joe Smith," she wrote, using the name as it generally appeared in the newspapers.

Her husband told her that they would show Prophet Joseph Smith all respect due him. He explained that Prophet Smith had received, directly from angels, messages directing the establishment of his church and added that the messages were written on golden tablets. Joseph Smith had translated them. Mary Ann herself firmly believed in angels and did not doubt their visitation to Joseph Smith. She herself always set her table with an extra place for the uninvited stranger, "angels unaware" as the Bible directed.

They took dinner the following noon at Nauvoo House with Prophet Smith, whom Mr. Hubbard addressed with great respect, as he had recommended. Smith was tall and dark-haired, a handsome, intense man, a few years younger than Mr. Hubbard. Joe Smith was pleasant enough, but Mary Ann disliked him. Mr. Hubbard told Joe Smith that President Jefferson believed the Indians had come to America from Europe, and Joe Smith seemed pleased to hear of it. Mary Ann thought her husband would ask about "celestial marriage and plural marriage," which she had heard was a practice of the Mormons, but nothing was said of such religious matters. They discussed instead the troubles of the Mormons in Missouri, where Joe Smith and his brother Hyrum ". . . they had a strange way of misspelling it . . ." had been taken prisoner, court-martialed by Missouri militiamen, and ordered shot. When the order was given to Col. Alexander Doniphan, Smith told the Hubbards, he refused to execute it. "This is cold-blooded murder," Doniphan had told his superior officer. "I will not obey this order . . . if you execute these men, I will hold you responsible before an earthly tribunal, so help me God!" The Smiths were saved, but imprisoned for six months. "There was no charge against us, they were forced to concede that," Joe Smith declared. "We were not criminals and we were not engaged in rebellion."

Mary Ann was astonished to learn that the Saints, as they called themselves, had been so badly treated. "Mr. Hubbard said that the people of Illinois might not understand why the Nauvoo Legion was required," Mary Ann recalled. "He pointed out that any militia in the state of Illinois was to be under the control of the governor." Joe Smith had replied that they had been well treated in Illinois, for the most part, but he added that "the enemies of God are everywhere." There was a long silence. Mary Ann felt that the men would have gone further in their talk had she not been present. She was glad to leave.

She realized finally that she had accompanied her husband to visit Mr. Smith for a reason, possibly as a witness to what was said. Mr. Hubbard then told her he would return alone to talk with Prophet Smith on the day following, and she was glad not to be required to accompany him. "I told him I did not care to see Joe Smith ever again," she said. While her husband was away, Mary Ann locked herself in their room. She was frightened her entire time in Nauvoo, she remembered. Her husband had said after their meeting with the Prophet, "I may become converted" but she assumed he was joking. "I told Mr. Hubbard I hoped a second sermon would not convert him." Her husband shook his head. Then he said he believed a devout man could be visited by angels; Abraham had been so visited and he expected that God would continue to send angels to those ready to listen. Mary Ann knew her husband was not pleased to learn she had locked herself in the room. "He said Mormons were most law-abiding unless they became threatened." Surely she was no threat. The Saints did not want trouble but felt required to protect themselves. But she had read otherwise about them. Mr. Hubbard showed a flash of anger. Mormons were feared mostly because they worked hard and gathered great wealth and power unto themselves and because they were well organized and disciplined, he explained. He thought that, unfortunately for the Mormons, "Nauvoo is no better place for a great city than Green Bay is." He pointed out to his wife that it had been a great honor for them "to dine with a man who has become a candidate for President of the United States." She felt chastized, but nevertheless she locked her door tight while her husband was away.

The next day it rained hard. Late in the day her husband took Mary Ann to the museum which, she said, was kept by Mrs. Smith, "Joe Smith's mother." They were shown various relics, including several mummies, said to have come from Egypt. She asked Mrs. Smith if she had "the golden tablets" in the museum. "No," Mrs. Smith replied. "They was stole, but they have now been taken back by the angels." Mary Ann mocked the old woman's use of language, but acknowledged that Mrs. Smith was gracious to them. "I thanked Madam Smith for showing us the relics," Mary Ann recalled. "Mr. Hubbard purchased some Mormon books." Back at the hotel, when she criticized Mrs. Smith's manner of speech, her husband again flared. " 'That is what is miraculous about Prophet Smith,' " he said. " 'He too had no education, but the language of *The Book of Mormon* is the language of the Bible.' "

*

They took a boat to Quincy and the stage to Springfield, Mr. Hubbard continuing deep in his thoughts most of the way. After he had gone to see Governor Ford, he took Mary Ann on a true holiday, down to St. Louis, seeming much at ease. "I greatly enjoyed that part of the trip," Mary Ann recalled. "Your uncle had many good friends and they made us welcome." Then the Hubbards went up river to Burlington, Iowa, where they saw Mrs. Alfred Hebard and learned her husband was away, making a survey for a projected railroad through Iowa. They went down river to the place where they had left their carriage and horses and drove back to Chicago.

*

Mary Ann had become interested in Prophet Smith and the Mormons, and began reading about them, for they were much in the newspapers. The people of western Illinois were being aroused by the critical writings of John C. Bennett, a former follower of Joe Smith and former mayor of Nauvoo. Bennett's charges had caused some Mormons to leave the church, it was said, and they inflamed people who already hated the Mormon movement. "There could be great trouble," Mr. Hubbard told her. She found it hard to believe that Joe Smith, a man who sat across the table from them at the Nauvoo House, was so important, and actually was an announced candidate for President of the United States.

Bennett's charges were printed in Nauvoo itself and the Chicago newspapers reported that Joseph Smith had ordered Bennett's writings confiscated and burned and the press destroyed. Smith also was said to have called up his militia to protect Nauvoo from possible attack. Governor Ford issued a statement defending the Mormons, declaring they had proved themselves to be law-abiding citizens of Illinois, though perhaps overzealous in defending those among their number who were accused of offenses by other citizens of Illinois. The Mormons were living within the law and their militia was no threat, Ford had said. After Prophet Smith took action against Bennett's publisher in Nauvoo, however, Governor Ford went to Nauvoo himself and there learned that Smith had mobilized his militia, and, with drawn sword, had called upon the Nauvoo Legion to fight to the death "in defense of their rights."

Nauvoo had become divided by Joseph Smith's actions. Many of his own people pleaded with him to surrender into the custody of the state after Governor Ford promised there would be a fair trial. Prophet Smith and Hyrum gave themselves up and were taken to the Carthage jail to await the promised trial. On June 27, 1844 men from an Illinois militia company, which had been ordered disbanded by Governor Ford, "daubed their faces with mud and gunpowder, rushed the jail, and quickly overpowered the cooperative guards," wrote historians Allen and Leonard. Hyrum was shot dead. Joseph Smith, mortally wounded, plunged through a window, crying, "Oh Lord . . . my God!" his final words.

Gurdon Hubbard did not then, nor any time later, discuss publicly his visit to Nauvoo or his conferences with Joseph Smith. The history section of the Mormon church has no record of the visit. Governor Ford was severely criticized for mishandling the defense of the Mormon leaders. Brigham Young took over the direction of the Saints, restoring order at Nauvoo and improving relations with the state government. But the populace of nearby towns and counties continued to fear Mormon prosperity and the effects of Mormon mass voting. In the fall of 1845, the Illinois militia was again called out, and in 1846 a force of vigilantes moved on the city of Nauvoo. There was fighting and casualties. By that time the Mormons had made their decision to depart Illinois for the Far West. They again crossed the Mississippi, under loaded cannon pointed their way, en route to lands the Elders were purchasing from the Indians. The first contingent of the persecuted group reached the Salt Lake valley in what would become the state of Utah, July 24, 1847.

*

Gurdon Hubbard was back in politics again, hoping to help the Whigs carry Illinois for Henry Clay, staying loyal to Clay, the Whig, despite the fact that Stephen A. Douglas, the young Democrat spellbinder downstate, had called for the nomination of Lewis Cass, Gurdon's other national political hero. Cass lost the Democratic nomination to James K. Polk, the dark horse candidate from Tennessee, and Polk carried Illinois by 13,000 votes and went on to win the national election, defeating Clay by a margin of 38,181 votes. Governor Ford, despite his Mormon troubles, was re-elected and Congressman Douglas was re-elected, both with Mormon support. Gurdon and his friends, including Lincoln, were dismayed by Clay's defeat, though Lincoln had doubted Clay could win. In May, 1846, Abraham Lincoln was elected to Congress and Governor Thomas Ford called for Illinois volunteers for the war with Mexico. Lincoln and the Whigs in Congress questioned the justice of the Mexican war. Gurdon Hubbard, in Chicago, made no public statement of record, nor did he volunteer for service, though his close friend Richard J. Hamilton raised a company and served as its colonel, and John Kinzie made speeches, supporting the war.

*

The Illinois and Michigan canal had been saved by actions of

Governor Ford that alienated him from the Illinois Democrats. Ford sent commissioners to New York and Europe to arrange further loans and in 1845 was able to promise $1,600,000 to carry the canal to completion. Ford blamed Douglas for some of the criticism of his actions, furthering the split among the Democrats, providing new hope to the shattered Whigs. By July, Chief Engineer Gooding had reorganized his canal forces, a steam pumping plan devised by Ira Miltimore to lift water into the locks was approved, financiers in New York, London and Paris paid up their subscriptions, and canal digging again got under way.

In November, 1846, as the canal work entered its final phase, William Ogden switched his interest to the beckoning profits possible from the other mode of transportation doing well in the eastern states, steam railroads. Ogden wrote optimistically to an eastern correspondent on the 20th: "The health of the country is improving again and the canal will now progress more rapidly. It has been much retarded by sickness and somewhat by contractors who took their work too low or have not been able to perform it." Ogden was now ready to proceed with "other interests." He indicated in his letters that he and Gurdon Hubbard were working together in real estate deals as the panic of 1837 and the following depression ended in 1844. The two had formed a land-buying syndicate with Bronson and Butler as Ogden's eastern partners and Henry and Elijah Hubbard, close associates of Gurdon. But a coolness developed between Ogden and Gurdon as the former mayor moved into his railroad project—one they had discussed years before—the Galena and Chicago Union. The trouble arose over charter rights to build such a line. Ogden had purchased lapsed rights to the 1836 Illinois state charter authorizing such a road. Gurdon and Elijah Hubbard believed they had acquired the rights in 1838, "rights" rendered nebulous at best because of non-performance by the original holders and then by the Hubbards. The railroad had not been built under charter terms and therefore lapsed a second time. The feuding would result in Gurdon's estrangement from Ogden and disaster for Hubbard's railroad plans.

Chicago was booming again by 1847. The town arranged a spectacular Rivers and Harbors convention that summer to preview its anticipated canal triumph, bringing in 3,000 delegates and thousands of visitors from 18 of the 29 states. Similar conventions had been held by other cities to promote their markets and to attract immigration and federal aid, but Chicago's show was the first in the far west, the biggest, and the best. Dignitaries from the east who attended included Thurlow Weed, Albany editor and boss of the New York Whigs; Erastus Corning, president of the New York Central, and Horace Greeley, editor of the New York *Tribune.* The visitors were welcomed with artillery salutes, parading bands, military companies and marching clubs and 16,000 cheering spectators lining a parade route along Randolph street. The delegates heard speakers tout western lands and attack President Polk, the Democrat from Tennessee, for opposing internal improvements such as those at Chicago. Polk feared they would make the northwest dominant over the south in the fight for western trade, speakers asserted, charges indicating President Polk possessed a considerable prescience. When Thurlow Weed returned home, he told the Albany *Journal* readers, "In ten years Chicago will be as big as Albany . . . on the shores of this lake (Michigan) is a vast country that will in fifty years support a city of 125,000 inhabitants." Erastus Corning advised his friends to invest in western lands. Senator Tom Corwin of Ohio promised that Chicago would get federal attention to its harbor needs. Among the politicians present was recently elected Congressman Abraham Lincoln of Springfield, visiting Chicago for the first time.

The ceremonies marking the actual canal opening in 1848 were somewhat less impressive, but spectacular in their own way. On April 10, the canal barge *General Fry,* under tow by the *Rossitor,* reached Chicago from Lockport. On April 16, a fleet of sixteen canal boats arrived and was greeted by marching clubs, bands and speeches, while steamboats in the harbor tied down their whistles and the town's bells sounded. Chicago knew well enough its importance and future prospects. Now farmers could haul their grain to port towns accommodating the canal barges. Manufactured goods arriving from New York via the Erie canal, and from Liverpool by the way of Montreal, would transfer in Chicago to the barges going south and west. Sugar and rum would be received from New Orleans; cotton, coal and hardwoods from the river ports along the Mississippi, Ohio and Illinois rivers. The great water route from the Gulf of St. Lawrence to the Gulf of Mexico, envisioned by the French explorers, was at last a reality, opening the spraddling town astride the Chicago Portage to the world. Henceforth Chicago would serve prairie corn farmers, cane raisers in Louisiana, cotton planters in Arkansas and Mississippi, pig growers in Illinois, and the wheat and cattle growers of the far west as well as the mill and banking towns of the east. All would buy and sell in Chicago.

The Illinois and Michigan canal for which Gurdon Hubbard and his associates had labored would itself become a solid financial success, paying its own way through the next century as Chicago grew. It was less than Gurdon Hubbard and others had envisioned, a shallow cut, but it worked from the start. "Narrow and shallow, it could not handle steamboats; and a complicated lock system slowed the passage of barges through its 97 mile course," historians Harold M. Mayer and Richard C. Wade would say in *Chicago: Growth of a Metropolis* in 1969. "Yet, despite these limitations, the canal was a major factor in the extraordinary growth of Chicago in the next two decades." Some would suggest a century later that the railroads were really responsible for the astonishing growth of Chicago. Traffic into the Chicago harbor, however, quadrupled from half a million tons of freight at the time the canal opened to two million tons annually before the railroads eclipsed water traffic; each mode of transportation served the other. By the end of 1848, Chicago had ten miles of railroad, William Ogden's Galena and Chicago Union. It remained the only railroad entering the city in 1850, but within eight years Chicago would be served by ten trunk lines—3,000 miles of track—as well as the waterway from Montreal to New Orleans and New York City via the Erie to St. Louis. "Chicago is the greatest primary market in the world," booster William Bross of the Chicago *Press-Democrat* exulted in 1851, "we have the world's greatest pork, lumber and grain market. We exceed St. Louis by 250 per cent, Milwaukee by 400 per cent." The town by that time had a population of more than 30,000.

*

Gurdon Hubbard had no part in William Ogden's railroad. He long had planned to get into the construction of a line of his own but he had been too preoccupied elsewhere and had left the project to Elijah Hubbard, who in 1837 started a railroad to run due west of Chicago, but abandoned it during the panic that year. Gurdon's other ventures survived the panic, except for the grandiose Lake House, which sold under the auctioneer's hammer for $10,000, a tenth of its original cost. Gurdon had signed over his insurance policies to his creditors the year Eleanora died, but grimly held onto his remaining businesses, freight forwarding, warehousing and docking, packing, steamships and insurance. By the late 1840s he had recovered, paying off his debts. He joined Devillo Holt in the lumber business along the south branch of the river and expanded his own large packing plant on the north branch to a capacity of 200 cattle and 1,000 hogs daily. Hubbard now sold most of his pack in eastern markets. Chicago's dozen packing plants killed 1,765 cattle and 9,000 hogs daily and shipped beef and pork to England as well as Canada. "It is expected 18,000 to 20,000 barrels of beef will be packed this season," the Chicago *Democrat* said in September, 1848. "Chicago competes in Boston with the best beef from Maine, and in England with the best beef from Ireland."

*

In 1848 the Chicago boom was well under way. To accommodate the trading needs of the business community, Hubbard and eighty-six other Chicagoans attended a meeting in March called by W.L. Whiting, the town's first grain broker, to discuss "an organization for the regulation and expedition of business affairs, to be called the Chicago Board of Trade." The response overflowed Whiting's office. Those present agreed that a constitution should be written and they elected Thomas Dyer, associated with Ogden's railroad project, as president. Gurdon Hubbard was named a director of the Board of Trade and chosen also to head a board of inspectors to investigate alleged irregularities in the fish, provisions and flour markets. Gurdon had no liking for Tom Dyer, and no wish to take on an obviously thankless task, but he remembered the havoc that occurred when traders hiked flour prices from $9 to $25 a barrel a few years previously, a "corner" he helped to break by using his *voyageurs* and mackinaw boats to bring in flour from ships anchored in the lake. He agreed to serve and promptly won from the city council an ordinance giving the board the power to enforce its rules, thus demonstrating that the Board of Trade could regulate business as promised.

The pleased and surprised board members then formed a similar committee on banking, launched a campaign for further harbor improvements, induced the new telegraph companies to provide daily reports of business and commodity activity in New York and Boston, and by February, 1849 had reorganized under a charter from the Illinois legislature, extending the scope of the board's work and influence. The board began a campaign to promote "free navigation of the St. Lawrence river" and the improvement of Illinois navigation. Gurdon Hubbard was a member of this committee also, with William Bross, editor of the *Press-Democrat,* and George Steele, a canal builder. When Bross demanded that a Georgian Bay canal should be constructed, Hubbard dissented. Since the canal would be in Canadian territory and completely under control and direction of the Canadian government, Gurdon considered such a proposal, coming from Chicago, improper. He declined to accompany Bross and Steele, both old friends, to Canada to press the idea. They made the trip nevertheless, were coldly received by Canadian officials and their canal plan was soon forgotten.

*

That summer Shabona and his wife Wiomex Okono arrived in Chicago with a story of white perfidy that infuriated Gurdon Hubbard and John Kinzie. Most of Shabona's land, granted to him by the Treaty of Prairie du Chien, July 29, 1829, had been seized by white squatters while Shabona was absent in Missouri and Iowa on tribal matters. Chief Shabona had farmed the land for many years, seeking to set an example to his people, but in his absence Ansel and Orrin Gates, asserting the land had been abandoned, laid claim to 1,200 acres. The federal government then put up the acreage for sale, as provided by law should the land cease to remain under cultivation, and the Gates brothers, according to James Dowd, a Shabona biographer, "sent a large mob of ruffians to bid on the lands at the minimum price, $1.25 an acre. . . . They went, armed to the teeth, to the Dixon land office, and defied any bid against them.''

Gurdon joined John Kinzie in protesting to the government this wanton theft from an Indian who not only was farming the land, but who also had remained a steadfast friend of the white settlers, for whom he had risked his life in the Black Hawk war days. Nonetheless, according to Henry Hamilton, ''the lands remained sold, the money going into the government treasury,'' James Dowd, checking the records of the case more than a century later, found that the government repurchased the land, for $1,600 in 1852, restoring it to Shabona. The old chief and his family meantime was living on his remaining acres at Paw Paw Grove, having returned there in 1849 after dwelling some weeks with the Hubbards.

*

Gurdon's railroad venture, resumed in the early 1850s, became the great failure of his life. He unwisely sought vengeance against his old friend Ogden, who had ignored his claim to rights in the railroad charter he and Elijah had acquired in 1837. Thus Gurdon entered into a legal fight with his own lawyer. The State of Illinois issued the first railroad charter affecting the Chicago area January 16, 1836, to Ebenezer Peck and T.W. Smith, with the provision construction must start within three years. Peck and Smith abandoned their efforts during the 1837 panic. E.K. Hubbard, who had joined Gurdon in land, banking, and insurance ventures in 1835, acquired rights to the charter for the Hubbards in 1838, or so they thought, and began the construction of a new line, representing an extension of Madison street, ''piles being driven and stringers placed upon them,'' according to Andreas' history. These operations ceased that year, shortly after Hubbard had sent surveyors along a route to St. Charles, due west of Chicago. So, the Hubbard rights, too, would have lapsed.

On August 10, 1847, William Ogden and J. Young Scammon, also a Chicago lawyer, opened subscription books for the Galena & Chicago Union. They asserted ownership of charter rights but Gurdon Hubbard didn't agree, nor did Edwin C. Litchfield, the experienced railroad builder who had been successful in Michigan, Ohio and Indiana in reviving "failed" railroads and restoring lapsed charters. He called his firm, based in New York, The Railroad Charter & Insolvent Railroad Purchasing Company. By the early 1850s, Litchfield had restored a defunct state-owned railroad in Michigan and had acquired rights to the Northern Indiana railroad, once called the Buffalo & Mississippi, and brought his railroad to the Illinois line, heading for Chicago, as the Michigan Southern. When Litchfield approached officials of Ogden's Galena & Chicago Union, proposing a connection through the city, he was rebuffed. The Galena & Chicago Union intended to build its own line through the city he was told.

Litchfield then approached Gurdon Hubbard with a plan to connect the Michigan Southern with a Dixon Airline railroad that did not yet exist, along a proposed short line from Chicago to the Mississippi river. Such a railroad would parallel the Galena & Chicago Union part of the way. Hubbard and Litchfield formed an alliance. By 1852, Gurdon was pushing this venture, ordering a survey of the line from West Madison street due west toward Dixon via St. Charles. He obtained a considerable amount of Chicago subscriptions and was working with businessmen in Ogle and Kane counties, with a view to an extension of his still non-existing line.

The Hubbard and Litchfield plan was vigorously opposed by the Ogden people, although Ogden himself had been temporarily ousted from control of his railroad by dissident directors. On January 17, 1853, Gurdon crisply summarized the situation in a letter to James Waterman, an Ogle county stockholder, who evidently also served as Gurdon's agent: "E.C. Litchfield is now here to make arrangements for the immediate commencement of the grading of our line from this point (Chicago) 40 miles west . . . . This I know to be good news to you, but, at the same time, I have to inform you that we are having the worst kind of opposition at every step from the Galena & Chicago Union RR whose directors are each an unofficial committee (for) active denunciation of our inter-line and make it a daily business to visit our stockholders & use every argument possible against construction of our road. . . . Their object is to break us down and thus secure to themselves a monopoly with their own lines and branches. Should they succeed in this you can understand

411

how they will obtain exhorbitant rates. . . . If your citizens feel like putting themselves in the jaw of a lion I don't know that we in Chicago have any right to object. . . ."

Gurdon was angry but obviously did his cause little good with implied threats. His fear of Will Ogden's people and the expectation that the residents of Ogle and Kane and Cook counties might not rise to support his airline railroad project were fully justified. The Galena & Chicago Union filed lawsuits to stop the Hubbard-Litchfield project and Hubbard's stock subscriptions languished. The legal actions restraining Hubbard became moot in 1857 when Litchfield's New York company, badly overextended by the acquisition of steamship companies while it also was buying and building railroads, withdrew support from the Michigan Southern and Northern Indiana companies. They crashed October 1. Gurdon Hubbard's railroad dream was ended.

*

In 1853 Gurdon and Mary Ann moved into their fine new house on South Michigan avenue, facing the lake, after a decade in their 300 Indiana home. She described their happy life together in later years. "Chicago was a much pleasanter place then," Mary Ann recalled. "The people we associated with were all friendly and kind, sharing each other's joys and sorrows, and enjoying simple pleasures. The Sabbath was kept holy. . . . If we wanted to give a party, we borrowed lamps of neighbors, sometimes spoons, and, as we had to make our own ice cream, those of us who kept cows would send cream, others sent flowers in season . . . kindly neighborly acts were offered and often accepted and reciprocated.

"I took two nieces of Mr. Hubbard's to live with us, they were daughters of a dependant, widowed sister of Mr. Hubbard, and wholly untrained and un-educated, and grew to be lovely Christian girls and a comfort to us. . . ." Mary Ann did not refer to the education of Gurdon, Junior, but indicated he was living at home, since he helped with preparations for a party: "Some Detroit friends of Mr. Hubbard came to Chicago and your uncle wanted to show them some attention. . . ." As was his custom, Gurdon sent a messenger to Mary Ann that afternoon, mentioning his friends and several Chicago people who should be invited that evening. Mary Ann had one servant then, and she also had guests, "Mrs. Morison of New York and her little girl were visiting. . . . We decided . . . the weather was very hot . . . to invite the friends to come about 8 o'clock—after tea, we all had dinner about one o'clock and tea at six. So the invitations went out verbally by Gurdon Junior and the girls, and were accepted." Before the guests arrived that night, Mary Ann added, " Your uncle started for New York on urgent business."

"We entertained a good deal," Mary Ann continued. "The practice had been to bring visitors to our one o'clock dinners without notice. I always aimed to have things in order and the table well set, and plenty of well-cooked food. We were not forgetful to entertain strangers—angels unawares—giving up our own room if necessary. When I first went to house-keeping I took a highly recommended Irish girl at the highest price, $1.50 a week, but she was so impressed with her own importance I kept her only about two weeks. Then I had a good English girl for $1.25 a week. . . . We always kept a man and a horse and cow. . . . Food was cheap, eggs six cents a dozen, butter ten to fifteen cents. . . . Water was bought by the barrel for cooking and drinking. . . ."

The Hubbards evidently did not subscribe to the hollow-log water distribution system in which Gurdon owned shares and had been a director, possibly for good reason. Some Chicagoans, like Deacon Bross, thought the logs were unsanitary, passing along germs. The company suffered a setback when James Long installed a powerful new hydraulic pump to take water from Lake Michigan and pumped thousands of small fishes into the kitchens of many outraged housewives. In 1852, Chicago erected its own pumping station and absorbed the private hydraulic company.

Her husband was away much of the time, but Mary Ann was happy in her life with him. Sometime prior to 1852 she added a fourth child to their household, Alice Tinkham, daughter of her late sister, Paulina, for whom, she noted, Paulina street was named. Alice was much interested in Mary Ann's church life and aided her with the gardening, and they both taught in the mission school which trained Italian immigrant children. Mary Ann read many of Mr. Hubbard's books, observing that he inscribed his own views, often in dissent, in the margins. She thought he must have been joking when he stated in a margin of the Mormon Bible that he almost had been converted by Joseph Smith.

Mary Ann had close women friends, some less prim than she. While she was describing her own idyllic life in Chicago, "the Garden City," her friend Caroline Kirkland wrote of it: "Chicago is the grandest, flattest, muddiest, coldest, wettest, driest place in the world. . . . It has the most elegant architecture, the meanest hovels, the wildest speculation, the solidest values. It is proudest in self-esteem and loudest in self-disparagement. . . . Chicago, the wondrous, sits amid her wealth, like a magnificent Sultana, half-reclining over a great oval mirror . . . but we are told the Oriental beauties, with all their splendor, are not especially clean. . . ." Kirkland observed that the streets of Chicago "are very peculiar in not having a lady walking in them . . . but there are great crowds of men."

Mary Ann rarely went out, except to Second Presbyterian or the mission school, unless Mr. Hubbard escorted her. Chicago was indeed somewhat mean and dirty. Many of Mr. Hubbard's friends irked or bored her, even William Bross of her church, who bragged on Chicago's greatness and wonders, and John S. Wright, the bold speculator known as Chicago's greatest booster. "Chicago's trade territory is bigger than 23 states," Bross would roar. "We can pack enough beef and pork to feed the eastern states and have enough left for all of Europe!" And Mr. Wright would state solemnly, "Chicago will become the first city of the world!" Mr. Hubbard appeared to appreciate such talk, but it wearied Mary Ann. She knew that Chicago was a great trade center with fine retail and wholesale stores, factories and packing plants, ships and railroads, fifty-seven hotels and seven daily newspapers, two of them profaning the Sabbath with their intrusive editions. She knew also that Chicago was a city of evil and of lost souls, and poor, suffering immigrant women unable to feed and clothe their children properly. She sought graciously to serve her husband well, welcoming all whom Mr. Hubbard asked to their home, the Kinzies, the Wrights, the Mark Skinners, Deacon Bross and his daughter; and of course their relatives, the Hubbards and the Holts. Mr. Hubbard liked theatrical entertainment, so they occasionally went to Rice's new theater or to concerts in the Saloon building. They rarely danced any more, Mary Ann wasn't sure such frivolous diversion was proper for truly Christian people.

Despite her severe outlook on life, and an occasional pettiness, Mary Ann Hubbard was a kind and gracious woman, who always arose to emergencies, her friend Caroline McIlvaine, librarian of the Chicago Historical Society, would write. She tolerated much from her indulgent but often thoughtless husband, especially his practice of inviting guests on short notice, or no notice at all, and his practice of welcoming Indians to his home whenever they chose to come. Mary Ann and most Chicagoans understood the need for consideration and kindness to the poor immigrants, and they were organizing abolitionist societies to stop slavery and to assist freed black men and women, but they had no organized arrangements for the care of indigent Indians, generally preferring to ignore them. Mr. Hubbard and John Kinzie and his wife Juliette were conspicuous exceptions. They were eager to praise the Indians. Juliette Kinzie, with whom Mary Ann got on less well than with the other writing ladies she knew, the Carolines, McIlvaine and Kirkland, was writing a book about them. Mary Ann herself sought always to be considerate to her husband's Indian friends and she understood that Chief Shabona and his family would always have a place in their carriage house and woodshed whenever they came to Chicago.

On one occasion, Mary Ann told Caroline McIlvaine, she was entertaining a party of eastern women when Shabona and his wife Wiomex Okono and their grandchild wandered into the parlor. The old chief was dressed for the road in his buckskins and blanket. He no longer resembled the sturdy, handsome Indian brave of whom Mr. Hubbard so often spoke. He was fat and gross like his Indian wife. Shabona had come in to inform Mr. Hubbard that he expected to occupy "the woodshed" for the next several days.

Mary Ann Hubbard presented her unexpected Indian guests to each of the startled ladies from the east, though Wiomex held back stolidly and then disappeared with her grandchild into the hall. Shabona, to his credit, bowed slightly to each lady he met, his beads and silver medals rustling pleasantly as he murmured soft Potawatomi words. Chief Shabona and his wife and grandchild then departed for the woodshed. "To him," wrote McIlvaine, "the woodshed was a palatial dwelling, in which he remained in state for weeks."

July 12, 1858
Delightful day, cool and pleasant. Lincoln and I took tea
with Gurdon S. Hubbard.
Orville Browning Diary

For the purpose of giving a sketch of my history in Illinois,
I have from time to time laid aside letters and documents
touching the early settlement as well as my own diary of
events, and from 18 mo. previous to our great conflagration had written as I had leisure . . . and had at the date of
the fire some 800 pages. Most unfortunately, all were destroyed.
Gurdon S. Hubbard
to Dr. John Goodell

The Whigs were laid low in Chicago in the Spring of 1855.
Strong anti-slavery sentiment turned many voters from both the
Whig and Democrat parties to the Native American (Know-
Nothings) movement. Dr. Levi Boone, a descendant of Daniel
Boone, was elected mayor of Chicago and a Know-Nothing city
council took over. Gurdon was too dismayed by the national
elections and too involved in his business ventures to be much
concerned with the 1856 outlook. His heroes, Henry Clay, the
Whig, and Lewis Cass, the Democrat, had both gone down, Clay
losing to Polk for the presidency in 1844, Cass to Zachary Taylor in 1848. The Whigs had nominated General Winfield Scott
in 1852, while Cass fell before Franklin Pierce of New Hampshire at the Democratic national convention, the President-elect
carrying all but four states. In 1856 the Whigs, turned Republican in part, Know-Nothing for the rest, would lose to States-
Rights Democrats who elected James Buchanan.

The issue became that of the extension of slavery, but in
Chicago, both Republicans and Know-Nothings, the latter so-
called because it was said they would not or could not answer

417

any questions about their position, were not only against slavery but also were strongly anti-foreign and anti-Mormon. Hubbard approved of Dr. Boone's strict law and order position, he had himself complained often enough about the evil conditions along the north side of the river, where criminals and prostitutes infested The Sands, living in shacks and hovels near the Lake House and Hubbard's warehouse. He opposed the extension of slavery, but, like Abraham Lincoln, he doubted slavery could be exterminated by fiat. In 1852 he had no liking for General Scott, who commanded the forces standing at the ready when the Indians were forced into exile, though he knew General Scott was only obeying orders. His own Whig party was anti-slavery, but also anti-foreign and anti-Mormon. He could not remain a loyal Whig and he could not abide the Know-Nothings, so he joined the new Republican party. Like most men of the frontier, he was fiercely independent, often placing his friends ahead of party and even church. In 1855 he became involved in an Episcopalian controversy, supporting the Reverend William Cooper in an obscure dispute with the church hierarchy. "It was because Mr. Hubbard admires Mr. Cooper so much," Mary Ann explained, but Gurdon insisted that he acted from principle, believing that servants of the church had the right to free speech and thought like everyone else. Later Gurdon would be the presiding layman at the "Chicago Protest," in which Episcopalian clergy from several states would join.

In 1856, however, Gurdon appeared to stay clear of church quarrels and national politics, the latter possibly because the Republican platform that year was stridently anti-Mormon. Senator Douglas and the Democrats sought to woo old-line Whigs by nominating Senator James Buchanan, the Conservative Democrat from Pennsylvania, for president and then undertook to link him with President Harrison, the Whig victor in the "Tippecanoe and Tyler too" campaign, by arranging a giant rally on the Tippecanoe battlefield in Indiana. Though Hubbard's Democratic hero Lewis Cass occupied the speaker's stand and had urged Gurdon Hubbard to join them, he refused to be lured. The Republicans nominated John C. Fremont; the Know-Nothings named ex-president Millard Fillmore. Buchanan won, though his combined opponents out-polled him.

Gurdon hoped the Republicans had learned a lesson. He fervently admired Lincoln and believed that he was the man to unite the Republicans and northerners generally, as well as the voters of the border states, by his moderation on the slavery issue. He agreed with Lincoln that slavery should not be permitted to spread into the Territories; if not allowed to grow, it would become extinct. With Lincoln he rejected Douglas' position that the people of a territory or state should decide for or against slavery, a solution destroyed in any event by the Supreme Court's Dred Scott decision. At the same time he preferred Douglas' position on Mormonism to that of his own party. He hated slavery, whether whites enslaved blacks or Indians enslaved whites, or one another, as they once did. Like his friend Dr. Fifthian, Gurdon feared that the slavery issue could bring civil war to Kansas, where southern filibusters opposed with guns the armed northern abolitionists. He wanted compromise, but believed it possible only on Lincoln's terms, no slavery in territories seeking statehood. He subscribed to the Chicago *Democratic Press,* published and edited by William Bross, who also sold Gurdon his books, and read it daily, as he did his Bible. When his friend Deacon Bross merged his paper with the Chicago *Tribune,* edited and owned by Joseph Medill and Dr. Charles Ray, Gurdon went along with it. But he was not as much abolitionist as Bross or the *Tribune's* Dr. Ray, but rather pragmatic like the *Tribune's* Medill, who had helped to establish the Republican party in Ohio. Medill reputedly was the secretary of the underground railroad in Illinois, yet he did not call for outright extinction of slavery in his paper, since he knew that was not the way to the political power needed to stop slavery. When it became clear that Abraham Lincoln would challenge Senator Douglas and Lyman Trumbull, the anti-Nebraska Democrat, for Douglas' United States senate seat, Gurdon returned enthusiastically to politics. This included endorsement of the principles set forth by the Republican party organized at Ripon, Wisconsin, and those of Medill, as stated in his Prospectus for the Chicago *Tribune.* The new Republican party would be strongly anti-slavery, it would attempt to gather up the pieces of the shattered Whig party, and to win over Know-Nothings and anti-Nebraska Democrats, and "the foreign vote."

*

On the evening of July 8, 1858, Gurdon arrived home a bit early, bringing with him, as he had promised Mary Ann by messenger that afternoon, his friend from Springfield, Abraham Lincoln. Mary Ann had met Lincoln previously and was ready. Mr. Hubbard was always fetching guests for tea at the last minute, but this time he at least had told her. They had ample ice from Mr. Hubbard's packing plant, so Mary Ann's girl served lemonade on the porch, overlooking Lake Michigan. While Mary Ann had gone in to supervise the final preparations for tea, as she persisted in designating their usually elaborate evening meal, there was a bit of excitement on the Hubbard porch.

Their next-door neighbor was Judge Corydon Beckwith. He and his wife also were having a guest and had taken him to the verandah because the heat of the summer evening persisted indoors. Unlike Lincoln, who as usual entered Chicago quietly and alone, Senator Stephen A. Douglas had come back to his adopted home town with fanfare, aboard his special train from which a cannon carried on a flat car fired a noisy salute, signifying that the Illinois senate campaign was under way. Douglas had brought along his new wife, Adele, twenty-two years younger than himself—Douglas was then forty-two—a southern belle, whose wealth included a Mississippi plantation complete with slaves. Douglas had been welcomed to Chicago by gunfire salutes, marching clubs and bands, and a parade. He was scheduled to open the political campaign the night of July 9 by speaking from the balcony of the Tremont hotel and would be followed the next night by Lincoln.

Evidently that evening Douglas, like Lincoln, slipped away from the Tremont to enjoy the cool air of the lake with a trusted friend and political advisor. Frederick Francis Cook, a writer for the Chicago *Times,* owned by Senator Douglas, recalled the incident in later years: "In the cool of the evening both families, as was their wont, sought relief from the sultry interiors on their ample piazzas . . . neither knowing that the other had a famous guest present. When the antagonists, to their surprise, caught

420

sight of each other, they bridged the chasm with hearty, friendly greetings. . . .''

Whether Adele Douglas was present, Cook did not say. Nor did the Hubbards include the incident in their extant writings. Mary Ann had no particular liking for Lincoln, and didn't mention him or Mary Lincoln at any time. Frederick Cook, however, was without doubt correct in his facts, he was employed by Douglas, and recorded in his book *Chicago By-Gones* that he often had interviewed Hubbard, Lincoln and Douglas. Lincoln frequently stayed at the Hubbard home, Gurdon's relatives would say in their memoirs, and Lincoln included Hubbard among his principal advisors in Chicago in a letter to Norman Judd, Republican party chairman in Illinois, and manager of Lincoln's successful campaign for the presidency.

Gurdon had more than a political interest in Senator Douglas that evening in July, 1858, when the two candidates met. He had known Douglas many years, they got on well. He credited Douglas with being among the first to call for a shallow cut Illinois-Michigan canal, because of the cost, and Douglas had been right. He knew of Douglas' aid to the Mormons. And he was aware that Douglas, like himself, had married a much younger woman who reputedly was making him into a new man, sartorially by helping him to choose his clothes; morally by curbing his addiction to alcohol and tobacco. Gurdon must have been curious about that. Mary Ann had tried ending Gurdon's own tobacco habit without much luck. Adele Douglas had done better. Senator Douglas was superbly garbed in a summer suit made for him by a New York tailor under Adele's direct supervision. The senator was a bit thinner and he looked somewhat wan and worn. But he obviously was stone cold sober, and there were no thin lines of tobacco stain at the corners of his mouth. The senator's care-worn appearance undoubtedly resulted from his long struggle with President Buchanan and members of his own party as well as with the Republicans over the state's rights slavery issue in the session just ended; then he had gone on an enervating eastern political tour. Now, back in Chicago, his adopted town, he would have to put down the foes in his own party while taking on the lanky, smiling opponent who firmly shook his hand on their surprise encounter. "I shall have my hands full," Douglas had said in Washington when he learned Lincoln would oppose him. Abe Lincoln, towering over his younger foe, his hair touseled, his clothes wrinkled, his tie and collar loosely awry, appeared the man at ease, though he was the challenger.

"Twenty-two years ago Judge Douglas and I became acquainted," Lincoln would say on the Tremont balcony two nights later. "We were both young men, he a trifle younger than I. . . . Even then we were ambitious. I perhaps as much as he. With me the race of ambition had been a failure—a flat failure; with him it was one of splended success. . . ." But Lincoln was poised and sure, in his homely way. Gurdon Hubbard felt close to him in the days and nights when Lincoln's struggle for national attention began, and as he fought to define and limit the slavery issue.

"Hubbard, the judge don't look well," Lincoln remarked of Douglas at some point during their meetings that summer.

"Well, Lincoln," Gurdon answered, "he probably looks about as well as a man can who has to do without tobacco."

*

The evening of July 9 a great crowd gathered in the street below the Tremont House balcony. Abraham Lincoln and his friends were in the throng below. When Senator Douglas learned of it, he invited his opponent to sit on the balcony. Douglas was in full strength and vigor as he addressed the crowd, estimated at 30,000 by his own Chicago *Times,* and at 12,000 by the newspaper supporting Lincoln, the *Press and Tribune.* Douglas asserted that he had ended the threat of war in Kansas over the slavery question and again enunciated his belief, which he said would be the great issue of the campaign, that "the people have the right to form the constitution under which they are to live. . . . I go for the great principle of the Kansas-Nebraska bill, the right of the people to decide for themselves. . . . My opponent goes for uniformity in our domestic situations, for a war of sections, until one or another is subdued."

The following night, when Lincoln spoke from the Tremont balcony, the crowd was smaller, the newspapers agreed, though Lincoln himself thought it was as large and more enthusiastic.

422

The enthusiasm peaked early when a uniformed German marching band swept into the street before the Tremont House in a blare of sound. "The crowd gasped in astonishment when the German *Turnverein* marching club and band, from Chicago's newest ward, the 7th, tramped to a special spot under the balcony," the *Press and Tribune* reported. When the crowd grasped the significance of the Germans' arrival, and their special place, it erupted with shouting, cheers and applause. The appearance of the *Turnverein* club signified to all that Republicans had parted completely with any anti-foreign bias of the past. Gurdon Hubbard, present with his friends to hear Lincoln, may have had a bit to do with that. The Chicago strategists were worried that the Republicans were not making an appeal to the foreign communities within the city, especially the large German settlement on the north side in the 7th ward. Gurdon Hubbard was building his new home in the 7th ward and in the following year would become an alderman from the new 7th ward. However the appearance of the German marchers was arranged, it was most propitious and pleased Lincoln, who had urged his advisors to pay special attention to the German vote.

The cheering of the Germans continued as Lincoln himself was presented. He stood smiling above them in the smoky light of torches and burning tar barrels, tall and spare, six feet five in his boots, his black hair unkempt as usual, his long arms showing lengths of white cuffs and sleeves as he raised them asking for quiet. "Honest Old Abe" they called him. He gazed somewhat wistfully down upon them, 12,000 hoarsely yelling men and a few women standing in the half light of the torches and burning tar barrels, and they shouted harder. He began speaking, in a high-pitched, thin voice that contrasted with the deep, dramatic tones of Douglas the previous night, and the crowd promptly grew quiet. Lincoln wore a dark, ill-fitting coat, his shirt collar had already collapsed under his black cravat, and newsmen saw that his too short, baggy pants exposed rusty boots, in contrast to Douglas, turned out in a natty blue jacket with brass buttons, white ruffled shirt, well-pressed trousers and well-shined shoes. But when Lincoln settled in the crowd was fervently with him.

He attacked Judge Douglas' claim to have led the fight in Con-

423

gress to defeat the LeCompton constitution, adopted by Kansas. It was true that Judge Douglas had broken with the Democratic leader, President Buchanan, and had voted against the admission of Kansas to the Union. But Douglas had brought but three votes in the Senate to his cause, and 20 votes in the House. It had been the Republicans, Lincoln said, who provided the decisive margins. Douglas' popular sovereignty solution of the slavery issue would not work, and had been doomed by the Supreme Court's Dred Scott decision that states could not constitutionally bar slavery. Judge Douglas had drawn wrong inferences in attacking Lincoln's House Divided speech, Lincoln declared. He restated his position: "I have said a hundred times that the people of the north should not meddle with slavery in the states where slavery existed . . . but should demand that slavery be confined to present boundaries, which would lead to its ultimate extinction . . . the intention of the founding fathers. Let us then turn this government back into the channel in which the framers of the Constitution originally placed it . . . let us discard all this quibbling . . . about this race and that race and the other race being inferior . . . and unite as one people throughout the land, until we shall once more stand up declaring that all men are created equal."

*

Lincoln's task was a formidable one. The Illinois legislature would elect the senator, and its composition would be determined by the fall election. Many of the downstate seats in the legislature were held by Democratic veterans. They would be difficult if not impossible to dislodge. The anti-Democratic tide running in the west was not likely to sweep across southern Illinois, pro-south in sentiment. Lincoln's Chicago advisors, Norman Judd, William Brown, George W. Dole, and the three editors of the *Press and Tribune,* Joseph Medill, Dr. Charles Ray and William Bross, and Gurdon Hubbard believed that Lincoln won the seven downstate debates with Douglas, as well as the Chicago encounter on differing nights. Lincoln did in effect win the popular vote, 125,430 for Republican candidates to 121,609 for the Democrats. But the Democrats continued to control the Illinois legislature, and on January 6, 1859 the legislature re-elected Stephen A. Douglas to a third term in the United States senate.

Douglas had won, but the campaign would cost him the presidency. At Freeport Lincoln had required him to answer the famous "Freeport questions" relating to the Dred Scott decision by the Supreme Court, making slavery legal in all the states, regardless of popular views or state proscriptions. Lincoln had presented Douglas with a dilemma, he must either accept the Dred Scott decision, agreeing that slavery could go anywhere, contrary to his Kansas-Nebraska solution, or he must stop urging the sanctity of Supreme Court decisions. "Douglas was as discouraged as he was fatigued" by the Illinois campaign, Robert W. Johannsen, his biographer, would write. "The opposition he encountered away from Chicago, and the arguments against the Kansas-Nebraska act, were more impressive and persuasive than he had anticipated."

Yet, when Lincoln did not take advantage of Democratic defeats in Indiana, Ohio and Pennsylvania, and his own popular vote victory in Illinois, by announcing early that he would seek the Republican nomination in 1860, Gurdon Hubbard and most of Lincoln's other Chicago leaders chafed and wanted action. They blamed Norman Judd, whom Lincoln himself had once called "a trimmer," for equivocating on policy and encouraging Lincoln to go slow. Then they were aroused by Joseph Medill of the *Press and Tribune* who wrote Congressman Schuyler Colfax of Indiana suggesting that Senator Douglas might be persuaded to move into the Republican camp. "Douglas will never be reinstated in the Democratic church . . . ." Medill had said. "He will gradually drift around to our side and finally be compelled to act with us in 1860."

This caused further dissention among Lincoln's Chicago advisors. Norman Judd disagreed with Medill, he wanted no part of Douglas. Hubbard, always pragmatic, would lure Douglas to the Republican camp if possible, but not until Lincoln had announced for the presidency. Judd disagreed with that stand, too. Judd believed that Senator Douglas intended to run for the presidency himself, on a combined Republican-northern Democrat ticket if possible. Had Douglas not already split with pro-slavery President Buchanan in the Congressional debates and in the Illinois Senate race? They should leave Douglas alone, and give Lincoln time, Judd believed. Give Lincoln time. . . .

Lincoln clearly agreed with Judd. When Thomas J. Pickett, editor of the Rock Island *Register,* proposed that Illinois editors should get together early to endorse Lincoln, "Uncle Abe" wrote Pickett, "I really think it best for our cause that no concerted effort, such as you suggest, be made." When Horace Greeley, in his New York *Tribune,* urged that Republicans should adopt Senator Douglas, obviously for the purpose of running him for the presidency, the Chicagoans told "Uncle Horace" to keep his nose out of Illinois politics, though Joseph Medill, in his letter to Colfax, in effect had suggested the same possibility earlier. Said the Chicago *Press and Tribune* of Greeley's proposal, "The New York *Tribune* supported Douglas for reelection against one of the noblest and purest Republicans in our Union," and was in no position to tell any Republican what to do.

*

The Lincoln leaders in Chicago were a loyal but contentious lot. Lincoln was there often in 1858, on legal business which also allowed him opportunity to form a campaign staff without public announcement of his decision to run. Norman Judd, now a member of the Republican national committee and a power in the Illinois legislature, was a careful and cautious advisor. The influential newspaper editors, Joseph Medill, Dr. Charles Ray, and William Bross were the outspoken Chicago leaders for Lincoln; Gurdon Hubbard remained a staunch friend and advisor who knew both downstate Democrats and New England abolitionists in northern Illinois, and dared to tell Lincoln what he needed to know, sometimes angering Uncle Abe in doing so. The Chicagoans worked with Lincoln's downstate leaders, Senator Orville Browning, Jesse Fell and Judge David Davis among them, Fell and Davis also voicing criticism of Judd. But Lincoln continued confident in Judd, the wise and careful attorney who provided Lincoln with work that brought him often to Chicago, and won him fame as a lawyer in northern Illinois. While he was general counsel for the Rock Island railroad, Judd hired Lincoln to defend the company in a suit filed by owners of the steamer

Effie Afton after it crashed into the railroad's new bridge over the Mississippi river, burned and sank. The case was tried in the federal court in Chicago in September, 1857, receiving wide newspaper coverage since giants of old and new transportation systems were battling. It ended in a hung jury, in effect a victory for Lincoln and his client.

On January 5, 1858, Lincoln wrote Robert Kinzie for information needed for the celebrated "sand bar land case" which would help to establish land titles on the north side of Chicago as the Beaubien case had done on the south side. Lincoln asked Kinzie several questions "in re your land attached to your addition on the north side of the harbor." Kinzie referred Lincoln to Hubbard, who had pushed Robert and his mother into filing a claim to that land at the Palestine land office years earlier. Lincoln called Gurdon Hubbard as his expert witness in the case, Johnson vs Jones and Marsh, although Gurdon had told him that Johnson was his cousin. "I am interested in your knowledge and your integrity, not your relatives," Lincoln replied. While in Chicago for that case, Lincoln talked politics with Gurdon, Norman Judd, the *Tribune* editors, and George Dole. As usual, the suave and experienced Judd urged caution and delay in any such decisive step as candidacy announcement. Gurdon suspected that Norman Judd intended to bring ex-Congressman Long John Wentworth, the powerful Democrat, into the Lincoln camp, an idea that exasperated him and Bross, of the *Democratic Press.* They were sure that Wentworth was scheming to take control of the Republican party in Chicago in order to run for governor. But Lincoln himself insisted that Wentworth should be made welcome among the Republicans.

Throughout the year and into 1859, the Chicago friends of Lincoln continued to squabble. Meantime Norman Judd organized his political forces, including Gurdon Hubbard and other critics in his Illinois Republican Central committee. Medill, Ray and Bross had solved their newspaper financial problems for the time by merging their publications into *The Chicago Daily Press and Tribune.* Gurdon had put his own financial problems, arising from the panic of 1857, behind him. But Norman Judd continued to be plagued with troubles, some of them arising from continued criticism in John Wentworth's news-

paper, the *Chicago Democrat.* The reason, Wentworth's biographer Don E. Fehrenbacher would write, was that Long John
regarded Judd "as a leader of the *Tribune* clique, which included
most of Wentworth's deadliest enemies in the city."

*

Finally, on December 1, 1859, Chaiman Judd, furious at the endless sniping and criticism, and Long John's rejection of his friendship, turned on his tormentor, newly arrived into the Republican
party, by filing a lawsuit against Wentworth and his *Democrat.*
He fired off an angry letter to Lincoln. "I am berated in the
newspapers . . . and slandered in private conversation," Judd
complained, "and all this without any public defense by you
or any of your friends." Judd now demanded that Lincoln
should disavow Wentworth, who had in fact taken over the
Republican municipal political apparatus in Chicago, as Gurdon
Hubbard and others had predicted he would. "Wentworth must
be silenced or driven from the party," Judd concluded . . .
"kicked into his kennell (sic) with the rest of the curs."

On December 14, Lincoln replied to Judd, enclosing the copy
of a letter he had written to "Messrs. Dole, Hubbard, and
Brown"—William Brown, who, with Judd, had accompanied
the Hubbards to Springfield in 1855. Lincoln's enclosure scolded
his three supporters and advisors for their criticism of Judd,
denying that he believed that Judd had failed him in 1855 or had
given him "half-hearted support" in 1858, the year in which
Dole, Hubbard and Brown had been especially critical of Judd's
tactics, which they considered dilatory and inadequate. Lincoln
assured Chairman Judd of his general approval of Judd's conduct at all times, adding, "I find some of our friends here (he
had written the letter in Chicago) attach more consequence to
getting the national convention to our state than I did, or do.
Some of them made me promise to say so to you." Lincoln had
seen Hubbard, Dole and Brown just prior to writing his letter
to Judd. Probably they had disclosed to him that it had been a
part of Judd's strategy to urge at meetings of the Republican national committee that Chicago should be chosen as the convention city because Illinois was a neutral state, having no
announced candidate for the presidency.

Chapter 14

Senator Orville Browning of Quincy indicated that he and Lincoln had visited the Chicago malcontents before the letter to Judd was written. They had provided plenty of reason for opposing Judd's efforts to get along with the irascible Wentworth. On February 28, 1858, when the Chicago Republican committee had nominated Mayor Wentworth, the Democrat, for re-election, a course urged by Lincoln himself, Brown had written, "It is a bitter pill we have to swallow," but Hubbard and Dole refused to take such medicine, even after Wentworth was elected mayor on the Republican ticket. On April 20, 1857, Mayor Wentworth sent his police to raid and level "The Sands," a course long urged by Hubbard, but this did not appease Gurdon, nor the *Press and Tribune.* They insisted Wentworth had not solved the crime and vice problem. The thieves and prostitutes merely re-settled to the south of the river, creating an epidemic of robberies and assaults there. "The city has been delivered into the keeping of thieves and house breakers," the *Press and Tribune* charged. Even Democrats attacked Long John. "In the columns of Senator Douglas' *Times* Wentworth was portrayed as a despicable villain," wrote Fehrenbacher. "The Douglas organ repeatedly charged him with spitefulness and dishonesty . . . along with drunkeness, lechery, and the habitual use of vile language."

Then, in the spring of 1859, Long John Wentworth had infuriated further not only Gurdon Hubbard, Brown and Dole, but Norman Judd himself. The bizarre incident, recorded by Fehrenbacher, dismayed ardent Wentworth loyalists. "On a Saturday evening in April,"according to Fehrenbacher, "a Republican meeting in Metropolitan hall was interrupted by the sounds of bagpipes. Down the center aisle marched a bagpiper, followed by Long John, who took over the platform, and for one and a half hours denounced Peck (Ebenezer Peck, party leader and banker), Judd, the 'Pressed Tribune' and other assorted adversaries." Norman Judd was at the meeting. He angrily replied to Wentworth, calling him "a most corrupt liar and a knave." The fighting between Wentworth and Judd had gone on through 1859, Wentworth's *Democrat* asserting that Judd had twice betrayed Lincoln, and would do it a third time. "Judd is one of the most selfish and avaricious men living," the *Dem-*

ocrat declared. It was after the paper accused Judd of stealing Republican funds that the harassed Lincoln leader filed a $100,000 libel suit and wrote his complaining letter to Lincoln, supporting all the charges against John Wentworth that Hubbard and others had made earlier.

Lincoln himself then mediated the trouble between Mayor Wentworth and his Chicago leaders. Lincoln was emerging as a presidential contender and urgently needed a united Republican party, one that could include the fiesty Long John. In the mayoral campaign of 1860, Norman Judd, at last mollified, withdrew his lawsuit against the *Democrat* and sat on the platform with Wentworth. Gurdon Hubbard on his part agreed to run for alderman from the 7th ward to help give Chicago a Republican administration in the year of the Republican national convention. In 1861 Wentworth again was sued for libel, this time by a bank president, and he lost. He sold his *Democrat* to Joseph Medill, Charles Ray and William Bross, who took over its circulation list for their *"Pressed Tribune."*

*

Hubbard had pledged himself to the candidacy of Abraham Lincoln and remained loyal, asking no personal preferment for his political labors. He told John Kinzie and other friends that he would undertake to include in the Republican platform a statement calling for recognition of Indian treaties and rights. His bitterness about the Indian situation had been intensified early in 1859 by another experience of his friend Shabona, again the victim of vicious whites. Shabona had gone to the Iowa lands of the Potawatomis, called there by the death of his son, Smoke. When he returned to Illinois, there were further squatter depredations to his remaining lands. Fences had been destroyed, trees, some of them sheltering the graves of members of Shabona's family, had been cut down, his crops damaged. Again Shabona had come to his friend Hubbard, in Chicago, and stayed in the combined woodshed and guest house that had once been Billy Caldwell's cabin.

This time Hubbard solicited friends of Indians in Chicago to join Sheriff George E. Walker, Lucien Sanger and others of the downstate Illinois communities near Shabona's home to raise funds to buy land and a new home for Shabona. When the funds were obtained, a grand ball was given by the people of Ottawa, Morris and Seneca to celebrate the accomplishment. It was attended by Shabona, his wife, who had grown fat and could not ride a pony to Ottawa as Shabona did but was brought by wagon, and fifteen members of their family. As the grand march was about to begin, Chief Shabona was asked to choose the prettiest woman present. "The old chief," wrote Henry R. Hamilton, "examined each one critically, noting her looks, her dress and her gait." Shabona put Wiomex Okona, weighing 300 pounds it was said, through her paces also. "When the parade was over," Hamilton wrote, "he approached his wife and, slapping her on the shoulder, said, 'Much heap prettiest squaw.' "

"The money was raised," Hamilton concluded, "the house was built but Shaubenee (he used Hubbard's spelling) and his wife never lived in it. They were utterly opposed to the white man's way of living, and they lived in a wigwam, while their house was occupied by children and grandchildren." Shabona died July 17, 1859, "called to the Happy Hunting ground beyond the Evening Star."

*

Gurdon, always pragmatic, was one of those who believed that Chicago must be the site of the national convention if Abraham Lincoln was to be the Republican nominee for president. If Judd delayed Lincoln's announcement of candidacy to forward Chicago as the convention site, he did not win Hubbard's agreement to his policy, nor the others among his critics. One of those who concurred with Judd's strategy was Joseph Medill of the *Press and Tribune*, who named himself the paper's Washington correspondent to push both Lincoln's candidacy and Chicago as the convention city, without urging Lincoln to formally announce. Gurdon liked what Medill wrote from Washington and the *Press and Tribune* endorsement of Lincoln February 16. On the 26th, Medill disclosed that he found many Republicans in Washington who favored Chicago for their national convention, but few who wanted Lincoln for more than vice president. New York Senator Seward was preferred, Medill said, but he viewed Seward as "too radical." Then he added,

"I hear the name of Lincoln mentioned for president in Washington circles ten times as much as one month ago." This exasperated Senator Seward. "You have stunned me!" Seward protested. "You advocate Lincoln in preference to me for reasons that are wide of the truth."

The Lincoln men in Chicago knew that Seward was the man Lincoln must beat. He was politically powerful and well known, cultured, elegant, and suave. Abraham Lincoln was none of these. He was almost unknown to the eastern editors, whose papers were widely read and copied throughout the Union. Horace Greeley, editor of the New York *Tribune,* had been outraged when the Illinois Republican convention endorsed "Abe Lincoln the Rail Splitter" for president in June, 1858. "You have repelled Douglas, who might have been conciliated and attached to our side," he wrote Joseph Medill. "You knew the almost unanimous desire of the Republicans of other states, and you spurned and insulted them." Horace Greeley and Thurlow Weed, the New York Republican boss, wanted to unite the North behind the Repulican party. An unknown man, offering no more than a record of brief service in Congress and the Illinois legislature, would not do.

The Republican national committee, meeting in New York, chose Chicago for its convention city on December 29, 1859. In the spring of 1860 Long John Wentworth was again elected mayor on the Republican ticket and Gurdon Hubbard, who had moved into his elegant new home at Locust and La Salle streets, was named alderman of the 7th ward, gamely accepting Wentworth as his municipal leader. Mayor Wentworth in turn held his nose and appointed Gurdon Hubbard chairman of the committee on arrangements for the Chicago convention hall, then non-existent. Hubbard, it appeared, was the only experienced builder among the Lincoln leaders. Hubbard had put up the first multi-storied brick building in Chicago in 1834 and had erected several large buildings since, the newspapers said in announcing the appointment. Senator Douglas' *Times* accepted Hubbard's appointment as well advised, but noted that his associates had limited experience. Charles N. Holden, city treasurer, was an insurance man; Edward Ransom was an engineer specializing in railroad construction; Peter Page, a gas company official, had been a brick contractor who helped to build St. Mary's church in 1847. Sylvester Lind owned the Lind Block, and, the *Times* added, "he helped to build a church in a cornfield." That was Third Presbyterian, to the west of the south branch of the river. Lind was on the church building committee.

Gurdon assembled his convention hall committee on a site provided by the city, at Lake and Market streets, where the famed Sauganash hotel once stood. Time was short. Hubbard, according to Alfred Holt, delivered a short lecture on Chicago history: "It was here I watched the last war dance of the Potawatomis from the balcony of Mark Beaubien's inn." He proposed a two-story building of wood studdings and scantling to be set upon a stone foundation, Chicago balloon-style. It would look "like an enormous barn, or the first St. Mary's church," Gurdon declared. St. Mary's, at State and Lake streets, was the town's original "balloon-style" structure, introducing that architectural manner to Chicago in 1834. The convention hall would also look like an Indian longhouse "where chiefs and headmen held their tribal councils," Gurdon explained. "We could call it the Longhouse."

"Why not call it the Wigwam?" someone suggested.

Gurdon grinned. "Good! That will honor the Indians and tell our friends in the east that we here in the west are going to have something to say about this election. Gentlemen, unless there is objection you have just named our convention hall. We now have about three months to get the Wigwam ready."

Once the preliminaries were cleared, Chicago's new Wigwam convention hall was built in eight weeks.

*

Chicago, calling itself "The Garden City" and "The Queen City of the Lakes," prepared that spring for its greatest week since the memorable Rivers and Harbors convention of 1847. The town, grown from "four and a half houses and a fort" as Hubbard described it in 1818, now was the ninth largest city in the United States, with a population of 110,000, fifteen railroads, the world's largest railroad station, seven first-class hotels, and, as May arrived, a spanking new convention hall. The Wigwam was strictly utilitarian, a wooden structure of two stories, 100 by 180 feet, built around a huge platform large enough to accommodate the 400 convention delegates and the speakers and required officials and clerks. The alternates, newspaper writers, telegraphers and other functionaries were accommodated on the ground floor, while honored guests and the ladies would have seats in a large balcony extending around the interior walls. It was built at low cost and didn't look like much, said the *Press and Tribune,* but it was built in part with taxpayers' money and the paper was pleased that this forced pro-southern sympathizers to help shoulder the burden.

Early visitors to Chicago's new convention hall were impressed. Dr. Humphrey W. Wood, from Hillsboro, Illinois, sent his observations to the *Free Press* of that town: "The Wigwam is well ventilated, well lighted, and for speaking and hearing as well arranged as such a building could be. One third of the space is assigned to the use of the convention (delegates), and is divided into a platform and two spacious committee rooms, one at either end. All the delegates have seats on the platform, placards designating space for each delegation. The speaker's chair is at the rear of the platform and toward it all seats look." Women of Chicago had decorated the interior, Dr. Wood noted. They draped American flags over the speakers' platform and hung paintings of Greek goddesses amid sylvan scenes and red and blue bunting on the walls, "and festooned the entire auditorium with plants and flowers, all symbolic of Chicago, which calls itself 'The Garden City.' There is space at the front of the platform for alternate delegates, the press, and telegraphers. Outside of this railing (surrounding the press) are excellent standing accommodations for gentlemen not fortunate in holding tickets and not accompanied by ladies." Dr. Wood was one of those. Around three sides of the vast auditorium were wide galleries restricted to guests holding prized convention admission tickets, mostly women and their escorts. "On the front of the galleries were painted the coats of arms of all the states," Dr. Wood wrote. The roof was arched and well-supported by posts and braces, as were all the galleries, and "around these were twined evergreens intermingled with flowers." Atop the Wigwam, on a sturdy platform was mounted a cannon which could be used to fire salutes and signals at appropriate times.

This gun would announce the outcome of the voting anticipated late the second day of the convention.

While Hubbard and his committee readied the convention hall, Chicagoans generally prepared to receive the convention delegates. The leading hotels, such as the Tremont House and the Sherman hotel, both built after a major fire in 1847, and the Briggs and Richmond, charging $2.50 a night for their "sumptuous accommodations," had long since closed off reservations, as had most of the second class houses, fifty in number, charging $1.50. There were a hundred hotels at a dollar a night, the convention housing committee said, and thousands of rooms were available to delegates and visitors in rooming houses and private homes. The town expected 30,000 guests and they began arriving early the second week of May, aboard boats, via railroads and on the plank roads and muddy trails. Abraham Lincoln remained in Springfield. The Lincoln leaders had rooms and campaign headquarters in the Tremont House, with Judge David Davis, a friend of Lincoln from circuit-riding days, in charge; at the Richmond Hotel, Michigan and South Water street, the Seward delegation was housed. Seward, hailed by his supporters as "the candidate of the thinking people," was represented by Thurlow Weed, the Albany editor and New York Republican leader, directing convention strategy. Weed was known for his political wisdom and his ability to wheel and deal. He was a friend of Chicago, supporting the city's aspirations ardently since his visit there to attend the Rivers and Harbors convention.

The New York delegation under Weed arrived in town aboard a special train. Mayor Wentworth chose Gurdon Hubbard, the man responsible for the convention hall, to join him in welcoming the powerful New Yorker. It was important to have his good opinion of Chicago's convention facility and to get it early. Boss Weed, tall, handsome, courtly, led his New Yorkers into town the morning of May 14. Gurdon Hubbard was not fond of Mayor Wentworth or Boss Weed, but he knew his duty. Thurlow Weed was pleased to have an invitation to inspect the convention hall in advance of the opening session. First they would stop at the Richmond House where Weed invited them to watch the maneuvers of his "Irrepressibles," the pro-Seward marching club, resplendent in their green and red dragoon uniforms and high beaver hats. Senator Seward had stated in a campaign speech in October, 1858 that the North, with its free labor, and the South, basing its economy on slave labor, were bound for "irrepressible conflict," a warlike premise which frightened many, and was used against Seward by his critics and enemies. The nation could not endure half slave and half free, Seward had implied, and later Abraham Lincoln said it in milder words and tones. Boss Weed astutely emphasized what some considered Seward's political mistake. Mayor Wentworth, having anticipated the exhibition by the "The Irrepressibles," then presented Chicago's famed marching club, Elmer Ellsworth's "Zouaves," the crack drill team of the northwest, which welled into view, splendidly garbed in beaded blue jackets, red vests, yellow sashes, white pantaloons and gaiters and blue cadet caps.

"They're Mr. Lincoln's favorite marching club," Gurdon told Weed. "Well, then," said Weed smiling, "enjoy them while you may, Mr. Hubbard."

Following lunch, Hubbard took Weed to the Wigwam, where the New York boss was impressed and gracious. "This is the finest convention hall in the United States!" Weed told the newspaper reporters. He disclosed that he had retained the Wigwam for the following night, and would rally the Seward supporters there.

The night of the 15th, most newspapermen in town thought that William H. Seward would surely win the Republican nomination. Some of the close supporters of Abraham Lincoln, Gurdon Hubbard among them, were worried. Horace Greeley of the New York *Tribune* and Murat Halstead of the Cincinnati *Commercial* were known to have telegraphed their newspapers that Seward appeared unbeatable. The leaders of states other than Illinois were worried too. They had favorite sons to put forward for the nomination and didn't want Boss Weed to wrap it up before the convention got under way. Great principles were at stake, and needed discussion. Deals were planned and the delegates were eager to have them considered. Seward delegates outnumbered the combined other delegates when Boss Weed's rally got under way, the newsmen estimated, but Illinois and Pennsylvania and some other states were also well

represented, being ordered there by Judge Davis and various
state leaders. The Pennsylvania delegation seized control of the
floor late in the evening, refusing to relinquish it. The crowd,
said to have been more than 10,000, packed the galleries and
standing room area, howling, cheering, chanting and sweating,
and creating general disorder until William (Pig Iron) Kelly of
Pennsylvania, whose voice, it was said, could be heard across
Lake Michigan, shouted everyone down and began an oration
that lasted until near midnight. By that time the wearied and
bored Seward delegates had departed to see what went on in
downtown Chicago, which had begun to amass a reputation for
unabashed wickedness.

*

In the Tremont hotel, the Lincoln strategy committee under
Judge David Davis, "300 pounds of political wisdom and guile,"
was at work, Gurdon Hubbard among them. Davis realized that
the Pennsylvania and Illinois delaying tactics at the Wigwam
meant little, or Boss Weed would never have announced his rally
plans in advance. Probably Weed wanted most of the delegates
occupied that night, except those he invited, a few at a time,
to the Richmond House. There Boss Weed was trading and
promising. Davis gave his lieutenants assignments to call on delegations they might influence. Joseph Medill took Ohio, he had
been publisher of the Cleveland *Press;* Gurdon Hubbard had
Vermont and Connecticut delegates to visit, and also he was to
keep in line his political friends from downstate Illinois; Judge
Davis took for himself the Pennsylvania delegation, which he
could not see until after midnight, since it was preoccupied at
the Wigwam. He returned later in triumph, saying "Damned if
we haven't got 'em!" "How?" asked Medill. "By paying their
price," Davis said. He sputtered over a telegram which had arrived from Lincoln, at home in Springfield, "I authorize no bar-
gains and will be bound by none." Norman Judd had cussed
when he saw it. Judge Davis merely sighed. "Lincoln ain't here
and don't know what we have to meet," he said.

A crowd well over the 10,000 capacity of the Wigwam waited
in Market and Lake streets the morning of May 16 as formal sessions were to begin. Throngs pushed in when the doors opened

at 11 o'clock, most to be disappointed. Speeches of welcome, challenges, the seating of 606 delegates and alternates, platform proposals and various resolutions occupied the convention through the morning and afternoon. In the evening orators appeared to urge unity while presenting their own divisive proposals for the guidance of the platform builders, most of whom were absent. Clearly the work of the convention was going on in smoke-filled rooms, especially at the Tremont and Richmond hotels.

All leaders and delegates were at the convention hall the second day, especially the Sewardites who appeared to be picking up large delegations, such as Pennsylvania and Ohio. The platform committee was ready to report. It would be a bland document, side-stepping the slavery issue and making a wide appeal to the economic interests of the voters. The farmer was the backbone of the nation. Manifest destiny and free land were to be the issue. The platform urged a homestead act providing free land for settlers. It called for a protective tariff, and a railroad to the Pacific. Kansas was to be admitted as a free state. Gurdon Hubbard's effort to include a recommendation of adherence to Indian treaties was laid on the table, his own favorite tactic in the past for dealing with insoluble or unwelcome problems.

When the platform had been adopted and hailed as one which could unite the country and usher in an era of prosperity and good feeling, the convention moved toward the time of nominating speeches and the balloting. The great hall was again packed and the expectant crowd grew noisy as the hundreds of Sewardites began to chant for their man. Hubbard, in a group of Lincoln men near the podium, moved to Senator Orville Browning and shouted through cupped hands into his ear: "I think Abe will be licked if we vote today!" William Maxwell Evarts, a New York lawyer famed as an orator, had arrived in the hall with Boss Weed and other Seward leaders to make the nominating speech for Senator Seward.

"I think I'll move for adjournment," Browning said.

"It would look better coming from the floor, wouldn't it?" Gurdon responded.

Browning nodded. He slipped away, talked briefly with Norman Judd, who made his way to George Ashman, the presiding officer. Soon an Illinois delegate, whose name was not recorded, arose from his seat among the Illinois delegation and obtained the chairman's recognition. "Mr. Chairman," he shouted, "I move that we adjourn until 10 o'clock tomorrow morning."

The delegates were caught off guard but all were in a good mood and Thurlow Weed made no move to question the proceedings. Most delegations had been caucusing long and hard and had unfinished work, and the task of inspecting their host town, to complete. Their platform labors had gone well. They were ready for play. Chairman Ashman called for "ayes" and the motion carried, even Seward men voting for it. They expected to be back in full force in the morning.

Thursday morning, May 17, the Illinois Lincoln forces were ready and waiting for Boss Thurlow Weed and the Sewardites. Balcony tickets for a May 17th session had not been sent out in advance. Early that morning Ward Hill Lamson had obtained them from the printer and handed hundreds to the Lincoln leaders for distribution to Wide Awake marchers, Lincoln's Illinois supporters, who had been given free rail passes to Chicago by the convention committee. They were instructed to go early to the Wigwam entrances. During the night Joseph Medill and convention hall managers rearranged the convention seating to keep the New York and Pennsylvania delegations as far apart as possible, since they feared Pennsylvania might yield to Thurlow Weed blandishments. "It was the meanest trick I ever did in my life," Medill said later. Boss Weed, the strategist and power broker, had been out-maneuvered. When the Seward shouters reached the convention hall that morning, they found all balcony seats and standing room taken. The shouting Lincoln supporters dominated the hall.

"Imagine all the hogs ever slaughtered in Cincinnati giving their death squeals together, and a score of big steam whistles going together and you have the Lincoln boys' yell at the convention," Murat Halstead wrote in his newspaper. When Maxwell Evart, the New York lawyer, famed for his prolix and florid oratory, heard the unruly galleries he knew they couldn't hear him. He waited grimly for a second of silence, then shouted:

"Mr. Chairman, I take the liberty, sir, to name as candidate to be nominated by this convention for the office of president, William E. Seward of New York!"

The simple statement, miraculously heard by all in the rift of silence, stunned the great crowd into further quiet. Then the Seward delegates on the floor and their alternates rose and shouted inside, while a thousand angry Seward partisans kept outside yelled their anger at the Lincoln men who had tricked them. Norman Judd of Illinois rose and followed Evart's example of brevity: "Mr. Chairman, I desire, on behalf of the delegation from Illinois, to put in nomination as candidate for president of the United States, Abraham Lincoln of Illinois." The "yawp" of the Lincoln people shook the hall. For minutes the wooden walls of the Wigwam rocked with sound. Bates, McLean, Cameron and other favorite sons were nominated. Finally the clerk was able to begin the roll call of the states. Seward led the first ballot 173 ½, Lincoln 102, Simon Cameron of Pennsylvania 50½, Ohio's Salmon P. Chase 49, Edward Bates of Missouri 48, others scattering. Needed to nominate, 233.

Seward picked up 11 votes on the second ballot, Lincoln gained 79. As the third roll call proceeded, Lincoln steadily gained until his vote totalled 231½. Joseph Medill, sitting with the Ohio delegation, whispered to his friend David Cartter, the Ohio chairman, "If you can take Ohio to Lincoln, Chase can have anything he wants." Cartter arose, stuttering in his excitement: "Mr. Chairman!" he shouted, "I-I-I a-rise to announce a ch-change of f-f-four votes, from Mr. Ch-Chase to Mr. Lincoln!"

Abraham Lincoln was nominated. Again the Wigwam shook with sound. Men stomped, shouted and sang, women in the balconies cheered. Hats and canes were thrown in the air, and handkerchiefs and scarves fluttered down from the balconies. The signal cannon atop the Wigwam fired a salute that was answered by boat whistles along the river. The city's bells joined in. Reporters scribbled, the battery of telegraphers calmly tapped their keys. The uproar continued a full ten minutes, Dr. Wood wrote. When a lull came, Norman Judd arose to read a telegram from New York City: "One hundred guns being fired in honor of the nomination." New York state moved to make the nomination unanimous and Lawyer Evarts hoisted high in the New

York delegation a life-size portrait of Honest Old Abe. Again the crowd went wild.

*

The Democrats had failed to name a presidential candidate when they convened in Charleston, South Carolina in April. They met again in Baltimore June 18, Senator Stephen A. Douglas of Illinois winning the nomination after delegates from the deep south withdrew. The Democrats were split, dissident southerners choosing John C. Beckenbridge of Kentucky as their candidate. But the Republicans were divided also, their defectors forming the Constitutional Union party, that nominated John Bell of Tennessee. That summer Senator Douglas stump-campaigned and was criticized for such unseemly political conduct. Abraham Lincoln stayed home in Springfield, attending his law business, conferring with advisors and receiving the press. While he was in Chicago in April, following the final days of Johnson vs Jones and Marsh, in which he was awarded the verdict for the defendants, Lincoln again took tea with the Hubbards. He complained to Gurdon that he was "an old man,"—he was fifty-one. Gurdon had grown a beard and suggested to Lincoln that he should do the same. "It will give you dignity," Gurdon said.

Lincoln smiled. "On you, Hubbard, a beard looks fine," he said. "But, for me, now at this time, it would seem an affectation." In October, however, Lincoln also grew a beard, responding to a letter from Grace Bedell, eleven years old, assuring him that, since ladies liked whiskers, "they would tease their husbands to vote for you."

*

On September 8, 1860 Gurdon Hubbard received news of the first of a series of crushing disasters destined to befall him in the following decade. His finest steamer, the side-wheeler *Lady Elgin,* which with a sister ship, the *Superior,* he owned with A.S. Spencer, had gone down in a storm, with a loss of 297 lives. The *Lady Elgin,* named for the wife of Lord Elgin, governor-general of Canada, had taken on passengers and freight at her Chicago river dock the previous afternoon for her regular run to the upper Great Lakes. Towards seven o'clock in the evening, two hundred members of the Union Guards, a Milwau-

441

kee marching club, came aboard, to join other passengers and a crew of forty-five. Some of the passengers were bound for Lake Superior ports, but the vessel was scheduled to stop at Milwaukee to disembark the Union Guards, a popular drill team on a holiday excursion to Chicago. In the ship's saloon, bright with polished brass and gleaming furniture under festive greenery and bunting, lighted by kerosine lamps, an orchestra played for dancing. The Lake Michigan sky was heavily overcast as the *Lady Elgin* cast off shortly before seven-thirty. Captain Wilson, a veteran of Great Lakes navigation, had been advised that foul weather lay ahead.

As the steamer emerged from the narrow Chicago channel into the lake, Captain Wilson watched the squall line to the northeast. The wind began to build, rain fell heavily, but the ship moved smoothly northeasterly through the rollers, her engines pulsing steadily.

The night was black, yet passengers on the port side could distinguish the shoreline, where the lights of Evanston were seen shortly before midnight. Thereafter the ship veered slightly away from shore, moving through heavy seas and a steady rain. At two-thirty a.m., September 8, the *Lady Elgin* was ten miles offshore, between Winnetka and Waukegan. The saloon was still alight and the orchestra still played but most passengers had gone to their staterooms. The ship's running lights were on, and shafts of light slanted from portholes and opened cabin doors. As the wind picked up, the big steamer began to roll slightly. Captain Wilson ordered a turn to starboard, into the seas.

A jolting, groaning crash told Wilson, his crew and some of the passengers that the *Lady Elgin* had been rammed on the port side, just aft of the wheelhouse, by a powerful, heavy ship. The offender was the lumber schooner *Augusta* of Oswego, heavily loaded, low in the water, running silently under full sail, without lights. The hull of the *Lady Elgin* was ripped open below the water line. Wind and wave tore the vessels apart. The schooner *Augusta* drifted away, and then was able to continue on course until she reached Chicago, some forty miles distant. There Captain D.M. Malott, her skipper, megaphoned the bridge tender, saying they had struck a steamship southeast of Waukegan.

Chapter 14

Captain Wilson meantime had ordered two veteran seamen into a small boat to survey the damage and to attempt to cover the hole with canvas. The high wind tore away their canvas taking the small boat with it. The *Lady Elgin* listed and began sinking. Wilson ordered cattle carried on a freight deck to be pushed overboard in an attempt to lighten the ship while he sought to head for shore. Lake water entering the gash in the hull reached the engine room, extinguishing the fires. The *Lady Elgin* stopped dead in the water, going down by the bow.

Horrified passengers emerging from their staterooms partly grasped the situation as jagged flashes of lightning tore across the eastern sky. On the port side the crew sought to launch half-filled life boats. Within thirty minutes the hull of the *Lady Elgin* was below the waves. Some passengers made the boats, others clung to life rafts, and a few clutched wreckage of the upper cabin deck which had torn loose in the storm and continued to float. Life boats capsized as they were turned in toward shore. Captain Wilson, who had been pushing bits of wreckage toward passsengers in the water, finally grasped a floating cabin door and sought to get a woman and her child aboard this makeshift raft, but they went down and Captain Wilson drowned with them.

As the storm continued, news of the accident spread along shore. Students from Northwestern University in Evanston formed rescue teams. One of them, Edward W. Spencer, a student at Garrett Bible Institute, a part of the university, was an expert swimmer. Seventeen times he went into the pounding waves, each time making his way back to shore with a rescued person. He fell exhausted on the beach as he tried to go out again, crying out as others came to his aid, "Did I do my best?"

There was heavy loss of life when the *Lady Elgin* went down. Gurdon Hubbard came to the scene of the rescue attempts the following morning. The ship was gone, the rescue effort ended. Gurdon walked silently along the beach, staring out at the gray water. He asked men who accompanied him, and who had been there much of the night, about the loss of life and was told 300 had died; the actual number lost was 297. Gurdon moaned softly, shaking his head in bewilderment. He learned of the heroism of young Spencer, immediately wondered if the young man

443

was related to Spencer his partner, and learned later he was not. Gurdon stated he would pay the young man's hospital bill and said he would place a plaque honoring Spencer at Garrett. He continued to ask about details of the disaster, the loading of the passengers, the life boats, the running lights, the behavior of the crew. He seemed lost, groping, dry-eyed but almost suffocating in misery. Gurdon Hubbard aged ten years that morning, Alfred Holt would write.

The formal inquiry at Chicago ended in exoneration for Captain Wilson and the co-owners of the *Lady Elgin* in what had been the worst ship disaster in the history of the Great Lakes. Said the Board of Inquiry on May 2, 1865: "The cause of this most horrifying disaster on the night of September 7-8, 1860 was two-fold: the failure of the *Augusta* to observe the brightly-lighted excurison steamer, the *Lady Elgin,* in time to change course, and the failure of the *Augusta* to stand by and lend assistance. We do hereby exonerate the owner and the captain of the *Lady Elgin* from all blame in this catastrophe." The board added that while it did not find that the *Lady Elgin* had been overcrowded, more life boats should have been provided and launched. It commended Captain Wilson for his personal gallantry.

Gurdon Hubbard did not recover from the *Lady Elgin* catastrophe. Alfred Holt, his grandnephew, recorded that later at a school musicale, which the Holts and Hubbards attended, a child came out to sing the popular ballad *"Wreck of the Lady Elgin,"* that began: "Lost on the Lady Elgin, Sleeping to wake no more, Numbered in that three hundred, Who failed to reach the shore." "Uncle Gurdon sat through it with grim, staring eyes, then excused himself and left the room," Holt recalled. "When we boys caught up with him he continued to shake with sobs." No one spoke as they returned to the Hubbard home. For a time thereafter, Gurdon kept to his house as much as possible. Two years later his *Superior,* sister ship of the *Lady Elgin,* went down in a storm, but no lives were lost.

*

"The prairies are on fire," the *Chicago Tribune* reported in the fall of 1860. This time the paper referred to the presidential campaign, predicting Lincoln would carry Illinois by 20,000 votes. On November 7 when the votes were counted, Lincoln had garnered 1,866,452, Douglas 1,365,976, Beckenbridge 849,781, Bell 588,870, the combined opponents receiving nearly a million more votes than Lincoln. Douglas carried Lincoln's home county. Lincoln carried Illinois, but received no votes in any state in the deep south. That night Chicago celebrated, with two hundred guns fired from the Randolph street bridge and a parade of 10,000 led by Wide Awakes, a procession the *Tribune* said was ten miles long.

Senator Douglas, much worn by his stumping campaign, nevertheless continued to tour the south after his defeat, seeking to find a way of compromise that might save the Union. On December 27, the South Carolina militia occupied Fort Moultrie at Charleston after Major Robert Anderson abandoned that post for Fort Sumter, considered safer. Early on April 11, 1861, General Pierre Gustave Toutant Beauregard, commander of the Confederate forces at Charleston, called upon Major Anderson to surrender, and the first cannon shot of the Civil War was fired.

On April 17, at a mass meeting of Chicagoans in Bryan hall, the Union Defense Committee organized, consisting of Gurdon Hubbard, A.E. Kent, Charles Walker, Jr., J.L. Hancock and Philip Conly, all but Conly members of the Chicago Board of Trade. The board announced it would fund $10,000 for the equipment of a battery of mounted artillery and would raise $15,000 more for bounties to recruit men. The city at the time had no military arms nor a capability for defense though there were many organized militia groups, now found to have existed chiefly for social and parade purposes. On April 19, at another mass meeting, the Union Defense Committee was enlarged to twenty-eight members. Major Julian Rumsey, commanding the Board of Trade militia company, contributed a building for use of the committee, and fund raising began, the committee pledging additional money for enlistments. Gurdon Hubbard himself, then fifty-nine years old, provided funds for the Second Board of Trade regiment, 88th Illinois, and commanded as captain in a home guard capacity until August 27, 1862 when it was mustered into national service. Gurdon by then had been commissioned a colonel by Governor Richard Yates. His son Gurdon

Jr. became captain of "G" company, known as the Hubbard Guards.

Gurdon and other members of the Union Defense Committee discovered in those April days of 1861 that while money and men could be raised, there were few guns to be had for the defense of Illinois, which, Hubbard believed, might become a battlefield because of strong southern sentiment within the state. The federal arms were mostly in the eastern and southern port cities, and in the west, where a line of forts had been established from Minnesota to Texas officially for the purpose of keeping whites out of Indian territories, but actually to keep the Indians from re-entering their former eastern lands. Now, in the emergency, there were inadequate arms for the Illinois militia, in Chicago or downstate.

The Chicago committee was called upon by Governor Yates for immediate action of high strategic importance. As commander-in-chief of the militia, Yates ordered General Richard K. Swift, a Mexican war veteran who commanded the Chicago military district, and the Union Defense Committee, to at once raise a military force for a mission "that must remain a profound secret," to protect and hold the port and town of Cairo, at the confluence of the Ohio and Mississippi rivers. Swift and the committee went promptly to work, borrowing muskets from a Milwaukee militia company as well as gathering up effective weapons in Chicago, mustering 400 men, forty-four horses and four cannon. Agents of the committee in Chicago commandeered all working shotguns, squirrel rifles, single-barreled pistols and antique revolvers that could be found and went even to Canada, seeking more guns and ammunition.

At eleven o'clock the night of April 21, the expedition under General Swift boarded a military train at the Illinois Central station on Chicago's lakefront. The departure of the militia force was no secret, though its mission remained so. A cheering crowd was present, the locomotive engineers tied down their whistles, which were answered by steamboats in the harbor, church bells rang, and the special train puffed along the Illinois Central trestle, its destination still unknown to all but those in command and the members of the defense committee. The Chicago committee had wanted to seize the telegraph offices along the line to safeguard secrecy, since both Governor Yates and General Swift feared the train might be stopped in pro-southern areas of Illinois. Railroad, telegraph and newspaper officials pledged secrecy however, a pledge kept. The regular trains were dispatched on their usual runs that night, then pulled onto sidings to allow the special train to pass. "We were surrounded by traitors in Chicago and a large proportion of southern Illinois sympathized with the south," Augustus H. Burley of the Defense Committee told the Chicago Historical Society after the war. "The wooden trestle bridges over the rivers could have been destroyed within an hour. There was fear that the rebels would seize Cairo as being a point of great strategic importance . . . it was later learned that Cairo would have been seized within 48 hours, had (our) occupation been delayed."

The Chicago force under General Swift was in control of Cairo the day following. Redoubts were dug. Cairo later became the base from which General Ulysses S. Grant, commander of the Union forces in the West, took control of the Mississippi and Ohio rivers, insuring the fall of Vicksburg and the defeat of the Confederacy in the west.

While the Chicago militia units were en route to Cairo, and agents of the Union Defense Committee continued to seek arms from other states without much luck, Governor Yates obtained the desperately needed guns from under the noses of a "rebel" force which surrounded the federal arsenal in St. Louis. Yates dispatched his aide, Captain James A. Stokes, southern-born but loyal to the Union, to get modern guns not only for Cairo but also to equip 3,000 militiamen the governor had called up. Stokes knew that the arsenal was surrounded. He arranged with the Alton and St. Louis Steamboat Company to send a steamboat to St. Louis, its true mission to be known only to its captain. Stokes himself went into St. Louis, walked to the arsenal gate alone, and there showed Captain Nathaniel Lyons his warrant from Governor Yates for the federal guns. Lyons, a loyal officer, at first suspected Stokes, known to be a former southerner, was scheming to get the guns for the rebels, who had not dared to attack the arsenal. Finally convinced by Captain Stokes, Lyons ordered his force to crate all the obsolete and faulty guns on hand for shipment by wagon to a St. Louis railroad station. The crates were promptly seized by the pickets around the arsenal. Meantime, the *City of Alton* was met by Captain Stokes and guided to an arsenal dock. There it was loaded with 2,000 boxes of modern muskets, plus ammunition, and a complete artillery battery, in all about 23,000 stands of arms. Six "rebel spies" were seized within the arsenal as the loading proceeded and held until the *City of Alton* had cleared the dock. The ruse was completely successful. The Cairo militiamen and Governor Yates' forces got arms immediately needed. The Union Defense Committee, according to Burley's report, served through 1861-62, chiefly aiding Union forces in Missouri after Cairo had been secured. "The first shot fired in the West for the Union," Burley boasted, "was from a Chicago cannon, by a Chicago Boy."

In addition to his Union Defense Committee and home guard duties, Colonel Hubbard was named to the Chicago Sanitary Commission which organized the town's famed Sanitary Fairs, to raise money for the assistance of federal troops in the field. Scores of such commissions were created around the country, and provided services contributed in later years by the American Red Cross. On December 23, 1863, Gurdon resigned his militia commission. The war in the West was won. He was sixty-one years old, his hair was thinning and fading, his trim beard was white. Gurdon served on the public committee named to honor martyred President Lincoln when his old friend came back to Illinois to rest in state in the Cook county courthouse in Chicago on May 2, 1865. Thereafter he was not often seen in public.

15

Chicago, 1870
The growth of this city is one of the most amazing things
in the history of modern civilization.
> Sara Jane Lippincott
> *New Life in New Lands*

My Dear Anna
As I have promised you to write some account of our experiences during the Chicago fire of Oct. 9, 1871, I will begin, although memory brings back so many circumstances
that I do not think I have the strength to write it all. . . .
> Mary Ann Hubbard to
> Anna Holt Wheeler

In the boom days following the war, Chicagoans again came to
know their city, quadrupled in population in a decade, from
58,000 in 1854 to 235,000 in 1864, a roaring factory and shipping town long preoccupied with the job of supplying the northern forces with war goods and food. The Queen City of the
Lakes now called itself the Queen City of the Northwest. It had
seized commercial leadership from Cincinnati and St. Louis. It
sprawled north and south for almost five miles along Lake Michigan, spreading west past sand dunes, over marshes and prairie,
more than two miles, into the thick woodlands ringing the town
and its new suburbs. It announced itself to visitors and eager
immigrants with smoking stacks of factories, tall red elevators
loaded with wheat and corn, the masts and spars of half a thousand ships, some three hundred of them arriving and departing each twenty-four hours, and the black scudding plumes of
ten railroad trunk lines sending forty freight trains and fifty-eight
passenger trains across the prairies to hundreds of tributary
towns, cities and hamlets. The Hoosier wagons still thundered
north, now over planked highways as they approached the city.
Canal barges from New Orleans, lumber schooners from Michi-

gan and Wisconsin, and sleek freighters from Liverpool and Hamburg mingled in the Chicago harbor, that handled three million tons of cargo, including sixty million bushels of wheat and fifty million sawn pine boards a year. Their town, they saw, had grown rich and powerful in military trade, in trade with newly liberated states of the south, and in trade with the growing west. It had become crime-ridden and over-run with seekers of employment, though a hundred thousand newcomers had been provided with jobs. To the west of the mansions of the newly rich along Prairie avenue, between the railroad tracks and the south branch of the river, and in the southwestern area of the 7th ward north of the river, were the shacks and hovels of immigrants who could not find adequate housing even if they found jobs, some finding neither, and the jobless derelicts and refuse of the war, from both north and south.

Yet Chicago promised all a great future. It had become the world's greatest lumber market, even shipping mail-order houses, cut, planed and packaged and ready for nailing, to any customer in the country with cash or credit and a two cent stamp. It was the nation's biggest shipper of grain and the leading butcher of hogs and cattle. In the booming town of pork packers twenty new plants had sprung up around the mile-square stockyards on the southwest side. Chicago in 1865 slaughtered enough hogs to reach all the way to New York City if laid in line, single file, visiting historian James Parton of *Atlantic Monthly Magazine* was told. "It would depend," said Gurdon Hubbard when newsmen asked him about the estimate, "on the size of the hogs."

Chicago, arsenal of the north during the war, supplier of provisions to the southern states after Grant opened the Mississippi and took them from the Confederacy, seller of reaping machines and plows and railroads to the new West, had become world-famous and was said to be the fastest-growing city on earth. "On every street one sees new buildings going up, immense stone, brick and iron business blocks, marble palaces and new residences everywhere," said the Chicago *Tribune*. It was a hustling but ugly town where fortunes could be made, visitors reported as the post-war boom roared on. The established residents, owning houses with yards about them, plowed their land and planted gardens and flowers all through the war, and insisted Chicago should be called, "The Garden City." But the newcomers working twelve-hour days six days a week, had no time nor place for gardens. Some made money and played rough at night in the segregated district adjoining the business area, taken over by riverboat gamblers, army deserters from both sides, and indigenous criminals and prostitutes during the course of the war. There was squalor and evil in the city. The preachers cried out against such iniquities, warning that Chicago would know the fate of Sodom and Gomorrah. The police force under Mayor Long John Wentworth seemed helpless against the rising tide of vice and crime.

Gurdon Hubbard, alderman from the 7th ward, was among the Republicans joining together to deny Long John Wentworth nomination for mayor in 1863. When Francis Sherman, a Democrat, won the mayor's office and promptly named John Wentworth to the Chicago Board of Police, the Republicans in the city council were stunned. Mayor Wentworth's war and anti-crime record had both been bad. Wentworth was forty-six in 1861, but did not volunteer in any war effort. "His enemies had often charged him with cowardice," wrote his biographer Fehrenbacher. Mayor Wentworth's *Democrat* had campaigned against the old-line Whigs in the Republican party before he lost the paper as the result of a libel suit. Gurdon Hubbard was one of those Republicans. When his party, convening in Metropolitan Hall September 1, 1864, nominated John Wentworth for congress, Hubbard, who already had given up his aldermanic post, withdrew from politics in disgust. Union soldiers stood guard at the polls that November 8, since William Bross, Gurdon's old friend, had disclosed a plot to free southern soldiers held prisoner at Camp Douglas on the south side, in an effort to take over the polls and control the election. The plot, thus exposed, failed. Wentworth won a seat in congress, returning for the sixth time, as Chicago voted for Lincoln.

Gurdon Hubbard turned to his business ventures, shipping, packing, the Board of Trade, where he continued as head of the provisions committee; banking and real estate. In 1866 he was lured back into political activity for a time as the Lincoln supporters in Chicago sought to elect Norman Judd to Congress.

Again John Wentworth won, though he would retire in 1867 to live on his farm southwest of Chicago. Mary Ann began talking seriously to her husband about his retirement in 1868, and proposed the celebration of their silver wedding anniversary and his fiftieth year in Chicago that fall. She thought Mr. Hubbard had earned a rest, time for travel and enjoyment. She had read that Prince von Bismarck of Prussia had stated that sixty-five was the proper retirement age.

"I may be well past sixty-five, wifie," Gurdon responded, "but you are only forty-eight; so it is no time for me to retire. Besides, Judd tells me Prince von Bismarck has said that if he should travel, the place he wants to visit is Chicago. We're here now." Norman Judd had served Lincoln as American minister to Prussia. But Mr. Hubbard compromised, allowing Mary Ann to plan any kind of silver wedding party she wished, and since she insisted it should also celebrate his arrival in Chicago in October, 1818, he suggested a few names of those he'd like to see included. When Mary Ann completed her list, she had almost four hundred names on it, the magic number set by Mrs. Astor, social arbitress of New York City. The party, properly catered, Mary Ann noted in her diary, was given in the Hubbard home at Locust and LaSalle. "The guests were requested to register their names with the date of birth and their arrival in Chicago," said an account of the affair accompanying the gift of the guest album to the Historical Society. "This album is now in possession of the society and will serve future generations not only as a roster of Chicago's 'four hundred' of that time, but as a roll of honor of those who made possible the Chicago of today."

*

The days preceding the glittering anniversary party were a time of happiness for Gurdon and Mary Ann. His business activities were going well, he had recovered from the losses of his biggest ships, and the repeated financial panics, and had formed still another company, for the importation and sale of tea from China. He had reconciled with Gurdon, Jr. who was said by the newspapers to be a leading man in the real estate business, and his one-time friend William Ogden, before Ogden departed Chicago to end his extended bachelorhood by marrying his childhood sweetheart in his fifty-third year, and retiring to his country place, Boscobel, on the Harlem river, New York. Ogden's letterbook would become property of the Chicago Historical Society, after the former mayor's death in 1875, and would disclose the details of his long friendship with Hubbard, and also that Gurdon, over the years, had used Ogden's good offices in directing business opportunities to both his son and his brother, Christopher.

While Mary Ann prepared for their party, following their 1868 summer trip to Mackinac Island, Gurdon went often to his office near the dingy rooms of the Board of Trade in South Water Street, and spent the rest of his time working on his memoirs in his study in their Locust street home, described as one of the grandest in Chicago, situated a few blocks west of the new Lincoln park and a few blocks northwest of the mansions of William Ogden and his brother Mahlon, where the Newberry library would later rise. In the quiet of his study Gurdon read the books he liked and could now afford, mostly about Indians and the history of the Northwest, and received old friends and blasé young men from the newspapers, and Captain Alfred Andreas' history book staff, who interviewed him about the pioneer days in the northwest. Gurdon was glad to help. He answered questioners not only from Chicago, but throughout the northwest, describing his own activities and the deeds of others, generally, as Frederick Francis Cook noted, allocating to those others much of the credit he might have claimed for himself. Gurdon's recreation in Chicago in the late years of his life included talk with friends, his intense interest in research and church affairs, occasional attendance at the theater, and the enjoyment of his "nieces and nephews" constantly around the house, Alice Tinkham, Mary Ann's niece, and children of his close friends, the Hamiltons, who lived two blocks away, and the Holts. One or two of the children accompanied the Hubbards north to "Mackinaw" each summer. He liked a game of croquet with them, Henry R. Hamilton would remember, and he enjoyed reading to them from his Indian books. "Sometimes Uncle Gurdon would speak in the Indian tongue for us as he showed us the pictures in his Indian books, and he even did war dances."

Mary Ann too enjoyed the quiet life. While her husband was

busy with his reading and research, preparing his papers and writing his recollections, she was heavily involved in her church work, as a member of the New England Congregational church where she had taken a pew. She and Alice Tinkham taught in the Sunday school and at the mission school for the children of the foreign-born. Mary Ann always welcomed preachers to their home, particularly if they had been missionaries. She took in Sarah Marsh, the daughter of the Reverend Cutting Marsh, a missionary among the Indians, to be her companion, when Alice left to become the wife of a minister, the Reverend Edward Williamson of Oak Park.

Mary Ann was proud of their home on Locust street. "It is comfortable," she wrote. "All of our homes have been happy, comfortable ones." The house was three stories, of brick and stone, Victorian in style, and was described by the newspapers as one of the finest in the city. It stood among gardens and orchards, facing Locust street at LaSalle, with stables and a large woodhouse, the latter intended for Shabona, though the old chief did not live to see it. With its mansard roof, wide verandah, green shutters, and ivy-covered red brick walls, in the center of a city block, the Hubbard home was described by Caroline McIlvaine as "the finest in Chicago when it was built. . . . It was one of the best-known places." Frederick Cook, the journalist who often wrote about Hubbard for the *Times,* and later the *Tribune,* agreed with McIlvaine. "It was one of Chicago's most splendid residences, rivaling that of William Ogden." he wrote.

Mary Ann complained when they first moved to Locust street that they were too far out of town, but she meant it was too far from the Second Presbyterian church, then in a handsome new edifice to the south of the business district, not far from Prairie avenue where many of the town's newly rich dwelled. For a while Mary Ann continued to attend Second Presbyterian, Deacon Bross' church, and she and Gurdon kept their membership in the exclusive Calumet Club on the south side. But in time she made her break. "When I said 'goodbye' to dear old Second Presbyterian, I was undecided where to make my church home," she wrote, but she then found New England Congregational congenial. Her husband, however, persisted in attending St. James, though he often grumbled about the services and told her he intended to leave it. He and Mary Ann sometimes did attend church together after they moved north, but on neutral ground, as when they visited Grace Methodist to hear Dr. Theodore Parker, the famed Boston abolitionist, preach on the evils of slavery.

Gurdon was content with his relative seclusion. He and Mary Ann did not attend the Old Settlers ball, though they both once loved social affairs and dancing. But when the sponsors of the ball decided to organize formally in 1871, and insisted the Old Settlers Association would not be authentic without the Hubbards as members, they agreed to join and Gurdon became a director. Both were active in the Chicago Historical Society and Gurdon served as a director of City hospital on LaSalle street and on the committee to welcome President Grant to Chicago. But generally he stayed away from crowds. Some said that Gurdon Hubbard was ostracized by his peers for his pro-Indian attitudes, and, more especially, his heretical stands in church controversy. If he was being excluded, he didn't appear to notice it. He was too preoccupied with his own affairs, and the lore of the past. The success of Mary Ann's anniversary party in October appeared to dispel such talk.

*

Late in the fall of 1868 the second of a series of disasters befell Gurdon. The Hubbard Packing Company plant on the north branch of the river was razed by fire. A decade earlier the *Gem of the Prairie* had described Hubbard's as one of the largest packing houses in the city, with extensive patronage on the eastern seaboard. Gurdon was the pioneer packer in Chicago, recognized as such by Sylvester Marsh, who credited Hubbard with being well established when he engaged in packing in Chicago in 1834. But newcomers during the war years had opened for business some twenty-six new plants, most of them in the stockyards district on the southwest side. They were more aggressive and efficient than Gurdon Hubbard. One, Philip Armour, would by the 1880s employ 10,000 men and manufacture packing products valued at $50 million annually. These newcomers "used everything of the pig but the squeal," Finley Peter Dunne of the Chicago *Times* would write, his famed "Mr. Dooley" observing, "a cow goes lowin' softly into Armour's and comes out glue, gelatine, fertilizer, celoolid, joolry, sofy cushions, hair restorer, washin' sody, soap, lithachoor, and bed springs. . . ." Gurdon's plant still produced mostly meat products, no gelatin, jewelry, or book bindings. He found his workmen and markets quickly snapped up by competitors when his plant burned. So he simply went out of the packing business.

In the spring of 1869, Gurdon was jolted from his tranquil pursuit of history and his own past by another controversy involving his friends in the Episcopal church, especially the Reverend William Cooper, who, according to historian Raymond W. Albright, "had come from the Church of England and served several parishes in this country, and become an ardent evangelical advocate. Reverend Cooper had served as a missionary in Spain, where he married a Spanish woman, and later was a missionary in Mexico." He was pastor at Lockport, according to Mary Ann Hubbard; her husband met him there and admired him. "Mr. Cooper published a series of articles in the *Protestant Churchman,* calling for a conference of evangelicals and a committee for revision of liturgy and canons to push toward a pure Reformed Church," wrote Albright in his *History of the Protestant Episcopal Church.* The minister influenced George David Cummings, assistant bishop of Kentucky, and Charles E. Cheney of Christ Church, Chicago to join his reform movement. The Reverend Mr. Cooper was saying in print precisely what Gurdon Hubbard over many years had said in his letters home and to Chicago church friends, as well as to Mary Ann.

The Reverend Mr. Cheney in Chicago agreed publicly with Cooper that Episcopal churchmen should exchange pulpits with Protestant preachers and should themselves revise the prayerbook and church office when they felt it was required, such as "omitting objectionable words in the Baptismal service, and such words as oblation in the office of Holy Communion." The Reverend Mr. Cheney did exactly that in Christ Church in Chicago. For this he was brought to a hearing by Bishop Henry J. Whitehouse of the Chicago Diocese. And, publicly on Cheney's side, was Gurdon S. Hubbard, asserting Cheney's right to modify the liturgy as he chose, something Gurdon's ancestor, the Reverend Gurdon Saltonstall had done for the Congregational church a century earlier, and made it stick. "We should have the right to think for ourselves, with only God as our judge," Gurdon Hubbard now said.

When a convention of dissident churchmen took place in Chicago in June, 1869, Gurdon Hubbard served as lay chairman of the proceedings, according to Andreas' history. Andreas and Albright recorded the details of the Chicago Protest, as the insurgency movement was called. Some fifty-seven clergymen and laymen from several states attended the sessions in the Young Men's Christian Association building June 16. Precisely what Gurdon Hubbard said to them beyond welcoming them to Chicago is not of record. Charles E. Cheney stressed the need for greater liberty of the clergy and Stephen Tyng, Jr., already under fire in New York for having preached in a non-Episcopal church, urged complete secession "from the sacramental system of the church."

Little was accomplished by the Chicago Protest, however. "The meeting became hopelessly snarled by filibuster," according to Albright. "It was even impossible to adopt the prepared agenda." Individual clergymen did have the opportunity to say they believed the Reverend Mr. Cheney was right in what he had done. Following the conference, Cheney returned to his duties as pastor of Christ Church, but after trial was suspended in February, 1871. Cooper, who had gone to Reformed Episcopal church in Chicago, resigned in 1872. Meantime Gurdon Hubbard had left St. James to join Reformed Episcopal because, wrote Mary Ann, "he admired Mr. Cooper so much." The Reverend George Savage, former assistant rector at St. James, became pastor at Reformed Episcopal, succeeding Cooper. It was Savage who finally offered an objective explanation of Gurdon Hubbard's action after Gurdon's death: "It was with much pain and a large sacrifice to himself that he left her (St. James) communion. He had been one of the founders and an officer of St. James, and a liberal supporter. He left her communion when dissatisfied with what he believed to be the unscriptural and ritualistic doctrines and practices which had crept into the church of his love. Yet, when the time came for action, he did not hesitate to leave it, and join the then small and despised Reformed Episcopal church cheerfully, giving his influence, counsel and pecuniary aid to this new and struggling organization." Christ Church, too, owed much to Hubbard from an earlier day, Reverend Savage said. He gave the ground on which it stood to the church when it was organized in 1856. Gurdon himself left few records of his beneficences; if any were kept prior to 1871 they were destroyed in the Chicago fire.

*

In August, 1871 Mary Ann and her husband were on Mackinac Island where they observed Mr. Hubbard's sixty-ninth birthday. He was busy as usual, filling their small suite with his papers and books as he worked on his memoirs. It was a task she sometimes shared and she was much pleased with his progress. In her opinion, Mr. Hubbard was far too modest about his accomplishments and she was glad to read his work, finding that now and then he did take personal credit for accomplishment. She aided him with his research, as did his favorite nephew, young Henry Raymond Hamilton, who accompanied her husband wherever he went that summer and ran his errands. Mary Ann had become interested in the history of Illinois, the Northwest and the Indians, and was a loyal supporter of the Chicago Historical Society with her husband. Though he was sixty-nine and she was fifty-one they got on well together after twenty-eight years of marriage. They had their own interests, but were much closer in their outlook than their friends and some relatives supposed. Mary Ann agreed with her husband that there was no need for storing up riches in the world. It was true that she felt he was overly generous with his friends, somewhat too trusting of the unworthy, and that he had a strange affinity for radical preachers like Reverend Cheney and Reverend Cooper. Mr. Hubbard, in turn, had made it clear to her that he considered her gifts to foreign missions excessive. He thought mission money should be kept at home. Well, Pacific Gardens mission in Chicago was her favorite.

Gurdon, on his part, was well satisfied with Mary Ann. His wife took good care of him, Henry Hamilton and the Holts believed. "He and Aunt Ann were devoted to each other," Hamilton wrote. "In the main they had the same ideas. Uncle Gurdon showed little interest in keeping money. He seemed ever ready to let others reap where he had sowed." Hamilton understood that Aunt Ann's austerity was sometimes a bit hard for her husband to take. "During the last twelve years of his life he came to our house almost daily, being glad, I think to exchange, for a brief time, the somewhat puritanical rigors of his own establishment for the more liberal atmostphere of ours." Gurdon loved to play cards, but Mary Ann thought of cards as the Devil's Pasteboards. At the Hamilton's, however, someone always was ready to join Uncle Gurdon in a game of Seven-Up. He came there also to read the Sunday newspapers. Sometimes while reading he would reach for his tobacco pouch, then absently realize it had been filled with camomile leaves by Mary Ann. Henry Hamilton Sr., noticing, would hand over his well-filled pouch to his friend.

Mary Ann accepted people like the Reverend Dr. Cooper, with reservations and obvious resignation, because Mr. Hubbard so wished. She professed not to understand her husband's admiration for such religious deviates. Gurdon was therefore much amused when one of Mary Ann's preacher friends, the Reverend David Swing, generally called Professor Swing by the press, of Fourth Presbyterian, was put under attack by *Interior,* a Presbyterian magazine edited by the Reverend Francis L. Patton and owned by Cyrus McCormick, the Reaper King, on charges of heresy. Swing allegedly had declared there was no such specific place as Hell. Later in 1874, Professor Swing would be charged in an ecclesiastical court with condoning atheism. As a result, he left the church and formed his own, which met Sundays in McVicker's theater. Gurdon approvingly helped to support Swing's new church, even though he did not especially like Prof. Swing on his occasional visits to the Hubbard home.

Mary Ann had cared well for him, Gurdon readily acknowledged, and also Gurdon Junior, though the young man seemed singularly unappreciative, and for their various young women, Gurdon's own nieces, who had died in young adulthood, her niece Alice Tinkham and the young Holts and Hamiltons. But by 1871 she was pestering her husband to hurry and finish his manuscript so they could travel. She wanted to go south for the winter. She wanted him to work less and to start by being less considerate of those who plagued him with interviews and letters asking questions about the past. Let them wait to read his book.

"Wifie, you should write your own book," Mr. Hubbard told her. He promised her they would go to California soon. Then he turned back to his desk to write an unknown correspondent: "I was not a trader at Peoria, but was at Bureau, a mile above Hennepin," and went on to provide details. And, to a second letter writer: "I came to Chicago in 1818. We went down river and did not meet a white man, nor any signs of civilization, 'til reaching the village about 18 miles above St. Louis." He said something of St. Louis and Cahokia, and his meeting with John Reynolds, later governor of Illinois. And, to a third: "Yes, I built the dam at Marseilles (on the Illinois river, near Ottawa) but it turned out to be a mistake."

*

The Sabbath of October 9, 1871 was dry and hot, Mary Ann would recall in her memoirs. Mr. Hubbard had planned that she would accompany him to the morning services at the Reformed Episcopal church at Center and Dayton streets, then they would drive downtown to have dinner with Mr. Hubbard's cousins, the Alfred Hebards, from Red Oak, Iowa, at Potter Palmer's new, elegant Palmer House. Afterward they would return north along the lake front, where they might find a cooling lake breeze, past the new water tower and into Lincoln Park, where they would see Swan Lake, as the new lagoon being created there was called. Since Mary Ann's mother, who lived with them, declined to join them, she instructed her maids to prepare an icebox lunch for the old lady. Her maids were not asked to do other than absolutely required work on the Sabbath.

It was unusual for Mary Ann to go to Mr. Hubbard's church, she wrote in her manuscript, intended for her entire family, and she explained: "Your uncle believed as Dr. Cooper did and wanted to go there."

Since William, their coachman, had been given the Sabbath off, Mr. Hubbard himself drove their carriage. "It was very unpleasant, exposure to the hot, dusty wind, and I had hard work to keep my bonnet on," she wrote, or dictated to her companion, Sarah Marsh. She was pleased that she and her husband were to be together the entire Sabbath day. Usually on that day Mr. Hubbard found an excuse, after church and their dinner, to go over to the Hamiltons where she knew he read the Sabbath newspaper and probably chewed on that vile weed, tobacco, to which he and Mr. Henry E. Hamilton were addicted. Mary Ann had confided to Anna Holt, to whom her recollections were primarily directed, that she knew her husband much better than he supposed. She knew that he kept plugs and bags of tobacco hidden somewhere at home, probably in the wood house. He still carried a tobacco pouch, but she kept that filled with camomile leaves. She sorrowed for those who tempted Mr. Hubbard, who bought the Sabbath newspapers and supplied him with the odious weed, for they would someday be called to answer to a Higher Power for it. Meantime, Mary Ann considered it her Christian duty to pray for them as well as for Mr. Hubbard. For a time, all that Sabbath day in fact, she was beginning to believe that her prayers were being answered.

Following dinner at the hotel, they met a cousin who told them there had been a large fire in the lumber district Saturday night. "His home had been threatened. He put out the fire near by but did not do anything to avert the same danger again." Mary Ann was convinced that the Saturday night fire left embers which ignited leaking gas, creating the October 9th conflagration. "I have always thought that the story of Mrs. Leary's (sic) cow tipping over the lamp was a newspaper lie," she wrote. Mary Ann would maintain her conviction even after a coroner's jury found that the great Chicago fire was started when neighbors of Mrs. Catherine O'Leary, of 137 De Koven street, had gone to the O'Leary barn late that night, after Mrs. O'Leary was in bed, to milk her cow in order to replenish their supply for a milk punch. Since Mrs. O'Leary had herself milked her cow earlier that evening, the outraged animal kicked over the lantern, starting the flames that spared the O'Leary home, but destroyed Chicago.

The evening of October 9 the Hubbards again went to church together, this time to Grace Methodist, at Clark street and North avenue, where the huge Moody Bible church later would stand. It was not far south of the Hubbard home. Again Mr. Hubbard drove. Following the service, they returned home and sat for a time in the library, chatting while they ate some grapes, their first food since their dinner with the Hebards. Mary Ann was serenely content and happy. Never had Mr. Hubbard behaved more circumspectly on the Sabbath. They went to their room on the second floor where Mr. Hubbard promptly went to bed and fell asleep. Mary Ann sat in her dressing room, combing her long blonde hair still completely free of any trace of gray. She then raised a shade of her dressing room window, which looked across the gardens toward the south and southwest and she saw "a vast conflagration, whipped by high winds, spreading across the city.

"It seemed fearful. The wind blew a gale, and soon the air seemed full of flying cinders. I called your uncle and begged him to come and look at the fire. He said, 'It is the old fire of last night kindled again; we can do nothing; you had better go to bed.' "

Mary Ann sighed and returned to her dressing table to prepare for bed, possibly remembering the time when Mr. Hubbard was a young volunteer fireman she had just married. Then he sprang from bed at the slightest alarm and raced his buggy to every fire in town, whether or not his own company was called. Mr. Hubbard loved fires, he had been a fire fanatic. But, after the blaze that destroyed his packing plant, and caused such a loss, even after the insurance was paid, and Mr. Hubbard had cautioned her about building any more chapels for the poor for a while, he didn't want to hear any more about fires. Poor Mr. Hubbard! Her dear man was growing old. Mary Ann returned to the window. "The sight of the clouds of smoke and flaming boards driven by the wind filled me with alarm; I could not leave the window nor cease watching it. Finally Mr. Hubbard arose at my entreaties and was extremely alarmed. He was not in the habit of using strong language, but his exclamation was, 'My God, we are all going to be burned up!' "

*

Gurdon then dressed, called William his coachman, only to remember he had been given the day off. He went next door to the McGregor Adams house but found his neighbors were not at home. He returned to instruct Mary Ann to awaken her mother, help her to dress, and pack a few necessities for her. He would harness the horse and take her to son Gurdon's home in the west division of the city, beyond the north branch of the river. That would also enable him to judge the extent of the fire and its direction. Soon Mary Ann had the old lady on the verandah "dressed in everything she owned," her daughter recalled. Her husband drove off into the night. Since Gurdon Jr. lived considerably west of the river, Mr. Hubbard evidently assumed the flames to the south would not head in that direction. In parting he told Mary Ann that he felt they too would be safe, at least for a time.

As Hubbard returned east from his son's home, he was not so sure. The fire had started on Chicago's west side and crossed the river to the east, feeding on the lumber yards there. Gurdon saw that the intense heat was causing flames to leap the river and over streets toward the east. The entire business section of Chicago was menaced; the whole of the western area was already burning. He could hear the roar of the flames, driven by high winds, the sounds of bells and alarms, shouting, and the screaming cries of frightened horses. He almost yielded to the temptation to go nearer for a closer look, but instead turned resolutely back north. He wondered about his relatives, the Hebards and their daughter, whom they had met that afternoon, who were staying in the Palmer House. He assumed the fire would not cross north of the Chicago river, the flames seemingly traveled almost due east, but then he observed that the wind appeared to change direction, to the northeast, and was driving embers and fireballs ahead of it, and he was no longer sure they would be safe at Locust street.

When he reached home near midnight, he found that William had returned, and the Hebards also were there, badly frightened, with a story of horror to tell. They had seen the flames from the room high in the eight-story Palmer House and had concluded they ought to attempt at once to seek safety to the north. They left the hotel carrying their trunk, no baggagemen were available at the entrance, people were rushing about and shouting, all attempting to attract a coach or a dray. Alfred Hebard found a drayman who agreed to take them and their trunk north across the river, but then he drove off, leaving them in the street, when a shouting man in their way made him a better offer. Frantic, Hebard found two boys with a cart, who agreed to take them all the way to the Hubbards for $10. They had to fight their way through a panicked crowd to get aboard the wagon, others wanted it, but the boys got them clear. By this time, the Hebards said, it seemed all downtown was burning, and the fireballs sailed high ahead of them. Years after the fire, Mary Ann, recalling the scene, was still appalled at the $10 payment Alfred Hebard made to the young men who helped him.

Soon others arrived at the house, among them young Henry Hamilton, whose family lived two blocks away. Henry's father was out of town. His mother had awakened him and sent him over to Uncle Gurdon's to find out what they should do. Henry ran the two blocks and through the Hubbard grounds where he discovered that several carts were drawn up, the drivers shouting at their horses. Inside the house, Henry recalled, "my uncle was surrounded by a group of people, some of whom had been burned out and others who had fled their homes because they expected to be. Some of the women were crying and some of the children were wailing. They had come to Gurdon Hubbard for help because they always had come to him for help and did not know where else to go."

Gurdon may have exclaimed profanely when Mary Ann called him the second time to see the extent of the flames to the south, but he was himself by the time Henry saw him, "Calm and unruffled, as if he were the host at a garden party, he was comforting the women and directing the men to tear up the carpets in the house, wet them in the cistern and spread them on the mansard roof. He had a light station wagon and directed his man to harness one of the horses and go back to our house with me and bring whatever household effects we could."

Gurdon obviously had concluded that although the fire was heading north, it might not leap the river in great force, or it might lose some of the force before crossing the open areas of the north side, thus reducing heat and pressure. He had much experience fighting fires. The grounds of his place were extensive. If they protected the roofs, they might save all. Even so he directed the men present, which included some of his former packing plant employees who had come to his aid, to haul their own possessions, and anything they could add to their carts, farther north. All available wagons were soon being loaded. Gurdon knew fires well enough to see that the winds whipped up by the flames themselves would continue their spread so long as there was dry wood on which to feed. His own house was of brick. He did not take the precaution to bury in the grounds their valuables which could not be carried. Clearly, he did not expect to lose the house.

*

To the south the sky itself seemed ablaze. The thud of explosions could be heard in the distance. Giant fireballs were thrown into the night above the ring of radiance surrounding all the downtown area. Burning embers and sheets of flaming tar paper swirled out of a vortex of flames into the surrounding darkness where new flames soon spurted. The hot breath of fire had reached across the Chicago river, igniting buildings on the north side before the main fire itself leaped over. The new waterworks buildings next to the water tower on Chicago avenue were thus set ablaze, their tar-papered roofs igniting, stopping any flow of water from any source. A woman in Hubbard's house asked Mr. Kelly, their new neighbor grown rich in the liquor business, if he thought the fire would spread all the way north.

"Hell, yes, madam," replied Mr. Kelly politely. "We'll all burn up."

By early Monday morning the flames extended north to the Ogden school at the corner of Chestnut and LaSalle. To the south the city still flamed, some areas a mass of burning, smoking ruins, brick and stone walls alone standing. The flames were now racing north, leaping across streets so fast they could not be stopped. The north side streets were filled with panic-stricken people hurrying north, crushing one another in their haste to get away. Alfred Hebard, who had come from town near midnight, was sure the fire would reach Locust street. "The State street bridge must have been burning just after we crossed it," he told Gurdon. George Holt, who had been staying at the Hubbard home, and Alice, their adopted daughter, returned home to help and brought fresh news of the spreading flames.

At some time during the early morning, the Reverend Dr. Cooper and his sons arrived to help the Hubbards. They had not saved anything from their own home.

"Mayor Ogden's house is going down in flames," Dr. Cooper said. "It can't be saved. But his brother's house, right behind it, hasn't been touched by the fire that's gone two blocks past it!"

Cooper was right. William Ogden's handsome mansion was razed by the flames, but Mahlon Ogden's equally fine home in the block adjoining to the north was barely scorched by the fire.

Dr. Cooper, still awed by this miracle occurring a few blocks away, turned to with his sons to help those now swarming through the Hubbard house in an attempt to save what they could. Dr. Cooper called to Mary Ann for a hammer. Without question, she obediently dashed to Mr. Hubbard's study, returning with an Indian tomahawk. Minutes later she saw that Dr. Cooper was using it in an effort to remove a large mirror from the reception room wall.

"Reverend Cooper, don't bother with that!" she exclaimed. "We can't save that!"

"Mrs. Hubbard, it's valuable," he told her, and went on with his work.

"I told him again to leave it," she wrote. "Men from your uncle's plant were helping to pack the goods they hoped to save. Mr. Hubbard had gone on north with some men to help other families."

She returned to the kitchen where she and her two maids had kept tea and food ready on the table for all who might have arrived thirsty and hungry. She looked in, saw her girls still putting food on the table, and sitting there calmly at the table was the Reverend Mr. Swing. "He was eating cold chicken, as if nothing at all were going on," she marvelled.

Mary Ann had been directing the women's work in the house throughout the night and early morning. Now she told her maids to fill all the containers in the house with water. "See that you take only clear water, we'll want to drink it," she said. She still hoped that the house might be saved. She saw that men had been dipping carpeting into their cisterns and were spreading over the roofs cut-up strips of her costly floor coverings, well soaked with their supplies of water, as ordered by Mr. Hubbard.

Chapter 15

The maids disappeared. Mary Ann was joined by Alice and some of the other women. She told them to fill picnic baskets with the remaining food, in case they did have to depart the house and to fill with water any jars that could be carried.

Mary Ann at last paused wearily. She had been working at top speed for hours. Now she hoped that Mr. Hubbard would soon return to tell them what next to do. She glanced at Mr. Swing, who was gnawing on a chicken leg. He noticed her, rose and bowed his thanks, then resumed eating.

"At the fire one thing impressed me very much," Mary Ann remembered. "It was the calm, courteous way in which people talked, if all had been serene and normal they could not have been more respectful. I remember meeting one man coming down the attic stairs with a new pair of winter boots your uncle had laid up for the cold weather . . . he politely asked if he could have them. I said yes, for the certainty of the wholesale destruction of our posessions made us very generous. Alice had a very handsome and expensive winter suit—royal purple with a hat to match, trimmed with a long, white $14 feather. She took it out, looked at it, and replaced it, having decided that in our changed circumstances she would have no use for such an extravagance, so she let it burn."

In the hall, Mary Ann saw that Cooper's work with the tomahawk had been rewarded. He and his boys had removed the huge mirror from the wall without shattering it. Later, after the fire, she was astonished to learn that her fine Venetian importation had been put into a wagon and hauled to safety. Several large chests of tea had been saved, but Mr. Hubbard's manuscript, on which he had worked for two years, his papers and his books were all lost, as well as most of the rest of their household goods. The mirror, Mary Ann recalled, was unscratched, but turned out to be much too large for the next home they were able to afford.

*

The wagons were filled and ready for departure. To the south the morning sky glowed red and the smoke pall hung low above them like a velvet canopy, completely obscuring the sky and stars directly overhead. Mr. Hubbard, after directing the men to put soaked carpet strips over the roof, had gone north to help other families and Dr. Cooper had gone to find him, to report the situation at home. Mary Ann persuaded the men remaining with them to stop their attempts to remove furniture from the house, to gather up the women and children, and to get under way. The house could not be saved. She had seen flame and smoke on the roof.

In the hall she had found a young woman with her infant, sitting forlornly on a bench, staring at the activity about her. " 'You must get out!' I told her," Mary Ann remembered. "She replied that she did not know where to go. I spoke with authority, telling her again to leave the house and to go north, that we all were leaving, that others had gone and if she remained she and her child would be burned alive; so she went. I never saw her again. There was plenty of time for her to get beyond the reach of the fire."

Mary Ann returned to the kitchen to check whether all the food had been taken out to the wagons. Someone she didn't know was drinking the last of their sherry. "I do not think our family tasted a mouthful of food that night or morning," she wrote. "We were all too busy."

Mr. Hubbard returned with Dr. Cooper and their small wagon train got under way, heading north, all of them walking because the wagons were fully loaded. Behind them their roof was burning. Within a few blocks they would be safe, her husband assured her. They were cold in the October dawn as they moved north and Mary Ann was bone-weary and hungry. They dragged themselves into a bivouac area Mr. Hubbard and his helpers had created for the refugees. There they found Alice Tinkham and George Holt.

They had saved themselves from the Great Chicago Fire, but little else. Shortly after daybreak their Locust street home burned. The wet carpeting on the roof no longer withstood the flying embers. "The hot gale flapped the water out as if the heavy Brussels carpet had been a pocket handkerchief," Mary Ann Hubbard wrote. Most of the household goods they attempted to save, sending it with friends, relatives, in hired carts or with former employees, became lost in the confusion. The men with the hired wagons they never saw again. Some of their possessions abandoned in the yard, near the house, were burned, the rest, scattered through the gardens and orchard, were stolen. They spent most of Monday finding the members of their family, their maids, and the Holts and Hamiltons who had not come to the Hubbard house. Gurdon and the men with him shaped up their refugee camp north of Fullerton avenue, beyond the northernmost devastated area, and sent out their wagons to obtain supplies of food and water. Gurdon Junior found them late in the day, and urged his parents to come to stay with him, reporting that Mary Ann's mother was much concerned about them. His father thanked him, pointing out that they had too many people to attempt to keep them in supplies on the west side. Instead he proposed to haul their remaining goods to their summer cabin on the bluffs overlooking Lake Michigan near Lake Forest. But he accepted his son's offer of cash and promised to return to the city as soon as possible.

Early Tuesday the fire burned itself out, after twenty-nine hours of fury. Two hundred fifty bodies of fire victims were found, an estimated hundred thousand Chicagoans were made homeless and dependent on the relief stations and refugee camps organized by those more fortunate. Soon food and money began to arrive from neighboring towns and cities, a total of $5,000,000 was provided in relief funds from cities as far away as London. The property losses, including 1,600 stores, 28 hotels and 60 major manufacturing companies totalled over $200 million, less than half covered by insurance. Less than half the $100 million of insurance in force was paid, since some insurance companies were bankrupted by the disaster.

Gurdon Hubbard lost his fortune in the fire and was near bankruptcy. A pioneer in the insurance business in Chicago, he not only had written policies over a half century, but was heavily invested in several of the companies. Both Henry Hamilton and Alfred Holt wrote of his decision to undertake to pay off all the insurance losses for which he was directly responsible by having underwritten them personally. This Mary Ann agreed they must do. It might require them to sell all they owned, her husband told her. She nevertheless agreed, her nephews said. "Mr. Hubbard lost a great many buildings in the fire and the widespread failure of the insurance companies crippled him," Hamilton wrote. "In spite of his far-flung business activities, Mr. Hubbard never ranked as one of Chicago's wealthiest families."

In the next several months, Hubbard advanced toward a slow recovery, while Chicago itself rebuilt with remarkable speed. Gurdon was not heavily invested in land, he had given away much of what he owned during his lifetime, but he continued to own the property at LaSalle and Locust, lots on Mackinac, and holdings in the west and downstate Illinois, as well as his steamship interests, in which young Henry Hamilton would eventually find his career. His son Gurdon Jr. was doing well and able to help his father, and the tea business continued to thrive. He sold most of the block in which his mansion had stood and built a row apartment building at 143 Locust street for himself and Mary Ann and three tenant families, one of them the Henry E. Hamiltons, who also had been burned out. He used some of the brick from his burned house to put up the new building, though thieves had arrived in wagons to carry much of it away to sell as building materials in other parts of the town before Hubbard and his men could get at it.

Their apartment was a modest one, Mary Ann said, with a large study for her husband and a sitting room for herself, and rooms for their nieces when they should visit. The Hamiltons, Holts and Hubbards were still welcome, and Mary Ann continued to find money for contributions to the soup kitchens operating in Chicago through that winter, for her church work and mission charities. Gurdon worked the next five years to pay off his obligations. He ignored his literary endeavors. All his eight hundred pages of manuscript, his papers, and his books were gone. He had no plans to return to the story of his life. "The fire had been a blessing to some," wrote Alfred Holt, "but to Gurdon Hubbard it was a catastrophe. His resilience was gone."

*

Chicago itself rose again, as Joseph Medill, editor of the *Tribune,* insisted it would in his first post-fire edition of the paper on Wednesday, October 11, his editorial concluding: "Let the watchword henceforth be: Chicago shall rise again!" George F. Root, writer and publisher of songs, took up the slogan in his ballad on the fire. Mayor Roswell B. Mason, who proclaimed martial law to protect the fire victims from looters, named DeWitt Cregier, the city engineer, to direct the clean-up of the ruins, while Col. Nelson A. Miles, the former army Indian fighter, commanded the Fifth army patrolling the stricken city. All three were friends of Gurdon Hubbard but this time he did not volunteer for civic duty. Within a year or two, when his home had been built and the Hamiltons had moved in next door, Gurdon again turned to the books he had acquired and thoughts of the past. Young Henry Hamilton, then about twelve, urged his Uncle Gurdon to get back to the writing of the story of his life, and promised to help.

"When I first met Gurdon Hubbard I cannot tell any more than I can tell when I first met my father and mother," Henry R. Hamilton would write in his autobiography years later. During the twelve years the Hubbards and Hamiltons lived next door, young Henry was with Uncle Gurdon almost every day. The Hamiltons and the Holt children also would join the Hubbards at Mackinac in summers. Gurdon felt able to keep his promise to Mary Ann to take her to California when he had recovered from the fire losses. She covered the trip in a single sentence in her own recollections: "En route to California, we went through Red Oak, Iowa. . . . It is a beautiful little town laid out by Mr. Hubbard's relative." The reference was to the Hebards, whom they visited at Burlington when they were also calling upon Joseph Smith at Nauvoo, and who came to the Hubbard's the night of the fire. Mary Ann, too, had grown a bit weary and provided few details of their later life.

It was DeWitt Cregier, the city engineer and Democrat who would become mayor of Chicago, who did more than anyone outside Gurdon's own family to bring the tough but momentarily beaten old pioneer back into the Chicago mainstream. Cregier had been water commissioner and knew Gurdon both for his work with the Hydraulic company and as an alderman. Cregier was a busy man in the re-construction days but he eventually found time to look up Colonel Hubbard, whom he found at work in his study on Locust street. "I went to cheer him up and he cheered me up," Cregier would remember. Thereafter Cregier visited Gurdon at home with some regularity. On one such occasion, Gurdon had just read in the newspapers that Cregier had been promoted to commissioner of public works.

"Cregier, I congratulate you," Gurdon said. "Now that you are responsible for it, I can tell you I don't like the way you are maintaining the streets. The streets hereabouts are a mess."

Public Works Commissioner Cregier, a tall, lean, white-haired man noted for his courteous and diplomatic ways, promised Colonel Hubbard he would have something done with the unpaved streets in the neighborhood. Back in city hall he summoned his superintendent of streets and an official in charge of the disposal of fire debris being dumped on the Lake Michigan shore directly off the downtown business area. Cregier suggested that they should use the ashes, stone and brick left by the fire to surface some of the town's worn streets, since the mixture of mud and aggregate made a rather substantial surface. He ordered some loads of the refuse to be distributed along Locust street off LaSalle on the far north side.

But Cregier's plan backfired when the foreman in charge of a street gang detailed to the Locust street phase ignored a part of the instructions. His men began dumping loads largely comprised of ordinary trash in Locust and that soon brought out a six-foot, ramrod-straight, fierce old man, brandishing his cane. The Irish boss intervened when Gurdon Hubbard sought to drive off the street crew and Hubbard turned on him, "You dump that trash here and I'll thrash you," he stormed. "Now git the hell outa here, all of you!" The foreman ordered the wagon away from the street and reported personally to Commissioner Cregier at City Hall. "He said he'd whip us with that cane," the foreman told Cregier. The commissioner heard him out. "Now, Mike, take it easy," Cregier then advised. "That old man is Gurdon Hubbard and he does exactly what he says he'll do. If you hadn't been wise enough to leave you'd be in the hospital now. I'll talk to him. Dump only ashes and broken stone there and let him inspect the loads before you do it. You are a good man, Mike. Do as I say about this. I don't want to lose you."

*

In the course of his visits to Locust street, Cregier asked Gurdon why he didn't join his old friend and relative by marriage,

Devillo Holt, in building houses on Mackinac Island. "You've got some land up there, haven't you? Mr. Holt has got plenty of lumber in Michigan and Wisconsin. Why don't you two get together again?"

"Well, God-a-mighty, how do you know all this?" Gurdon demanded. It was the first time Cregier had ever heard the old man cuss.

"Mr. Holt is an old friend of mine, too. He wants to do it."

"Why don't Devillo come to me, instead of running around talking about it?"

"Because you are getting to be a cranky old man, Colonel. He's afraid you'd be insulted if he proposed to finance it. You have the land, you love Mackinac, and you love building. Devillo is out of the Board of Trade now. He wants something to do. He remembers those good summers he had with you. It's time you get together again. I think Ann would like to have you out of the house now and then."

Gurdon grinned. His large gray eyes rested gratefully on his friend. He pulled at his graying beard. "Thanks, Dewitt," he said softly. "Ann's been talking to you too, has she? Why don't you tell Devillo to talk to me himself."

*

Young Henry Hamilton helped Gurdon when the work of writing memoirs was resumed, collecting such papers as could be found, searching for books to replace those lost in the fire. He had enjoyed the freedom of Gurdon's library throughout his boyhood and was familiar with Uncle Gurdon's practice of writing his commentary in the margins of the books and recalled many of the notations, especially those relating to Shabona and Black Hawk and Gurdon's views of the conduct of the Black Hawk war and the dispersion of the Indian tribes. In the summer of 1875, when Henry Hamilton was fifteen his uncle took the boy with him on a trip along Hubbard's Trail. They visited a town once called Old Middleport that long-since had been renamed Watseka. There, or in Danville, Henry heard his uncle's answer to Hiram Beckwith, a writer he respected for his contributions to the *Fergus Historical Series* in Chicago, and to various historical societies, who, in concluding his interview about

473

Gurdon's Iroquois river trading days, asked about the Indian girl, Watseka. Hamilton remembered the reply and read Beckwith's report in his Iroquois and Vermilion county histories, but did not himself use the information until he wrote his own life story, in 1931, after Gurdon and his wife and son had died.

In 1877 Gurdon was busy with his recollections, exchanging letters with Dr. John Goodell on some phase of this work. He wrote Goodell on March 27: "Yours of the 7th received in my absence, greatly obliged for the document enclosed. . . . My time the last three weeks has been wholly taken up with business of my own and in particular my connection with the Reformed Episcopal church, being one of the trustees and chairman of the executive committee. I have not been able to do much else than settle with Mr. Martin (probably Samuel Martin, wealthy lumberman) the conditions of his magnificent grant of 160 acres of land adjoining out city . . . for a geological and medical college. . . ." He then referred to the problems with his autobiography. "I had laid aside letters and documents as well as my own diary of events, and for 18 months prior to our great conflagration had written as I had leisure . . . and had at the date of the fire 800 pages . . . intending when I had got up the whole to have revised and published it. Most unfortunately all was destroyed.

"I had over 100 letters from gent. in high positions in our own and other states, such men as Daniel Webster, Henry Clay, Gen. Jackson . . . covering the period from 1820 to 1833, asking for information on various subjects connected with these western states. . . ."

"I have now commenced again but somewhat doubtful if I shall complete it, for the reason of the loss of data for a correct account. I find in this respect (memory) fails me, not being fixed, because I supposed I had it in my papers."

Gurdon did begin again, writing 107 pages of his *Recollections* in his own hand, taking him to near the time of Watseka, when again he was stopped, this time by illness.

In 1878, Gurdon learned of the death of Watseka at Council Bluffs, Iowa. Hamilton indicated that an Indian visitor brought the news and that his uncle spoke with him in Potawatomi. When the visitor had departed, Gurdon, evidently forgetting that Beckwith had asked of Watseka in Henry's presence, said to his young helper: "He brought me news of Watseka, and some day I will tell you of her." On December 14, 1879, Gurdon read a dispatch to the Chicago *Tribune* reporting the death of his friend and associate of fur trade days, Noel Le Vasseur, at Bourbonais Grove. Le Vasseur was a leading Republican politician in the Kankakee area, the report said. "He was educated in the Catholic church and lived and died in the venerable faith. St. Viatus College at Bourbonais was largely built through his efforts and influence. Le Vasseur was with his friend Gurdon Hubbard at Chicago Creek long before it was deemed possible to build a village in such a quagmire."

Gurdon became critically ill in May, 1883, suffering from chills and fever. Work on his manuscript ended and he still had not written of his life with Watseka. Later in the year he was afflicted with intense eye pain, especially behind the left eye. Doctors said abscesses or blood-poisoning were responsible for the excruciating pain; at a later time the diagnosis might have been glaucoma. In April, 1884, Gurdon's left eye was removed. "True to his Indian training he resolutely refused an anesthetic or to let anyone hold his hands," Hamilton wrote. "He simply lay down without a murmur or tremor and let doctors cut out his eye." His long-time friends came to see him, among them Judge Grant Goodrich, who recalled Gurdon's final years. "The atrocious pains did not end," Goodrich said. "He suffered without complaint, and called out cheerfully to a visitor entering his darkened room." In 1885, Gurdon's second eye was removed.

Gurdon was totally blind more than a year prior to his death September 14, 1886, at the age of eighty-four. His nephews, nieces and friends who visited him found Mary Ann constantly at hand, and, on a few occasions saw Gurdon Junior with him. Gurdon continued cheerful and uncomplaining, they said. Each day he heard read a chapter of the Bible and he led the morning prayers at breakfast. He did not lose his zest for the life of his exciting city, now grown to a million population, exceeding even the wild speculations of the 1836 canal celebration. He avidly followed the news and relished his opportunities to talk of old days with friends, though there were no more known Chicago survivors about from the fur trade days. Gurdon heard read some of the sections of the first volume of A.T. Andreas' momumental *History of Chicago from the Earliest Period to the Present Time,* published in 1884, in which he was extensively profiled and to which he contributed. Mary Ann or Henry Hamilton surely would have read to him Andreas' estimate of Gurdon S. Hubbard: "Only a single man became identified with modern commerce and trade of the city who had been connected with the rude Indian trade. . . . He stands pre-eminent as one of the foremost merchants . . . besides carrying on one of the largest shipping, commission and forwarding trades . . . he held nearly every office of trust that his fellow citizens could thrust upon him. It may be said here that he never violated any trust bestowed . . . his character is above reproach and reputation untarnished by the business vicissitudes of half a century." They might have passed reading Andreas' report on street names, stating that Hubbard street was named for Henry, not Gurdon; only a suburban area a day's canoe trip north of Chicago, where Gurdon once built a summer cabin, would memorialize him, calling itself Hubbard Woods.

*

Funeral services for Gurdon Saltonstall Hubbard were held at New England Congregational church, where Mary Ann continued to worship, because it could accommodate the large crowd expected. "It was the most remarkable gathering of early residents ever assembled there," Caroline M. McIlvaine would write. The Reverend J.D. Wilson, pastor of St. John's Reformed Episcopal church, met the funeral party at the door; on a platform in the nave sat Dr. R.W. Patterson, of Second Presbyterian; Dr. Flavel Bascom who had married the Hubbards in 1843; Dr. George Savage, formerly of St. James; and the Rev. Arthur Little. Dr. Patterson offered prayer, Dr. Little read from the Scriptures, the choir sang *Rock of Ages,* Gurdon Hubbard's favorite hymn; Dr. Bascom and Lt. Gov. William Bross delivered eulogies. "The congregation was an assemblage such as is seldom gathered in this or any other city," said the Chicago *Times.* "It was a sea of white heads, representing men who had come to Chicago when there was no Chicago, and have lived to see the results they began." Burial was in Graceland cemetery.

 # Chapter 15

In the days immediately following the service, Judges Henry
Blodgett and Grant Goodrich eulogized Gurdon Hubbard before meetings of the Chicago Historical Society, Judge Blodgett
urging that citizens should always remember that Hubbard
brought the canal to Chicago; Judge Goodrich saying: "Those
who believe that in the world's history its crowned heroes and
benefactors are those who win the bloodless victories of peace,
and who, by their acts of self-sacrifice and beneficence, scatter
the widest blessings . . . will hold Gurdon S. Hubbard as a prince
among them, in highest honor and esteem." The newspaper
editorialists also praised Gurdon, leading Dr. Savage to mildly
scold them. The newspapers, he said, missed an important aspect of Gurdon's character, "his strong Christian faith . . . his
love of the Bible . . . his uncomplaining submission to the will
of God. . . . He loved life, but met death without fear or anxiety."

The Hamiltons and Holts sought to keep alive in the public's
mind the memory of Gurdon Hubbard. Henry E. Hamilton
edited the new beginning of Gurdon's memoirs, written after
the Chicago fire, published by Rand McNally in 1888. Anna Holt
Wheeler encouraged Mary Ann to write her recollections of life
with Gurdon. Three years before her death Mary Ann commissioned Julia Bracken-Wendt to create "a massive bronze tablet
with a finely sculptured head of Mr. Hubbard between two oak
trees," as described by McIlvaine, to replace the Leonard Volk
sculpture of her husband that was lost when Volk's studio
burned in the fire. In 1911, R.R. Donnelly republished Gurdon's
recollections of his early years, entitled *The Autobiography of
Gurdon Saltonstall Hubbard* with extensive notes by Caroline
M. McIlvaine. In 1931, Henry R. Hamilton completed his book
about life with Uncle Gurdon, including the 1888 text of Gurdon's recollections, his own experiences with Uncle Gurdon,
and the story of Watseka and some details supplied by Gurdon
relative to the Black Hawk war. Caroline McIlvaine, in providing the introduction to Hamilton's work, wrote: "Gurdon Hubbard was the most useful citizen Chicago ever had. During his
lifetime and at the time of his death, this was conceded to him
by his contemporaries. . . ." Earlier, in 1911, McIlvain had written: "Hubbard looms up in history like the survivor of some
former race . . . a giant whose youthful adventures might have

477

been passed on by tradition, as of being more than human. Something he undoubtedly imbibed from the Indians, which, added to his own firm fibre, made him the hero he was in the estimation of his contemporaries and rendered him, in a very true sense, a representative American. That he was able to adapt himself to civilization, and to infuse in others something of the fire which burned within him, is, in large part, we believe, the secret of much of Chicago's extraordinary advance. If we have moved at a rapid pace, it is perhaps because that pace was set by Pa-pa-ma-ta-be, 'The Swift Walker'.''

Henry Holt also wrote of Uncle Gurdon, using some new material provided by Mary Ann, his aunt, but essentially basing his work on the 1888 text. In subsequent years the Chicago Historical Society gathered together some of Hubbard's letters and papers that escaped the Chicago fire. His diary, said to have survived the fire, has not been found. Gurdon himself did not have the use of it, nor the letters now in the archives, when he wrote in the early 1880s. The great Chicago fire that razed most of the city and left thousands homeless and penniless, destroyed most of what Gurdon Hubbard possessed, except for his indomitable spirit.

*

In 1891, Mary Ann Hubbard and her companion, Sarah Marsh, moved from the 143 Locust street apartment to the new Marquette apartment building at Rush and Ohio. There, according to Anna Holt, ''for the next 18 years the sunny library of Ann's cozy home was the gathering place of the Hubbard clan, and others of all nationalities who knew where to find sweet welcome and generous response to the appeal of need.'' Mary Ann's last notable public appearance was at her presentation of the bronze memorial to her husband at the Chicago Historical Society April 15, 1907.

Mary Ann died July 19, 1909, at age 89. She bequeathed the bulk of her estate, a modest $113,000, to Mrs. Alice Williamson, her niece, formerly Alice Tinkham, $1,000 each to Ellen and Marion Holt, and the rest to church and charities, the Second Presbyterian, the Pacific Garden Mission, the Chicago Foundlings Home, and to a fund for retired ministers and their families. Gurdon Hubbard, Jr., unmentioned in Mary Ann's will, died eleven years later, July 23, 1916. Mary Ann and Gurdon Junior were buried with Gurdon Hubbard at Graceland. The Chicago newspapers referred to Gurdon Junior as a respected Chicago businessman also active in the Illinois National Guard, in which he had served as Lieutenant Colonel of the First Regiment.

The visitor to Chicago today will discover only two "memorials" to Gurdon Saltonstall Hubbard, one, the city itself, skyscraper-tall along the windy shore of the great lake, bustling, vigorous, an American city as robust and distinctive as those sturdy, daring pioneers and their enduring women who founded it, Gurdon Hubbard foremost among them. The other, Fire King No. 1, the little red hand-pumper that Gurdon bought for the town of Chicago more than a century and a half ago. After serving Chicago long and well, it was sold in 1860 to Stevens Point, Wisconsin, and then was rescued from oblivion by purchase from the City of Stevens Point for the museum of the Chicago Historical Society, where it now stands, fully restored in bright red and gleaming brass, ready for action. Gurdon would like that.

Sources and Acknowledgements

Gurdon S. Hubbard began writing his life story in 1870 when he was sixty-eight years old, relying on papers, diary and marginal notes in his collection of history books and biographies as well as his recollections. He wrote Dr. John Goodell on March 27,1877 that he had completed eight hundred pages when all his papers and books were destroyed by the Chicago fire of 1871. (Hubbard Papers, Chicago Historical Society). In 1875, Gurdon took Henry Raymond Hamilton, his next door neighbor, then fifteen on a trip down Hubbard's Trail to Danville to refresh his recollections of the past for a new beginning of his memoirs. In Danville they saw Hiram W. Beckwith, whose writings were appearing in CHS proceedings, the Fergus Historical Series, No. 7, and the Wisconsin Historical Collection, Hubbard and Beckwith both writing on the Winnebago and Black Hawk wars. Young Henry Hamilton heard Beckwith question Hubbard about his life with "the Princess Watseka", the Indian woman who bore him two children, though at the time Gurdon mentioned only the daughter who survived for eight months. A few years later, as "Uncle Gurdon" and Henry began the writing of the new series of recollections, Gurdon evidently had forgotten the Beckwith interview, or that Henry had been present, and he promised, "Some day I will tell you about Watseka." But he never did.

The actual rewriting of Hubbard's recollections did not begin until about 1879, after he had recovered from his heavy losses in the Great Chicago Fire. He then lived in one of the four apartments in the row he had built on Locust street, with Henry's family, also burned out in the Fire, occupying the unit next door.

He had recouped a part of his fortune, repaid all his debts, and, with the help of Henry, had replaced many of his books. But his diary and papers were lost and he relied on his memory of the past. He had completed one hundred and seven pages of his memoirs prior to his illness, total blindness and death in 1886. This manuscript, written in a firm, bold hand on lined foolscap, may be found in the CHS manuscript rooms, together with letters and papers written by Gurdon but assembled after his death, plus the privately-printed recollections of Mary Ann Hubbard, his third wife. In our study of this material, and the background Chicago history, Martha Wendt and I were greatly helped by Archie Motley, Curator of Manuscripts, Assistant Curator Linda Evans, and members of the CHS staff.

Gurdon Hubbard's second manuscript, edited and slightly amended by Henry E. Hamilton, father of Henry R. and the son of Judge Richard Hamilton, Gurdon's lifelong friend, was published by Rand McNally and Company in 1888, entitled *Incidents and Events in the Life of Gurdon Saltonstall Hubbard.* I am indebted to the Rand McNally library for the opportunity to study a copy of this privately-printed edition. The Hamiltons generally adhered to Gurdon's original ms. The prose is terse, sturdy, factual, the account of a man of action, modest and reticent. Occasionally Gurdon forgot a date or two, or slightly altered an incident, since he did not have at hand his diary and letters to his mother and sister, Elizabeth, nor did the Hamiltons. The story carried up to Gurdon's twenty-ninth year, but omitted any mention of his liason with Watseka, nor was any dialogue recalled beyond his Mackinac Island days. This text was republished by R.R. Donnelley & Sons in 1911, again a limited edition, one of the Lakeside Press series. An introduction by Caroline M. McIlvaine, librarian of the Chicago Historical Society, and the sub-title, PA-PA-MA-TA-BE, "The Swift Walker," were added. McIlvaine provided later Hubbard data and her appraisal of Gurdon. The Publishers of *The Autobiography of Gurdon Saltonstall Hubbard,* in their Preface, stated that the text was precisely that "taken from the ms of the original diary now in possession of the Chicago Historical Society as it appeared in the memorial volume compiled by Mr. Henry E. Hamilton in 1888 for circulation only among the immediate friends of Mr.

Hubbard's own family." The preface is in error on this point. The Chicago Historical Society did not have the diary, nor did Gurdon when he wrote his hundred and seven post-fire pages. The CHS however in subsequent years gathered up Gurdon's letters to his family from the time he left Montreal in 1818 until about 1828, as well as some business correspondence thereafter. A.T. Andreas' history staff also acquired some of Gurdon's papers relating to the fur trade, according to the Preface to Andreas' *History of Chicago, Vol. 1, P4,* which, appearing in 1884, carried an excellent profile of Hubbard and scores of references to him.

Henry Raymond Hamilton, son of Henry E., went into "Uncle Gurdon's" shipping business. In 1932, following his retirement, when he was 72, Willett, Clark & Company, Chicago and New York, published *The Epic of Chicago,* Hamilton's story of his own life and much of the 1888 text of Gurdon's recollections, as well as data about Black Hawk and Shabona which probably came from Gurdon Hubbard. Hamilton also dipped into the Hubbard data in Andreas' *History* and the writings of Roland Tinkham, whose daughter, Alice was reared by the Hubbards. Hamilton did not however make use of the Hubbard letters and papers which by the time he wrote must have been available to him in the CHS archives. He drew from his own considerable experiences with Gurdon, those of his father, and the recollections of his grandfather, Judge Richard Hamilton, Hubbard's friend since Black Hawk war days. He described Hubbard's long relationship with Lincoln, stating that "Abraham Lincoln was the intimate friend of Gurdon Hubbard and often stopped at his house when he was in Chicago and here the boy (Henry E. Hamilton) became well acquainted with him." Judge Hamilton often visited in the Hubbard home prior to the Civil War and evidently took his son Henry, with him.

I have relied upon Gurdon's manuscript, his letters to his mother, Abigail, and his sister, Elizabeth, his business correspondence, his interviews with A.T. Andreas, the writings of Henry R. Hamilton and Hiram W. Beckwith, and the *Letter Books* of William Ogden, his friend and attorney (CHS) and the Charles Butler Papers (The Library of Congress) for the story of Gurdon's life. Also the writers of local history, from Windsor, Vt. to Montreal, from Mackinac and Green Bay to St. Louis and Danville, from New York City to Chicago, and Astoria, Oregon, who recounted the era of the trade in furs, then America's most profitable export, rivaling tobacco and cotton. There was a minimum of record keeping on the frontier, the Indians, for the most part, relied on their women, who often sat in the councils for such purpose, to keep an oral history account. Some practitioners of the craft fortunately were debriefed by writers of their time. These histories have preserved fragments of Gurdon's story and a lifestyle that endured for three centuries before the westward expansion of land-hungry populations destroyed it. I am indebted to local historians, missionaries who recorded their experiences, soldiers and pioneers for data on Gurdon Hubbard's life and times, the background of the fur trade, and the record of the conquest of the West. A portrayal of Chicago as it appeared in 1818, including a camp of *voyageurs,* shown by a series of dioramas at The Chicago Academy of Sciences was most helpful to the recreation of early Chicago scenes.

In writing Gurdon's story I have sought to provide relevant facts in narrative style against the background of formal history. Nothing set down is contrary to facts of history, though much of the dialogue has been created. The characters and events are true, the dialogue evoked from the known views, postures and actions of the individuals portrayed. Historical figures such as Lincoln, Black Hawk, Governor Reynolds and others, express in dialogue only what they had said on the record, though perhaps in a different context. Antoine Deschamps was Gurdon's teacher as well as *le bourgeois* of the Illinois Brigade—precisely what he said on a given occasion is not known, only his general views and attitudes on history, his management of the fur trade, his dealings with the Indians, his relations with his church. Gurdon's writings, his known statements, the commentaries of his third wife, Mary Ann, and others close to him, and the known utterances of those with whom he talked and conferred, motivate the fictional interludes that mostly concern Gurdon's personal life, especially his life with Watseka, on which no legal record exists. Indian customs and mores among the Potawatomis and Delawares with whom Gurdon lived in the Iroquois River area have been described in detail by missionary David Zeisberger and others, including Black Hawk and Daukayray, the Winnebago chief. I have used Zeisberger's *History of the Northern American Indians,* edited by Archer Butler Hulbert and William Nathaniel Schwarz, Ohio State Archaeological and Historical Society, Marietta, O., 1910, and *Black Hawk: an Autobiography,* edited by Donald Jackson, University of Illinois, Urbana, 1955, as chief sources for the fictionalized scenes of Gurdon's involvement with Watseka, in addition to Hiram Beckwith's account in his *History of Iroquois County,* H.H. Hill & Co., Chicago, 1880. Hamilton, op. cit., provides some information concerning Watseka and Hubbard. Alfred Hubbard Holt, however, in *Hubbard's Trail,* his fictional appreciation of "Uncle Gurdon", published by Erie Press, Chicago, 1952, carries the Watseka legend somewhat beyond credibility, though he sticks to the Hubbard recollections, as edited by Hamilton, for most other details of his story.

*

Chapters one through three, principal sources: Gurdon reported his early life in considerable detail. At Windsor, Vt., his birthplace, we probed for additional details with the assistance of Mrs. Gail Furnas and Mrs. Beverly Laptos, Windsor Public Library. At Bridgewater, Mass. we were aided by Mrs. Evelyn Nourse, town historian. That Gurdon read and remembered details of Alexander Henry's *Travels and Adventures in Canada and the Indian Territories,* published in Montreal and New York in 1809, is attested by his references to *Travels,* a book he carried with him, together with his Bible, into the wilderness. Our search for details of his life in Montreal and at Lachine, and the conditions of his employment in 1818, was made easy by Mrs. Nellie Reiss, Lande Librarian, Laurence Lande Collection of Canadiana, Department of Rare Books and Special Collections, McGill University Libraries, Montreal, and her aides, Lillian (Lu) Rider, Reference Librarian, and Carol Marley, Map Curator, Rare Books Department. *This was Montreal in 1814-1817,* a privately printed mongraph; *The Early History and Present State of the City and Island of Montreal,* Newton Bosworth, editor, published by Wm. Grief, Montreal 1839; *Montreal, Island City of the St. Lawrence,* Kathleen Jenkins, Doubleday, Garden City, N.Y. 1966, were most useful as was Thomas Doige's *Guide to Montreal,* 1819, in recreating for us the city as it was in Gurdon's days there. For information on the *voyageurs* and mackinaws, we found helpful the papers and maps of the Lande Collection, and books relating to *voyageurs* and the fur trade, especially Nicholas Garry's *Diary,* published by the Royal Society of Canada: *The Encyclopedia Canadiana,* Canadian Co., Ltd., Ottawa, 1958, vol. 9; *Dictionary of Canadianisms on Historical Principles,* W.J. Grace, Toronto, 1963; the works of French explorers, who set down such details as the exact number of steps required to portage freight canoes on the various routes from Montreal through the Indian territories, and Alexander Henry's *Travels.* Also useful in providing information on the fur trade and the life of the people in it, Grace Lee Nute, *The Voyageur,* Minnesota Historical Society, 1955; Charles Larpentur, *Forty Years a Fur Trader,* (M.M. Quaiffe,ed.) Lakeside Press, Chicago, 1933; *Mackinaws Down the Missouri,* (Glen Barret editor), Utah State University, Logan. Gurdon Hubbard himself has been the best source of data on the true Mackinaw, a craft pioneered by the Mackinac Island builders as a combination of the Hudson's Bay *canot du maitre* and the Missouri river trade boats. It was Hubbard who supplied such information to Andreas for vol. 1 of his *History of Chicago* and to Rufus Blanchard for his *Discovery and Conquest of the Northwest and the History of Chicago,* 2 vols., Chicago, 1898, as evidenced by Andreas' Preface and Gurdon's response to Blanchard's queries, Hubbard Papers, CHS.

For background on the general history of the fur trade, I found Paul Chrisler Phillips, *History of the Fur Trade,* 2 vols. University of Oklahoma Press, Norman, 1961, of great help. Data on John Jacob Astor's American Fur Company came from the Ramsey Crooks' letters supplied by Gurdon Hubbard to Andreas; from Washington Irving's *Astoria,* 2 vols. Lee and Blanckard, Philadelphia, 1841; Kenneth Wiggins Porter, *John Jacob Astor, Business Man,* which refers to Hubbard's letters to Astor; and the local history collections at Brown County Library, Green Bay, and Stephenson Library, Marinette, Wis. Some references to Antoine Deschamps' activities with Astor, and before him the

St. Louis trader, Sara, may be found in *The Parish Register of Michilimackinac - 1741-1821,* in the Wisconsin Historical Collections, vol. 18. Andreas, vol. 1, op. cit. p. 92, provides further details of Deschamps' life as a trader. The opposition of Astor and his people to the government factory system is related by Phillips, vol. 1, p. 85.

The Mackinac area museums and restorations are an excellent source of fur trade lore. The buildings where Gurdon Hubbard worked still stand in excellent condition, as does Fort Mackinac on the island and Fort Michilimackinac on the mainland where the fur trade town is being restored; also the mission of St. Ignace. Deschamps' dissertations as teacher of Gurdon and John Kinzie are imaginary, inferred from Gurdon's later writings and Deschamps' recorded role as tutor and guide to John Kinzie, Jr. The story of John and Eleanor Kinzie, who had great influence on Hubbard, is told in Andreas and by Juliette Magill Kinzie, wife of John Jr. in her *Wau Bun,* first published in 1856, and reprinted, with excellent notes by Louise Phelps Kellogg, by The National Society of Colonial Dames in Wisconsin, 1968. Gurdon's letter defending Kinzie in the Lalime slaying case is found in Andreas, vol. 1, p. 164; also Mrs. Victoire Porthier's eyewitness account. Lalime, interpreter at Fort Dearborn, reputedly had a fur trade agreement with Joseph Le Mai, from whom John Kinzie bought the Du Sable place in 1803, and Lalime claimed an interest in the property that Kinzie refused to pay. The feud continued into 1812. Mrs. Porthier and her husband, blacksmith at Fort Dearborn, were observers when Lalime followed Kinzie from the north gate of the fort on a day in 1812. "It was sunset," the Ottawa Indian woman told Andreas. "Lalime and Kinzie came out together, and we heard Lt. Helm (Lainai Helm, husband of Margaret Kinzie) call out to Kinzie to look out for Lalime, as he had a pistol. We saw the men come together, we heard the pistol go off, and we saw the smoke. Then they fell down together." Lalime was fatally wounded by his own knife. Kinzie sustained a flesh wound from the pistol shot. John Kinzie, Jr. told Gurdon he saw his mother dress the wound. Indians hid Kinzie until an army court, after hearing Lt. Helm and the Prothiers, cleared him. Lalime's friends, including Jacob Varnum and other government factors, insisted for years that Kinzie should have been criminally charged at Detroit, county seat for Chicago. Kinzie was taken prisoner by the British in the War of 1812, however, and held with his family in Canada. Some asserted he was actually a British agent and had been seized for his own safety.

Whether Jean Baptiste Point du Sable (also de Sauble and au Sable) was the first permanent resident of Chicago may never be unassailably established. Hubbard related to Andreas details of his visit to the site of the Gaurie cabin on the "Gaurie River" with Deschamps, who recalled visiting Gaurie there in about 1776 (he heard of the American Declaration of Independence later that year). Andreas, op. cit., p. 92. *The Wisconsin Historical Collections,* vol. 18, pp. 374-399 provide reports of Major A.S. De Peyster's speech to his soldiers, describing du Sable as "a handsome Negro, very much in the French interest, living at Chicago" in the summer of 1779. That year, Aug. 13, Lt. Thos. Bennett "of ye King's 8th Regiment," who had been sent to find du Sable at Chicago, reported to De Peyster, "I had the Negro Baptiste Point au Sable brought prisoner from the River du Chemin (Trail Creek—near Michigan City, Indiana) and taken to Mackinac." In a second message, Lt. Bennett said of Du Sable, "he is in every respect behaving as becomes a man in his situation . . . he hopes to make his conduct appear to you spotless." Andreas, op. cit., page 71, states that Point du Sable arrived in Chicago in 1779, leaving permanently in 1796 to live with his friend, Glamorgan, near St. Louis. His abrupt departure was unexplained. However, it was in that year that the British, under the Jay Treaty of 1794, abandoned posts in the Northwest to the Americans. Du Sable had been under British protection after serving Sinclair as a fur trader in the Detroit area. Augustin and Perish Grignon's recollections of Du Sable, whom Perish knew in Chicago, may be found in WSC, Vol. 3, pp. 197-235. Blanchard, op. cit. declares that "Point du Sable was a Haitien black, brought to Fort Chartres by the French. Jacques Glamorgan, from Santo Domingo, was in the Spanish interest, and received a grant of land from Spain." Spain had taken over French interests at Fort Chartres in the Louisiana Territory under a secret treaty with France. Du Sable died while a guest of Glamorgan. Milo M. Quaiffe, in his *Checagou, from Indian Wig-*

wam to Modern City, 1673-1835, University of Chicago Press, Chicago, 1933 suggests that the trader Gaurie may have been Jean Baptiste Guillory (also spelled Guyari), concluding "until more facts are found, the title (first resident) . . . still belongs to Point Sable." Father Marquette's journal, lost until about 1800, was found in the Jesuit college in that year and given to the nuns in charge of the Hotel Dieu, a hospital in Quebec. Deschamps evidently saw the page of the journal and an accompanying map. Father Marquette wintered in trader Pierre Moreau's cabin, about six miles south of the forks in the Chicago river, according to his journal. Andreas, op. cit., p. 44.

*

Chapters four through six. Deschamps' discussions en route to St. Louis are evoked, based on his known teaching relationship to Gurdon, and details of Deschamps' background. That Gurdon himself learned early a fondness for history is evidenced by the fact that he searched Indian mounds for artifacts with Chief Waba and explored the Tippecanoe battleground, guided by Indians and General Harrison's report. (*Autobiography,* 1911—pp. 61 ff.); he also accompanied Deschamps on a search for the site of the Gaurie cabin, Henry's cave, the ruins of Fort Michilimackinac, etc. according to his recollections and letters home. Deschamps, in addition to reading Father Marquette's *Journal,* kept by the nuns at the Hotel Dieu, may have read the book by Bartolome de las Casas, *A Relation of the First Voyages and Discoveries Made by the Spaniards in America,* published in Spain and in London in 1699. Deschamps himself referred to the fact that he had served in the fur trade under four ruling nations, Spain, France, England and the United States, and he did not approve of the treatment of the Indians by any except France. Though Deschamps' dialogue is fictional, the assertion that millions of Indians had been slaughtered or died of disease during the course of the conquest of Indian lands in America was known by 1818, even though an estimate of pre-Columbus population of the continent cannot be precise. According to C.S. Ceran, who cites Bishop la Casas in his book, *The First American,* Harcourt Brace Janovich, Inc., New York, 1971, pp. 30 ff., later non-Spanish research suggests that between 15 and 19 million Indians were killed in North and Central America by the white invaders.

Gurdon's experiences with the Indians at Fort Clark probably resulted from the great enmity of the Peorias for Americans, a fact well known to Deschamps, who was long based among them. For an account of the Peoria troubles, I relied on Robert P. Howard, *Illinois, a History of the Prairie State,* Erdeman Publishing Co., Grand Rapids, 1978, and *Concise Dictionary of American History* (Wayne Andrews and Thomas C. Cochran, editors) Charles Scribner's Sons, New York, 1962, *John Reynold's History of Illinois,* 2nd edition, Fergus Co., Chicago, 1887 and Gurdon's own account. Elizur Hubbard's letter to his wife, Abigail, fixes the time of Gurdon's arrival in St. Louis as November 12, 1818, Hubbard Papers, CHS. The St. Louis and Cahokia scenes are from Gurdon's recollections, Washington Irving's description of St. Louis in that period, James Neal Prim's *Lion of the Valley, St. Louis;* John Reynold's *My Own Times,* Belleville, 1855, and his *Pioneer History of Illinois,* Belleville, 1852; and John Francis McDonald's *Old Cahokia,* Joseph B. Donnelly's *The Parish of the Holy Family, Cahokia, Illinois 1699-1949,* and Adolph B. Guess' *The Romantic Story of Cahokia,* all locally published. I am indebted to Librarian Loretta Lopenot of the Cahokia Public Library for research assistance.

In recounting details of Gurdon's life among the Indians, I have sought to use the simplest form of Indian names, or that established in history, as in the case of Shabona. There are eleven versions of the name of this young Ottawa chief, who married into the Potawatomi tribe, became chief lieutenant to Tecumseh, the great Shawnee chief, fighting with him against the whites, and who later risked his own life to save white settlers. He was known as Stone Burner to many Indians, and was called Chaubonner, or Charbonner by the French, evidently a phonetic approximation of the Ottawa pronunciation, and almost literally meaning Coal Burner in French. Shabona was said to be the first man to use the coal found in plenty in his part of Illinois, as the source of warmth and cooking energy. Juliette Kinzie, in *Wau Bun,* wrote that Shabona, or Shaubenee, as Gurdon spelled it, should be pronounced Shawbonay, near to the French. It was Shaubenee, phonetically, to Gurdon, but survives on maps and in history as Shabona, Shabbona (the Illinois town) and Shabonna (the Illinois lake). In the case of Black Hawk, it was not difficult to decide that the Sac (or Sauk) version, *Makataimeshekiakiak,* meaning Sparrow Hawk, should be used infrequently.

While chapter five is based largely on Gurdon's recollections and his letters home, his vague treatment of his encounter with the woman and girl who nursed him back to health somewhere in the Iroquois country induced me to use a fictional approach to the incident. He may have had the kind of mystical experience occurring to Potawatomi boys who fasted in the forest until a vision directed them in the choice of besons, or good luck charms, and a name. It may have been a hallucination induced by illness. Undoubtedly two St. Louis duck hunters started with Gurdon for St. Louis, then abandoned him some thirty-five miles from his base at Sugar Creek, leaving him to die. Who saved him? Gurdon wrote only that a white woman and her sister, or daughter, did. Hiram Beckwith, a careful historian, said in his *History of Iroquois County* that the first white man to dwell in the area was Gurdon himself, and the first white woman was Mrs. Allen Baxter, who arrived five years later, as the wife of Gurdon's farmer. "I cannot conceive why I have lost from my memory the names of those hospitable people," Gurdon wrote years later. (Lakeside edition, *Autobiography,* p. 123). He added that he saw the woman who cared for him "but once more afterward." Why didn't he then speak to her to thank her and ask her name? Possibly, if she had been the captive or wife of an Indian, it would have been unwise for him and his benefactress to acknowledge one another at the time. The reason can be conjectured only, and this I have done.

*

Chapters six through nine. Gurdon continues to tell his own story in letters home and his recollections, though any mention of Watseka is omitted. Beckwith, op. cit. reports on Gurdon's life in this period, including the "Princess Watseka" romance, and some details of her work in her husband's trading post and store, and the settlers' attitude towards her. I am indebted to Hiram W. Beckwith, one of the best of local historians flourishing at that time, for his excellent accounts of life in downstate Illinois in both his Iroquois and Vermilion county histories, and his *The Winnebago Scare* in the Fergus Historical Series, No. 7, p. 45 ff. The total story of Gurdon and the Indians comes from such local histories, based on the recollections of pioneers, and the collections of the libraries in the area where Gurdon traded in the decade 1818-28: I am grateful to Eleanor Yeomans, Adult Service Librarian, Danville Public Library, Barbara Sunderland, Watseka Public Library, and Librarian Carl Heidenblad, Putnam County Library, Hennepin. Henry A. Ford's *History of Putnam and Marshall Counties,* Lacon, Illinois, 1860; John Spencer Hunt's *The Past and Present of La Salle County, Illinois;* Henry Le Baron's *The History of Will County, Illinois,* Chicago 1878 and Leslie C. Swanson's *Canals of Mid-America,* Moline, Illinois undated, were especially useful, as well as the exhibits and papers at the La Salle County Historical Society Museum at Ottawa, Illinois.

Hiram Beckwith and Col. Gurdon Hubbard contributed reports on the Winnebago Scare, as they called it, or the Winnebago War as it was later termed, to the Fergus Historical Series, No. 7, and the Wisconsin Historical Collections, No. 5. Gurdon's letter to his mother on the eve of his daring ride details the situation at Fort Dearborn and describes the Fort Dearborn fire. Two excellent histories of the Potawatomi nation, James A. Clifton's *The Prairie People,* The Regents Press of Kansas, Lawrence, 1977 and R. David Edmunds, *The Potawatomis, Keepers of the Flame,* University of Oklahoma Press, Norman, 1978 provide background material on the Potawatomis and their allies. Edmunds describes, from National Archives sources, the secret meeting Big Foot (*Mawgebset*) held with the Potawatomis at Chicago at the time of the 1827 treaty sessions, when he presented them "with an invitation from the Winnebagos and the Sioux to join in a war against the Long Knives." I have relied for general Indian history of the period on Henry R. Schoolcraft's *Personal Memoirs of a Residence of Thirty Years with the Indian Tribes,* Lippincott, Grambo and Co., Philadelphia, 1851; and his *History of the Indian Tribes,* 1857; and the memoirs of Zeisberger, the Moravian missionary who lived forty years among Indians, for details on Indian customs and mores. Black Hawk's views, recreated in the dialogue with Gurdon, are to be found in his *Autobiography,* edited by Donald Jackson, University of Illinois Press, Urbana, 1955; and in Henry R. Hamilton, op. cit. Hamilton evidently got his Black Hawk information from Gurdon Hubbard, as well as Benjamin Drake's *The Life and Adventures of Black Hawk,* Cincinnati, 1838. Kinzie, in *Wau Bun,* quotes Chief Daukayray, a Winnebago, as expressing views similar to Black Hawk's.

Gurdon's letters to Dr. William Fifthian indicate their close relationship, Hubbard Papers, CHS. Dr. Fifthian's biographical data is found in Beckwith's histories, his second home in Danville, a fine mansion, has been restored and is maintained as a museum. Gurdon's return to Danville and his trip east to see his family, and to New York, are recounted in letters to his mother. The account of his initial meeting with Eleanora Berry is fictional, but their marriage certificate, stating they were joined in matrimony in Danville May 17, 1831, may be found in the Danville Public Library. Gurdon's election to the 8th Illinois General Assembly is recorded by Beckwith, *History of Iroquois County,* pp. 342-6, it convened December 3, 1832; his data on Hubbard's Trail may be found on the pages following. Representative Hubbard's career in the Assembly is recorded in the House and Senate *Journals.* The restored capital at Vandalia and its exhibits provide background for the fictionally evoked scenes, including his meetings with Governor Reynolds. Gurdon's appointments to house and joint select committees are of record, though the secret assignment to report on Black Hawk is inferred from Gurdon's activities. Edmunds, op. cit. states that the Indian tribes of the area asked Hubbard to seek help in delaying their eviction from their lands; Black Hawk's agreement to stay west of the Mississippi is of record, but Gurdon's discussions with Black Hawk are created. Gurdon's reward from Governor Reynolds, his commission as colonel and paymaster of the Illinois militia, is of record.

*

Chapters ten through twelve. I am indebted to Roger D. Bridges, Director of Research, Illinois State Historical Society Library at Springfield and his staff for assistance to us in researching Gurdon's activities in the Black Hawk war and as an Illinois and Michigan canal commissioner. *The Letters and Papers of the Black Hawk War,* edited by Ellen M. Whitney, provide data, orders and correspondence, including the courier and scouting activities of G.S. Hubbard. That he served and reported to Governor Reynolds, commander of the Illinois militia forces, General Henry Atkinson, commanding the United States troops, and Col. Richard Hamilton, commander of militia at Fort Dearborn, is shown by the record, (vols. 1-3). His additional duties relating to the gathering of tactical and strategic intelligence can be inferred from his movements. Examples of his orders may be found in the *Black Hawk War papers* pp. 270 ff. Beckwith's *History of Iroquois county* provides the background of Hubbard's Rangers in the Danville area, pp. 343 ff. Beckwith credits Hubbard with supplying horses, food and guns to the company that proceeded to the relief of Fort Dearborn. I have used Henry R. Hamilton's account of Black Hawk's meeting with the Potawatomis and describing Shabona's ride; for Black Hawk's report of the war, I have gone to his *Autobiography;* for the Army version, General Robert Anderson's *Reminiscences of the Black Hawk War,* WHC, vol 19, pp. 169 ff; James Patrick Dowd *Built Like a Bear,* Ye Galleon Press, Fairfield Wash., 1979 is the source of some of the Shabona material; also Edmunds, op. cit. pp. 236 ff. John Reynolds, in *My Own Times,* refers to unnamed spies and secret agents he sent into the Indian villages during the Black Hawk war. "I was well apprized, long before, of the difficulties," he wrote. Gurdon Hubbard replying to questioning by J.T. Kinston, WHC, stated his own Black Hawk War record succinctly: "I was on Gen. A's campaign from the time we left the Illinois River . . . and personally conversant with every movement. The young warriors of the Potawatomis did not plan to seize Fort Dearborn. Shaubenee sent some of his young men to Gen. Atkinson." Hubbard was mustered into Col. I.R. Moore's regiment May 23, 1832, mustered out June 23, 1832; continued to serve as a private attached to Captain Jacob Early's company, and received orders directly from General Atkinson, as shown by *Black Hawk War Papers.* "When (his) battalion disbanded, he reenlisted as a scout in the field until Black Hawk was caught," says Beckwith.

494

The description of the 1833 Potawatomi treaty gathering in Chicago is from eyewitness reports in the Fergus Historical Series, and the extensive report in Andreas' *History*. Gurdon himself described the scene in letters to his family and to Dr. Fifthian. Latrobe's account of his 1833 visit to Chicago appears in *The Rambler in America*, London, 1836, and was reprinted in Henry H. Hurlbut's *Chicago Antiquities*, Chicago, 1881. A Bureau of Indian Affairs report, National Archives, shows Hubbard paid nineteen dollars for service as a clerk. Harriet Martineau's report from her *Society in America*, 6 vols. London, 1837; other sketches of Chicago life are provided by B.J. McClure, *Stories and Sketches of Chicago*, Rhodes & McClure, Chicago, 1880; Frederick F. Cook, *Bygone Days in Chicago*, A.C. McClurg & Co., Chicago, 1910, (from Chicago *Times* 1875-76), Charles S. Winslow's *Early Chicago*, published by the author, 1947 (CPL), *Richard J. Hamilton's Letter Book*, CHS; Charles Butler's *Letters*, Library of Congress; also *Reminiscences* by Edwin O. Gale, Chicago, 1902; Charles Cleaver, *Reminiscences*, Fergus Papers No. 19; Elias Colbert, *Chicago Historical and Statistical*, Chicago 1868; Charles Fenno Hoffman, *A Winter in the Far West*, 2 vols. London, 1835.

The history of the Illinois and Michigan canal begins in the writings of the French explorers and the reports of Army engineers, all well covered in Andreas, vol. 1. For the legislative history, including Hubbard's activities, I used the Assembly *Journals*, the *Illinois Fact Book* and the *Illinois and Michigan Canal Papers*, IHSL, Springfield; Hubbard and William Ogden Papers, CHS, and James Williams Putnam, *The Illinois and Michigan Canal: a Study in Economic History*, University of Chicago Press, Chicago, 1918.

Mary Ann Hubbard wrote her *Family Memoirs*, privately printed in 1912, CHS, providing an account of her wedding and carrying through her vivid description of the Chicago fire ordeal. Caroline M. McIlvaine provided a biographical sketch of Mary Ann in her introduction to the 1911 edition of Hubbard's memoirs and in the 1909 annual report of the CHS. Mary Ann, a close friend of McIlvaine, Caroline Kirkland, and Juliette Kinzie, and kin of Harriet Hubbard Ayer, a Chicago social leader of the '70s, was a highly respected, responsible woman, recognized for her devotion to her church, charitable works, and her own position as a leader in Chicago society of her time. Hers is the only account of the Hubbards' visit to Prophet Joseph Smith, the Mormon leader, at Nauvoo. Mary Ann did not share Gurdon's confidences in the way Eleanora did; she was not sent on any secret missions by Gurdon as Eleanora was. She evidently did not know precisely why they made the difficult trip to Nauvoo some five weeks before Joseph Smith and his brother Hyrum were killed by a mob at the Carthage jail. The sequence of events, Gurdon's conferences with Governor Ford, the issuance of Ford's statement saying "my investigation" of charges against the Mormons indicated "there was no more crime at Nauvoo than at St. Louis" was issued soon after Hubbard's visit. "I think the Mormons sometimes erred in protecting members of their community under the belief that accusations against them was a persecution of their religion," Gov. Ford added. I have inferred that Gurdon visited Nauvoo at the request of Governor Ford and reported to him the information used by Ford in his statement. Ford himself, in his posthumously published *History of Illinois,* S.S. Griggs & Co., Chicago, 1854, allocates much of his book to a defense of his actions in the Mormon crisis, called by some the Mormon War. While Ford did not name his confidential agents who visited "the Holy City of Nauvoo", he indicates that a late report by one of them, just prior to his own visit to Carthage, June 21, inspired his statement exculpating Mormons of many of the charges against them. Gurdon Hubbard and Mary Ann were in Nauvoo just five weeks prior to the murder of Prophet Smith and his brother at Carthage. The historical department of the Church of Latter-day Saints at Salt Lake City has no record of the Hubbard visit, but Mary Ann's account is undoubtedly true. Potawatomi chiefs had been summoned by Prophet Smith to Nauvoo shortly before the Hubbard visit. Both Governor Ford and Hubbard were friendly to the Mormons. I have used Leonard J. Arrington and Davis Britton, *The Mormon Experience: A History of the Latter-day Saints,* Alfred A. Knopf, New York, 1979, and James B. Allen and Glen M. Leonard, *The Story of the Latter-day Saints,* Deseret Books, Salt Lake City, 1976, as background sources.

Henry R. Hamilton and Alfred Holt state that Gurdon Hubbard and Abraham Lincoln were "intimate friends", Hamilton declaring that Judge Richard Hamilton, his grandfather, first met Lincoln in Hubbard's home and saw him there several times. Hubbard was a Chicago advisor Lincoln mentioned in his letter to Judd. Frederick Cook, a *Chicago Times* employee presumably knew the whereabouts of the paper's owner the evening prior to the start of the senatorial campaign in 1858. Senator Orville H. Browning's *Diary* notes that he and Lincoln had "tea", i.e., the evening meal, with the Hubbards three days later, suggesting that Lincoln was a house guest at the Hubbard's July 8-12, 1858. Alfred Holt states that he studied the record of "The Sand Bar Case" and found that Hubbard was Lincoln's expert witness. Joseph Medill of *The Chicago Tribune* described the rearrangement of the seating at the Chicago 1860 Convention the night before nomination. Mary Ann Hubbard stated to Holt that her husband told her he urged Senator Browning to take action to delay the 1860 convention proceedings a day, as was done. "I don't suppose anyone will remember," Gurdon said. Historians generally agree that the 24-hour delay greatly improved Lincoln's chances for the nomination. Data on the *Lady Elgin* disaster are from Hamilton and Holt, the Chicago newspapers, and Dana Thomas Bowen's excellent account in his *Shipwrecks of the Lakes,* published by the author, Daytona Beach, Fla., 1952. The activities of the Chicago Defense Committee were reported in a paper read before the Chicago Historical Society by Augustus Harris Burley, which later appeared in *Reminiscences of Chicago During the Civil War,* The Citadel Press, New York, 1967, pp. 51-70.

The final years of Gurdon's life are recounted in his letters, his wife's memoirs, and Hamilton's and Holt's recollections. Cregier's visits to Gurdon are related by Henry Raymond Hamilton, who himself visited "Uncle Gurdon" almost daily in that period. I also am indebted to E.B. Cregier, great grandson of Mayor Cregier, for his account to me of his ancestor's activities. Mary Ann Hubbard discussed her husband's participation in the Episcopalian liturgical dispute. Andreas, in reporting the Chicago Protest meeting in his *History,* vol. 2, p. 412, states that Gurdon S. Hubbard was the lay chairman. The background of the dispute is provided by Raymond W. Albright, *A History of the*

Protestant Episcopal Church, Macmillan Company, New York, 1964. The Reverend Mr. Savage's statement, explaining Hubbard's action, appears in *Incidents and Events,* Rand McNally, 1888. Dr. Cheney's letter of October 24, 1871, Gurdon Hubbard's letter to Dr. John Goodell, relating to his church activities as well as the fate of his first manuscript, and the eulogies by Judges Goodrich and Blodgett may be found in the Chicago Historical Society Collections.

Mary Ann Hubbard provided a fascinating narrative of her experiences in the Great Chicago Fire, in her *Family Memoirs,* pp. 102-139, CHS. Her story, and that of Henry Hamilton, op. cit, pp. 298-307, and Mrs. Hebard's recollection, in Andreas, vol. 2, p. 728, provide a vivid and complete story of personal experience at the Hubbard home during the catastrophe of 1871. For background history I have used Elias Colbert and Everett Chamberlain, *Chicago and the Great Conflagration,* Cincinnati and New York, 1871, the first and best journalistic account, and Herman Kogan and Robert Cromie, *The Great Chicago Fire 1871,* G.P. Putnam's Sons, New York, 1971, the most vivid and complete modern account.

The work with the life of Gurdon Hubbard has extended over several years. Throughout I have received the generous help of librarians and workers in the field of local history. I am indebted to all. I also thank Harold M. Finley and Professor John Lamb, of Lockport, Illinois, who assisted my wife Martha and me in finding the old portage route and the various scenes of Gurdon's canal and trading activities in northern Illinois; Herman Kogan, Kenan Heise and Virgil Peterson, authors of books on Chicago, who made their collections of Chicago research materials available. I am grateful to Carl Guldager, who not only provided editorial guidance as the book was being completed, but also edited *Swift Walker* for publication; to Henry Regnery, for his personal interest and guidance; to Bette Wendt Jore for editorial assistance; and to Mildred Morrison for Chicago research aid and manuscript preparation.

Lloyd Wendt

Index

Index

Clay, Henry, 261, 262, 404, 417, 474
Cleveland Press, 437
Clifton, James A., 238
Clybourne, Archibald, 231
Clybourne, Jonas, 245, 246, 275
Collins, James H., 369
Cooper, Rev. William, 418, 456, 459, 466, 468
Corning, Erastus, 406
Cook, Daniel P., 307
Cook, Frederick Francis, *Chicago By-Gones,* 363, 365, 366, 367, 420, 421, 453, 454
Courtright, Isaac, 309
Crafts, John, 65, 75, 77, 82, 84, 88, 110, 112, 272
Creiger, Dewitt, 471, 472
Crooks, Ramsey, 12, 40–1, 42, 104, 130, 136, 153, 166, 188, 193, 214, 224, 270, 272, 343, 354, 358
Cummings, George David, 456
Cunningham, Hezekiah, 234–7

Davis, Judge David, 426, 435, 437
Davis, Jefferson, 304, 306
Davis, William, 297
Dearborn, Fort, 7, 147, 247, Massacre, 48–51, 71, 78–80
Dedmon, Emmett, *Fabulous Chicago,* 387
de Champlain, Samuel, 23
de Soto, Hernando, 100
de Tonty, Henri, 259
Deschamps, Antoine, 42, 49–50, 60, 64, 69, 74, 82, 92, 101, 103, 114, 126, 136, 156, 166, 175, 179, 182, 187, 189, 193, 255, 319, 355, 388
Dodge, Gen. Henry, 301, 304, 306
Dole, George W., 275, 276, 327, 332, 335, 336, 337, 339, 356, 374, 376, 385, 424, 427, 428, 429
Doniphan, Col. Alexander, 400
Doty, James Duane, 355
Donnelly, R.R., *The Autobiography of Gurdon Saltonstall Hubbard,* (1911), 477
Douglas, Adele, 420, 421
Douglas, Camp, 451
Douglas, Stephen A., 336, 357, 359, 375, 386, 397, 404, 418, 419, 420, 421, 422, 423, 424, 425, 426, 429, 441, 445
Dowd, James, 409, 410
Dredd Scott decision, 419, 424
Dufrain, Jacques, 139–43, 145–53
du Sable, Jean Baptiste Point, 57–8, 83

Duncan, Joseph, 306, 324, 356, 357, 358, 359, 360, 362, 372, 396
Dunham, Capt. Joshua, 15
Dunne, Finley Peter, 455
Dyde, John, 10, 24, 25, 29, 45, 62, 136
Dyer, Thomas, 408

Early, Col. Jacob M., 300, 302
Edmunds, R. David, 227, 238
Edwards, Ninian, gov. of Illinois Territory, 101
Egan, Dr. William B., 362, 371, 377
Ellsworth, Elmer, 436
Episcopal Church (St. James), 313, 328, 370, 457
Erie Canal, 341, 357
Evarts, William Maxwell, 438, 439, 440

Fallen Timbers, Battle of, 119
Fehrenbacher, Don H., 428, 429, 451
Fell, Jesse, 426
Fergus Historical Series, 473
Fifthian, Alethea, 261, 268, 274, 378, 382
Fifthian, Dr. William, 255, 260, 262, 263, 309, 314, 320, 323, 326, 337, 377, 396, 419
Filmore, Millard, 418
Fonda, John H., 247, 317, 319, 327
Ford, Thomas, 306, 369, 395, 397, 398, 402, 403, 404
Forsyth, Thomas, 226
Fourth Presbyterian Church, 459
Fowle, Capt. John, 256, 257, 258, 259, 265, 280
"Freeport Questions", 425
Fremont, John C., 418
Frothingham's, 20
Fry, Jacob, 375

Gaines, Maj. Gen. Edmund P., 287, 301
Gale, Edwin O., *Reminiscences of Early Chicago,* 328, 349
Garrett, Augustus, 345, 346, 350
Gates, Ansel, 409
Gates, Horatio, 18
Gates, Orrin, 409
Ghent, Treaty of (1815), 21
Gillespie, Joseph, 398
Godell, Dr. John, 417, 474
Gooding, William, 359
Goodrich, Judge Grant, 475, 477
Grace Methodist Church, 461

Mrs Abby

DETROIT
JUN
6
MIC. T.